WM9 PSY.

WITHDRAWN 19/06/24.

PSYCHOPATHOLOGY: EXPERIMENTAL MODELS

A Series of Books in Psychology

Editors: Richard C. Atkinson
Jonathan Freedman
Gardner Lindzey
Richard F. Thompson

PSYCHOPATHOLOGY:
Experimental Models

Edited by

Jack D. Maser
National Institute of Mental Health

Martin E. P. Seligman
University of Pennsylvania

W.H. FREEMAN AND COMPANY
San Francisco

Indication of one editor's affiliation with the National Institute of Mental Health does not constitute its endorsement of any of the material contained herein. Authors themselves are responsible for any views they express.

Library of Congress Cataloging in Publication Data

Main entry under title:

Psychopathology: experimental models.

Bibliography: p.
Includes indexes.
1. Psychology, Pathological—Addresses, essays,
lectures. I. Maser, Jack D. II. Seligman, Martin E. P.
RC458.P78   616.8'9'07   77-5032
ISBN 0-7167-0368-8
ISBN 0-7167-0367-X pbk.

CONTRIBUTORS

Lyn Abramson, Ph.D.
Department of Psychology
University of Pennsylvania
Philadelphia, Pennsylvania
19104

Louise DeWald
Department of Psychology
Bryn Mawr College
Bryn Mawr, Pennsylvania 19010

Gordon G. Gallup, Jr., Ph.D.
Professor
Department of Psychology
State University of New York at
Albany
Albany, New York 1222

Harry F. Harlow, Ph.D.
Resident Professor
University of Arizona, and
Resident & Emeritus Professor
Department of Psychology
University of Wisconsin
Madison, Wisconsin 53706

**Isaac Marks, M.D., MRCPsych.,
DPM.**
Reader in Experimental
Psychology
Institute of Psychiatry,
The Maudsley Hospital
De Crespigny Park, Denmark
Hill,
London, England

Jack D. Maser, Ph.D.
Clinical Research Branch
National Institute of Mental
Health
Rockville, Maryland 20857

William R. Miller, Ph.D.
Assistant Professor of Psychology
and Psychiatry
University of Pennsylvania
School of Medicine
Philadelphia, Pa. 19104

Steven M. Paul, M.D.
Laboratory of Clinical Science
National Institute of Mental
Health
Bethesda, Maryland 20014

Judith Rodin, Ph.D.
Department of Psychology
Yale University
New Haven, Connecticut 06510

Robert A. Rossellini, Ph.D.
Department of Psychology
University of Pennsylvania
Philadelphia, Pennsylvania 19104

Gary E. Schwartz, Ph.D.
Associate Professor
Department of Psychology
Yale University
New Haven, Connecticut 06520

Jeri A. Sechzer, Ph.D.
Associate Professor
Department of Psychiatry
Cornell University Medical
College and the Edward W.
Bourne Behavioral Research
Laboratory
The New York Hospital-Cornell
Medical Center
White Plains, New York 10650

Martin E. P. Seligman, Ph.D.
Professor
Department of Psychology
University of Pennsylvania
Philadelphia, Pennsylvania 19104

Richard L. Solomon, Ph.D.
Professor
Department of Psychology
University of Pennsylvania
Philadelphia, Pennsylvania 19104

Stephen J. Suomi, Ph.D.
Assistant Professor
Department of Psychology and
Primate Laboratory
University of Wisconsin
Madison, Wisconsin 53706

Earl Thomas, Ph.D.
Department of Psychology
Bryn Mawr College
Bryn Mawr, Pennsylvania 19010

Ingeborg L. Ward, Ph.D.
Associate Professor
Department of Psychology
Villanova University
Villanova, Pennsylvania 19085

Jay M. Weiss, Ph.D.
Associate Professor
The Rockefeller University
New York, New York

CONTENTS

PREFACE

We ask the reader to consider two popular points of view: that the clinical method has taught us nothing about psychopathology; and that the experimental method is artificial and irrelevant to clinical reality. The first of these views has been expressed by some experimentalists, the second by some clinicians. We subscribe to neither, and we hope that the range of approaches we have chosen for this volume reflects our lack of commitment to either extreme. Rather, this book represents a synthesis of these opposing views: it provides scientifically based accounts of psychopathology that have (or have the potential for) applicability to the clinical setting.

This book is intended for undergraduate and graduate students and researchers in psychopathology. In particular, the book is for students who find the experimental method sterile unless it has proper regard for clinical reality and for those who find clinical intuition unreliable and capricious unless it is firmly grounded on empirical evidence. The twelve models discuss recent advances in a dynamic field. They concentrate on the work of leading scientists who want their work to be applied to psychopathology but who are not committed to any particular clinical approach.

Each model was chosen to represent the prejudices of its author; none of the contributors was told to be eclectic. The authors were asked to write with the undergraduate in mind. The result of this is a book that presents advanced ideas without being difficult to read.

The book could be used to supplement a textbook of abnormal psychology or experimental psychopathology. It was originally conceived as an ancillary text for these courses, but the result is a book that also can be used in other ways. Teachers of courses more limited in scope, such as seminars in animal models or experimental psychopathology, will find the book useful. The models we have chosen—obesity, addiction, depression, phobias and obsessions, neurosis, ulcers, psychosomatic disorders, minimal brain dysfunction, catatonia, schizophrenia, sexual diversity—while not exhaustive of the many models used in the study of psychopathology, are of current interest and are widely studied.

A model of behavior, pathological or normal, is not necessarily identical to the behavior it models. Yet, to be useful for exploring a given phenomenon and for generating new research ideas, the model must have symptoms, causal events, and even anatomical structures in common with the pathology. The more exact the match, the greater the likelihood of our understanding the cause of the symptoms in question, the more rational our treatment, and the more enduring the model will be. However, behavioral homology alone is not sufficient in the study of behavioral phenomena. That the behavioral homology can be manipulated in a predictable fashion does not guarantee its equivalence to a given psychopathology. The answer to the question of equivalence is an empirical one, and, at any given time the "state of the science" yields an approximate answer. For now, these models appear to represent forms of psychopathology more or less adequately. Twenty or even ten years from now, we would be surprised to find the twelve models still intact. Models change as new knowledge is assimilated, or they are abandoned when they prove unable to accommodate important clinical or experimental findings.

Knowledge in all areas of medical and behavioral research has advanced through the use of models. We are speaking not only of animal models, although these are certainly prominent, but of computer simulations, mathematical models, mock-up constructions, psychodrama, and drug-induced psychosis in humans. For example, children may be shown a violent film and later allowed to act out an aggressive scene, perhaps against a large, air-filled doll. Some psychologists view this as a model of aggression. One of us (Seligman) has developed a model of depression based on an effect of inescapable shock administered to animals and men. The other (Maser) helped to develop a model of catatonia/catalepsy from research on a widespread defensive reaction of animals to predation.

Are these models really "theories"? Not long ago, the distinction between model and theory would have been certain to be discussed in every course on systems and theories. Today that distinction is less well defined, and we will not argue that some of the models in this volume are really theories.

As with any effort of this nature, the editors did not act alone and we would like to acknowledge the aid of others. The contributing authors were magnificent in meeting deadlines. Someone, of course, was first and someone last, but all fell within our projected timeline. The staff at W. H. Freeman, especially W. Hayward Rogers and Linda Chaput, were cooperative at every turn. Their editorial suggestions greatly improved the text. Irma Maser read most of the manuscripts and retyped many sections. Many times she called our attention to terms or phraseology that might have proven difficult for someone just out of introductory psychology.

Jack D. Maser
Martin E. P. Seligman

January 1977

PSYCHOPATHOLOGY: EXPERIMENTAL MODELS

OVERVIEW

Modeling Psychopathology in the Laboratory: History and Rationale

Lyn Y. Abramson
University of Pennsylvania

Martin E. P. Seligman
University of Pennsylvania

On Method and Madness

For as long as man has been confronted with madness, he has sought to explain it. This book is about a new and powerful method for understanding insanity: investigations using laboratory models. In essence, the *modeling* is the production, under controlled conditions, of phenomena analogous to naturally occurring mental disorders. Its goal is to understand the disorders. In the last decade, scientists have made enormous strides in understanding psychopathology through laboratory investigation. The research described in the chapters that follow is of relatively recent origin. It is the latest step in the evolution of the field of psychopathology from case history, observation, and speculation toward a controlled setting in which a particular symptom or constellation of symptoms is produced in miniature to test hypotheses about cause and cure. Confirmed hypotheses can then be further tested in situations outside the laboratory.

How and why did the attempt to model madness in the laboratory begin? The laboratory study of psychopathology began as a reaction to the futility of existing explanations. The study of insanity has taken many turns: supposed causes have ranged from those as exotic as demonology to those as quasi-scientific as humoral imbalance. Many hypotheses have neither been discarded nor verified in any way; they simply have accumulated over the years. Let us look at one persistent explanation of insanity for the light it casts on the pitfalls of generating and evaluating causal hypotheses.

The publication in London early in the eighteenth century of a book entitled *Onania, or the Heinous Sin of Self-Pollution* by an anonymous author led to the proposal of the Masturbatory Insanity Hypothesis. As recently as World War II, the hypothesis that masturbation was a frequent cause of mental disorder still appeared in a few psychiatric textbooks.

E. H. Hare (1962) traced the development of the Masturbatory Insanity Hypothesis and suggested several reasons why the hypothesis was proposed and readily accepted. First, a correlation between masturbation and insanity stood out: whereas many patients in asylums masturbated openly and freely (before the wide use of antipsychotic drugs), sane persons rarely masturbated where they could be seen and rarely admitted to doing so at any time. Furthermore, masturbation was most often practiced during adolescence, and it is precisely at the end of this period that certain forms of insanity most often appear in males. Finally, the idea that masturbation caused insanity suited the religious and moral Victorian attitudes of the time. For these reasons, Hare believes, the correlation between insanity and open masturbation generated a false hypothesis that has only recently been abandoned.

This brings us to a question: how do we assess which of two or more correlated phenomena is indeed the causal one? The history of the study of psychopathology is littered with explanations based on observed correlations between phenomena such as masturbation and psychiatric disorders. For instance, Gall (1825, 1835), the founder of phrenology, hypothesized that "prominences" on the head caused psychopathology. According to Kretschmer (1925) psychopathology was a function of body type; he observed that schizophrenics tended to be asthenic, narrow in build, thin, and delicate, whereas manic-depressives tended to be rounded pyknik types and he suggested using body type to predict what disorder a person would have if he became mentally ill.

However, correlations between two events do not necessarily mean that one caused the other. A person's insanity may have caused him to masturbate; prominences on the head may have been the cause of or have been caused by the psychopathology; and a state of manic-depression may have induced a particular body build. On the other hand, perhaps none of these relationships is a causal one. A third factor, unknown to the investigator, may be the cause of both body build and schizophrenia. Perhaps some chemical is present in abnormally high concentration in the hypothalamus. This chemical might depress eating (leading to a thin, delicate appearance) and simultaneously induce a tendency to hallucinate and misinterpret sensory information.

Experimental methods in the laboratory are a solution to the correlation and cause dilemma. They have recently come into use as a means to unravel the determinants of psychopathology. One popular method is comparing responses by psychiatric and "normal" groups to controlled situations. The comparisons often are designed to test deductions from hypotheses about the determinants of the disorder. For example, one might compare the performances of schizophrenic and nonschizophrenic people on dichotic listening tasks in order to test hypotheses concerning disordered attention in schizophrenia.

An alternative laboratory method, the experimental model, has been pursued by the contributors to this book. In this method, psychopathology is not merely brought into the laboratory for study; it is modeled and reproduced there. The advantage of studying a model over observing and comparing two groups is that because the disorder is produced in a lab, we can specify what causes it. The model is rarely an exact replica of the spontaneous psychopathology, and it is useful only to the degree that it mimics the phenomenon in question or suggests interesting experiments (Minsky, 1968).

Three constraints preclude attempts to reproduce phenomena in the laboratory that are identical to naturally occurring psychopathologies. The first is ethics. Imagine a scientist who discovers that he had indeed manipulated the correct variable: Toxin X caused such profound depression that all of his experimental subjects committed suicide after being injected with it. The second constraint is knowledge; at the outset, a laboratory modeler simply may not know how to duplicate the psychopathology in question. Third, animals used in modeling experiments obviously are incapable of expressing certain features of psychopathology.

Consequently, instead of producing phenomena identical to naturally occurring psychopathologies, experimental modelers usually study phenomena that are *analogous* to them. Furthermore, the variables used to produce experimental disorders are often analogous rather than identical to the natural causes of a disorder.

The logic behind modeling is that the important aspects of etiology, cure and prevention of the naturally occurring psychopathology can be illuminated through examination of the model. As mentioned earlier, the burden is on the modeler to determine whether the answers the model provides to questions agree with those the natural environment provides. This issue of demonstration of similarity will be dealt with more explicitly in a later section of the model.

Experimenters must consider four points in evaluating any laboratory model of psychopathology. First, they must make a thorough analysis of the model. This requires that they know exactly the essential features of the variables used to produce the experimental psychopathology. The experimental design techniques available to the laboratory modeler allow definition of these conditions with a great degree of specificity. For instance,

Miller, Rosellini, and Seligman say they have a laboratory model of human depression (see pp. 104–130). They have found that dogs and rats administered electric shocks from which they cannot escape develop a behavioral debilitation similar to that observed in human depression.

To evaluate the relevance of the paradigm for the production of human depression, we must know its essential features. If shock itself is essential, then the paradigm may be relevant only to the production of psychopathology in concentration camps and interrogation rooms. If, on the other hand, aversive uncontrollable events in general impair dog and rat behavior, then the paradigm may have far-reaching significance for human depression. Therapy and prevention techniques must also be evaluated cautiously; their essential features must be discovered.

In addition to analyzing the laboratory model thoroughly, investigators must demonstrate *similarity* between the experimental model and the real-world disorder it imitates; both phenomena must be measured. In other words, clinical patients should be studied in the laboratory to determine whether their behavior and physiological responses are similar to those of the laboratory subjects. Ideally, similarity of cause, symptoms, prevention and cure should be determined.

This is a difficult task because these areas are not well-defined for many psychopathologies. For example, an enumeration of the physiological symptoms *necessary* for an adequate model of schizophrenia is premature in light of the lack of existing data on the physiology of schizophrenia. However, because the laboratory disorder is often well defined and the real disorder often poorly defined, the former can suggest properties to look for in the latter. Therapies that are effective for an experimental disorder can be tested on the naturally occurring disorder. Cause is a more difficult issue to examine. Within the laboratory, researchers can completely control it. Outside the lab, researchers can only attempt to note whether the events that caused the model disorder occur with the onset of the naturally occurring disorder. If a laboratory phenomenon and some psychiatric disorder are similar in a few of these areas, researchers can further test the model by looking for similarities in other areas.

Early literature on experimental models of psychopathology indicates that many investigators ignored the problem of *demonstrating* similarity between the experimental model and the natural disorder. Frequently the evidence of similarity was merely that one or more symptoms of the laboratory disorder looked like a few of the symptoms of the natural form of the psychopathology. Unfortunately, because the natural psychopathology was rarely studied under controlled conditions and the experimental disorder often given only cursory examination, the analogies were very crude and often inaccurate.

The preceding discussion has implied a third point: demonstration of a causal relationship between an experimental procedure and the production of certain symptoms does not prove that every naturally occurring instance of the symptoms has that same cause. Suppose sensory deprivation procedures are effective in producing behavior that resembles schizophrenia in laboratory volunteers. Such a demonstration would suggest that sensory deprivation causes schizophrenia. But if long-term studies of schizophrenics did not support this notion the laboratory model would have little relevance for explaining the nature of schizophrenia. Alternatively, the sensory deprivation phenomenon might be true for some types of schizophrenia but not others. Perhaps one subgroup of schizophrenics has a history of sensory deprivation, whereas a second subgroup does not. Such results would suggest different etiologies for the two types of schizophrenia. The laboratory model of a clinical disorder may ultimately reshape the very concept of the disorder itself.

Fourth, various naturally occurring psychopathologies should be compared with the laboratory phenomenon. Similarities may be found between several clinical disorders and a laboratory phenomenon, so before concluding that any specific clinical disorder is being modeled, experimenters must take care to determine whether the laboratory phenomenon is not just modeling *general* features of all psychopathologies.

Admittedly, the strategy of demonstrating similarity between a laboratory event and a natural disorder is tedious. It is necessary, however, because no rules now exist for relating the two. An engineer can use a small-scale bridge to predict weight capacity of the actual bridge but in the study of mental disorders, no model is related in a well-defined way to the thing it represents. One rationale for modeling psychopathologies is construction of such rules.

We can use these criteria in evaluating laboratory models of psychopathology with either human or animal subjects.

1. Is the experimental analysis of the laboratory phenomenon thorough enough to describe the essential features of its causes as well as its preventives and cures?

2. Is the similarity of symptoms between the model and naturally occurring psychopathology convincingly demonstrated?

3. To what extent is similarity of physiology, cause, cure and prevention found?

4. Does the laboratory model describe in all instances a naturally occurring psychopathology or only a subgroup? Is the laboratory phenomenon a model of a specific psychopathology, or does it model general features of all psychopathologies?

By now, it should be clear that a laboratory model represents a theory of a naturally occurring psychopathology. In discussing the logic of computer simulation, Fodor (1968) argued that a machine program of a behavior is a psychological theory and thus explains the simulated behavior only insofar as it satisfies the usual methodological and empirical constraints upon such theories. We argue that the same logic applies to laboratory models of psychopathology; the theory realized in the laboratory model is subjected to the usual rules for confirmation of scientific theories.

With these guidelines in mind, let us examine the significant historical attempts to model various psychopathologies in this century.

Human Models of Psychopathology

Little Albert: Learning a Phobia in the Laboratory

Little Albert is the most famous subject of a psychology experiment. He had the dubious fortune of participating in the first study in which an attempt was made to produce psychopathology, in this case a phobia, in a human subject under laboratory conditions. Albert was a healthy child whose mother was a wet nurse in the Harriet Lane Home for Invalid Children. He began his career as an experimental subject at eight months and 26 days of age.

Imbued with the behavioristic spirit, Watson and Rayner (1920) were unhappy with the psychoanalytic formulation of phobias. They thought that a conditioning model was more appropriate for phobia acquisition. In their now famous study of conditioned emotional reactions, Watson and Rayner put their conditioning hypothesis to the test by pairing a startling noise with a white rat in Albert's presence to make him afraid of the white rat.

Watson and Rayner were aware of the ethical problem of their experiment but they justified the experiment in this way: "We decided finally to make the attempt, comforting ourselves by the reflection that such attachments would arise anyway as soon as the child left the sheltered environment of the nursery for the rough and tumble of the home." (Watson and Rayner, 1920, p. 3).

Before initiating the conditioning regimen, Watson and Rayner confronted Albert with a white rat, a rabbit, a dog, a monkey, masks with and without hair, and cotton wool. Albert displayed no fear reaction to any of these stimuli. Next, Albert was presented a very loud sound made by striking a hammer on a steel bar. As expected, the loud sound elicited fear in Albert; he started violently, raised his arms, and cried.

The crucial part of the experiment was the deliberate pairing of the white rat (CS) and the aversive sound (UCS). The conditioning made Little Albert fearful of rats, and the fear generalized to other furry objects such as rabbits and fur coats as well. Unfortunately for science and Little Albert, Watson and Rayner never had the chance to discover a technique to remove the conditioned emotional response because Albert was taken from the hospital on the day of the generalization tests.

Watson and Rayner's study is often considered the "classical" learning model of phobia acquisition. Although Watson and Rayner did not attempt to demonstrate similarity between their laboratory phobia and naturally occurring phobias, other investigators have attempted to do so. Clinical anecdotes support the model with respect to etiology. For example, many people become intensely afraid of driving an automobile after a serious automobile accident. However, other clinical anecdotes suggest that phobias often develop in the absence of traumatic experience with the feared object.

Anecdotes are not persuasive evidence for an experimental science of psychopathology. A more sophisticated strategy is that of bringing a phobic into the laboratory and comparing the properties of his phobic reaction with those of the experimentally induced phobic response. It is difficult to model by ordinary classical conditioning of fear the relatively limited set of phobic objects in nature (Marks, 1969; Seligman, 1971). All objects do not have an equal chance of becoming objects of phobias. Bregman (1934) and English (1929) found that common household objects and a wooden duck do not become phobic objects when paired with loud noise. Artificially-induced fear and naturally occurring phobias also demand different treatment. Laboratory-conditioned fear seems far more easily extinguished than phobias. In summary, the simple classical conditioning model of phobia acquisition suggested by Watson and Rayner leaves much to be desired in demonstrated similarity to naturally occurring phobias (see Marks, pp. 174–213).

Watson and Rayner disposed of the ethical problem in their experiment in a rather cavalier manner. Unlike most laboratory modelers of psychopathology, they did not attempt to produce an attenuated version of some psychopathology. Instead, they attempted to produce a full-blown phobia in Little Albert. Modelers are morally obligated to consider potentially harmful or long-term consequences to laboratory subjects before experimenting with them. One useful tactic to circumvent this problem is induction of a *temporary* psychopathology in the laboratory subject. This tactic was used in the following model.

Psychedelic Drugs: Models of Psychoses?

Fascination with psychedelic drugs did not originate with Timothy Leary. During the 1950s, more than a decade before Leary began his crusade, scientists and psychiatrists were studying the psychotogenic properties of these drugs (Snyder, 1974b). Both lysergic acid diethylamide (LSD-25) and mescaline were thought to cause disorders that modeled schizophrenic reactions. The impetus for drug models of psychoses was Kraepelin's (1910) experimentation with drug-induced effects on psychomotor tasks, perception, and work performance.

The logic behind a drug-induced model of psychoses is clear. If the symptoms produced by the psychedelic drugs are similar to schizophrenia, then the physiological or biochemical mechanisms of their action may provide clues about the cause of schizophrenia. Perhaps some LSD-like or mescalinelike chemical is produced in the brains of schizophrenics. Osmond and Smythies (1952) proposed a biochemical theory of schizophrenia that attributed the disorder to an aberrant mescalinelike byproduct of norepinephrine.

The notion that psychedelic drugs model schizophrenia was predicated on comparisons between schizophrenic patients and laboratory subjects who had ingested LSD or mescaline. The early phases of some schizophrenic reactions seemed similar to the psychedelic experiences of laboratory volunteers (Bowers and Freedman, 1966). Many patients described an early state in which they experienced themselves, others, and the world in an altered way. They experienced more intense perceptions and emotional responses.

The clinical syndromes produced by LSD-25, mescaline, and psilocybin seem to resemble each other (Hollister, 1962). Patients experienced hallucinations as well as psychic changes such as anxiety and depersonalization. Then psychiatrists began to examine differences between schizophrenic symptoms and the reaction to psychedelic drugs. Feinberg (1962) compared the hallucinations of schizophrenic patients with those of normal people who had taken LSD and found that whereas the hallucinations induced by LSD were primarily visual, those of the schizophrenics were primarily auditory: schizophrenics heard "voices." Furthermore, even when visual hallucinations occurred in schizophrenic patients, they differed from those induced by LSD in several ways. Their onset was more sudden in schizophrenics; and certain visual forms such as lattice-work, cobwebs, tunnels, alleys and spirals that were almost invariably present under LSD were almost invariably absent from schizophrenic hallucinations.

Hollister (1962) also contended that psychedelic drugs did not produce a schizophrenia-like state. In a well-controlled study, he asked a group of mental-health professionals to listen to tape-recorded interviews conducted with schizophrenic subjects and with normal subjects taking LSD and to guess which were which. The raters were quite accurate in discriminating the tapes made by schizophrenics from those made by drugged subjects. One rater summed up the difference by suggesting that the primary disturbance of the schizophrenics was in their thought, whereas the primary disturbance of the drugged subjects was in their perception. The hallucinogenic drugs, then, appear to produce some of the accessory, perceptual but not the fundamental, cognitive symptoms of schizophrenia (Bleuler, 1964).

Snyder (1974a), a critic of the drug model, reported that LSD given to schizophrenic subjects did not simply make their schizophrenia worse. The drug produced the typical psychedelic effects. The patients themselves were aware of the differences between the drug's action and their own illness.

Hollister (1962) has pointed out that it seems unlikely that a mescaline or LSD-like substance could produce a *chronic* psychosis because after repeated doses tolerance develops for these chemicals.

Finally, is there any evidence that some toxic agent chemically similar to psychedelic drugs is produced in the bodies of schizophrenics but not in the bodies of normal people? Friedhoff and van Winkel (1962) reported that they isolated such a substance, dimethoxyphenylethylamine (DMPE), from the urine of 60 percent of their schizophrenic subjects and from none of their control subjects. Numerous investigators have attempted to replicate this finding. Some have confirmed the original finding whereas others have not. In the absence of appropriate controls in many of these studies, we find it difficult to evaluate them.

Understandably, in the context of the evidence just presented, many researchers have become disenchanted with the idea that psychedelic drugs model schizophrenia. One could quibble about the drug dosages employed in various studies as well as the differences in expectancies between schizophrenic patients and laboratory subjects who fully understand that they are in an experiment deemed permissible by an ethics committee. The fact remains, however, that similarity of symptoms, etiology, and physiology between drug-induced psychoses and schizophrenia has not been proven.

Animal Models of Psychopathology

> We have definite experimental neurosis in our animals (dogs) and in the same animals what is analogous to human psychoses, and we know their treatment. (Pavlov, 1941, p. 39)

Pavlov's assertion that he was able to reliably produce and cure "neuroses" and "psychoses" in laboratory dogs marked a turning point in the history of man's attempt to understand psychopathology. In essence, Pavlov argued that we could come to understand human psychopathology by the study of animal models.

The advantages of using animals in the study of psychopathology are enormous. Great precision of control over experimental variables can be obtained. Both life history and heredity can be controlled. The experimenter may isolate cause by systematically introducing traumatic events into the subject's life and continuously monitoring consequent behavioral and physiological symptoms.

However, there are disadvantages. It is much harder to demonstrate that a laboratory disorder is similar to a naturally occurring psychopathology when the former is produced in one species and the latter observed in another. To compensate, greater care must be taken to make convincing similarity arguments with animal models. Many investigators have overlooked this.

Another disadvantage is that some human psychopathologies (e.g., stuttering, existential neuroses?) and symptoms (e.g., suicide, "clang" associations?) may have no animal counterparts.

Various investigators have wrestled with the problem of just what constitutes psychopathology in an animal. Hebb (1947) suggested a set of criteria by which the "neuroticism" of any form of animal behavior could be evaluated. He derived these criteria by defining human neuroses in behavioral terms that do not require the neurotic patient's report of his emotional state. According to Hebb, neurosis is defined by the following six criteria: it is (1) undesirable, (2) emotional, (3) generalized, (4) persistent or chronic, (5) statistically abnormal, and (6) not caused by a specific, gross neural lesion. He derived the criteria of undesirable and statistically abnormal from his general notions of psychopathology. Reviewers have applied these criteria to the animal models we discuss in this chapter and have found the models lacking (Broadhurst, 1960). But to apply Hebb's criteria to any animal behavior you must adopt implicitly his definition of human neuroses. More recent theorists on psychopathology have challenged many of his notions. Wishner (1969) has cogently argued that behavior that is statistically deviant or socially unacceptable is not necessarily psychopathological. Moreover, psychopathology is not necessarily manifested in socially undesirable ways. For example, compulsive studying may be socially acceptable in medical school. Hebb's second criterion—emotionality—is so vague that it is difficult to use. According to Hebb, the third criterion—that it be generalized —would mean that fear responses to a conditioned stimulus adequately reinforced in the past are not neurotic, whereas current textbooks of psychopathology (e.g., Davison and Neale, 1974) include such examples as instances of phobias. The persistence criterion rules out transient reactive depressions, which are also classified as neuroses today.

Because of these questions about Hebb's general notions concerning neuroses, we will not use them in evaluating the animal models. Instead, we will use the criteria set out earlier in this chapter. Our criteria are neutral: they do not suggest which instances of behavior should be classified as psychopathological. Rather, they merely tell us when we have an adequate laboratory model of a state deemed psychopathological in humans. For example, if a currently accepted definition of psychopathology required "passivity" as a symptom, then we would need to devise some means of assessing the passivity of both animal and human behavior to evaluate laboratory models of psychopathology. The laboratory model method avoids the morass of defining psychopathology; it is merely a technique for assessing whether a laboratory phenomenon models a phenomenon that occurs in nature.

Although medical research is regularly conducted on animals, psychological research on animals has been scorned on the assumption that insanity is uniquely human. We believe that this assumption is false, and much of the evidence presented in this book supports the idea that certain animal phenomena capture the essence of human psychopathology.

Let us now turn to Pavlov's ground-breaking work on animal models of psychopathology.

Pavlov: Experimental Neurosis

During the course of Pavlov's work on the conditioned reflex, two dramatic "accidents" occurred that persuaded him to devote the last decade of his life to applying conditioning principles to psychiatric problems. In the famous circle-ellipse experiment of Shenger-Krestovnikova (1921) a dog exhibited an apparently neurotic breakdown. Here is what happened:

A luminous circle was projected onto a screen in front of the dog, repeatedly accompanied by food. When the salivation to the circle had become well established, the dog learned to discriminate the circle from an ellipse twice as long as it was wide. Discrimination was then made more difficult by making the ellipse successively more similar to the circle by changing the ratio of its axes. The dog successfully discriminated between circle and ellipse until a 9 : 8 ratio of axes was reached. Then the dog's discrimination became poor. After three weeks of training on 9 : 8, the dog's discrimination broke down. More dramatic than the failure to maintain the discrimination was the abrupt change in the dog's behavior. The once-quiet dog began to squeal in its stand and to destroy the experimental apparatus. Whereas the dog previously had gone willingly each day to the experimental room, he now barked violently and resisted going into the room. Even easy discriminations (a 2 : 1 ratio) were also disrupted.

Rather than being annoyed by the misbehavior of one of his laboratory animals, Pavlov was deeply impressed. Pavlov reasoned that perhaps an analogy existed between this "experimental neurosis" produced in the laboratory and the various neuroses of man. Another accident stimulated his interest in psychopathology: the great Leningrad flood of 1924. The building that housed Pavlov's dogs was flooded, and the dogs were trapped in a room slowly filling with water. The water rose until the dogs were swimming around with their heads at the tops of the cages. Luckily, at the last second a laboratory attendant discovered the dogs' plight and pulled them through the water to safety. Upon testing, the conditioned reflex activity of the rescued animals was poor. After the dogs' conditioned reflexes were restored, Pavlov let a trickle of water run in under the door of the laboratory. The sight of the water again disrupted some dogs' conditioned reflexes (Sargant, 1957). So, at the age of 80 Ivan Petrovich Pavlov decided to enter the field of psychiatry. He was convinced that the application of his principles of higher nervous activity to psychopathology would illuminate the questions of etiology, mechanism, and treatment of such disorders.

What, exactly, was Pavlov's notion of experimental neurosis? By neurosis, he meant chronic deviations from normal in "higher nervous activity." In Pavlov's system, higher nervous activity is seen in conditioned positive and negative reflexes. A positive reflex is the conditioned response (CR) to the stimulus predicting food, and the negative reflex is the CR to the stimulus predicting no food. Pavlov inferred that there was excitation in the cerebral cortex from the presence of salivation during a positive stimulus and that there was inhibition from its absence during a negative stimulus. He saw neuroses in a weakening of the excitatory and inhibitory processes, in chaotic nervous activity, and in stages of the 'hypnotic' state (Pavlov, 1941; 196–).

In accounting for experimental neurosis, Pavlov looked to the *type* of animal as well as the situation. Thus, Pavlov did what every investigator of human psychopathology would like to do; he looked at both constitution and environment as determinants of psychological breakdown. He found that whether a dog broke down, and in what way, depended upon the situation as well as the dog's nervous system.

Although not remembered as a personality theorist, Pavlov was very interested in the study of individual differences in his dogs. Ultimately, he used *type* to refer to differences in properties of the nervous system rather than differences in patterns of behavior (Teplov, 1964). Pavlov's classification of types coincided very closely with the classical Hippocratic grouping of temperaments. He distinguished four different types. Two were extreme—excitable (choleric) and inhibitory (melancholic). The two more balanced types were calm (phlegmatic), dominated by the process of inhibition, and lively (sanguine), dominated by the process of excitation. In addition to strength of nervous system, another organic determinant of type was the state of equilibrium between the processes of excitation and inhibition as well as the mobility (ease with which a stimulus produces a response) of both processes. Pavlov observed that the balanced sanguine and phlegmatic types did not ordinarily break down. The extreme groups, choleric and melancholic, on the other hand, were likely to break down either in the direction of excessive excitation or excessive inhibition. Pavlov grounded his definition of types in various experimental indexes: the speed of formation of positive and negative conditioned reflexes, the stability of both kinds of reflex, the magnitude of positive conditioned reflexes, the rapidity of extinction with nonreinforcement, and the capacity to form conditioned reflexes to "ultra-strong" stimuli (Pavlov found that for each dog there existed a maximum stimulus beyond which massive inhibition intervened).

Pavlov considered four factors important in the production of experimental neurosis. In general, susceptible dogs developed neuroses when given tasks too difficult for their nervous systems—stimuli that were too strong or complex. For instance, some dogs developed neuroses after receiving strong noxious stimuli, such as electric shock. A second factor was how much strain was produced by inhibition—the more difficult the negative CR, the more strain. Third, he thought collision of excitatory and inhibitory processes produced breakdown. Finally, Pavlov considered castration a factor in experimental neurosis (Pavlov, 1941).

Although Pavlov's experimental analysis of animal neurosis was reasonably thorough, it is rather difficult for Western psychologists to interpret. The problem in interpretation revolves around some of his explicit and implicit notions of neurophysiological functions. Some of these notions are out of date, and others have no Western counterparts.[1]

The analogy between the maladaptive behavior of Pavlov's dogs and human neuroses seems to us to be the weakest part of his endeavor. He failed to demonstrate similarity between the laboratory phenomenon and human neuroses in nature. In general, Pavlov was concerned with only the grossest similarities between "symptoms" obtained in the laboratory and symptoms observed in the clinic. With the exception of his work on schizophrenia (Pavlov, 1941), he made little attempt to bring clinical subjects into the laboratory for similarity studies. Furthermore, Pavlov often made very specific assertions about which forms of neuroses he had produced in his dogs. Some dogs supposedly developed neurasthenia, a syndrome characterized by vague aches and fatigue, whereas others became compulsive. Such assertions were premature in the absence of compelling evidence indicating that behavioral disturbances in his dogs modeled any human neuroses. Perhaps Pavlov modeled general features of psychopathology rather than specific disorders in the laboratory. The strength of Pavlov's animal models of neuroses would be increased if it were shown that closer parallels between symptoms existed and that those situations that produce human neuroses contained elements important in the production of animal neuroses. It should be noted, however, that bromides, sedative drugs used widely for the treatment of neuroses in the latter half of the nineteenth century (Sharpless, 1965), were effective in the treatment of experimental neuroses in Pavlov's dogs (Pavlov, 1941).

Experimental Neuroses in Children

One of Pavlov's colleagues, N. I. Krasnogorski (1925), applied the experimental neurosis model to humans, in particular to children. Krasnogorski attempted to produce neuroses in a six-year-old boy, I.N., employing a difficult discrimination procedure similar to the circle-ellipse experiment. I. N. formed a conditioned response when 144 beats of a metronome were accompanied by food. When it was well learned, Krasnogorski differentiated the presentation of 92 beats from 144 beats by presenting no food with 92

---

[1] Gray (1964) has reinterpreted the Pavlovian notions concerning strength of nervous system in light of more recent neurophysiological findings on arousal.

beats. Then he made discrimination increasingly more difficult. When a response was required between 144 and 120 beats, the discrimination deteriorated. Concurrently, the child's behavior underwent an abrupt change. Whereas I.N. previously had been easy to work with during the experiments, he now became irritable and refused to enter the laboratory. When the discrimination was 144 beats versus 132 beats, the child's behavior became still more disordered; I.N. cried often and beat other children.

Although this experiment demonstrates that "experimental neuroses" can be produced in humans, we are still in the dark about whether these behaviors are similar to natural, neurotic symptoms and whether the same process underlies the two phenomena. Again, it should be noted that bromides were somewhat effective in relieving children's neuroses in Krasnogorski's experiments, as they had been with the dogs.

Pavlov and his colleagues were not the first to report experimental neurosis. The first known subject in an experimental neurosis paradigm was Victor, the 12-year-old wild boy of Aveyron captured in the Caune Woods in France in 1799 (Itard, 1932, 1962). In an attempt to help Victor exercise his intellectual faculties, his teacher, Itard, employed a discrimination procedure similar to those employed over a century later by Pavlov. When the discrimination became difficult, Victor became very destructive and bit the sheets, blankets, and mantelpiece. Furthermore, he scattered the ashes and fire irons over the floor and fell into convulsions like those of an epileptic.

I.N. and Victor are dramatic and reliable experimental phenomena, but we await more convincing arguments that they model human neuroses (See Thomas and De Wald, Model 7).

The Pavlovian Conception of Schizophrenia

After Pavlov became convinced that the study of experimental neurosis in animals would illuminate human psychopathology, he began to make regular visits to the psychiatric hospital near Leningrad to observe patients, hoping to explain schizophrenia in Pavlovian terms. His attention was captured by certain symptoms of the patients: apathy, dullness, immobility, stereotypy, and negativism on the one hand, and playfulness, unconventionality, and childish behavior on the other. Immediately he was reminded of the "hypnotic" phenomena he had studied in his dogs. By hypnosis, Pavlov meant an intermediate state between wakefulness and sleep. Whereas the cortical processes of excitation were presumed to be constantly at work during the waking state, sleep was characterized by inhibition that spread in waves over the cortex. Hypnosis referred to an incomplete sleep, a partial cortical inhibition. Pavlov found that he could induce hypnosis in his laboratory dogs by continuously presenting to them the same stimulus.

Pavlov noted that in the early phases of laboratory hypnosis the dogs lost their reactions to strong stimuli but continued reacting to the weak. This laboratory phenomenon had an analogue in the clinic: a schizophrenic patient might fail to respond to questions stated in usual voice but respond to whispered questions. The dog's refusal of food when it was offered and its turning toward food when it was removed was a parallel to schizophrenic negativism.

One of the most extreme symptoms of schizophrenia, stereotypic repetition of the same movements, also had its analogue in dogs. Most alert, conditioned dogs habitually licked the front of their bodies and paws during a food experiment. Early in hypnosis, this licking was prolonged greatly; sometimes it lasted until the next feeding. Other stereotypic movements were also repeated by the animal.

Theoretically, Pavlov viewed chronic hypnosis, characterized by inhibition, as an integral component of schizophrenia. According to Pavlov, intense or prolonged stimulation of the nervous system induces a state of protective inhibition. The term *protective* is used because the inhibition protects the cells from further stimulation, which would be harmful to them. The price paid for this protection is schizophrenia. Protective inhibition can be caused by situations (e.g., stress) as well as by constitutional weakness of the nervous system. A weak nervous system is more likely than a strong one to become overstimulated, to defend itself with protective inhibition, and to eventually succumb to schizophrenia. The notion, popular in the 1930s, that sleep therapy should benefit schizophrenics followed directly the Pavlovian notion of schizophrenia (Lynn, 1963). Various Western investigators have suggested disorders of arousal that are conceptually similar to Pavlov's theory of schizophrenia (Lynn, 1962; Venables, 1960).

The Pavlovian hypothesis has provided the impetus to many Russian investigators for studying schizophrenics in the laboratory. These are their principal empirical findings (Lynn, 1963):

1. Two types of schizophrenics appear to exist, a majority characterized by low sympathetic tone and hyporeactivity, as measured by pulse rate, respiration rate, blood pressure, and pupil diameter, and a minority with unusually high sympathetic tone and hyperreactivity. The first group consists mainly of catatonic and simple schizophrenics, whereas the second group consists of acute and agitated patients, particularly paranoids.

2. Electroencephalogram (EEG) patterns indicate lower arousal in schizophrenics than in normal people. However, many investigators in the West have failed to find EEG differences between schizophrenics and normal people (Brackbill, 1956).

3. Various motor conditioning procedures have been employed in which the subject was instructed to respond to a stimulus and was reinforced verbally for correct performance. Speed of conditioning was impaired in all schizophrenics and was more greatly impaired in catatonics than in paranoids.

The Russian research on schizophrenia represents one of the most concerted efforts to appraise an animal model of psychopathology. The degree to which we wish to accept the model depends on the degree to which we accept the Pavlovian theory of brain function. According to Lynn, the Russian researchers think the results fit reasonably well with Pavlovian notions of schizophrenia. Unfortunately, because of the inaccessibility of much of the Russian literature, this is difficult for us to evaluate.

Gantt: Schizokinesis and Autokinesis

Pavlov's work on experimental neurosis inspired American contributions to this field in the early 1940s. W. Horsley Gantt (1944), like Pavlov, became interested in experimental neurosis as the result of a laboratory accident. One weekend, about 15 dogs escaped from their cages and roamed the building, barking and fighting. Following their escapade, several dogs showed disturbances of their conditioned reflexes and of other behavior such as passivity. Gantt then decided to study the experimental procedures that had caused the disturbances. Nick, the neurotic dog, was a subject in one of these studies.

Nick was a normal, playful male mongrel, three years old, when he first was studied in the laboratory. He was slow to acquire conditioned salivation. Then he began to refuse food when he was required to make an auditory discrimination. Eventually, all conditioned reflexes deteriorated and the dog's behavior became quite bizarre. Although Nick would not eat in the experimental room, the farther he was moved from it, the more readily he would eat. His sex behavior became abnormal. For no apparent reason, when Nick was in the presence of people who had previously experimented with him, or when he was given food of the kind used in the original experiment he experienced penile erections and ejaculations. Furthermore, he urinated frequently—20 times in 30 minutes—when brought into the experimental room.

Nick's abnormalities were studied for 12 years. Rests in the country seemed therapeutic because his anxiety and stereotyped responses were subsequently lessened in the experimental room. Nick died in a fight in 1944, but he was studied more closely than any other animal in the conditioned reflex literature. The anecdotal nature of this report, however, makes it little more than a well-documented case history.

Gantt's more recent research has led to his formulation of two principles of psychopathological development: *schizokinesis* and *autokinesis* (Gantt,

1953a, 1962, 1971). The concept of schizokinesis evolved from experiments on dogs that showed that cardiac components of conditioned responses are often formed more rapidly and are more resistant to extinction than motor or secretory ones. Schizokinesis refers to discrepancy between the emotional (visceral) components of the conditioned response and the external, skeletal components. Such a discrepancy might be maladaptive when, for example, an animal or person appropriately refrains from making a skeletal response but persists with an emotional response such as rapid heart beat to a stimulus that no longer predicts danger. Edwards and Acker (1962) found that World War II veterans retained a galvanic skin response (GSR) to their wartime battle signals for as long as 15 years after the war.

Autokinesis is a progressive, internal development of responses in the absence of further external stimulation. Strictly speaking, negative autokinesis refers to downhill development and positive autokinesis to improvement. Gantt inferred negative autokinesis because Nick developed new neurotic symptoms such as respiratory difficulties long after the original experimental manipulation. A single therapeutic experience that profoundly influenced someone's life would be an example of positive autokinesis. Because Gantt focused experimentation on schizokinesis rather than autokinesis, the remainder of this section will be devoted to schizokinesis.

Unfortunately, Gantt's formulation of the theoretical relationship between schizokinesis and psychopathology was rather imprecise. For example, he did not specify whether schizokinesis itself causes or predisposes one to psychopathology. Nor is it clear whether schizokinesis is merely a symptom or a correlate of the psychopathological process—or neither. Has schizokinesis been shown to have a role in psychopathology? Bridger and Gantt (1956) attempted to answer this question by administering mescaline to dogs and looking for evidence of schizokinesis. Because mescaline was thought to produce schizophrenia-like behavior in animals and men, they thought that study of schizokinesis in dogs under the influence of mescaline would illuminate the role of schizokinesis in human schizophrenia.

They used a simple differential conditioning paradigm with four dogs for their study. The conditioned stimuli (CS) were two tones, T_{256} and T_{512}, separated by an octave. The unconditioned stimulus (US), a shock applied to the skin, produced flexion of the foreleg and cardiac changes—the unconditioned responses (UR). T_{256}, the positive stimulus, was always followed by shock, whereas T_{512} was never followed by shock. Conditioning was soon established, and the four dogs learned to flex their forelegs and to undergo cardiac changes to T_{256} and never to T_{512}. These responses remained stable during control periods of saline injection.

When the dogs were injected with mescaline, marked changes occurred. Although the motor CR remained relatively intact, the cardiac response dropped out completely. This example of schizokinesis is unusual in that the motor response persisted longer than the emotional response. To ensure that this result was specific to mescaline, two of the dogs were injected with morphine. Under morphine the cardiac response persisted while the motor response dropped out.

Given the more recent abandonment of mescaline psychosis as a model of schizophrenia, Gantt's study does little to illuminate the role of schizokinesis in schizophrenia. Broadhurst (1973) recently suggested that the value of the concept of schizokinesis was that it led to testable deductions concerning the speed of development of visceral versus skeletal conditioning, a dichotomy that has assumed importance in the context of current attempts to operantly condition autonomic functions. (See Schwartz, this volume, pp. 270–307).

Liddell: Conditioned Reflex Method and Experimental Neurosis

Like Pavlov and Gantt, H.S. Liddell at Cornell University became interested in experimental neurosis as the result of serendipity in the laboratory (Liddell, 1944; 1956). Having found that thyroidectomy had little effect on maze learning in sheep and goats, he turned to conditioned reflex methods. Because these animals slobbered continuously, the salivary reflex was difficult to use. Liddell used instead a motor response to an electric shock applied to the animal's foreleg.

During the first experiments on the effect of thyroidectomy on the conditioned reflex, a sheep began to exhibit abnormal behavior similar to that of the experimental neurosis Pavlov had described. As time passed, Liddell became less interested in the effects of thyroidectomy on conditioning and more preoccupied with experimental neurosis per se.

The longer Liddell studied the conditioned reflex method, the more convinced he became that the method itself was traumatic. According to Liddell, the daily period of "self-imposed restraint" by the sheep in the conditioning laboratory, and the monotonous repetition of stimuli followed by trivial reinforcement, were sufficient to lead to breakdowns in behavior. To support his claims, Liddell made daily observations of his sheep, watching some for as long as 14 years. The following account illustrates the progressive change in the laboratory and barnyard behavior of an animal subjected to prolonged conditioning.

On the first day of conditioning the sheep or goat was placed in the Pavlovian frame with loops under its limbs that allowed movement but prevented locomotion. Shocks that were startling but not painful were applied to its foreleg. Early in training the animal's behavior was irregular; the animal experienced bursts of activity during shock stimulations as well as between them. As training progressed, however, the animal's behavior became more episodic. Flexion occurred in response to the signal predicting shock. The animal's physiological responses such as respiration and pulse also changed. Following shock, a state of quiet ensued, and breathing and pulse returned to resting levels.

When it was this well trained, the animal came willingly to the laboratory. In fact, among the goats, those that were in training customarily separated themselves from the other animals at testing time. As training continued, the animals began to engage in rather strange behavior—they stiffened their tested limb, they became very agitated, and they resisted entry to the laboratory. Signs of their experimental neurosis ranged from somnolence, inertness, and immobility to hypersensitivity and overactivity.

Vacations from the laboratory proved therapeutic for some of Liddell's animals. Various sedatives produced beneficial, but transient, effects. Finally, "spontaneous remission" was observed in some animals (Anderson and Parmenter, 1941).

It is difficult to evaluate Liddell's view that "self-imposed restraint" with subsequent "loss of freedom" caused experimental neurosis. Because the theory is formulated in such vague terms, it is difficult to design experiments to test it. Parmenter (1940) did show that lack of the restraining harness changed responses in a normal veteran sheep. The idea behind abandoning the restraining harness was to increase the sheep's freedom. Whereas the response of the sheep was episodic and stereotyped when restrained, it became *less* episodic when the animal had liberty of locomotion. We would still want to know whether lack of the restraining harness reduced the experimental neurosis of a neurotic sheep. In general, Liddell's experimental analysis was not thorough enough and his conceptual framework not clear enough for us to evaluate his theory adequately.

Although Liddell was rather hesitant about calling the maladaptive behavior of his animals *neurotic*, it is clear from his later writings that he thought it had relevance for human psychopathology (1944, 1956). He undertook one major study to ascertain whether the experimental neuroses of his animals were similar to human neuroses (Liddell, 1956). Theoretically, breakdowns should occur in humans subjected to conditions of self-imposed restraint in monotonous environments. Humans should go through the same or similar stages as did the sheep. Liddell noted that three signs in his animals presaged the approach of breakdowns. The first sign was the stage of "prophylactic caution," in which the animal "feared to do the wrong thing." Another sign of impending breakdown was "oscillating" emotional behavior. For example, a middle-aged formerly inoffensive ewe snatched off the experimenter's spectacles as he knelt to attach the electrodes to her foreleg. The third sign, which consisted of "peculiar" behavior, occurred almost at the point of breakdown. Unfortunately, Liddell was not very explicit in defining "prophylactic caution," "oscillating" emotional behavior, and "peculiar" behavior, and it is difficult to distinguish one from the other.

In the fall of 1952, Liddell interviewed officers and enlisted men who had completed their service in Korea—"self-imposed restraint"[2]—and were about to board ship for home. Later, Liddell interviewed soldiers at a mobile army surgical hospital unit near the central front and at other medical installations. His goal was to determine whether soldiers approaching their neurotic breakdowns went through the same three stages as did the animals.

Liddell said he found that combat veterans recognized certain warning signs of emotional difficulties in their comrades. These appeared to be the same signs that the animals exhibited preceding emotional breakdown. The counterpart of prophylactic caution in animals was the excessive caution exhibited by front-line soldiers during their last month of duty. Oscillation of emotional behavior was often seen in soldiers going into combat for the first time. Finally, according to Liddell's information, after protracted exposure to the combat zone and repeated combat experience, the soldier's behavior sometimes became "peculiar" or unfamiliar.

The study is wholly unconvincing in demonstrating similarity between the animal and human phenomena. But at least it is an attempt to find similarity between animal and human neuroses. Etiology is not addressed directly by the study, but a useful design would have included comparison of settings in which self-imposed restraint and monotony were present and were absent. If Liddell's theory of neurosis were correct, a lower incidence of neuroses would be expected in the second setting. Furthermore, it is not clear from the study what percentage of soldiers exhibiting the three signs of impending breakdown actually broke down and what percentage of soldiers who broke down did not exhibit the three signs. No compelling evidence exists that Liddell's animal phenomenon models any human neurosis.

Masserman: Motivational Conflicts

Jules Masserman (1943, 1971) approached experimental neurosis in animals from a psychoanalytic viewpoint. According to Masserman (1943), four biodynamic principles guide behavior: (1) all behavior is fundamentally motivated by the physiologic requirements of the organism, (2) behavior is adaptive, (3) behavior is symbolic, and (4) when physical inadequacies, environmental stresses, or motivational conflicts exceed an organism's capacities for adaption then behavior becomes hesitant, inefficient, inappropriate, or excessively symbolic. In short, the behavior becomes neurotic.[3] Masserman studied experimental neuroses in cats in an attempt to test Principle 4.

---

[2] Perhaps the reader would not call military service "self-imposed". As with sheep, however, Liddell used the phrase "self-imposed restraint" for situations in which the subject had to exercise restraint regardless of whether he chose to be there.

[3] More recently Masserman (1971) has made the neurosis-generating conflict conditions of Principle 4 part of the broader category of unpredictability and uncontrollability.

To produce experimental neuroses in cats, what he here called "phobias," Masserman (1943) devised a laboratory conflict between two motivations. To do this he subjected cats to an air blast or a grid shock at the moment of feeding. First, the cats were taught to associate a signal with the delivery of food into the food box of the apparatus. Blasts of air were then applied across the food box either at the moment the animal opened the lid or immediately afterward, as the cat was about to feed. In other experiments, several electric shocks were given through the grid floor of the cage during the feeding signals or at the moment of food taking. Finally, some cats were subjected to both air blasts and grid shocks simultaneously. Under these three conditions of conflicting motivations, the cats showed a number of changes in behavior: changes in spontaneous activity; phobic responses to the feeding signals such as crouching, hiding, attempts to escape from the apparatus, and pulse and respiration patterns indicative of fear; "counterphobic" behavior patterns consisting of stereotyped behaviors; and "regressive" behaviors such as preening and playing.

Control observations were made to determine whether hungry cats become neurotic if their path to the box was blocked, if the lid was locked, or if food rewards were presented randomly. The observations suggested that under these conditions the animals did not become neurotic. In other control experiments, six cats were exposed to an unsignaled air blast at irregular intervals. Although the cats showed anxiety and fear—they tried to escape from the apparatus, they experienced rapid and irregular pulse and respiration, and they trembled—these disturbances eventually dissipated.

The so-called neurotic behavior patterns persisted for many months if they went untreated, but various procedures were found somewhat effective in ameliorating them. Therapy techniques consisted of lowering the hunger drive; handling and petting by the experimenter ("transference therapy" according to Masserman); forcing the cat to eat the food after it is mechanically moved closer and closer to the food box with no avenue of escape; modeling a normal cat eating in the presence of the food signal; and allowing the cat manipulative control over some relevant aspect of the experiment. Although formal control groups were not used in the therapy studies, 30 of 37 neurotic cats showed the same abnormal behavior after rest periods when not given therapy as they had on the last day of the experiment. Mere passage of time did not appear therapeutic.

In later studies, Masserman and his colleagues demonstrated therapeutic effects of alcohol (Masserman and Yum, 1946; Masserman et al., 1944), electroconvulsive shock (Masserman et al., 1950; Masserman and Jacques, 1947), and brain lesions (Masserman and Pechtel, 1956).

Questioning the experimental analysis employed by Masserman, Wolpe (1958) conducted similar experiments. In brief, Wolpe argued that the neuroses of Masserman's cats were not produced by motivational conflicts, but by shock alone. He was able to show that a cat shocked in the apparatus developed the same behavioral changes regardless of its motivation at the time of shock.

In turn, Wolpe's conclusions were questioned because the cats that experienced no conflict had received a greater number of shocks than the cats that experienced conflict. Smart (1965) trained groups of cats to press a lever to obtain food and subsequently gave them four equal shock sessions. There were three groups: (1) a conflict-preconsummatory group, shocked as they approached food, (2) a conflict-consummatory group, shocked one second after they began eating, and (3) a non-conflict group, not shocked for 30 seconds while eating on a given trial. Smart found that all groups became equally neurotic and therefore concluded, as Wolpe had, that conflict was not essential for the development of experimental neuroses.

Recently, Dmitruk (1974) reopened this issue and argued that the relationship of conflict to experimental neuroses in cats was unresolved by Smart's experiment because all three of Smart's groups can be considered conflict groups. Dmitruk also questioned the very existence of the experimental neurosis by suggesting that any abnormal behavior observed in the conditioning apparatus might be an artifact of confinement. In order to conclude that some experimental manipulation produces neurotic behavior it is necessary to know the normal activities of animals confined in a conditioning apparatus. Dmitruk contended that responses emitted by cats following lever training for food reward were not representative of their customary responses in confinement. Specifically, unreinforced responses would be extinguished during training. The introduction of aversive stimulation might have increased the frequency of these responses (i.e., disinhibited them). Dmitruk speculated that because Masserman, Smart, and Wolpe recorded their baseline measures *following* lever training for food, disinhibited normal responses may have been mistaken for symptoms of neurosis. To test his confinement hypothesis, Dmitruk compared the behavior of cats exposed to the sort of conflict specified by Masserman to that of cats simply confined (neither shocked nor fed) in the conditioning apparatus for the same length of time. All cats were observed on five separate occasions before the conflict to determine base rates of the behaviors subsequently used as indexes of neurosis. No differences existed between the groups. Dmitruk concluded Masserman's findings had resulted from artifacts of the experimental procedures. In its experimental analysis, great controversy surrounds Masserman's phenomenon.

What evidence favors the notion that Masserman modeled real human neuroses in his laboratory? Masserman's data demonstrating that treatments effective in human neuroses were also effective with neurotic cats is the main body of support. The preventive action of certain drugs, such as alcohol, certainly has a human analogue in the "bracer" effect! But the model's etiology is hardly analogous to that of human neuroses. Furthermore, claims of symptom similarity between cat and human neuroses generally were unpersuasive. Are the properties of the "phobic" response of cats really similar to the properties of the human phobias? For example, are some objects more likely than others to become phobic? Such questions have not been addressed in experiments; and the model is lacking both in experimental analysis and in proof of similarity to the human case.

Maier: Experimental Neurosis and Frustration Concepts

N. R. F. Maier attempted to explain the experimental neuroses described by Pavlov, Gantt, Liddell, and Masserman as frustration-instigated behavior (Maier, 1949). Maier argued that a clear-cut distinction exists between frustrated (without a goal) and motivated behavior. According to Maier, "abnormal fixations" produced by frustration cannot be explained by traditional learning theory. Once an animal or human has been frustrated, its behavior becomes very rigid and incapable of modification by conventional learning techniques.

Maier's theory developed from a series of experiments in which insoluble problems were presented to laboratory rats. In most experiments the Lashley jumping stand was used. Here the rat is placed on a stand in front of two cards between which he must learn to discriminate. During the course of training, the rat learns to express a preference for one of the cards by jumping at and striking it. If the rat strikes the correct card, it falls over and he gains access to food. If the rat jumps at the incorrect card, it remains locked in place and the rat, having suffered a bump on the nose, falls to a net below (punishment). The rat soon learns and consistently chooses the card leading to reward. Rats can also be taught to learn to always strike one location. Because the jumping is determined by its consequences in these two cases, Maier said it was goal motivated.

In the insoluble problem, rats are forced with an air blast to respond on the Lashley jumping platform even though the cards are locked in random order (no particular card or position is consistently rewarded). No response can consistently avoid punishment. The rats' behavior typically becomes rigid and stereotyped, and jumps come to be made in only one direction. When the problem is then made soluble, many rats fail to recognize the solution and continue to jump to a given side. Maier referred to this behavior as "abnormal fixation" and regarded frustration as its cause. Because not all rats faced with the insoluble problem developed fixations, Maier inferred individual differences in frustration thresholds. Maier made extensive use of this bimodal distribution in attacking his critics.

In reviewing the experimental neurosis literature, Maier (1949) concluded that the experiments contained methods for inducing frustration. Like responses produced by recognized frustration paradigms, the behavior of experimentally neurotic animals was unadaptive in that it was compulsive and lacked goal orientation. Rather than assert that all frustrated animals were neurotic, Maier argued that the frustration established in the experiment generalized to other situations and reduced the threshold for future frustration in the animals.

Predictably, a flurry of papers attempting to explain "frustration-instigated" behavior by conventional learning principles soon appeared after publication of Maier's book *Frustration* (1949). Taken together, the papers argued that in explaining the development of abnormal fixations Maier overlooked the possible contribution of factors familiar to learning theory.

Dollard and Miller (1950) contended that fixations were caused by rats' attempts to escape punishment (air blast) on the jumping stand. They noted that rats in the insoluble condition were rewarded on every trial by escape from the air blast regardless of where they jumped. Because the air-blast schedule was retained in the soluble phase, it maintained a response now deemed incorrect by the experimenter, but still reinforced from the rat's point of view.

Maier's (1956) reply to the escape-from-punishment argument was that it could not account for the bimodal distribution of scores. Why would only some rats be affected by escape from punishment?

In another attempt to explain Maier's data with conventional learning principles, Wilcoxon (1952) argued that in addition to nondifferential reinforcement (which frustrated the rat, according to Maier), a partial reinforcement factor was involved in the insoluble problem since a response was rewarded 50 percent of the time (and punished 50 percent of the time). Wilcoxon designed an experiment to isolate the effects of partial versus non-differential reinforcement using the same apparatus and general method as Maier. Three groups of rats were trained on an initial habit under different training conditions. The first group was trained to hold a position under conditions of invariable reward for the correct response and invariable punishment (the rat bumped his nose on the card and fell into the net) for the incorrect response (continuous reinforcement). The second group was trained to hold a position under conditions by which the correct response was rewarded half the time and punished the other half, and the incorrect response was punished when it occurred (partial reinforcement of the correct response). The third group received training in which any response resulted in reward on half the trials and punishment on the other half (insoluble problem). All rats were then tested on a new response that required them to abandon what they had learned. Whereas Maier ignored the contribution of the partial reinforcement to the development of abnormal fixations, Wilcoxon found it to be of primary importance—more rats fixated in the partial reinforcement condition than in the insoluble condition. Finally, fixations were unlearned by techniques based on learning principles without use of the manual guidance Maier had used.

Maier (1956) argued that Wilcoxon's experiment was not crucial because the partial reinforcement group received more punishment than the other two groups and thus, according to frustration theory, should develop more fixations. Maier contended further that partial reinforcement could not account for the bimodal distribution of scores obtained with groups because partial reinforcement effects should apply to all members of a group.

A word in general is necessary about Maier's bimodal distribution argument. Although, as Maier pointed out, neither escape from punishment nor partial reinforcement predicts the bimodal distribution, it is not clear that frustration theory does either: the notion of individual differences in frustration threshold was inferred from the bimodal distribution itself. The distribution phenomenon seems a weak argument against the more traditional interpretations.

More recently, Karsh (1970) has convincingly shown that fixations develop in the absence of frustration. She trained three groups of rats on a reversal learning procedure. Rats were trained to respond by choosing one of two levers presented simultaneously and pressing it. Pressing the correct lever was always followed by food, but the consequences of pressing the incorrect lever differed for the three groups. In the extinction (E) group, the incorrect response was followed by neither reward (food) nor punishment (shock). In the punishment-extinction (PE) group, shock followed the incorrect response. Finally, both shock and food followed the incorrect response in the conflict (C) group. Rats in all groups learned to press the correct lever. However, when the reward lever was reversed, all rats in the conflict group perseverated with the now incorrect lever whereas none of the rats in the other two groups developed fixations. Karsh argued that strong frustration, which presumably caused fixations in Maier's rats, was absent here because the rats had free choice between a rewarded alternative and an alternative both rewarded and punished.

Maier's basic work raised many issues that have not yet been resolved satisfactorily. The relationship of his work to experimental neuroses is even less clear. In the absence of an adequate account of frustration-instigated behavior, speculation about generalized frustration and lowered frustration thresholds in the experimental neuroses paradigms is premature.

Summary

Over the course of the twentieth century a new approach to the study of psychopathology, that of the experimental model, has emerged. The legacy left by early modelers of psychopathology is not their specific models, but rather the approach they forged. Indeed, our historical survey suggests that the early attempts to model psychopathology in the laboratory were not very convincing. The methods used to evaluate human models seemed adequate; however, much of the early animal experimentation was disappointing. The dangerous temptation to many animal modelers of psychopathology has been to gain hasty satisfaction with crude similarities between a dramatic breakdown of animal behavior and some human psychiatric disorder. Perhaps because the animal's behavior appeared so strikingly maladaptive, experimenters were convinced of its relationship to human disorders. In retrospect, general features of psychopathology, such as aggressiveness and passivity, rather than specific disorders, probably were modeled by the early animal studies. More sophisticated approaches are called for because animal models have the virtue of allowing both precise control over heredity and experience and the opportunity to constantly monitor the disorder. Relative ease of modeling various human psychopathologies in animals may offer clues about what aspects of human functioning are unique to humans.

Bidirectional Influences of Emotionality, Stimulus Responsivity, and Metabolic Events in Obesity

Judith Rodin
Yale University

Description of Obesity

Hunger

To understand obesity, we must begin with a brief review of hunger and the regulation of feeding. As anyone who has gone without food for any length of time can attest, hunger can be a powerful motivator. The body needs an adequate supply of essential nutrients in order to function efficiently. But what mechanisms determine the proper regulation of food intake?

Brain Centers. Many of the neural control systems that regulate feeding are integrated in a region of the brain called the hypothalamus. Two hypothalamic areas appear to be most directly a part of food intake: a region near the ventromedial hypothalamus (VMH) influences satiety by signaling that enough has been eaten. Destruction of this region leads to gross obesity in humans and animals (Anand, 1961; Brobeck, 1946; Brooks, Lockwood, and Wiggins, 1946; Hetherington and Ranson, 1940). A lateral but less well-defined region anatomically—the lateral hypothalamus (LH)—is responsible for integrating food seeking behavior. Its destruction leads to a loss of appetite. Rather than there being two anatomically distinct centers that

The author's research reported here was supported in part by NSF Grant GS-37953.

regulate feeding, however, recent neurochemical evidence has suggested that the monoamine pathways that travel through these regions and extrahypothalomic sites as well play a crucial role in food intake (Marshall, 1975).

Inputs to the Brain that are Important for Feeding. What is the nature of the information relevant to feeding used by brain regions to initiate and terminate eating? First, constituents of the ingested diet may influence feeding by changing the rates at which certain neurotransmitters are synthesized. The two neurotransmitters that now appear to be most dependent on food are acetylcholine and serotonin. For example, the consumption of a single meal containing carbohydrate but lacking protein markedly accelerates serotonin synthesis (Wurtman and Fernstrom, 1974). These diet-induced changes in neurotransmitters might provide channels by which the brain could couple feeding strategies to nutritional state.

Second, sensory stimuli such as the taste and sight of food have been shown through electrophysiological studies by Rolls et al. (1975) to trigger firing of hypothalamic neurons. The brain regions that regulate feeding may be directly responsive to sensory, food-relevant stimuli.

Third, the brain is sensitive to chemical stimulation. Anand, Sharma, and Dua (1964) and Oomura (1975) have reported glucosensitive neurons in the VMH and LH. The functional role of these glucosensitive neurons in feeding behavior has not been well established, however. A comparable statement can be made about the role of temperature. Although there are "thermoreceptors" in the hypothalamus, it is not clear whether changes in brain temperature before and during feeding are correlated with food intake (Grossman, 1975).

Fourth, the brain may sense information about adipose tissue stores, directly by means of neural or chemical feedback from fat deposits or indirectly through the influence of fat stores on metabolic events.

Peripheral Factors in the Regulation of Feeding

Gastrointestinal (GI) factors. The ingestion of food may inhibit food intake in one of three ways. First, distention of the GI tract during ingestion of food may activate neural pathways to the brain. If food is injected directly into the stomach of a hungry animal (without passing through the mouth and throat) the animal eats much less than it would otherwise (Smith and Duffy, 1955). Experiments suggest that cells in the VMH respond to distention of the stomach by inhibiting further eating (Kennedy, 1953). An empty stomach produces periodic contractions of muscles in the stomach wall that we identify as hunger pangs. This increased movement of the stomach wall has been shown to activate cells in the LH. Second, ingestion of food may trigger the release of hormones from the GI tract or elsewhere. Gibbs, Young, and Smith (1973) have recently suggested that the GI hormone cholecystokinin may function as a satiety signal. Third, early absorption of nutrients may signal an end to eating. After digestion, the macro and micro nutrients are absorbed across the GI tract and they enter the portal circulation. Glucose might then influence subsequent food intake. Recent findings (Novin, VanderWeele, and Rezek, 1973) have suggested that glucoreceptors in the liver may transmit messages related to acute changes in nutritional state to the brain through the vagus nerve. There also appear to be glucoreceptors in the duodenum and the hypothalamus.

Hormonal Factors. Woods, Decke, and Vasselli (1974) have reviewed the possible role of insulin in the control of food intake. They found that if rats are injected regularly with insulin, their food intake and body weight increase. The effect of insulin could result from peripheral hypoglycemia or from a direct action of insulin on the central nervous system. Evidence of the latter, however, is conflicting (cf., Oomura, 1975; Panksepp, 1974). Estrogens and growth hormone also appear to influence food intake.

Nutrients. Food intake is influenced directly by a variety of qualitative and quantitative changes in diet composition. Among these are changes in the caloric density of the diet (Adolph, 1947), changes in the osmotic pressure exerted by diet components (Harper and Spivey, 1958), and changes in the proportions of major nutrients in the diet (Cowgill, 1928). Deficits of essential nutrients (Chesters and Will, 1973; Frazier et al., 1947), excesses of some nutrients (Harper, Benevenga, and Wohlheuter, 1970), and the presence of unpalatable or toxic substances in the diet (Richter, 1953) also influence food intake.

Environmental and Social Variables

Taste and smell play an important role in our eating enjoyment and food preferences. They may also contribute to the physiological regulation of food intake by actually changing perceived pleasurability in response to changes in short-term satiety cues (Cabanac, Minnaire, and Adair, 1968; Jacobs and Sharma, 1969; Rodin, Moskowitz, and Bray, 1976).

Stimuli outside the organism can also influence hunger and eating behavior. We walk past a bakery right after a meal and find ourselves hungry for the piece of cake in the window. The signal for hunger in this case is unrelated to the depletion of nutrients in the body or to stomach pangs. The actual sight of food (external stimuli) can arouse hunger even when there is no physiological need. Responsiveness to external stimuli plays an important role in obesity and we shall consider it at length later in the chapter.

Habits and social customs can also influence feeding. If we are accustomed to eating lunch at 12 P.M. we may suddenly feel hungry when the clock strikes noon. Great quantities of food are consumed at a Thanksgiving dinner because the occasion itself is centered on the meal. Food selection by humans is also greatly determined by cultural constraints or cuisine. Cuisines are sets of practices concerning basic foods, the flavors added to these foods in preparation, and special constraints such as taboos.

Long-term Control of Food Intake

Most wild animals maintain about the same weight throughout their adult lifetimes, despite the fact that food may be plentiful one week and scarce the next. Human beings have greater difficulty maintaining a constant weight, presumably because their eating behavior is more strongly influenced by emotional and social factors. Even so, studies (Comstock and Stone, 1972; Chinn, Garrow, and Miall, 1974) have indicated that many people stay at about the same weight from year to year, and it has been proposed that total energy reserves are regulated over the long term (Baile and Forbes, 1972; Hirsch, 1972; Lepovsky, 1973). The mechanism by which this would occur is not yet clearly understood but the way in which the regulatory control goes awry in obesity must be due to at least one of three factors: regulation of food ingestion, the distribution and storage of calories, and the control of energy expenditure.

Obesity

Obesity is essentially the easiest of all pathologies to describe and recognize. It can simply be defined as an excess quantity of fat in the body. Obesity is a visible consequence of ingesting more calories than the body uses for energy.

Of all human frailties, obesity is perhaps the most perverse. The penalties are so severe, the gratification so limited, and the remedy so simple, that obesity should be the most trivial of aberrations to correct. Yet it is among the most recalcitrant. Almost any fat person can lose weight; few can keep it off. It is this fact that makes the study of obesity so intriguing.

There must be an optimal amount of fat in the body, and this optimum is determined in interaction with the environmental conditions: fatness is a conditional state. For example, a person preparing for an emergency trek, or a population preparing for famine, has physiological advantages from excess stored fat. However, in a food-abundant society such as ours, excessive storage of fat is nonadaptive and pathological. In this society, obesity is associated with a number of chronic physical diseases and several psychopathological symptoms. Insurance statistics show that heavier people have a higher mortality rate than lighter peers. This suggests that excess weight has a detrimental impact on longevity. The psychological effects of obesity are as disabling as any physiological effect, because they often are the major cause of an obese person's unhappiness. The effects range from mild feelings of inferiority to serious incapacities that occur when obesity acts as a bar to normal social and sexual activity. Many consequences of obesity are the direct result of negative social views, for obesity is commonly regarded as a mark of poor self-discipline and chaotic personality structure; in short, a state verging on crime, rather than a disease.

How many people are obese? The U.S. Public Health Service (1966) reports that from 25 to 45 percent of the adult American population over 30 years of age is more than 20 percent overweight and therefore classified as obese. For childhood obesity, defined as 40 percent or more above the median weight for a given height, there is an incidence of 2 to 15 percent. Obesity is not equally prevalent among all segments of society. Studies (Moore, Stunkard, and Srole, 1962; Srole et al., 1962) have shown that obesity is seven times more common in the lowest socioeconomic group than in the highest, and the difference is particularly marked among women. Variations in the prevalence of obesity among different social classes are more likely to reflect general social attitudes and the high caloric value of cheaper food than individual metabolic disorders or psychological disturbances. There is evidence showing that at any time twice as many women in the upper social classes as in the lower are dieting to lose weight (Dwyer, Feldman, and Mayer, 1970; McKenzie, 1967).

Differences in patterns of distribution of obesity also highlight the point that obesity is far from homogeneous; instead, it is a manifestation of several abnormalities. These may be categorized as environmental, psychodynamic, and physiologic (including metabolic, neural, and genetic). As an added complication, these abnormalities frequently interact. Consequently, obesity has been described by specialists in so many diverse areas that the literature on it reads like the blind men describing an elephant, each touching a different part of the elephant's body. Yet each of these elements—emotional reactivity and depression, metabolic and endocrine disorders, adipose tissue composition, genetic propensity, and heightened responsiveness to environmental food cues coupled with inattention to internal hunger and satiety signals—characterizes the pathology known as obesity. Laboratory models of obesity and more sophisticated techniques to study the spontaneously occurring state through change allow us to consider critically the contribution of each element to the development and maintenance of obesity.

In the following sections, I will describe the elements presumed to be of etiological significance and then review the major efforts to study them experimentally. The difficulty with this research lies in the fact that there are different kinds and degrees of obesity. Therefore, sampling is always a problem. If a moderately overweight group is studied, will the results necessarily apply to the massively obese? One way to reduce this problem is to test several different weight groups in order to see to whom the findings apply. This technique allows us to determine not only how generalizable the experimental results are but also whether the causes of obesity are unitary.

Many good studies use within-subject designs, in which the same person is tested at least twice. For example, obese people can be studied before and after weight reduction, normal weight people before and after weight gain, or newborn infants, at birth and then again later. Variation due to individual difference can thus be controlled.

Work with animals is also crucial to the understanding of human obesity because it allows so many more experimental interventions. Again, we must question whether results can simply be generalized to include humans. However, except for psychodynamic factors, many of the variables correlated with human obesity are also present in animals.

Concepts of Psychological Disturbance

In 1816, Wadd wrote:

> If the increases of wealth and the refinement of modern times have tended to banish plague and pestilence from our cities, they have probably introduced the whole train of nervous disorders and increased the frequency of corpulence.

The view that obesity is related to psychological and social factors is by no means recent. The present position of those who hold emotional factors paramount in the etiology of obesity has recently been summarized by Kiell (1973):

> However obesity may be defined, there is now general agreement that persistence in overeating has its basis in unresolved emotional problems and that the overeating serves as a substitute for other satisfactions . . . [A] more enlightened outlook perceives the adipose person as the victim of social and unconscious forces which compel him to persist in a repetitive, self destructive pattern.

Several attempts have been made to categorize the specific types of emotional disturbances related to overeating and obesity. Hamburger (1951) suggested that there are people who overeat in response to emotional tensions that are essentially nonspecific—when they are lonely, anxious, or bored. Another group overeats during chronic states of tension and frustration, using food as a substitute gratification. These people live in unpleasant or intolerable conditions that continue over a long period of time. For a third group, overeating is a symptom of an underlying emotional illness, most frequently depression. For a fourth group, the overeating takes on the proportions of an addiction, and is characterized by compulsive, intensive craving for food, that does not seem related to external events or emotional upheavals.

These categories are in keeping with the psychoanalytic view that overeating probably represents an attempt to achieve substitute gratification or a defense against real or imagined anxiety resulting from various emotional conflicts (Burdon and Paul, 1951; Kaplan and Kaplan, 1957; Shorvan and Richardson, 1949). Berblinger's (1969) analysis of child development suggests that "the infant derives his first meaningful interpersonal contact with his mouth. The situation in which early nursing takes place may remain a distant memory trace and lead to the formation of habits that are maintained throughout one's life." Clinical studies report that the obese often experience psychological and social difficulties such as feelings of considerable social anxiety, alienation, low self-worth, mistrust, behavioral immaturity, and hypochondria (Craddock, 1969; Werkman and Greenberg, 1967).

Because not all obese people show signs of psychopathology, Bruch (1961, 1973) has categorized her obese patients according to their psychological adaptation. Each patient was evaluated for the functional significance of the obesity to his whole development, in particular to ability to adjust to life stress. She divided her observations into three main groups. First, there were many competent people who were overweight but whose weight excess was not related to abnormal psychological function. There were also patients in whom the obesity was related to psychological problems, the nature of which constitute the second and third groups: developmental obesity—where obesity was intrinsically interwoven with the whole development and was characterized by many features of personality disturbance—and reactive obesity—where people became obese as a reaction to some traumatic event.

Developmental obesity has its onset in childhood and Bruch contends that in this syndrome the disturbances result from problems in early learning. She says that a functional deficit in the perceptual and conceptual awareness of hunger can develop because the experience of hunger is not innate, but partly learned. Incorrect and confusing early experiences can interfere with a person's ability to recognize hunger and satiation, and these experiences make it difficult to differentiate hunger from other signals of discomfort unrelated to food deprivation or from emotional tension aroused by a variety of conflicts and problems. Such people also have difficulty identifying not only hunger but also other bodily sensations.

Reactive obesity, in contrast to developmental, is the pattern of a more mature person. Instead of expressing or even experiencing emotions like anger or depression, the person overeats as a defense against deeper negative affect. People who use food to combat anxiety and loneliness are apt to become depressed when dieting is enforced. The immediate enjoyment of food serves as their reassurance that life still holds some satisfactions. People who have reactive obesity are apt to eat between meals, often quite impulsively, as soon as the idea strikes them that something might be tasty or enjoyable. Bruch calls the obesity of middle age typically reactive—it develops in response to psychological stress. Crisp (1970), and Mayer (1968) also think that reactive obesity stems from overeating as a compensating response for frustration and tension. Thus, whatever a handicap obesity may become, as a defensive reaction it is less destructive than suicidal, paralyzing deep depression. Psychological assessments often indicate that the obese score higher on measures of anxiety and emotionality than do people of normal weight (Pliner, Mayer, and Blankstein, 1974; Rodin, Elman, and Schachter, 1974). Burdon and Paul (1951) reiterate that obese people are not necessarily anxious or depressed, as eating tends to relieve feelings of anxiety or depression before they become organized. Therefore, eating is seen as a defensive behavior that helps keep potential depressives stable.

According to Stunkard and Mendelson (1967), of the many behavioral disturbances to which obese people are subject, only two seem specifically related to their obesity. The first is overeating, and the second is a disturbance in body image. The term *body image* refers to a person's perception of the physical appearance of his body. Disturbances of body image may range from gross depersonalization to distorted thoughts and feelings about the body (Cappon and Banks, 1968; Orbach, Traub, and Olson, 1966; Traub and Orbach, 1964). Stunkard and Mendelson say that body image disturbances do not occur in emotionally healthy obese persons. Instead, they are found only in a minority of neurotic obese people. The disturbance essentially is one of a negative self-image. For example, an obese woman says, "I call myself a slob and pig. I look in a mirror and I say 'You're nothing but a big fat pig.'" The private views that some obese people have about their bodies are frequently paralleled by an intense self-consciousness and even misperception of how others view them; they see weight as determining how other people respond to them (Rodin and Slochower, 1974). Obese people are particularly self-conscious with members of the opposite sex. However, disturbances in body image seem to be a consequence, rather than cause, of the obesity, for they occur primarily in people for whom obesity began in childhood and for whom there is real evidence of emotional disturbance (Stunkard and Mendelson, 1967). In fact, these disturbances appear comparable to disturbances reported among people suffering from deformities of the face, breasts, and genitals (MacGregor et al., 1953; Schonfeld, 1962).

Stunkard and Mendelson (1967) conclude that as they learn more about obesity they become more impressed with the need for specificity in linking neurosis and obesity. Many obese persons have serious neurotic problems; consequently, it has often been inferred that neurosis is the cause of the obesity. On methodological grounds alone, this is a shaky inference. Many studies reviewed by Louderback (1970) suggest that the majority of overweight people are quite psychologically normal. His review of the literature suggests that there is no positive correlation between overeating and neuroticism, although one exists between fear of obesity and neuroticism, often exemplified in anorexia nervosa. In lower socioeconomic groups where the norm is a mild degree of overweight, there is almost no association between obesity and mental ill health. Such an association occurs more frequently among women of the middle and upper classes, where the pressure to reduce is very intense. Shipman and Plesset (1963) found that their obese groups of subjects were not significantly more anxious or depressed than the normal samples with which they were matched, and Silverstone and Solomon (1965) showed over two-thirds of an obese population of women in England to be emotionally stable.

Even the work of people who favor psychiatric explanations of obesity suggests that psychodynamic causes are far from uniform, if they exist at all. It is not possible to speak of one basic personality type as characteristic for all obese people. Obesity may be associated with every conceivable psychiatric disorder, psychosis as well as neurosis. Furthermore, it is necessary to differentiate between psychological factors related to the development of obesity and those that are created by the obesity. Finally, certain emotional conflicts are precipitated by reducing. As mentioned before, in each phase, physiological and psychological factors interact and influence each other.

Let us summarize these descriptions in this way: no figures are available about the incidence, whether rare or frequent, of obesity associated with severe personality problems. In talking about obesity, whatever other subdivisions we choose to apply, there is need to differentiate between two basic groups, those who can follow a diet and function normally while doing so, and others who encounter serious difficulties or find it intolerable. The latter cases of obesity most typically come to a psychiatrist and therefore appear in psychiatric studies dealing with obesity. When studies are done using random sampling procedures, (not limiting the sample to people who come to a psychiatrist for help, and even avoiding those who come to a diet clinic or other diet group for help), there is no correlation between emotional disturbance and obesity (Stunkard and Mendelson, 1967). There are several types of disturbed obese people, but there are also several types of disturbed people of normal weight. Furthermore, most of the data collection on obesity and mental disorders is made through case histories or interviews rather than using laboratory procedures. In the following sections, we will investigate some of the laboratory studies devoted to examining three aspects of reported emotional differences between overweight and normal weight people: first, that overweight people are more emotionally reactive than normal weight people; second, that anxiety and depression lead to overeating and that eating reduces anxiety; third, that overeating and elevated body weight act to prevent depression and that when obese people reduce weight depression and other psychological disorders ensue.

Emotional Reactivity. To determine whether overweight people are hyperemotional, Rodin, Elman, and Schachter (1974) tested Columbia undergraduates—half obese, half of normal weight. The obese ranged from 15 to 63 percent overweight and normal participants from −9 to 8 percent overweight. In one experiment, subjects listened to one of two kinds of tapes: emotionally disturbing tapes, which for 10 minutes detailed either the bombing of Hiroshima or the subject's own death of leukemia, or emotionally neutral tapes, which were concerned with either rain or seashells. A few typical excerpts will allow the reader to judge the effectiveness of these tapes.

From Hiroshima:

Picture how the eyebrows of some were burnt off, and skin hung from their faces and hands. Others were vomiting as they walked.

Imagine trying to help someone, reaching down and grabbing him by the hands but not being able to hold him because his skin slipped off in huge, glovelike pieces into your hands.

From leukemia:

Imagine how you would feel if you could feel your body degenerating—a constant deterioration going on inside you that no one was able to stop or even slow down. You would have to be fed because you would be too weak to hold a fork. You would have to lie in bed because you would be too weak to hold up your own head.

Think about who in your family would help you, which of your friends would stand by you . . . How would your illness affect their lives. Who would feel inconvenienced and put upon? . . . Who would be glad to see you dying in great pain and suffering?

From neutral tapes:

Think about all the varied shapes and colors of shells you've seen. Think about seeing them along the beach, about picking them up and saving an unusual one . . . Some are rough with spiny and irregular edges that tingle when you pick them up.

Think about the rains that come in the spring and fall. Remember how sometimes it rains so hard that the sewers plug up within minutes. You may be outside and before you can reach cover you are soaked and the ground is turned to mud.

One set of tapes is concerned with deeply disturbing material; the other could be expected to leave the auditor untouched or in a lyrical, somewhat abstracted mood.

Immediately after listening to the tape, all subjects answered a series of questions about the task on which they had worked and about their perceived physiological and emotional state. The questions relevant to emotionality are the following:

1. Are you experiencing any palpitation?
2. Do you think your breathing rate is faster than usual?
3. Are you feeling generally upset?
4. Are you experiencing any anxiety?
5. Do you feel emotionally aroused?

Each of these questions was answered on an appropriately labeled version of the following scale.

0	10	20	30	40	50	60	70	80	90	100

Not at all   Extremely

On each of these questions, obese subjects reported that they were significantly more disturbed by the emotional tapes than were subjects of normal weight. The difference does not simply reflect a tendency of the obese to exaggerate their responses because after listening to the undisturbing material the obese described themselves as significantly less emotional than normal subjects.

Pain and the threat of pain are disturbing and unsettling experiences bound to make a subject edgy and tense. If the obese are more reactive and emotional than are normal people, the experience and anticipation of pain should be more disruptive for obese than for normal subjects. In part to consider this hypothesis, an experiment was designed to test the effects of pain on the ability of obese and normal males to learn a rather complex maze.

To measure learning, we employed Lykken's (1957) electronic maze, which is a 20-step maze with 4 alternatives at each step. The maze was housed in a small metal box with four levers mounted in the front. The subject's job was to thread his way through the maze by pressing the correct sequence of levers. At each step, when the subject pressed the correct lever, a green light flashed and he automatically moved on to the next step. If the subject pressed one of the three incorrect levers, a red light flashed and an error was recorded on a counter visible to him. A light signaled when the subject had worked his way through the maze, the machine was reset, and the subject began working again until he went through the maze three times without making an error or had completed 21 trials.

Subjects experienced one of three experimental conditions—severe shock, mild shock, or no shock. Electrodes were fastened to the second and third fingers of the subject's nondominant hand to administer shock. The experiment had been explained as a study of the effects of "partial reward and punishment" on learning, and the subject was told, "You will occasionally receive a shock when you make an error. We have set up the apparatus to randomly give a shock on every few errors." In fact, the shocks were not administered randomly but were linked to one of the three incorrect levers at each step. Theoretically, a subject could learn to avoid shock by not pressing the shock lever at a given step, even if he had not learned to press the correct lever to advance. Because we wanted to minimize the possibility of upsetting the subject in the no-shock condition, electrodes were not fastened to his hand and no mention was made of shock.

Table 1-1   Effects of Electric Shock on Learning

Subjects	Total number of errors			No vs. severe-shock
	No shock	Mild shock	Severe shock	
Normal	228.7	163.4	198.1	nonsignificant
Obese	189.9	228.8	286.5	$p < .05$
p	n.s.	n.s.	$< .05$	

Interaction $p < .03$

The effects of electric shock on learning are presented in Table 1-1. The figures in the table are the average of the total number of errors, shocked and unshocked, made by the subjects in the course of learning (or not learning) the maze. It is evident that shock had a disruptive effect on the learning ability of obese subjects and no such effect on normal subjects. The obese made somewhat fewer errors in the no-shock condition than normals and considerably more errors in the severe-shock condition. It does appear that pain interfered more with the ability of the obese to learn a complex task than with that of normal subjects. Altogether, three experimentally garnered facts support a view of the obese as more emotional than people of normal weight.

1.   In response to a threat of painful shock, the obese describe themselves as more nervous than do normals.
2.   Emotionally distressing audio tapes are more upsetting to obese than to normal subjects.
3.   Painful shock interferes with the ability of the obese to learn a complex task.

If overweight people are more emotionally reactive than normal people, is it this emotional state that leads to overeating or is emotionality simply a correlate of the obesity? A set of experiments was designed to consider this question.

Relationship between Emotionality and Eating.   In each study designed to test the relationship between emotionality and overeating participants were again selected from a college population on the basis of degree of overweight. The important experimental question is *whether emotional arousal leads to overeating in the obese and whether eating in turn reduces the arousal.* In the first experiment, Schachter, Goldman, and Gordon (1968) were concerned with the effects of fear on eating behavior. Subjects were threatened with either very painful or very mild electrical stimulation and then given the opportunity to eat from a bowl of crackers under the guise of a taste test. Because anxiety inhibits gastric contractions and releases sugar into the bloodstream, high arousal actually decreased eating in subjects of normal weight whereas the obese ate slightly, but not significantly more when they were aroused than when they were not. Schachter, Goldman, and Gordon concluded that the psychosomatic hypotheses of obesity, which assert that the obese confuse hunger with negative affect (Bruch, 1961, 1973) and that overeating is a conditioned response to aversive emotional states (Kaplan and Kaplan, 1957), were not confirmed. Obese subjects did not eat much more when they were anxious and did not exhibit significant anxiety reduction as a consequence of eating.

In a subsequent study, McKenna (1972) suggested that the psychosomatic hypothesis would perhaps only be expected to apply when tasty food was available. Schachter, Goldman, and Gordon had employed crackers as their food, but they admit that crackers are a rather neutral food, neither liked nor disliked by most people. McKenna predicted that the replacement of crackers with extremely appetizing and tasty chocolate chip cookies would elicit significant overeating in the anxious state. Even using these cookies, however, McKenna found only an insignificant increase in eating in the obese under conditions of anxiety and no evidence of differential anxiety reduction after eating. However, McKenna argued that the temporal arrangements of his experiment may have prevented accurate measures of eating-induced anxiety reduction. He suggested that anxiety reduction might be an ephemeral effect that had dissipated by the time he attempted to assess it. In the next experiment, Herman and Polivy (1974) incorporated both a good-tasting food—ice cream—and an immediate assessment of anxiety reduction effects. In their study, conducted under the guise of a study on sensory psychology, subjects were threatened with severe electric shock and then given ice cream to rate, presumably in order to determine the effect of tactile stimulation on taste. Actually the experimenters were only interested in the amount subjects ate. A control group of subjects was offered food in the same way, but was not threatened with severe electric shock. This study also showed that anxiety did not significantly increase eating in a group of subjects who by their own admission considered themselves unrestrained eaters. Second, there was no decrease in reported anxiety as a result of their having eaten the ice cream.

The Herman and Polivy experiment essentially demonstrated what Schachter, Goldman, and Gordon and McKenna also found; that is, a very small increase in consumption for subjects experiencing extreme anxiety. But although no single study has demonstrated a substantial effect, the consistency of results across studies necessitates caution before this aspect of the psychosomatic hypothesis is dismissed. The seond component of the psychosomatic hypothesis involves a purported anxiety-reducing effect of eating. None of the three studies reported provided any evidence to support this notion.

However, one implication of the psychosomatic notion that obesity is a manifestation of internal conflicts is that the experiential anxiety state that triggers eating may be diffuse, and its source frequently not understood by the obese person. It seems plausible that it is precisely the vague and undefined nature of some emotional responses that triggers eating in the obese person. Tests of the psychosomatic hypothesis have thus far employed manipulations of the external environment that allowed subjects to label and appropriately interpret their emotional state (as, e.g., fear of shock). Because obese subjects are highly responsive to external cues, they should be even more likely than normal subjects to label their internal state according to available external information. However, if the obese subject experienced a *diffuse, or free-floating arousal state* for which there was no perceived stimulus, his idiosyncratic eating response to arousal might emerge. Slochower (1975) tested this and found that aroused obese subjects ate more when they could not identify the cause of their arousal than when a clear cause was known. When obese subjects were calm, the presence or absence of a label did not affect their eating.

Even if some form of free-floating anxiety does increase consumption for obese persons, it is still unnecessary to invoke an anxiety-reducing effect of eating to account for such increased consumption. Anxiety may be regarded as a disrupter of behavior, including self-control, which then might disinhibit hunger-motivated eating behavior. Increased consumption during anxiety may reflect a person's chronic hunger, which is normally suppressed in an attempt to achieve emotional homeostasis. The notion of the obese person as someone in a chronic state of hunger will be considered later.

It seems fair to conclude that thus far experimental attempts to study the psychosomatic hypothesis of eating have been relatively unsuccessful. However, it remains an open question whether a more powerful anxiety manipulation—such as a threat to ego—might succeed in significantly increasing consumption.

Depression and Dieting. One set of findings has been very influential in linking obesity to emotional pathology. These studies demonstrated that depression during dieting is very severe, and that affective responses to dieting produce anxiety and apathy in some subjects and responses bordering on psychotic episodes in others (Glucksman and Hirsch, 1968; Grinker et al., 1973; Kollar and Alkinson, 1966; Robinson and Winnik, 1973; Swanson and Dinello, 1970). These results have been taken to suggest that for many people, overeating is related to psychological disturbance in that obesity maintains the distorted psychological image intact, and thus that with the removal of the obese condition the person's adjustment deteriorates.

The most salient characteristics of the dieting depression syndrome are weakness, nervousness manifested in anxiety and restlessness, irritability, fatigue, difficulty in concentration, general apathy, and downheartedness (Stunkard, 1957). Although several investigators have attributed this dieting depression to a loss of overweight body image (Glucksman and Hirsch, 1968; Glucksman, Hirsch, and McCully, 1968; Leon and Chamberlain, 1973), especially among people obese since childhood, Stunkard (1957) has made an interesting comparison that he says disconfirms this notion. He cites an earlier study in which Keys et al. (1950) investigated 32 healthy young men of *normal* weight who lost 25 percent of their body weight in six months. These rigid dieters experienced very similar psychological symptoms to those that have been most characteristic of dieting depression. Stunkard suggests that severe emotional disturbance seldom occurs before the patient has lost a certain amount of weight, usually 15 to 20 pounds, or has been on the regimen more than 10 days. He says that these disturbances may at least in part be precipitated by metabolic changes.

Before concluding that metabolic changes precipitate the depression, we must consider the possibility that it is simply depressing to be without food, especially for people who love to eat. They feel deprived and crave foods that they can no longer have. They see a future in which dieting will always be a way of life, and this in itself is very depressing. Finally, it is possible that weight loss does produce a change in body image that is debilitating and depressing for some overweight people. Surgical treatment of obesity, using a jejuno-ilial bypass that short-circuits most of the intestine, provides a unique opportunity to study the psychological consequences of relatively rapid reduction of body size. The intestinal bypass produces a controlled malabsorption state and leads to a substantial and lasting weight loss in which weight stabilizes after one to two years.

Surgically induced weight loss has a number of advantages for evaluating the psychological impact of diminished body size. Weight loss is rapid and reliable, while allowing for continued oral gratification. It does not make prolonged demands on the patient's willpower, and it usually takes place in his or her home and work environment. In a study of the psychosocial effects of intestinal bypass surgery for severe obesity, Solow, Silverfarb, and Swift (1974) demonstrated an improvement after surgery and weight loss in mood, self-esteem, interpersonal and vocational effectiveness, body image, and activity level. There were a decrease in depression and also improvements in ego strength and body image that were directly proportional to the magnitude of weight loss. The findings in this study fail to support the view (Glucksman and Hirsch, 1968; Glucksman, Hirsch, and McCully, 1968) that behavioral abnormalities regularly accompany substantial reduction of adipose tissue in the obese. Instead, their results suggest that disturbance is associated with the mode of weight loss or related to factors other than weight loss itself. Oral deprivation, or the constant stress of resisting the temptation to eat, may be one such factor.

Many attributes described as central in the constellation associated with obesity (i.e. low self-esteem, passive dependence, vulnerability to depression, marked self-consciousness, and a sense of helplessness and ineffectiveness) appear surprisingly reversible in bypass patients. The distortion of body image seems to be substantially ameliorated by surgically induced weight reduction. For this reason, the bypass operation provides an important experimental technique: it allows an opportunity to compare the consequences of weight loss with the manner in which that weight loss was achieved. This study leaves one more impressed than ever with the profound psychological *consequences* of being obese. The impact of years of physical disability, social stigma (Cahnan, 1968; Kalisch, 1972), and dieting failure become all the more apparent when the effects of weight loss are assessed.

The obese personality, to the extent that it exists, seems to have been as much the result of obesity as it was the cause in massively obese patients. If obesity is viewed as a symptom of psychological conflict, surgically induced weight loss seems to be a prime example of symptom removal, without resolution of the antecedent conflict. The lack of any convincing evidence of the emergence of substitute symptoms is another challenge to a simplistic psychogenic concept of obesity. Even when patients initially manifest emotional disturbance, weight loss seems to facilitate and catalyze evolution of more flexible and helpful modes of coping. Rather than an obligatory defense, obesity would be more usefully viewed as an unfortunate result of an imperfectly understood interplay of biological, psychological, and social factors.

If there is psychopathology associated with obesity, it may be the obsession that many obese people have with food and eating and their weight. In our society, the fat are chastised for their lack of self-control. Many of our norms suggest that fat people should be stigmatized and made to feel mortified and ashamed. They are rejected and disgraced for a condition viewed as both a physical deformity and a behavioral aberration. Studies have shown that people do react negatively to overweight. Many fat people are full of self-disparagement and self-hatred, because they are discriminated against and because they are made to feel that they merit such discrimination (Cahnan, 1968). A fat person perceives himself in a way that is indicated by dominant values and expectations. The state of imprisonment in the role of fatty seems to alter the overweight person's personality, a finding also true for other minority groups.

Thus, as Bruch (1973) suggests, overweight people are caught in a paradox; they symbolize to a large extent the fulfillment of the great American dream of a life of ease and abundance, the natural consequence of which is more than ample nutrition. Yet at the same time society makes every effort to fight overweight, calls it undesirable, and labels it "the unsolved health problem of the nation." We have made excessive slimness the ideal of health and beauty. Perhaps the real pathology with relation to overweight is a social pathology, rather than one inherent in an obese person. At the extremes of eating disorders, in massively obese people and in people who suffer from anorexia nervosa, there are real psychological disturbances. However, among the largest percentage of people who have earned the label obese because of a deviation of their weight from the statistical norm, psychiatric disorders are no more prevalent than they are in a comparable number of people of normal weight. Thus we can conclude that psychopathology often is secondary or coincidental to the development of obesity.

Metabolic and Endocrine Disturbance

Increased body weight is correlated with a variety of metabolic and endocrine abnormalities including decreased glucose tolerance, increased basal and stimulated insulin levels, elevated triglyceride and blood choles-terol levels, increased cortisol secretion rate, and blunted growth hormone secretions (Bortz, 1969; Forsham, 1974; Rabinowitz, 1970).

The elements of obesity correlated with these abnormalities are fat use, carbohydrate use, and hormonal factors. It is plausible to propose that obesity might reflect an inability to burn fat. This proposal has been widely debated. The inability could be a result either of failure in the transfer or mobilization of fat from its stores or failure of the target organ to burn the fat for energy. Numerous investigators have observed that when obese people are starved, their plasma-free fatty acid level does not rise so strikingly as does that of lean individuals (Newburgh, 1944). These observations seem to indicate that obese people have a diminished capacity to mobilize their fat stores.

Several convincing experiments demonstrate that rather than exhibiting a decreased capability for the mobilization and utilization of adipose tissue stores, obese people are actually subsisting on a fat-enriched substrate mix-ture. Dole (1956) has shown that the obese still have higher plasma-free fatty acid levels when fed or after a simple overnight fast, and Hanley, Lewis, and Knight (1969) have shown that for each 10 percent weight gain, the plasma-free fatty acid level rises proportionately. If fat use is not defective in the obese, perhaps fat synthesis is disproportionately increased. The high plasma level of insulin, a fat-forming hormone, seen in obesity, seems to support this suggestion. Obviously fat formation must exceed fat use during weight gain. However, now clear biochemical data suggest that an accelerated fat formation is not a characteristic of steady-state obesity (Shreeve, 1964).

Next let us consider carbohydrate use. Defective glucose use is the most frequently reported metabolic abnormality in obesity. It has been associated both with severity and duration of the obesity (Newburgh, 1944; Olgilvie, 1935; Sussman, 1966). Not only does glucose use affect fat metabolism, but fat use can profoundly affect glucose metabolism (Randle et al., 1963; Seyffert and Madison, 1967). Therefore, defective glucose use may be both a partial cause and a consequence of the higher plasma-free fatty acid levels.

Finally, no endocrine gland has been so implicated in obesity as the thyroid. It is a rare fat person who has not been given thyroid extract at some time in his life. However, repeated studies have failed to demonstrate any abnormality of thyroxin secretion or any universally affected organ in fat people (Newburgh and Conn, 1939). More important are the endocrine secretions of the pancreas. Numerous reports attest to elevated plasma insulin levels in the obese (Kreisberg et al., 1967; Solomon, Ensinck, and Williams, 1968; Yalow et al., 1965). High levels of insulin have been shown to be associated with increased food intake (Hoebel and Teitelbaum, 1966).

The research demonstrates clearly that there are serious metabolic correlates of obesity. Again, we must ask whether these are causes of consequences of increased food intake and adiposity. It is now generally agreed that this question has been answered by the elegant work of Sims and his colleagues, who studied the induction of obesity in a group of volunteers in a Vermont state prison (Sims and Horton, 1968; Sims et al., 1968, 1973). These subjects ingested two or three times their normal daily caloric intake and gained an average of 26 percent over their initial lean weight. The proportion of carbohydrate to fat to protein in the diet was left unchanged. The investigators point out that some subjects reached their goal only with great difficulty. Others failed to gain, even though they consumed more calories than the successful volunteers. As the subjects became obese, the following metabolic alterations were noted. First, amounts of serum cholesterol and triglycerides increased, and amounts of plasma-free fatty acids decreased. Second, plasma insulin levels during fasting were raised, and following oral or intravenous administration of glucose the rise of insulin was greater than that observed before weight gain. Third, despite the rise in fasting and post-glucose insulin levels, there was a significant reduction in oral and intravenous glucose tolerance. Fourth, with weight gain there was a progressive impairment in the rise of plasma growth hormone levels, which is usually observed four to six hours after ingestion of glucose. Fifth, the production rate of cortisol was increased in every subject.

These studies have contributed greatly to our understanding of obesity. Although numerous endocrine and metabolic alterations have been observed in obese humans, before this work it was not clear which if any of the deviations might be primary abnormalities that promote or perpetuate the obese state, and which were secondary changes that occurred in association with such factors as enlargement of the size of the adipocytes, increased intake of calories, diet composition, level of physical activity, or other factors commonly associated with the obese state. The Sims study demonstrated that with few exceptions lean people develop endocrine and metabolic changes like those observed in spontaneous obesity when they overeat and thus increase adipose tissue mass.

Only three major differences were observed between this experimental obesity and spontaneously obese states. First, the subjects with experimentally induced obesity increased their adipose tissue mass by increasing only adipose cell size, without any change in the total cell number. Many spontaneously obese people have a greater number of fat cells as well. Second, in all subjects who gained weight by increasing all elements of the diet, there was a marked increase in the daily caloric requirement necessary to maintain the obese state. Spontaneously obese men can maintain a constant weight on a daily intake of as little as 1,300 kilocalories per meter squared (Bray, 1970a), whereas subjects with experimental obesity required approximately 2,700 Kcal/M^2 to maintain their gained weight, an increase of 50 percent over that required for maintenance of their usual lean weight. Finally, in contrast to the increased plasma concentration of free fatty acids frequently found in spontaneous obesity, subjects with experimental obesity had a decrease. This has subsequently been attributed to diet composition; suppression of plasma-free fatty acids is associated with the high carbohydrate intake, rather than with the development of obesity. In all other respects, the changes observed in experimental obesity paralleled those found in spontaneous obesity.

A second way to examine the contribution of metabolism is to look at the hormonal and metabolic consequences of extreme weight loss. For example, the most striking endocrine alteration in obesity is the combination of hyperinsulinemia and the presence of peripheral insulin resistance. The research of Horton and his coworkers (Horton et al., 1972) demonstrated that hyperinsulinemia and insulin resistance can be reversed in spontaneously obese subjects by caloric restriction and weight reduction. Similarly, after a restriction in caloric intake, most of the other metabolic and hormonal consequences of obesity are similarly diminished. Thus, we can conclude that most forms of obesity occur because food intake exceeds the rate at which foodstuffs are burned. We assume that a person initially has normal responsivity, but that during active weight gain there is enhanced activity and metabolic and endocrine change. The studies of Sims and Horton and their colleagues clearly establish that obesity is not caused by changes in hormonal economy but rather is the cause of many of them.

Adipose Tissue Cellularity

Because obesity is an excess accumulation of fat, it is essential to examine how excess fat may be retained in the body. Fat can be stored in the body by one of several means: the size of the preexisting adipose tissue cells can increase, the number of adipose cells can increase, or both can occur at once. Hirsch and Knittle and their coworkers (Knittle, 1975; Knittle and Hirsch, 1968) have found in several investigations that fat cell volume is increased threefold in grossly obese patients and that body weight and fat cell size are significantly and positively correlated even in normal-weight and moderately overweight people. In other words, the more overweight the subject, the larger the fat cells. Enlarged fat cells seem to be a common phenomenon of both moderate and gross obesity.

An increase in fat cell number is a mechanism of fat storage seen primarily in the grossly obese, but whether the slightly and moderately obese also have an increased number of fat cells is an unsettled question. In general, extremely obese people with a childhood history of obesity tend to display the most marked increase in adipose cell number, whereas those whose obesity occurs after puberty have a greater contribution of adipose cell enlargement. However, weight reduction is accomplished by alteration in adipose cell size, without any appreciable effect on cell number (Bray, 1970b; Hirsch and Knittle, 1970; Salans, Cushman, and Wisemann, 1973).

The apparent constancy of adipose cell number in obese people, even after marked weight reduction, is striking; indeed, a similar constancy of adipose cell number is encountered in animals (Hirsch and Han, 1969; Knittle and Hirsch, 1968). Adult adipose cell number is unaffected by dietary manipulation. In addition, decreases in adipose cell size in the adult are not permanent; starved cells are quickly restored to predeprivation size when feedings are reestablished.

Both human and animal studies suggest that for treatment of obesity to be completely effective, weight reduction may have to occur before the number of fat cells is permanently increased. The reduced subject must continue to restrict calories long after ideal weight has been achieved, perhaps for the remainder of his life. This may be due in part to the inability to lose adipocytes (Hollenberg, 1970) and the consequences of altered metabolism in the fat cells of formerly obese subjects (Knittle and Ginsberg-Fellner, 1972; Salans, Knittle, and Hirsch, 1968). Two series of experimental investigations have pursued this question. The first investigated animals in the early stages of development, and the second studied obese and normal-weight humans ranging in age from infancy to their early twenties.

Recent evidence indicates that adipose cellularity can be traced to a great extent to eating patterns established in infancy and childhood. To study and manipulate the development of adipose cell tissue, Knittle and Hirsch (1968) investigated the effects of early nutrition on the development of rats. By separating 26 newborn rats from two nursing mothers, they varied litter size before weaning. They allowed four rats to nurse from one mother and the other 22 to nurse from the second mother. Hirsch and Knittle found that by this treatment they had influenced the body weight of weanling rats. Those animals sharing food with 21 siblings were significantly lighter than those sharing with only three. In addition to this significant difference in body weight between the two groups, there were also important differences between the epididymal fat pads of the two groups. The epididymal fat depots of animals raised in small litters were both absolutely and relatively larger than fat depots of those raised in large litters.

The average adipose cell number and size for each group of animals were then studied. At all ages, animals raised in large litters had fewer and smaller fat cells than those raised in small litters. During early development, these differences were both in cell number and cell size, but cell size was clearly secondary. Once cell number was established—that is, by the 15th week of life in rats—further changes in the size of the tissue occurred only in cell size. These large-litter rats who were nutritionally deprived during the first 21 days of life were stunted, and their adipose depot remained small. They had a low number of cells and small cell size, in spite of complete freedom to feed following the weaning. Hirsch and his colleagues suggested that there are a fixed number of mature adipocytes unaffected by changes in depot size; and that the adipocytes or their precursors are formed early in life, and during a finite postnatal period certain influences, primarily nutritional, may determine adipose cell number.

Although these findings are consistent with the concept that the observed differences were mainly due to differences in infant caloric intake, we cannot attribute all the changes observed solely to differences in caloric intake during the suckling period. Animals raised in litters of varying sizes have markedly different early experiences in feeding and socializing that could alter later feeding patterns and contribute to changes in energy balance. The continued increase in differences in cell size and number observed after weaning might have resulted from differences in caloric intake during this later period. However, the fact that dietary manipulation in untreated animals after the age of ten weeks failed to affect permanent changes indicates that some time limit does exist after which food consumption cannot effectively alter adipose tissue cellularity.

The striking similarity between these results and those previously reported for obese and normal human subjects is significant. Because the Hirsch and Knittle findings clearly show that early nutritional experiences can permanently modify adipose cell number and size in the rat, it is postulated that similar nutritional experiences in man have prime importance in producing the hyperplasia and hypertrophy of adipose tissue found in obese humans. The treatment of obesity may therefore lie in a prevention early in life through the control of factors that influence adipose cell division and enlargement.

Knittle (1975) has demonstrated that critical adipose tissue development does occur somewhere between birth and age two in obese children, and that this time has important consequences for the future development of the adult fat depot. By age two, obese children have more and larger fat cells than normal children. After that age there is a rapid proliferation of cells without enlargement that continues to approximately ages 12 to 16 in obese people. Normal subjects do not have significant increases in total fat until age 10, the adolescent period. After age two, weight loss in obese children does nothing to alter the number of adipose cells. Decreases in body fat are accomplished solely by a reduction of adipose cell size without significant changes in cell number. Thus even in children, once a particular adipose cell number is achieved it cannot be decreased by dietary restriction. This permanent excess of fat-making machinery and high lipogenic capacity that the once-obese child always carries with him may be the physical underpinning for the high rate of recidivism in weight reduction programs.

The importance of these studies is great. The total number of fat cells that we carry into adult life is at least partially dependent upon early childhood feeding behavior. However, what makes some people overeat and others not is still not answered by this research. For further answers we must next consider genetic and then environmental factors.

Genetic Contributions to Obesity

It is a commonplace observation that the tendency to gain weight runs in families. Sixty percent of overweight people have at least one overweight parent. However, between these simple observations and a more precise genetic statement, there are relatively few studies and many problems. Human obesity tends to be familial because of either genetics or early training. Withers (1964) and others (Angel, 1949; Seltzer, 1969) examined the correlation of parent-child weights, comparing natural children with adopted children. The correlations in body weight between mother and father and an adopted child were very low. In contrast, there were higher correlations between the weight of a father and mother and their natural child.

If heredity plays a direct role in obesity, it may be that some people are predisposed to developing a greater number of adipose cells, or lack some metabolic substrate for the conversion of food to energy, and that this predisposition can be transmitted to offspring. Eating patterns are familial, however, so these questions are sometimes difficult to answer. Rather than using the descriptive approach of geneticists, the experimental method of examining the nature-nurture question uses studies of twins reared together or apart. It has been reported that identical twins have closely correlated body weights (von Verschuer, 1927). The mean adult weight difference of identical twins was 4.1 pounds, that of fraternal twins 10.0 pounds, and that of other siblings 10.4 pounds. Identical twins reared apart show somewhat larger weight variation than those reared together, but they are more similar than either fraternal twins or siblings. Clark (1956) estimates the heritability of body weight as 0.69, meaning that 69 percent of what produces differences in body weight between individuals may be accounted for by heredity. Obesity in humans surely has some genetic contribution, but the influence of environmental factors, that is, of nurture, still obscures a true understanding of how genetic influences operate.

Investigators have used animal models to study the genetic component more clearly. Several strains of obese rodents transmit the obese trait in one of three systematic patterns (Bray and York, 1971; Schemmel, Mickelson, and Gill, 1970): (1) a single gene dominant, (2) a single gene recessive, or (3) polygenic. For example, rodents that transmit obesity by means of a single dominant gene develop hyperphagia and obesity with variable hyperglycemia at about four weeks of age. Thermoregulation is defective, and there are signs present of hyperinsulinemia and a moderate degree of hypercorticism (Carpenter and Mayer, 1958; Dickie and Woolley, 1946).

Hypotheses put forward to explain the abnormalities in inherited forms of obesity name four types of defects (Bray and York, 1971). First, there may be a primary defect in adipose tissue. However, it appears that most tissue abnormalities result from either the obesity itself or from the accompanying hyperinsulinemia. Second, there could be a deficit in the release or peripheral action of steroid hormones. Third, there could be a defect in secretion or action of insulin. Obesity, whether regulatory or metabolic, is generally accompanied by hyperinsulinemia. Although hypersecretion of insulin is present in all genetic syndromes, it may simply correlate with increased body weight rather than reflect a primary genetic defect in the pancreas. Fourth, the hypothalamus might be performing defectively. A number of studies have suggested that some forms of genetically obese mice have hypothalamic impairments. The disorder in carbohydrate metabolism, depressed activity, hyperphagia, and inefficient food utilization could indicate disturbed hypothalamic function.

Rodent obesities are so varied in their causes that we can easily find a model to apply to the enormously more complicated human disorder. To what extent this application is appropriate remains to be learned. Obese mice eat excessively, tend to hypoactivity, and have large fat cells. Whether they have larger total number of adipocytes is uncertain. One attempt has been made to generalize from animal models by speculating that in some humans obesity is an inherited disorder, due to a genetically determined defect in an enzyme (Astwood, 1962). Astwood suggested that people who cannot metabolize fats properly become overweight and that somehow this may be useful for the body because it insures that there is enough fat available. At the present time this hypothesis has not been subjected to experimental tests.

An understanding of animal models of genetic obesity may well provide significant clues towards classifying the biochemical and metabolic varieties of human obesity that at present defy our understanding, but for now there is very little evidence of a strong genetic endocrinological or metabolic dysfunction in human obesity. Genetically obese mice reflect metabolic forms of obesity, whereas human obesity seems to be more a problem of regulation (Mayer, 1953). Other methods for inducing experimental obesity, such as the ventromedial-lesioned animal which will be described in the next section, seem to provide better analogues to human forms of obesity. Again, studies of these methods stress that no single explanation can account for all forms of obesity.

Environmental Factors in Obesity

In human eating behavior, where habits and preference play so great a role, short- and long-term biological regulation may be either influenced or determined by environmental influences. Eating behaviors influence biological regulation in several ways. For example, it is now clear that eating one meal per day, as opposed to three or more, has metabolic consequences independent of total caloric intake. Amounts of cholesterol in the blood are elevated, so to control cholesterol it would seem important to eat several meals during the day. Glucose tolerance is impaired by eating only one meal a day rather than eating the same quantity of food in several meals through the day (Young, Scanlan, and Topping, 1971). Adipose tissue shows enhanced lipogenesis—that is, increased fat synthesis—when food is ingested in one large meal instead of several small meals (Bray, 1972). Finally, epidemiological studies have shown a clear negative correlation between the number of meals and obesity. The fewer the meals, the greater the tendency toward obesity and increased skin thickness (Fabry, Hejda, and Cerny, 1966). Several studies (summarized by Schachter and Rodin, 1974) indicate that overweight people eat fewer meals and more food per meal than their normal-weight counterparts. The frequency with which food is ingested could be a factor in controlling subsequent metabolic events that contribute to obesity.

Environmental food cues also directly control food intake. All people are responsive to the sight of well-prepared food, fragrant aromas, and delicious tastes, but whereas everyone occasionally overeats in the presence of tempting external food cues, it appears that many obese people are highly and sometimes uncontrollably responsive to external food-relevant cues. This behavior might cause them to ignore internal regulatory signals to a greater extent than normal weight people. It has been shown that the eating behavior of many obese people is largely determined by cues associated with food and with the eating routine and ritual (Schachter, 1971). Because obese people are so responsive to external cues their eating may be initiated primarily in response to factors outside their own bodies. It actually may not matter if and when they are physiologically hungry. What experimental evidence supports this description?

The first study that suggested that the obese were unresponsive to their internal state was conducted by Stunkard and Koch (1964), who asked food-deprived subjects to swallow an intragastric balloon that would continuously record stomach contractions. Every 15 minutes subjects were asked whether they were hungry. For normal-weight subjects, there was a strong correlation between contractions and self-reported hunger; for overweight subjects the correlation was far weaker.

Schachter, Goldman, and Gordon (1968) showed that not only self-reports of hunger but actual food consumption by the obese were relatively unrelated to manipulations of internal state. All subjects were requested to refrain from eating for several hours before the experiment, and immediately before testing half of them were fed two roast beef sandwiches. The others remained hungry. All subjects were then asked to complete a lengthy taste questionnaire evaluating a variety of crackers for qualities such as cheesiness and saltiness. During this tasting session, subjects of normal weight ate far more crackers when they were hungry than when they were full from the sandwiches. Overweight subjects ate slightly more when they had just eaten than when they were deprived.

If obese people do not respond to internal physiological cues arising from food deprivation, what signals tell them when to start and stop eating? Quite likely external cues play this role. Nisbett (1968b) first demonstrated this by having subjects taste one of two ice creams: an excellent and expensive French vanilla and a vanilla that had been adulterated with quinine. Overweight subjects ate more of the tastier and less of the bad-tasting ice cream than did normal subjects. The taste of the ice cream determined the amount consumed and the obese subjects were more reactive to taste.

The passage of time is another external cue that should influence eating. Schachter and Gross (1968) persuaded subjects by means of a clock rigged to speed or move slowly that it was either dinnertime or almost an hour earlier at the conclusion of the experiment. At this time, the investigator returned, nibbling from a box of crackers. He asked subjects to complete a final questionnaire and offered them crackers, which he left on the table.

Only 30 minutes had actually elapsed in the study but when they thought that an hour had passed and it was dinnertime, obese subjects ate twice as many crackers as when they thought the experiment had lasted 15 minutes. Normal-weight subjects ate somewhat fewer crackers when they thought an hour had elapsed, many saying that they did not want to spoil their dinner.

Studies such as these suggest that obese people are strongly influenced by external factors. With great consistency, where external, food-related cues for eating were manipulated, the obese were affected. The preceding experiments seem to suggest that fat people are responsive to all food-relevant stimuli in their environment. We might expect that they would eat almost constantly then, for the world is abundant with food cues. However, several studies have shown that the obese actually eat fewer meals than normal people (Beaudoin and Mayer, 1953; Johnson, Burke, and Mayer, 1956; Ross et al., 1971).

To rectify this apparent disparity, Schachter and Rodin (1974) postulated that eating behavior in the obese is triggered only when food cues are highly potent. This formulation suggests that if stimuli are weak or entirely absent, obese people will eat less than normal people. In fact, there is evidence that in an environment entirely devoid of food-relevant cues, the obese may abstain from eating more easily than normal people. Consider, for example, Yom Kippur—the Jewish Day of Atonement—which is a day of fasting and prayer. External food cues are extremely sparse for those who remain in a synagogue. Goldman, Jaffa, and Schachter (1968) found that obese Jews were more likely to fast than equally religious Jews of normal weight and that the longer the time spent in the synagogue, the easier the fast. However, normal weight Jews, responsive to their internal deprivation state, found fasting painful whether they remained in the synagogue or not.

One other piece of evidence suggests that the obese may be more likely than normal people to forego eating when food cues are unavailable or weak. According to Schachter and Gross (1968) food cues are routinely present and absent during the week for college students, especially at lunch hour. "Come noontime, all students are up and about, surrounded by hordes of colleagues on their way to lunch, inevitably passing lunch counters, delicatessens and dining halls" (p. 104). With this abundance of potent, food-relevant stimuli, most obese people should be expected to eat lunch. However, weekends provide no comparable routine. Students may engage in a variety of activities, some of which will undoubtedly remove them from food-related cues. On weekends, then, the obese should be more likely to skip lunch than normal students, for whom eating is unrelated to the salience of food cues. The investigators found precisely this pattern of results. On weekdays, relatively few fat or normal students went without lunch, whereas on weekends 54 percent of the obese skipped lunch and only 11 percent of the normal students did so. This difference has also been reported by Ross and coworkers (Ross et al., 1971) in their survey of the eating habits of college students. Moreover, both Schachter and Gross and Ross and coworkers reported that the obese were more likely to skip breakfast than any other meal during the week. They argued breakfast was the meal for which external food cues were least salient.

To directly manipulate food-relevant external stimuli, Ross (1969) exposed subjects to cashews that were prominent and brightly illuminated or were remote and dimly lit.

As shown in Figure 1-1, Ross found that obese subjects ate twice as many cashews when the lights were bright (high cue salience) as when they were dimmed (low cue salience). For normal-weight subjects a slight reversal was found. Actually, obese subjects consumed fewer cashews than normal subjects when the nuts were not salient. Thus, as predicted, when external cues are weak or remote, they exert no more influence on the eating behavior of the obese than on that of people of normal weight. Externality—the heightened responsiveness of obese subjects to food-relevant stimuli— appears limited to conditions of high cue salience.

Cognitive salience also appeared to affect the eating behavior of the obese. Obese subjects told to think about cashews ate many more nuts than obese subjects who were permitted to think about anything. Normal subjects ate the same amount whatever they were told.

The results of these studies may be summarized as follows. In all cases, the eating behavior of the obese appears highly stimulus-bound under conditions of high cue or cognitive salience. A food-relevant cue, above a given degree of prominence, appears more likely to trigger an eating re- sponse in an obese than in a normal person. In addition, eating behavior is likely to reflect heightened responsiveness when it is elicited. The obese do not simply eat; they overeat, at least after they are aroused by potent stimuli. Ross et al. reported that obese subjects ate more than normal subjects at each meal, when food cues are undoubtedly most prominent. However, they ate fewer meals, presumably because food-relevant stimuli must be sufficiently potent before eating is elicited.

The compelling tendency of the obese to respond to prominent food cues has led researchers to suspect that overweight people may be simply more reactive than normals to potent stimuli in general. Rodin (1973) has sug- gested that these various findings about eating behavior are simply a spe- cial instance of a much broader phenomenon of generalized stimulus sensitivity. Our studies on shock avoidance behavior (Rodin, 1974) and emotional responsiveness (Rodin, Elman, and Schachter, 1974) lend support to this assertion. When subjects listened to either neutral or emotionally

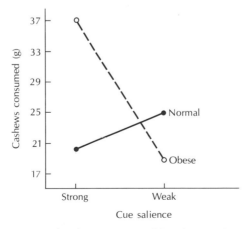

Figure 1-1. Mean grams of cashews consumed by obese and normal weight subjects under conditions of high and low cue salience. (From Ross, 1969.)

disturbing tape recordings, the obese behaved more emotionally and reported more emotional responses than normal subjects when the tapes were
upsetting (and less emotional than did normal subjects when the tapes were
neutral). In addition, overweight subjects worked more to avoid shock than
did normal subjects.

Further experiments were designed to test the hypothesis of a more
broadly-based stimulus sensitivity and its implications in contexts unrelated
to consummatory behavior. First, Rodin, Herman, and Schachter (1974) put
together a variety of tests, dictated by notions of what generalized external
sensitivity might mean. The authors reasoned that if the obese are in general
more sensitive to external stimuli, they should react more to external cues,
take in more cues, and remember them better. To test these predictions,
Rodin et al. measured the reaction-time latencies of obese and normal
subjects, their immediate recall for items presented briefly on a slide, and
their thresholds for the recognition of tachistoscopically presented stimuli.
The authors found that although the obese appeared somewhat slower than
normal subjects on simple reaction time, their reaction times were faster
when the response required a choice between stimuli. Obese subjects also
recalled significantly more items presented briefly on a slide than did
subjects who were not obese. Finally, when subjects were asked to identify a
word flashed briefly in the visual field of a tachistoscope, the obese tended to
recognize words at significantly shorter exposures than did normal subjects.

Despite the fact that these results were statistically reliable, we felt that
their interpretation was questionable. The data may indicate differential
stimulus sensitivity but they might also show differential motivation. Certainly there is consensus on what constitutes good performance on the
measures employed in this study. In selecting subjects according to degree of
obesity, we may have inadvertently selected subjects who were differentially
eager to please. Because of this ambiguity, the next set of experiments was
deliberately designed to test interaction predictions—to specify the conditions under which obese subjects should do worse than normals as well as
the conditions under which they should do better. These experiments were
designed to test implications of the interaction hypothesis suggested for
eating; that is, that the relationship of cue prominence to responsiveness is
considerably stronger for obese than normal subjects.

First, I (Rodin, 1973) examined the effects of distraction on performance.
I predicted that salient, distracting stimuli should be more disruptive for
obese than normal-weight subjects when they were performing a task requiring concentration. Prominent irrelevant stimuli did distract the obese and
caused them to proofread less accurately, as shown in Figure 1-2. They also
had longer reaction times than normal subjects. Under conditions of no
distraction or when presented minimal cues, the obese performed better
than normal subjects on both measures. Rodin and Slochower (1974) used
an incidental verbal learning paradigm in which performance was evaluated

in the absence of intent to remember—that is, in the absence of explicit motivation to learn—and found that even in a task that minimized conscious compliance, obese subjects were still distracted.

These experiments all strongly support the hypothesis that the responsiveness of many obese subjects to external food cues is only one aspect of a more general responsiveness to external stimuli. What is it that makes many obese people more responsive than normal people to external influences? Answering this question will help us to understand the causal relationship between obesity and externality. There are several possible explanations. First, externality may simply be a consequence of diminished internal responsiveness. Or it may result from adiposity. External responsiveness may be an indication of chronic deprivation in obese people. Or externality may be a learned behavior pattern that derives from early feeding experience. Finally, externality may derive from functional neural differences between individuals. Let us consider the experimental evidence for each of these in turn.

The possibility that externality is simply the result of less attention to internal cues is relatively unsupported. Even normal-weight people show far from perfect internal regulation (Jordan, Stellar, and Duggan, 1968; Spiegel, 1973; Wooley, Wooley, and Dunham, 1972) and studies have demonstrated that when regulation was required for 15 days through internal cues, some obese subjects were as responsive to caloric changes as normal subjects (Wooley, 1971). Finally, Griggs and Stunkard (1964) attempted to modify overeating of obese patients by increasing their awareness of internal hunger signals from stomach contractions. Although all subjects learned to correctly identify contractions and label them as hunger signals, none lost much weight. Presumably greater attention to internal cues was unable to counteract their external responsiveness and they continued to overeat when they encountered salient food cues.

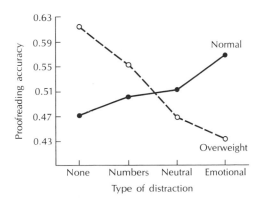

Figure 1-2. Accuracy of proofreading under conditions of no distraction and increasingly interesting distractions.

The second hypothesis says that the fatter people are, the more responsive they are to external stimuli. In other words, the obesity causes the externality. To test this notion we compared the external responsiveness of 90 people who varied in degree of overweight. In addition, we tested them before and after weight loss so that we could also determine whether a change in degree of obesity within a person would affect external responsiveness. Subjects were females between the ages of 12 and 28 who were campers and counselors attending a weight reduction camp for overweight girls (Rodin, 1976). At the time of the first test (week 1 of the camp season) the overweight girls ranged from 14 to 122 percent overweight and the normal-weight girls ranged from 3.4 percent underweight to 7.5 percent overweight. Weight loss was subsequently accomplished by a combined program of daily exercise and restriction of intake. The summer camp provided an ideal experimental setting because everyone was fed identical types and quantities of food at the same hours, engaged in comparable activities, and lived in the same environment for eight weeks. All participants were tested during the first and final weeks on those measures of heightened external and lowered internal responsiveness that had most clearly discriminated between overweight and normal weight in previous experiments. These were: (1) amount eaten before and after a uniform preload, (2) immediate recall of objects and words briefly presented on a slide, and (3) extremity of affective responsiveness to positive and negative stimuli.

The overweight sample was divided into thirds and the heaviest and lightest groups compared to the data obtained from the six normal weight counselors. A composite externality score was devised, based on the sum of the individual measures, each standardized on the entire sample. As indicated in Table 1-2, moderately overweight subjects were significantly more responsive to external stimuli than either the normal subjects or the extremely obese. Normals and the most obese group were not significantly different from each other. Furthermore, considerable weight loss did not influence these response differences. When the means were compared within weight groups before and after weight loss, there were no significant changes. The week 1 to week 8 correlation of standardized externality scores, summed across measures, was .76 ($p < .001$), for the heaviest group and .74 ($p < .001$) for the lightest overweight sample. The correlation for the small normal weight sample was .78. In addition, degree of weight loss was not significantly related to any changes in externality which did occur after weight loss.

We concluded from this study that externality is not simply a consequence of overweight because the most obese subjects were not the most responsive to external stimuli and externality remained stable even after weight loss. Decke (1971) confirmed these findings by measuring whether the subjects who gained weight in the Sims metabolic studies (discussed earlier) also showed increases in responsiveness to external stimuli as they become more overweight. She found little evidence of greater responsiveness with increased adiposity.

A third hypothesis recently advanced by Nisbett (1972) contends that overweight people are responsive to external stimuli because they are actually in a state of physiological deprivation. Nisbett argued that neural regions adjust food intake to maintain adipose tissue cells at a baseline or "set point." Because these centers may set different baselines in different people, it is possible that some people have higher set points that maintain greater quantities of adipose tissue. If overweight people with higher set points diet, they are actually in energy deficit and their behavior should be like that of any starved organism. Nisbett suggested that the physiological and behavioral responses of many overweight people are comparable to those of normal people when they are deprived of food.

Our summer camp data question this hypothesis because deprivation occasioned by long-term weight loss did not increase external responsiveness in overweight or in normal-weight people. It is quite possible that overweight people are physiologically hungry but this does not appear to be a sufficient explanation for their responsiveness to external stimuli.

The hypothesis that externality is the result of early feeding experience might suggest the possibility of obtaining heightened responsiveness through manipulation of the conditions to which neonates are exposed. The finding that relatively short exposure to conditions of scarcity results in modification of the characteristic eating pattern of the rat lends credence to the view that experiential factors play a large role in the development of eating behavior

Table 1-2 Mean Performance Scores on Measures of External Responsiveness for Subjects Divided by Weight

	Overweight		Obese		Normal		
	Before weight loss	After weight loss	Before weight loss	After weight loss	Before weight loss	After weight loss	$F(2,88)$
Percentage correct on slides	.45	.41	.37	.39	.34	.36	2.37
Affective responsiveness							
Positive	2.35	2.31	2.07	2.14	1.81	1.75	3.86*
Negative	1.58	1.84	1.12	1.13	1.02	1.01	3.51*
Time perception	1.88	1.83	1.71	1.63	.93	1.06	3.94*

*$p < .05$

(Jacobs and Sharma, 1964; Hunt, 1941). Gross (1968) tested the effects of scarcity and unpredictability of food directly by exposing rats to conditions of both constant and random deprivation. Random deprivation for varied intervals was expected to produce a state in which relatively constant energy depletion would be complicated by continual uncertainty regarding the future availability of food. To maximize the effects of scarcity and unpredictability, the researchers exposed them to these conditions for a considerable length of time. Evidence by Bruch (1961) and Keys and coworkers (1950) with humans indicates that exposure to prolonged deprivation often results in a persistent tendency to overeat.

Gross created three groups of experimental animals immediately after weaning. One group was allowed to feed freely, the second group was placed on a 22-hour deprivation schedule in which they were fed once every 22 hours, and the third group was placed on a random deprivation schedule in which they were fed on the average every 22 hours, with the time of deprivation ranging from eight to 48 hours. All animals were kept on these schedules for 100 days. Gross found that rats maintained under conditions of randomly varied deprivation were highly responsive to variations in the taste and caloric density of their diet. This was interpreted as an increase in external control in the randomly deprived rats as compared to animals having regularly available food.

After 100 days, the animals were allowed to feed when they chose and Gross (1968) found that even under conditions of abundance the randomly deprived animals continued to exhibit externally oriented responses to dietary variations. Most interesting, the rats that had been randomly deprived also demonstrated a pattern of external control reflected in a measure of responsiveness to external food cues that did not involve eating. Gross tested this by measuring the amount of time that they remained in contact with food in an open field, although they were not allowed to eat the food. This is reminiscent of the observations of nonconsummatory food-relevant activity reported by Nisbett and Kanouse (1969), who showed that the supermarket shopping of obese humans was unrelated to deprivation state. Like these human shoppers, Gross's randomly deprived rats exhibited an interest in food independent of internal state, depletion, or satiety. The animals seemed to have hungry eyes.

What then can we conclude from Gross's study about the ontology of external control of obese humans? An externally imposed schedule, combining both scarcity and unpredictability, might be expected to encourage dependence upon external cues for the regulation of eating. Given the uncertainty of such a schedule, it would be best to eat whenever possible, regardless of internal needs. For a neonate, these conditions might well produce a lasting pattern of external control. Bruch (1973) suggests that the early environments of many obese people may have created psychological conditions that override the testimony of internal feedback. This speculation leads us to suppose that in societies where food is normally scarce, a large proportion of the population would exhibit external control of eating. The presence of this pattern in ecologies of scarcity would not necessarily have the same association with obesity that has been found in our society. The expectation of patterns of external control among people living in conditions of constant scarcity and unpredictability has been confirmed in observations of the Yanamamo Indians of Brazil. When food is available, they eat continuously. Social life is largely centered on food and when food is plentiful, the Yanamamos feast even to the point of vomiting. Yet the males of the tribe also seem able to spend days hunting without food in the jungle without being discomfited by pangs of hunger.

The conclusions drawn from Gross's (1968) study are that regardless of factors such as heredity, the imposition of irregular feeding and scarcity should facilitate external control and internal insensitivity. Although most human neonates in our society do not live in an environment of scarcity, many may live in a very unpredictable food environment. The implications of this notion merit further research, and we are currently investigating these issues.

The fifth possible explanation focuses on a neural region known to be directly involved in the regulation of food intake—the hypothalamus—and in the monamine pathways that run through it. Investigations have been advanced by the demonstration that after bilateral destruction of the ventromedial hypothalamus (VMH), animals practically double their weight in a relatively short period of time (Brobeck, 1946; Brooks et al., 1946) by compulsive overeating. For several weeks after surgery voracious eating continues, and very rapid weight gain ensues. This is called the *dynamic phase* of hyperphagia. Finally a weight plateau is reached, and food intake drops to only slightly more than that of the normal animal. This is called the *static phase*. During both the static and dynamic phases, the lesioned animal is characterized by marked inactivity and finickiness towards food; it is also hyperemotional. This general hyperphagic syndrome has been demonstrated in rats, cats, mice, geese, monkeys, rabbits, goats, dogs, pigs, and sparrows.

In contrast to the normal animal, the lesioned animal is remarkably sensitive to cues in its diet, for it will eat large quantities of tasty food, but almost nothing of somewhat unpleasant food, an eating pattern also characteristic of obese humans. Both VMH-lesioned rats and obese humans appear to share hyposensitivity to the internal physiological cues associated with eating and hypersensitivity to the external cues associated with food proper. Although these similarities are striking, attempts to push the parallel may be capitalizing on an occasional resemblance between two otherwise remotely connected sets of data. Therefore, Schachter and Rodin and their associates (Schachter and Rodin, 1974) designed a set of experiments to explore this parallel in detail.

First, we considered finickiness. Though the lesioned animal is obese, it is also particularly sensitive to the effects of the texture or taste of its diet (Carlisle and Stellar, 1969; Corbit and Stellar, 1964; Teitelbaum, 1955). If quinine is added to its food, it eats far less than a normal animal whose food has been similarly tainted. On the other hand, if dextrose or lard is added to its normal food (they are apparently tasty to a rat) the lesioned animal eats far in excess of its regular intake or that of a control rat whose food has also been enriched. This is also true for obese humans (Decke, 1971; Nisbett, 1968a; Rodin, 1975).

The eating habits of lesioned animals have been thoroughly studied as well. Static obese rats eat on the average slightly but not considerably more than normal rats (Teitelbaum and Campbell, 1958). They also eat fewer meals per day, eat more per meal, and eat more rapidly than do normal animals (Teitelbaum and Campbell, 1958). For each of these facts there is parallel data for overweight humans (Beaudoin and Mayer, 1953; Ross et al., 1971; Schachter and Rodin, 1974). In addition, Schachter and Rodin (1974) identified behavior unrelated to food consumption, in which it was possible to draw somewhat more fanciful, though still not ridiculous, comparisons between the species. For example, studies of gross activity using stabilimeter cages or activity wheels have demonstrated that the lesioned animal is markedly less active than the normal animal (Teitelbaum, 1957). This does not indicate only that the lesioned animal has trouble dragging its immense bulk around the cage. The dynamic hyperphagic rat, though not yet fat, is quite as lethargic as his obese counterpart (Teitelbaum, 1957). Chirico and Stunkard (1960) used a pedometer to measure the distance walked each day by obese and normal humans who were matched for occupation, and found that the obese were far less active than normals. The mean distance walked per day by normal-weight subjects was 5.96; for the obese it was 3.74. Mayer and his coworkers (Bullen, Reed, and Mayer, 1964; Johnson, Burke, and Mayer, 1956; Mayer, 1965) report similar findings for participation in scheduled athletic activities in a summer camp.

Schachter and Rodin (1974) then identified still other types of behavior that were described in the literature for ventromedial lesioned animals and tested for these in obese humans. These were: (1) that the VMH animal is hyperemotional, easily startled, excitable, and difficult to handle (Eichelman, 1971; Wheatley, 1944), (2) that the lesioned animal is better at avoidance of painful stimuli than its normal counterpart (Grossman, 1972a; Levine and Soliday, 1960; McAdam and Kaelber, 1966; Sechzer, Turner, and Liebelt, 1966), (3) that the lesioned animal appears to be more sensitive to pain (Kaada, Rasmussen, and Kveim, 1962; Turner, Sechzer, and Liebelt, 1966), (3) that although the lesioned animal will eat large quantities of easily available food, it will not always work to get food (Miller, Bailey, and Stevenson, 1950). For each type of behavior a parallel was found in obese humans.

The striking parallels could be taken to suggest that something is awry with the hypothalamus of the obese humans. But although a few humans have specific anatomical or functional derangements, knowledge of such a condition is quite rare. What then, can we learn from this exercise in science by analogy? First we must ask, as we did for the obese human, whether these types of behavior are simply a consequence of the obesity in the lesioned animal. Graff and Stellar (1962) demonstrated clearly that finickiness could exist independent of obesity and that the occurrence of either finickiness or obesity was related to the size and placement of the hypothalamic lesion. Second, Schachter and Rodin (1974) compared the behavior of rats early in the dynamic stage—that is, well before their obesity had reached a plateau—to that of obese lesioned animals. By comparing dynamic to static VMH-lesioned animals, the effects of the lesion can be evaluated independent of obesity. Schachter and Rodin found that on measures of finickiness, eating habits, effort, activity, and emotionality, dynamic and static animals behaved very much the same. On amount eaten per meal and amount eaten when animals were unrestrained, the responses of only the dynamic animal were exaggerated; and it would appear, as Corbit and Stellar (1964) have maintained, that the degree of obesity does exert some inhibitory influence on consumption of ordinary food. Our analyses supported the findings of Corbit and Stellar regarding food consumption but we suggest that their conclusion is limited to this domain. On virtually all other dimensions the two groups of animals were quite similar. It would appear that obesity qua obesity is not the cause of most of the behavior associated with the hypothalamic-hyperphagic syndrome.

If obesity does not produce the changes in eating behavior typical of lesioned animals or of overweight humans, possibly heightened external responsiveness contributes to obesity. To test this hypothesis in humans, we again selected an eight-week summer camp for girls (Rodin and Slochower, 1967). This was not a diet camp, so food was abundant, attractively prepared, and served family style. Treats sent by parents were plentiful in each cabin, and the girls could buy candy at any time at the camp canteen. We predicted that the more external a child was, the more her eating behavior would be influenced by the shift to abundant food cues that coming to camp provided. This, in turn, would affect her weight. In contrast, nonexternal children were expected to be more responsive to internal physiological signals and thus to maintain a relatively constant body weight independent of alterations in the environment. The strong test of this hypothesis was provided by studying normal-weight people with no overweight history.

The same measures of external responsiveness used in the earlier study (Rodin, 1976) were given to all campers during the first week. Standardized externality scores for each subject were then correlated with weight change from the first to final week divided by starting weight. A significant positive correlation between externality and this weight change measure suggested that the children who were most external subsequently gained the most weight. Activity and emotional adjustment were not related to weight change.

As indicated by their weight gain, many external children must have found camp an environment with more novel, abundant, or tasty food cues than home. It is also possible, however, that for others camp actually offered fewer food cues. If this were true, then some external children may have lost weight at camp as a consequence of their externality. The mean standardized externality scores can be divided for children who lost weight ($\bar{x}$ = −1.94), those whose weight remained relatively constant ($\bar{x}$ = −4.423), and those who gained weight ($\bar{x}$ = 4.22).[1] As the means indicate, the weight gainers and the weight losers were more external than the "stables".

That there are externals of normal weight who behave like the moderately obese lends further support to the theory that externality is not purely a function of overweight but rather reflects an underlying tendency toward hyperresponsiveness. Yet degree of overweight is not significantly related to degree of externality. Although externality is related to amount of weight gain in the short run, it apparently is not related to *degree* of long-term weight regulation.

This distinction may help to explain why some external children were already overweight when they arrived at camp and others were not. Perhaps people responsive to external stimuli who maintain normal weight are influenced by major shifts in food cues. Such shifts produce short-term weight gain, but their long-term regulation is responsive to other factors. On the other hand, overweight externals may have long-term regulatory mechanisms that do not inhibit continued weight gain resulting from heightened responsiveness. Although we have no data that directly test this issue, some patterns of weight gain differences are suggestive. Of the overweight campers who gained weight, 86 percent reached their highest weight at week 8. Among girls of normal weight who gained, 70 percent reached their highest weights before week 8 and then began to lose. The novelty of the food environment diminished over time, but it is also possible that long-term regulatory mechanisms were taking over. Such mechanisms could be biological, psychological, or both.

In summary, the data suggest that on the basis of pretested differences in external responsivity we can predict with some degree of accuracy whose weight will change in a novel external environment. We can predict to a lesser degree the direction of the change. In fact, it might be expected that when those responsive to external stimuli are exposed to a novel food setting for a sufficient period of time their weight should be affected. For example,

---

[1] The scale of standardized scores ranged from −8 to +9.

in the first year of college, there are typically large weight changes among freshmen living away from home. This experience could parallel summer camp. Because the present data were obtained for a sample of subjects with no present or past history of overweight, we can conclude that externality is not simply caused by corpulence.

This causal relationship also finds support in the ventromedial-lesioned animal. We assume that some consequence of the lesion produced heightened responsiveness to external cues that in turn led to overfeeding. Grossman (1966) produced a reversible lesion by implanting cannulas in the VMH. This made it possible to release atropine into the cannula and produce a functional lesion of brief duration (i.e., deactivate the region chemically). Grossman showed that when the VMH was temporarily blocked, the rat's characteristic unwillingness to work and the emotional lability often attributed to it were very much in evidence. When the atropine was metabolized, the behavior of the animals became practically the same as that of control animals that had received saline through their cannulas. Grossman did not report any experiments in which functionally lesioned animals were allowed to eat freely for long periods, and it cannot be said that such animals would have become fat had they been given unlimited access to very palatable food. But it seems likely.

More current evidence from a different procedure provides the strongest support for the hypothesis that responsiveness to external stimuli leads to overeating and weight gain. Marshall (1975) gave his animals unilateral (i.e., on only one side of the brain) VMH lesions. Because the neural region on one side of the brain is responsive to the external environment on the contralateral side, Marshall varied the location of the food dish. He found that when the lesion was on the right side of the ventromedial hypothalamus, animals ate primarily from the left food hopper; when the lesion was on the left side they fed primarily at the right food hopper. This suggests that the lesion itself enhances cue responsiveness. Marshall reported that these animals were also hyperresponsive to a variety of tactile and sensory stimuli unrelated to food. Gibson and Gazzaniga (1971) noted a comparable finding in split-brain monkeys with unilateral hypothalamic damage. Such monkeys overate only when using the eye that projected to the hemisphere with the ventromedial lesion, which suggests that external visual cues influenced feeding behavior. These findings—that unilateral damage can produce overeating and general stimulus reactivity largely lateralized to stimuli in the contralateral field—provide important clues to the role of the ventromedial area in the development and maintenance of obesity.

Ultimately, the production of external control of eating in the rat by means of surgical lesions may not aid our understanding of the genesis of such behavior in normal animals or in humans. Nonetheless, it is certainly possible that humans may differ in certain central nervous system activities, either because of genetics or development, and thus be differentially responsive to external stimuli. Marshall's work suggests that hyperresponsiveness might be related to increased activity within catecholamine-containing systems that run through the hypothalamus. Central neurons containing catecholamines have been identified as contributing to broad, nonspecific components of arousal that are associated with homeostatic imbalance and conditions of excitement or alarm (Stricker and Zigmond, 1976). The neurochemical link between responsivity, arousal, and feeding systems has exciting implications for the study of external responsiveness and obesity. Peripheral states of deprivation and arousal may also give chemical information that goes into this pathway, which would explain why hungry organisms could also be more responsive to external stimuli.

Future Implications

Although experimental evidence supports the view that responsiveness to external stimuli contributes to the development and maintenance of obesity, the data do not support an extreme environmentalist position. If obesity is not inherited, body frame does appear genetically linked. Inherited metabolic abnormalities have been extensively studied, but they probably do not account for much human obesity. But a genetic predisposition to form adipose tissue or to be more aroused by external stimuli may exist. Clearly we must not overlook the importance of a genetic contribution to obesity, although the specific nature of the inheritance has yet to be clearly identified.

Next, early experience may also play a crucial causal role in obesity. Obesity developed in childhood appears the most resistant to treatment; the odds against successful weight reduction are 28 to 1 (Bray, 1970) if a child remains obese until the end of adolescence. The mechanisms that maintain obesity once it is developed in childhood are not yet fully identified, but one crucial factor is the number of fat cells. The number of fat cells, in turn, is determined at least in part by high-calorie diets during infancy and childhood. Feeding patterns may not only influence adipose cell development and consequent metabolic processes but may also be directly linked to the development of patterns of responsiveness to external stimuli.

Finally, although we have not discussed it in this model, physical inactivity can play a role in the development and maintenance of obesity. Energy expenditure consumes calories, either from ingested food or from body stores. In modern affluent societies, energy-sparing devices reduce energy expenditure and may enhance the tendency to caloric accumulation. Although obese people are apparently less physically active than normal people, we do not know the extent to which inactivity is important in the etiology of human obesity.

We have also gone a long way towards understanding which factors do *not* cause obesity. Most metabolic abnormalities are now known to be primarily caused by adiposity rather than to be its cause. The severe psychological disturbances, so often presumed to be associated with obesity, cannot be proven to exist with any great frequency. Emotional difficulties that do exist appear to be a consequence of attempts to lose weight and of a negative self-image. If food were not a positive reinforcement for some obese people, they would not overeat. It is not surprising that these people overeat under conditions of distress and unhappiness. However, other obese people overeat when they are especially happy, and for some there is no apparent association between overeating and emotional state. Psychopathological factors are not generally the cause of most common forms of obesity.

The crucial studies remain to be done. They should determine the factors that predispose a person to obesity, and define which are genetic, which are related to early experience, and what the contribution of each may be. Prospective developmental studies should provide these answers, and several independent laboratories including our own are undertaking them.

An Opponent-Process Theory of Acquired Motivation: The Affective Dynamics of Addiction

Richard L. Solomon
University of Pennsylvania

Introduction

Drug addiction is a powerful form of acquired motivation. It often pulls into its vortex most of the everyday behaviors and concerns of the addict. In spite of this very conspicuous feature, drug addiction has no special properties which require it to be classified as an illness. Indeed, a major theme of this chapter is that drug addiction is too much like many other kinds of acquired motivation, such as love or attachment, to be profitably classified as psychopathological. We will argue that drug addiction reflects the operation of a normal and general motivational principle.

A person's use of drugs progresses through stages. The reasons for drug use are obvious after a user has developed tolerance for a drug, and has come to suffer intense withdrawal symptoms during abstinence from it. But the initial reasons for having used the chemical are usually complex and obscure. Probably as a consequence of subtle social forces and personality

This research was supported by USPHS Grant MH-04202. I am grateful to Dr. Luci Paul for her thorough criticism of an earlier draft. I wrote this article in 1974 while I was at the Psychology Department, Princeton University. (A later article on this same topic was published in 1977.) The helpful criticisms of many Princeton colleagues are gratefully acknowledged.

predispositions, a person will become a drug sampler, a *tentative* user. No one has yet convincingly established the necessary or sufficient conditions that cause a person to try a drug. The single best predictor of drug sampling is drug availability (Bourne, 1974). For example, in England in 1962, 15 percent of all opiate addicts were nurses and physicians (Jaffee, 1965). Curiosity, unhappiness, vague cravings, frustration, anger, loneliness, and peer group social pressures have all, at one time or another, been thought to precipitate drug sampling.

Though these influences may be antecedents for the subsequent development of a drug addiction, they certainly are not sufficient to explain most of the salient features of addiction. Drug use is too widespread and drug addiction too infrequent for the mere sampling of a drug to be a major cause of subsequent addiction. In a report by Chambers (1971) for the New York State Narcotic Addiction Control Commission, projections based on actual interviews with drug users yielded this information: in the state of New York (population 18,241,266), barbiturates were used at least six times per month by 377,000 people; sedative hypnotics (i.e., Doriden) by 173,000 people; tranquilizers (i.e., Librium) by 525,000 people; Thorazine by 85,000 people. Pep pills (i.e., Dexedrine) were used by 110,000; diet pills (Dexamyl and similar drugs) by 225,000; prescribed narcotics (i.e., Demerol) by 21,000; marijuana by 485,000; and heroin by 41,000 people. Add to this veritable army of drug users the 46 percent of the population who drink alcohol and we have a pool of millions of users who, in New York state, are potential drug addicts.

Yet the addiction rate is relatively low for users of drugs, and among the drugs there are large differences in the proportion of regular users who eventually become addicts. For example, about 8 percent of regular drinkers of alcohol are addicts (U.S. Department of Health, Education and Welfare, 1971, p. 31). Sniffed and smoked heroin of high purity were not very addictive to American soldiers in Vietnam. Only about 7 percent of the regular users still used heroin after a year back in the United States (Robins, 1974). For "mainlined" heroin, the addiction rate is undoubtedly higher, sometimes estimated to be 75 percent. The differences could be attributed to the psychoactive properties of the drugs themselves or to the kind of person who selects a specific drug for regular use after extensive drug sampling.

Of the psychoactive properties of drugs, the most crucial for their addictiveness are their initial pleasure-giving and their later abstinence unpleasantness. Some people experience much pleasure when they first take heroin. Others don't. Indeed, some go through an agonizing experience and never take heroin again. These differences in drug effects have been attributed to physiological-constitutional differences among people. They have been attributed to enduring personality traits acquired as a consequence of life's experiences. Some clinical studies have purported to show that initial drug experience is related to specific emotional problems. Thus, a neurotic may report that he or she tried a drug in order to relieve anxiety, or a psychopath may report that he or she was seeking a new thrill. A depressive may report that the drug was a possible way to mitigate intense depressed moods. Some psychologists have characterized *all* drug users as "schizoid, depressed, dependent, hostile, and sexually immature" (Jaffe, 1965, p. 286). Our skepticism is appropriate here, because addicts are assessed for personality attributes *after* they are identified as addicts. Nevertheless, the users of a particular kind of drug often do show common patterns of behavior. We don't know whether such patterns are a consequence of, or one of the causes of, drug use because most psychological studies of drug users are retrospective and correlational in design.

It would, however, be foolish to ignore the ideas emerging from retrospective studies. For example, it has been speculated that most alcoholics solve their sex, aggression, and dependency conflicts by using alcohol as an aid to "acting out." Opiate users have been described as personalities whose major anxieties stem from pain, sexuality, or aggression conflicts. The anxieties are handled passively, aided by the opiate and not by "acting out." However, these psychological attributes exist among nonaddicts too, and their frequency is unknown. Thus, we cannot now know the correlation between these traits and opiate use. On the other hand, the opiate user infrequently turns to alcohol when in trouble, and the alcohol user rarely turns to opiates. Because many drug users have sampled numerous drugs, such preferences may indeed be significant; for now we can only guess at the behavioral laws generating them.

Most drug use is probably *instrumental* in nature at the outset. That is, in addition to solving temporarily some social problem, the drug may relieve or reduce the unpleasantness of a variety of recurring emotional and motivational states. However, after a user has dosed many times, the motivation changes radically. The problems that initially encouraged drug use now become relatively trivial beside the new, major problem: *abstinence agony and drug craving*. Once this shift in motivational control has occurred, the user is lost in a new world. Instead of coping with problems that potentially could be ameliorated by a variety of *instrumental* behaviors, the user must cope with abstinence agony and drug craving itself, the amelioration of which is a long, torturous and often hopeless affair. Drug craving can become so powerful that most of the other major concerns of living (sex, food quality, achievements, social obligations, social rewards, aesthetic pleasures, liquids, family pleasures, and needs) become trivial by comparison. They may become ignored.

In this chapter some of the affective dynamics of addiction will be discussed. The description will be behavioral and psychological. Biochemical and neurochemical dynamics will be omitted for the most part, as a matter of convenience. It will be argued that a theoretical model for addiction solely in behavioral and psychological terms can be useful at the present stage of our understanding. The model may be useful in suggesting new directions for the investigation and interpretation of drug addiction.

We first assume that drug addiction is only one of many types of acquired motivation, all sharing common features. We describe a new theory of acquired motivation, the *opponent-process theory* (Solomon and Corbit, 1973; Solomon and Corbit, 1974; Hoffman and Solomon, 1974, D'Amato, 1974, pp. 97–99), the features of which generate the facts of drug addiction. The theoretical model will enable us to specify the behavioral attributes of addiction and the mode of action of addictive drugs in a new and simple way.

The Opponent-Process Theory of Acquired Motivation

a-Processes and b-Processes

Assume that the brains of all mammals are organized to oppose and suppress many types of affect (emotional arousal, hedonic reaction, strong feeling), whether they are pleasurable *or* aversive. The opposing affective or hedonic processes are automatically set in motion by events that psychologists have identified, through defining experiments, to be effective Pavlovian UCSs or operant reinforcers (rfts).

All *primary affective processes* elicited by strong UCSs or rfts are postulated to correlate closely with the stimulus intensity, quality and duration of the reinforcer. These primary, stimulus-induced processes are phasic and sensitive to small stimulus changes. They rarely show very much sensitization or habituation. We call these *a-processes*. By Pavlov's definition, they are emotional or affective UCRs. For example, a snake (UCS) elicits a reflex fear pattern (UCR). The taste of chocolate syrup (UCS) elicits salivation (UCR) and a pleasure state (UCR).

A primary (UCR) process arouses a *b-process* which then opposes and suppresses the affective strength of the a-process. In contrast to the a-processes, b-processes (the opponent-processes) are thought to be sluggish and inertia-laden. They are (1) of relatively long latency or reaction time; (2) slow to build up to maximum amplitude; and (3) slow to decay after the stimulus input (UCS) is terminated and the a-process (UCR) has ceased. Because the b-process is an opponent-process, it must have an affective or hedonic quality *opposite* to that of the a-process. The implications of this assumption are far-reaching, and so we will describe them in detail.

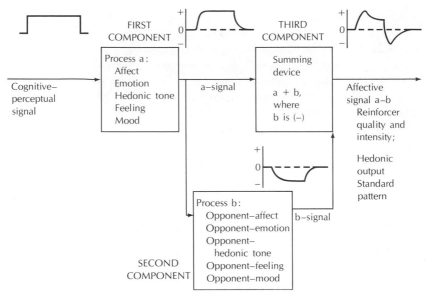

Figure 2-1. A box diagram of the interactions between a-processes and b-processes. The b-processes are activated by a-processes, and the resultant [a-b] is determined by a sum-mator. (From Solomon, R. L., and Corbit, J. D., 1974.)

Interaction of a-Processes and b-Processes

The affective or hedonic condition of the organism at any moment is postulated to be the sum of the intensities of the a-process and b-process, where the b-process has a negative sign (because it opposes the a-process). Whenever a is greater than b, the organism is in State A. Whenever b is greater than a, the organism is in State B. States A and B have affective and hedonic qualities and intensities dictated by the residual a-process or b-process sum. If being in State A is *positively* reinforcing, then being in State B will be *negatively* reinforcing, and vice versa.

The Processing System

Figure 2-1 is a box diagram of the opponent-process system. It reflects the simplicity of the model.

For illustration, the incoming signal is categorical (a dog), depicted as a square wave. Its side effect is the arousal of a primary affective or a-process. For example, suppose the subject is a cat, and the categorical information is "a dog is there." Assume that the UCR is fear. When the fear is aroused, then the b-process will be aroused. It will have an affective sign *opposite* to

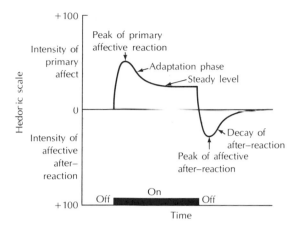

Figure 2-2. The standard pattern of affective dynamics, showing the five distinctive features of affect resulting from a typical, square-wave input. The B-state becomes manifest after the A-state is terminated. (From Solomon, R. L., and Corbit, J. D., 1974.)

that of the a-process. At this point, we can only guess what an affect opposite to fear might be. (When the dog is removed, we will see what the oppositeness implies).

The a-process and b-process amplitudes are now fed to a summator that will compute [a-b] at any moment, thus determining the quality and intensity of the resulting A-state. At UCS onset, most a-processes are more intense than their opposing b-process which, as we have said, has a slow onset. The subsequent slow buildup of the b-process will then produce a gradual decrease in the amplitude of the A-state, even while the UCS is still present. In this case, therefore, the cat will look less fearful as time goes on. It will appear to become accustomed to the dog's presence.

Then the dog goes away, removing the categorical stimulus for the a-process. According to the model, the a-process amplitude will go quickly to zero, but the b-process, being sluggish, will decay slowly. Therefore, directly after UCS termination, the peak amplitude and hedonic quality of the b-process will be revealed in the B-state, which, because the a-process is now zero, will be only b-process. In the example, the cat will look "relieved," "pleased," or some pleasure reaction will ensue a few seconds after the dog is gone. Then this B-state will slowly die away.

Standard Pattern of Affective Dynamics

This complex sequence of events, precipitated by the square-wave, categorical input, has *five distinctive features*. They are labeled in Figure 2-2. This complex function is called the *standard pattern of affective dynamics*. It is composed of (1) the peak of A; (2) the adaptation phase of A; (3) the steady level of A; (4) the peak of B; and (5) the decay of B back to the original baseline state.

In the affect-control system we have described, there is no need eventually to guess what is opposed to what. You merely observe the quality and intensity of the affective reaction directly following the termination of the UCS or rft. The peak of B will occur. This then must be the opponent of the affective reaction aroused by the onset and maintenance of the UCS or rft. Consider an analogy from color vision. If the presentation of a saturated red light is suddenly terminated, a human subject sees a green after-image that peaks in quality and intensity and then slowly dies away and is gone. This is the *negative* afterimage. Green is, therefore, the opponent color for red in current opponent-process color theory (Hurvich and Jameson, 1974). Our attention, then, is on negative, affective or hedonic afterimages which occur when UCSs are terminated.

Two examples of affect will illustrate the almost ubiquitous nature of such affective after-reaction phenomena.

Imprinting. A newly hatched duckling is exposed to a moving object or mother surrogate. The duckling looks at the object and follows it with its eyes, showing general excitement. We know that presentation of the moving object is a positive reinforcer (Hoffman et al., 1966). Its onset and maintenance will suppress distress-calling in uncomfortable or frightened ducklings, and the ducklings will acquire a variety of new, arbitrary operants if presentation of the mother surrogate is contingent upon those operants. If the mother surrogate is now removed, after three to 10 seconds there is a burst of distress calling that peaks in frequency and intensity and then gradually declines and disappears. The distress calling may index a state of loneliness, disappointment, abandonment or frustration. We don't know. But we can assume that the distress calls reflect an aversive B-state caused by the b-process that has been opposing the a-process previously elicited by the presentation of the positively reinforcing mother surrogate. Therefore, it is not surprising that we can easily train ducklings to perform arbitrary operants to obtain presentations of the mother surrogate. Nor would it be surprising if we successfully should train the duckling to perform operants to prevent the removal of the mother surrogate. Such events establish the aversiveness of the B-state which underlies the distress calls (see Hoffman and Solomon, 1974).

Habituation to Aversiveness: Dogs Receiving Shocks of Long Duration. A naive dog is placed in a Pavlov harness and 10-second, high intensity shocks are delivered to its hind paws. At shock onset the dog yelps and its head tilts back; its eyes bulge and its pupils dilate fully. Its hair stands erect and there is profuse defecation and urination. As the dog struggles, its heart rate and blood pressure increase. Figure 2-3 shows a typical heart rate

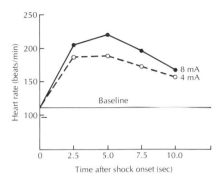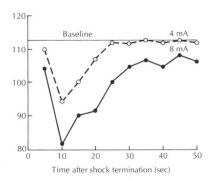

Figure 2-3. Typical course of heart-rate reaction to intense foot shocks in the dog. While 10-second shock is on, heart rate increases and then decreases. When shock is terminated, heart rate falls significantly below the base line or resting level. Then it slowly returns to base line, but more slowly after the 8 mA shock than after the 4 mA shock. (After Katcher, A. H., et al., 1969.)

reaction: it peaks at 2.5–5 seconds and then declines even while the shock is still present. This is true for both 4 and 8 milliampere (mA) shock intensities. After 10 seconds, shock is turned off, and in the bottom portion of the figure we see a cardiac rate decrease to a below baseline level, followed by a slow return to baseline. The deceleratory reaction is greater after the 8 mA shock is terminated than it is for the 4 mA shock. Both decelerations peak at a level far below the baseline. Many of the gross behavioral events are loosely correlated with heart rate changes. Vocalization is most intense directly after shock onset, and it decreases even while the shock is still on. This is sometimes true of struggling, pupillary dilation and piloerection.

Notice that this example differs from that of imprinting because the presence of the UCS is aversive and its response-contingent removal can be shown to constitute negative reinforcement. However, in both examples, the five distinctive features of the standard pattern of affective dynamics (Figure 2-2) are manifested. The onset of each UCS produced a marked change in the subject's behavior. The change then mitigated. When the UCS was terminated, the behavior of the subject did not simply subside. Instead, after termination of the stimulus a *new* state revealed itself, one which could *not* have occurred had the arousing UCS *not* been presented and then terminated. This new state is State B. In the first example, termination was aversive. In the second example, it was the onset that was aversive. In the first example, the onset was positively reinforcing. In the second, the termination was positive reinforcement (see Weisman and Litner, 1969a, b, for the positive effects of events coming after shock termination; see also Moscovitch and LoLordo, 1968). The standard pattern of affective dynamics can be readily deduced from the opponent-process model for acquired motivation, as shown in Figure 2-1.

Strengthening the b-Process by Frequent Use

So far, our attention has been confined to the initial stimulations. Now we look at what happens when the same UCS is *repeatedly* presented. In the imprinted duckling, two phenomena occur. First, the veteran imprinted duckling no longer spends as much time looking at or staying constantly close to the mother surrogate. Second, when the mother surrogate is arbitrarily removed, distress calling and frantic activity is more intense and long lasting than it was at the start. This fact is illustrated in Figure 2-4 (from Hoffman et al., 1974), in which minutes of distress calling during a 60-second absence of the mother surrogate are shown as a function of repeated, 60-second presentations and removals of the mother surrogate. There is an orderly growth in the amount of distress calling, which we assume to reflect an intensification of the b-process caused by repeated occurrences of the UCS. Imprinting is, therefore, *not* an all-or-none phenomenon (see Hoffman et al., 1974; Hoffman and Ratner, 1973). The duckling becomes more and more attached to, or dependent upon, the presence of the mother surrogate, as measured by the lengthier bouts of distress calls when the mother surrogate is removed. (It will be helpful for the reader to think about the distress calls as an index of abstinence agony or mother craving).

Analogous changes occurred in the dogs' responses to shocks to their hind feet as they became veterans of this stressful treatment. The intensity and frequency of yelps in response to shocks decreased. There was no further defecation or urination. Struggling was sporadic. Heart rate increases became small and infrequent. The dogs had become accustomed to the

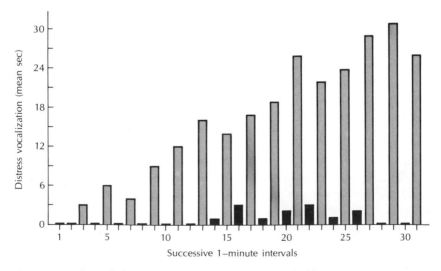

Figure 2-4. The orderly growth of distress calling in the duckling as a consequence of repeated exposures and removals of the imprinting stimulus. (From Hoffman et al., 1974.)

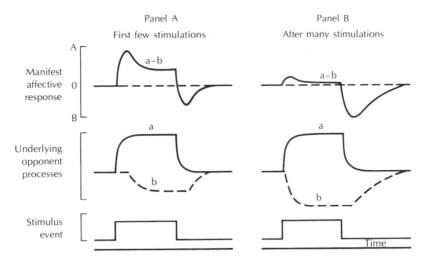

Figure 2-5. The consequences of subtracting the b-process from the a-process when the b-process is weak and when it is strengthened by repeated use. The resultant A-state is small after the b-process is strengthened, but the B-state is more intense and longer lasting. (From Solomon, R. L. and Corbit, J. D., 1974.)

shocks. However, when a shock was terminated, the decrease in heart rate was very large and long lasting. Whereas the rate initially declined to about 80 beats per minute as is shown in Figure 2-3 (with a baseline of about 110 beats per minute), and required about 2 minutes to return to baseline, after many days of experimentation the same dogs showed a decrease to 45–50 beats per minute, and required about 5–10 minutes to return to baseline after the same 8 mA shocks (Katcher et al., 1969).

The generalization we can draw from our two examples of potent UCSs repeated many times is that as the subject appears to become more accustomed to, or less reactive to, the *onset* and *presence* of the UCS, it also becomes *more* intensely and enduringly reactive to the cessation of that UCS. Our theoretical model leads us to infer that A-states *decrease* in amplitude with repeated elicitations, but that the consequent B-states *increase* in intensity and duration with repeated elicitations. Assume, then, that *b-processes are strengthened by use and weakened by disuse.* This postulate, taken with the other features of the theoretical model, generates the comparison of outcomes shown in Figure 2-5. There we see a representation of the summing process subtracting the b-process from the a-process for initial UCS presentations and for the same UCS after many repeated presentations. The UCS is represented as a square wave event (such as shock going on and off, or a mother surrogate being presented and taken away). The changes in the standard pattern of affective dynamics are brought about by the strengthening of the b-process. The resulting A-state is seen to be small, but the B-state is large and enduring.

Temporal Variables in Strengthening b-Processes

The important conditions for strengthening the b-process are illuminated by recent experiments carried out by Starr (1974; 1976). Ducklings were assigned to four groups. Each group was exposed to a different temporal arrangement of stimulations by, and absences from, a moving mother surrogate. The experimental conditions are summarized in Table 2-1.

Notice that for each group the total length of exposure to the surrogate mother was six minutes. Familiarity with the mother surrogate was therefore equated across all four groups. What differed among groups was the duration of the repeated absence intervals, or interstimulus intervals (ISIs). Distress calling was recorded during each absence period. Figure 2-6 shows for each of the four groups the amount of distress calling during the first 30 seconds of each absence period. The rate of growth of amount of distress calling was lower when the stimulus exposures were widely spaced in time. The apparent asymptote also was lower when exposures were widely spaced in time. For the 5-minute absence group there was no growth at all in amount of distress calling.

Distress calls are assumed to measure the magnitude of the B-state. Therefore, it is reasonable to assume that one important condition for the strengthening of the b-process is an interval short enough to prevent the complete decay of the b-process between stimulus presentations. This *critical decay duration* (Starr, 1976) must have been between two and five minutes in the duckling experiment of Table 2-1. Your awareness of the critical decay duration concept will later make the analysis of drug addiction much simpler.

Another condition for the strengthening of the b-process is the duration of exposure itself. Eiserer and Hoffman (1973), in a series of experiments on the "priming" of ducklings by the presentation of a mother surrogate for different continuous durations, showed a strong positive correlation between amount of distress calling after removal of the stimulus and the duration of

Table 2-1 Experimental Conditions Used to Strengthen the b-Process

	Time of exposure to mother surrogate			Time-out interval	
Group	Length (sec)	Number	Total	Time	Number
I-0	360	1	6 min	0	1
I-1	30	12	6 min	1 min	12
I-2	30	12	6 min	2 min	12
I-3	30	12	6 min	5 min	12

*From Starr, Mark D. Unpublished doctoral thesis. University of Pennsylvania, 1976.

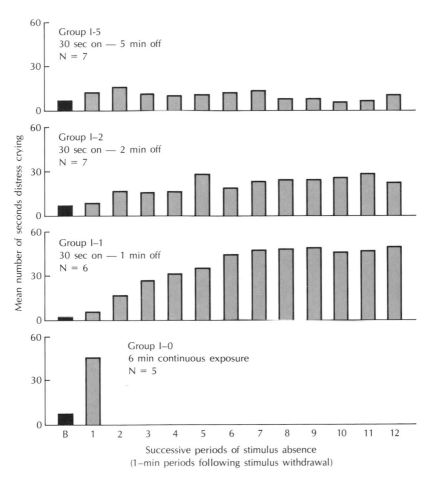

Figure 2-6. The growth of distress calling in imprinted ducklings as a function of the duration of the time-out period. All four groups received the same total exposure to the mother surrogate, and in groups I-5, I-2, and I-1, each exposure was of 30 seconds duration. In Group I-0, the mother surrogate was presented continuously, and the distress calling was recorded for the first 30 seconds of the first time-out period. When the time-out period was five minutes long, there was no growth in distress calling. (From Starr, 1976, unpublished doctoral thesis, University of Pennsylvania.)

the preceding exposure to the stimulus (see Figure 2-7). This relation might imply that the b-process is continuously strengthened while it is being exercised, or, alternatively, that it is more fully elicited when given an adequate time of arousal.

It seems reasonable to infer that for every UCS or rft there is a critical decay duration sufficient to prevent the strengthening of the b-process *despite* repeated stimulations, when we hold constant the duration of each

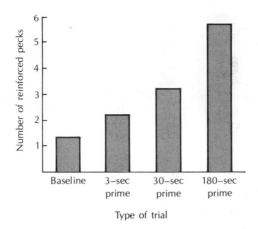

Figure 2-7. The increasing amount of distress calling in ducklings as a function of the duration of the prior exposure of the duckling to the mother surrogate. This is the "priming" effect. (From Eiserer, L. A., and Hoffman, H. S., 1973.)

exposure. If we increase exposure duration, then we should see the critical decay duration increase. For *any* UCS intensity and duration, there should exist a critical decay duration that will both allow the b-process to decay completely and prevent the strengthening of the b-process when stimulations are repeated. Later it will be apparent that such a conception helps us to understand the conditions under which drug addiction will or will not develop with repeated use.

If we hold an interstimulus interval constant, the strengthening of the b-process will depend on two variables, the *intensity* of the a-process (see Figure 2-3) and the *duration* of each UCS presentation (see Figure 2-7). A precise mathematical model of the interrelations between UCS intensity and duration and the ISI and the strengthening of the b-process is now needed.

The Opponent-Process Theory, Reinforcement, and Conditioning

Motivation and Reinforcement

By this time, a psychologically sophisticated reader may have noticed that even though our theory is called a motivational one, the motivational status of the A and B states has not been considered. In addition, even though behavior has been demonstrated to be importantly changed by repeated experiences (see Figures 2-4, 2-5 and 2-6), there has been no mention of associative processes (conditioning or learning).

First, consider the motivational properties of A and B states. The simplest assumption is that organisms act vigorously and purposefully only in the presence of an aversive state. Pleasure-seeking may appear to occur, but what actually is occurring is behavior that removes or decreases either an aversive A-state or an aversive B-state (see Brown, 1961). Behavioral arousal occurs whenever an aversive A-state (fright, pain, disgust, irritation) is precipitated by the onset and maintenance of an aversive UCS or rft or whenever an aversive B-state is precipitated by the termination of a positive UCS or rft (loneliness, grief, disappointment, drug craving, loss, depression, and taste craving).

If organisms are being strongly stimulated by positive reinforcers, they initially ought to just relax and enjoy the stimulation. There is nothing to do, unless the reinforcer becomes less pleasurable. However, positive reinforcers, by their onset and maintenance, selectively reinforce the operants upon which they are contingent. They determine which operants in a huge array of operants will be selected when a specific, aversive B-state occurs again. Thus, aversive B-states are the cues for, and selectors of, appropriate operants, just as aversive A-states are the cues for, and selectors of, appropriate operants in escape and avoidance learning. In the same vein, the sudden termination of an aversive A-state will reinforce the operant that immediately preceded its termination.

This simple system of motivation and reinforcement can both arouse and select appropriate behaviors. For opponent-process theory, an appropriate behavior is one that has been effective in preventing or terminating aversive A-states or B-states. Pleasurable B-states are able only to reinforce or select operants; initially they are unable to energize operants selectively. Because pleasurable B-states occur directly after the termination of those UCSs that arouse aversive a-processes, the possibility exists that after much repetition the associative mechanisms can render the two processes equivalent. One could become a "symbol" of the other. Therefore, we need to look closely at the evidence on the associative processes relevant to an opponent-process theory of acquired motivation.

Pavlovian Conditioning and Opponent-Processes

Assume again that b-processes are strengthened through repeated use and weakened by prolonged disuse. Could associative mechanisms be responsible for this? The evidence is still equivocal on this point. Perhaps some of the strengthening of the b-process is associative and some non-associative. Our initial assumption was (Solomon and Corbit, 1974) that the process is non-associative, and that conditioning and learning are not involved. There were reasons for this. First, consider Starr's ducklings in the group that received 6 minutes of continuous exposure to the mother surrogate. Upon removal of the mother surrogate, the distress calling was as intense as for the group receiving 12, 30-second exposures, with a 1-minute ISI. Evidently conditioning trials, which would allow the associations between environmental stimuli and UCSs to be formed, were not necessary for the distress calling to become intense. Only one long exposure to the UCS was necessary.

Consider infants born of methadone mothers. Even though the environment is radically altered at birth, the infants are tolerant to opiates and they suffer severe withdrawal disturbances when opiates are withdrawn. If conditioning processes were necessary for the strengthening of the b-process, then birth should remove most of the controlling CSs, and the infants should lose their opiate tolerance and suffer no withdrawal symptoms. Not so.

On the other hand, consider Siegel's (1975, 1977) recent findings on the control of morphine tolerance in rats by environmental stimuli. The pain thresholds of rats can be measured by the temperature of a hot plate just hot enough to elicit paw withdrawal. Injections of morphine raise the threshold, demonstrating the analgesic effect of morphine in rats. However, if the morphine injections are repeated each day, the hot plate threshold decreases. Siegel takes this as evidence of tolerance to morphine. Moreover, this tolerance is situation-dependent. It can be eliminated by altering the experimental setting or procedures in a discriminable way. Siegel believes that some type of compensatory mechanism is being conditioned to the situational cues, and that this mechanism produces the lowered effect of morphine (tolerance).

Within the framework of opponent-process theory, Siegel's view could mean that the b-process is being elicited on the first trial, is being conditioned to environmental cues, and the well-conditioned subject in the presence of the controlling CSs will have a small [a-b] sum. It will have drug tolerance. However, remove the CSs and the [a-b] quantity will be large, or tolerance will be small. Siegel's evidence is, at present, quite compelling.

It seems safe to assume that conditioning processes will occur whenever effective UCSs are contingent upon reliable environmental CSs. Based on what we already know about fear conditioning and salivary conditions, the conditioning of a-processes is a fact. When we pair a CS with a fear-arousing UCS, the CS assumes some of the arousal properties of the UCS. Such CSs are usually called CS^+. If we use a pleasure-arousing UCS and pair a CS with it, we see the CS acquire some of the properties that the UCS has. We also call that a CS^+. In opponent-process theory, such CSs are called CS_A, meaning that they tend to evoke A-states similar to the A-states originally evoked by the UCS.

An important question is whether B-states are conditionable. Siegel's work suggests that the answer is yes, and that this process proceeds more rapidly than does the conditioning of the a-process in the case of morphine use in rats. Siegel's finding is remarkable, because in many other cases of Pavlovian conditioning, such as fear conditioning, salivary conditioning, heart rate conditioning or eyeblink conditioning, the initial development of the CR usually is characterized by the growth of A-state properties in response to the CS, not B-state properties. With the use of drugs as a UCS, this may not be the case. For example, Siegel (1975) has shown that the CR given in response to a cue paired previously with insulin injections will be a hyperglycemic reaction, even though the original effect of the insulin is to produce a phasic hypoglycemia. Here again, we see a compensatory CR rather than a CR with UCR-like properties. There is some evidence that CRs of a compensatory type occur with CSs paired with epinephrine injections (Lichko, 1959).

Compensatory CRs may be taken as evidence for the rapid conditioning of b-processes. However, there is more direct evidence. In Pavlovian fear conditioning, a stimulus paired repeatedly with the peak of B acquires properties opposite to those acquired by a CS presented directly prior to the onset of A. Because the peak of B comes right after UCS termination, such a stimulus arrangement fits the Pavlovian *backward conditioning* paradigm. In fear conditioning, such a backward CS becomes a conditioned *inhibitor* of fear (Moscovitch and LoLordo, 1968; Maier, 1976). In opponent-process theory, such a CS, established in the backward conditioning paradigm, is called a CS_B, a CS that elicits a B-state.

During the first few conditioning trials, when the subject is relatively unfamiliar with the UCS, the b-process should be weak in comparison to the a-process. Therefore, if we pair a CS_A with UCS onset and a CS_B with the peak of B, we should see a relatively rapid growth of the excitatory properties of CS_A but a relatively slow growth of the opponent-process properties of CS_B. However, after a large number of conditioning trials, the quantity [a-b] should be small due to the strengthening of the b-process, State A should be therefore of low amplitude, and increments in the excitatory CR should be very small as a function of conditioning trials. In contrast, at this later stage of conditioning, the increments of an opponent CR, caused by the pairings of CS_B with the peak of State B, should be relatively large. If, before the introduction of the Pavlovian CS-UCS contingency, the subject is habituated to the UCS, we should see, on the subsequent conditioning trials, the slow conditioning of CS_A but rapid conditioning of CS_B. Evidence on human GSR-fear conditioning tentatively suggests that this is so (Kimmel, 1971). In addition, Weisman and Litner (1969b) traced the growth of fear inhibition to a CS_B by training rats to spin a wheel to avoid unsignaled shocks. Then the rats were exposed to a CS_A that predicted the occurrence of shocks and a CS_B that predicted the nonoccurrence of shocks. The abilities of the CS_A to arouse fear and the CS_B to inhibit fear were measured by increases or decreases in the rats' rate of wheel-spinning. The CS_B function developed more slowly than did the

CS_A function. These findings are matched by some events seen in the phenomena of addiction (Wikler, 1971). The environmental events surrounding the self-injection of opiates often arouse some of the components of the primary reaction to the drug itself. Sham injections of saline can sometimes produce a temporary "high." Such placebo reactions would be expected if CS_A is established rapidly during frequent self-administration of drugs.

The standard pattern of affective dynamics (see Figure 2-2) tells us to expect recovery after the presentation of a CS_A to be very different from recovery after presentation of a CS_B. Recovery after the CS_A should be biphasic, but recovery after the CS_B should be monotonic. This is our reasoning. A CS_A should elicit a conditioned A-state, and because the a-process will be opposed by the b-process, the termination of CS_A should be followed first by the peak of B and then its slow decay. In contrast, elicitation of State B by a CS_B *cannot* arouse the a-process (the block diagram in Figure 2-1 shows why this is so: there is no feedback loop from the opponent-process to the primary process). Therefore, termination of CS_B will be followed only by a slow, monotonic decay of the b-process to some baseline. We will later use these expectations from the theory to organize some of the clinical findings on pitfalls in the cure of addiction.

Summary of The Opponent-Process Theory

The major details of an opponent-process model for motivation and reinforcement have been described. Many UCSs and rfts are postulated to arouse affective and hedonic a-processes that are opposed by affective and hedonic b-processes in a simple, dynamic affect control system. The a-processes are assumed to be phasic, relatively stable, and to follow the UCS quite closely. In contrast, the b-processes are of longer latency, are slow to build up strength, and are slow to decay. Furthermore, the b-processes are strengthened by repeated elicitation of their a-process opponent, provided that the properly short intervals occur between elicitations. Finally, resultant A-states and B-states are postulated to be conditionable to previously neutral stimuli.

These postulates constitute a broad theory of acquired motivation. The phenomena they explain are quite common both in nature and in the laboratory. One such phenomenon is drug addiction. The postulates construct a conceptual brain system for minimizing the affective and hedonic impact of UCSs and rfts, whether pleasureable or aversive. This system represents the assumed *normal* or usual way in which the brain copes with potent stimuli through its automatic, hedonic control mechanisms.

Why, then, is this theory applicable to the phenomena of drug addiction? Drug addiction is usually considered to be *pathological*. The title of this book, and the inclusion of the topic of addiction in it, attests to this assumption. However, in terms of the theoretical model, drug addiction cannot in principle be different from many other opponent-process motivational systems (e.g., attachment-loneliness, love-grief, taste pleasure-taste craving, sex pleasure-sex craving, or satisfaction-depression). Addiction ought to reflect the same kind of normal control system, of the opponent-process type. Therefore, addiction is *not* profitably labeled as pathological (unless we are willing to attach the pathology label to love, affection, love of power, love of money, social attachment or aesthetic interests).

Although our theoretical model is included in a book on behavioral pathology, it is not a model for pathology. Indeed, the model was induced from findings in a wide variety of laboratory experiments on normal subjects showing normal behavioral adjustments to potent UCSs and rfts. Analysis of the facts of addiction in such terms makes addiction easier to understand. Even a satisfactory definition of addiction will become easier to fashion, and it will be compatible with motivational theory at the same time that it is stripped of much of the confusing psychiatric and sociological language that has burdened previous definitions. We will be able to define the psychological attributes of an addictive substance or event as well as those of addictive behavior.

First, let us outline some of the major aspects of addiction to specific drugs and point out similarities and differences between drugs whenever possible. Then we can formulate some generalizations that seem to be true of all addictive drugs. Finally, we will relate these generalizations to the opponent-process model for acquired motivation.

The Major Addicting Drugs

Alcohol

According to the U.S. Department of Health, Education and Welfare, alcohol is considered by many drug experts to be a more significant problem than all other forms of drug abuse combined (1971, p. 21). Yet society's opinion of alcohol differs greatly from its posture toward other drugs. Alcohol is widely accepted as a good substance in many countries, as a satisfier of thirst, a way to enliven conversation, a part of good living, a food, a religious experience, a general nostrum for illnesses, and a psychedelic agent and intoxicant. Two-thirds of all adult Americans drink alcohol at least once a year. More than half drink alcohol at least once a month, and over 10 percent of the population drink alcohol every day. The distribution of alcohol intake in the population is skewed; most people drink very little and a minority drinks large amounts.

In a report published in 1975, the U.S. Department of Health, Education and Welfare said:

> Most people drink alcoholic beverages to obtain feelings of pleasure as well as relief from fears and tensions. Undoubtedly this is the basic reason for the widespread popularity of alcohol as a social beverage. This typical response is not universal, however. For some people, the same small amounts of alcohol result not in relaxation but in increased anxiety, not in happiness but in suspicion and distrust. These atypical responses may lead to belligerent feelings or actions, or episodes of confusion and disorientation. With the drinking of larger amounts, however, individual differences in behavior tend to decrease, and the pharmacological depressant effects of alcohol begin to predominate. As this occurs, a typical sequence of tiredness, sleepiness, and ultimately stupor occurs, although feelings of tiredness may nevertheless be accompanied by irritability on the one hand, or by mellowness and warmth on the other, depending on the individual and the circumstances. . . . The concentration of alcohol in the blood which affects the functioning of the brain is lower than that which would affect other tissues. The observable effects of alcohol intoxication, such as slurred speech and unsteady gait, are not due to the direct action of alcohol on the tongue or legs, but are caused by its effect on the parts of the brain which integrate and control their activities. . . . Some studies have shown that alcohol tends to decrease fear and increase the likelihood that an individual will accept risks. When a group of bus drivers were given several drinks, for example, they were more likely to try to drive their buses through spaces that were too narrow—and seemingly more likely to risk failure—than when they were sober. . . . Studies with rats, mice and cats tend to confirm this fear-and-anxiety-reducing property of alcohol. . . . For example, cats that became afraid to eat after receiving several electric shocks lost their fear after they had been given alcohol (p. 39).

Alcohol probably has other effects of instrumental significance. Some are legendary. For example, alcohol can reduce sexual suppressions. Indeed, some people are able to engage in sexual activity only after drinking alcohol. However, large doses of alcohol will prevent sexual activity. Alcohol precipitates sleep, but causes fitful tossing and turning, morning fatigue, impaired concentration and vigilance, as well as increased irritability. Many of these effects of alcohol have been verified in both human and animal subjects (see Mello, 1973).

The chronic use of large amounts of alcohol produces *tolerance*, a progressive change in the relation between dose size and response to that dose, so that progressively larger doses are required to produce the same response. Another way of defining tolerance is a progressive decrease in the response to a given dose size when the same dose is repeatedly administered. Thus, if alcohol has been used instrumentally (instrumental in suppressing anxiety or guilt feelings, for example), it will become less and less instrumentally effective, while increasingly larger amounts of it are required to achieve the same instrumental outcome. The growth of tolerance is believed by some pharmacologists to be the cause of addiction. Certainly, tolerance to alcohol is correlated with the intensity of disturbances seen during subsequent alcohol abstinence. Sporadic or casual drinkers experience only a hangover during withdrawal from alcohol. Heavy drinkers, tolerant to alcohol, experience tremulousness, confusion, hallucinations, sweating, nausea, and intense alcohol craving. They may also experience vague dread and fear of dying during withdrawal. Very heavy drinkers or alcoholics experience *delirium tremens*, accompanied by psychomotor agitation, hallucinations, memory loss, and severe autonomic nervous system disturbances that sometimes are lethal. For such alcohol users, withdrawal symptoms usually emerge between 12 and 48 hours after heavy drinking has ceased. However, drinkers who have developed a great tolerance for alcohol may actually experience withdrawal symptoms when still drinking when some unmetabolized alcohol is still in their bodies. This can happen especially when the tolerant drinker is drinking only small amounts relative to the tolerance level.

The withdrawal agony of the alcohol addict has been attributed to "denervation supersensitivity" (Jaffe and Sharpless 1963, 1968), which is a mechanism to account for the seemingly heightened level of CNS excitement (thought to be a kind of CNS "rebound" phenomenon) manifested during withdrawal.

Eventually, even though the alcoholic may have initially used alcohol for instrumental reasons, he or she will enter a phase of alcohol use during which drinking occurs only to alleviate his or her withdrawal agony. Each successive drinking bout, although it alleviates the aversive symptoms, engenders the next siege of abstinence agony, which in turn motivates the next drinking bout. This *addictive cycle* is similar to that of opiate use. However, only a very small proportion of alcohol users enter this cycle, whereas a large proportion of opiate users do so. This fact has led pharmacologists, psychiatrists and sociologists on an extensive search for predisposing personality and constitutional and social variables that might produce alcohol addiction. It has been purported that such predispositions are very weakly correlated in the United States with being male; being single, separated, or divorced; having no religious affiliation; being a beer drinker; condoning drunkenness in others and believing that drunkenness is funny and enjoyable (U.S. Department of Health, Education and Welfare, 1971). It is, of course, possible that these attributes are correlated with alcohol addiction only through their relationships with other, unidentified variables. The major event, however, the one that forecasts an enduring craving for alcohol, is the stage during which the alcohol-tolerant drinker begins to suffer from alcohol abstinence symptoms and relieves them with more alcohol rather than allowing the symptoms to subside. Why one path rather than the other is chosen is, at present, a mystery.

The number of alcohol addicts in a given population is related to the mean alcohol consumption of that population. France has a mean consumption of 6.53 gallons of alcohol (not the volume of the beverages, but the volume of alcohol content of those beverages) per person per year. The U.S. has a mean consumption of 2.61 gallons of alcohol per person per year. Although the number of alcohol addicts is difficult to estimate accurately, there are probably many more per 100,000 in France than in the U.S. In the U.S., about 15 percent of the men who drink regularly, and about four percent of the women who drink regularly, have alcohol-related problems, such as frequent intoxication, alcohol-caused illnesses, problems with family or friends, and on-the-job problems.

It is only a guess, but it seems safe to assume that about 10 percent of the regular drinkers in the U.S. are alcohol addicts enmeshed in the addictive cycle. They are an enormous burden to our society. The National Institute of Alcohol Abuse conservatively estimates the annual cost of alcohol addiction to be about 25 *billion* dollars, a figure that includes lost productivity, health and medical costs, costs of motor vehicle, aircraft, and industrial accidents, costs of alcohol treatment programs and research, hours entailed in the criminal justice system, the value of the alcohol consumed, and the efforts of the social welfare system.

Strong motivation to abstain exists among most alcohol addicts, and many social, economic, and personal forces strengthen this desire. Often the alcohol addict begs for help after unsuccessfully trying to abstain. Try as he or she may, the typical alcohol addict usually is unsuccessful in abstaining for long periods of time. It has been estimated that about 50 percent of alcohol addicts seeking professional assistance remain in therapy. The others disappear, often to appear later. Of those who remain in treatment, a large percentage are able to abstain for a few months, but at the end of a year about 80 percent have resumed drinking (Hunt and Matarazzo, 1973). Relapsed alcoholics quickly resume their old behaviors, drinking in the same places, with the same people, procuring alcohol from the same sources, and consuming the same large amounts. The typical alcohol addict is never really cured. The data on temporary cures and relapses for alcohol match closely those for nicotine and for heroin, and from such evidence one may conclude that it is equally difficult to abstain from either alcohol, nicotine, or heroin for a period of more than one year, after one has become addicted.

Laboratory animals have been used to study the psychological effects of alcohol (see Mello, 1973). They have been induced to drink large quantities of alcohol in one way or another. For example, rats have been given a series of electric shocks and then given access to fluids that contain alcohol. Such rats develop a preference for alcoholic fluids over nonalcoholic ones. However, when the shock stress is terminated, the preference usually declines. Such preferences probably are instrumental, indicating that alcohol will decrease subjective stress. Such experiments do not usually produce the withdrawal syndrome or the addictive cycle. Other methods have purported to produce addiction, but the data are conflicting. For example, the operant conditioning of lever pressing that results in intravenous injection of alcohol in monkeys usually produces withdrawal symptoms after about three weeks. Blood alcohol levels in these laboratory monkeys are equivalent to those found in human alcohol addicts. These monkeys will show alternation of bouts of infusion with periods of abstinence. With dogs, forced administration of alcohol through nasogastric intubation produces withdrawal symptoms within a few weeks. However, it is not at all certain that such dogs would tend to use alcohol if given the choice after the alcohol is terminated.

Experimental findings with laboratory animals have not been consistent. For example, experimenters have given alcohol solutions to infant rhesus monkeys as their only source of liquid. The alcohol concentration was gradually increased over an 18 month period, but no signs of withdrawal illness were exhibited when alcohol was taken away. In contrast, other experiments showed a withdrawal syndrome in rhesus monkeys after large alcohol doses had been administered to them orally for 10 days. In rats, about 20 days of forced alcohol administration can produce withdrawal symptoms. In mice, such symptoms seem to occur only during starvation. According to many experimenters: "These findings serve to re-emphasize that the crucial determinants in the development of the signs of physical dependence upon alcohol are unknown and the nature of the addictive process remains a matter of conjecture" (U.S. Department of Health, Education, and Welfare, 1971, p. 62).

Even if withdrawal symptoms were to be demonstrated reliably for alcohol, an animal model of addiction could be adequate only if the animal could be shown to enter the addictive cycle. The animal would have to learn to dose itself and would reliably do so at the times when the withdrawal syndrome would usually be manifested. According to Mello (1973), this demonstration is still lacking in animals.

An important feature of alcohol use in human subjects is *cross-tolerance* between alcohol and barbiturates. This means that the development of tolerance for alcohol will cause tolerance for barbiturates, even though the alcohol user has not been taking barbiturates. Large doses of barbiturates then are required to produce a given effect in people who drink alcohol heavily. For example, an alcohol addict may require a huge dose of Seconal to produce sleep. We are not aware of experiments on cross-tolerance in animal subjects. The cross-tolerance phenomenon must have significance for motivation theory, and we will consider it when evaluating the common features of the various kinds of addiction.

Opiates

The opiates (opium, laudanum, codeine, Percodan, Demerol, morphine, heroin, dilaudid, metopon, methadone) are highly addictive drugs. In the correct doses, all can produce pleasure and quick relief from pain, followed by sedation and then sleep. Although each opiate has its own special hedonic and affective aspects, most will produce the pleasurable and analgesic effects. Very disagreeable physiological and psychological withdrawal symptoms tend to emerge after relatively few strong doses of these drugs. It has been asserted that certain "addiction-prone" people experience intense pleasure from opiates, whereas normal people do not. The prone people supposedly have a vivid pleasure experience (rush, ecstasy) even though there are some accompanying, unpleasant symptoms occurring on initial use. Normal people have less pleasure, more unpleasant symptoms, is the supposition. However, the evidence for two such classes of people is not convincing. There are, however, huge individual differences in initial reactions to a dose of an opiate. Apparently, the more intense the pleasures, the more intense will be the abstinence aftereffects. This correlation has its analogue in Figure 2-2, where the aftereffects of 4 mA and 8 mA shocks are compared. Intravenous injection of an opiate in solution is usually effective in giving pleasure. Abstinence then produces craving and a general feeling of malaise.

With repeated use of an opiate, the pleasure invariably becomes less intense and finally does not occur. This high degree of tolerance can be somewhat overcome by an increase in dosage amount or by a period of total abstinence. After repeated use, withdrawal agony intensifies and the craving becomes pervasive and enduring, overshadowing other kinds of human motivation.

Many opiate addicts are willing to suffer *temporary* abstinence and withdrawal agony because they can partially restore the rush and at the same time save money (the high price of opiates is a serious problem for most users). In trying to restore their "lost euphoria" addicts will sometimes increase their dose to amounts larger than the maximum amounts utilized physiologically (about 20 grams of morphine in 24 hours). Thus "there appears to be an emotional need to consume increasing amounts of the drug, over and above the increase accounted for by the development of tolerance" (Maurer and Vogel, 1967).

The dramatic symptoms of opiate withdrawal in an addict are now almost legendary:

> When an addict misses his first shot, he senses mild withdrawal distress ("feels his habit coming on"), but this is probably more psychological than physiological, for fear plays a considerable role in the withdrawal syndrome. At this stage, a placebo may give relief. During the first eight to sixteen hours of abstinence, the addict becomes increasingly nervous, restless and anxious, and close confinement tends to intensify these symptoms. Within fourteen hours (usually less) he will begin to yawn frequently; he sweats profusely and develops running of the eyes and nose comparable to that accompanying a severe head cold. These symptoms increase in intensity for the first 24 hours, after which the pupils dilate, and recurring waves of goose flesh occur. Severe twitching of the muscles (the origin of the term 'kick the habit') occurs within

36 hours, and painful cramps develop in the backs of the legs and in the abdomen; all the body fluids are released copiously; vomiting and diarrhea are acute; there is little appetite for food, and the addict is unable to sleep. The respiratory rate rises steeply; both systolic and diastolic blood pressure increase moderately to a maximum between the third and fourth day; temperature rises an average of about one degree, subsiding after the third day; blood sugar content rises sharply until the third day or after; and the basal metabolic rate increases sharply during the first 48 hours. These are the objective signs of withdrawal distress which can be measured; the subjective indications are equally severe, and the illness reaches its peak within 48 to 72 hours after the last shot of the opiate, gradually subsiding thereafter for the next five to ten days. . . . Complete recovery requires from three to six months, with rehabilitation and, if needed, psychiatric treatment. The withdrawal syndrome proper is self-limiting, and most addicts will survive it with no medical assistance whatever (this is known as kicking the habit "cold turkey"). Abrupt withdrawal is inhumane, but with the development of drugs such as methadone, it is possible to reduce the distress of withdrawal very considerably. . . . The symptoms described above vary with the individual, the length of time he has been addicted and the quantity of drugs he has been taking. As a rule, the more opiates he has been taking, the more severe his withdrawal illness, and the less he has been taking, the lighter will be the distress (Maurer and Vogel, 1967, pp. 95–96).

According to Maurer and Vogel (1967, p. 96),

Fear of withdrawal distress is undoubtedly one of the very strong factors in sustaining addiction and eventually apparently supersedes the desire for pleasure which the addict originally felt on taking opiates; nevertheless, as tolerance develops, most addicts cannot support the large habits which they build up and must withdraw themselves or be withdrawn so that they can start over on a smaller dosage" (see also Jaffe, 1965, and Lindesmith, 1968).

Withdrawal symptoms are subject to Pavlovian conditioning. Through use of Nalorphine, a potent morphine antagonist, the withdrawal syndrome can be abruptly precipitated in monkeys. After several injections the syndrome can then be elicited by an injection of saline (Irwin and Seevers, 1956). Wikler and his colleagues have demonstrated conditioned opiate withdrawal symptoms in the rat ("wet-dog" shakes, hypothermia, loss of appetite, and increased emotionality). This syndrome could be conditioned to "withdrawal cages" in which rats experienced forced morphine abstinence. After long, drug-free periods in their home cages during which abstinence signs were no longer seen, these rats showed a recurrence of withdrawal symptoms when they were abruptly returned to the withdrawal cages. Such recurrences could be induced many months after the original withdrawal episodes.

Wikler and Pescor (1967) showed, however, that the conditioning effects were not necessary (though they were sufficient) for the rearousal of withdrawal symptoms and subsequent relapse. Only a long history of opiate addiction was sufficient to predispose a rat to relapse. The relapse process could be either associative or nonassociative, or perhaps both. For example,

Weeks and Collins (1968) rendered rats physiologically dependent on morphine by repeated doses over relatively long intervals. The rats were then trained to press a lever to receive morphine intravenously, only to be later withdrawn from it during the next four weeks. When returned to the lever, they promptly resumed self-dosing. They relapsed. A comparison group of rats were also rendered physiologically dependent on morphine, but they were trained to press a lever for water, not morphine. After four weeks of abstinence, the rats were allowed to lever press to receive morphine intravenously. Although they did do a little self-dosing, they did much less than did the first group (originally trained to lever press for morphine). Thus, prior morphine exposure alone can predispose a rat to self-dose after a long abstinence period, but prior operant conditioning in self-dosing produces an even greater tendency to redose after a protracted abstinence. The associative process seems to be involved here, but a nonassociative one is also operating.

What is needed now is a set of experiments in which the relative contributions of *two* associative processes (Pavlovian conditioning of withdrawal symptoms and operant conditioning of self-dosing) and *one* nonassociative process (prior drug habituation, without correlated cues or operants) are assessed for their relative contributions to the tendency to relapse after a period of total abstinence. The findings from such an experiment would be relevant to the condition of the human opiate addict. Most opiate addicts do relapse, even after long periods of abstinence. Furthermore, when the relapse occurs, the addict quickly resumes his self-dosings in the amounts and frequencies of his past usage. The buildup of intake is very fast compared with the initial buildup, and tolerance is quickly reestablished. In studies of associative learning, this phenomenon is often called *savings*. We do not know, however, whether the savings phenomenon for the reestablishment of opiate tolerance reflects an associative or nonassociative mechanism.

In thinking about the differences between alcohol addiction and opiate addiction, several aspects stand out. First, a much higher percent of regular users of opiates become addicts than do users of alcohol. Second, it has been so far impossible to produce a satisfactory animal model for alcohol addiction, although we have several good animal models for opiate addiction. Finally, the human alcohol addict is a very sick person, often having hepatitis and liver damage, congestive heart failure, kidney dysfunction, and brain damage. The opiate addict is not a sick person when he has a good supply handy and uses it. A rationale for these differences has been emerging. We now know that the metabolism of alcohol generates some very poisonous aldehydes and that these substances can severely damage body organs. The development of tolerance to alcohol does not give the alcohol addict any protection against organ damage from toxic metabolic products. Indeed, organ damage may be one of the costs of tolerance. Why doesn't opiate use involve the same threats to health? Recently, it has been found that the brain itself secretes morphinelike substances when the organism is put under aversive or painful stress. These substances have an analgesic effect. Therefore, when one takes morphine, one is excessively increasing the amounts of already present substances of a physiologically normal and compatible kind. Perhaps the constant presence of such compounds (they are now called *endorphins*) implies that there are compensatory, homeostatic mechanisms for modulating the amounts of the substances when they become too voluminous. These mechanisms could conceivably be involved in the establishment of tolerance, intense withdrawal symptoms and addiction. Certainly the discovery of the toxic products of alcohol metabolism and the existence of the endorphins will help us to understand some of the differences between an alcohol addict and an opiate addict.

Barbiturates

Barbiturates are derived from barbituric acid. Over 20 are in use, and each has its typical latency and duration of affective reaction. In general, the longer the onset latency, the greater the subsequent duration of the reaction. Latencies may vary from a few seconds to 30 minutes, depending on dose and route of administration. Two slow-acting barbiturates are Veronal and phenobarbitol. Pentathal sodium and Seconal are two of the fast-acting drugs.

Barbiturates are manufactured in huge amounts in the U.S. (probably over 5 billion one-grain doses per year). They are usually prescribed by physicians when sedation or sleep is medically or personally desirable. They are also prescribed for nervousness, anxiety, and emotional upsets, as well as for a variety of diseases like asthma and gastric ulcers. Barbiturates are not analgesics, but they can be effective anesthetic agents. They are effective also in removing some inhibitory influences on behavior, just as alcohol does.

Everyday use of barbiturates, or a series of very large doses, can lead to tolerance and to aversive withdrawal symptoms. When used with alcohol, barbiturates intensify the typical effects of alcohol. Death through overdosing is common when alcohol and barbiturates are taken together. Death through overdose is also common with barbiturates taken alone, partly because large quantities produce nervousness, irritability, and insomnia. These side-effects in turn cause further self-dosing while the user is still completely intoxicated. There is also a marked cross-tolerance between barbiturates and alcohol which can easily result in lethal overdosing.

The psychological effects of barbiturates are similar to those of alcohol. Barbiturates induce a short period of pleasurable excitement, followed by sedation, depression, and sleep. There is a barbiturate hangover (nervousness, irritability) during withdrawal. However, a large margin exists between the usual, prescribed doses of barbiturates and those doses of barbiturates large enough to produce the development of tolerance, abstinence agony, and drug craving.

The abstinence syndrome for users of large doses of barbiturates emerges about 24 hours after the last dose, peaks at about two or three days, and then slowly subsides. The symptoms of withdrawal agony include anxiety, muscle twitches and tremors, dizziness and weakness, nausea and vomiting, and sometimes convulsions similar to those of alcohol delirium tremens. Chronic use of barbiturates in large doses will cause ataxia, confusion, emotional outbursts, and bizarre (psychotic) symptoms prior to withdrawal and during the peak of action of the drug. Craving for barbiturates during complete abstinence probably lasts as long as does alcohol craving in those people who have been taking intoxicating doses for extending periods. This time period varies from a few weeks to a few years for reasons that remain obscure (see Maurer and Vogel, 1967).

Bromides

Bromides are compounds of sodium, potassium, and ammonium. They have a sedative effect and they suppress anxiety, fear, and emotional distress. After chronic use bromides accumulate in the body. Bromide intoxication includes loss of appetite, confusion, slow speech, memory lapses, sluggish reflexes, bizarre behavior, and delirium. Such intoxication rarely occurs with one dose, even a large one, but depends rather on chronic dosing over a long period. Bromides are insidious because intoxication builds up slowly until a stuporous state ensues, and then the withdrawal symptoms can be very intense and long lasting.

Before the body is intoxicated with bromides, withdrawal symptoms are relatively mild, though aversive. They include drug craving, nervousness, tremors, and a feeling of malaise. The mildness of withdrawal symptoms is due to the fact that bromides accumulate and are secreted very slowly. The violent physiological disturbances seen in opiate, alcohol and barbiturate abstinence are not seen in bromide users. Furthermore, tolerance for bromides is never very great. Treatment, therefore, usually consists of total abstinence, which presents no dangers to the body (Maurer and Vogel, 1967).

Tranquilizers

Tranquilizers came into wide use relatively recently in medical history, and we don't yet know their long-term action. They can produce tolerance, cross-tolerance with barbiturates, and serious withdrawal symptoms. The withdrawal syndrome for many tranquilizers mimics that for barbiturates. Hallucinations and convulsions may accompany abrupt withdrawal from highly addictive tranquilizers (such as Miltown, Equanil, Librium, and Valium). The evidence is not yet in, but there probably will be a new, large group of drug addicts as a consequence of the use of these readily available compounds.

Amphetamines

Amphetamines include Benzedrine, Dexedrine, and Methedrine, drugs that are similar in structure to ephedrine and epinephrine. The amphetamines act as CNS excitants. They induce euphoria, a sense of well-being, feelings of self-confidence, wakefulness and alertness, and a sense of control over events. Amphetamines block the subjective awareness of physical fatigue. They also reduce appetite. They can be administered orally, nasally, or intravenously.

Large doses of amphetamines produce intoxication characterized by restlessness, insomnia, rapid speech, hyperactive reflexes, and dilated pupils. Sometimes they cause hallucinations and paranoia, with intense fear or violent aggressiveness.

Surprisingly, the withdrawal from amphetamines is free of severe physiological symptoms despite the fact that drug tolerance can rapidly develop to several times the early dose levels. The major withdrawal symptoms are emotional and motivational. There are feelings of general fatigue, lassitude, deep depression and drowsiness, along with craving for the drug. Many suicidal episodes have occurred during withdrawal from amphetamines.

Nicotine

Although very frequent use is required to establish addiction to cigarettes, cigars, or pipes, the behavioral patterns for nicotine consumption are similar to those for alcohol and opiates. Tolerance occurs, frequency of self-dosing increases, the pleasure during smoking decreases, and the intensity and duration of craving increases with protracted, repeated use of nicotine. Abstinence has very few physiological effects, but the aversive craving state is often accompanied by headaches, irritability, increased motor activity, anxiety, tension, increased food intake, and a general feeling of dissatisfaction.

The treatment success rate for nicotine is about the same as that for opiates and alcohol. About 50 percent of those voluntarily entering a treatment program stay with it. Of those who appear to have kicked the habit, about 80 percent relapse within a year (Hunt and Matarazzo, 1970; 1973). Thus, by a treatment success criterion, cigarette smoking is as powerfully addictive as heroin and alcohol.

Generalizations about Drug-Controlled Behavior: Their Significance for the Opponent-Process Theory of Motivation

Earlier in this chapter we briefly reviewed the knowledge about the addicting properties and symptom characteristics of some major addicting drugs. Some compounds, such as marijuana, cocaine, and LSD, are absent from the list, because their capacity to produce addiction is very low. Although each addictive drug has its own special features and physiological consequences, it is still possible to identify attributes that seem common to addictive drugs and to relate such attributes to the postulates of the opponent-process theory.

The hedonic, affective, and behavioral phenomena of drug addiction emerge slowly during repeated self-dosings and the intervals between them. The first self-administration of any drug that noticeably changes the affective state of the user may also induce some aversive symptoms. For example, opiates and alcohol can cause nausea, vomiting, and headache. Yet coexistent with these aversive symptoms many positive effects may exist. Anxiety-ridden people may suddenly experience complete freedom from anxiety for several hours. A frustrated, angry person may lose his anger. In addition, part of the experience may be intensely pleasant, euphoric or satisfying. Thus, the first experience with an affect-arousing drug is often a blend of several kinds of aversive and pleasurable feelings. If the aversiveness is very intense, a person will probably not use the drug again. This is described dramatically by Claude Brown (1965), who credited to an agonizing, 24-hour headache his subsequent rejection of heroin in a cultural setting in which many of his talented acquaintances were becoming addicted.

However, if the pleasurable components outweigh the aversive ones, it is possible that sufficient craving will ensue and the user will repeat the self-dosing. This is especially likely to occur if the drug has an instrumental escape feature, such as the alleviation of anxiety or frustration. Nevertheless, even if a drug does serve this instrumental escape function effectively, it may not subsequently lead to addiction. Taking the drug may be limited only to counter an already existing aversive state. This is the way most of us use aspirin in relation to headaches. The so-called casual user is often following this course of action. Many mild sedatives and most barbiturates are used casually, as is alcohol. These users are not addicts because their drug use is still contingent upon the occurrence of events that are not attributable to the effects of the drug itself.

How, then, do we identify an addict? By frequency of drug use? By the magnitude of worldly goods and pleasures sacrificed in the service of a drug habit? By the degree of preoccupation with obtaining the drug? By criminal acts committed in securing a drug? By the level of pleasure the user experiences when taking a drug? By the degree of disorganization introduced into a person's life by drug-taking? By alterations in basic personality structure? By extent of derangement of social interrelationships? No. The affective dynamics postulated in the opponent-process model for acquired motivation strongly suggests that the adequate psychological criteria for addiction do not include these features at all. Nor do the past attempts to define addiction touch on its most crucial features. The most elegant definition probably was that of Jaffe (1965, p. 286), who wrote that addiction is "a behavioral pattern of compulsive drug use, characterized by overwhelming involvement with the use of a drug, the securing of its supply, and a high tendency to relapse after withdrawal." The major terms in this definition are undefined (compulsive, overwhelming involvement).

The opponent-process model, together with the laws of Pavlovian and operant conditioning, suggest an entirely different set of defining criteria for addiction. Consider these facts. Often, during the time between doses of a drug, an aversive state slowly emerges. The labels for this state are: withdrawal syndrome, abstinence syndrome, abstinence agony, withdrawal illness, and drug craving. Like most aversive states, this one has both affective and physiological attributes, the natures of which depend on the drug. However, one psychological feature is common to all the abstinence syndromes: *an aversive state of craving.* This state, if given the time needed, will die out slowly and disappear. Just as we have described for the imprinted ducklings, the state will have its own particular *critical decay duration.*

According to the opponent-process model, the intense pleasure of the opiate "rush" for an opiate user reflects an a-process and the aversive withdrawal symptoms, both physiological and psychological, reflect the b-process, the opponent. Should instrumental self-dosing occur during or at the peak of magnitude of withdrawal agony, the user will usually discover a very dramatic effect: the new dose produces complete cessation of craving and discomfort, and at the same time it reinstates the pleasurable attributes of the hedonic state aroused during the previous self-dosage. In terms of opponent-process theory, when the user is still inexperienced, the a-process is strong enough to overwhelm the decaying b-process so that a is greater than b and [a-b] will yield State A.

Drugs with a *long* critical decay duration present a fine opportunity for the user to discover that a new dose will eliminate State B. If a given dose of a drug has a very *short* critical decay duration, then it will be much harder for the user to discover this effective source of relief. However, should this be discovered, the user then has only two ways of coping with abstinence agony. Either he can stoically suffer through the critical decay duration, or he can dose himself again.

Alternative 1: If the user chooses to suffer through the decay period, there will be no further motivation for self-dosing stemming from the drug-engendered aversive symptoms. There still may exist reasons independent of the drug's aversive effects for using the drug again in an instrumental fashion. In our view, this does not constitute addiction.

Alternate 2: If the user does dose again during the most intense periods of withdrawal, he falls victim to the *addictive cycle*. He will then be using the drug in order to produce a quick cessation to current withdrawal symptoms. Once this occurs, the user is probably doomed, because frequent repetitions of self-dosing at time intervals shorter than the critical decay duration will bring about three motivational changes.

First, the intensity and duration of withdrawal agony will gradually *increase* (just as distress calling did in those ducklings whose interstimulus interval was short; see Figure 2-6). This will occur because, as the b-process is strengthened by repeated use, the quality and intensity of state B will increase.

Second, the positively reinforcing, pleasurable state associated with the onset of a new dose will gradually *decline* in quality and intensity. This is assumed to occur because the quantity, [a-b], decreases as the b-process is strengthened; State A will therefore decline in quality and intensity. In opiate users this has been called "loss of euphoria." The intense pleasure of the "rush" gradually disappears. The affect system appears to have habituated to the onset and maintenance of the drug. The user now has drug *tolerance*: increasing amounts of the drug are required to induce a pleasurable state, and eventually no dose will be able to produce this state. According to the theoretical model, tolerance reflects [a-b] whenever b has been strengthened. At best, all the user can then expect is alleviation of withdrawal discomfort with each new dose.

The third motivational change is the development of partial immunity to the physiological and affective symptoms caused by certain other drugs. This is cross-tolerance. Those drugs whose affective or hedonic qualities are similar are the ones most likely to share cross-tolerance. Such drugs do not necessarily have similar chemical structures. Consider alcohol use. When the alcohol addict requires large doses of alcohol in order to terminate his current withdrawal agony, he also will require a relatively large dose of a barbiturate to produce a desired effect such as sleep. In becoming tolerant to alcohol he has become tolerant to a barbiturate (which he may never have taken before). For opponent-process theory, this means that the b-process elicited by a specific a-process must contain elements in common with the b-process generated by a completely different a-process. Therefore, we expect that for some drugs there will be b-process generalization gradients, but for others there will be b-process specificity. The principles underlying such differences are unclear.

It is relatively simple to define the behavioral phenomenon of addiction within the confines of the opponent-process model and to distinguish it satisfactorily from other kinds of motivation (such as hunger, thirst or conditioned fear states). Addiction is the use of a specific drug for the effective alleviation of craving and withdrawal discomfort. In addiction, the drug used is the same one whose subsequent absence is sufficient for the occurrence of the next episode of craving. The psychological preconditions for addiction will have affective and cognitive features. The user must discover the correlations that exist between (1) abstinence from the drug and presence of an aversive state and (2) current use of the drug and the quick termination of the aversive state. The drug must be used frequently and at intervals shorter than the critical decay period for the dose size. The user cannot become an addict if intervals between doses of drugs are longer than the critical decay period, because neither would he have the opportunity to discover the correlation between current use of the drug and the quick termination of the aversive state, nor would the opponent-process be strengthened by repeated self-dosage.

Thus, if you use aspirin in order to alleviate an alcohol hangover, you are not strengthening an opponent-process nor entering into the addictive cycle for alcohol. Nor are you setting up an addictive cycle for aspirin. But if you use alcohol to remove an alcohol hangover then you are initiating an addictive cycle by strengthening the b-process for alcohol and by knowledge of the correlation between drug use and the termination of the aversive state. The notion of "the hair of the dog that bit you" is, therefore, very danger-ous. If you use heroin to alleviate an alcohol hangover, you are not starting an addictive cycle for alcohol. Nevertheless, you might be laying the foun-dation for an eventual addictive cycle for heroin, because the subsequent absence of heroin, for one who has used it recently, produces its own aversive craving state, and one might then choose to dose with heroin again in order to get rid of the craving state. Indeed, the history of many so-called drug cures is replete with such cases. Heroin was once used to alleviate morphine withdrawal, and methadone is currently in wide use for the alleviation of methadone-withdrawal agony. The opponent-process model suggests that the opponent-processes for morphine, heroin, and methadone are quite similar.

Even if there were no Pavlovian conditioning processes operating in drug addiction, it would be very difficult for an addict to abstain because of the severity and long duration of the intensified b-process (abstinence agony and craving). The most effective relief is redosing and not waiting for the craving to subside. To make matters worse, Pavlovian conditioning mechanisms operate only to intensify and prolong the suffering of an addict who tries to abstain. We have already described the establishment of CS_A and CS_B for aversive conditioning with shock UCSs. Now let us examine the implica-tions of Pavlovian conditioning for the intensity of the A-states and B-states in drug addiction.

For A-states precipitated by pleasurable events, the CS_A is a stimulus that regularly precedes the onset of the A-state. The CS_B is a stimulus that regularly precedes or accompanies the most intense periods of the B-state. The CS_A will acquire positive reinforcement properties but the CS_B should be aversive and will be able to select and energize operants that produce

State A and CS_A. Indeed, because the operants associated with drug self-dosage regularly precede the onset of the A-state, the perceptual aspects of those operants should become part of the CS_A complex. They should become secondary positive reinforcers, especially *early* in addiction when the quantity [a-b] is quite large.

Late in addiction, when tolerance is large and asymptotic, or the quantity [a-b] is small or perhaps zero, the major conditioning effect should be confined to CS_B. Because the b-process is so strong, the conditioning of CS_B should proceed rapidly, establishing an effective complex of aversive conditioned stimuli. Early in addiction we should see the rapid establishment of CS_A but very little of CS_B. Late in addiction, most of the conditioned reactions should be aversive, controlled by CS_B complexes. If tolerance is truly a consequence of [a-b], then Siegel's (1975, 1977) findings are contrary to these theoretical expectations. His rats quickly developed tolerance to morphine, and the tolerance was under the control of a CS_B complex very early in the dosing sequence. It may turn out that the conditioning of opponent-processes by stimuli close to the onset of the A-state requires special temporal relationships. At present, we are ignorant about the conditions for bringing this about.

Wikler's (1971) review of the conditioning phenomena reflected in human opiate addiction showed clearly that CS_A and CS_B stimuli can be strongly established. Sham or placebo dosing can have a reinforcing effect, can reduce abstinence discomfort and craving, especially if the placebo is self-administered. The effect of CS_A is to subtract from the intensity of the B-state for a short time. Stimuli forecasting State B have an aversive effect and select and energize those operants previously effective in terminating the B-state. These stimuli can therefore induce premature dosing, arouse anxiety and dread, and intensify the discomfort of abstinence. One way of demonstrating this effect is to inject Nalorphine, an opiate antagonist, contingent upon the regular presentation of CS_B. The antagonist will come to precipitate the user from State A into State B, and any situational stimuli correlated with this switch become aversive. Given some degree of regularity in the social stimuli that have been correlated with drug use in any person, an array of CS_A and CS_B events becomes established. According to the opponent-process model, the CS_B events should be strengthened more slowly than are the CS_A events in their capacities to evoke conditioned b-processes and a-processes, respectively.

The addict who attempts to abstain is battling powerful motivational forces that tend to defeat his mission. Although the environmental CS_A events may, at any time, mitigate the severity of craving for the moment, they should also arouse the opponent-process, and so when CS_A is terminated there should be a short period of intensified b-process. Or, if CS_B stimuli are encountered, a temporary intensification of the b-process will occur, and any intensification of the b-process may then activate behaviors culminating in a redose.

An example from cigarette addiction illustrates the Pavlovian principles. The nicotine addict may resolve to stop smoking. To help himself through the most difficult times, he may sniff other people's smoke, may put an unlit cigarette in his mouth, suck on it, and draw deep breaths of air into his lungs. This helps momentarily by producing a conditioned a-process arousal that reduces the chronic B-state intensity for a short time. However, the end of the episode will be marked by increased craving, more intense than the chronic level, because when CS_A arouses the conditioned a-process, it must also arouse the opponent b-process. (Remember that the recovery from presentation of a CS_A is biphasic, as demonstrated in fear conditioning experiments).

Consider the smoker who isn't trying to abstain. He smokes on the average of every 45 minutes. However, he suddenly discovers while smoking a cigarette that the pack is empty and he doesn't have another. That event is a CS_B event, the perceptual properties of which predict the subsequent absence of nicotine. This is aversive and it energizes operants leading up to the next smoke. Our smoker goes down the hall to a cigarette vending machine and buys a new pack. He then lights up a cigarette from the new pack, even though it is only a few minutes since his last smoke. The CS_B events can energize drug use operants and increase the dosage rate over short time periods.

Given that the world of the addict is full of both CS_A and CS_B events, abstaining becomes an almost impossible task. The addict is hemmed in. Redosing is the only sure way to alleviate quickly any suffering due either to nonassociative or associative processes, or to both. Thus, the opponent-process theory deduces, from a simple set of assumptions about normal motivational and Pavlovian conditioning processes, the great improbability of abstinence in an addict (inability to abstain is thought by many to be psychopathological).

The motivation to cease drug use must be at least as strong as the B-state intensity in order for an abstention to occur. Such motivation does not occur with high frequency in any sample of addicts. Indeed, the social circumstances often protect the drug user from such conflicting motives. Of course, a vivid example is nicotine addiction, but it is also true that many alcohol and heroin addicts have no desire to quit.

The data on cessation of drug use are not very helpful. The only solid information we have is for those who are: (1) arrested for the use of an illegal drug or (2) strongly motivated to quit for a variety of health and social reasons, but who have failed and then have sought help of a treatment agency that keeps good records. We know very little about those who tried to quit and failed (because they did not seek the help of a treatment agency that keeps good records); very little about those who tried to quit and succeeded (there must be thousands of nicotine addicts who have done this); very little about those who have never tried to quit and have no intention of doing so. We don't even know whether treatment for addiction is generally voluntary or involuntary. Because of legal and social sanctions, the circumstances preceding and surrounding treatment are correlated with the type of drug that is used. Many opiate addicts and some alcoholics are forced into treatment, but almost no nicotine addicts are. We don't know, therefore, whether the low success rate in addiction treatment programs is an index of how difficult it is in general to cure an addict, whether the people in such treatment programs are a peculiarly difficult group to treat, or whether lack of control over complex environmental events during treatment precludes our obtaining an accurate picture. We do not have base rates on self-cures.

Given that empirical findings on drug treatments are not of much help to us and that current treatment programs for all the addictive drugs cure relatively few of their participants, it is of some practical interest to consider some implications the opponent-process theory might have for a cure regimen, either imposed by others or self-imposed. The opponent-process theory focuses on nonassociative and associative (cognitive and affective) features that intensify the b-process at a given time, because the b-process is the aversive motivation plaguing all addicts. The ameliorative task, then, is to reduce the strength of the b-process as a nonassociative process while at the same time reducing to a minimum the occurrence of associative influences (CSs) that might arouse a conditioned b-process.

One deduction is painfully straightforward. Abrupt, involuntary withdrawal (cold turkey), in a physically and socially unfamiliar environment, should be optimal for obtaining the lowest possible levels of b-process magnitude and for weakening the b-process at the maximum rate. The strange environment would, however, quickly become a symbol for drug absence, and episodes of intensified b-process induced by these new CS_B events should occur. Nevertheless, there would be no exposure to CS_A events (which if they were to occur could restrengthen the decaying b-process and also would cause short bouts of B-state as a consequence of the biophasic recovery from CS_A). If prolonged and forced abstinence is successfully imposed, it would be foolish to return the addict to his old environment and its myriad CS_A and CS_B cues: relapse would probably occur.

The consequences of the usual treatment regime, when the addict is finally returned to his familiar environments, are shown in Figure 2-8. The relapse curves for alcohol, opiate, and nicotine addiction appear to be about the same. If we assume that at the end of formal treatment programs, the nonassociative b-process is quite weak, then other events are controlling the relapse. For the sake of argument, and to highlight the theoretical stance taken here, assume that the 50 percent of temporary successes *within* a treatment program are mainly due to the gradual weakening of the nonassociative b-process due to disuse. Then relapses *after* treatment is over are mainly due to the evocation of the conditioned b-process, either by exposure to CS_A or CS_B events or both. Therefore, directly after formal treatment, the addict should be placed in an environment calculated not to contain such

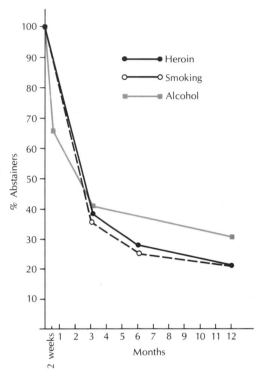

Figure 2-8. The relapse curve for nicotine, heroin and alcohol addicts, as a function of months after "cure." These data cover those subjects who were "cured" during treatment. In the usual treatment program, only about half of the subjects are "cured." The asymptote at 20–30 percent represents the most responsive addicts. (From Hunt, W. A., and Matarazzo, J. D., 1973.)

CSs. How practical or accurate would this social engineering actually be? There are no grounds for optimism.

Another very important route to relapse is not necessarily implied in the previous argument. The action of *generalization gradients* across *aversive* b-processes must be considered. We have previously emphasized the occurrence of cross tolerance. In the opponent-process model, cross-tolerance means that sometimes a b_1-process can combine, in the quantity $[a_1-b_1]$ with a different a-process $[a_2-b_1]$. For instance, the strong b_1-process for alcohol can subtract from the barbiturate a_2-process. Psychologically, this means that some b-processes have generalization functions. If so, then there probably is yet another type of a-process and b-process generalization: perhaps certain *aversive* b-processes can be confused with, or substituted for, certain *aversive* a-processes as well as with other *aversive* b-processes. The effect of these substitutions would be disastrous for the addict who has been successfully abstaining. Consider these hypothetical cases:

1. Aversive a_2 generalizes to aversive b_1. Assume b_1 is heroin craving and a_2 is influenza and its malaise. Relapse in an abstaining addict would then be potentiated by influenza malaise. For another instance of an aversive a_2 generalizing to an aversive b_1, assume b_1 is heroin craving and a_2 is the addict's estranged spouse. Relapse would be potentiated by the presence of the spouse.

2. Aversive b_1 generalizes to aversive b_2. Assume b_1 to be nicotine craving and b_2 to be loneliness for an absent loved one. Then nicotine abstinence might increase loneliness. Or perhaps increased loneliness might intensify nicotine craving and smoking rate.

3. Aversive b_1 generalizes aversive a_2. Assume b_1 to be nicotine craving and a_2 some painful experience (toothache, headache, gastritis). Here, absence of nicotine would enhance the aversiveness of the painful experience. Such a case is interesting, because we are not subtracting opponent-processes of different kinds to obtain a quantity $[a_2-b_1]$; instead, a_2 is *added* to b_1 along some appropriate *aversiveness continuum*. This cannot be consistent with our analysis of cross-tolerance, which we said was the resultant of $[a_2-b_1]$. We are lamentably missing the generalization laws for opponent-processes. One important difference between the generalization of aversive b_1 to aversive a_2 and the case of cross-tolerance is that in the latter b_1 is aversive and a_2 is pleasant, but in the former case both b_1 and a_2 are aversive.

These are new questions generated by the opponent-process model, and the model can't tell us yet the answers to questions about generalization functions. For example, should a stomach upset increase heroin craving in the abstaining addict? Should loneliness? Should guilt, or anger, or jealousy? Should these aversive states (some are A and some are B) potentiate relapse in alcohol or nicotine addicts who are now abstaining? We can reasonably assume, however, that the potential generalization of aversive qualities of a_1- and b_2-processes may be a vast source of difficulty for drug addicts. A variety of emotional, hedonic or motivational processes might be substitutable for the b-process of a given addiction. The presence of any one of these might add to the total aversiveness being experienced at any time. That in turn might energize the drug-use operants. For any addict and his drug, relapse might be more dependent on seemingly irrelevant hedonic and affective processes than on the drug b-process itself. Therefore, an argument can be made for protecting abstaining addicts after treatment from as many aversive affective influences as possible. This includes not only aversive a-processes but also the aversive b-processes engendered by highly pleasurable a-processes that are to be terminated or diminished.

Taken together, all the nonassociative, associative, and generalization processes seem to conspire to trap the addict. In this sense, his addictive operants are overdetermined. His abstinence is assaulted from all sides. It is the central thesis of this essay that this is true for many kinds of pleasurable reinforcers. Drug addiction is only one of many subclasses of normal, acquired motivation systems of the opponent-process type. It is hardly a pathological phenomenon, though it presents a very difficult therapeutic challenge because of the variety of determining influences that maintain it.

Though the opponent-process theory of motivation suggests the means of preventing addiction, it also suggests that the grave difficulties in curing an addict are not necessarily due to our failure to find a good cure. Instead, the difficulties may be indigenous and normal for any opponent-process system for affective and hedonic regulation.

Learned Helplessness and Depression

William R. Miller
University of Pennsylvania

Robert A. Rosellini
University of Pennsylvania

Martin E. P. Seligman
University of Pennsylvania

Each year, 4 to 8 million people in the United States suffer from debilitating depression, which is possibly the most common major mental disorder. Many people recover from depression, but unlike most other forms of psychopathology it can be lethal. One out of every 100 persons afflicted by a depressive illness dies by suicide (Williams, Friedman, and Secunda, 1970). The economic cost is also enormous. Loss of productivity and cost of treatment among adults in the United States amount to between $1.3 and $4 billion a year (Williams, Friedman, and Secunda).

Most of us have experienced some sort of depression—we are sad, we cry without knowing why, we feel helpless, worthless, or unsure, we lose interest in our own lives. Yet in spite of being a universal experience, depression has remained a mystery. This chapter highlights qualities that depression and the phenomenon of learned helplessness have in common. It suggests that learned helplessness can provide a model for understanding *reactive* depression, or depression caused by environmental rather than internal events.

The term *learned helplessness* describes what happens when prior exposure to uncontrollable aversive experiences interferes with escape and avoidance learning (Overmier and Seligman, 1967; Seligman and Maier, 1967). The

Research reported here was supported by a grant from the National Institute of Mental Health (MH-19604) and a Guggenheim Fellowship to Martin E. P. Seligman.

main behavioral symptoms of learned helplessness—deficits in response initiation and in association of reinforcement with responding—are seen as resulting from learning that reinforcement and responding are independent. Such learning is said to lower performance by reducing the incentive for instrumental responding, which results in lowered response initiation. In addition, learning that reinforcement and responding are independent interferes with learning that responses later control reinforcement (Seligman, Maier, and Solomon, 1971).

In order to compare learned helplessness and depression, let us look at their similarities in four areas: symptoms, cause, treatment, and prevention. Learned helplessness and depression have not been convincingly demonstrated to be similar in all four areas as yet, but making the form of the argument explicit has two virtues: it enables us to test the model and it can help us to narrow the definition of depression. As the two phenomena overlap in one area, we can then test the model by looking for other similarities. Say, for example, that learned helplessness in animals and men presents similar symptoms to reactive depression. If the etiology of the two is similar, and if we find that learned helplessness can be cured by forcibly exposing subjects to responding that produces relief, we can make a prediction about the cure of depression. The recognition that responding is effective in producing reinforcement should be the central issue in successful therapy. If this is tested and confirmed, the model is strengthened. Strengthening our model is a two-way street: if Imipramine (a tricyclic drug) helps reactive depression, does it also relieve learned helplessness in animals?

In addition to being easier to test, the model can help sharpen the definition of depression. The laboratory phenomenon of learned helplessness is well defined. Depression is not so easily defined. Rather, it is a convenient diagnostic label that denotes a constellation of symptoms, not one of which is necessary. The relationship among phenomena called depression is perhaps best described as a family resemblance (See Wittgenstein, 1953, paragraphs 66–77). Depressed people often report feeling sad, but sadness is not a necessary symptom of depression. Consider a patient who does not feel sad, but who experiences verbal and motor retardation, cries a lot, is anorexic, and whose symptoms can be traced to his wife's death. Depression is the appropriate clinical label for his condition. Some of these symptoms may be absent in different types of depression; other symptoms may take their place. Clinical labels can best be seen as denoting "a complicated network of similarities overlapping and crisscrossing" (Wittgenstein, 1953). A well-defined laboratory model does not mirror the openendedness of the clinical label; rather it imposes necessary conditions on it. Thus if a particular model of depression is valid, some phenomena formerly classified as depression may be excluded. We as psychologists are engaged in an attempt to refine the classification: learned helplessness does not model all phenomena now called depression. Rather, we think there will some day come to be "helplessness depressions"—embodied in passive people who have negative cognitive sets about the effects of their own actions, who become depressed upon the loss of an important source of gratification. The disorder will have a given prognosis, a preferred set of therapies, and perhaps a given physiology. Some phenomena not now called depression—such as the catastrophe syndrome (Wallace, 1957)—will be included. Others, now called depressions, will be excluded—manic depression, for example. Learned helplessness attempts to understand depressions like that of the man whose wife had died. His slowness in initiating responses, his belief that he was powerless and hopeless, his negative outlook on the future all began as a reaction to having lost his control over gratification and relief of suffering.

Let us now examine learned helplessness in the laboratory and depression in nature.

Symptoms

Learned Helplessness

When an experimentally naive dog receives escape-avoidance training in a shuttle box, it usually responds in this way: at the onset of the first traumatic electric shock, the dog runs frantically about until it accidentally scrambles over the barrier and so escapes the shock. On the next trial, the dog, running and howling, crosses the barrier more quickly than before. Eventually, the dog learns to avoid shock altogether. Overmier and Seligman (1967) and Seligman and Maier (1967) found a striking difference between this pattern of behavior and the pattern exhibited by dogs first given inescapable electric shocks in a Pavlovian hammock. Those dogs resemble a naive dog in their first reactions to shock in the shuttle box. In dramatic contrast to a naive dog, a dog that has experienced uncontrollable shocks before avoidance training usually soon stops running and sits or lies, quietly whining, until shock terminates. The dog does not cross the barrier and escape from shock. Rather, it seems to give up resisting and to passively accept the shock. On succeeding trials, the dog continues to fail to make escape movements and it accepts as much shock as the experimenter chooses to give.

Dogs that have first experienced inescapable shock demonstrate another peculiar characteristic. They occasionally jump the barrier early in training and escape, but then they revert to taking the shock; they appear to learn nothing by jumping the barrier and so avoiding the shock. In naive dogs a successful escape response is a reliable predictor of future successful escape responses.

We studied the escape-avoidance behavior of over 150 dogs that had received prior inescapable shocks. Two-thirds of these dogs did not escape shock; the other third escaped and avoided shock in normal fashion. Clearly, failure to escape is highly maladaptive—it means that the dog is experiencing 50 seconds of severe, pulsating shock on each trial. In contrast, only 6 percent of experimentally naive dogs fail to escape in the shuttle box. Dogs either fail to escape on almost any trial or learn normally; an intermediate outcome is rare.

We use the term *learned helplessness* to describe the interference with adaptive responses produced by inescapable shock and also as a shorthand to describe the process that we believe underlies the behavior (this will be discussed further later in this model.) Learned helplessness in the dog is defined by two types of behavior: (1) dogs that have had experience with uncontrollable shock *fail to initiate responses* to escape shock or are slower to make responses than naive dogs, and (2) if the dog does make a response that turns off shock, it has *more trouble than a naive dog learning that responding is effective.*

This example of learned helplessness is not an isolated phenomenon. In addition to the reports of Overmier and Seligman (1967), and Seligman and Maier (1967), such interference was also reported in dogs by Carlson and Black (1957), Leaf (1964), Seligman, Maier, and Geer (1968), Overmier (1968), Maier (1970), and Seligman and Groves (1970). Nor is it restricted to dogs: deficits in escaping or avoiding shock after experience with uncontrollable shock has been shown in rats (Seligman and Beagley, 1975; Katzev and Miller, 1974; and Shurman and Katzev, 1975), cats (Seward and Humphrey, 1967), dogs (Overmier and Seligman, 1967), fish (Behrend and Bitterman, 1963), chickens (Maser and Gallup, 1974), and mice (Braud, Wepman, and Russo, 1969). Similar deficits are found in humans following experience with uncontrollable noise (Hiroto and Seligman, 1975).

We have worked extensively with rats and have found one procedure to be successful (Seligman and Beagley, 1975; Seligman, Rosellini, and Kozak, 1975). We expose them to 80 trials of 15 seconds of inescapable shock. Twenty-four hours later we test them to see whether they will press a bar to escape shock on a Fixed-Ratio 3 (FR-3) schedule. The behavior of a rat that has experienced inescapable shock is very much like that of a similarly shocked dog. Even though it may successfully escape shock on the first few trials of the test, the rat eventually sits passively in one corner of the experimental chamber and receives the total amount of scheduled shock. Maier, Albin, and Testa (1973) have also found similar behavior in rats. After 64 exposures to 5 seconds of inescapable shock while restrained, their rats showed a deficit in acquiring a shuttling escape response. Rats were required to cross from one side of the two-way shuttlebox to the other and then back again (Fixed Ratio-2) to terminate shock. Few of them could complete the task. In addition, the more trials of inescapable shock (Looney and Cohen, 1972), or the higher the intensity of the inescapable shock (Seligman and Rosellini, unpublished data) the poorer was the subsequent performance.

When inescapable shock is given to weanling rats, the rats also exhibit escape learning deficits as adults (Hannum, Rosellini, and Seligman, 1976). Both our research and that of Maier and his coworkers have indicated that only a relatively difficult voluntary testing response yields large deficits in rats (Maier, Albin, and Testa, 1973; Seligman and Beagley, 1975). Helplessness does not seem to undermine reflexive responses.

However, if we are to propose a model of depression in man, we must have proof that learned helplessness occurs in man. And it does.

Hiroto (1974) used an analogue of the shuttlebox, a finger shuttle, to test for the symptoms of learned helplessness in human subjects. A finger shuttle is a rectangular box with a handle protruding out from the top. With one finger a subject can move the handle from one end of the box to the other to stop noise. Hiroto found that subjects who had listened to inescapable loud noise were severely impaired in their ability to learn to shuttle to escape noise. Groups who had experienced escapable noise and no noise showed no impairment. It is important to realize that a well-designed helplessness experiment always consists of these three groups: one that experiences some inescapable event, a second that experiences exactly the same event but can do something to control it, and a third that does not experience the event. The symptoms of helplessness, as opposed to the symptoms produced by the event itself, occur only in the first group. Interestingly, impairment in learning was greater among subjects who were instructed that the task was a chance rather than a skill task and for subjects who perceived that their lives were determined by outside forces (Externals) rather than caused by their own actions (Internals).

Rascinskas (1971) has also reported such impairment in human responses following inescapable electric shock. Hiroto and Seligman (1975) reported that people who had experienced inescapable noises or who had worked unsolvable problems were impaired both in learning to finger shuttle to escape noise and in solving five-letter anagrams such as EBNOL. Subjects who had listened to escapable noise or who had worked solvable problems and subjects who had no experience were unimpaired in shuttlebox and anagram performance.

These findings have been replicated (Miller and Seligman, 1975), as has the Hiroto and Seligman (1975) study of unsolvable problems and anagrams (Klein, Fencil-Morse, and Seligman, 1976). Klein and Seligman (1976) replicated the inescapable noise-shuttlebox observation. These replications make us confident that our findings for humans are not due only to chance.

Miller and Seligman (1976) and Klein and Seligman (1976) found that subjects who had been exposed to inescapable noise perceived reinforcement in a skill task as more response independent than subjects who had been exposed to escapable noise or no noise. Roth and Bootzin (1974) and Roth and Kubal (1975) have also found deficits in learning and tendency to continue trying to solve cognitive problems following noncontingent reinforcement with concept formation problems. These authors have also found improved performance (facilitation) on cognitive problems following noncontingent reinforcement. Roth and Kubal (1975) identified two factors that seem to determine whether helplessness or facilitation occurs: task importance and amount of helplessness pretreatment. Subjects who have performed seemingly trivial tasks or who have received small amounts of noncontingent reinforcement are likely to experience facilitation. Helplessness seems to result when the pretreatment task is defined as important and when subjects receive noncontingent reinforcement over many trials.

Inability to control trauma not only disrupts shock escape in a variety of species, but also interferes with many types of adaptive behavior. Both Powell and Creer (1969) and Maier, Anderson, and Liberman (1972) found that rats that had received inescapable shocks responded to pain with less aggression toward other rats. McCulloch and Bruner (1939) reported that rats given inescapable shocks were slower to learn to swim out of a water maze, and Braud, Wepmann, and Russo (1969) reported similar findings in mice. Brookshire, Littman, and Stewart (1961) reported that when inescapable shocks were given to weanling rats, their food-getting behavior was still disrupted when they were adults, even when the rats were very hungry. And we have found that rats that had experienced inescapable shock failed to hurdle-jump escape from frustration (Rosellini and Seligman, 1975).

Uncontrollable events other than shock can produce effects that may be related to failure to escape shock. Escape deficits can be produced by inescapable tumbling (Anderson and Paden, 1966), as well as by unsolvable problems, loud noise (Hiroto and Seligman, 1975), and by defeat in fighting (Kahn, 1951). Harlow, Harlow, and Suomi (1971) reported that 45-day old monkeys that were confined from birth to a narrow pit showed deficits later in locomotion, exploration, and social behavior. A more detailed discussion of the generality of the effects of various inescapable USs across species is presented by Seligman (1975).

Besides passivity and retarded response-relief learning, four other characteristics associated with learned helplessness are relevant to depression in man. First, helplessness has a time course. In dogs, inescapable shock produces transient as well as permanent interference with escape (Overmier and Seligman, 1967) and avoidance (Overmier, 1968): 24 hours after *one* session of inescapable shock, dogs are helpless; but after 48 hours their response is normal. This is also true of goldfish (Padilla et al., 1970). After multiple sessions of inescapable shock, helplessness is not transient (Seligman and Groves, 1970; Seligman, Maier, and Geer, 1968). Weiss (1968) found a parallel time course for weight loss in rats given uncontrollable shock, but other than this no time course has been found in rats or in other species (e.g., Anderson, Cole, and McVaugh, 1968; Seligman, Rosellini, and Kozak, 1975).

In spite of the fact that permanent learned helplessness does occur in dogs and rats, one session of inescapable shock may produce a physiological depletion that is restored in time. Weiss, Stone, and Harrell (1970) and Weiss, Glazer, and Pohorecky (1975) found smaller amounts of whole-brain norepinephrine in rats when shock was inescapable than when they had experienced escapable shock or not shock. Thomas and DeWald, Model 6, found that blocking cholinergic activity with atropine, which released inhibited noradrenergic neurons, broke up learned helplessness in cats. Weiss, Glazer, and Pohorecky (1975) hypothesized that depletion of norepinephrine may partly cause the transient form of helplessness by creating a "motor activation deficit." According to this hypothesis, as a consequence of norepinephrine depletion, which occurs following inescapable shock, the amount of activity an animal is capable of is lowered. Reduced activity results in the failure to perform or learn the escape-avoidance response required on a subsequent test. Weiss and his coworkers have performed a series of studies to test the applicability of this hypothesis to the learned helplessness phenomena. They report a deficit in FR-1 shuttlebox escape after treatment either with a very large amount of inescapable shock or with exposure to a cold (2° C) swim task, both of which produce norepinephrine depletion. In an interesting study reported by Weiss, Glazer, and Pohorecky (1975) rats failed to show a deficit in escape-avoidance after repeated exposure to stress. Rats were given either a cold swim or 15 sessions of intense shock. Control rats received one session of shock. As expected, the controls showed the typical deficit in escape-avoidance learning. However, no deficit was found in the rats that had experienced repeated exposure to the stress. Weiss says that such a finding is not expected in view of other evidence about learned helplessness. This result is seen as supportive of the motor activation deficit hypothesis, since the noradrenergic system is known to recover after repeated exposure to a stress. We have recently replicated this procedure using our own means for producing helplessness. Rats were exposed to 15 sessions (one per day) of 80 trials of 1.0 mA of inescapable shock and were subsequently tested in FR-3 bar press shock escape. In direct contrast to Weiss, we found that repeated exposure to inescapable shock does produce a profound escape deficit (Rosellini and Seligman, 1976). This finding, the lack of a time course of helplessness in the rat, and Maier's repeated failure to obtain helplessness on an FR-1 shuttle response indicate that the escape-avoidance deficit obtained by Weiss, Glazer, and Pohorecky (1975) may not be a representative result. Thus, although norepinephrine depletion may be a consequence of uncontrollability, there is no strong evidence that such depletion causes the behavioral deficits of learned helplessness. The interested reader should consult Maier and Seligman (1976) for the details of this and other hypotheses.

Weiss (1968a, b) reported that uncontrollable shock retarded weight gain more than controllable shock in rats. Mowrer and Viek (1948), and Lindner

(1968) reported more cases of anorexia in rats given inescapable shock than in rats given escapable shock.

In summary, uncontrollable trauma produces a number of effects found in depression. The two basic effects are these: animals and humans become *passive*—they are slower to initiate responses to alleviate trauma and may not respond at all; and animals and humans are *retarded in learning* that their behavior may control trauma. If a response is made that does produce relief, they often have trouble realizing that one causes the other. This maladaptive behavior has been observed in a variety of species over a range of tasks that require voluntary responding. In addition, this phenomenon dissipates in time in the dog, and it causes lowered aggression, loss of appetite, and *norepinephrine depletion*.

Depression

Depression is not well defined; for this reason it needs a model. The clinical "entity" has multifaceted symptoms, but let us look at those that seem central to the diagnosis *and* that may be related to learned helplessness. The symptoms of learned helplessness that we have discussed all have parallels in depression.

Lowered Response Initiation. The word "depressed" as a behavioral description denotes a reduction or depression in responding. It is, therefore, not surprising that a prominent symptom of depression is failure or slowness of a patient to initiate responses. In a systematic study of the symptoms of depression, Grinker, Miller, Sabshin, Nunn, and Nunally (1961, pp. 166, 169, 170) described this in a number of ways:

> Isolated and withdrawn, prefers to remain by himself, stays in bed much of the time . . .
> Gait and general behavior slow and retarded . . .
> Volume of voice decreased, sits alone very quietly . . .
> Feels unable to act, feels unable to make decisions . . .
> [They] give the appearance of an "empty" person who has "given up . . ."

Mendels (1970, p. 7) describes the slowdown in responding associated with depression as:

> Loss of interest, decrease in energy, inability to accomplish tasks, difficulty in concentration, and the erosion of motivation and ambition all combine to impair efficient functioning. For many depressives the first signs of the illness are in the area of their increasing inability to cope with their work and responsibilities.

Beck (1967b) describes "paralysis of the will" as a striking feature of depression:

> In severe cases, there often is complete paralysis of the will. The patient has no desire to do anything, even those things which are essential to life. Consequently, he may be relatively immobile unless prodded or pushed into activity by others. It is sometimes necessary to pull the patient out of bed, wash, dress, and feed him.

The characteristic passivity and lowered response initiation of depressives have been demonstrated in a large number of studies (see Miller, 1975, for a review of these studies). Psychomotor retardation differentiates depressives from normal people and is a direct example of reduced voluntary response initiation. In addition, depressives engage in fewer activities and they show reduced interpersonal responding and reduced nonverbal communication. Finally, the intellectual slowness and learning, memory, and IQ deficits found in depressed patients may be viewed as resulting from reduced motivation to initiate cognitive actions such as memory scanning and mental arithmetic. These deficits all parallel the lowered response initiation in learned helplessness.

Recent experiments in our laboratory demonstrate a striking similarity between the lowered response initiation of learned helplessness and depression (Klein, Fencil-Morse, and Seligman, 1976; Miller and Seligman, 1975). In each of these studies, depressed and nondepressed students were first divided into three groups: group 1 experienced inescapable loud noise (or unsolvable concept formation problems), group 2 heard the loud noise but could turn it off by pressing a button (or was provided with a solvable problem); group 3 heard no noise (or did not work on any problems). All subjects then worked on a series of patterned anagrams. Half of all subjects were depressed; half were not depressed. As in the earlier study by Hiroto and Seligman (1975), nondepressed subjects in group 1, who had previously been exposed to inescapable noise or unsolvable problems, showed response initiation deficits on the anagrams, while nondepressed subjects in groups 2 and 3 exhibited no deficit. Moreover, depressed subjects in all groups, including those in group 3 who had no pretreatment, showed poorer response initiation on the anagrams than the nondepressed subjects in group 3. Nondepressed subjects given a helplessness pretreatment showed response initiation deficits wholly parallel to those found in naturally occurring depression. Klein and Seligman (1976) showed the same parallel deficits between depressed subjects and nondepressed helpless subjects on tasks involving noise escape.

Negative Cognitive Set. Depressives not only make fewer responses, but they interpret their few responses as failures or as doomed to failure. This negative cognitive set directly mirrors the difficulty that helpless subjects have in learning that responding produces relief from an aversive situation.

Beck (1967b, pp. 256–257) considers this negative cognitive set to be the primary characteristic of depression:

The depressed patient is peculiarly sensitive to any impediments to his goal-directed activity. An obstacle is regarded as an impossible barrier, difficulty in dealing with a problem is interpreted as a total failure. His cognitive response to a problem or difficulty is likely to be an idea such as "I'm licked," "I'll never be able to do this," or "I'm blocked no matter what I do . . ."

Indeed, Beck views the passive and retarded behavior of depressed patients as stemming from their negative expectations of their own effectiveness:

The loss of spontaneous motivation, or paralysis of the will, has been considered a symptom *par excellence* of depression in the classical literature. The loss of motivation may be viewed as the result of the patient's hopelessness and pessimism: as long as he expects a negative outcome from any course of action, he is stripped of any internal stimulation to do anything.

This cognitive set crops up repeatedly in experiments with depressives. Friedman (1964) observed that although a patient was performing adequately during a test, the patient would occasionally reiterate this original protest of "I can't do it," or "I don't know how." This is also our experience in testing depressed patients.

Experimental demonstrations of negative cognitive set in depressed college students were provided by Miller and Seligman (1973) and Miller, Seligman, and Kurlander (1975). These studies showed that depressed students view their skilled actions very much as if they were only chance actions. In other words, depressed subjects, more than nondepressed subjects, tend to perceive reinforcement in a skill task as independent of their behavior. Miller, Seligman, and Kurlander (1975) found this perception to be specific to depression: anxious and nonanxious students matched for extent of depression did not differ in their perceptions of reinforcement contingencies.

Miller and Seligman (1975; 1976), Klein, Fencil-Morse, and Seligman (1976), and Klein and Seligman (1976) more directly demonstrated the parallel between the negative cognitive set in learned helplessness and depression. While replicating the findings of Miller and Seligman (1973) and Miller et al. (1975) mentioned before, Miller and Seligman (1976) and Klein and Seligman (1976) found that nondepressed subjects who had been exposed to inescapable noise perceived reinforcement as less response contingent than did nondepressed subjects who had been exposed to either escapable or no noise during a skilled task. Pretreatment had no effect on perception of reinforcement in chance tasks. So, the effects of learned helplessness and depression on perception of reinforcement are parallel.

Cognitive deficits were also found in the previously mentioned studies of Miller and Seligman (1975), Klein et al. (1976), and Klein and Seligman (1976). These studies measured the degree to which subjects were able to benefit from successful anagram solutions or escapes from shuttlebox noise. As with response initiation, depressed subjects in the untreated groups showed cognitive deficits relative to nondepressed subjects, and nondepressed subjects who had experienced inescapable noise or unsolvable problems exhibited cognitive deficits relative to nondepressed subjects in the control groups. So, learned helplessness and depression produce similar effects on measures of cognitive functioning.

Some studies indicate that negative cognitive set may also explain poor discrimination learning by depressives (Martin and Rees, 1966), and may be partly responsible for their lowered cognitive abilities (Payne, 1961; Miller, 1975).

Time Course. Depression, like learned helplessness, seems to have its time course. In discussing the "disaster syndrome," Wallace (1957) reported that people experience a day or so of depression following sudden catastrophes, and then they again function normally. It seems possible that multiple traumatic events intervening between the initial disaster and recovery might exacerbate depression in humans considerably, as they do in dogs. We should also note that endogenous or process depression is characterized by fluctuations of weeks or months between depression and mania. Moreover, it is commonly thought that almost all depressions dissipate in time, although whether they last days, weeks, months, or years is a matter of some dispute (see Paskind, 1929; 1930; Lundquist, 1945; Kraines, 1957).

Lack of Aggression. According to psychoanalysts, the lowered aggression of depressives is due to introjected hostility. In fact, psychoanalysts view introjection of hostility as the primary mechanism producing symptoms of depression. We do not believe that the increased self-blame in depression results from hostility turned inward, but it seems undeniable that hostility, even in dreams (Beck and Hurvich, 1959; Beck and Ward, 1961), is reduced among depressives. This symptom corresponds to the lack of aggression in learned helplessness.

Loss of Libido and Appetite. Depressives commonly show reduced interest in food, sex, and interpersonal relations. These symptoms correspond to the anorexia, weight loss, and sexual and social deficits in learned helplessness.

Norepinephrine Depletion and Cholinergic Activity. According to the catecholamine hypothesis of affective disorders proposed by Schildkraut (1965), depression is associated with a deficiency of norepinephrine (NE) at receptor sites in the brain, whereas elation may be associated with its excess. This hypothesis is based on evidence that imipramine, a drug that increases the NE available in the central nervous system, causes depression to end. Klerman and Cole (1965) and Cole (1964) experimented with imipramine and placebos on depressed patients and reported positive results of imipramine over placebos. Monoamineoxidase (MAO) inhibitors, which prevent the breakdown of NE, also may be useful in relieving depression (Cole,

1964; Davis, 1965). Reserpine, an antihypertensive medication that depletes NE, often produces depression as a side-effect in man (Beck, 1967). There is also some suggestion of cholinergic mediation of depression. Janowsky et al. (1972) reported that physostigmine, a cholinergic stimulator, produced depressive affect in normal people. Atropine, a cholinergic blocker, reversed these symptoms. So NE depletion and cholinergic activation are implicated in both depression and learned helplessness (see Thomas and DeWald, Model 6). However, Mendels and Frazer (1974) reviewed the behavioral effects of drugs that deplete brain catecholamines and they contend that the behavioral changes associated with reserpine are better interpreted as a psychomotor retardation-sedation syndrome than as depression. Moreover, selective depletion of brain catecholamines by alpha-methyl-para-tyrosine (AMPT) fails to produce some of the key features of depression, despite the fact that this drug produces a consistently greater reduction in amine metabolate concentration than occurs in depression. So depletion of catecholamines in itself may not be sufficient to account for depression.

Feelings of Helplessness, Hopelessness, and Powerlessness. Although this is a discussion of the behavioral and physiological symptoms of depression, we cannot avoid mentioning the subjective feeling states and self-evaluations that accompany the passivity and negative expectations of depressed people. Depressed people say they feel helpless, hopeless, and powerless, and by this they mean that they believe they are unable to control or influence those aspects of their lives that are significant to them.

Grinker and coworkers (1961) describe the "characteristics of hopelessness, helplessness, failure, sadness, unworthiness, guilt and internal suffering" as the "essence of depression."

Melges and Bowlby (1969) also characterize depressed patients in this way and Bibring (1953) *defines* depression "as the emotional expression [indicative] of a state of helplessness and powerlessness of the ego."

There clearly are considerable parallels between the forms of behavior that define learned helplessness and major symptoms of depression.

Differences. But there are substantial gaps.

First, there are two symptoms found with uncontrollable shock that may or may not correspond to symptoms of depression. Stomach ulcers occur more frequently and severely in rats receiving uncontrollable shock than in rats receiving controllable shock (Weiss, 1968b; 1971a, b, c). We know of no study examining the relationship of depression to stomach ulcers. Second, uncontrollable shock produces more anxiety, measured subjectively, behaviorally, and physiologically, than controllable shock (see Seligman and Binik, 1976). The question of whether depressed people are more anxious than nondepressed people does not have a clear answer. Beck (1967) reported that although both depression and anxiety can be observed in some people, only a small positive correlation was found in a study of 606 patients. Yet, Miller et al. (1975) found very few depressed college students who were not also anxious. We can speculate that anxiety and depression are related in the following way: when a man or animal is confronted with a threat or a loss, he initially responds with fear or anxiety. If he learns that the threat is wholly controllable, anxiety, having served its function, disappears. If he remains uncertain about his ability to control the threat, his anxiety remains. If he learns or is convinced that the threat is utterly uncontrollable, depression emerges.

A number of facts about depression have been insufficiently investigated for parallels in learned helplessness. Preeminent among these are the depressive symptoms that cannot be investigated in animals: dejected mood, feelings of self-blame and self-dislike, loss of mirth, suicidal thoughts and crying. Now that learned helplessness has been reliably produced in man (Hiroto, 1974; Hiroto and Seligman, 1975; Klein et al., 1976; Klein and Seligman, 1976; Miller and Seligman, 1975; 1976; Racinskas, 1971; Roth and Kubal, 1975; Thornton and Jacobs, 1970; Dweck and Reppucci, 1973), we can determine whether any of these states occur in helplessness.

Finally, we know of no evidence that *disconfirms* the correspondence of symptoms in learned helplessness and depression.

Etiology

Learned Helplessness

The cause of learned helplessness is reasonably well understood: it is not a trauma itself that produces interference with later adaptive responses but rather trauma that we cannot control. The distinction between controllable and uncontrollable reinforcement is central to the phenomenon and theory of helplessness, so let us now examine it.

Learning theorists usually use a line depicting the conditional probability of reinforcement following a response, designated p (RFT/R), to explain the relationship between instrumental responses and outcomes about which organisms could learn. This line ranges from 0 to 1. At 1, every response produces a reinforcement (continuous reinforcement). At 0, a response never produces a reinforcement (extinction). Intermediate points on the line represent various degrees of partial reinforcement.

However, a single line does not exhaust relations between response and outcomes to which organisms are sensitive. Rewards or punishments sometimes occur when no specific response has been made. Only a woefully maladaptive S could not learn about such a contingency. Rather than

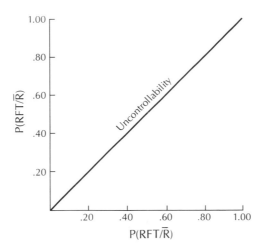

Figure 3-1. The instrumental training space. The ordinate and abscissa represent the relationships between the subject's response and a reinforcer. They are conditional probabilities or contingencies arranged by the experimenter. The 45-degree line represents a special condition in which the reinforcer is uncontrollable because the probability of reinforcement for responding is equal to the probability of reinforcement for not responding.

representing instrumental learning as occurring along a single dimension, we can better describe it using the two-dimensional space shown in Figure 3-1. The x-axis (p[RFT/R]) represents the traditional dimension, conditional-probability of reinforcement, following a response.

At a right angle to the conditional probability of reinforcement, given a response, is the conditional probability of reinforcement, given the absence of *that* response (p [RFT/$\overline{R}$]). This dimension is represented along the y-axis. We think that Ss learn about variations along *both* dimensions at the same time. Thus, S may learn the extent to which relief occurs when it does not make a specific response at the same time as it learns the extent to which relief occurs when it makes the specific response. Systematic changes in behavior occur with systematic changes along both dimensions.

There is considerable convergence of opinion and evidence among learning theorists today that organisms can learn about the contingencies within this instrumental training space, including the crucial 45-degree line (e.g., Catania, 1971; Church, 1969; Gibbon, Berryman, and Thomson, 1974; Maier, Seligman, and Solomon, 1969; Poresky, 1970; Premack, 1965; Rescorla, 1967, 1968; Seligman, Maier, and Solomon, 1971; Wagner, 1969; Watson, 1967; and Weiss, 1968a).

The traditional training line has been thoroughly explored (e.g., Ferster and Skinner, 1957; and Honig, 1966). The points in the line that are of special concern in the study of helplessness are those that line along the 45-degree line, (where x = y). Whether or not the organism responds, it still gets the same amount of reinforcement. The conditional probability of reinforcement, given a specific response, *does not differ* from the conditional probability of reinforcement in the absence of that response. Responding and reinforcement are independent.

The concept of control is defined within this instrumental training space. Any time there is something the organism can do or refrain from doing that changes what it gets, it has control. Specifically, a response, stands in control of a reinforcer *if and only if*:

$$p(RFT/R) \neq p(RFT/\overline{R})$$

That is, the probability of reinforcement given a response is different from the probability of reinforcement in the absence of that response. Furthermore, when a response does not change what S gets, the response and reinforcement are independent. Specifically, when a response in independent of a reinforcer, $p(RFT/R) = p(RFT/\overline{R})$. When this is true of all responses, S cannot control the reinforcer, the outcome is uncontrollable, and nothing the organism does matters.

The passivity of dogs, rats and men in the face of trauma and their difficulty in benefiting from response-relief contingencies result, we believe, from their having learned that responding and trauma are independent— that trauma is uncontrollable. This is the heart of the learned helplessness hypothesis. The hypothesis states that when shock is inescapable, the organism learns that responses and shock termination are independent (the probability of shock termination given any response doesn't differ from its probability in the absence of that response). Learning that trauma is uncontrollable has three effects.

(1) A motivational effect. It reduces the probability that the subject will initiate responses to escape, because part of the incentive for making such responses is the expectation that they will bring relief. If the subject has previously learned that its responses have no effect on trauma, this contravenes the expectation. Thus the organism's motivation to respond is undermined by experience with reinforcers it cannot control. We think this motivational effect underlies passivity in learned helplessness, and, if the model is valid, in depression.

(2) A cognitive effect. Learning that responses and shock are independent makes it more difficult to learn that responses do produce relief when the organism makes a response that actually terminates shock. In general, if we have acquired a cognitive set in which As are irrelevant to Bs, it will be harder for us to learn that As produce Bs when they do. By the helplessness hypothesis, this mechanism is responsible for the difficulty that helpless organisms have in learning that responding produces relief, even after they respond and successfully turn off shock. Further, if the model is valid, this mechanism produces the "negative expectations" of depression.

(3) An emotional effect. Although it does not follow directly from the helplessness hypothesis, we have mentioned that uncontrollable shock also has an emotional impact on animals. Uncontrollable shock produces more conditioned fear, ulcers, weight loss, defecation, and pain than controllable shock.

We have tested and confirmed this hypothesis in several ways. We began by ruling out alternative hypotheses. It is unlikely that our dogs have either become adapted (and therefore not motivated enough to escape shock) or sensitized (and therefore too disorganized to escape shock) by pretreatment with shock; because making the shock very intense or very mild in the shuttle box does not attenuate the phenomenon. Further, it is unlikely that the dogs have learned during inescapable shock, by explicit or superstitious reinforcement or by punishment, some motor response pattern that competes with barrier jumping in the shuttle box because interference occurs even if the dogs are paralyzed by curare and can make no overt motor responses during shock. Seligman and Maier (1967) performed a direct test of the hypothesis that not the shock itself but rather its uncontrollability causes helplessness. Three groups of eight dogs were used. Dogs in the escape group were trained in the hammock to press a panel with their noses or heads to turn off shock. Dogs in a yoked group received shocks identical to the shocks delivered to the escape group. The yoked group differed from the escape group only with respect to the degree of instrumental control it had over shock; pressing the panel in the yoked group did not affect the programmed shocks. Dogs in a naive control group received no shock in the hammock.

Twenty-four hours following the hammock treatment all three groups received escape-avoidance training in the shuttle box. The escape group and the naive control group suffered no impairment in shuttle box performance. In contrast, the yoked group showed significantly slower defenses than the naive control group. Six of the eight Ss in the yoked group failed to escape shock. It was not the shock itself but rather not being able to control the shock that produced failure to escape.

Maier (1970) provided more dramatic confirmation of the hypothesis in response to the criticism that what is learned during uncontrollable trauma is not a cognitive set as we have proposed, but rather some motor response, reinforced by shock termination, that antagonizes barrier jumping. Maier reinforced the most antagonistic response he could find. One group of 10 dogs (passive-escape) was tied down in the hammock and panels were pushed to within one-fourth inch of the sides and top of their heads. Only by *not* moving their heads, by remaining passive and still, could these dogs terminate shock. Another group of 10 (yoked) received the same shock in the hammock, but the shock was independent of their responses. A third group received no shock. A response-learning theory of helplessness would predict that when the dogs were later tested in the shuttle box, a test situation requiring active responding for successful escape, the passive-escape group should be the most helpless since it had been explicitly reinforced for not moving during shock. The cognitive-set view made a different prediction: these dogs could control shock, even though it required a passive response. Some response, even one that competed with barrier jumping, produced relief, and they should not learn response-reinforcement independence. As predicted by the cognitive-set theory, dogs in the yoked group were predominantly helpless in the shuttle box escape, and the naive controls escaped normally. The passive-escape group at first looked for "still" ways of minimizing shock in the shuttle box: failing to find these, they began to escape and avoid. Thus it was not trauma itself nor interfering motor habits that produced failure to escape, but having learned that no response at all could control trauma.

Maier and Testa (1975) have shown that the escape deficit seen in rats after exposure to inescapable shock partly results from associative interference and not from a motor deficit. In a lucid series of studies, they have found that it is the contingency between the response and shock termination that is crucial in determining the effect of prior inescapable shock, and not the amount of motor response required of the animal to execute the response. In the first experiment, they simplified the typical FR-2 shuttling contingency by briefly terminating shock after the first response of the FR-2. Rats that had experienced inescapable shock showed no learning deficit. In a second experiment, they made the escape contingency more difficult to see, but not to perform, by interposing a delay between shuttling and shock termination. Only one crossing of the barrier (FR-1) was required of the rats (usually, inescapably shocked rats do not show a deficit in FR-1 shuttling). However, a deficit was obtained when shock termination was delayed after escape. Changing the complexity of the escape contingency in no way altered the amount of motor response required of the animals but it drastically affected the animals' behavior. (See Maier and Seligman, 1976, for a more exhaustive discussion of motor response theories of learned helplessness.)

Learning that responses and reinforcement are independent causes retarded response initiation, but does it also cause a negative cognitive set that interferes with later formation of associations? Evidence from four different areas in recent literature supports the idea that independence between events retards learning that events are correlated: Seligman (1968) reported that when stimulus and shock were presented independently, rats were later retarded in learning that a second stimulus preceded shock. Bresnahan (1969), and Thomas et al. (1970) reported that experience with the value of one stimulus dimension, presented independently of food, retarded a rat's ability to discriminate among other dimensions of the stimulus. MacKintosh (1965) reviewed substantial discrimination learning literature and concluded that when stimuli are presented independent of reinforcement, animals are retarded at discrimination learning when these same stimuli are later correlated with reinforcement (see also Kemler and Shepp, 1971, and MacKintosh, 1973. N. Maier (1949) reviewed a set of related results.) Gamzu and Williams (1971) reported that when pigeons are exposed to independence between a lighted key and grain, they later are retarded in learning when the lighted key signals grain. Engberg, Hansen, Welker, and Thomas (1972) found that noncontingent food presentations produced deficits in the pigeon's ability to autoshape, a phenomenon they referred to as *learned laziness*. This result is an unsatisfactory demonstration of learned laziness, however, because autoshaping may be under Pavlovian as well as operant control. Welker (1974) also reported rats were deficient in learning to bar press for food after the rats had prolonged exposure to bar pressing which was independent of food. Recently, we have obtained some preliminary data that suggest that prolonged presentation of noncontingent food may produce a deficit in learning to escape shock (Rosellini, Bazerman, and Seligman, 1976).

In summary, one cause of laboratory-produced helplessness seems to be learning that one cannot control important events. Learning that responses and reinforcement are independent results in a cognitive set that has two effects: fewer responses to control reinforcement are initiated, and associating successful responses with reinforcement becomes more difficult.

Depression

The etiology of depression is less clear than are its symptoms. A dichotomy exists between kinds of depression and it will be useful for our purposes: the "exogenous-endogenous" or "process-reactive" distinction (e.g., Kiloh and Garside, 1963; Kraepelin, 1913; and Partridge, 1949). Without agreeing that a dividing line can be clearly drawn, we can observe that one type of depression occurs cyclically with no identifiable external event precipitating it (e.g., Kraines, 1957), and that it may swing regularly from mania to depression. This so-called *endogenous* or *process* depression and its immediate etiology are presumably biochemical or genetic or both. On the other hand, depression is also sometimes clearly precipitated by environmental events. This form of depression—*reactive* or *exogenous*—is the primary concern of this paper. It is useful to regard the process-reactive distinction as a continuum rather than a dichotomy. On the extreme of the reactive side, strong events of the kind discussed in following passages are necessary. In between may lie a continuum of preparedness to become depressed when faced with helplessness-inducing external events. The most mild events set off depression at the extreme process end.

Let us enumerate some of the events that typically precipitate depression: failure in work or school; death or loss of loved ones; rejection by or separation from loved ones; physical disease, and growing old. What do all of these have in common?

Four recent theories of depression seem to be largely in agreement about the etiology of depression, and what they agree on is the centrality of helplessness and hopelessness. Bibring (1953), arguing from a dynamic viewpoint, sees helplessness as the cause of depression:

> What has been described as the basic mechanism of depression, the ego's shocking awareness of its helplessness in regard to its aspirations, is assumed to represent the core of normal, neurotic, and probably also psychotic depression.

Melges and Bowlby (1969) see a similar cause of depression:

> Our thesis is that while a depressed patient's goals remain relatively unchanged his estimate of the likelihood of achieving them and his confidence in the efficacy of his own skilled actions are both diminished . . . the depressed person believes that his plans of action are no longer effective in reaching his continuing and long range goals . . . From this state of mind is derived, we believe, much depressive symptomology, including indecisiveness, inability to act, making increased demands on others, and feelings of worthlessness and of guilt about not discharging duties.

Beck (1967b, 1970a, b) sees depression as resulting primarily from a patient's negative cognitive set, largely about his abilities to change his life.

> A primary factor appears to be the activation of idiosyncratic cognitive patterns which divert the thinking into specific channels that deviate from reality. As a result, the patient perseverates in making negative judgements and misinterpretations. These distortions may be categorized within the triad of negative interpretations of experience; negative evaluations of the self; and negative expectations of the future.

Lichtenberg (1957) sees hopelessness as the defining characteristic of depression:

> Depression is defined as a manifestation of felt hopelessness regarding the attainment of goals when responsibility for the hopelessness is attributed to one's personal defects. In this context hope is conceived to be a function of the perceived probability of success with respect to goal attainment."

We believe what joins these views and lies at the heart of depression is this: the depressed patient has learned or believes that he cannot control those elements of his life that relieve suffering or bring him gratification. In short, he believes that he is helpless. Consider a few of the common precipitating events. What is the meaning of job failure or incompetence at school? Frequently it means that all of a person's efforts have been in vain, his responses have failed to bring about the gratification he desires: he cannot find responses that control reinforcement. When a person is rejected by someone he loves, he can no longer control this significant source of gratification and support. When a parent or lover dies, the bereaved person is powerless to produce or influence love from the dead person. Physical disease and growing old are obvious helplessness experiences. In these conditions, the person's own responses are ineffective and he must rely on the care of others. So, we would predict that it is not life events per se that produce depression (cf. Alarcon and Cori, 1972), but uncontrollable life events.

The previously mentioned studies by Miller and Seligman (1975, 1976) and Klein, Fencil-Morse, and Seligman (1976) are of interest here. These studies all involved the same 3 (controllability) × 2 (depression) design—depressed and nondepressed subjects were first exposed to controllable reinforcement, uncontrollable reinforcement, or no pretreatment and then asked to perform on a test task where reinforcement was controllable. In all three studies, strikingly similar test task performance deficits were found for depressed subjects who had no pretreatment and for nondepressed subjects who had uncontrollable pretreatment. With a slightly different design, Klein and Seligman (1976) obtained parallel results. Clearly, the fact that noncontingent reinforcement results in behavioral deficits similar to those of naturally occurring depression does not *prove* that the depression was also produced by experiences with uncontrollable reinforcement. However, if experiments using the 3 × 2 design continue to demonstrate a variety of similarities in the effects of helplessness and depression, the hypothesis that learned helplessness and depression are parallel phenomena with the same etiology will be strengthened.

Ferster (1966, 1973), Kaufman and Rosenblum (1967); McKinney and Bunney (1969); and Liberman and Raskin (1971) have suggested that depression is caused by extinction procedures or the *loss* of reinforcers. There is no contradiction between the learned-helplessness and extinction views of depression; helplessness, however, is more general. Extinction commonly denotes a set of contingencies in which reinforcement is withdrawn, so that the subjects' responses (as well as lack of responses) no longer produce reinforcement. Loss of reinforcers, as in the death of a loved one, can be viewed as an extinction procedure. In conventional extinction procedures the probability of the reinforcer occurring is zero whether or not the subject responds. Extinction is a special case of independence between responding and reinforcement. Reinforcement, however, may also be presented with a probability greater than zero, and still be presented independent of responding. This occurs in the typical helplessness paradigm and causes responses to decrease in probability (Rescorla and Skucy, 1969). Therefore, a view that talks about independence between responses and reinforcement assumes the extinction view and, in addition, suggests that situations in which reinforcers still occur independent of responding also will cause depression.

Differences. Both learned helplessness and depression may be caused by learning that responses and reinforcement are independent. But this view runs into several problems. Can depression actually be caused by situations other than extinction in which reinforcements still occur but are not under the individual's control? To put it another way, "Is a net loss of reinforcers necessary for depression, or can depression occur when there is only loss of control without loss of reinforcers?" Would a Casanova who made love with seven new women every week become depressed if he found out that women wanted him not because of his amatory prowess but because of his wealth or because his fairy godmother wished it? We can only speculate.

It seems appropriate to mention "success" depression in this context. When people finally reach a goal after years of striving—being promoted or getting a PhD—many become depressed. This puzzling phenomenon is clearly a problem for a loss of reinforcement view of depression. From a helplessness view, success depression may occur because reinforcers are no longer contingent on present responding: After years of goal-directed instrumental activity, the reinforcement automatically changes. One now gets his reinforcement because of who he is rather than what he is doing. The common clinical impression that many beautiful women become depressed and attempt suicide also presents problems for the loss of reinforcement theory: positive reinforcers abound not because of what they do but because of how they look. Would a generation of children raised with abundant positive reinforcers that they received independently of what they did become clinically depressed?

We do not wish to maintain that helplessness is the only cause of reactive depression. The absolute quality of life also alters mood. Holding the quality of one's life constant, even when events are uncontrollable, will push mood in the *direction* of euphoria or dysphoria. Controllable events will be less depressing or more cheering than uncontrollable ones, and uncontrollable events more depressing or less cheering (Klinger, 1975).

Cure

Learned Helplessness

We have found one behavioral treatment that cures helplessness in dogs and rats. According to the helplessness hypothesis, the dog makes no attempt to escape because he expects that no instrumental response will produce shock termination. By forcibly demonstrating to the dog that responses produce reinforcement, you can change this expectation. Seligman, Maier, and Geer (1968), moreover, found that forcibly dragging the dog from one side of the shuttle box to the other so that changing compartments terminated shock for the dog cured helplessness. The experimenters pulled three chronically helpless dogs back and forth across the shuttle box with long leashes. This was done during CS and shock, with the barrier removed. After being pulled across the center of the shuttle box (thus terminating shock and CS) 20, 35, and 50 times respectively, each dog began to respond on its own. Then the barrier was replaced, and the subject continued to escape and avoid. Recovery from helplessness was complete and lasting, a finding that has been replicated with more than two dozen helpless dogs.

The behavior of animals during the time they were pulled by a leash was noteworthy. At the beginning of the procedure, a good deal of force had to be exerted to pull the dog across the center of the shuttle box. Less and less force was needed as training progressed. Generally, a stage was reached in which a slight nudge of the leash would drive the dog into action. Finally, each dog initiated its own response, and thereafter failure to escape was very rare. The problem seemed to be one of motivating the dog.

We first tried other procedures with little success. Merely removing the barrier, calling to the dog from the safe side, dropping food into the safe side, kicking the dangerous side of the box—all failed. Until the correct response occurred repeatedly, the dog was not effectively exposed to the response-relief contingency. It is significant that so many forced exposures were required before the dogs responded on their own. A similar "therapy" procedure has also been successfully used with rats (Seligman, Rosellini, and Kozak, 1975). Helpless rats were forcibly exposed to FR-3 bar press escape by being dragged onto the operant lever. After many forced exposures, the rats began to escape on their own. Their behavior was much like that of the dogs. During the early part of training, a fair amount of force was needed to drag the rat to the lever. As therapy progressed, less and less force was required to induce the animal to escape. Finally, after repeated exposure to escape, the rats started escaping without any intervention from the experimenter. This observation supported the twofold interpretation of the effects of inescapable shock: (1) the motivation to initiate responses during shock was low, and (2) the ability to associate successful responses with relief was impaired.

Time (Overmier and Seligman, 1967), electroconvulsive shock (Dorworth, 1971), atropine (Thomas and DeWald, this volume, Model 7), and the antidepressant drug pargyline (Weiss, Glazer, and Pohorecky, 1976) have all been reported successful in alleviating learned helplessness.

Depression

According to the helplessness view, the central theme in successful therapy should be having the patient discover and come to accept that his responses produce the gratification that he desires—that he is, in short, an effective human being. Some therapies that reportedly alleviate depression are consonant with a learned helplessness model. However, it is important to note that the success of a therapy often has little to do with its theoretical underpinnings. So, with the exception of Klein and Seligman (1976), the following "evidence" should not be regarded as a test of the model, but merely as a set of examples that seem to have exposure to response-produced success as a cure for depression.

Consonant with their helplessness-centered views of the etiology of depression, Bibring (1953), Beck (1967a, b), and Melges and Bowlby (1969) all stressed that reversing helplessness alleviates depression. For example, Bibring (1953) has stated:

> The same conditions which bring about depression (helplessness) in reverse serve frequently the restitution from depression. Generally one can say that depression subsides either (a) when the narcissistically important goals and objects appear to be again within reach (which is frequently followed by a temporary elation) or (b) when they become sufficiently modified or reduced to become realizable, or (c) when they are altogether relinquished, or (d) when the ego recovers from the narcissistic shock by regaining its self-esteem with the help of various recovery mechanisms (with or without any change of objective or goal).

In their review of therapies for depression, Seligman, Klein, and Miller (1976) indicated that most of the therapies have strong elements of inducing the patient to discover that responses produce the reinforcement he desires. In antidepression milieu therapy (Taulbee and Wright, 1971), for example, the patient is *forced* to emit one of the most powerful responses people have for controlling others—anger—and when this response is dragged out of his depleted behavior repertoire, he is powerfully reinforced. Beck's (1970a) cognitive therapy is aimed at similar goals. He sees success manipulations as changing the negative cognitive set ("I'm an ineffective person") of the depressive to a more positive set, and argues that the primary task of the therapist is to change the negative expectations of the depressed patient to more optimistic ones. In both Burgess's (1968) therapy and the graded task assignment (Beck, Seligman, Binik, Schuyler, and Brill, unpublished data), the patient makes instrumental responses of gradually increasing complexity, and each is reinforced. Similarly, all instrumental behavior therapy for depression (Hersen, Eisler, Alford, and Agras, 1973; Reisinger, 1972), by definition, arranges the contingencies so that responses control the occurrence of reinforcement; the patient's recognition of this relationship should alleviate depression. Lewinsohn's therapy also has this element: participation in activity and other nondepressed behavior controls therapy time (Lewinsohn, Weinstein, and Shaw, 1969). In assertive training (Wolpe, 1969), the patient must emit social responses to bring about a desired change in his environment.

As in learned helplessness, the passage of time has been found to alleviate depression. Electroconvulsive therapy, which alleviates helplessness, probably alleviates endogenous depression (Carney, Roth and Garside, 1965), but its effects on reactive depression are unclear. The role of atropine is largely unknown (see Janowsky et al., 1972).

In a recent series of human helplessness studies, Klein and Seligman (1976) demonstrated that the behavioral deficits of both depression and learned helplessness are reversed if subjects are exposed to success experiences. Three groups of college students were used—nondepressed students who had experienced inescapable noise, and depressed and nondepressed groups, both of whom had experienced no noise. Following the pretreatment, subjects were allowed to solve 0, 4, or 12 discrimination problems. Then, subjects performed in either the noise escape task of Hiroto (1974) or the skill and chance tasks of Miller and Seligman (1973). As in the human helplessness studies reviewed above, the nondepressed subjects that had experienced inescapable noise and depressed subjects who had experienced no noise showed similar deficits on noise escape and skill expectancy changes relative to the nondepressed subjects that had experienced no noise when the subjects were not allowed to solve the discrimination problems. However, when subjects successfully solved 4 or 12 discrimination problems following the pretreatment, those groups did not exhibit test task deficits relative to the nondepressed subjects who had experienced no noise. Experience in controlling reinforcement reversed the behavioral deficits of both learned helplessness and mild depression.

We think that the study provides a useful method for testing the effectiveness of *any* therapy for depression in the laboratory. Because we can bring depression into the laboratory both in its naturally occurring state and in the form of learned helplessness, we can see what reverses it in the laboratory. Will assertive training, emotive expression, or atropine given to helpless and depressed subjects in the laboratory reverse the symptoms of depression and helplessness?

Some comment is in order on the role of *secondary gain* in depression; that is, on the tendency to use symptoms for inducing others to display sympathy and affection. In order to explain depression, Burgess (1968) and others have relied heavily on the reinforcement the patient gets for his depressed behaviors. It is tempting to seek to remove this reinforcement during therapy, but caution is in order here. Secondary gain may explain the persistence or maintenance of *some* depressive behaviors, but it does not explain how they began. Helplessness suggests that failure to initiate active responses originates in the perception that the patient cannot control reinforcement. Thus, there can be two sources of a depressed patient's passivity: 1) patients are passive for instrumental reasons, because they think staying depressed brings them sympathy, love and attention, and 2) patients are passive because they believe that *no* response at all will be effective in controlling their environment. In this sense, secondary gain, although a practical hindrance to therapy, may be a hopeful sign in depression: it means that there is at least some response (albeit passive) that the patient believes he can effectively perform. Maier (1970) found that dogs who were reinforced for being passive by shock termination were not nearly as debilitated as dogs for whom all responses were independent of shock termination. Similarly, patients who use their depression as a way of controlling reinforcement are less helpless than those who have given up.

Psychologists can cause learned helplessness to end by forcing the passive dog or rat to see that his responses produce reinforcement. A variety of techniques and theories suggest that therapy aimed at breaking up depression should center on the patient's sense of efficacy: Depression may be directly antagonized when patients come to see that their own responses are effective in alleviating their suffering and producing gratification.

Difficulties. Many therapies, from psychoanalysis to T-groups, claim to be able to cure depression. The evidence presented here is selective: only those treatments that seemed compatible with helplessness were discussed. It is possible that when other therapies work it is because they reinstate the patient's sense of efficacy. However, evidence on the effectiveness of therapy in depression that is less anecdotal and selective is sorely needed. The recent study of Klein and Seligman (1976) may provide a laboratory procedure for evaluating the effectiveness of *any* therapy suggested for learned helplessness and depression.

Prevention

Learned Helplessness

Dramatic success in medicine has come more frequently from prevention than from treatment, and we would hazard a guess that inoculation and immunization have saved many more lives than any cure. Psychotherapy is almost exclusively limited to use as a cure, and preventive procedures rarely play an explicit role. In our studies of animals we found that behavioral immunization provided an easy and effective means of preventing learned helplessness.

The helplessness viewpoint suggested a way to immunize animals against inescapable shocks. Initial experience with escapable shocks should do two things: it should interfere with learning that responses and shock termination are independent, and it should allow the animal to discriminate between situations in which shocks are escapable and those in which they are inescapable. The relevant experiment was done by Seligman and Maier

(1967). One group of dogs was given 10 escape-avoidance trials in the shuttle box before it received inescapable shocks in the hammock. The dogs that began by learning to escape shock in the shuttle box pressed the panels four times as often in the hammock during the inescapable shocks as did naive dogs, even though pressing panels had no effect on shock. Such panel pressing probably measures the attempts of the dog to control shock. Seligman, Marques, and Radford (unpublished data) extended these findings by first letting the dogs escape shock by panel pressing in the hammock. This was followed by inescapable shock in the same place. Experience with control over shock termination prevented the dogs from becoming helpless when they were later tested in a new apparatus, the shuttle box.

Other findings from our laboratory support the idea that experience in controlling trauma may protect organisms from the helplessness caused by inescapable trauma. Recall that among dogs of unknown history, helplessness is a statistical effect. Approximately two-thirds of dogs given inescapable shock become helpless, and one-third respond normally. Only 6 percent of naive dogs become helpless in the shuttle box without any prior exposure to inescapable shock. Why do some dogs become helpless and others not? Could it be that those dogs that become helpless even without any inescapable shock have had a history of uncontrollable trauma? Seligman and Groves (1970) tested this hypothesis by raising dogs singly in cages in the laboratory. Relative to dogs of variegated history, these dogs had very limited experience controlling anything. Cage-reared dogs proved to be more susceptible to helplessness; although it took four sessions of inescapable shock to produce helplessness in dogs of unknown history, only two sessions of inescapable shock in the hammock were needed to cause helplessness in the cage-reared dogs. Lessac and Solomon (1969) also reported that dogs reared in isolation seemed prone to experience interference with escape. Thus, dogs that are deprived of natural opportunities to master reinforcement in their developmental history may be more vulnerable to helplessness than naturally immunized dogs. We have been able to immunize rats against the debilitating effects of inescapable shock. Rats first exposed to one session of escapable shock did not become helpless when subsequently exposed to inescapable shock (Seligman, Rosellini, and Kozak, 1975). More recently we have found lifelong immunization against helplessness: rats, given inescapable shock at weaning, did not become helpless when given inescapable shock as adults (Hannum, Rosellini, and Seligman, 1976).

Even less is known about the prevention of depression than about its physiology or cure. Almost everyone at some time loses control over the reinforcements that are significant to him—parents die, loved ones reject us. Everyone also becomes at least mildly and transiently depressed in the wake of such events. But why are some people emotionally paralyzed and others resilient? We can only speculate about this, but the data on immunization against helplessness guide our speculations in a definite direction. The life histories of those persons who are particularly resistant to depression may have been filled with mastery. These people may have had extensive experience controlling and manipulating the sources of reinforcement in their lives, and they may therefore perceive the future more optimistically. Those people who are particularly susceptible to depression may have had lives relatively devoid of mastery. Their lives may have been full of experiences in which they were helpless to influence their sources of suffering and gratification.

The relationship of depression in adults to loss of parents in youth seems relevant. It seems likely that children who lose their parents experience helplessness and may be more vulnerable to later depression. The findings on this topic are mixed. So it is possible, although not established, that losing a parent in youth may make one more vulnerable to depression.

A caveat is in order here, however. Although it seems reasonable that extensive experience controlling reinforcement might make one more resilient from depression, how about the person who has met *only* with success? Is a person whose responses have always met with success more susceptible to depression when confronted with situations beyond his control? It seems reasonable that too much experience controlling reinforcers might not allow the development and use of coping responses against failure, just as too little control might prevent the development of ability to cope.

One can also look at successful therapy as preventive. After all, therapy is usually not focused just on undoing past problems. It also should arm the patient against future depressions. Would therapy for depression be more successful if it were explicitly aimed at providing the patient with a wide repertoire of coping responses that he could use in future situations where he found he could not control reinforcement by his usual responses?

Finally, we can speculate about child rearing. What kinds of experience can best protect our children against the debilitating effects of helplessness and depression? A tentative answer follows from the learned helplessness view of depression: a childhood of experiences in which one's own actions are instrumental in bringing about gratification and removing annoyances. Seeing oneself as an effective human being may require a childhood filled with powerful synchronies between responding and its consequences.

Testing the learned helplessness model of depression requires the demonstration of similarities in symptoms, etiology, cure and prevention of learned helplessness. The current evidence, reviewed in this model, indicates that in many respects the major symptoms of helplessness parallel those of depression. In addition, we have suggested that the cause of both reactive depression and learned helplessness is the belief that responses do not control important reinforcers. Finally, we have speculated that the methods that succeed in curing and preventing learned helplessness have their parallels in the cure and prevention of depression. Much remains to be tested, but we believe that a common theme has emerged: both depression and learned helplessness have at their core the belief in the futility of responding.

Production and Alleviation of Depressive Behaviors in Monkeys

Stephen J. Suomi
University of Wisconsin

Harry F. Harlow
University of Wisconsin

Research employing nonhuman primate subjects has always occupied a special niche in the hierarchy of behavioral sciences. On one hand, it provides investigators with subjects whose physical, cognitive, and behavioral characteristics are more similar to humans than those of traditional laboratory animals. We would expect the findings from primate studies to be more applicable to direct human concerns than findings gleaned from rodent or canine data. Moreover, because nonhuman primates are not furry little men with tails but rather "merely" animals, research utilizing them for subjects is not restricted by the same ethical constraints that properly limit what an experimenter can directly investigate in a human subject or patient. In short, nonhuman primates are attractive as subjects for research related to human concerns that cannot be performed on human subjects.

One research topic to which we at the Wisconsin Primate Laboratory have directed much of our recent attention is study of behavior in rhesus monkeys that closely resembles human depression. Underlying much of this work is the basic assumption that human disorders such as depression can be simulated or *modeled* in nonhuman subjects. This assumption requires some clarification and qualification.

This research was supported by USPHS Grants MH-11894 and MH-18070, from the National Institute of Mental Health to the University of Wisconsin Primate Laboratory, and by the Grant Foundation.

Animal Models of Human Disorders

There can be little argument that mankind would be spared considerable suffering if valid and usable models of all human disorders could be developed in nonhuman subjects. If this were the case, both somatic and psychosomatic human ailments could be studied, cured, and perhaps even prevented under controlled conditions in certain animals. The findings could then be applied to man, potentially reducing the incidence and intensity of disease and misery throughout the world. Unfortunately, this is not the case now, and probably it never will be. As of today, there do exist many useful and beneficial animal models for human disorders (McKinney, 1974). However, for a vast number of human somatic and psychosomatic syndromes there are no realistic animal models. Furthermore, there likely exists an entire family of disorders that are totally and exclusively human, for which no animal model is possible because no other species possesses the capability to express the definitive human syndromes physically or mentally. Numerous animal models exist—the problem is to determine which are accurate and appropriate and which are not. For this, some criteria are needed.

First, criteria must be developed to determine the *validity* of any animal model. One set of such criteria that we have found useful is described in detail by McKinney and Bunney (1969). Basically, they argue that to be valid, animal models should possess at least the following three characteristics: (1) the objectively definable symptoms of the disorder in man should be mirrored in the animal under study; (2) known predisposers and direct causes of the dysfunction in humans should effectively and consistently produce the parallel dysfunction in the animal species; (3) finally, procedures that reverse the disorder in humans should be therapeutic to the species upon which the model is based. If these criteria can be successfully met by the animal model, then arguments for the validity of the nonhuman data for the human disorder become convincing, even compelling.

A different set of criteria concerns the *utility* of an animal model for diagnosing, understanding, and ultimately curing the corresponding human disorder. A model may be totally valid for a particular human disease, yet useless in the practical sense. For example, suppose that a certain disease can be modeled perfectly in a macaque species, that all physiological symptoms are identical in both man and monkey. Further suppose that there exists an infallible diagnostic test for this disorder in monkeys, one that will enable an investigator to determine long in advance whether the disorder will disable a given individual. However, what if such a test is conducted through chemical assay of the entire frontal lobe, which necessitates its surgical removal. Such an animal model would then be valid, but it would have definite practical limitations inasmuch as few humans would be willing to give up their frontal lobes for a mere diagnosis. Similarly, a rehabilitative procedure that is totally effective for monkey subjects but that requires several years of solitary incarceration in a padded room, will probably generate little enthusiasm among either human therapists or patients. Thus, when considering the utility of any animal model for human disorders, one must weight not only the empirical validity of the model but also the practical consequences of its adaptation for a human population.

A case in point from our own laboratory is the "total isolation syndrome." This form of psychopathology can be consistently produced in rhesus monkeys and other primates by separating infants from their mothers within a few hours of birth and subsequently rearing them for at least the first six months of life in chambers where they can neither see nor make physical contact with other monkeys. Monkeys so reared fail to develop species-appropriate social behaviors. Instead, they exhibit a peculiar constellation of self-directed activity—self-orality, self-clasping, rocking, and other stereotyped patterns of behavior—seldom if ever exhibited by monkeys reared in normal social settings (Harlow, Dodsworth, and Harlow, 1965). Moreover, monkeys reared in total isolation from birth generally remain socially incompetent throughout their entire lives. They continue to exhibit inappropriate aggressive behavior and are incompetent sexually (Harlow and Harlow, 1969). Recently, we have developed procedures that socially rehabilitate isolate-reared monkeys (Suomi and Harlow, 1972b; Suomi, Harlow, and Novak, 1974). We exposed socially incompetent isolates every day to younger, socially competent "therapist" monkeys. Results to date indicate that the isolates can recover almost completely. Thus, the total isolation syndrome clearly is a psychopathological disorder whose cause, symptomology, and cure have been reliably established. The question is: does the isolation syndrome in monkeys provide a suitable model for any known human psychiatric disorder?

Some researchers have pointed out the similarity between elements of the isolate monkeys' behavior and specific behavior patterns exhibited by autistic human children. Anyone who has had the opportunity to observe both autistic children and isolate monkeys would feel compelled to consider them as examples of similar phenomena—particularly with respect to stereotypic rocking activities. Does this mean that keeping in mind the basic behavioral differences between the species the social isolation syndrome in monkeys serves as an effective model of childhood autism?

We doubt it. It is our belief that the social isolation syndrome in monkeys can serve as an adequate model for only one human disorder—the human total social isolation syndrome (Itard, 1932). If one could systematically separate human infants from mothers at birth and maintain them for the first two to four years in physical and visual isolation from other humans, the infants probably would exhibit the same reactions as monkeys reared in isolation. Perhaps the rehabilitative procedures successfully employed for monkeys would also be effective in reversing human children's social deficits as well. We hope such a study will never be conducted, although evidence that such predictions might hold can be gleaned from reports of developmental deficiencies seen in children raised in sterile orphanage environments (Yarrow, 1961). The point is that the consequences of rearing infants in social isolation are probably quite similar in monkey and man.

However, it has not been established that autism in children is caused by total social isolation from birth. Indeed, the opposite is probably true. It is highly unlikely that the disorders of isolated monkeys and autistic children share the same etiology. Because this fact violates a major criterion concerning animal model validity, we believe that the social isolation syndrome represents an inappropriate, possibly misleading, model for human autism. Furthermore, even if it were a valid model for autism, it is doubtful that the procedure used to rehabilitate isolate monkeys would be practical for human children. During therapy the monkey isolates are exposed to socially normal infant monkeys. Presumably, the corresponding human therapy would consist of exposing autistic children to normal human infants approximately one year of age. The practical problems inherent in such an approach, such as finding parents who are willing to expose their normal infants to potentially destructive autistic children, are apparent. Thus, there are serious shortcomings for the monkey isolation syndrome as a model of human autism.

We have employed this example to illustrate the point that animal models must satisfy stringent requirements in order to be of real value in the study and treatment of human disorders. Some researchers, such as McKinney and Bunney (1969), have argued that some animal models may have great heuristic value even if they are not entirely valid. We prefer to keep our requirements rigorous. Use of inadequate animal models may lead to inaccurate or misleading conclusions about the human ailment being modeled. In that event, they would be more useless than no model at all. In fact, they might be dangerous.

Depression in Humans

Our choice of depression as a psychopathological disorder to model in monkeys was not made indiscriminately. Depression is one of the most widespread psychiatric problems known to man. It has been estimated that 12 percent of the adult population in the United States will experience at least one depressive episode during their lifetime serious enough to require professional attention. The disorder affects people of every age (beyond the neonatal state), sex, race, and culture (Williams, Friedman, and Secunda, 1970).

The fact that depression is so exceedingly widespread is sufficient practical justification for its study. In one way this aids us in our attempts to model it. If rhesus monkeys are capable of developing depressive disorders, it is likely that these disorders are potentially reproducible in a wide sample of subjects, not only those possessing a particular genetic makeup. In other words, if depression occurs in virtually every segment of the human population and if it generalizes to monkeys, then it seems reasonable to assume that it can be produced in most segments of the monkey population as well.

The nature of the overt symptoms of depression is important in establishing animal models. The disorder is almost universally classified as one of *affect*, even though the conditions under which it appears, as well as the behavioral forms that it takes, vary considerably. Symptoms labeled as depressive include melancholy, grief, apathy, loneliness, and despair. People who are diagnosed as clinically depressed typically have sad, morose facial expressions and sometimes exhibit weepiness and crying. They often exhibit psychomotor retardation, and disturbances in eating and sleeping. Because depression is a disorder of affect, its occurrence invariably has social consequences, most often a disruption of ongoing patterns of social behavior (Becker, 1964). Hence, if depression is to be modeled in another species, it would not be advantageous if the species providing the model failed to possess complex social repertoires. An enormous body of research has clearly demonstrated that rhesus monkeys possess complex and varied social behavioral repertoires, analogous in several respects to that of man, particularly when social *development* is concerned (Harlow, Gluck, and Suomi, 1972).

The development of viable animal models of depression has been hindered by a general lack of definitive knowledge concerning the disorder in humans. The symptomology and etiology of depression remain subjects of considerable contention. Some theoreticians and clinicians maintain that depression is a unitary phenomenon, whereas others argue that it is binary in nature, with one form being *endogenous* (or bipolar or psychotic) and the other *reactive* (or unipolar or neurotic). An alternative classification scheme has been recently proposed by Winokur (1973). He differentiates "normal grief," "secondary depression," and "primary affective disorder," which itself can be further divided into unipolar (depressive) and bipolar (manic-depressive) types.

There is parallel confusion concerning the *basis* for a classificatory scheme for depression. Some choose to classify on the basis of the presence or absence of a genetic predisposition (Reich, Clayton, and Winokur, 1969; Gershon, Dunner, and Goodwin, 1971). Others focus upon differences in observable etiology or upon clusters and constellations of symptoms (Mendels, 1970). Still other workers classify by the forms of therapy that have been found effective—for example, electroconvulsive therapy (ECT), tricyclic antidepressants, or talk therapies (Ollerenshaw, 1973).

Much of the disagreement stems from the fact that there is no universally accepted theory or model of human depression. For example, Akiskal and McKinney (1974) describe in detail ten distinctly different models of depression that reflect five dominant schools of thought—psychoanalytical, behavioral, sociological, existential, and biological. Any researcher who wants to develop an animal model of depression must decide which human approach to take.

Anaclitic Depression

Occurrence in Human Infants

One form of depression exists for which cause, course, and one form of effective cure are relatively well known and documented. It is *anaclitic depression,* also known as dependency depression. It was first described in full by Spitz (1946) and it gained widespread recognition from the work of Bowlby and his coworkers (Robertson and Bowlby, 1952; Bowlby, 1960; 1973). Anaclitic depression occurs primarily in children who are between six months and six years of age. Reportedly, it most often occurs as a consequence of a child's prolonged separation from his mother.

Anaclitic depression as described by Bowlby (1960; 1973) begins with protest. An infant or young child typically behaves as if in a severe tantrum. Vocalizations, particularly crying and screaming, and random activity, including occasional stereotypic behavior, characterize young children's initial reaction to separation from their mothers. The protest phase of the anaclitic depressive syndrome rarely lasts more than a few days, and is usually terminated almost immediately when and if the mother returns.

However, if separation continues, a different pattern of behavior may emerge. This phase of the reaction has been termed "despair" by Bowlby, and it includes the behavioral reactions and responses that most clearly resemble symptoms exhibited by adult humans who are depressed. Spitz described the reactions of his six- to twelve-month-old subjects as including "increasing lack of contact, rejection of the environment . . . retardation of development, retardation of reaction to stimuli, slowness of movement, dejection, stupor, and the physiognomic expression which . . . would in an adult be described as depression" (Spitz, 1946, p. 316). Bowlby (1960) has noted withdrawal, mourning, and reduction of activity during the despair phase. Despair usually persists as long as the infants or young children remain separated from their mothers.

In most cases of anaclitic depression, the disorder disappears as soon as mother and child are reunited. In his original reports Bowlby described a reaction to reunion that he called "detachment." Children would show indifference and sometimes hostility toward their parents, often not returning to "normal" behavior for several months. However, in his original observations Spitz (1946) reported recovery to be almost always immediate and complete upon reunion, and recently Bowlby (1973) has agreed that detachment is not an invariant step in the anaclitic depression sequence. At present the basis for occurrence of detachment is not known.

Because anaclitic depression has a documented etiology, a well-defined sequence of symptoms, and at least one form of therapy that appears to be generally successful it is perhaps the most easily modeled form of depression. Anaclitic depression can be precipitated by separation from mother, its symptoms include protest and despair, and it can be terminated effectively by reunion with mother.

However, anaclitic depression is not totally free of problems for modeling. First, it is *not* an inevitable consequence of separation from mother. Even in Spitz's original definitive report only approximately 20 percent of his institutionalized subject population experienced anaclitic depression, despite the fact that most infants had entered that population under similar circumstances. Observations by Robertson and Robertson (1971), among others, have confirmed the fact that not all separations from mother, even lengthy separations, produce anaclitic depression in young children. (This is fortunate for humanity—child-rearing practices in today's society would lead to chaos if all maternal separations did indeed result in severe and prolonged depression.)

Second, as was previously mentioned, reunion with mother does not always yield immediate return to preseparation behavior. Detachment occurs commonly enough that Bowlby postulated that it was a principal component of the syndrome. To date, conditions sufficient and necessary for the appearance of detachment are not well defined. Again, these facts tend to limit the efficacy of anaclitic depression for modeling in animal subjects.

Finally, there exists some question about whether anaclitic depression is representative of adult depressions. Rie (1966) presented an extensive review of some of the relevant literature and concluded that such a generalization may not be valid. Rie's assertion, if correct, would definitely limit the desirability of anaclitic depression as a basis for development of an animal model of the more prevalent adult depressions.

Nevertheless, anaclitic depression remains an attractive starting point for pursuit of a viable monkey model. One obvious reason lies in diagnosis. Although most adult depressions have readily observable behavioral concomitants, they are usually diagnosed on the basis of verbal reports by the patient. Anaclitic depression, on the other hand, usually occurs in preverbal patients. Hence, the diagnosis must be made because of behavior rather than because of subjects' describing how they feel in words. This fact can be used to great advantage in developing models which employ rhesus monkeys as subjects.

Anaclitic Depression in Nonhuman Primate Subjects

In theory, the viability of monkeys as subjects for a model of anaclitic depression should be relatively easy to test. Because rhesus monkey infants develop strong attachments to their mothers over the first six months of life (Harlow and Harlow, 1965), an obvious approach would be to rear infant monkeys with their mothers for a period of time sufficient to insure that strong attachments have been formed, then separate mother and infant from each other and observe the reactions of the infant. If there is a basis for anaclitic depression in monkeys some of the infant monkeys should exhibit symptoms of protest and despair.

There have been numerous reports, some documented and some merely anecdotal, that deal with the consequences of natural separations of infant nonhuman primates from their mothers that occurred usually through the mother's death. For example, Hamburg, Hamburg, and Barchas (1974) have pointed out that depression in young chimpanzees is a common consequence of loss of the mother. The pattern of behavior is similar to the reports of Spitz, Bowlby, and others for human children: they experience a period of active protest followed by a period of despair, characterized by inactivity, social withdrawal, and apathy. Most of the young chimps that lost their mothers died within a few months, even though some of them had been "adopted" by older siblings. Apparently, severe anaclitic depression is well within the capability of young chimpanzees, given appropriate precipitating conditions.

Observations of other species have yielded similar findings. Esser (1974) has described the reaction of a feral-born adolescent gibbon that had lost its mate. The young gibbon rapidly fell into a deep depression, separated itself from the rest of the gibbons and died shortly thereafter. We have observed similar depressive reactions in infant rhesus monkeys living in nuclear families (M. K. Harlow, 1971) whose mothers died of illness or old age. When the mother died a rapid, rather than a lingering, death the infants showed clear indications of a protest-despair reaction to maternal loss. Apparently, anaclitic depressive reaction to loss of mother is not an exclusively human characteristic.

This fact has been used as a basis for numerous studies of mother-infant separation in several macaque and other monkey species, under carefully controlled laboratory conditions. The first of these studies was performed at Wisconsin by Seay, Hansen, and Harlow back in 1962. These investigators raised infant rhesus monkeys with their mothers in a playpen apparatus that allowed the infants to interact not only with their own mothers but also with other adult females and their offspring. At six months of age each infant was separated from its mother for a period of three weeks, during which time each subject could see and hear but not physically contact its mother and could interact with peers. After the three-week separation mothers and infants were reunited.

The results of this study indicated that the responses of the infant monkeys paralleled symptoms seen in human anaclitic depression. The monkeys' initial behaviors included high-pitched screeching and crying, disoriented, random locomotion, and repeated attempts to break through the Plexiglas barriers that separated them from their mothers. Mothers exhibited similar protest behaviors, although they were not as intense or persistent as those of their infants.

The vocalizations of the infants, as well as visual contact with their mothers, declined as the separation progressed. Moreover, the infants showed drastic decreases from preseparation levels of most complex interactions, particularly play, as Figure 4-1 illustrates. Indeed, simple mutual contact among separated infants was seldom observed, contrary to the expectation of the investigators. These behaviors appeared to be compelling analogs to Bowlby's report of despair and Spitz's description of social withdrawal among depressed human children.

Finally, the data indicated that generally reunion resulted in greater incidence of mother-infant interactions than that recorded immediately before separation. For example, in three of the four pairs, clinging behavior and

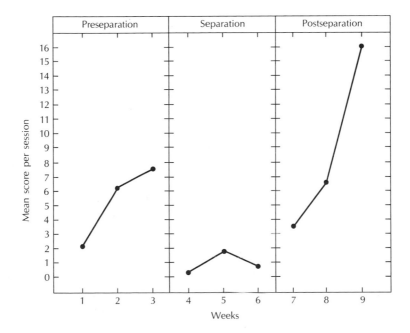

Figure 4-1. Infant approach-withdrawal play responses before, during, and after separation from mother. (From Seay, Hansen, and Harlow, 1962.)

nipple contacts occurred more frequently after reunion than before separation, despite the fact that most monkeys of this age stop these activities as they become more independent of their mothers (Hansen, 1966). However, these differences from preseparation baselines all but vanished after three weeks of reunion. Moreover, during this period infant-mother play resumed near-normal frequency. The fourth subject exhibited what the authors described as "partial detachment." In short, the reactions of the monkeys in the Seay et al. study were similar in almost all respects to human anaclitic depression.

Several other researchers have examined the consequences of mother-infant separation in monkeys since the original Wisconsin studies were completed. These efforts have varied considerably in both species and separation procedures employed. For example, Hinde, Spencer-Booth, and Bruce (1966) raised infant rhesus monkeys in pens containing their mothers and one adult male. When each subject was approximately six months of age, its mother was removed from the social group for a six-day period and then returned. Kaufman and Rosenblum (1967) reared pigtail monkey infants (*Macaca nemestrina*) in similar social groups for the first five to seven months of age, then removed each of their mothers from the group pen for a 28-day period. Schlottmann and Seay (1972) employed a variation of the original Wisconsin housing and separation procedure, using another macaque species, the Java monkey (*Macaca iris*). All these investigators found the reactions of their infant macaque subjects to be basically similar. Each form of maternal separation brought a protest-despair reaction, followed generally by recovery shortly after reunion. There is nothing unique about the anaclitic depressive reaction to maternal separation in human infants—the syndrome can be readily induced in a number of nonhuman primate species by means of a variety of experimental paradigms.

However, anaclitic depression is not an invariant consequence of all mother-infant separations among nonhuman primates. Investigators have been unable to produce a depressive phenomenon in some species by means of maternal separation. For example, Kaufman and Rosenblum (1969) removed bonnet macaque (*Macaca radiata*) mothers from a pen environment essentially identical to that of their earlier study with pigtail mothers and infants. The bonnet infants were scarcely affected by the separations. Following a mild protest they increased their contact with remaining members of the bonnet group, showing little if any indication of depression. Studies of primate species other than the macaque have revealed a similar lack of depressive response to separation from their mothers. Preston, Baker, and Seay subjected patas monkeys (*Erythrocebus patas*) to a maternal separation paradigm similar to that of Seay et al. (1962) and Schlottmann and Seay (1972). They observed initial protest but little indication of macaque-like despair in these subjects. Instead, like bonnets the patas infants intensified their interactions with remaining group members following departure of their mothers. After reunion the infants exhibited detached behaviors. Kaplan (1970) and Jones and Clark (1973) studied the reactions of squirrel monkeys (*Saimiri sciureus*), a species of New World monkeys, to separation from their mothers. Both groups reported that squirrel monkeys exhibited well-defined agitation immediately after separation, but that they did not exhibit prolonged despair behavior.

These reports do not preclude the possibility that anaclitic depression can be produced in these species. It may be argued that the investigators did not use the most appropriate experimental manipulations for their studies. For example, Harlow and Suomi (1974) have said that a more appropriate procedure for bonnet macaques might be to separate the infants, not their mothers, from their social group. They reasoned that because bonnet macaque infants have multiple functional mothers—other adult females interact extensively with offspring that are not their own progeny—true "maternal separation" should involve blocking access to all "mothers," not merely the genetic one. In addition, because behavioral repertoires differ considerably across species, it may be argued that perhaps the specific behavioral manifestations of "depression" in one species are outside the repertoire of a second species. Taken to its logical limit, this argument would say that a monkey is not incapable of exhibiting depression as we know it in humans simply because it cannot say "I feel depressed."

It is nevertheless true that classic anaclitic depression has been sought but not yet found in several nonhuman primate species. This fact is not necessarily a critical flaw for generalizing data from one species, such as the rhesus macaque, to another species, such as man. Hinde (1976) has convincingly argued that the value of generalization across species lies not only in the similarities between species but also in the nature of the differences between them. It is likely, Hinde believes, that between-species variation in reactions to a given manipulation or event parallels variation within each species in reactions to the same manipulation or event. If this is true, then it may be possible to identify the factors underlying within-species variation by examining ways in which members of other species differ from one another with respect to their patterns of social behavior.

Returning to an earlier example, let us assume that following loss of their mothers, bonnet macaques do not exhibit despair because they are comforted by other adult female bonnet macaques. Pigtail macaques do exhibit despair because other adult female pigtails ignore their protests. If this is true and if we believe in generalizing these phenomena, then we might predict that human infants are more likely to exhibit a depressive reaction to loss of their mothers if they are left alone than if they are cared for by a close friend or relative. Actually, numerous data on humans support such a prediction (see Bowlby, 1973).

Moreover, recent research has suggested that as much variation exists in reaction to separation from mother among rhesus monkey infants as exists across the several primate species whose reactions to maternal separation have been studied empirically. In rhesus monkeys, as in humans, not all separations from mother yield anaclitic depression. For example, Young, Lewis, and McKinney (1975) reported a series of five studies involving physical separation of mother and infant monkeys. The subjects were diverse in age, ranging from four and one-half to eight months at time of separation. Some were housed in single cages with their mothers before separation, and other subjects were housed with their mothers in large pens containing several other mother-infant pairs. Housing during separation varied considerably from study to study. Some infants were housed next to their mother, while other mothers and infants were housed in separate rooms. In addition, duration of separation varied from study to study, with six days being the shortest and 20 days the longest. In one study the infants were also returned to their mothers for a 12-hour period midway through the separation.

Not surprisingly, Young, Lewis, and McKinney reported considerable variation in the reactions of their infants to separation from their mothers. Some subjects responded with a typical protest-despair sequence. Other infants exhibited considerable agitation but little or no subsequent despair. Still other infants showed no sign of protest or upset immediately after separation but did exhibit all behavior patterns associated with despair—they engaged much more frequently in self-clasping and huddling and less frequently or not at all in locomotion, exploration, and social play. Some subjects exhibited only partial patterns of either stage; for example, they might be very vocal during their protest stage without increasing locomotion and during despair they might become much less active without exhibiting increased self-clasping and huddling. Finally, a few subjects showed little, if any, behavioral disruptions following separation from their mothers.

One might assume that such diverse findings in response to separation reflected the methodological or procedural differences across the five studies. Unfortunately, it is not that simple. Apparently, there was almost as much variation among subjects separated under similar or identical conditions as there was across the five different studies. Young, Lewis, and McKinney were thus unable to account systematically for this diversity of response to separation from mother. They concluded that separation from mother in rhesus monkeys did not provide a particularly practical model for human depression because monkey depression was hardly an invariant consequence of the model's basic manipulation.

Perhaps a more precise view would be that *maternal separation* in monkey infants provides an appropriate, and probably an excellent, model of *maternal separation* in human infants. Clearly, not all human mother-infant separations yield depression, but then not all mother-infant separations are without severe consequences. Rather, there appears to be enormous variation both in human response to maternal separation (Bowlby,

1973), and in rhesus monkey reaction to separation from mother. It would be useful to know which variables determine or influence the response of a given infant rhesus monkey to separation from mother, the underlying assumption being that some or all of the variables would generalize their influence across species. In other words, it seems likely that if we could pinpoint variables that enabled accurate prediction of the course of monkey mother-infant separation, then knowledge of these same variables would help predict the course of a given human mother-infant separation. More specifically, if one can determine which monkey separations result in depression, then perhaps this information can be used to predict which human separations are likely to result in depression as well. Consequently, recent work on separation of infant rhesus monkeys from their mothers has been directed toward identification and examination of such variables.

For example, the *age* at which the infant monkey is separated from its mother has been systematically varied (Spencer-Booth and Hinde, 1967; Abrams, 1969; Suomi, Collins, and Harlow, 1973). The general finding from these studies has been that age of infant at time of separation seems to be relatively unimportant if the subjects are over 60 days and under a year old and all other variables are held constant. The one exception to this rule occurs among subjects *three months old* at time of separation—such infants exhibit a quantitatively more severe reaction to separation from mother than either older or younger monkeys. This finding has been attributed to the fact that at three months of age the *fear response* has matured in developing monkeys, and they are particularly sensitive to *any* changes in their physical or social environment (Sackett, 1966; Griffin and Harlow, 1966; Suomi and Harlow, 1976). *Sex* of the separated infant has also been examined as a relevant variable, but the findings to date have not been definitive. There is little evidence that male infants are more prone to depressive reaction following separation from mother than young females, or vice versa.

However, several studies have indicated that the nature of an infant's *attachment relationship* may affect the nature of its response to removal from mother. For example, Hinde and Spencer-Booth (1970) found that within their sample of mothers and infants, those infants most active in maintaining proximity to their mothers and least likely to leave them to explore the environment tended to exhibit the greatest disturbance following separation. The investigators also found that offspring of permissive mothers—those that neither punished their infants for approaches nor restrained them from interaction with other monkeys—were unlikely to exhibit depression following separation if they had access to other monkeys when their mother was absent. Ainsworth (1976) has reported similar findings about human mothers and infants. Such intraspecies differences in patterns of mother-infant interaction parallel species differences in mother-infant relationships found between pigtail and bonnet macaques (Kaufman and Rosenblum,

1969). The resulting differences in reaction to separation from mother are parallel as well. Thus, the nature of the attachment before separation apparently is an important variable in determining the reaction to maternal separation in both monkey and man.

The separation environment also influences an infant's reaction to separation from mother. For example, *duration* of separation has been shown to be an important variable in determining both the course of separation reaction and the extent of long-term consequences on the infant's behavioral development. Generally speaking, the longer the separation between mother and infant is maintained, the more severe are both the immediate and long-term consequences (for a review of the relevant data, see Suomi, 1976). This finding generalizes to humans. In Spitz's original data (1946) the prognosis for recovery was poorer the longer infants who were anaclitically depressed remained apart from their mothers.

The form of separation has also been found to be a relevant variable in a number of monkey studies. In the early Wisconsin researches it was found that subjects who could still see their mothers throughout the period of physical separation (Seay, Hansen, and Harlow, 1962) generally exhibited more severe and persistent reactions than infants whose mothers were housed in other rooms, out of sight and hearing (Seay and Harlow, 1965). Rosenblum, Coe, and Bromley (1975) reported similar data for pigtail macaque infants separated from their mothers.

In another series of studies, Hinde and his coworkers (Hinde and Spencer-Booth, 1971; Hinde and Davies, 1972) compared the reactions of infants whose mothers were removed from a group pen, leaving the infants with an adult male, other adult females, and other infants, to the reactions of infants who were taken from the group cage, their mothers remaining in the social unit. The investigators reported qualitatively similar reactions among both sets of infant subjects; however, they did find that "the fear and associated immobility of some infant-removed subjects was more marked than anything seen in the mother-removed infants. . . . Furthermore the searching behavior and/or hyperactivity was more marked and longer-lasting in the infant-removed group: perhaps for this reason the onset of depression was somewhat delayed" (Hinde and Davies, 1972, p. 231).

Further supporting evidence is found in the results of a study by Schlottmann and Seay (1972) involving mother-infant separation of Java monkeys. During the three-week period of separation from mother, half the macaque infant subjects were provided a "substitute," an adult female with no infant of her own. The other half of the infants had only a peer with whom to interact. Schlottmann and Seay reported few differences between subjects that had substitutes and those that did not in behaviors during separation, but said that "the effects of separation would have been less severe [for those infants with substitutes] if the mother substitutes had behaved in a more maternal manner" (p. 340).

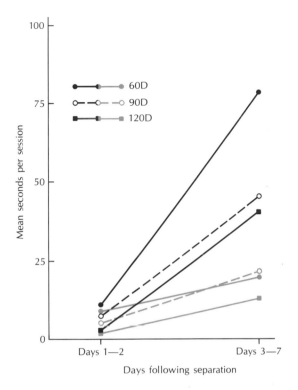

Figure 4-2. Self-clasping and huddling behaviors during the first week of permanent separation from mother. 60, 90, and 120D indicate age in days at time of separation. Dark lines are for subjects housed individually; light lines are for subjects housed in pairs. (From Suomi, Collins, and Harlow, 1973.)

An even more extreme example of this principle can be found in a study by Suomi, Collins, and Harlow (1973). In this study infant rhesus monkeys were permanently separated from their mothers and housed in small cages, either alone or in pairs. All separated infants exhibited strong protest in response to separation from their mothers, but by the end of the first week only those housed by themselves still exhibited despair behaviors, including more frequent self-clasping and marked passive disturbance (Figure 4-2). Subjects housed in pairs soon recovered. They exhibited almost no passive disturbance and they began to engage in social contact, exploration, and play interactions by the end of the first postseparation week.

These data make it clear that variation in the *nature of the postseparation social environment* can profoundly influence the infant's reaction to loss of mother. The influence need not necessarily be adverse. Those infants that were left in the company of adult female caretakers ("aunts") that showed interest in them seemed least likely to suffer deleterious consequences from the separation (for a review of the relevant literature, see Harlow and Suomi,

1974). These findings also appear to generalize to man. Both Spitz (1946) and Bowlby (1973) have described conditions in the separation environments that exacerbate the infants' reaction, while Robertson and Robertson (1972) have described social environments that tend to ameliorate the adverse effects of loss of mother.

The *nature of the infant's environment following reunion* with its mother can influence the long-term consequences of separation from mother. Generally, the more similar the reunion environment is to the preseparation environment, both with respect to its physical characteristics and to the social behavior of the individuals within it, the more rapid and complete will be the infant's return to its previous pattern of social development. This principle was elegantly illustrated in the studies of Hinde and coworkers (Hinde and Davies, 1972), in which the reactions of infants removed from their social group were compared with those of infants whose mothers were removed from the group while they remained in it. During separation the monkeys that had been removed showed the most severe reactions, but following reunion, their behavior soon returned to what it had been before. Infants whose mothers were removed continued to exhibit excessive disturbance activity for at least several weeks and occasionally several months after they had been reunited with their mothers. Although they acknowledged that alternative explanations existed, the authors offered the interpretation that mothers that had been removed from the group were less like their preseparation selves than were mothers that stayed in their group and thus did not have to reestablish their dominance. Their infants encountered mothers more like the one lost during separation than did the infants whose mothers, upon return to the group, had to spend a larger proportion of time and effort reestablishing their dominance position.

Further evidence for this point was presented by Kaufman (1973), who compared the reactions of pigtail and bonnet macaque infants to the reunion activities of their mothers. Pigtail infants spent more time in close proximity to their mothers than they did before separation, and this lasted for several months after reunion. In contrast, bonnet macaques soon left their mothers following reunion and continued their normal course of social development. Part of this disparity can be attributed to the differential behaviors of the returning mothers. Pigtail mothers were more protective and restrictive, discouraging infant forays from the range of the group, whereas bonnet mothers let their infants play and explore as they pleased.

Factors in the overall environment affecting the infant monkey's adjustment following separation were also found in data from the long-term study of permanent mother-infant separation by Suomi et al. (1973). Mothers could not influence their infants because they were never reunited. Instead, each subject remained housed alone or with a peer. The long-term consequences of such postseparation environments were readily apparent (see Figure 4-3). By six months of age monkeys housed alone had not recovered;

instead their levels of self-clasping were higher and their exploration and locomotion more reduced than they had been one week following maternal separation. In contrast, the monkeys housed in pairs developed a social behavioral repertoire by six months that was sufficient to permit them to serve as normal stimulus animals in subsequent experiments. It seems clear that the quality of the long-term social environment following separation from mother can markedly affect the degree to which debilitating consequences of the separation continue to be shown. Again, the monkey data are consistent with the clinical literature (Bowlby, 1973) on humans.

It is difficult to escape the conclusion that there is enormous generality among higher primates in the reaction of infants to separation from mother. In particular, it seems that very similar or identical factors predict the consequence of any given mother-infant separation in both humans and monkeys. This suggests that results from controlled studies of mother-infant separations of monkeys can be used to predict the effects of potential mother-infant separation in humans. Where necessary and possible, appropriate remedial procedures can be taken. In this sense, the monkey model of maternal separation is both valid and useful.

However, as we said earlier, models of separation from mother and models of human depression are not necessarily analogous for two reasons. First, as has been shown, not all maternal separations, human or monkey, result

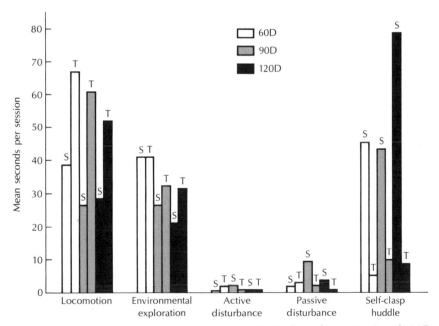

Figure 4-3. Mean levels of nonsocial behaviors, 150-180 days of age. 60, 90, and 120D indicate age in days at time of separation. *S* indicates monkeys housed individually, and *T* stands for monkeys housed in pairs. (From Suomi, Collins, and Harlow, 1973.)

in depression. The conditions that apparently precipitate and foster depressive reactions to separation from mother are rather specific, and it is thus misleading or inaccurate to equate mother separation per se with depression, anaclitic or otherwise.

Second, it is also clear that not all human depressions are a direct result of separation from mother. Beside the incidence of true anaclitic depression, theorists have attributed to maternal separation at best a predisposing capability for depression later in life (Bowlby, 1973; Freud, 1950; Granville-Grossman, 1968); no clinician in his or her right mind would argue that most adult human depressions are the direct result of separation from mother. Hence, a viable monkey model for depression must be able to transcend the paradigm of mother-infant separation. One possible approach, consistent at least with a number of theoretical views concerning human depression, is separation from objects of attachment other than the mother (see Akiskal and McKinney, 1974 for a review of the relevant literature about studies on humans). In other words, some adult depressions have followed loss of a loved one who was not the mother. Is it possible to reproduce such phenomena in monkey subjects?

Nonmaternal Social Separation in Rhesus Monkeys

Recent research has indicated that the mother-infant bond is not the only affectional relationship whose disruption may lead to depression for rhesus monkeys. For example, Novak (1973) demonstrated that infant monkeys reared with inanimate surrogate mothers developed attachments strong and persistent enough to yield a protest-despair reaction to separation from the surrogate at eight months of age. Numerous studies have reported considerably more severe reactions in young monkeys to separation from *peers* with which they have been reared from birth (for a review, see Suomi, 1976). Actually, these findings should come as no surprise. Evidence that young animals can become upset if nonmaternal attachments are broken has been available for years, both from controlled experimental studies (e.g., Cairns, 1966) and from widespread anecdotal reports (Senay, 1966).

At any rate, infant monkeys reared with then separated from peers will under certain circumstances exhibit biphasic protest-despair reactions at least as severe and persistent as any that are exhibited after mother-infant separation. Furthermore, recent research has consistently demonstrated that *those variables that determine the nature and course of mother-infant separations have similar or identical effects for peer separations.* For example, Suomi (1971) and Erwin, Brandt, and Mitchell (1973) demonstrated that the nature of the attachment, as well as the behavioral repertoires of the subjects before separation, are significant determinants of the form of the peer separation reaction, just as they are for maternal separations in monkey and human infants. Suomi, Harlow, and Domek (1970), Suomi (1973), Suomi and Harlow (1975), and Erwin, Brandt, and Mitchell (1973) found that variables that characterize the separation environment are as important in determining the course of peer separation as they are for maternal separation. The more prolonged and socially restricted the environment is when peer bonds are broken, the more it is likely that depression will result. Finally, Suomi (1973) and Suomi and Harlow (1975) have demonstrated that the more socially disruptive the reunion environment, the greater the probability of long-term depressive symptomology.

In short, virtually all variables found to influence reaction to separation from mother have been demonstrated to have similar effects in peer separations, at least among monkeys under one year of age. This is not to imply that the mother-infant bond is identical to an infant's attachment to a peer. As Harlow and Harlow (1965) have pointed out, the two affectional systems can be distinguished in a number of ways, including chronology, course, duration, and specificity. Moreover, Suomi, Harlow, and Domek (1970), and Suomi, Collins, Harlow, and Ruppenthal (1976) have shown that different reactions to separation from mother and from peers can be readily elicited from the *same* subjects over a relatively short span of time. Monkey infants were first separated from their mothers at six months of age; after exhibiting protest and despair reactions, they were separated from each other. In both studies the infants responded to the peer separation with a second protest-despair sequence that was quantitatively different from, although qualitatively similar to, the initial reaction to removal of mother.

It is this very fact—that the young monkey's affectional relationship with peers is different from that with its mother, yet it tends to react in similar fashion to separation from either mother or peers, given comparable preseparation, separation, and reunion conditions—that makes peer separation a particularly attractive means to develop a practically useful model of depression. What are these differences and why should they be attractive?

First, the strength of the relationship between mother and infant changes far more rapidly than it does between peers. Under normal circumstances the mother-infant bond, strongest during the first three months of the infant monkey's life, begins to wane from three to six months, and by the end of the first year of life the attachment bond is usually too weak for depression to result from separation of mother and infant. In contrast, peer bonds begin to become established by three months of age and become increasingly strong throughout the rest of the first year of life (Harlow and Harlow, 1965). Peer bonds among rhesus monkeys continue to predominate at least through adolescence. Thus, peer bonds are stronger, and hence susceptible to separation for longer periods than are mother-infant attachment relationships in rhesus monkeys.

Second, peer bonds in rhesus monkey subjects are more amenable to experimental manipulation than are mother-infant bonds. Infants reared with peers require less space than those housed with their mothers, and they allow their mothers to be free earlier for additional breeding. Moreover, peer separations require less time and physical effort on the part of caretakers than do maternal separations (Suomi, Harlow, and Domek, 1970). In a laboratory with limited space and personnel these practical advantages are of considerable importance. For example, Suomi, Harlow, and Domek (1970) subjected peer-reared monkeys to brief, *repetitive* separations from each other between three and nine months of age. They found that depressive reactions similar to those reported to result from mother-infant separation generally could be induced by the repetitive separations. During each 4-day peer separation, all subjects exhibited protest-despair reactions, and during reunion periods they showed extraordinary levels of peer-directed clinging (Figure 4-4). A striking cumulative effect of the separations was *maturational arrest* of behavioral development, despite the fact that the six-month period during which subjects were repetitively separated is chronologically the period of maximal positive social development in unseparated subjects similarly reared (Harlow and Harlow, 1965). This finding is illustrated in Figure 4-5. In short, Suomi, Harlow, and Domek demonstrated that many protest-despair depressive responses could be elicited from the same subject, that the biphasic reactions did not differ significantly from one another, and that long-term effects of the separations were clear-cut and easily quantifiable.

Such results argue strongly for use of peer separation paradigms in producing a monkey model of depression. If a phenomenon can be produced repeatedly and if its consequences, both immediate and long term, can be readily measured and evaluated, then the phenomenon becomes amenable to experimental manipulation. Also, if peer separation can be used to produce depressive reactions in older subjects, then the generality of the phenomenon to adult human depressions directly attributable to loss of a loved one becomes more compelling.

Unfortunately, the initial efforts to produce depression in monkeys over one year of age by means of peer separations have not been very fruitful. For example, Bowden and McKinney (1972) housed feral-born adolescent rhesus monkeys (31 to 48 months of age) in pairs for six to eight months, a period of time the investigators felt sufficient for development of mutual attachment bonds. Pair members were then physically and visually separated from each other for two weeks, then reunited. All subjects responded to peer separation with active protest during the first few days, but there was little indication of subsequent despair. Excessive self-clasping and rolling into a ball, characteristic of despair seen in infant monkeys, was not observed. Instead, these subjects returned to preseparation levels of most nonsocial activities, except for a gradual but slight increase in self-directed activity and occasional stereotypic rocking. The authors also reported a biphasic reaction to peer reunion. Initially, they found responses "remarkable for the variety and intensity of three forms of behavioral interactions: sexual, aggressive, and grooming" (p. 358). However, by the second day of reunion virtually all behaviors had returned to their preseparation levels.

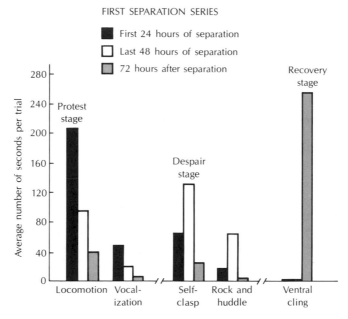

FIRST SEPARATION SERIES

■ First 24 hours of separation
□ Last 48 hours of separation
▨ 72 hours after separation

Figure 4-4. Levels of behavior during 12 peer separations and reunions. (From Suomi, Harlow, and Domek, 1970.)

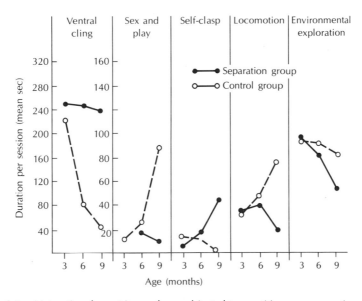

Figure 4-5. Maturational arrest in monkeys subjected to repetitive peer separations. Control levels are for monkeys reared with peers from birth but not subjected to any separations.

In a second study, McKinney, Suomi, and Harlow (1972a) studied the responses of well-socialized adolescent monkeys to repetitive peer separations. The subjects were 3-year-old male monkeys that had been reared with their mothers and peers for the first two years of life and then housed individually for the third year. Two groups of four monkeys were formed, and members of each group were permitted unlimited interactions with each other for four weeks, a period McKinney, Suomi, and Harlow felt sufficient to establish strong social bonds. Members of one group were then subjected to four separations, each two weeks in duration, during which time they could neither see nor physically contact each other. The other group of adolescent monkeys remained intact throughout the study. Reactions to peer separations among these subjects were very similar to those described by Bowden and McKinney. The monkeys showed clear-cut protest behaviors, but little evidence of despair—at least of the form exhibited by younger subjects following maternal or peer separation. Also, upon reunion, the adolescent male pairs exhibited temporary increases in socially directed behavior but rapid return to control levels of most behaviors. A third study of peer separation of juvenile-aged rhesus monkeys (Erwin, Mobaldi, and Mitchell, 1971) reported essentially the same findings.

What do these results suggest about a monkey model of depression based upon social separation—either mother, peer, or both? At first glance, they are scarcely favorable. In commenting upon their essentially negative results, McKinney, Suomi, and Harlow said:

> Our experimental understanding of separation reaction has been based almost exclusively on young organisms. In the case of humans most of the theorizing about separation effects with respect to depression is based on observations of young children. Perhaps unfounded extrapolations have been made to more mature organisms. The presence of a biphasic response to separation either in young animals or in young children in no way means that the same response will be seen at later developmental stages (p. 202).

Arguments that anaclitic depression caused by separation is akin to adult forms of depression are probably undermined by these data, which indicate that a depression-inducing manipulation for infants is ineffective for adolescents or adults.

An Alternative View of Social Separation and Depression

Perhaps we have been overly critical of the separation approach to study of depression in monkeys. On the basis of the adolescent monkey separation data alone, there are at least three reasons why we should not dismiss all monkey separation data as unrelated in any meaningful form to adult human depressions. First, it is possible that some studies failed to yield despair in adolescent monkeys because the manipulations rather than the subjects were inadequate. After all, even among infants, not all social separations result in depression. It may well be that the "necessary ingredients" for depressive reaction were missing here. It is unlikely that the adolescent attachment bonds developed during only one month of mutual exposure before separation were as strong as those developed by infants who had spent their entire lives in the company of the social objects from which they were separated. Adolescent and adult monkeys may not be immune to depressive reaction to social separation if the appropriate conditions exist. We will shortly present some data that clearly indicate that this is indeed the case.

Second, it is conceivable that the adolescent monkeys suffered as much from the separations internally as did infants in earlier studies but had different ways of displaying their depressed state. In other words, it is conceivable that the proper phenomenon was produced but the wrong dependent measures taken. Carrying this argument further, it may be that the internal state of anaclitically depressed infant monkeys is synonymous with the inner state of depressed adult humans, even though the precipitating circumstances are not necessarily identical. Such an argument may not be as vaporous as it seems. It is clear that the overall behavioral repertoires of infant and adolescent monkeys are vastly different, just as the behavioral repertoires of infant and adult humans differ considerably. Certainly, children's and adults' expressions of joy or fear are not always identical to each other; why should behavioral expressions of depression be identical?

Such an assumption is, in fact, almost basic for the assumption of genetic or biochemical causes of human depression. A given chemotherapy is effective, it is argued, because it counters the biochemical dysfunction which characterizes the depression, rather than directly influencing the "external" or "resultant" behaviors. This argument can be tested in monkeys, if one accepts as valid indexes of "internal state" such commonly used physiological measures as EEG, urine metabolites, or levels of certain amines in certain areas of the brain. Such data are now being collected on young monkeys separated from mothers. For example, Reite, Kaufman, Pauley, and Stynes (1974) have recorded EEGs of monkey infants before and during separation from mother. They reported reliable changes in EEG that paralleled the protest-despair separation reaction. In addition, Young and coworkers (Young, McKinney, Lewis, Breese, Smither, Mueller, Howard, Prange, and Lipton, 1973) have performed brain assays on monkeys sacrificed during behavioral protest following separation from mother and have compared the results to those obtained from unseparated control animals. The same research group is currently examining brains of infant monkeys sacrificed while exhibiting despair (McKinney, 1974). The different sets of brains to date have yielded different results. It is not beyond belief to expect corresponding data to be available from humans in the near future (not obtained in the same manner); at that time, direct comparisons between monkeys and humans could then be made and the assumptions tested empirically.

A final reason for not dismissing monkey anaclitic depression out of hand concerns the nature of separation itself. What is separation exactly? How does a subject perceive a given separation and its consequences? As has been pointed out, there are many different forms of separation. Let us consider mother-infant separation as an example. We can leave an infant in its rearing environment and remove the mother. The mother may be placed in an environmental within the infant's reach (Suomi, Collins, Harlow, and Ruppenthal, 1976), or out of reach but within sight and sound (Seay, Hansen, and Harlow, 1962). She may be placed out of reach and sight but still within the infant's range of hearing (Young, Lewis, and McKinney, 1975), or out of reach, sight, and sound (Seay and Harlow, 1965). We can leave the mother in the infant's rearing environment and move the infant to a new environment, as Hinde and Davies reported (1972). Obviously, the new environment can vary considerably in its similarity to the rearing environment and in its social complexity for the separated infant. Finally, as we have pointed out, the reunion environment—that is, the situation in which mother and infant are brought together—can vary. In short, we can describe numerous forms of mother-infant separation that are considerably different from one another in terms of what the infant actually experiences. Obviously, the same holds for other forms of social separation. One can be homesick for a variety of reasons in a variety of situations.

If we carefully examine those experimental separations *in which a depressive reaction was exhibited as a consequence of the separation*, certain consistencies appear. Each time, the monkey (a) loses a salient portion of its environment; that is, it no longer has that part of its social world toward whom a majority of its previous interactions were directed, (b) has nothing in its separation environment that can replace what it lost through separation, and (c) has no power or ability to change its current social situation. In other words, depression results from social separation when the subject loses something of significance, has nothing with which to replace that loss, and is incapable of altering this predicament by its own actions. We might say that the subject in these situations is *helpless* and *hopeless*, and we can perhaps assume that it perceives its predicament.

Most current views of human depression center on these very terms— helplessness and hopelessness. According to *cognitive* theories of depression (e.g., Beck, 1967), depressed people are characterized by feelings or perceptions of helplessness, lowered self-esteem, and "negative cognitive set." According to behavioral views of depression (Ferster, 1965; Lazarus, 1968), patients find themselves in situations in which their actions are independent of any environmental changes; that is, they experience a "loss of reinforcement." Examining those cases of separation in which depression results, it can be argued that the subjects' activities fit either a cognitive or a behavioral model of helplessness. In other words, it is not the separation itself that is crucial for depressive reaction, but rather the subject's perception of the consequences of the separation.

Continuing this theme, it can be argued that separation is only one of several events that can precipitate depressive reactions in certain individuals—human or monkey. This, of course, is consistent with a large body of data on human depressions. It is also consistent with the results of studies of both human and nonhuman subjects placed in "learned helplessness" experimental paradigms (see Seligman, Klein, and Miller, 1976). If monkeys are capable of exhibiting depression—and the separation studies strongly indicate that they are, at least under certain circumstances—then a question crucial to the generality of monkey depression can be readily raised: Is it possible to induce depressive reactions in monkeys without using social separation?

Vertical Chamber Induced Depression in Monkeys

One alternative to social separation as a basis for a monkey model of depression has involved a vertical chamber apparatus designed by Harlow (illustrated in Figure 4-6 and fully described by Suomi and Harlow [1969]). The vertical chamber is basically a stainless steel trough, wide at the top with

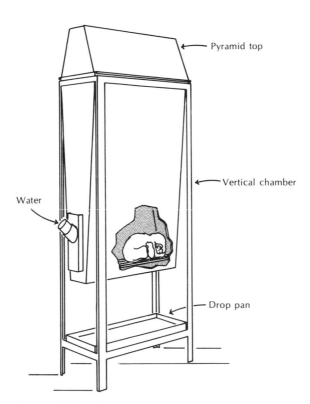

Figure 4-6. The vertical chamber apparatus.

Figure 4-7. Typical behavior of subject immediately after placement in the vertical chamber.

sides that slope downward and inward to form a rounded bottom. A mesh false bottom and holes drilled in the real bottom of the device protect an incarcerated monkey from its feces and urine, and a food box and water bottle holder permit a subject to be fed and watered within the chamber. The apparatus has an overall volume approximately equal to that of a standard 2.5 x 2 x 2 foot nursery cage. It can be fitted with a variety of tops, ranging from wide mesh to pyramid-shaped and covered with fine mesh, which discourages monkeys from hanging from the top of the apparatus.

Why a vertical chamber? As Harlow and Suomi (1971) have explained, "Depression has been characterized as embodying a state of helplessness and hopelessness, being sunken in a well of despair. It was our intention to create such a well for our monkey subjects, physically as well as psychologically" (p. 246). Monkeys placed within the chambers typically spend the first day or two actively moving about, trying to escape, viewing the world outside, as Figure 4-7 illustrates. Such activity requires considerable effort because of the slippery stainless steel sides of the apparatus, and most subjects give up searching and escape behaviors within a few days. Thereafter, they typically assume a hunched posture in a corner of the bottom of the apparatus, as is illustrated in Figure 4-8. One might presume that at this point, they have found their situation to be hopeless and that they are unable to alter their environment by their own effort.

Data obtained from monkeys housed in the Harlow vertical chambers have demonstrated that confinement in the chambers induces depressed behavior—more frequent self-clasping and huddling and less frequent movement and exploration among socially unsophisticated monkeys.

Figure 4-8. Typical posture of subject after several days of vertical chamber confinement.

Moreover, subjects that have been separated from social groups and placed in the chambers exhibit exaggerated forms of typical separation reactions. These subjects, when reunited with the objects of attachment from which they have been separated, continue to exhibit residual depressive reactions for longer periods than would be expected to result from "simple" separation.

For example, Harlow and Suomi (1971) placed socially naive monkeys ranging in age from six to thirteen months, that had been reared in partial isolation, in vertical chambers for a total of 30 days each. Data were collected in the home cage before the period of confinement and for two months after return from the vertical chambers. The results are shown in Figure 4-9. Self-clasping and huddling behaviors increased significantly over baseline levels; locomotion and exploration declined significantly. In a second study, Suomi and Harlow (1972a) placed six-week-old socially naive infants in vertical chambers for a six-week period, then compared their subsequent behavioral development for the remainder of the first year of life both with control monkeys that had been reared with peers and with monkeys reared in partial isolation. Some of the results are plotted in Figure 4-10. The differences between the chambered subjects and each of the control groups were overwhelming. Furthermore, these differences were maintained throughout the first year of life.

The results of these two studies indicated that depressive behaviors need not have their origin in separation from an object of attachment. The monkeys we have just discussed could not have experienced social separation for

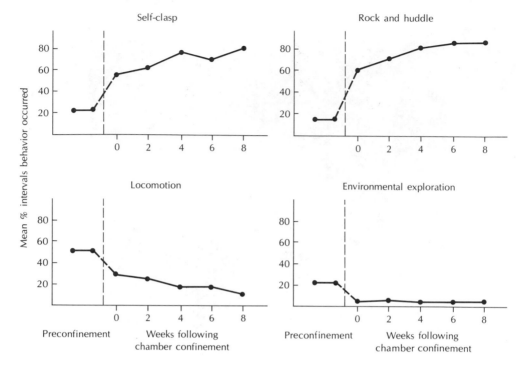

Figure 4-9. Mean levels of subject behavior prior to and following 30 days of vertical chamber confinement. (From Harlow and Suomi, 1971.)

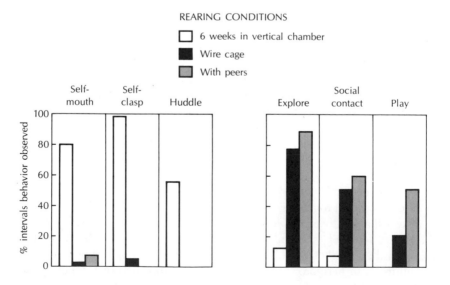

Figure 4-10. Playroom behaviors at 11 months of age in chamber-confined, single cage-reared, and peer-reared monkeys.

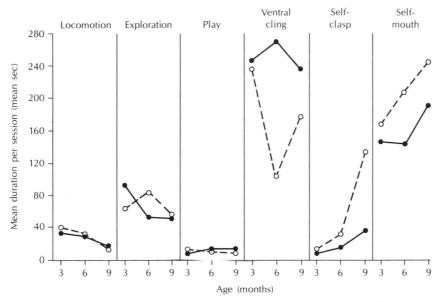

Figure 4-11. Levels of behavior prior to (3 months), during (6 months), and following (9 months) repetitive peer separations: chamber-confined versus cage-confined monkeys. (From Suomi, 1973.)

the simple reason that they had not established any social bonds before chamber confinement, having lived alone in cages their entire lives. Nevertheless, they responded to chamber confinement with persistent exhibition of behavior patterns qualitatively identical to those shown in the despair phase of separation reaction of well-socialized young monkeys. The implications of this set of findings will be discussed shortly.

When used in conjunction with social separation, vertical chamber confinement has tended to intensify depressive responses of well-socialized monkeys. For example, Suomi (1973) compared the reactions of peer-reared monkeys repeatedly separated from each other to those of infants subjected to an identical separation procedure but confined to vertical chambers during each separation period. Both groups of subjects exhibited protest-despair reactions to each separation, but they differed in their reunion behaviors, as Figure 4-11 illustrates. Subjects that had been confined to vertical chambers displayed significantly less ventral clinging with peers and significantly more frequent self-clasping than the monkeys housed in individual cages during the repeated separation periods. Self-clasping was the predominant activity of socially naive subjects that were confined to vertical chambers in previous studies.

Other research efforts have yielded similar findings. Suomi and Harlow (1975) examined the effects of a 30-day period of solitary separation versus separation with concomitant vertical chambering on each member of groups of four monkeys, and compared their behaviors during the first year of life with those of a control group that experienced no separation. All separation groups exhibited a steady deterioration of social interactions, such as grooming, play, sex, and aggression, as group members were subjected to separations. Those monkeys that had been put in a chamber during separation showed significantly more severe response to group removal and significantly greater deterioration in group activity than subjects that were only confined to cages during separation. Members of the control groups showed normal social behavioral development and a marked absence of self-clasping and huddling behavior.

A second example of the exaggeration of reactions to social separation through confinement in a vertical chamber may be found in McKinney, Suomi, and Harlow (1972b). Here, juvenile rhesus monkeys (3-year-old males) were separated from their group once for sixty days in vertical chambers. Then their reactions were recorded. As previously mentioned, juvenile monkeys that are separated repeatedly typically display only protest and not a trace of despair, and they engage in active social behaviors following reunion. The chambered juvenile monkeys, in contrast, exhibited behavior patterns during separation and following reunion that might well be interpreted as depressive. When chambered, they soon ceased trying to escape and subsequently assumed the posture of younger incarcerated subjects. Upon reunion, these monkeys moved significantly less than they did before separation. Moreover, they failed to exhibit the active reactions to reunion shown by juvenile monkeys subjected to simple social separation. Instead they displayed a passive form of social contact, termed "contact clinging" by McKinney, which is a most unusual behavior for three-year-old male rhesus monkeys that are socially competent. As Figure 4-12 illustrates, it is not unlike the immature mutual clinging exhibited by infants following repeated peer separation.

Whether these behavior patterns are equivalent to the despair stage of infant reaction to social separation has yet to be satisfactorily determined. McKinney's 3-year-old subjects did not show appreciable self-clasping following two months in a vertical chamber. Self-clasping has been reported to be a major characteristic of infant monkey despair following separation, and it certainly is the predominant behavior in younger monkeys removed from vertical chambers. But as we have said before, the behavioral repertoires of juvenile and infant monkeys differ considerably from one another, even among social isolates (Suomi, Harlow, and Kimball, 1971). Thus, it is conceivable that these behavior patterns were, in fact, representative of depression in juvenile subjects. Further data are needed before a definite conclusion can be reached.

The results of these various studies that employ a vertical chamber are generally supportive of a helplessness interpretation of monkey depression. The activities of subjects placed in the chambers are consistent with reports

Figure 4-12. "Contact clinging" among 3-year-old adolescent males following vertical chamber confinement. (From McKinney, Suomi, and Harlow, 1972b.)

by other investigators of the behavior of nonprimate subjects placed in learned helplessness paradigms—for example, exposure to inescapable shock or noise (Seligman, Klein, and Miller, 1976). The monkeys initially exhibit considerable activity, and the activity appears directed toward escape from the apparatus. Within a short period of time, however, the subjects typically give up, retreat to a corner, and roll up into a passive ball of fur. When subjects are removed from the vertical chambers and returned to their previous environments, they tend to remain passive, inactive, and withdrawn. At this point, they are less responsive to external stimuli, both social and nonsocial, than they were before they were confined in a vertical chamber. As such, their activities meet both the cognitive and the behavioral theorists' criteria for helplessness.

Reinduction of Depressive Behaviors

One of the most long-standing and rarely questioned assumptions regarding depression is that traumatic separations experienced early in life can predispose adults to depressive episodes following periods of stress. Analysts from Freud (1917) to Bowlby (1973) have emphasized the importance of early social experiences as the basis of adult psychopathology. Further, an enormous body of data on animal behavior has demonstrated that adverse early environments usually have measurable effects later in life (see Scott et al., 1974, for a recent review).

However, it has been difficult to find direct evidence that separation experiences in childhood predispose humans to depression following social separation in adulthood. It is true that numerous reports have supported this contention, but most of these reports are retrospective in nature and are replete with methodological inadequacies. A closer examination of the data on humans reveals that the empirical basis for such a proposition is ambiguous at best (Akiskal and McKinney, 1974).

The hypothesis that early separation sensitizes people to depressive reaction to later separations can readily be tested in monkey subjects. One need only subject monkeys early in life to separation or vertical chambering or both, permit the monkeys to recover, and then maintain them in social environments until they are older. These monkeys can then be subjected to a second separation or chambering manipulation and their reactions compared to those of peers that had no previous separation experiences. To date we have performed two such studies at Wisconsin.

The data are relatively straightforward, but the implications and interpretations of these results are less clear. In the first study (Young, Suomi, Harlow, and McKinney, 1973), monkeys that had been reared with surrogates and peers from birth, but each separated and placed in vertical chambers for 30 days in the last half of the first year of life, formed the experimental group. Members of a control group, similar in age, were reared with mothers and peers and were weaned from their mothers at one year of age. When they were two years old, members of each group were separated daily from each other for 23 hours, spending one hour together each day, for a total of 28 consecutive days.

The results indicated clear differences in both separation and reunion reactions among the two groups of subjects. The previously separated and chambered monkeys exhibited more frequent self-clasping, huddling, and rocking than control monkeys and much less frequent locomotion and stereotypy. During the hour-long reunion periods control subjects showed considerable contact clinging, seeking activity, and locomotion. The experimental subjects exhibited more frequent self-mouthing and self-clasping. The authors concluded that early separation and vertical chambering predisposed the experimental subjects to "despair" reactions to stress, explaining that "our imposition of the stress of separation from peers in these older monkeys appears to have unmasked or at least intensified a response to stress that probably developed in very early life. . . . What remains to be decided is not whether such a relationship exists but how it comes to be" (Young, Suomi, Harlow, and McKinney, 1973, p. 404).

Yet in a second study conducted by some of the same investigators

(McKinney et al., 1973), a predisposing consequence of early vertical chambering was not found. The monkeys were two or four years of age. All had been placed in chambers for 45 or 90 days one or one and one-half years before beginning the study. For the second study they were placed in vertical chambers for an additional period of 90 days. Their reactions to vertical chamber confinement were compared with those of control monkeys of the same age that had never before been confined to vertical chambers.

McKinney and coworkers found that experimental subjects differed from control subjects, but only in behaviors exhibited *before* the latter period of chamber confinement. These differences disappeared or at least declined during and after the period of vertical chambering, which clearly had deleterious effects on experimental and control subjects alike. There was no evidence that the early chambering predisposed experimental subjects to more severe reactions shown by the control monkeys. The researchers could only conclude that "It seems likely that certain types of stresses will [sensitize subjects to adverse response to similar or related experiences later in development] and others will not" (p. 634).

Clearly, the issue remains unresolved for monkey subjects, just as it does for humans (Akiskal and McKinney, 1974). There is much evidence indicating that adverse early experiences can have lingering consequences. It has not been established whether the early experience sensitizes an individual to all, or at least a wide variety of, subsequent stressful situations. Nor is it known whether adverse early experiences are "imprinted" upon the individual so that only reoccurrences of the original stimulus complex precipitate reactions similar to those exhibited originally. Further research is needed before the precise relationship between early experience and predisposition to later psychiatric disorders can be firmly established.

Nuclear Family Separations

Recently, we have utilized a somewhat different approach to produce and study depressive behavior in adolescent and adult monkeys. In contrast to previous studies conducted on subjects that had experienced adverse manipulations early in life, this approach utilizes monkeys raised from birth in the most socially enriched laboratory environment we have been able to produce at Wisconsin. For the past several years we have been rearing monkeys in *nuclear families*, designed by the late M. K. Harlow, in which subjects have continual access from birth to their fathers, mothers, and siblings. As these monkeys grow up they also have considerable access to other adult pairs and their offspring. A nuclear family unit is illustrated in Figure 4-13; a complete description of the social environment may be found in Harlow (1971). Data collected on over 50 offspring have consistently indicated that monkeys reared in a nuclear-family are certainly equivalent to and quite

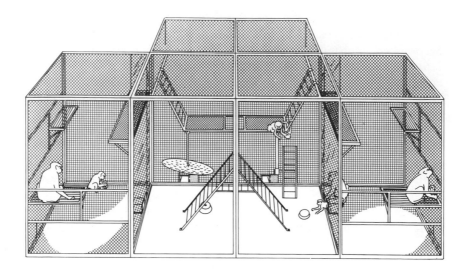

⊢————⊣ = 1 foot

Figure 4-13. The nuclear family apparatus. Adult male-female pairs are confined to the four outer living cages (on both sides and in rear of apparatus), while offspring are free to enter the central play area and/or visit adults other than their parents.

possibly superior to laboratory and ferally reared peers in their social sophistication (Ruppenthal et al., 1974; Suomi, 1974) and performance on complicated tests of intellectual capability (Gluck, Harlow, and Schlitz, 1973). Further, there is strong evidence that they retain lasting attachments with both parents (Suomi et al., 1973).

Ten first-born offspring of nuclear family adult pairs were removed from their family environments when they were five years of age. This was the first time in their lives that they had left their home environment for any appreciable period of time. Separation lasted a total of 18 weeks, after which time each subject was returned to its family. During separation the monkeys were housed under one of three conditions: (1) with friends, (2) in pairs with strangers, or (3) in individual cages permitting only visual contact with strange monkeys. The results of this small study (Suomi, Eisele, Grady, and Harlow, 1975) are instructive and intriguing.

Major differences across separation conditions were observed, even though the young adult subjects exhibited similar behavior before separation. Those monkeys housed with friends and those housed with strangers showed little, if any, adverse reaction to removal from their family environments other than a mild and brief period of initial protest. In contrast, subjects housed alone reacted to family separation in a manner strikingly similar to that shown by monkey infants following mother or peer separation. As can be seen in Figure 4-14, these young adults exhibited significantly higher levels of stereotypy than the other subjects. They groomed themselves significantly less during the later weeks of the separation, and as a result, their physical appearances deteriorated. Most important, during separation the monkeys that were housed alone exhibited self-clasping behavior, a pattern shown by none of the young adults that were housed in groups. As we have indicated earlier, self-clasping behavior has not been reported for any subjects of comparable age following a social separation.

In addition, residual effects of separation were apparent among the solitary monkeys long after reintroduction to their family units. All of the subjects separated with groups were smoothly integrated back into their families, and within a few weeks returned to preseparation levels of most behaviors. In contrast, solitary monkeys became passive and relatively unresponsive to social initiations from other nuclear family members. Before separation they had been among the most socially active and dominant of the nuclear family offspring.

We must be cautious in generalizing the results of this study. The sample of separated monkeys was small—only two solitary subjects and four in each of the other two groups—and the study was limited to subjects that had been reared in nuclear families. However, the findings are provocative. First, they are consistent with some previous separation data. Certain variables found to influence separation reactions in younger animals appeared to be operating in much the same fashion among these subjects. Only those subjects whose separation environment provided no compensation for the social loss incurred by removal from family and only limited opportunity to develop meaningful social behaviors showed adverse reaction to separation. Second, the reactions shown by these subjects were consistent with a helplessness hypothesis. Only subjects placed in an environment where no social activity was possible, no matter what they might do, displayed any sign of depressive reaction. Those subjects that could maintain at least some forms of social interactions were scarcely affected by the separations.

The present data indicate that, given the proper conditions, depressive behavior can be elicited in semi-adult, socially sophisticated rhesus monkeys by means of a separation manipulation. Moreover, the data support the position that variables important in determining the consequences of mother-infant separation tend to generalize to other forms of social separation. Furthermore, they are consistent with a helplessness interpretation.

We are confident that other techniques can be developed for production of depressive behavior in adolescent and adult rhesus monkeys. It is conceivable that procedures used to develop nonprimate models of depression might well yield depressive behavior in monkeys. For example, it is possible that if monkeys were subjected to inescapable shock, they might exhibit reactions that could be termed depressive. It would be interesting to see how similar such behaviors might be to those resulting from separation or vertical chambering.

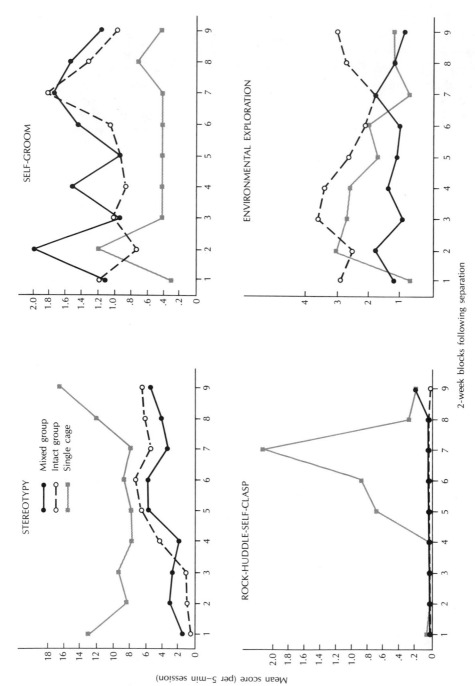

Figure 4-14. Levels of separation behavior among nuclear family reared semi-adult monkeys. (From Suomi, Eisele, Grady, and Harlow, 1975.)

Alternatively, one might take a pharmacological approach to animal models, as has been done in the "reserpinized rat" model of depression (McKinney and Bunney, 1969). Many theorists (e.g., Schildkraut, 1965) have argued for a biochemical etiology of depression, usually implicating one or more of the amine systems of the brain. Consequently, some researchers have attempted to produce depressive phenomena in animals by injecting them with compounds that block synthesis of specific amines—for example, reserpine, alpha-methylparatyrosine (AMPT), or 6-hydroxydopamine (6-0HDA) for norepinephrine and parachlorophenylalanine (PCPA) for serotonin synthesis.

In fact, several such studies have already been performed in macaque subjects, using not only reserpine (McKinney et al., 1971) but also AMPT (Redmond et al., 1970), PCPA (McKinney, 1974), and 6-0HDA (Breese et al., 1972). The results of such studies to date have been mixed. Behavior patterns somewhat similar to those exhibited by monkeys subjected to separation have been observed. However, there are also many side effects seemingly unrelated to depression. Further, the crucial behaviors themselves are often chronologically independent of physiological measures of the drug's activity in brain or in urine. We are hardly surprised by these data, as it is our position that a biochemical interpretation of depression that presumes to be independent of environmental conditions is misleadingly simplistic. This is not to say that such approaches are without merit. Indeed, we think that important data could be obtained if pharmacological manipulations could be simultaneously performed on monkeys being subjected to depression-yielding behavioral manipulations such as peer separation.

Rehabilitation of Induced Depression in Monkeys

One of the most potentially valuable assets of any animal model of a given disorder is its capability to be used to develop effective therapeutic strategies and procedures. In keeping with this principle we have recently initiated a series of studies designed to rehabilitate monkeys that had become depressed as a result of controlled manipulations. We are utilizing both sociobehavioral and somatic approaches to therapy.

The first of these rehabilitative procedures (Suomi, Sprengel, and Harlow, 1975), social in nature, has been employed for a group of together-together reared infants that were subjected to a series of peer separations of a form and sequence identical to that of Suomi et al. (1970). In other words, these monkeys were reared with peers from birth. Then, from three to nine months of age, they were subjected to a total of twenty 4-day-long separations from each other. As in the previous study the subjects exhibited protest-despair reactions to each of the first twelve peer separations, and by six months of age they were showing clear signs of maturational arrest. Unlike the subjects of the 1970 study, however, these monkeys were given "therapists" for the final eight separations. The therapists were socially normal peers, chosen specifically for their propensity to initiate active social behaviors such as play. The rationale underlying the choice of therapists was that the therapist "model" used in previous studies of isolate monkey rehabilitation—that is, younger, clinging, socially unsophisticated infants —would be totally inappropriate for the present subjects. We feared such therapists would merely reinforce the immature social behaviors, such as excessive clinging, that characterized the depressed monkeys' reunion repertoires. Instead, socially hyperactive peers were chosen as therapists in the hope that they would force the depressed peers out of their social withdrawal, discourage clinging responses, and initiate and perpetuate play interactions.

In two-hour daily interactions with the subjects, both during separation and reunion periods, the therapists repeatedly drew the depressed subjects into active social interactions. As a result, protest was abated and despair diminished in each of the final eight separations, while behavior during reunion periods became more appropriate. However, recovery by the separated monkeys was not complete. As Figure 4-15 illustrates, they showed considerable improvement over the behavior exhibited by monkeys that had been repeatedly separated and had received no therapy. Yet they were inferior to both unseparated controls reared with peers and the therapists themselves. For this reason, it was decided to continue the therapy sessions in somewhat revised form.

For the next six months the subjects were exposed to therapists for two hours per day in a variety of subject-therapist combinations (one subject to two therapists, four subjects to four therapists, etc.) in different test environments (quad cage, group pen, playroom). They were also periodically separated from each other. By the end of this six-month period, the formerly depressed subjects were indistinguishable from the therapists in most behaviors while separated, reunited, or in interaction sessions with their therapists. The lack of control data limits the degree to which we can attribute the observed improvement to effects of the therapy sessions as opposed to what one might term "spontaneous recovery." What data do exist for both unrehabilitated repetitively peer-separated and nonseparated peer-reared monkeys over the second year of life, however, strongly suggest that the subjects that received therapy were superior to those animals in frequency and sophistication of social behavior.

Further support for the effectiveness of the therapy procedure can be found in follow-up data. These subjects were subsequently tested with valium-treated social isolates of the same age, normal mother-peer-reared animals, and monkeys reared in nuclear families. The results of playroom interaction tests indicated that the behavioral advances made by formerly depressed subjects had generalized; they were decidedly superior to subjects

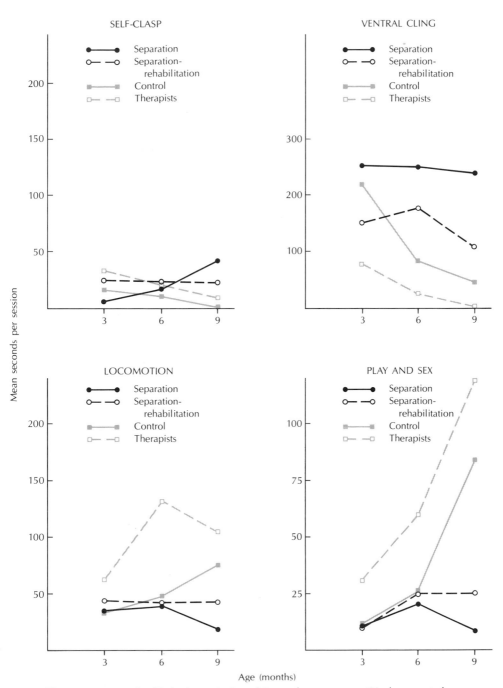

Figure 4-15. Levels of behavior at 3, 6, and 9 months among repetitively separated, rehabilitated repetitively separated, nonseparated control, and therapist monkeys. (From Suomi, Sprengel, and Harlow, 1975.)

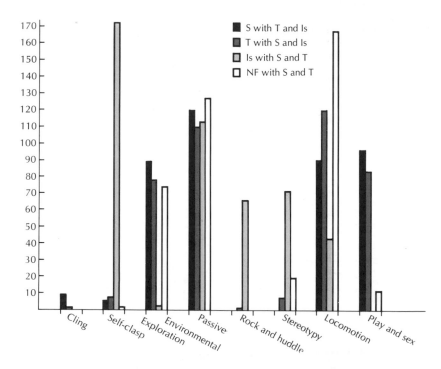

Figure 4-16. Play behaviors of monkeys in different groupings. S = separated subjects, T = therapists, Is = partially rehabilitated isolates, and NF = nuclear-family reared monkeys.

reared in isolation, slightly dominant to mother-peer-reared subjects, and could at least hold their own in interactions with nuclear family offspring (Figure 4-16). Recovery appeared to be complete.

We plan to conduct further research to see whether the procedure can be improved, particularly with respect to length of the therapy. More effective therapist models or more efficient therapy schedules may exist. It is also of interest to determine whether this therapy procedure is appropriate for other behaviorally induced depressions; for example, those following vertical chambering or removal from nuclear families. Presumably, if consistent drug-induced depressions could be achieved, such a social therapy could be tested on these forms as well. We assume that successful procedures developed for monkeys might well be of interest to imaginative clinicians dealing with depressed human patients.

However, we are well aware that there already exist numerous forms of therapy practiced upon human depressives. One attribute of a viable animal model of any human psychiatric disorder is that therapies should be effective across species. Concurrently, we have been subjecting some of our depressed subjects to procedures more commonly utilized in the treatment of human depression. For example, electroconvulsive therapy (ECT) has been employed both in pilot and in ongoing studies (Lewis and McKinney, 1976). The approach involves testing experimentally depressed and socially normal control monkeys in a playroom to establish baselines, subjecting each group to repeated administrations of electroconvulsive treatments in the standard human clinical manner, and monitoring both immediate and long-term effects. Results to date suggest that ECT is partially effective in reversing some depressive behavior. For example, chambered monkeys showed increased locomotor and exploratory activity following four weeks of thrice-weekly ECT. However, they did not exhibit substantial gains in social reactivity following shock treatments. Instead, they wandered about the test area apparently indifferent to the other monkeys sharing the test environment. When equivalent shock sessions were administered to socially normal control monkeys, their social interactions in the test environment also deteriorated, although their activity remained relatively constant.

These findings, while provocative, are certainly preliminary. Before they can be appropriately applied to the evaluation of consequences of ECT applied to humans, they must be replicated. However, monkey models of depression may prove very helpful in evaluating both the pros and cons of ECT, as well as in determining what constitutes an appropriate patient population for ECT and what does not. For example, amnesia is a common, albeit undesirable, consequence of electroconvulsive shock therapy. Considerable research with lower mammals (e.g., Meyer, 1972) has determined what might effect selective amnesia following electroconvulsive shock. Appropriate primate research might enable human therapists to predict and presumably avoid uses where undesirable amnesia was likely to be a major concomitant of ECT.

We are also investigating the efficacy of various antidepressive drugs currently employed in human clinical practice. For example, in an ongoing study, infant monkeys are reared for the first four months of life with peers, then subjected to three three-week separations. Subjects receive antidepressant drugs or placebo on a daily basis beginning midway through the second three-week separation and continuing through the final reunion. Such a paradigm permits comparisons of drug effectiveness both between and within subjects.

Data to date suggest that the tricyclic antidepressant imipramine is effective in reducing depressive behavior in monkeys, at least within the experimental paradigm we have described. However, it is not immediately effective, but takes 10 to 14 days to have therapeutic consequences for most subjects. It is notable that the form of improvement, as well as the delay in therapeutic effectiveness, is virtually identical to reports of its usage in the human clinical literature. We are presently investigating the capability of other agents to reverse these depressions in monkeys.

Perspectives

In the beginning of this model we devoted considerable space to the need for effective criteria for determining the validity and utility of animal studies of human disorders. Important criteria included cross-species similarity with respect to etiology, symptomology, and therapy, as well as practicability. We then described an animal model that we think is a good one: rhesus monkeys modeling human depression. Let us examine the model that has been presented for its present viability, its current limitations, and its future promise.

To begin, events or situations that have been found to precipitate some forms of depression in humans have been applied to monkeys—and monkey depression has been a common result. The data regarding anaclitic depression are most clear cut. Separation from mother produces depression in some human infants, and separation from mother produces depression in some monkey infants. Further, the variables crucial for precipitating a depressive reaction are most likely similar or identical across these species.

With respect to loss of other attachment objects, the data—about both humans and monkeys—are considerably less clear. Melancholy following loss of a loved one provided the basis for Freud's original formulations regarding depression. However, as pointed out by Akiskal and McKinney (1974), as well as by many others, such a reaction is not always the rule in human society. For monkeys, it has been convincingly demonstrated that nonmaternal social separations can yield severe depressions under some circumstances, particularly when the monkeys are infants and they are separated from peers. However, depression is not an inevitable consequence, just as it is not in humans. Although the specific variables that influence such separations for humans are not as well known as they are for monkeys, it seems likely that they are similar. Convincing evidence to the contrary has not yet been reported.

Research designed explicitly to produce a condition of "helplessness" in monkey subjects has been demonstrated to induce behaviors that are similar to those described as "depressive" in other situations. On the other hand, in situations where the human data provide ambiguous support for a theoretical presupposition—for example, that early separations predispose to later depression—there has also been only limited support in the primate data. In view of what is known in behavioral and environmental terms, the various etiologies for human depressions appear to be basically reproducible in monkeys.

The second criterion necessary to establish an animal model's validity is similarity of symptoms between man and model. In anaclitic depression, the nature and course of the disorder across species are virtually identical. In other disorders, particularly those for which the patient's verbal reports provide the basis for diagnosis, it is more difficult to compare symptoms between monkeys and men. Yet such problems seem less severe than those encountered in models that employ nonprimate subjects.

Finally, although the data to date are limited, therapies shown to be of some use for humans appear to reduce or alleviate depressive behavior in monkeys. Of course, the data to date are preliminary and do not establish a firm case for the equivalence of effective therapies across species. But disconfirming data for this view are noticeably lacking, at least at this point in time.

Thus, the monkey data that we have presented appear to satisfy in large measure the criteria crucial to the validity of any animal model. But what of practicability—of what use are the data obtained from depressed monkeys for clinicians currently working with depressed patients? We have a considerably more difficult time establishing a strong case, since so much monkey work to date has been based upon existing human data and theories. Certainly, one can argue that the variables that govern separation reactions can be more directly disclosed and their interactions more clearly evaluated with monkeys than ever would be possible with humans. These data are bound to be helpful if any clinician wishes to use them for understanding separation-induced disorders. Probably more relevant is the now existing vehicle for testing the efficacy of drugs proposed to be antidepressive. At the very least, they can be compared for rate and degree of effectiveness using criteria that are more valid than reversal of reserpine-induced hypothermia in rats, a commonly used technique at present.

One reason the monkey model in its current state does not have greater immediate practical applicability is that it is far from fully developed. One can readily point out a number of areas where additional data are clearly desirable. For example, the precise relationship among the various "depressions" produced by maternal separation, peer separation, and vertical chambering has not yet been firmly established. Are these depressive states identical, similar, homologous, or unrelated? On what level can or might they be equated—behavioral, cognitive, physiological, biochemical, or for responsivity to particular therapies? These questions cannot be adequately answered on the basis of today's data. However, most of these questions are not beyond empirical solution. They can be tested experimentally.

Because such questions can, in theory, be answered by additional research and because the data to date are promising, the potential of a monkey model of human depression is enormous. It is possible that facilitation of diagnosis, prescription of appropriate therapy, perhaps even preventative approaches could be achieved, given the appropriate monkey data. We are perhaps overly optimistic in our evaluation of the potential of nonhuman primate research for dealing directly with human clinical depression. However, the data have been anything but discouraging, and it would be unrealistic to deny that we, as human beings, need all the assistance we can get in order to further our understanding of human depression.

Clinical Phenomena in Search of Laboratory Models

Isaac Marks
Institute of Psychiatry
The Maudsley Hospital

To be useful, models of psychopathology must bear strong resemblance to their natural counterparts. In this chapter I will first outline the main features of normal fears and obsessions and of phobic and obsessive-compulsive syndromes found in the clinic (Marks, in press). Thereafter I will examine possible models for the generation and extinction of such behaviors. Similarities and differences will be noted between the natural syndromes and their experimental simulations. I will show that current models are at best pale reflections of clinical phobias, and that adequate models for obsessive-compulsive disorders do not yet exist. Finally, I will discuss research that might improve our models.

Naturally Occurring Phenomena

Phenomenology of Fear and Related Emotions

Normal fears and obsessions shade imperceptibly into clinical disorders and share with them important features that viable experimental models need to simulate in order to be useful. We will begin with normal fears and emotional phenomena.

Fear is an emotion produced by present or impending danger. It is "normal" in appropriate situations and has obvious survival value in leading an organism to avoid the danger. Fear and anxiety are very similar. When the cause of the worry is readily apparent—a charging lion or footsteps behind you in a dark alley—then we call the evoked emotion fear. When the cause is vague or less understandable—a trivial examination that is months away or "ghoulies and ghosties and long-legged beasties and things that go bump in the night," we call the emotion anxiety. Fear and anxiety often overlap. The word *fear* derives from an Old English term for sudden calamity or danger, and the term *anxious* comes from the Greek root meaning "press tight" or "strangle."

Because most people have minor fears of one kind or another it might be considered normal to have them. Many children are afraid of being abandoned by their parents, of noise, strangers, animals, and unusual situations. Many adults are frightened by heights, elevators, airplanes, spiders, mice, and taking examinations. Adults and children express fear of a variety of superstitions, from voodoo curses to having a black cat cross their path. These minor fears seldom lead to total avoidance of the situations concerned and may decrease with time or explanation. They rarely require professional treatment.

Two obvious changes in behavior caused by fear are in striking contrast to each other. One is the tendency to freeze and become mute. Rats sometimes freeze in an open field and feign death (play possum). The opposite trend is to become startled, scream, and run away from the source of the fear. Freezing and flight can occur close together in time. As yet, we know little of the antecedent conditions that decide which behavioral pattern will occur. Possibilities include the intensity of the fear (Sartory and Eysenck, 1976), proximity of the predator, and prior experience.

Strong fear and anxiety cause unpleasant feelings of terror, irritability, a strong desire to run and hide, to cry, and sensations of faintness or falling. There may also be a sense of unreality or being "distant from the event," as well as desperation and a tendency to lash out. Feelings of tingling in the hands and feet, of weakness, or even paralysis are reported. Even more commonly mentioned during states of terror is an urge to discharge urine or faeces. An objective observer could also see increased muscle tension, readiness to be startled, and trembling.

Many physiological changes accompany these sensations. These include paleness of the skin, sweating, hair standing on end, pupillary dilation, rapid breathing and heart rate, rising blood pressure, increased blood flow through the muscles, contractions of the bladder and rectum, and decreased electrical resistance of the skin. Like other emotions, fear produces many biochemical changes, including secretion of epinephrine (adrenalin) by the adrenal glands and norepinephrine at peripheral nerve endings of the autonomic nervous system. If the fear and anxiety continue for extended periods even healthy people become depressed, tired but unable to sleep, inactive or restless, and anorexic, and they begin to avoid novel and tension-producing situations.

Although fear and anxiety are usually considered unpleasant, many people actively seek experiences that such emotions produce and enjoy mastering dangerous situations. Racing car drivers, bull fighters, and mountaineers willingly expose themselves to extreme hazards. Thousands of spectators throng to experience vicariously the tensions produced by dangerous sports. Thriller films and books earn millions of dollars from the pleasure derived from the suspense they create. In their less extreme forms anxiety and fear can be not only enjoyable but also useful. They may lead to rapid action in the face of threat and maintain our alertness in difficult situations. Moderate fear normally accompanies activities like taking examinations, parachuting, and public speaking. Fighter pilots report that feeling afraid makes them better at their jobs.

There seems to be an optimal amount of fear for good performance: too little and we risk being careless, too much and we react clumsily (Lader and Marks, 1972). Trainee parachutists perform poorly if they are overly frightened, and even trained paratroopers may become too afraid to jump. Soldiers under bombardment have been known to vomit, defecate, and become so paralyzed with fear that they failed to take shelter or to move those people for whom they were responsible into safer areas. Actors and public speakers can be so terrified that they forget their lines and become speechless.

Anxiety may sometimes follow rather than precede danger. In a sudden crisis rapid action may be required to avert disaster, and we may only become aware of fear after the worst danger has passed. This interval between the onset of danger and the start of fear can take up to several hours. It is well documented in soldiers and air crew after combat and in civilians who have coped with bad accidents, fires, and earthquakes.

Terminology

Although the subjective experience that accompanies phobias and obsessions usually includes fear or anxiety, it can be absent or variable in quality. Some phobics experience the autonomic components of fear without calling them frightening. Obsessive-compulsives may feel disgust or vague discomfort rather than anxiety, and occasionally have no subjective emotion accompanying their compulsive rituals.

Definitions may help to clarify for purposes of this discussion, a number of confusing and ambiguous terms. We have already discussed anxiety and fear. Anxiety is the unpleasant emotion associated with a feeling of impending danger, which is not obvious to an observer. Fear is a similar feeling that arises as a normal response to realistic danger. *Timidity* indicates a lasting tendency to show fearful behaviors easily. *Panic* denotes a sudden upsurge of acute terror. *Phobic anxiety* is anxiety that occurs only in contact with a particular situation or object. A *phobia* is a special kind of fear that is out of proportion to the reality of the situation, can neither be explained nor reasoned away, is largely beyond voluntary control, and leads to avoidance of the feared situation. *Superstitious* fears and taboos are collective beliefs shared by members of a culture about danger shared by other members; like, for example, the notion that bad luck follows walking under a ladder. *Obsessions* are the insistent recurrence of unwanted thoughts despite active resistance against their intrusion; for example, a mother may be plagued by urges to strangle her baby in its sleep. Obsessive thoughts are often associated with *compulsive rituals*, recurrent repetitive actions that some people feel compelled to carry out, usually against their better judgment. A man might wash his hands several hundred times a day because he feels dirty, although he knows that his feeling and action are irrational. *Preoccupations* are repetitive ideas against which someone has no sense of resistance; for example, an adolescent may worry incessantly that he is sexually inadequate.

Aversions are interesting cousins of fear. Price and Kasriel (1973) reported that although many people were not actually afraid of certain situations, they did have an intense dislike of touching, hearing, or tasting things that in most of us arouse either indifference or only mild aversion. For people with aversions, contact with such stimuli may produce severe feelings of revulsion, or of their teeth being on edge, or cause shivers down their spines. Everyday minor examples are the awful feelings many people have when they scrape their knife against a plate, or hear the screech of chalk against blackboard, or scrape their fingernail along the blackboard. People who have extreme touch aversions may be unable to touch wool, velvet, or similar textures. Some people have aversions to the taste of certain foods. Aversions usually are the pinpricks rather than the burdens of life, but they may affect choice of career and work around the home.

Normal Fears and Obsessions

Like other species, human beings appear programmed to respond to certain situations with anxiety and fear (Marks, 1969). As with emotions in general, fear and anxiety develop through the interaction of three influences: genetic, developmental, and learned. Human infants take a long time to mature. As they do so, the experiences they have or observe greatly modify those innately programmed mechanisms that originally triggered their fears. By adulthood the traces of these inborn mechanisms are largely obscured by learned behavior.

Timidity was defined earlier as the enduring tendency to react in a frightened way. Some animal species are very timid; this presumably is genetically determined for its survival value. Rabbits are more timid than tigers. In addition, however, some rabbits are more timid than other rabbits. There are inevitably individual differences within a species, as there are for any biological function. This is true for humans as well as other animals. Identical twin infants resemble each other in the amount of fear they show toward strangers over the first year of life. Adult twins are also similar on a distant correlate of timidity—the number of neurotic symptoms they express.

Fears Humans Are "Prepared" to Develop. Although animals and humans may show fear of any situation at some time or another, some situations are generally feared much more than others. These prepotent or low-threshold fears may develop with little or no prior exposure to the relevant situation. Many of the fear stimuli appear related to special dangers that were important during evolution of the human species. At birth human infants are startled readily by noise and other unexpected, intense, or novel stimuli. Most infants avoid heights as soon as they are old enough to crawl and be tested. Between six and twelve months of age, shortly after they learn to distinguish between strangers and family members, most infants begin to fear strangers. Fear of strangers is a special example of the well-known fact that the novel, strange and unfamiliar is apt to provoke fear in many species. Hebb and Thompson (1954) documented the fear of mature chimpanzees in the presence of a plaster death mask made of one of their number that had died; younger chimpanzees showed no fearful behaviors. Young humans are often afraid of strange masks or other slightly unfamiliar objects.

Though novelty may provoke fear, those same novel stimuli can, on other occasions, cause pleasure and come to be eagerly sought out or produce alternating attraction and repulsion. The last is seen in small children, who look curiously at strangers but quickly hide their faces when their glance is returned. The shy, covert glances of a demure young girl follow a similar pattern.

Writhing and jerky movements are known to frighten monkeys and men (Marks, 1969). This might explain the common fear of snakes in monkeys, which is pronounced from two to four years of age. A child's fear of animals becomes evident at about the same age. Animals are much more frightening to children if they move rapidly, with sudden stops and starts, or if they loom above the children. Young toddlers may handle live animals fearlessly. However, if the animal stalks or rushes toward them, this will precipitate immediate fear that only subsides when the animal is still again.

Staring evokes fear in both children and adults. From its earliest months an infant attends closely to another person's eye movements. The suckling infant fixes its gaze on its mother's eyes; by the age of two months, it will smile at a mask that has two eyespots painted on it. The drawings made by a young child emphasize eyes. Adults are extremely aware of another person's gaze, which can arouse intense emotion. In social phobics, gaze is an important trigger of fear (Marks, 1969).

As soon as infants can crawl they avoid heights. In experiments with a visual cliff apparatus infants are placed on a transparent surface so constructed that looking down from half the surface gives the illusion of suspension over a deep space, while looking through the other half gives the appearance of a shallow space beneath. On this surface infants crawl away from the "deep" side towards the "shallow" side (Gibson and Walk, 1960). This dislike of heights continues into adulthood. Most of us have experienced an urge to jump off the edge of a precipice and have drawn back in a protective reflex. Fear of heights commonly inconveniences people living in high-rise buildings. Both they and their guests feel uncomfortable in such buildings, particularly if there are undraped glass windows running from floor to ceiling (Marks, 1969). Some discomfort of these people may result from a lack of privacy or too much light, but many report feeling dizzy when they look down through full-length windows. The discomfort is eased if curtains are put in the windows. At daytime parties in apartments of this type, many guests retreat from the well-lit, window side of the room and gather in darker regions of the apartment (Marks, 1969).

Some stimuli seem to trigger fears and phobias more readily than others (Marks, 1969; Haslerud, 1939; Yerkes and Yerkes, 1936). Given equally painful experiences with automobiles, bricks, grass, animals and bicycles, humans are much more likely to become fearful of animals than of the other objects. In other words, certain stimuli seem to be like lightning conductors toward which our fears are directed.

Other Features of Normal Anxiety.   In general females tend to show more fears than males, and in both sexes fears tend to dissipate after puberty (Marks, 1969). The common fears change as children grow. Fears can come and go in children in a very volatile fashion. Fears of animals are more common in children at age two through four, but by age four to six fears of the dark and of imaginary creatures begin to predominate. After age six, children become resistant to acquiring new animal phobias, and their existing fears of animals diminish rapidly when they are between nine and 11 years of age. Other objects of fear common in children are thunder and lightning, cars, strong winds, and trains.

There are various explanations why particular fears come and go at particular ages. Children of all ages encounter many varieties of animals, yet they develop phobias of such stimuli primarily from age two through six. Presumably this reflects some maturational process. Some fears start at a given age simply because that age marks a child's first exposure to the frightening object. School phobias are a case in point. We expect some fear of school during the first term or when the child changes schools, but the child usually adapts rapidly. Complete refusal to go to school because of fear is uncommon.

Occasionally a child develops fear of an object immediately after some trauma. However, trauma-related onset of a phobia is the exception rather than the rule. This is damaging to the conditioning model for the origin of phobias, which will be discussed later.

Fears and rituals appear in children for little or no apparent reason and disappear just as mysteriously. Children regress during illness, and forgotten fears may reappear, but when they regain their health the fears disappear once more. Fears of adults are more stable. In a five year follow-up of people who had untreated phobias, a steady decline was noted for subjects under twenty years of age; phobias remained relatively unchanged in adults throughout the five-year study (Figure 5-1).

College-age females continue to report more intense fears than males on fear survey schedules (Hersen, 1973). Factors that may contribute to this continuing difference include innate and cultural influences over the experience and expression of fear in males and females.

Some children's fears are modeled after those of their parents. Many children develop the same fears as their parents and look at their parents before they react in emotional situations. If the adult shows fear, the child picks it up readily. Fears are associated in mothers and daughters (Agras, Sylvester, and Oliveau, 1969). Hagman (1932) found a correlation of .67 between the numbers of similar fears reported by mother and child, and John (1941) found fear of World War II London air raids by mother and child to correlate .59. Since we know that fear can be acquired by modeling, it is surprising that only about one-sixth of adults who have phobias have close relatives with a similar problem (Marks and Herst, 1970).

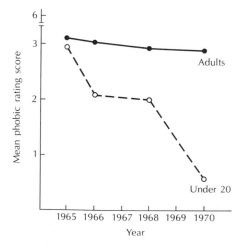

Figure 5-1. Untreated phobias tend to persist over five year follow-up in adults, but improve without treatment in younger subjects. (From Agras et al., 1972.)

In adults many situations produce anxiety. Examinations commonly cause stress in students. Stage fright can plague actors and public speakers. Anxiety regularly accompanies combat and parachute jumping, even among veterans. Dental and medical treatment produce qualms in many people, and before an operation it is common to feel more anxious as the hour of surgery approaches.

Separation anxiety is another normal response to stress of a special kind: the threatened loss of a loved object (see Model 4). Grief is separation anxiety that results from the actual loss of a loved object. The fear of losing one's own life is very common—not simply fear of the process of dying, but fear of the end to all opportunity to achieve one's goals or to pursue pleasure (Hinton, 1967).

Normal Obsessions.   Many children pass through a normal phase of development in which they engage in obsessive rituals. They may avoid stepping on sidewalk cracks, or tap alternate pickets in a fence, or engage repeatedly in a nonsense rhyme or game. Such rituals can be carried out in the hope of staving off some terrible disaster. A. A. Milne's "When We Were Very Young" provides an example:

> Whenever I walk in a London street,
> I'm ever so careful to watch my feet;
>   And I keep in the squares,
>   And the masses of bears,
>   Who wait at the corners all ready to eat
> The sillies who tread on the lines of the street,
>   Go back to their lairs.
>   And I say to them, "Bears,
> Just look how I'm walking in all of the squares!"
> And the little bears growl to each other, "He's mine,
> As soon as he's silly and steps on a line."

However, rituals and magic beliefs are usually under the child's control and do not impair other activities. They are a developmental phenomenon whose significance is unknown.

In adults meticulous tidiness is usually considered a normal feature of personality. Some people cannot bear to have their clothes disarranged or a hair out of place, and others could not care less. House-proud women are part of the cultural scene in Central Europe.

Normal fears and rituals share much with clinical phobias and obsessions, but they differ in intensity. For reasons that are unclear, a normal fear or obsession can grow in intensity to become a handicap. The pathology appears out of the blue without a trace of such characteristics. Because the normal repertoire is closely akin to the psychopathology outlined in the following paragraphs, good experimental models are needed to account for both.

Clinical Phobias and Obsessions

Minor fears and obsessions do not need treatment, though professional advice might be reassuring to someone who suffers from them. However, when phobias and obsessions begin to constrict one's life—when a phobia of sex prevents establishment of a normal marital relationship, or when cleanliness becomes such an obsession that six hours a day are spent washing one's hands until they are raw and bleeding—then treatment is indicated.

Data about the prevalence of phobias and obsessions are scanty. The only community survey available to date was conducted in Vermont by Agras et al. (1969). They estimated the overall prevalence of phobias at 7.7 percent of the general population. However, only 0.2 percent were thought to have severely disabling phobias. About 3 percent of all psychiatric outpatients have phobic disorders and another 2 percent have obsessive-compulsive disorders (Marks, 1965, 1969).

Syndromes in Children. Obsessions in children have similar features to those in adults. Phobias in children often start and stop for no obvious reasons; like most children's feelings, they fluctuate and can be more intense than those of adults. Because fears in children are so intense it is more difficult to separate their normal fears from abnormal phobias.

Although many children have fears, they rarely have handicapping phobias. In one survey, of more than 2,000 children living on the Isle of Wight in Britain, only 16 had troublesome phobias (Rutter and Hemming, 1970). In another study, out of 239 children referred to a psychiatric department only 10 had specific phobias (Graham, 1964). Yet when they do occur, phobias incapacitate children as much as adults.

Subnormal and autistic children have numerous fears, which linger for longer periods than those of normal children (Wing and Wing, 1971). A small incident may produce a lasting phobia of some harmless object or activity (Wing, 1970). Autistic children may be frightened by barking dogs, bathing, wearing shoes, entering a special room and many objects we consider commonplace. On the other hand, they are often unmindful of real dangers, and may run in front of moving cars or climb onto high roofs or window ledges (Wing, 1970).

School Phobia. Though most children are reluctant at times to go to school, only rarely does their reluctance culminate in outright refusal or become a school phobia. The peak age for refusal is that at which children move from one school to another. In England and the United States this is about 11 or 12 years of age, which coincides with the time when most children move from primary to secondary schools. School phobia is different from truancy. In contrast to truants, children who have school phobia do not show other delinquent behavior. Most have no history of their parents being absent from home, and most maintain a high standard of work and behavior at school. School phobics also have more physical symptoms of anxiety than truants, especially difficulties in eating and sleeping, abdominal pain, nausea and vomiting. They may fear separation from their parents.

Syndromes in Adults.   As we discussed earlier although phobias can occur in almost any situation, they tend to involve certain situations more often than others. They can also occur together with almost any other psychiatric problem, and accompany, for example, depressive illness or an anxiety state. When a phobia becomes a handicapping problem, it is called a phobic state or phobic disorder. Such states can occur in many forms— from an isolated phobia in an otherwise healthy person to widespread phobias occurring with many other psychiatric problems.

Agoraphobia is probably the most common and most distressing phobic reaction of which adults complain. Agoraphobia derives from the Greek *agora*, meaning an assembly or market place, and it describes those who fear going into stores, and crowds, and traveling alone in cars, trains, buses, and other public places. Some may simply have a mild travel phobia or fear of enclosed spaces. At the other extreme, agoraphobics may have multiple phobias plus free-floating anxiety, depression, and other difficulties. Though mild fear of open spaces is often seen in agoraphobia, it is *not* a central feature. Agoraphobia usually begins between ages 13 to 35 years. The onset can be sudden or gradual and the phobia may last a few days, months, years, or decades. For some unknown reason it rarely occurs in childhood. Occasionally, children who have chronic school phobias have agoraphobia in adolescence. About two-thirds of agoraphobics are women.

Main symptoms are fears of going out into the open; fears of entering closed spaces such as elevators, theatres, and churches; fears of travel on ships, trains and airplanes (but not usually cars); fears of entering tunnels and crossing bridges; having haircuts or hairdos; and of leaving or remaining at home alone. These fears occur in many combinations and are commonly associated with panic attacks, depression, obsessions, and feelings of unreality.

Social phobias are fairly common and they occur as often in men as in women, unlike most other phobias, which are more commonly reported in women. People who have social phobias may be afraid of eating and drinking in front of other people; afraid that their hands will tremble as they hold their fork or cup; they may become nauseated or feel a lump in their throats that hinders swallowing if they feel that they are being observed. Social phobics refuse invitations to dinner and restrict their social lives for fear of shaking, blushing, sweating, or looking ridiculous. They may refuse to sit facing another passenger in public transportation, or to walk past a queue of people, and may leave their house only when it is dark or foggy so that they cannot be seen easily. They avoid talking to superiors and refuse to appear in front of an audience. Self-consciousness may prevent them from wearing swimsuits in front of others. Parties are avoided and going to the bank and shopping are shunned for fear that their hands might tremble when writing a check or handling money in front of others. At the onset of such a phobia a secretary may become unable to take shorthand or type when others are in the room; a teacher may stop reading dictation or writing on a blackboard in front of the class; and an assembly line worker may become unable to assemble parts as rapidly as usual.

Some social anxieties center on excessive preoccupation about one's appearance. Plastic surgeons have numerous would-be patients who want their noses smaller, bigger or straighter, or their bat ears retracted, or rolls of fat removed from their abdomen.

Social phobias can be highly specific or diffuse. A phobic may simply avoid eating in one particular restaurant or may be driven to lead the life of a recluse. Extreme shyness may be a form of social phobia.

Fears of blood and injury are different from other phobias in that frequently they are accompanied by vasovagal fainting, which reflects a *slowing* of heart rate on contact with the blood phobic stimulus (Connolly, Hallam, and Marks, 1975). By contrast, the usual response to contact with other phobic stimuli is *increased* heart rate (Marks, Viswanathan, and Lipsedge, 1972). Fainting is a rare occurrence with most phobics, but is usual with blood and injury phobics. We might speculate whether the mechanism for fainting in blood and injury phobics is related to the mechanism that produces death feigning in certain animal species.

Illness phobias are common: many people worry endlessly that they may have heart or venereal disease—or any other illness that is being publicized. People who have illness phobias misinterpret bodily sensations as signs of fatal disease. Cancer phobias can cause people to avoid all mention of the illness as well as anybody who has been in remote contact with it. Fears of death cause some to shun cemeteries or to refuse to talk about death. Illness phobias differ from other phobias in that the stimulus that evokes fear is in the person's body rather than in his environment. Consequently, cues cannot be escaped or avoided in the way a travel phobic can avoid fearful experiences by staying at home. This feature makes illness phobias rather like obsessions in that subjective ruminations form a greater part of the disability than observable avoidance. When the fears are diffuse rather than fixed on one illness or part of the body, then we speak of hypochondriasis.

Other specific phobias can be brought on by a wide variety of stimulus situations—heights, darkness, wind, thunderstorms, or various animal species. *Obsessive-compulsive* phenomena shade into phobias to the extent that anxiety accompanies the thoughts or rituals, and there is frequent avoidance of situations that evoke them—for example, someone who has a washing ritual and avoids dirt. However, there are at least two important differences. First, the fear is not directed at a situation itself but rather at the *consequences* of contact with it—for example, having to wash or check for hours afterward. A man worried about dirt from dogs disliked touching a single dog hair as much as touching any live beast; the dog hair alone would initiate hand-washing for hours. Nevertheless, given freedom to conduct their ritual after contact, many compulsives will touch a "contaminated" object quite easily, but then immediately wash away the "dirt." In contrast, most phobics can be persuaded only with great difficulty to contact the stimulus that evokes their fear. Second, obsessives develop a more elaborate set of beliefs around their rituals than phobics develop around their fears. Cognitions seem to play a larger role in obsessives than in phobics. Minor changes in obsessives' perception of a situation can therefore produce a marked change in their behavior. As an example, obsessives who know that they can wash will make contact with "dirt" more readily than those not given this opportunity. Our man with compulsions about dogs would not enter a room in which he believed a dog had been present—even if several months had passed. But he would freely enter a similar environment that was believed to be "dog free."

Obsessive-compulsive problems take two forms: obsessive thoughts or ruminations (which some people think about repeatedly despite all attempts to banish them), and compulsive rituals that they usually know are silly but feel compelled to perform time and again. Obsessive thoughts can occur without rituals, and vice versa. Commonly, however, ritualistic motions are preceded by related ruminations; for example, a mother may repeatedly have the thought that she will kill her child, and then compulsively check the house to ensure that she has removed all knives and other sharp instruments.

Many obsessive thoughts of compulsives are often concerned with the contamination or harming of themselves or others, or going against some social taboo like swearing, or making inappropriate sexual advances in public. Fears of contamination usually occur together with compulsive washing and rituals of avoidance. Those who have obsessions may feel contaminated each time they urinate, defecate, touch the floor, or pet a dog, and this feeling may bring on a bout of washing and bathing for hours after each such occasion. Nor does bathing necessarily end the feeling of contamination, for they may then disinfect all objects in the house they contacted while feeling dirty.

Obsessives may have fears of killing, stabbing, strangling, beating or maiming others, and may avoid having potential weapons for this reason. A housewife may hide sharp knives and give up using needles and pins. Mothers may require constant company for fear they will strangle their babies if left alone. Yet the risk of translating obsessive ideas into terrible actions is in fact very small. It is rare for obsessive-compulsive patients to actually perform the deeds they dread.

Another compulsive ritual consists of endless hair combing, or checking for hairs throughout the home. People may make a ritual of checking hundreds of times for locked doors and windows in their homes. Obsessive-compulsives frequently involve their families, inducing relatives to watch them carrying out their self-appointed rounds, or to check for them. The lives of family members can be completely disrupted.

In compulsive *slowness* each particular sequence is delayed so that it can take hours to dress, have breakfast, or carry out everyday actions. The slowness is selective, so only certain activities are affected—one patient took seven hours to bathe, but talked and walked at normal speed.

Compulsive *hoarders* find it impossible to throw rubbish away; they spend hours sorting out kitchen scraps before throwing them away. They may store valueless papers for decades. Vast quantities of food, tins, and other objects might be bought when none are needed. Any attempt to remove some of the accumulations evokes great anxiety from a hoarder. It can become impossible to live and move in a house where rooms and passages become cluttered with thousands of unused items.

Obsessives often report increased desire to perform rituals when they are anxious or depressed. Some experimental evidence goes in the same direction. Horowitz (1975) found that normal people had more repeated intrusive thoughts after viewing a stressful film than after seeing a restful film.

Problems Associated with Phobic and Obsessive-Compulsive Syndromes

Depression seems especially frequent in phobias and obsessives, and it may assume a variety of forms. Often phobias or obsessions begin during a severe depressive phase. When the depression clears, the phobias or obsessions sometimes persist and sometimes go away. In some patients the onset of depression is not accompanied by any change in severity of obsessions and phobias and in rare cases depression coincides with a decrease in fears and rituals.

That depression is maintained by mechanisms different, at least in part, from those of fear or obsessions, is suggested by the fact that reduction in fears or obsessions has little effect on the course of depression. Marks, Hodgson, and Rachman (Figure 5-2) found that rituals in obsessive-compulsives decreased markedly after treatment and two years followup—yet the severity of depression remained constant. Loss of rituals did not produce loss of depression. But another sequence is quite common. After antidepressant drug treatment, depressed patients who also have phobias or obsessions often lose them as well as their depression.

Clinical observation of obsessives and phobics indicates they are complicated by an unusually high incidence of interpersonal problems. Marital, sexual and family problems are common in obsessives and phobics. Research is still needed to delineate the frequency of these complications and the role they play, if any, in etiology. In a tiny minority of phobics and

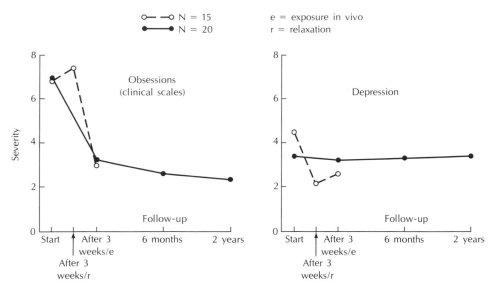

o— —o N = 15
●———● N = 20
e = exposure in vivo
r = relaxation

Figure 5-2. Improvement in obsessive-compulsive rituals is not necessarily accompanied by improvement in depression. (From Marks, Hodgson, and Rachman, 1975).

obsessives, schizophrenic or depressive *psychoses* occur temporarily, but it is not clear whether their incidence is more common than in the general population.

Treatment of Phobic and Obsessive-Compulsive Syndromes: The Exposure Principle

The basic behavioral approach to treatment was enunciated clearly by John Locke 300 years ago. If

> your child shrieks and runs away at the sight of a frog let another catch it, and lay it down at a good distance from him; at first accustom him to look upon it; when he can do that, to come nearer to it, and see it leap without emotion; then to touch it lightly, when it is held fast in another's hand; and so on, until he can come to handle it as confidently as a butterfly or a sparrow.

Today this principle is called *exposure in vivo*.

Phobias and obsessions can be treated effectively by bringing the patient into contact with those situations that evoke his phobias or rituals for a period long enough to allow him to get used to them (reviewed by Marks, 1975). Lengthy exposure is more effective than short, and improvement is much more rapid when contact is made with the real discomforting situation rather than a pictured or fantasied one. It does not matter whether patients are feeling relaxed or anxious during their exposure treatment; the level of arousal during exposure does not affect outcome (Marks, 1975). The patient may be shown what to do during treatment (modeling), though this may not contribute significantly beyond the effect of exposure itself. The same applies to systematic reward of a patient for approaching the phobic situation (operant conditioning).

Different facets of the psychopathology can improve with varying speeds during exposure treatment so that avoidance and physiological responses can be abolished long before the patient actually feels better; this delay in feeling better is sometimes called *cognitive lag*. Improvement often fails to carry over from hospital to home settings unless treatment is carried out in the home as well. Complications such as depression or interpersonal problems frequently need treatment in their own right, and family members may need to cooperate in treatment when their lives have been impaired by ramifications of the patient's phobias or rituals.

Perhaps 5 percent of patients do not habituate with exposure treatments but retain their phobias and obsessions in the face of prolonged exposure. Even more rarely exposure may result in sensitization instead of habituation. These exceptions are unpredictable, but theoretically important. They highlight our ignorance of those factors that decide whether exposure to a discomforting stimulus will be therapeutic or noxious.

Another phenomenon that requires explanation in an exposure model is the improvement of phobias and obsessions that can occur after exposure to an irrelevant fear stimulus (that is, a stimulus unconnected with the original phobia; see Watson and Marks, 1971)—or after the abreaction, or discharge, of intense emotion. These events could be accommodated within a wider exposure principle by assuming that exposure to unpleasant feelings teaches the patient to cope with them. Experimental testing of this idea is not easy, and useful animal models have yet to be discovered.

The exposure principle does not explain the improvement without systematic exposure of some phobias and obsessions when accompanying depression is treated effectively with antidepressant drugs (e.g., Klein and Fink, 1962; Klein, 1964; Gittleman-Klein and Klein, 1971; Solyom et al., 1973). Elucidation of the mechanisms involved requires more careful studies in which the drug and exposure variables are systematically varied and controlled, with separate measurement of phobias, obsessions, anxiety, and depression, not only during treatment but also during long-term follow-ups after drugs have been withdrawn. Such studies are currently in progress.

Experimental Models

A model can be defined as something that accurately resembles something else. Although this definition has the virtue of simplicity, it also presents problems. One such problem is that of deciding the meaning and limits of "accurate." The more closely the model approaches the real thing, the greater its heuristic value. An ideal model would enable us to predict features that are not obvious in the syndrome being modeled, but that can be found on closer examination. Models of psychopathology also enable experiments that cannot be conducted with patients to be done outside the clinic.

It is unrealistic to expect any single model to simulate a clinical syndrome completely. Models are inevitably incomplete, resembling only a few aspects of the natural psychopathology. With this caveat in mind we are less likely to overgeneralize to the point of serious error. We must ask, "Which particular resemblances are under discussion, and how far can we extrapolate from them?" The rest of this chapter will only concern *minimodels:* each concerning a few clinical features, but none by itself an adequate representation of the real thing. To design a reasonable model of psychopathological behavior, we would need to integrate all of the minimodels into a comprehensive framework. Biological ideas about the traits for environmental programming of the brain would have to be synthesized with the learning that occurs in response to the programming and much else besides.

The first part of this chapter delineated the main features of human fear, phobias, and obsessions. Let us summarize important aspects that experimental models should simulate or illuminate. Each will then be discussed in turn.

1.   Both phobias and obsessions focus on selected objects and situations. This is to some extent illuminated by studies of preparedness, and it reflects the phylogenetic boundaries of learning.

2.   Phobias and obsessions involve only certain people. An understanding of these individual differences might be gained from studies in behavioral genetics and the idiosyncratic experiences of individuals.

3.   Some phobias appear selectively at certain ages. Given constant exposure to the relevant situation at all ages, this argues for the role of maturational influences on the emergence of these phobias. The phenomenon is illuminated by experiments with animals.

4.   A good model should integrate the known biochemical and neurophysiological substrates of phobias, but other than Ungar's (1976) work on scotophobin, there is little basic research in this area. Those students who are interested can read the neuropsychological literature on fear, which is beyond the scope of this chapter.

5.   Family and cultural influences or modeling must be considered by model builders. Most phobics and obsessives do not have close relatives with similar problems, although the family incidence may be higher than would be expected by chance, The proportion of agoraphobics known to have agoraphobic parents or siblings whom they might model is only one out of six (Marks and Herst, 1970). Such findings suggest that though modeling

can play a part in the acquisition of phobias and obsessions, it can hardly be the dominant factor.

6.   Few phobias and obsessions begin with a clear history of trauma.

7.   Depression and interpersonal problems are common in persons who are either phobic or obsessive. It is unlikely that this issue is specific to phobias and obsessions alone, but its role requires elucidation. This important issue will not be discussed further here; relevant experiments are currently in progress whose results will not be available for some years.

Let us now consider these requirements for models of phobias and obsessions in more detail.

1. Selected Objects and Situations: Phylogenetic Influences

The limited range of phobias common in man may be partly explained by the concept of "prepotency" I have suggested (Marks, 1969) for human phobias, and by the related concept of "preparedness" elaborated by Seligman and Hager (1972) for learning in general. Prepotency and preparedness are similar ideas that are embodied in the phrase "doing what comes naturally." Phobias are not fears of stimuli picked at random from everyday life. Rather, relatively few stereotyped stimulus patterns are the usual prepotent targets for phobias.

Seligman noted the same phenomenon in many species other than man. He observed that all events are not equally associable in animals, and he defined a continuum of preparedness, along which, because of natural selection, organisms are more prepared to associate certain classes of events, unprepared to associate others, and contraprepared to associate still others. Nest building by birds is an extreme example of rapid learning through preparedness. A bird's first nest is built largely under innate or genetic control. The nest is built, but close examination reveals it is of poor quality. Birds' subsequent nests are stronger and are built with better materials and more protection from the elements.

An example of relative unpreparedness for learning comes from Konorski (1973). Investigators in his laboratory reported that if the sound source of a tone CS+ was not near the feeder, dogs that had been conditioned to eat at the sound of this tone would approach the source of the CS and not the feeder. We can better understand this if we realize that outside the laboratory, signals for food (sounds produced by prey) operate from the very place food awaits. Hungry animals that turned left when food-related sounds were coming from the right seldom survived to pass on their genes to the next generation. Learning to approach the feeder when the signal for food was in an opposite direction was difficult for dogs to learn.

As an example of contraprepared associations we may turn to a study designed to suppress by punishment an innate behavior of the gerbil—alert-posturing. Whereas shock punishment did suppress sand-digging, it served only to increase the frequency of alert-posturing (Walters and Glazer, 1971).

These data suggest that the laws of learning make evolutionary sense; that preparedness to make particular associations goes hand in hand with the evolutionary history and survival tactics of a given species. Fears of specific objects, such as snakes, spiders, dogs or cats, may develop because in the course of our evolution those people survived to pass on their genes who tended to be cautious or to become frightened easily in the presence of certain snakes, spiders, dog- and cat-like creatures. Today these fears are largely vestigial and irrelevant to our survival; nevertheless, some people learn them very quickly and these prepotent stimuli may be very resistant to extinction.

Taste aversion is a current topic of investigative interest, and it offers a classic illustration of prepared behavior by certain species (see review of Garcia's experiments in Seligman and Hager, 1972). The ability to develop taste aversion varies across species (Carroll et al., 1975). Although wild rats develop a profound aversion to foods associated with nausea, the laboratory rat develops an aversion that is far less intense, as judged by its duration.

Human taste aversions are similar to those of animals. More than one-third of a sample of people polled by Garb and Stunkard (1974) reported having had a taste aversion at some time, and one-quarter had one at the time of the poll. The learning was highly selective for these people, in that the taste produced nausea rather than some other sensation in more than 90 percent of them. Only rarely did the unpleasantness generalize to other systems. The taste aversion had generally been acquired after only one pairing of taste and aversive consequences, and sometimes there had been a delay of up to six hours between exposure to the taste of the food and subsequent nausea. Some acquired aversions persisted 50 years later. Novel foods triggered the aversion nearly half of the time, and were incriminated even when novel and familiar foods were eaten at the same meal prior to the onset of nausea. Most types of food toward which aversions developed and persisted the longest were foods previously disliked and eaten infrequently.

The Garb and Stunkard survey reported several new findings about humans. Taste aversions were more common in children than in adults. The common age for acquisition was 6 to 12 years of age, and from age 13 years onward many children lost their aversions. This is reminiscent of animal phobias in children, which generally are acquired before the age of six and lost by the age of eleven (Marks, 1969). Only six percent of the taste aversions studied generalized to other foods. Neither gender nor weight were related to taste aversions, which makes it unlikely that they are related to anorexia nervosa, the clinical syndrome that occurs generally in young women.

The fact that the subjective discomfort associated with taste aversions was *nausea*, not fear or anxiety—the usual concomitants of phobias—is also of interest. To the extent that taste aversions are similar to phobias, fear or anxiety should have been observed. That they were not indicates that sensory modalities are selectively involved with avoidance responses to different types of stimuli. Avoidance of taste is associated with nausea. Avoidance of sights, sounds, and tactile stimuli, which are the usual triggers for phobias, is accompanied by anxiety. There seem to be several forms of avoidance, each accompanied by different subjective states. The greater the feeling of anxiety, the more that avoidance resembles a phobia. However, this is not a sharp distinction. In my clinical experience, the treatment of taste aversions can be successfully accomplished by means similar to those used for more conventional phobias.

Experiments on preparedness in man have just begun. Öhman et al. (1974) found that skin conductance (SC) responses to pictures of snakes and spiders take longer to habituate than responses to neutral pictures of houses. The difference is small but consistent. However, presentation or threat of shock potentiate more SC responses to pictures of snakes than to pictures of houses. This evidence suggests that snakes and spiders, unlike houses, may be prepotent targets for phobias. Of course, we must consider the effects of cultural learning before we can conclude that biological factors are responsible.

The idea of prepotency or preparedness might explain why fears of heights and snakes are common, whereas fears of plastic, filing cabinets, or grass are rare. Preparedness is the lightning rod that conducts associations selectively along certain nervous pathways rather than others. The point is emphasized by two anecdotes about the acquisition of snake phobias. Both are reminiscent of the experiment of Öhman et al. A four-year-old girl was playing in the park. Thinking that she saw a snake, she ran to her parents' car and jumped inside, slamming the door behind her. Unfortunately, the girl's hand was caught by the closing car door, the results of which were severe pain and several visits to the doctor. Before this she may have been afraid of snakes, but not phobic. After this experience a phobia developed, not of cars or car doors, but of snakes. The snake phobia persisted into adulthood, at which time she sought treatment from me.

A similar case was reported by Larsen (1965). An 18-year-old woman was a passenger in a car that was involved in an accident. At the moment of the accident the women happened to be looking at a photograph of a snake. The sudden fear and noise became associated only with the snake and not the car or photographs in general. Why did these people, who have justifiable reasons for fearing cars, develop phobias of snakes?

Different stimuli may possess different capacities for evoking emotional responses. It would be worthwhile to use the techniques of Öhman et al. (1974) to chart a detailed map of S-R valencies in man, which could have uses such as those of Mendelyev's periodic table of elements. Such a map could potentially clarify clinical and experimental data that is otherwise unexplained.

In the classic case of Watson and Rayner (1920), an 11-month-old boy showed fear toward a white rat after a loud noise was made each time he approached it. From the third pairing of noise and approach to the rat, Albert showed fear responses in the presence of the animal. This fear then generalized to other furry objects, such as a fur neckpiece, a Santa Claus mask, cotton wool, and a white rabbit.

In 1929 English published a paper that put the Watson and Rayner study in perspective. He sat a 14-month-old girl in a high chair and presented a wooden toy duck to her. As soon as the child grasped it, a large metal bar behind her was struck a resounding blow (US). The duck was repeatedly presented, reached for, and withdrawn, but even after 50 trials no conditioned fear response had been established. The noise itself failed to evoke fear. English stated, "The writer must confess his surprise—and admiration—at the child's iron nerves. In a later trial, when the duck was grasped, the metal bar was struck such a tremendous blow with a 2-pound hammer that professors in remote parts of the building, students, and children able to make a verbal report spoke of the distasteful and alarming nature of the sound." Yet a month later the same child showed fear, not of a duck, but of new patent leather boots she had never seen before. This fear generalized to related objects. When English used the same US on another child, that child readily developed conditioned fear to a stuffed black cat.

In the Watson and Rayner experiment a furry moving animal became the object of a phobia. In the study conducted by English a wooden painted duck could not be associated with fear, but a stuffed black cat and leather boots could. Such findings led Valentine (1930) to suggest that fears might be much more easily conditioned to furry or leathery objects than to objects such as opera glasses. Another failure to condition fear was reported by Bregman, a student of Thorndike's (see Thorndike, 1935), who studied fifteen babies nearly a year old. When a baby reached for any of six objects (wooden shapes and colored cloths) an electric bell was rung behind the baby's back, frightening and startling it. However, the objects themselves did not become frightening.

Thorndike noted the difficulty of producing fear in children by contiguity conditioning, or what he called "associative shifting." He commented that Bregman's results

> are like what parents usually get who try to shift attitudes toward fear of matches, knives, bottles, dangerous spots, and the like. . . . Progress is slow. . . . There are occasional sudden and dramatic shifts from a few associations (often only one). . . but these are extremely rare. An observing parent would hardly find one per child per year. . . but they are not typical of the great bulk of associative shifting. To use them as explanations of changes in attitudes and interests in general or as the foundation of the theory of education is in every way unjustifiable. Indeed, it is perverse.

These points illustrate the limited preparedness of humans to develop phobias of most types of stimulus. They make a simple theory of contiguity conditioning (which will be discussed shortly) untenable as an explanation for the origin of phobias. In view of the argument against a simple contiguity model by a theoretician as eminent as Thorndike, it is surprising that the theory became so widespread. Its necessary modification by concepts like "stimulus prepotency" or "response preparedness" has long been obvious to ethologists, but acceptance of these concepts into general learning theory is recent and not without continuing controversy.

The role of preparedness in *obsessions* is more obscure. It seems plausible that the developmental phase of transient rituals through which so many children pass is based on phylogenetic mechanisms. Little is known about how these transient rituals relate to lasting obsessive-compulsive disorders, but the stimuli that evoke rituals seem nonrandom. There may well be some that are prepotent in the evolutionary sense. My clinical impression is that obsessive-compulsive behaviors are more diverse than phobic behaviors, and are more under the domination of cognitive components (i.e., beliefs about the rituals). This does not preclude the influence of preparedness on obsessions, because our cognitions are built on a biological base.

In summary, the stimuli for human phobias, and perhaps for obsessions, are fairly predictable and unrelated to the frequency of contact with them. Certain stimuli seem to act as magnets for phobias and for obsessions, as if human brains were preprogrammed to make these preferential connections easily. The evidence that animals readily learn selected S-R connections strongly supports this hypothesis. Experiments in man also confirm it. Prepared learning is selective, readily acquired, resistant to extinction, and unaltered by simple corrective information, and it makes evolutionary sense. All these features apply to phobias and obsessions.

2. Individual Differences: Genetic Influences

Individual differences in people's relative fearfulness and readiness to acquire phobias and obsessions may be partly explained by genetic factors. The evidence is strong for the influence of heredity on timidity in animals. Dogs, rats, and numerous other species have been selectively bred into separate strains of bold and timid animals (Murphree et al., 1966; Peters et al., 1966; Broadhurst & Bignami, 1965). Over successive generations, the animal strains came to differ increasingly in their fearfulness as measured by conditioned avoidance and other tests of emotionality.

How far these genetic studies apply to man is unclear. In the first year of life the development of the smiling response and later fear of strangers are more concordant in identical than in fraternal twins (Freedman, 1965). There is also evidence for a genetic influence on adult neuroticism. The similarity of identical twins reared apart was greater than that of those reared together (Shields, 1975). Environmental influences are unlikely to have produced concordance. Further research should strengthen our knowledge of the strength, range, and mechanism of genetic influences.

There is slight evidence for genetic influences on timidity. A carefully assembled series found phobias and obsessions to be less rare in homo- than in dizygous twins, suggesting a noticeable genetic contribution beyond that of the environment alone (Carey, unpublished). Physiological responses relevant to fear (SC habituation rate, number of spontaneous fluctuations in SC, pulse, and respiration rate) are more alike in identical than in twins (Lader and Wing, 1966; Vandenberg, Clark, and Samuels, 1965; Young, Lader, and Fenton, 1972).

3. Maturational Factors

The fact that certain fears, phobias, and rituals appear only at particular ages in humans suggests that maturational influences are at work. Such influences should exist in an experimental model, and they have been found in both avian and mammalian species. Several fears wax and wane at different ages in animals as in man, and it is reasonable to suppose that this is a reflection of developmental factors.

In ducks and other birds fear is not apparent immediately after hatching, but it becomes apparent after several hours or days have passed (Hess, 1973). Commonly it develops when ducks cease to follow a moving object. An experiment that has not received the attention it deserves was performed by Sackett (1966) on rhesus monkeys. This study demonstrated the influences of maturation on the development of avoidance behavior and it also showed how certain stimuli were prepotent in eliciting such avoidance. Sackett experimented with socially naive rhesus monkeys—that were reared in isolation from each other and from human contact after the first nine days of life. In daily test sessions, slides were projected by the experimenter onto one side of the cage. The monkey could also activate the slides by depressing a lever. These slides showed monkeys in poses of threat, play, fear, withdrawal, exploration, sex, and inactivity, and infant monkeys alone and with their mothers.

Throughout the nine months of testing, the monkeys were little disturbed by any of the pictures except those of threat. Beginning at 2–2½ months and peaking at 2½–3 months, the monkeys' behavior was markedly disturbed whenever pictures of threatening monkeys appeared on the screen. The disturbed behavior consisted of fear reactions, withdrawal, rocking, and huddling. All animals behaved similarly toward the threat pictures, and at 2½–4 months rarely pressed the lever to make them appear. Pictures of infants aroused more vocalization and play than did any of the other pictures but did not produce the agitated disturbance evoked by pictures of threat.

Sackett concluded that at least two kinds of socially meaningful visual stimuli—monkeys in threat postures and infant monkeys—have unlearned prepotent activating properties for isolated, socially naive infant monkeys. From the second month of life these two stimuli produced high levels of all measured behaviors in all subjects. According to Sackett, (1966), the visual stimulation of threat

> . . . appears to function as an "innate releasing stimulus" for fearful be-haviour. This innate mechanism appears maturational in nature. Thus, at 60–80 days threat pictures release disturbance behaviour, although they fail to do so before this age. These fear responses waned about 110 days after birth. This could be due to habituation occurring because no consequences follow the fear behaviour released by threat pictures—consequences that would cer-tainly appear in a situation with a real threatening monkey.

When Sackett's isolated monkeys were later brought into contact with normal monkeys, they neither withdrew nor became frightened when at-tacked, the response to threat having atrophied by then.

These results suggest innate mechanisms of recognition in monkeys that lead to social interaction and learned modifications of the innate reactions. Similarly, in humans, innate mechanisms lead to smiling and the onset of language. In isolated monkeys, the waning of fear responses to threat after four months of age could be due to lack of social reinforcement, as perhaps is the waning of the babbling of deaf infants when they are left without special training. In young animals approach and withdrawal are respectively evoked by fear and high-intensity stimuli.

In rhesus monkeys that are not socially isolated, avoidance behavior ap-pears after a period of approach to both novel and familiar objects (Harlow, 1961, p. 76). Very young rhesus monkeys approach almost all stimuli, and the larger, stronger, brighter and more mobile these stimuli are, the stronger their approach. This would be lethal if it were not checked by the mother monkey in the wild and by the experimenter in the laboratory. When they are 20–40 days of age, an internalized fear begins to act as a check on their tendency to approach novel objects. Stimuli, particularly large, mobile, strange stimuli, cease to call forth approach. They elicit avoidance instead. The same is true for new environments even though they contain no obvi-ously frightening stimuli. In human infants homologous periods occur in two stages: the smiling response—from 2–4 months—followed by a fear of strangers, which is greatest at about 8–12 months (Freedman, 1965; Ricciuti, 1974). Maturational effects are also evident in phobias of animals, which nearly always start in childhood and rarely begin in adult life (Marks, 1969).

Animal research reviewed in this section, especially that of Sackett, suggests a useful line of inquiry to refine animal models of phobias. It is worth studying rhesus monkeys at their critical age of showing fear to threat displays (2½–4 months); at this time they may be particularly prone to acquire new fears of neutral stimuli that are paired with innately fear-releasing stimuli like threat. Perhaps a program of "stress immunization" at this age could have more enduring therapeutic potential than at other phases of development. Research that recognizes the importance of developmental stages and stimuli relevant to them may produce phenomena more akin to enduring human psychopathology.

4. Biochemical and Neurophysiological Substrates

Knowledge of biochemical mediators of phobias and obsessions is rudimentary. When their influence and that of pharmacology become better understood relevant findings can be incorporated into experimental models. This would allow better explanation of the "anxiolytic" effect of psychotropic drugs like the benzodiazepines, the reduction of autonomic discomfort by beta blockers, and the occasional improvement of phobias and obsessions, that is obtained with antidepressant drugs of the tricyclic and monoamine oxidase class.

DeWied, Bohus, and Greuen (1968) found that adrenocorticotrophic hormone (ACTH) and ACTH-like peptides inhibit extinction of avoidance behavior, whereas gluco-corticosteroids facilitate it.[1] Several substances have been isolated from animal brains that are said to appear for the first time after certain kinds of behavior have been trained. Furthermore, when these substances are injected into naive animals without such training, similar specific behavior is said to be induced (Ungar, Desiderio, and Park, 1972; Ungar, 1976). The naturally occurring substances have been analyzed chemically and eight "learning-induced" peptides are said to have been synthesized, each with its own action (Ungar, 1976).

The most widely studied peptide is 'scotophobin' (Ungar, 1976), which is chromatographically similar to a pentadecapeptide that de Wied et al. (1973) found retards extinction of passive avoidance of a dark compartment. Scotophobin is absent in untrained animals, but was isolated from rats, mice, and goldfish trained to avoid the dark side of a light and dark apparatus by being shocked repeatedly while in the dark compartment. When natural or synthetic scotophobin was injected into naive animals it induced avoidance of the dark compartment too (Malin, 1974; Malin, Radcliffe, and Osterman, 1976).

It seems most unlikely that the brain functions according to "one peptide, one behavior," even though Ungar (1976) says that the number of possible

---

[1] ACTH is released by the anterior pituitary and it controls the activity of the adrenal cortex. Among the large number of steroid hormones secreted by the adrenal cortex are the glucocorticoids. The level of cortical steroids in the body feeds back information to the brain (hypothalamic area) and to the pituitary, thereby controlling further ACTH release.

peptides (3×10^{19}) exceeds the amount of information that the human brain can store in a lifetime (estimated at 10^{15} bits). He notes Roger Sperry's concept of "the chemospecificity of innate neural pathways," and suggests that peptides form the basis of a chemical recognition system for the labeling of memory storage circuits. It is too early to evaluate this work, especially its potential relevance for clinical problems like phobias and obsessions. However, consider the speed at which the genetic code formed at conception can over 9 months execute an orderly program of instructions for conversion of a zygote into a human being. There must be numerous chemical organizers that guide this process down ever more diverse one-way paths with a match somewhere between chemistry, structure, and function. Whether Ungar and his coworkers are nearing such a match remains to be seen.

Little is known about the *neurophysiological pathways* subserving phobias and obsessions and their relevance for a good model. There is reasonable evidence that the temporal lobe can play a part in the expression of fear. When a brief sensation of fear heralds the onset of an epileptic attack, the site of the epileptic discharge indicates at least one area of the brain where electrical activity can produce fear. In the great majority of patients who report fear as part of the epileptic experience, abnormal EEG discharge is found in the temporal lobe (Williams, 1956). Of 61 epileptic patients who described fear as part of the seizure, thirty-five had an anterior temporal lesion and 17 had a middle temporal disorder. Williams' observations were borne out by Weil (1959) who found that epileptic fear was associated with cortical temporal lobe pathology.

The only report of a phobia associated with temporal lobe pathology that I could find was the case reported in his book *Fears and Phobias* (1969, p. 52–53). A 51 year old lady had phobias of men and darkness that occurred for seven to 10 days after each temporal lobe seizure but were absent at all other times. Evidence from the case history indicated that psychologically significant events became linked in some way to her abnormal temporal lobe discharges, so that her phobias were reactivated repeatedly shortly after a seizure occurred.

In humans destruction by microcoagulation of the supraorbital region is said to relieve anxiety in patients with chronic anxiety states, and similar lesions in the paracingulate area are claimed to improve obsessive-compulsive states (Grey Walter, 1975). Such claims have to be regarded with caution until detailed controlled evidence is available on the subject. In retrospective controlled studies (Marks et al. 1966; Tan et al. 1970), it has been found that bimedial leucotomy, which destroys tissue in the supraorbital region, does improve chronic anxiety, phobias, and obsessions up to several years followup. Though significant, and greater over five years followup than in matched controls, the overall improvement was not marked.

These clinical findings accord with those of animal experiments that stimulation and ablation of several parts of the limbic system modulates fear states. The limbic system includes the amygdaloid nucleus, which is partly situated in the anterior temporal lobe, and has links with other limbic structures like the hypothalamus, cingulate gyrus and septum, and with the thalamus. The picture is complex and far from complete.

An intriguing 'kindling' effect is produced by intermittent regular stimulation of the amygdala (Isaacson, 1974) and it is just possible that this has some clinical relevance. When repeated stimulation periods are separated by hours or days, brief stimuli come to evoke increasingly intense and widespread discharges in the region concerned. Massing the periods of stimulation together prevents the kindling effect. 'Kindling' is reminiscent of two features of phobias. First, clinical phobias occasionally have a stuttering onset associated with intermittent contact with trauma. Second, in treatment by exposure in vivo, phobias are reduced more by continuous than by intermittent exposure. Work in this area might clarify such features in the incubation and extinction of phobias. Eventually models of psychopathology will have firmer roots in psychophysiology.

5. Family and Cultural Influences

Models of social learning may aid our understanding of phobias and obsessions, although it is unlikely they will be of major importance. Identical twins are very rarely concordant for phobias, and few pairs of twins who are concordant for obsessive-compulsive neurosis have been reported (Lader and Marks, 1972).

Certain subcultures may be model situations that predispose the development of sickness. Zborowski (1952) showed that responses to pain and disease take place within an elaborate cultural context in which patient, family, and community react in socially patterned ways; for example, Jewish and Italian Americans are emotional and they tend to exaggerate their pain experiences, whereas Irish and "old Americans" (Zborowski's phrase) are more stoical. Among immigrant Chinese in Southeast Asia, the phenomenon of koro, in which men fear that their penis is retracting into the abdomen, is prevalent (Ngui, 1969). Koro has been linked to cultural beliefs about the dire effects of semen loss. It would be intriguing to have data comparing the incidence of height phobias among people who live in the Himalayas with that among people who live on the steppes of Central Asia, or of snake phobias among Eskimos, who never see snakes, with that of Amazonians, who see them often.

Hypochondriasis in one's family during childhood could lower one's threshold for perception of bodily sensations, which might then be interpreted as signs of disease. Bianchi (1971) found that patients who had phobias for disease also had a lowered threshold for the sensation of electric shock and decreased pain tolerance to shock. More tended to report a dry mouth than control subjects matched for salivary excretion rate. Bianchi argued that disease phobics augment bodily sensations and pain as well as misinterpret their significance. Similarly, in patients who had phobias of dentists, Lautch (1971) found a significantly lower threshold of shock to the crown of the left upper incisor tooth. The dental phobics all insisted on being given general anaesthetia before undergoing dental procedures and were unable to look at the dental instruments.

6. Conditioning Variables in Fear and Avoidance

Perhaps the most apt minimodels for phobias and obsessions in animals are fear reactions. These include the responses of avoidance, escape, and freezing, and their autonomic concomitants. An important difference is that humans show phobias to many stimuli that animals never encounter as well as complicating features like depression and interpersonal problems, which have few animal counterparts.[2] In humans normal fears and rituals are minimodels for psychopathology.

Many animal experiments assume that conditioned fear and avoidance conditioned by trauma are models of human phobic reactions. Conditioned fear is usually inferred from autonomic responses like increased heart rate and defecation, or such motor responses as freezing and frantic attempts to escape. Such models, therefore, meet a major criterion of similarity with human phobias—they produce strong fear of relatively specific stimuli. In the laboratory, shock is the usual US used to condition fear. In Pavlovian conditioning, shock is paired with a hitherto neutral stimulus to evoke a CR of fear. That stimulus then becomes the CS. Escape and avoidance behavior are produced when the animal is allowed an opportunity of learning to escape or avoid the shock. Temporal pacing is a special form of avoidance conditioning in which the animal learns that a given behavior will delay the onset of unsignaled shock (Sidman, 1953).

These experimental techniques allow systematic study of which variables are important for the learning of fear—such variables as the species, age and sex of the animal, its physiological and psychological state, the quality of the noxious and neutral stimuli, the intensity and duration of such stimuli, the delay between the neutral and noxious stimuli, the maneuvers the animal has to learn in order to avoid or to escape from the feared situation, and the contingency between response and consequence. A major problem encoun-

---

[2]"Learned helplessness" studies on animals have not produced, to my satisfaction, important features of severe depression: insomnia, anorexia, guilt, suicidal behavior and ideas, and lasting mood changes. The success experiences that overcome learned helplessness have not yet been proven practically useful for clinical depression. The therapeutic evidence so far is based on single case experiments and incompletely controlled group studies without significant follow-up differences at 3-6 months. (See Model 3 for an alternative opinion.)

tered in conditioning experiments on fear acquisition is that clearly traumatic events—a definable US—can rarely be pinpointed at the start of human
phobias and obsessions. Even the biochemical studies of Ungar and others
must begin with an event that is clearly defined to the donor animal as a
US. Phobias that are known to begin with a real trauma, such as a serious
accident, can be regarded as similar to the animal's CR. One other clinical
situation resembles an animal pattern. Many obsessive-compulsive persons
feel that disaster will strike if they don't carry out their rituals. An analogy
could be between that and what an animal might feel on the temporal pacing of a Sidman avoidance schedule. Its response has the effect of postpon-
ing an unpleasant event—usually shock. But the only similarity lies in the
established behavior, and we cannot assume that the obsessive ritual has
been acquired in the same way as the animal analogue.

Extinction of Fear and Avoidance. Extinction of fear and avoidance
in animals parallels many patterns that appear during treatment of clinical
syndromes. For this reason experiments on extinction are given some prominence in this chapter. Extinction of fear is commonly said to depend on
repeated exposure of an animal to an aversive CS complex in the absence of
the noxious US. Extinction is slow when conditioning has been established
with an intense and painful stimulus and when fear is strong.

There are many methods of exposing an animal to a frightening CS. One
technique, desensitization, begins with weak stimuli that gradually increase
in strength. With another technique the subject is 'flooded' with the frightening stimuli until finally the fear subsides. In a typical active avoidance extinction procedure, the CS is presented without being followed by
the US, and the subject is allowed to escape from the CS when it carries out
the proper response. The animal usually escapes before it discovers that no
shock would follow if it simply did nothing. The animal may continue to
respond for many trials before learning that the contingencies between response and reinforcement have changed. In a similar way, once established,
human phobias and obsessions tend to continue unchanged for many years
if they are not treated. However, when experimenters expose animals for
prolonged periods to the CS, extinction of the avoidance response occurs
much more rapidly.

Several forms of exposure are called *flooding*. This term denotes confron-
tation with stimuli that the subjects have been conditioned to escape or
avoid, or that evoke freezing or other signs of fear. Other terms used to
describe this procedure are *forced exposure, forced reality testing* (Baum,
1970), *environmental press* (Masserman, 1943), *response prevention* (Baum,
1970), and *detainment* (Weinberger, 1965). In animal experiments the subjects are forced to confront the situation they fear, whereas patients endure
such exposure partly by their own will, though a therapist may encourage
and may exert social pressure.

Flooding in the form of response prevention has produced the extinction of avoidance by rats in shuttleboxes (Berman and Katzev, 1972); Reynierse and Wiff, 1973; Uno, Greer, and Goates, 1973; Delprato, 1973a) and in other experimental environments (Baum, 1970). Baum's extensive studies on the rat suggest animal parallels to human behavior that deserve detailed description (Baum, 1971, 1972a, b, 1973a and b, and 1976). In those studies, rats were placed on the grid floor of a cage; a few seconds later shock was delivered through the grid. The rats' only means of avoiding this shock was to jump on a ledge situated about four inches above the grid. The rats quickly learned to jump on the ledge before the shock was delivered. When the shock was finally turned off, the rats seldom stayed on the floor long enough to find this out. Baum then removed the safety ledge, forcing the rats to remain in contact with the floor without shocks. Initially they made strenuous attempts to jump towards a nonexistent shelf, but these attempts rapidly diminished and within a few trials the subjects remained placidly on the grid floor. Eventually the autonomic signs of fear were lost.

Now consider that in Baum's study the CS was contact with the grid floor and that when the ledge was removed a complete avoidance response was impossible. It could be argued, therefore, that the rat's initial attempts towards jumping the nonexistent shelf were abortive avoidance responses that were not prevented. The active therapeutic ingredient was not response prevention, but rather forced contact with the aversive CS (the grid floor) in the absence of the US.

The longer the duration of response prevention, the faster the avoidance response was extinguished (Baum, 1969a). When rats were trained to avoid low intensities of shock, one minute of response prevention had no effect, but three- and five-minute periods were quite effective. Thirty minutes of response prevention (or exposure to the CS) was necessary to extinguish avoidance if the US was strong, or if random shocks preceded avoidance training (Siegeltuch & Baum, 1971). Extinction testing in Baum's experiments consisted of brief periods on the grid floor with shock turned off. Massing of trials by shortening or eliminating the intertrial interval facilitated extinction (6, 30, or 54 seconds, Oler and Baum, 1968; no intertrial interval, Baum, 1973a).

In clinical work with phobias and obsessions, continuous exposure to the stimulus that evokes the psychopathology (henceforth called the *evoking stimulus*, ES) is followed by a decrease in avoidance of the ES and in accompanying discomfort. This is comparable to the extinction of avoidance in rats by exposure to the CS. In man, as in rats, longer is better than shorter ES exposure times for the reduction of phobias (Stern and Marks, 1973; Marks, 1975).

Extinction is quicker if rats are in the company of other rats that are not fearful (Baum, 1969b), or if response prevention is accompanied by opportunities to see other rats undergoing the same procedure (Uno et al. 1973). Uno et al. found that observational learning alone was less effective than just response prevention alone, (i.e. exposure to the CS), which was highly effective. These findings remind us that company also reduces the fear of agoraphobics, though it does not extinguish it, and group exposure of agoraphobics to their ES produces slightly better results than exposure of individuals. Extinction is also facilitated by forcing the rats to move around and explore the cage (i.e., to come into more intimate contact with the CS) (Lederhendler and Baum, 1970). Use of a loud buzzer was found to increase exploratory activity (Baum and Gordon, 1970). Conversely, confinement prevents the rat from exposure to many facets of the CS, (the grid floor) and hinders extinction (Baum and Myran, 1971). These findings accord with clinical experience that has shown the importance of bringing phobic and obsessive patients into contact with as many facets of the ES complex as possible.

Other experimental findings have no parallels in human disorders. Flooding efficacy is greater if accompanied by positive intracranial stimulation to the right lateral hypothalamus (Gordon and Baum, 1971). With repeated reacquisition and extinction, avoidance responses become steadily weaker, so that by the fifth extinction, performance is the same as that after flooding (Baum, 1972b). Similar observations were made by Akiyama (1968, 1969).

Many other experiments illustrate aspects of CS exposure that hasten extinction. Reynierse and Wiff (1973) showed that exposure to the CS between acquisition and extinction testing hastened the extinction of avoidance as effectively as prevention of the avoidance response for five minutes. However, 15 minutes of response prevention was maximally effective, whether or not there had been prior exposure to the CS between acquisition and extinction testing.

Continuing the CS after the avoidance response was executed helped to facilitate extinction of avoidance in rats. Continuing the CS beyond the moment of the avoidance response was found to hasten extinction (Katzev, 1967; Delprato, 1974), but exposure to the CS without the US for a few seconds after the avoidance response was made was even more effective (Berman and Katzev, 1972; Delprato, 1974). In several experiments Delprato added a positive stimulus such as eating (an analogue of desensitization) to the aversive CS, but this did not hasten extinction (Delprato, 1973a, b; Delprato and Jackson, 1974). Delprato concluded that the therapeutic effectiveness of his techniques in rats was primarily a matter of exposure to the CS without the shock and that counterconditioning was unimportant. The same applies in a clinical setting. Counterconditioning is not particularly helpful during exposure to the phobic stimulus (Benjamin, Marks, and Huson, 1972; Marks, 1975), but repeated, prolonged exposure to the ES produces lasting reduction of avoidance and fear in most human phobias and obsessions.

If a stranger observed an animal's conditioned avoidance responses without knowing its earlier history, he would be unable to surmise the unconditioned trauma that originally led to the avoidance behavior and accompanying emotionality. The same is true of phobic and obsessive-compulsive patients. One might conjecture that "treatment" of the animal's avoidance would be exposure to the evoking stimulus, hoping that a US wasn't being unwittingly supplied at the same time. However, this could never be proven unless one knew how the avoidance response was originally acquired—that is, what the original trauma was.

For unknown reasons, shocking an animal when it makes an avoidance response may, on rare occasions, increase rather than decrease the frequency of that response (Melvin, 1971). This is *vicious circle behavior*, and the question is whether this is related to the rare occurrence of sensitization of phobias in humans. Usually treatment by exposure to the ES results not in sensitization but in a decrement of phobias and obsessions. At times—rarely—this does not happen and the patient either does not improve or actually gets worse with continued exposure. Severe panic during escape from the phobic stimulus sometimes seems to make it more difficult for patients to come into contact with the phobic object on future occasions. Fortunately such sensitization seldom occurs; unfortunately, we have no means to predict when this will happen.

It is unclear why exposure treatments are generally so effective. Seligman and Johnston (1973) suggested a cognitive explanation that posits that the animal has a preference for no shock over shock and expects that avoidance will lead to no shock whereas not avoiding will lead to shock. Extinction is said to depend upon modifying this expectancy.

This explanation does not fit the sequence observed in clinical treatment. Phobics and obsessives expect to feel panic and discomfort when exposed to the ES during treatment. This expectation is confirmed during treatment, yet following treatment their psychopathology declines. Often the avoidance behavior is lost well before the cognitions change (cognitive lag). The expectancy of many patients is thus modified *after* they improve, not before. In them such a cognitive event can hardly be invoked as the main agent of change.

Shortcomings of Animal and Conditioning Models and Theories

One problem in extrapolating results from animal conditioning experiments to patients is the difference in time-span over which the events occur. Many animal experiments produce acquisition of avoidance, treatment, and extinction testing on the same day (Baum, 1970), although a few take several days to do so. Most investigations study only one sequence of acquisition and extinction in a given animal species; only a few examine repeated acquisition and extinction. There is evidence that repeating the sequence over a long period can produce an outcome different from that following a brief experience (Akiyama, 1968; 1971; Baum, 1972b). By the time many humans seek treatment, their phobias and obsessions have been present for years, running a fluctuating course with repeated partial reacquisition and reextinction. To mimic these forms of human pathology more closely, it is desirable to have animal experiments which extend over long periods of time with recurrent acquisition and extinction series. At present very few such experiments have been conducted.

General rules would be easier to deduce from animal experiments if more species were included in many more stimulus-response systems. It is dangerous to overgeneralize when the great bulk of experiments are based on a narrow range of stimuli and responses from one species—the rat.

Contiguity conditioning theories of fear and obsessions show serious clinical shortcomings on formal analysis. In brief, an S-S theory fits the clinical facts of extinction but not of acquisition, whereas S-R theory describes acquisition but not extinction.[3] An S-S (CS-US) theory requires that a neutral stimulus—for example, a bus stop (CS)—become associated with an unpleasant stimulus (US), such as being struck by a bus. The resulting unconditioned response (UR) is pain and an attendant CR of fear. This S-S theory predicts that fear is extinguished when the CS occurs without the US. However, a phobia as seen in the clinic usually develops without a known history of trauma, and the CS becomes aversive without initial pairing with any discernible US. Furthermore, extinction of fear of the bus stop should constantly be occurring in the absence of a US, yet before treatment agoraphobics report steadily increasing fear during repeated encounters with the bus stop. S-S theory thus fails to account for the acquisition of most clinical phobias. It may accord better with the facts of extinction, which are that repeated exposure to the CS (bus stop) without a known US, eventually leads to disappearance of the CR (fear).

To explain acquisition of a phobia of buses, an S-R theory associates the neutral bus stop (CS) with an unpleasant UR, which could be panic. The need for a US is disregarded. This accords with the clinical observation that those settings in which panic strikes (the bus stop) become the CS for phobias. So an S-R theory fits the clinical facts of acquisition, but not those of extinction, since extinction requires the CS (bus stop) to occur without the UR (panic). Unhappily for the theory, panic during exposure to the CS gradually disappears, as does avoidance of the CS. S-R theory predicts that exposure treatment will make the phobia worse, yet the opposite is generally true.

---

[3]Spence (1951) eloquently divided learning theory into two varieties. Sign-significant (S-S) theories held that reinforcement was unnecessary for learning, which was only one aspect of a larger problem, perceptual organization. The fact that in Pavlovian conditioning the CS and US are both stimuli that must be integrated perceptually makes this an S-S learning paradigm. Stimulus-response (S-R) theories emphasize the reinforced (instrumental) learning postulated by Hull and Thorndike. Spence noted that such distinctions were not always clear, and now this issue is often ignored.

Animal models for the reduction of avoidance behavior are more promising than the more global S-S and S-R theories. Continued exposure of both animals and humans to the stimulus that evokes discomfort (ES) usually leads to reduction of avoidance and fear: the patient eventually learns that the discomfort will gradually subside despite continuing contact with the ES. Avoidance or escape are therefore unnecessary for discomfort to be reduced, and gradually drop out. This explanation could be tested by seeing whether reduction of discomfort by the end of a treatment session (ending on a "good note") predicts improvement in avoidance. However, we would still not know why subjective fear or other discomfort was reduced by continuing exposure to the ES. Patients generally find the experience of fear noxious, and fear could be regarded as a US. Continued exposure to such a noxious stimulus should lead to increased, not decreased, fear. It is thus a mystery why most phobics and obsessives improve on exposure to situations in which their expectations of panic on contact with the ES are confirmed, at least in the first part of the treatment program. It is also difficult to explain why humans are often able to tolerate such exposure better in the company of a trusted therapist or a family member than by themselves.

Research on animals has little to tell us about human anxiety that exists internally and symbolically, often without observable motor or autonomic concomitants. Operational definition of such anxiety becomes very tricky. Cognitive avoidance and escape responses may follow rules rather different from those governing overt responses, and causal antecedents can only be inferred from what patients say or do. Such inference can be as much a projection of the therapist's fantasies as a reflection of reality. The same event can mean very different things to different people.

It is so easy to equate fear of snakes with fear of the penis, or impotence with castration anxiety: validating such an equation is a task fraught with difficulties. Even when the fantasies are clearly those of the patient rather than of the therapist, the question remains whether they are the product or the cause of his psychopathology. Consider a dog phobic who feels dogs are dirty. Does he feel this as a reflection of his distaste, or is the cognition of "dirty" a cause of his discomfort? This chicken and egg issue often bedevils interpretation of cognitions in psychopathology.

Conditioning Terms Can Confuse Clinicians

A crucial difficulty in the study of human psychopathology is the definition of "conditioned" and "unconditioned" stimuli. Because there is usually no history of a clearly traumatic onset to human phobias or obsessions, we cannot assume that they have been conditioned, only that they have been acquired. Traumatic conditioning is uncommon in humans, and experiments on this issue are understandably rare. In one such experiment a single traumatic experience of respiratory paralysis (the US) led to persistent autonomic responses to the CS, but these alone do not amount to a phobia (Campbell et al., 1964).

In a typical animal experiment a single CS and a single US are arranged to produce fear. In contrast, a variety of situations usually trigger a patient's clinical distress, and these are seldom traceable to particular traumatic experiences. No one knows the original US, or if indeed one ever existed. The phobia or obsession simply appears, and search for the equivalent of unconditioned shock is fruitless. Shock is an obvious (although unnatural) US in a rat experiment; what is its equivalent in the human phobic or obsessive? Are we to call anxiety the US, UR, CS, or CR? In clinical disorders it could be any or none of these. Clearly, an alternative terminology might be desirable.

To illustrate this problem of definition, we will try to use Pavlovian labels for the typical phenomena found in a woman who has agoraphobia. She complains that each time she waits for a bus she has a wave of panic, breaks into a cold sweat, and wants little else than to rush back home. Just thinking about the bus stop evokes panic, and any panic triggers fear that her fear will get even worse, which aggravates it further in an increasing spiral of anticipatory anxiety we might call fear of fear.

We are tempted to say that the bus stop is the CS that evokes the CR of panic. The panic could equally well be a UR. Had the woman once been attacked while waiting for the bus, we would know that this US produced a UR of pain. But such traumata are exceptional at the first onset of panic. Generally, panic just strikes suddenly. The phobics then blame their panic on those surroundings in which it chances to occur. Should we then call the panic a US? But we have already called it a CR. If we wished we could even label the panic a CS when the fear of fear comes into play, the first fear being a CS and the second a CR. The act of phobic avoidance could also be called a CR, but the "C" for "conditioned" implies an act of faith that conditioning in fact occurred. If by now the reader feels confused, he will be sharing the author's same confusion in trying to translate conditioning language into clinical practice. This confusion is compounded when conditioning labels are extended to obsessive-compulsive phenomena. In a man who repeatedly checks the locks on his house for an hour, what is the US, UR, CS, or CR? It is hard to say.

The operant (instrumental or Skinnerian) model is as unhelpful as the Pavlovian one. Operant language tells us little about the acquisition of phobias and obsessions. In this language the bus stop we considered before is a discriminative stimulus (S^D) for panic, but this simply means that the bus stop evokes panic. It is commonly assumed that avoidance is maintained (reinforced) by arrival in a neutral area that reduces panic (S^{R-}). Many patients describe this sequence, but they can be treated successfully despite continuation of their avoidance reactions. Therefore, other factors must play a part (Marks, 1975). Another operant assumption is that "histories of reinforcement" magically explain the psychopathology. In some cases such analyses do make sense, but often they do not, and one is left to search in vain for plausible reinforcing factors.

Toward a Clinical Language: The ES-ER Paradigm

Conditioning language and theory were developed as a means of describing and predicting experimental events in laboratory animals. In that context they are very useful, but when they are applied to clinical data serious flaws are found. In scientific work it is accepted practice to evolve different languages for different universes of discourse, even though we need to build as many links as possible between these universes. Let us reserve conditioning terms for behavior in the experimental laboratory that clearly has been conditioned (most such work is in animals). For clinical problems like phobias and obsessions let us evolve a simpler language that has clearer implications for treatment and for theory.

It is unnecessary to make an untestable assumption that phobias and obsessions are CSs. To do so would initiate a fruitless search for an unknowable US. Instead let us speak simply of the ES, the evoking stimulus that triggers phobias and obsessions. The phobias and obsessions are the ER, evoked responses. Neither ES nor ER make assumptions about antecedent conditions related to the psychopathology.

Analysis of phobias and obsessions with ES and ER has a major advantage for the clinician. It indicates at once the therapeutic strategy required— continued exposure to the ESs until the ERs subside. Why the ERs are extinguished when patients expose themselves to the ES during treatment is a vital and unsolved question, but this does not deter the clinician from mapping a successful treatment policy: to search for those situations (ES) that evoke the phobias and obsessions and then to maintain the patient in contact with them until he gets used to them. In an agoraphobic this ES may be complex—such as panic while being out alone in public places, crowds, elevators, stores, and the like. The ER they evoke is a cluster of events, like flight and its autonomic concomitants. In an obsessive the ES could be the discomfort brought on by the perception of dirt, disarray or uncertainty. This evokes the ER of compulsive washing, tidying up or checking. The therapist's task is to seek all components of the ES that evoke any ER, so that exposure of the patient to the appropriate ES complex can be contrived and continued until the ER no longer occurs. An agoraphobic may be persuaded to remain in a crowded store for an extended time despite his panic; the compulsive tidier and checker of windows might be asked to untidy his possessions and deliberately refrain from checking rituals. In time the resultant ES of discomfort will come to be tolerated without evoking rituals.

Is "panic" or "discomfort" an ES or an ER? When they *initiate* other phobic or obsessive components they constitute an ES. When they *result* from exposure to an ES, they are called ERs. They are defined by where they are found in the temporal chain of events. An early panic that acts as an ES to initiate a chain of phobic behavior later becomes an ER when the patient deliberately evokes panic by returning to a situation capable of triggering it. When the panic chases the patient it is an ES, but when the patient hunts the panic, it is an ER.

The ES-ER paradigm has a second advantage, a theoretical one that focuses on crucial questions about mechanisms of improvement. We do not understand why the same experience before treatment evokes dread, yet continued exposure to that experience during treatment leads eventually to loss of discomfort. We need to work toward specifying the differences, so far unknown, between exposure that is traumatic or sensitizing and exposure that is therapeutic. Our theoretical task is to discover these differences, which are likely to be multivariate. They may be biochemical; they may lie in duration of ES exposure or in duration of intervals between exposure trials. They may lie in modification of the ES during exposure because of distraction or change in the meaning of the ES for a person when he accepts the need for treatment and the license of the therapist to treat: that is, in the patient's definition of a situation as therapeutic instead of noxious. The type of ER emitted on contact with the ES may also be relevant.

Our aim should be precise statements of the necessary conditions that separate exposure (sensitizing) from exposure (therapeutic). Laboratory models of conditioning are inadequate because they do not simulate both onset and extinction of phobias or obsessions. For clinical work it is preferable to use the simpler notation ES (evoking stimulus) and ER (evoked response of psychopathology) rather than the traditional US, UR, CS and CR. The ES-ER paradigm indicates a therapeutic strategy without the dubious etiological connotations of conditioning models. It also focuses on the theoretical conditions that make the exposure therapeutic rather than sensitizing.

Future Directions for Inquiry

Elucidation of biochemical and neurophysiological mechanisms subserving fear and obsessions might eventually enable us to find better models of these behaviors. Current knowledge is still too scanty to indicate how this might aid prevention or treatment.

A neglected area of potential importance is delineation of the perceptual and physiological reflex mechanisms that are triggered in phobias and obsessions, and of the extent to which these mechanisms are present in normal people. The constant perceptual triggers for phobic reactions, such as fear of heights, open spaces, confinement, and social gaze, as well as the fact that many of these are present to a minor extent in normal people, suggest the operation of widespread reflexes. What factors elicit our normal feeling of being drawn off the edge of a cliff or onto a railway track? What produces dizziness when we turn around while simultaneously craning our neck to look up at a skyscraper? The questions have hardly been investigated.

In a pilot experiment women phobic patients experienced significantly more discomfort than normal women when a male experimenter stood near them under controlled conditions (R. Blumenthal, personal communication). No difference was found between the experiences of phobics and normal males. At this stage it is important to understand the thresholds of fear for normal people and for phobics when they are exposed to standardized perceptual situations such as heights (visual cliffs), open fields, enclosures, being stared at, standing on a shaking surface, and the like.

"Cinerama" rooms might be constructed so that these features could be simulated and manipulated, the thresholds of anxiety plotted, and a cohort followed to see which thresholds marked out individuals who eventually become phobic. Parameters of testing could be systematically varied when subjects were anxious or depressed. This might help us understand how phobic, compulsive, and other neurotic phenomena regularly begin in a depressive setting yet remain when the depression remits. For example, volunteers might remain in a standardized "cinerama" room with illumination and space around them specified. The floor could be vibrated beneath them or it could be left still while the light is made brighter. They could be shown different visual cliffs on a screen. All of these and other variables might be manipulated together.

Experiments exploring preparedness are overdue. These would systematically examine which stimulus-response associations are easy and which are difficult in the establishment of fear in humans and in animals, especially apes, our nearest relatives. Parameters governing extinction of these links could also be explored, and a map of S-R valencies could thus be produced. A start has been made by Öhman et al. (1974, Öhman, Erixon, and Lofberg, 1975).

The preparedness hypothesis could be tested in humans if ethical issues are overcome. Human volunteers could participate in experiments designed to identify differential speeds of acquisition of fear to different classes of stimuli in the manner described by Öhman et al. (1974, 1975). It should be simple to test whether subjects standing on a wobbly floor develop more rapid and enduring fears of heights (e.g. in a visual cliff apparatus) than of telephones, given both situations present while the subjects are shaken on the floor. Again, it might be demonstrated that fear of eating could be engendered more readily when one is stared at critically than when one is given a mild electric shock. To avoid circular reasoning, experimenters would need to predict in advance which fear-evoking stimulus would be the more "natural."

An issue related to preparedness is specificity of the link between aversion in a particular sensory modality and the unpleasant subjective state that accompanies that aversion. The majority of phobias that have the subjective accompaniment of anxiety or fear are to visual or auditory stimuli, which involve long-distance receptors. Anxiety or fear are not usually shown to stimuli we smell, taste, or touch; these stimuli, even smell, usually act over short distances in man. This relationship makes evolutionary sense, since anxiety or fear are associated with danger, which humans learn about far more through long- than short-distance receptors.

In contrast, touch aversions do not evoke anxiety, but rather different sensations expressed in such phrases as "setting one's teeth on edge," "sending shivers up the spine." These contrast with the common autonomic sensations of fear. Similarly, food aversions are not characterized by anxiety or fear, but rather by nausea or disgust, which occurs in the gastroenterological mode associated with eating. Obsessions and compulsions can be associated with variable kinds of discomfort, including anxiety, disgust, or a feeling of being dirty.

The contrasting patterns of autonomic arousal which seem to be associated with different versions in various sensory modalities could be confirmed experimentally by examining the physiological patterns of response evoked by these unpleasant experiences when they involve sight, sound, touch, taste, or smell. It would be surprising if specific patterns of response could not be demonstrated eventually among aversions to stimulation in different sensory modalities. Of course, the specificity to be expected is only relative, with appreciable overlap across modalities as part of a general withdrawal reaction.

Another problem is the clinical impression that phobics and compulsives habituate to noxious stimuli at different rates. Compulsives seem to show greater discrepancy between cognitive, motor, and physiological systems during habituation, the cognitive system usually lagging behind the others, whereas this lag seems less pronounced in phobics. Systematic study might check whether these differences are real. If real, these could further point to mechanisms that cause differences between phobic and obsessive-compulsive behavior.

Uncertainty is a common trigger for obsessive-compulsive rituals. Berlyne (1977) found that uncertainty can act as a stress stimulus which increases EEG desynchrony, and humans work to avoid such desynchrony. One variable making uncertainty rewarding is presumably boredom. Further experiments along these lines might delineate those conditions which decide whether uncertainty will act as a stressor or as a reward and thus illuminate aspects of obsessive-compulsive behavior.

Experiments about the nature of imitation learning might indicate those circumstances when observation of fear in others would likely result in the acquisition of phobias and obsessions. They could aid our understanding of that minority of people for whom modeling facilitates acquisition. Similar experiments could be on the extinction of fear. Current experiments confound the effects of modeling with those of exposure to the discomforting stimulus (ES). Work is needed that keeps the amount of exposure to the ES constant while varying only the parameter of modeling.

It is possible to test whether reduction in avoidance during exposure treatment is due to decrement in subjective fear and its concomitants. The experiment would need to test whether those patients who end their sessions on a good note—that is, with a reduction in subjective anxiety—show greater reduction of subsequent avoidance than patients who are just as anxious at the end of a session as at its beginning.

I don't know what experiments could be done to explain the reduction in subjective anxiety that occurs with continuing exposure to stimuli which evoke obsessive or phobic discomfort. Research into the means by which antidepressants and other psychotropic drugs can be combined with exposure treatment may illuminate the role of depression in phobias and obsessions. (It is also worth considering whether the effects of exposure vary at differing points, say, in circadian and other rhythms that are found in so many biochemical processes.) For example, does it make a difference whether exposure treatment is carried out during the daily high or low points of epinephrine or cortisol secretion?

Finally, experiments are needed about the mechanism of action of self-regulatory processes in fear reduction. What is the role of patients' commitment to grit their teeth and bear their anxiety until it diminishes during exposure treatment? We are still uncertain whether forced exposure treatment could be successful, even though this is ethically undesirable in practice. Of necessity, patients can only be treated when they agree to it.

This brings us to many cognitive conundrums. Meichenbaum (1974) has found value in "psyching oneself up" by thinking positive thoughts (e.g., "I can beat this fear; I must take deep breaths slowly and get nearer to that snake.") However, other patients feel helped by negative thoughts (e.g., "I know I might die any minute of a heart attack. Let's see if I can bring on such an attack.") It would be intriguing to compare the outcome effect of such negative statements with that of positive ones. If both types are equally therapeutic for phobias and obsessions, what is the role of self-statements? Do they aid people in committing themselves to therapeutic actions?

This topic must be explored. Why should obsessives find it easier to refrain from carrying out their rituals when so directed by a therapist, whereas they might fly into a rage when the identical suggestion is made by a spouse? Yet they might accept their spouse's suggestion when the therapist has, with the patient's agreement, enrolled the spouse as a cotherapist. How does the therapist's license to treat help the patient bear what is otherwise unbearable? Is this related to the attitude of resignation and submission that helps deeply religious people to be unscarred by trauma which might deeply wound many other people? How is such therapeutic resignation different from learned helplessness?

Stress immunization and *anxiety management training* are seductive constructs that have current appeal. Stress immunization is the notion that exposure to a mild noxious stimulus under controlled conditions that allow a person to cope increase his ability to deal with subsequent stresses. Anxiety management training describes self-regulatory maneuvers that reduce anxiety. These ideas might have value for child rearing practices that would reduce the prevalence of psychopathology. However, there is little evidence to guide us in these matters, and much work is needed to indicate what useful steps can be realistically undertaken for both children and adults.

Summary

In this model, I have described the features of human phobias and obsessions that occur naturally. At least seven of these features stand in need of explanation by an adequate model: (1) selection of phobic and obsessive situations—phylogenetic influences; (2) individual differences—genetic effects; (3) maturational changes; (4) biochemical and neurophysiological substrates; (5) family and cultural influences; (6) absence of a clear traumatic history, and (7) frequent complication by depression and interpersonal problems. No one model or classical theory of learning explains all of these features, but several minimodels suggest explanations: taste aversions, laboratory fear conditioning, avoidance learning, prepared learning, and fear changes in monkeys during maturation. Conditioning terms, while useful for experimental behavior in the laboratory, is misleading with clinical phenomena. Conditioning language makes assumptions about etiology and treatment that are not borne out in practice and its terminology is difficult to apply to clinical events. It is simpler for clinicians to describe an evoking event or stimulus (ES) and an evoked psychopathological response (ER). Such terms lead to clearer treatment strategies that are usually successful, and to better focused questions about clinical improvement.

Experimental Neurosis: Neuropsychological Analysis

Earl Thomas
Bryn Mawr College

Louise DeWald
Bryn Mawr College

Experimental neurosis refers to maladaptive behavior observed in learning situations. Such behavior may be produced by a variety of techniques that had their beginnings in the laboratory of Ivan Pavlov. Indeed, in this as in many areas of conditioning and learning, Pavlov distinguished the essential features. His early experiments still serve as prototypes for research in experimental neurosis. One of the most well-known early experiments was carried out by Shenger-Krestovnikova (Pavlov, 1927), who used a dog for a subject. In that experiment discrimination between a circle and an ellipse, when made progressively more difficult, resulted in breakdown of that discrimination, as well as in a variety of other, different discriminations that the animal had learned before. Furthermore, the normally quiescent behavior of the animal in the experimental situation was replaced by howling, biting, and struggling. From this experiment we may discern two distinctive properties of experimental neurosis. First, it interferes with previously elaborated conditioned reflexes or learned responses. Second, it is manifested in the appearance of various types of collateral behavior that are maladaptive in the experiment (e.g., howling and struggling in the Shenger-Krestovnikova experiment).

The maladaptive behavior of experimental neurosis is often a surprise to the experimenter. For instance, the experiment of Shenger-Krestovnikova

The research reported here was supported by grants MH 15946 and MH 27023 from the National Institute of Mental Health. The authors would like to thank Anna Rose Childress, Paul Hirsh, and Andrew Balter for their invaluable contributions to the research and ideas presented in this paper.

was initially designed for an entirely different purpose—to test the dog's ability to discriminate between the shapes of various objects. The neurosis represented a new form of behavior that was incompatible with efficient discrimination and that was interpreted by Pavlov as pathological. Moreover, some researchers, including the authors, became interested in experimental neurosis through their observation of pathological behavior in experiments designed to test the limits of discrimination ability in animals (see especially, Dworkin, 1939; Liddell, 1944). The emphasis on maladaptivity is the essence of the study of experimental psychopathology through experimental neurosis. That emphasis distinguishes it from a variety of other approaches, a number of which are represented in this book.

Pavlov suggested that the "neurosis" took two general forms, one characterized by excessive excitation, with an associated loss of inhibitory processes, the other by excessive inhibition, with an associated loss of excitatory CRs (Pavlov, 1927). The form of neurosis was presumably related to the dog's temperament or nervous system—that is, whether the nervous system was predominantly excitatory or predominantly inhibitory (Pavlov, 1927). In furthering Pavlov's work in experimental neurosis, Gantt (1971) compared these symptoms to manic and depressive states in humans.

In the Pavlovian typology, animals and humans could be categorized on the basis of three characteristics of the nervous system: (1) strength; (2) balance; and (3) tendency towards excitation or inhibition. Combinations of these characteristics, according to Pavlov, yielded four basic personalities based upon the traditional Hippocratic categories. The four types of temperament were: (1) sanguine—strong, balanced, with a slight tendency towards excitation; (2) phlegmatic—strong, balanced, with a slight tendency towards inhibition; (3) choleric—strong, unbalanced, predominantly excitatory; and (4) melancholic—weak, unbalanced, predominantly inhibitory. The first two types represented relative normalcy and relative unsusceptibility to neurosis. The choleric type supposedly was susceptible to excitatory manic neurosis, and the melancholic type supposedly was most susceptible to inhibitory depressive neurosis.

Whereas the Pavlovian theory of types has contributed a good deal to research on the conditioned reflex (e.g. Gray, 1964; Nebylytsyn and Gray, 1972), it apparently has not provided a useful framework for subsequent research on experimental neurosis. Perhaps, as Ivanov-Smolensky (1954) has suggested, the theory was abandoned as oversimplified, particularly because animals do not easily fit the typology and because the symptoms of breakdowns are often fluctuating or phasic. Ivanov-Smolensky found, moreover, that even strong, well-balanced (sanguine) nervous systems could be induced to psychopathological behavior under a variety of circumstances such as intoxication, endocrine disturbances, and brain intrusions.

The precipitation of a neurosis was related to a variety of occurrences such as these:

1. The administration of excessively strong stimulation. Perhaps the most famous case of this was a flood in Leningrad in 1924 in which several dogs were trapped. The flood had a profound effect upon the animals' behavior. They began to reject food in the conditioning apparatus. They lost established CRs to positive signals, and showed an increased tendency towards inhibition.

2. The elaboration of extremely difficult or numerous differentiations, as in the Shenger-Krestovnikova experiments.

3. Considerable prolongation of differential stimuli. An example of this is an experiment by N. K. Petrova. After six acoustic, optical, and tactile CSs were prolonged an unusual 3 minutes before the presentation or nonpresentation of food, a dog described as melancholic no longer salivated to previously positive stimuli. Excitable dogs began to salivate to negative and previously inhibited stimuli and they became more agitated.

4. A quick, direct transition from an inhibitory to a positive stimulus.

5. The breaking of a stereotyped chain of learned responses (the "dynamic stereotype" of Pavlov). The basic etiology of Pavlovian neurosis was presumed to be *"a difficult collision, an unusual confronting of the two opposing processes of excitation and inhibition* . . . which leads to a more or less permanent destruction of the normal balance between these two processes" (Pavlov, 1928, p. 361, italics are Pavlov's).

The Pavlovian tradition in experimental neuroses was continued in the United States by Gantt (1944, 1953, 1971) and Liddell (1944). At about the same time, Masserman (1943) derived his experimental approach to neurosis from Pavlov's experiments and psychoanalytic interpretation. Fundamental to all of these approaches was the emphasis on conflict as an important source of experimental neurosis.

Changes in the paradigms of these investigators have raised a number of questions about the mechanism and interpretation of experimental neurosis. One major paradigmatic change was from stimulus discrimination conflict to goal orientation conflict to produce the experimental neuroses. The major consequence of this change may best be demonstrated by a detailed example of each paradigm.

Consider first the Shenger-Krestovnikova experiment. In the final stages of that experiment the animal was required to discriminate between a circle and an ellipse with a major to minor axis of 9 to 8. During this stage the animal was essentially on a partial reinforcement schedule. Pavlov himself and, indeed, scores of others after him, have shown that animals tolerate a partial reinforcement schedule with few problems. We may presume, therefore, that the reaction in the Shenger-Krestovnikova experiment must not have been due to the fact that the animals were sustaining considerable nonreward. Indeed, a reasonable conclusion is that the reaction must have been a unique property of the difficulty of the discrimination and the conflict between the effects of the two stimuli. Moreover, the intense reaction must have occurred in the absence of any specific aversive archetypical stimulus in the situation. In this experiment, the neurosis was maladaptive and inimical to efficient food-getting behavior.

Now consider a classical experimental neurosis experiment performed by Masserman (1943). In the first stage of this experiment, a cat was trained to manipulate a device in order to obtain food until that response was thoroughly learned. In the second stage, as the animal was about to consume food it was subjected to electric shock through its paws or to an air blast across its snout. This represents a goal orientation conflict, and it is a conventional approach-avoidance or punishment paradigm. As a result of these procedures, the animal showed aberrant behavior, including changes of heart rate, pulse, respiration, blood pressure, sweating, piloerection, and other autonomic and somatic responses. The conflict also interfered with the learned behavior. Now, this experiment differs from the first in one very important aspect. There is an aversive stimulus—the air blast or the shock. The presence of such an aversive stimulus raises the question about whether the behavior is a result of the conflict or the built-in response of the animal to any aversive situation. In confirming the results of Masserman, Wolpe (1952) noted the similarity of the effects of using shock alone without any previous food reinforcement training. He therefore argued against the explanation of the abnormal behavior that stressed conflict in favor of an explanation on the basis of a learned reduction of anxiety drive. Watson (1954) has argued that the reaction is a "healthy, rather than pathological reaction to conflict." In a sense, the animal is behaving in an economic way, pitting the reward value of food against the aversion of shock.

Largely on the basis of the goal orientation conflict paradigm, most investigators have analyzed experimental neurosis as a particular instance of punishment and have viewed experimental neuroses as "anxiety" neuroses or phobias. These conclusions may be misleading as a model for experimental neurosis in general. In fact, using a variant of the Shenger-Krestovnikova experiments, we have found a somewhat different picture in which the majority of animals exhibit depression.

Although the original Pavlovian paradigm comes closest to the concept of neurosis as truly maladaptive, the use of it has been restricted to a very few laboratories in the West, and the research on it has been unsystematic. One major reason for the paradigm having fallen into relative disuse by those interested in experimental psychopathology is that the approach afforded by it has generally been idiographic and descriptive. Most of the data has been based upon gross observation, and a lack of precision and quantifiability seems inherent in its design. Nonetheless, it appeared to us that the Pavlovian paradigm, if it could be rendered quantifiable, could make invaluable contributions to the understanding of psychopathologic processes. Indeed, our interest stems from certain similarities between the depressive syndrome seems inherent in its design. Nonetheless, it appeared to us that the Pavlovian paradigm, if it could be rendered quantifiable, could make invaluable suggested to us a possible neural model for experimental neurosis. Because of this and because of the potential of the Pavlovian paradigm for understanding experimental psychopathology in general, we have sought ways of making the Pavlovian neurosis experiment amenable to more precise experimental analysis. Furthermore, because of the number of important similarities between experimental neurosis and the learned helplessness phenomenon of Seligman (1975), we have been examining the role of the nervous system in causing them. A single model may apply to both kinds of experimental psychopathology.

Experimental Neurosis

In order to examine experimental neurosis in the absence of an aversive archetype, we have adapted Pavlov's method of increasingly difficult discrimination to two paradigms, one for instrumental conditioning and the other for a combination of instrumental and Pavlovian conditioning. Both paradigms permit precise quantification of the behavior deficits that characterize experimental neurosis. We will present the objective learning data for each paradigm separately, but because the collateral symptoms were similar under both paradigms, they will be presented later together.

Paradigm 1

In the first paradigm cats were trained in a chamber measuring 76 centimeters long, 91 centimeters high, and 76 centimeters wide. Two retractable omnidirectional levers were located 61 cm. apart on the front wall of the chamber, and a liquid dipper mechanism for feeding was placed between them. Above each lever was a translucent disk illuminated by a variable intensity lamp. A third, nonretractable lever, was placed at the center of the rear wall. A large one-way glass mounted on the door of the chamber permitted unobtrusive observation of the animal. We have found that a very good reinforcement for cats is canned liver cat food mixed with a little milk and liquefied in a blender. We used this mixture in all of the experiments we describe. In general, the subjects were deprived of food for 22 hours and fed Purina Cat Chow freely for one hour each day following the experimental session.

In the first stage of the experiment the animals were taught a light-dark discrimination. They initiated the trials by pressing the center lever. Such a press presented to the animal the two front levers, one illuminated, and the other not. If the cat pressed the illuminated lever (S+) then both levers were retracted and the reinforcement was presented. If the unilluminated lever

(S–) was pressed, both levers were retracted but no reinforcement was presented. The next trial was again initiated by a press of the center lever at the rear of the chamber. The positions of the S+ and the S– were varied according to a two-position randomization method (Gellerman, 1933). Each session consisted of 60 self-administered discrimination trials and lasted approximately one hour. In the event that the cat stopped pressing, the session was terminated after 60 minutes. The animals were trained to a discrimination criterion of 85 percent correct and then given overtraining for up to 10 more days, after which Stage 2 was begun.

In Stage 2 the illumination of S– was gradually increased to the amount of illumination of the lever of S+ according to the following schedule. On the first day of Stage 2 the illumination of S– was increased to 30 percent intensity. On the following sessions the illumination was increased by 5 percent in each session, provided that the performance at each level was no lower than 85 percent correct. If after a given increment the performance fell below 85 percent, the illumination of S– was lowered by 5 percent to the previous day's amount. Following the example of the prototypical experimental neurosis experiments, we have concentrated on measuring what we consider to be the two important defining properties of experimental neurosis: interference with learned performance and collateral symptoms that emerge as a result of the conflict. The first of these measures provides an objective basis for assessing experimental neurosis. However, interference with learned performance is necessary but not sufficient to identify behavior as neurotic because a variety of factors may interfere with this behavior, such as, for example, the frustrating effects of nonreward. The observation of aberrant symptoms is required to lend credence to a "neurosis" interpretation of the effects of conflict.

In general, by the end of Stage 1 and through the beginning of Stage 2, the animals exhibited near perfect discrimination. Typically, at some amount of illumination of S–, (usually between 50 and 80 percent of S+ illumination), the animal would suddenly stop responding for reward and begin exhibiting the symptoms that characterize the neurosis. In our objective learning measure, neurosis was defined as 15 consecutive minutes of not responding in the experimental session. All the cats easily satisfied this criterion at some level of S– illumination. Disruption of behavior often occurred even though the large majority of previous responses were correct and reinforced. Indeed, the interruption of behavior appears unrelated to the occurrence of nonreinforcement. The course of events characterizing the neurosis in four animals may be seen in Figure 6-1. The figure plots each of the animal's performance after achieving a performance criterion. As may be seen, the effect of increasing the difficulty of the discrimination was similar for each animal: a modest increase in percentage of errors and a dramatic decline in the percentage of trials in which the animal pressed the lever to initiate further discrimination trials.

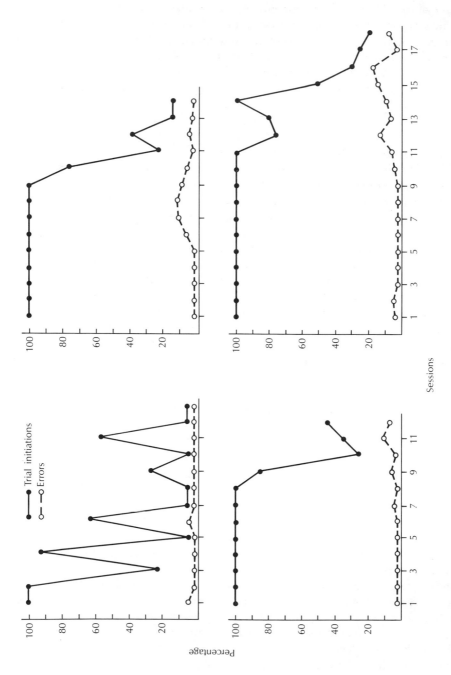

Figure 6-1. Percentage of discrimination trials initiated and errors for each of four neurotic animals during Stage 2. The responses depicted begin with the first session in which CS- was changed for each animal.

Paradigm 2

Paradigm 1 represents an attempt to produce experimental neurosis under conditions in which frustrative nonreward would be minimized by keeping the number of errors as small as possible as the discriminations were made more difficult. Even though the percentage of errors was small, it is not possible to completely rule out frustration as a reason for response termination. Perhaps as a result of considerable overtraining, the few errors made were very frustrating to the animals and they unintentionally served as punishment. To rule out this possibility, a second paradigm was devised in which the frequency of reinforcement for bar pressing was independent of the animal's performance. In this procedure the animal was required to press a lever in order to initiate Pavlovian discrimination trials. The lever press produced one of two CSs (either a 300 or 2,000 Hz tone of moderate intensity). The CS+ was followed, after a 20-second interval, by a food US presented in the food magazine. The CS− was terminated after 20 seconds and not followed by food. Half the trials were CS+ trials, and half CS− trials. The animals were on a 50 percent reinforcement schedule for lever pressing because a lever press produced CS+ and CS− equally often. The percentage of reinforcement for lever pressing did not change. After several days of training, we moved the CS− closer and closer to CS− by successively halving the frequency difference between them on successive sessions.

The results of this procedure were remarkably similar to those of the first paradigm. Four of six animals showed dramatic reductions in bar pressing, even though the percentage of reinforcement for bar pressing remained constant at 50 percent throughout the experiment. This may be seen in the columns labeled *Acquisition* and *Prestimulation* in Table 6-1. The drop in lever pressing is quite remarkable in light of the fact that there is absolutely

Table 6-1 Percentage of Pavlovian trials initiated by each of four neurotic animals

| Subjects | ICSS* | Total Responses | | |
		Acquisition	*Prestimulation*	*Poststimulation*
Fury	—	60	0	—
Dainty	1290	60	13	26
Bonnie	3015	60	26	36
Eve	3795	59	9	54

* Self-stimulation rates given in responses per hour.

Note: *Acquisition* refers to the performance on the final day of training before adjustment of CS similarity. It represents baseline preneurotic performance. *Prestimulation* refers to performance after neurosis had been established but before a session of MFB stimulation. *Poststimulation* refers to performance on the session immediately after the session of MFB stimulation.

no utility in ceasing to respond. Presumably, for lever pressing, there is no more frustration under the difficult discrimination than under the easy discrimination.

Collateral Behavior

All subjects in both paradigms showed a very similar sequence of collateral behavior concomitant with the interruption of responding. As a rule, subjects discontinued responding and suddenly became aggressive and attempted to escape. Many attacked objects within the chamber, such as the house light. The degree of emotionality may be inferred from the urination and defecation that often occurred in the chamber only during the specific periods of nonresponding. A number of the animals developed diarrhea after at least two days of experimental neurosis. The initial symptom, then, may be characterized as severe agitation. However, over a period of several successive days in the apparatus, the agitation abated and generally yielded to depression. Animals sat or lay immobile with their shoulders rigidly hunched in a distinctively depressive posture that is characteristic of experimental neurosis. Some animals crouched as if to urinate and remained in this position for long periods of time. The rigid posture was accompanied generally, by an absence of piloerection, miosis, and considerable lethargy. Three animals refused food when the food magazine was operated. The other three animals approached the food very lethargically and often waited for several minutes after the food was presented before approaching and eating.

Learned Helplessness

In addition to working on classic experimental neurosis, we have also been working with the learned helplessness syndrome described by Seligman, Overmier, and others (Overmier and Seligman, 1967; Seligman and Maier, 1967; Seligman, 1975). It seems clear to us that learned helplessness and experimental neurosis are highly related, if not virtually identical, phenomena. It is not within the scope of the present model to review the general data on the learned helplessness phenomenon; it is thoroughly covered in Model 3 of this volume. We will briefly describe our results with cats and relate our findings about learned helplessness to those on experimental neurosis.

In our initial experiment we adopted for cats with only minor variations the procedure employed by Overmier and Seligman (1967) with dogs. The procedure was as follows. On Day 1 animals received 64 15-second, 3 milliampere (mA) shocks that were unavoidable, inescapable, and unsignaled. The shocks were delivered to the rear footpad through Grass electrodes coated with conductive paste. During this procedure the animals were suspended in a cloth hammock. On Day 2 each subject experienced 20 trials of two-way avoidance training. Each trial consisted of the onset of the tone CS, followed 10 seconds later by the 3 mA footshock US scrambled through the floor grid. If the animal did not cross the barrier to the other side of the shuttle box, then the shock remained on for 60 seconds, both tone and shock terminating together. If the animal escaped by crossing the barrier during the 60 seconds of footshock, both shock and tone were terminated; and if the animal avoided shock by crossing the barrier, the tone was terminated and the animal received no shock on that trial. On the third day animals experienced a further helplessness training session identical to that of Day 1, and on Day 4 the animals received further avoidance training identical to that of Day 2. A control group received two days of avoidance training without any prior inescapable shock.

Effect on Avoidance

The effect of prior unavoidable and inescapable shock upon subsequent avoidance may be seen in Figure 6-2. In this figure the group labeled *Nonatropine* (for purposes of another part of the experiment to be discussed later) was subjected to helplessness training, whereas the group labeled *Control* was not. The data correspond substantially to that of Overmier,

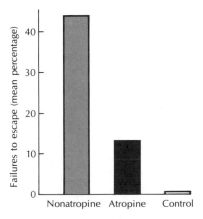

Figure 6-2. Mean percentage of failures to escape during avoidance testing after either helplessness training or control procedure. A comparison of the Nonatropine and Control groups provides an index of the effect of helplessness training. Comparison of the Atropine and Nonatropine groups provides an index of the ameliorative effects of the drug.

Seligman, and others. Approximately 50 percent of the animals with helplessness training withstood the full 60 seconds of shock in the majority of trials. None of the control animals either avoided or readily escaped.

Collateral Behavior

First of all, let us consider the animals' behavior during the original helplessness sessions. With the first few presentations of shock, the cats displayed considerable resistance—they struggled and cried. After several trials the vocalization and struggling greatly diminished and finally disappeared. By the end of the session the only evidence that shock was being received was a slight muscle twitch in the animals' shocked limb. Indeed, we found ourselves checking the shock circuit during the course of training to ensure that it was still functioning. This sequence is not easily explained by peripheral sensory adaptation, because it carries over into the second helplessness session.

The general demeanor of the animals in the avoidance situation after helplessness training is characterized by a striking lack of affect or overt signs of fear. For example, helpless cats at the beginning of the session never resisted being placed in the avoidance apparatus, nor did any of the helpless animals urinate or defecate in the avoidance apparatus. This stands in marked contrast to normal animals, which without exception struggled against being placed in the apparatus and often urinated and defecated. In addition to the striking lack of affect, animals with helplessness training displayed a general lethargy both in the experimental chamber and in the open field. Such animals often stood rigid and motionless in the open field for lengthy periods of time. The animals were very passive—they offered no resistance to handling and displayed a kind of "waxy flexibility," often remaining in whatever position they were placed.

Recently we have produced a symptom remarkably like the helplessness phenomenon by a different method. We first gave animals 20 one-way avoidance trials for 8 days. Because one-way avoidance is learned rapidly (in three or four trials), these animals received a great deal of overtraining. After the one-way avoidance, the animals were switched to a two-way avoidance in the same apparatus. In each case the sequence of events was rather similar. After about three or four escape responses, the animal stopped responding and began to take shock in the apparatus in a manner similar to that we described before. Furthermore, animals showed a similar lack of emotionality and also showed other collateral behavior described in helpless animals. The larger portion of the total shock was taken in the chamber that was previously safe during the one-way avoidance.

The animal that had previously learned an avoidance response was apparently helpless.

This represents a failure of avoidance training to immunize against helplessness (Seligman and Maier, 1967). It seems likely that immunization was offset by the switch of paradigms in the same apparatus and the conflict that presumably followed. It suggests that conflict may produce a syndrome highly similar, if not identical, to learned helplessness.

A Model for Neurosis and Helplessness

In attempting to understand the neural substrate of neurosis and helplessness we have been particularly impressed by the striking lack of affect associated with the terminal stages of both syndromes. Both syndromes seem to follow a similar course—a period of intense agitation followed by a stage of lethargy and depression. It is the curious lack of affect and unresponsiveness to reinforcers—food in experimental neurosis, shock in learned helplessness—that suggest that both syndromes share a motivational deficit or, perhaps more precisely, a loss of incentive.

Our interest in the role of incentive loss in the psychopathology we have described was generated by similarities we saw with a concept of general inhibition that we developed in our laboratory. This concept is related to the function of certain forebrain structures. Here we will describe some data on the function of these structures that are relevant to experimental neurosis and learned helplessness. We will then outline a model that has guided our search for the role of forebrain structures in these pathologies. Last, we will cite some of the relevant evidence about the model.

A number of forebrain structures including the septal area, the area of the diagonal band of Broca, the hippocampus, and others appear to function as general inhibitory areas. That is, they promote inhibition in many other areas of the brain. Stimulation of such areas—such as the septum—produces symptoms very similar to what we see in our experimental neurosis and learned helplessness paradigms, including behavioral arrest, lack of behavior initiation, and lethargy. Hess (1954) has termed this kind of response to brain stimulation as adynamia, which he described as "a state due to lack of volition." Adynamia perfectly describes the behavior of our neurotic animals.

The septum has important inhibitory connections to hypothalamic areas responsible for emotional behavior, including the lateral hypothalamic area generally implicated in reward, and the posterior hypothalamic area generally implicated in aversion (Beagley, 1972; Miller and Mogenson, 1971, 1972; Siegel and Skog, 1970). The fact that septal stimulation in the cat produces an apparent reduction of anxiety and fear was recently confirmed in our laboratory. We found that septal stimulation reduced both somatic and autonomic signs of emotionality (Beagley, 1972) and that animals were motivated to perform to obtain such stimulation when and only when they were also receiving stimulation of aversive sites in the hypothalamus (Evans, 1974). In the absence of aversive hypothalamic stimulation the animals were quite indifferent to septal stimulation, which by itself would not sustain intracranial self-stimulation.

The model of depression to be described is a preliminary one that serves a heuristic function for our research. The major presumption is that when an animal is subjected to conditions of unremitting stress, for which its behavior cannot provide relief, then an internal compensatory mechanism is activated through the forebrain inhibitory areas to inhibit downstream structures in the hypothalamus that are related to fear and anxiety and perhaps to reward. The symptoms of learned helplessness and experimental neurosis may be related to diminished activity in these hypothalamic motivation centers. As mentioned before, there is considerable anatomical and physiological evidence for these connections.

Mitigation of Helplessness Symptoms by Cholinergic Blockade of the Septum

One major presumption of the model is that by interfering with the functioning of forebrain inhibitory areas it should be possible to mitigate the depressive effects of experimental neurosis and learned helplessness. Thus far we have only tested the effect of such interference upon the learned helplessness phenomenon. There is considerable evidence that cholinergic blockade of the septum by atropine faithfully reproduces many of the effects of septal lesions and has the advantage of reversibility (Grossman, 1972b)—that is, the atropine is eventually removed from the system. If the septal area is implicated in the inhibition generated by learned helplessness in the manner in which we think, then functional blockade of the septal area should mitigate the effects of helplessness.

Animals were subjected to helplessness training as described. Half of the animals underwent a subsequent avoidance-escape session while under the influence of crystalline atropine methylnitrate, bilaterally administered to the septal area. No drug was given to the other half. You can see the results of these procedures by referring back to Figure 6-2 and comparing the groups labeled Atropine and Nonatropine. The percentage of failure to escape is appreciably decreased by drug administration. At the same time, animals showed a dramatic change in the collateral behavior characteristic of helplessness. Approximately 15 minutes after the administration of atropine they became much more active in the open field, showing little of their previous lethargy. When placed in the experimental chamber animals resisted being handled and appeared fearful—they cried, their hair bristled, and their pupils dilated.

If we are correct in our assumption that a similar substrate exists for both learned helplessness and experimental neurosis, then blockade of the septum should ameliorate experimental neurosis. We contemplate studying this in the near future.

Effect of Brain Stimulation on Learned Helplessness and Experimental Neurosis

According to the model we have outlined, septal inhibition results in diminished activity in important motivational centers in the hypothalamus and elsewhere. It seems reasonable that direct electrical stimulation of one of those centers might bypass septal inhibition and reinstate the appropriate goal-directed behavior. We have evidence that this occurs for both learned helplessness and experimental neurosis and that direct electrical stimulation of the *relevant* center can improve the symptoms associated with these pathologies.

Because of our observations, we think that in learned helplessness, sites concerned with fear or anxiety, which serve as the bases for escape-avoidance behavior, are inhibited. An experiment performed in our laboratory by Anna Rose Childress demonstrated that the mechanism that produces learned helplessness can be bypassed by electrical stimulation of the brain. The experiment was based on a technique for producing helplessness in rats developed by Seligman and Beagley (1975). Except for the physiological manipulation, the experiment replicated as closely as possible their technique. Basically, the design was this: Two groups of animals received helplessness training during one session. One group received helplessness training with peripheral shock and a second group received electrical stimulation of the dorsal midbrain. Stimulation of the dorsal midbrain has been shown in many studies to yield escape and avoidance behavior. The current was adjusted for dorsal midbrain stimulation so that it elicited behavior that was virtually indistinguishable from behavior produced by peripheral shock. A third control group was exposed to the experimental chamber during the first session but received no shocks. After the helplessness session, each of these groups was divided into two subgroups for subsequent testing in escape. Each subgroup received either peripheral shock or dorsal midbrain stimulation as the basis for escape training.

The results of these procedures were clearcut. The animals that received peripheral shock both during helplessness training and during subsequent escape training showed the typical helplessness effect compared with controls receiving no shock during the first session. Animals that received peripheral shock in helplessness training and dorsal midbrain stimulation on the escape day showed no signs of helplessness to the dorsal midbrain stimulation. Neither did the group that received dorsal midbrain stimulation on both

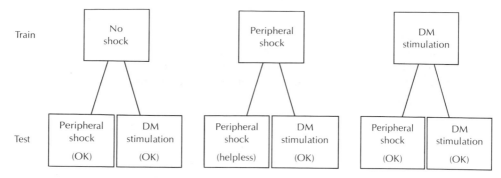

Figure 6-3. Diagram of the design and results of experiment comparing peripheral and dorsal midbrain (DM) stimulation in the production of learned helplessness.

days. Finally, the animals that received dorsal midbrain stimulation during the helplessness session and peripheral shock during the escape session escaped significantly better than the appropriate controls. A block diagram depicting the design of the experiment and the results may be seen in Figure 6-3.

It appears virtually impossible to produce helplessness when the source of aversive stimulation is in the dorsal midbrain. A reasonable conclusion is that the inhibition of affect seen in the typical learned helplessness experiment is afferent, or directed toward the motivational center.

There is evidence that electrical stimulation of the brain may ameliorate symptoms of conflict-produced experimental neurosis as well, although this has not been systematically explored. We have preliminary evidence of both short-term and longer-term improvement in the symptoms of experimental neurosis by electrical stimulation of the reward sites in the median forebrain bundle (MFB) of the cat.

We tested for short-term effects in cats made neurotic under Paradigm 1. Two of the cats that exhibited profound experimental neurosis were selected for chronic implantation with several electrodes in the hypothalamus, including the MFB. During the 60-minute discrimination session, 30 trains of MFB stimulation were given. Each lasted 1 minute or until the animal completed one entire sequence of the Paradigm 1 complex of behavior. The session was divided into 30 periods each of stimulation and nonstimulation. The average number of presses during the stimulation was 30, and the average number of presses in the absence of stimulation was 0 for both animals. Their behavior during the period of stimulation was quite remarkable. During each stimulation of the MFB the entire complex of behavior required by Paradigm 1 was reestablished in the correct order. Indeed, if you were unaware of the history of the animal, you might think that the entire complex of behavior was directly elicited by the stimulation. Immediately upon application of the stimulation, the behavior began; upon termination the animals resumed their former depressed posture. The electrodes for each animal that produced this dramatic effect sustained rates of intracranial self-stimulation of about 1,000 presses per hour, which is a moderate to low rate of responding for intracranial self-stimulation in the cat. At first it seemed to us that the effects of stimulation were extremely short because the animal only showed the appropriate behavior when under its influence. In the absence of stimulation they showed only the neurotic symptoms and lack of behavior. Unfortunately we did not test the long-term effects in these two animals. We did test for three of the animals made neurotic by Paradigm 2.

After several consecutive days of displaying neurotic symptoms and very depressed bar pressing, each cat received a session of MFB stimulation concomitantly with one-half of the trials. The animals were later tested, both after stimulation and in the absence of brain stimulation. Again the effects were dramatic. For each the initiation of Pavlovian trials was dramatically improved, as is shown in Table 6-1.

Let us summarize our physiological theory and data by referring to a schematic diagram of our model, Figure 6-4. This model is a somewhat simplified version of one we have developed for a paper we are preparing. Our initial presumption is that certain afferents directly activate aversive centers in the brain (presumably located in the hypothalamus and elsewhere). The activation is synonymous with psychological stress. When such stress is unmitigated and it reaches a critical threshold, we assume that the septum is activated by a pathway (+) and that it inhibits virtually all downstream centers, both appetitive (rewarding) and aversive. These pathways are represented by the two lines labeled (−). This inhibition accounts for the symptoms of experimental neurosis and learned helplessness. It should be clear from the diagram that alleviation of the pathological behavior should result from the removal of septal influence (as in septal blockade by atropine) or from direct stimulation of the appetitive or aversive centers

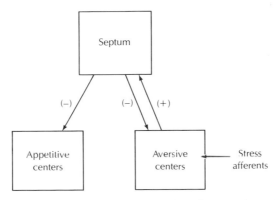

Figure 6-4. Diagram of hypothesized physiological mechanism of experimental neurosis and learned helplessness. The symbols (+) and (−) refer to excitatory and inhibitory influences, respectively.

that overcome septal inhibition. The latter method should produce more discrete effects; that is, stimulating appetitive centers should reinstate only appetitive behavior, and stimulation of aversive centers should reinstate only behavior based on aversion.

Summary and Conclusions

The results of our experiments to date have a number of specific, although tentative, conclusions.

1. It seems reasonable to presume that in addition to other factors, conflict can produce neurosis, even in the absence of any other sources of aversive stimulation. Considerable *indirect* evidence based upon the observation of collateral behavior suggests that conflict may produce an anxiety reaction that because of the very nature of conflict, the animal cannot relieve.

2. Experimental neurosis generally includes a stage of agitation followed by a stage of depression and lethargy.

3. There is a similar course in the reaction to inescapable or unavoidable shock.

4. The mechanisms underlying experimental neurosis and learned helplessness are similar, if not identical.

5. Both learned helplessness and experimental neurosis involve the inhibition of motivational centers and pathways by limbic forebrain inhibitory centers, especially the septal area.

6. The main function of this inhibition is compensatory; it relieves anxiety or distress that is not mitigable in any other manner.

It is always risky to compare maladaptive behavior of the kind that we have described to specific human pathologies, yet the similarities to certain kinds of human affective disorders such as reactive depression are compelling. We use parallel terms both in describing the behavior of our animals and in clinical descriptions of reactive depression—terms such as "loss of pleasure," "loss of motivation," "loss of interest," "low mood," and "stooped posture" (Beck, 1967a).

Finally, a quotation from Beck (1967a) in an important treatise on depression may help put our model into perspective. "The loss of spontaneous motivation or paralysis of will has to be considered a symptom par excellence of depression in the classical literature" (p. 263), and again "The loss of positive motivation is often a striking feature of depression. The patient may have a major problem mobilizing himself to perform even the most elemental and vital tasks such as eating, elimination, or taking medicine to relieve his distress" (p. 26). The similarity of these descriptions to the concept of adynamia that we have used in describing our animals is, indeed, compelling.

Questions and Future Prospects for Research

The major aim of the research described in this chapter is to develop an adequate and comprehensive model of one kind of human psychopathology—reactive depression. The value of such a model could be enormous, especially in helping us to understand the etiology of the syndrome. Animal experimentation in psychopathology must be able to answer at least two very important questions. First, is an animal model of human depression possible? And second, if it is possible, how do we know when we have achieved an adequate model? There is no easy answer to these questions, and the use of a nonhuman model for human psychopathology is exceedingly risky. Indeed many such models are proven to be inadequate or misleading. The adequacy of this model will be decided on a confluence of evidence, and it is towards that confluence that future research must be directed. As a beginning, we would propose several areas of possible similarity between the animal model of depression and human clinical reactive depression. These are:

1. Similarity of symptomology. We have pointed out many of the similarities we found in observing neurotic animals and depressed humans. Our own research will continue to be directed toward developing objective and quantifiable indexes of these symptoms.

2. Similarity of drug effects. Especially convincing evidence for the animal model would be a close correlation of the efficacy of drugs in the animal model and in the human clinical situation, especially for new drugs as they are developed. We are at present embarking upon a comprehensive examination of putative antidepressant and anti-anxiety drugs upon experimental neurosis at several stages in its development.

3. Generality of symptoms. A major symptom of human depression is a general lethargy. That is, lack of motivation becomes a personality characteristic of depressed people. It is useful, even essential, to test the generality of the motivational deficit in animals. We should ask the question: does the lethargic syndrome produced in one kind of learning transfer to other kinds? The usefulness of the model would be limited if the phenomenon only occurred in the particular situation in which the neurosis was produced. One particularly strong test of the generality of experimental neurosis as a general inhibitory phenomenon would be to test for the transfer from the appetitive to an escape situation, in tests of learned helplessness. This experiment is also planned in our laboratory in the near future.

Psychological and Behavioral Influences on Gastrointestinal Lesions in Animal Models

Jay M. Weiss
The Rockefeller University

This chapter will evaluate research on the use of animal models for the study of gastrointestinal lesions. The reason for the inclusion of a chapter on gastrointestinal lesions within a volume mainly devoted to disorders of behavior is that lesions of the gastrointestinal tract, particularly ulcers, are considered to be heavily influenced by behavioral and emotional factors (e.g., Alexander, 1934; Mittleman and Wolff, 1942; Weiner et al., 1957; Mirsky, 1958). This chapter will therefore focus on research that has explored how behavioral and psychological variables affect gastrointestinal pathology. Those studies that involve nonbehavioral manipulations, such as effects of physiological changes, will not be extensively considered here, although such findings may be described where they are particularly relevant for evaluation of a model.

Work described from the author's laboratory was supported by Hoffmann-La Roche, the Scottish Rite Schizophrenia Research Program and the Alfred P. Sloan Foundation. The author gratefully acknowledges the assistance of Daria Korzeniowski in preparation of this manuscript.

Types of Gastrointestinal Lesions:
Ulcers and Erosions

Of particular interest for those studying psychological and behavioral variables are two types of lesions that occur in the stomach and in the duodenum (the small intestine just below the stomach)—ulcers and erosions. Ulcers are chronic, or long-lasting, lesions that extend into the wall of the stomach and/or the duodenum. Figure 7-1 shows an ulcer in an opened human stomach. These lesions extend through the mucosa into the underlying muscularis mucosa and may even penetrate (i.e., "perforate") the outer layer (serosa) of the stomach and/or duodenum, thereby allowing the contents of the gastrointestinal tract to leak out into the peritoneum (see Figures 7-2 and 7-3). Such lesions are thought to leave a scar after healing. Erosions are acute, rapidly developing lesions that almost never extend into the muscularis mucosa or perforate (see Figure 7-4). Such lesions are thought to heal within a few days without scarring. Whereas ulcers most often occur as single, discrete lesions, erosions are often multiple and widespread throughout the organ.

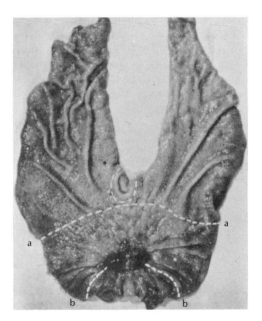

Figure 7-1. A human stomach (opened) in which there is an ulcer. The esophagus enters at the top center and is seen within the circle of dotted white lines. The point of esophageal entry is surrounded by cells similar to those in the rumen of the rat; the extent of this small region is demarcated by the same dotted circle. Between the two dotted lines, a and b, toward the bottom of the stomach lies the pylorus, and below the lowest dotted line lies the top of the duodenum. The ulcer can be seen at the border of the pylorus and the duodenum. (From Oi, Oshida, and Sugimura, 1959.)

Figure 7-2. The stomach of a rat and the duodenum below it (opened). A large perforated duodenal ulcer, which was produced by infusion of histamine and carbachol, can be seen in the duodenum. (From Robert, Stout, and Dale, 1970.)

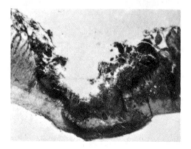

Figure 7-3. A histological section taken through a duodenal ulcer in a rat. Note how the lesion (loss of normal cellular structure) penetrates completely through the upper mucosa and into the underlying muscularis mucosa. (From Robert, Stout, and Dale, 1970.)

Virtually all of the experimental studies carried out with animals, and particularly those involving behavioral/psychological variables, have produced gastric erosions. Gastric erosions in humans, and the subsequent bleeding that they produce, are a most serious problem. Erosions are a major complication arising after burns, surgery, and head injury, although

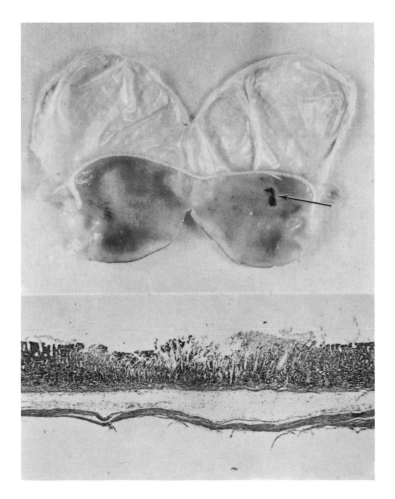

Figure 7-4. In the upper section of the figure is shown the stomach of a rat with a gastric erosion (indicated by the arrow). Note that the lesion occurs in the lower, glandular portion of the stomach. The rumen of the rat stomach is seen above the glandular section. In the lower section of the figure is shown a histological section taken through the lesion shown in the upper section. (From Weiss, 1971a.)

the lesions occurring in each of these instances are not identical (e.g., Skillman and Silen, 1970; Wangensteen and Golden, 1973). The bleeding that occurs from such lesions is often so severe that death ensues. Moreover, although these lesions are most often associated with the traumas listed in the previous sentence, psychological stressors in man apparently can play a role in their production (Wolf and Wolff, 1974; Wolff et al., 1948). What role psychological factors may play in the development of erosions following the traumas listed above is not known.

Although the problem of gastric erosions and the subsequent bleeding that they produce is a very significant one, the usual interest of persons concerned with psychosomatic issues has been with ulcers rather than erosions. It is ulcers that have been, in course of general medical practice, associated with psychological factors. For many reasons—such as the need for an animal model to study ulcers and the fact that gastric erosions are indeed readily produced by stressful conditions—there has been a tendency to consider erosions in experimental animals as synonymous with ulcers in man. Failure to distinguish between these lesions serves no useful purpose. On the other hand, the evidence indicates that there is considerable "crossrelevance" between ulcers and erosions. Erosions are widely referred to as *stress ulcers*, even within the gastroenterological literature (e.g., Grosz and Wu, 1967; Skillman and Silen, 1972). The issue of how experimentally induced erosions are relevant to human ulcers will therefore be discussed briefly.

Perhaps the first observation to be made in this regard is that the stomach of the rat, which is the animal used in virtually all of the experimental work to be described, differs in morphology from the stomach of man. The most striking difference is that the rat's stomach is clearly divided into two zones—an upper zone called the *rumen* or *cardiac* region, the cells of which do not secrete acid; and a lower zone called the *fundus* or *glandular* region, containing the parietal cells, which do secrete acid. Although the human stomach also has what is called a cardiac region in the upper portion, this region is not clearly demarcated from the rest of the stomach as it is in the rat. Comparison of Figure 7-1 with Figures 7-3 and 7-4 reveals that what is called the rumen in the rat is virtually absent from the human stomach, where it is restricted to a small region directly adjacent to the esophageal entry.

But more important than any morphological difference is the possibility that the stomach of the rat is physiologically different from the stomach of man so that it will not show similar pathology. We have no good evidence to suggest that this is the case. As indicated earlier, both the human and the rat develop erosions in the body of the stomach so that with respect to this pathological condition the organs are comparable. More important is the question of whether rats develop ulcers, particularly duodenal lesions that are often found in humans. As mentioned before, virtually all experimental studies with the rat have shown erosions in the glandular portion of the stomach. However, a series of important studies by André Robert and his colleagues has shown that duodenal lesions can be produced in the rat (see Figures 7-2 and 7-3) by injection of cholinergic stimulating agents, which presumably produce high acid secretion (Robert and Stout, 1969; Robert, Stout, and Dale, 1970). Thus, with respect to the question of whether the rat will develop duodenal ulcers, the stomach of the rat appears comparable to that of humans.

The issue of duodenal ulcers brings this discussion to another major question in evaluating the "cross-relevance" of ulcers and erosions. A major distinction that has been made between ulcers and erosions concerns the role of stomach acid. The evidence seems quite good that certain ulcers, specifically duodenal ulcers, are typically found where acid secretion is high (Bockus, Glassmire, and Bank, 1931; Vanzant et al., 1933; Baron, 1962; Dragstedt, 1967). In contrast, gastric erosions do not necessarily co-vary with stomach acid in this way. Evidence for this comes, for example, from studies showing that certain stressful conditions which decrease acid secretion will actually increase gastric erosions (Polish et al., 1962; Mikhail, 1971; Paré, 1972; Paré and Livingston, 1973). Thus, gastric erosions differ from duodenal ulcers with respect to the role of acid secretion.

However, any distinction between erosions and ulcers that is based on the role of stomach acid cannot be an absolute one. First, ulcers in man occur in the stomach as well as in the duodenum. These ulcers, called gastric ulcers, are in some cases associated with elevated stomach acid but in other cases are found to occur where acid is lower than normal or virtually absent. Consequently, some investigators have suggested that (a) there are different types of gastric ulcers, and (b) gastric ulcers are a disorder different from duodenal ulcers. (An excellent discussion of these issues can be found in Ackerman and Weiner, 1976.) Second, although erosions do not require elevated stomach acid in order for them to develop, there is much evidence that stomach acid increases the severity of gastric erosions. Factors that increase acid secretion, such as steroids (e.g., Robert and Nezamis, 1964), increase erosions, and factors that decrease acid secretion, such as vagotomy (cutting of the vagus nerve; see Bonfils, Rossi, Liefooghe, and Lambling, 1959; Brodie and Hanson, 1960; Hanson, 1963) and administration of acid-depressing drugs (e.g., Levine and Senay, 1970; Dai, Ogle, and Lo, 1975), decrease erosions. Thus, erosions are clearly affected by acid secretion in a manner similar to the manner in which acid affects ulcers. Certain investigators have, in fact, suggested that some acid is essential for certain types of erosions (Skillman and Silen, 1972). The distinction between ulcers and erosions with respect to the role of acid seems best described as a matter of degree. That is, certain lesions, such as duodenal ulcers, depend for their etiology more on high acid secretion than do other lesions, such as erosions and some gastric ulcers, but the evidence indicates that all types of ulcers and erosions are promoted by acid secretion.

The issue of how erosions and ulcers are related (or unrelated) should not be considered without directing one's attention to the basic causes of both ulcers and erosions. For many years, investigators have repeatedly emphasized that the genesis of gastrointestinal lesions is determined by those factors that alter the viability of the gastric mucosa. The gastric mucosa is specialized to coexist with corrosive elements (pepsin, acid) whose function it is to digest food matter, so that the lining of the stomach under normal conditions is prepared to withstand, without the development of pathology, those elements that would otherwise produce pathological changes. Lesions develop when the viability of the mucosa is compromised. Attention has for some time been focused on factors such as changes in blood flow and mucosal regeneration rate as primary in the production of lesions. Such studies stem from the view that a healthy mucosa will withstand virtually all challenges and that the development of pathology stems primarily from breakdown in the integrity of the mucosa. Even in the case of duodenal ulcer, where high acid secretion seems to be a most important agent in compromising the mucosa, mucosal impairment may also be necessary for the lesion to occur since we know that there are many persons who also secrete large quantities of acid do not develop lesions.

From this point of view, the key to understanding the production of both erosions and ulcers is seen as the need to discover those basic changes which compromise the viability of the mucosa. We are only beginning to discern these factors. Based on our knowledge of these processes, we may some day be able to make a much clearer distinction between ulcers and erosions. But what is perhaps more important for the present is that many of the basic processes in the development of erosions will inevitably be found to partici-pate in the development of ulcers, and the exploration of these processes is equally relevant to both pathologies. Clinical findings have revealed that ulcers are often found together with erosions (e.g., Schindler and Baxmeier, 1939; Thompson, 1959; Brito et al., 1961). Moreover, conditions that are well known to cause erosions, such as burns, can activate ulcer disease (e.g., Dragstedt et al., 1956), and, conversely, factors closely associated with ulcers, such as elevated acid, can also produce single, focal erosions that may be incipient ulcers (e.g., Polish et al. 1962). Thus, for those interested in the influence of psychological and behavioral factors on gastric pathology, it seems reasonably clear that much of fundamental significance will be learned about how psychological and behavioral factors affect a wide variety of gastrointestinal disorders, including ulcers, from the study of experimen-tally-induced erosions.

What Causes Gastric Erosions: Physiological Considerations

Before turning to the psychological and behavioral factors that influ-ence experimental gastric lesions, a few words will be said of the physiologi-cal etiology of such lesions. As was stated earlier, the attempt to understand gastrointestinal lesions has led investigators to focus on factors that com-promise the viability of the gastric mucosa. With regard to the experimental lesion described in preceding paragraphs, the evidence points to circulatory changes as being important in its genesis. Such lesions appear to begin development when the mucosa becomes ischemic—that is, when the mucosa is deprived of normal circulation of blood. In a particularly valuable study, Hase and Moss (1973) found that, as an initial response to stressful conditions, blood flow into the mucosa of rats is restricted by constriction of ascending arterioles, with much of the flow likely shunted through submucosal arteriovenous anastomoses. Precisely how the lesion subsequently develops, however, remains a question. An early view (see Ivy, Grossman, and Bachrach, 1950, pp, 184–186, 193–196) was that extreme constriction of blood vessels led to rupture of vessels followed by hemorrhage into the mucosa, and that it was this hemorrhage which impeded normal cell metabolism in the mucosa, leading to the cellular death (necrosis) that marks a lesion. Hase and Moss (1973) observed breakdown of the mucosal vasculature in conjunction with the ischemia. The work of Guth and Hall (1966) and Kristt and Freimark (1973) shows the pervasive nature and early development of hemorrhage (also called engorgement) in conjunction with gastric lesions. Similar phenomena have been noted in humans (Cushing, 1932, p. 13). On the other hand, it is quite possible that hemorrhage is secondary to lesion development. Both processes, in fact, seem likely. It has also been suggested that stomach acid, acting on an ischemic mucosa, is highly important in formation of erosions (Skillman and Silen, 1972). These investigators contend that some amount of acid is essential for the lesion to develop. The phenomenon of *back diffusion*, referring to acid diffusing back into the mucosa because of an impaired mucosal barrier, is hypothesized to be significant in this regard.

Knowledge of the neural inputs that mediate lesion-producing changes is presently rudimentary. It has long been known that activity of the vagus nerve promotes gastric erosions in experimental animals (e.g., Bonfils et al., 1959; Brodie and Hanson, 1960; Hanson, 1963) just as it does ulcers (Dragstedt and Woodward, 1951; Scott et al., 1960), an action that possibly occurs because vagal activity increases acid secretion, though other changes, such as increases in stomach contractions, may also play a role (Cho, Ogle, and Dai, 1976). Also, insofar as vasoconstriction is important in lesion development, sympathetic nervous inputs are also likely to participate in causing lesions. This is supported by recent work showing that adrenergic blocking agents can protect against development of gastric lesions (e.g., Djahanquiri, Taubin, and Landsberg, 1973). With regard to the central nervous system we know little beyond the fact that hypothalamic activity can influence lesions (e.g., French et al., 1957; Hall and Smith, 1969; Freimark, 1973), probably a ubiquitous finding in the relationship between brain and viscera.

Before leaving this topic, mention should be made of a different type of erosion that has also been produced experimentally in the rat, commonly called the *shay* ulcer after the investigator who led the team that discovered

Figure 7-5. The stomach of a rat showing multiple "Shay" lesions. These lesions appear as linear defects in the upper, rumenal area of the stomach. (From Ader et al., 1960b.)

it (Shay et al., 1945). This lesion is shown in Figure 7-5. It appears as multiple, usually linear, lesions located in the rumenal (upper) portion of the stomach. It was initially produced by ligating (blocking) the pyloric opening in the rat, thereby causing subjects to retain gastric contents. Shay and his coworkers suggested that this lesion is produced by prolonged contact of the rumen with unbuffered gastric juice, and this investigator knows of no evidence to contradict this original conclusion. Shay lesions have since been reported in normal (nonligated) rats in experiments in which the rats were deprived of food for a prolonged period (e.g., Mikhail, 1973; Paré and Temple, 1973).

The discussion now turns to how stressful conditions, and particularly how behavioral and psychological factors, affect experimental gastrointestinal lesions. First, the use of the immobilization technique is discussed, followed by examination of how lesions are affected by fear stimuli, conflict, predictability or unpredictability of stressful events, coping behavior, and finally aggression.

Immobilization

The technique used most widely for the production of experimental gastric lesions was first reported by Selye in 1936. Selye found that various forms of immobilization applied to rats (wrapping subjects in a towel or tying their legs together) produced gastric lesions in the lower, glandular section of their stomachs. Development of gastric lesions was one of three physiological changes, the other two being involution of the thymus and enlarging of the adrenal cortex, which Selye designated as the principle changes in the "stress syndrome." Selye's discovery that gastric pathology could be produced in this way was a very important one; his observation marks the genesis from which the research reported in this chapter has developed.

Selye was of the opinion that immobilization was a psychological or emotional stressor since the physical assault on the animal appeared to be negligible in comparison with that of other stressors such as injected toxins, trauma, and surgical operations that were used in studies of physiological stress reactions. The supposition that immobilization can be used to discern effects of an emotional stressor or psychological stressor is no longer accepted. For example, Feldman, Conforti, Chowers, and Davidson (1970) studied secretion of the pituitary hormone, ACTH, in animals in which the hypothalamus (and hence pituitary) was surgically isolated (by knife cuts) from the rest of the brain. The investigators studied the effects of various stressors on such animals. Immobilization, like ether anesthesia, produced an augmented ACTH response despite the lack of neural input from virtually all of the brain. Loud noise, which normally produces an ACTH response, had no such effect in these animals. Thus, the results indicate that immobilization does not depend on higher nervous integration or consciousness for some of its "stress" effects as does a noxious sensory stimulus. But, despite the shortcomings of the immobilization procedure as a way of studying emotional or psychological conditions, studies using this stressor have provided an excellent basis for our understanding of experimentally-induced gastric lesions.

In the late 1950s two groups of researchers, one led by Serge Bonfils and the other by David Brodie, defined many of the basic characteristics of gastric lesions induced by immobilization. Bonfils and his co-investigators generally immobilized animals by placing them in a wire cylinder with holes cut in the bottom so that the rats' legs protruded through the holes in the cylinder. Brodie and his colleague Harley Hanson initially used this technique but soon switched to one in which they immobilized animals within wire screen drawn closely around the animal.

The severity of gastric lesions was found to depend upon the closeness and the duration of the restraint. Bonfils and his coworkers (Bonfils et al., 1960) found that as the space within the restraining compartment decreased, the number of animals developing lesions increased. Both groups of researchers (Bonfils, Rossi, Liefooghe, and Lambling, 1959; Brodie and Hanson, 1960) reported that the number of animals developing lesions increased as the duration of exposure to the restraint increased. Both groups also reported that the lesions healed relatively rapidly and without scarring. Whereas 80 to 100 percent of the animals showed lesions after being restrained for 24 hours, the number of animals having lesions was found to be reduced to 60 percent 12 hours after they had been removed from restraint. By the third day after restraint, Brodie and Hanson reported that only 20 percent of the animals showed lesions, and Bonfils, Richir, Potet, Liefooghe, and Lambling (1959) reported a similar reduction by the ninth day.

Other factors found to play a significant role in development of gastric lesions were the age (or weight) of the animals and the degree of food deprivation prior to the immobilization. Both groups of investigators found that the younger (or more lightweight) animals were at the time of immobilization, the more likely they were to develop gastric lesions. Also, food deprivation before the restraining period was found to increase the ulcerogenic capacity of restraint and/or to prolong the time required for lesions to heal.

Since a much-used surgical treatment for ulcers in humans was to cut the vagus nerve input to the stomach (vagotomy), both groups tested the effects of vagotomy on the development of ulcers induced by immobilization. Vagotomy was thought to be effective because it reduced acid secretion, although it obviously had many other effects as well. Both groups of researchers found that vagotomy significantly reduced the incidence of gastric lesions produced by immobilization. Another surgical operation, removal of the adrenal gland, was found to increase the incidence of gastric lesions by Brodie and Hanson, while Bonfils and his collaborators reported no effect from this procedure.

Habituation also can apparently occur with respect to lesions induced by immobilization. Bonfils's group reported that repeated immobilization for 24 hours followed by 24 hours of rest between immobilization periods resulted in a progressive decline in lesions. Whereas 86 percent of the animals were found to have lesions after a single 24-hour period of immobilization, only 71 percent had lesions after two such periods, 51 percent after three such periods, and 25 percent after four such periods. Guth and Mendick (1964) reached a similar conclusion, showing that repeated periods of immobilization for four hours followed by 20 hours of rest produced a decrease in lesion development although there was an increase in mortality. On the other hand, Brodie and Hanson (1960) subjected animals to repeated immobilizations for 18 hours followed by six hours of rest, and found that this regimen resulted in an increase in gastric lesions. Such results suggest that habituation will occur provided that sufficient recovery time between exposure to immobilization is allowed, but that increased susceptibility will result if only a brief recovery time is allowed between exposures to relatively long immobilization.

Recently, Ackerman and his coworkers (Ackerman, Hofer, and Weiner, 1975) have uncovered an extremely powerful variable affecting immobilization-induced lesions. When animals were separated from their mothers 15 days after birth or earlier (pre-weaning), these animals later exhibited a very high vulnerability to gastric lesions in response to 24 hours of restraint. This increased vulnerability was evident until the animals were 100 days of age. On the other hand, animals that were separated from mothers at a slightly later time (21 or 25 days after birth) showed much less vulnerability to gastric lesions when restrained at the same age as the rats

separated at 15 days. Further experiments showed that 24-hour food deprivation alone was sufficient to cause marked development of lesions in the
early-separated group. As yet there is no adequate explanation for these
findings. The remarkable significance of allowing a young rat to remain with
its mother for a few more days during its early life is evident from this work.
The fact that profound changes may occur within a very short period of time
makes this model a potentially valuable one for studying the etiology of these
lesions.

Another interesting characteristic of gastric lesions produced by immobilization is the fact that lesions are related to the level of pepsinogen in plasma.
Pepsinogen is secreted into the stomach by the chief (or zymogen) cells and
is there converted to pepsin (which digests protein) at low pH. Since pepsin
is a digestive agent, it is not surprising that very high levels of stomach
pepsin, which could attack a compromised mucosa, would dispose an
individual to the development of ulcers. Some pepsinogen, presumably a
small percentage of that secreted into the stomach, enters the bloodstream.
Thus, the level of pepsinogen found in the circulatory system is one
predictor of vulnerability to ulcer. In one of the classic studies in psychosomatic medicine, Weiner, Thaler, Reiser, and Mirsky (1957) showed
that pepsinogen level in humans was indeed a predictor of duodenal ulcer
development. Working with rat subjects, Ader and his associates found that
(a) the distribution of plasma pepsinogen in a population of rats was similar
to the distribution in humans (Ader, 1963a), and (b) rats with high plasma
pepsinogen were also more likely to develop lesions as a consequence of
immobilization than were animals with low plasma pepsinogen (Ader,
Beels, and Tatum, 1960a).

Another approach toward understanding gastric lesions was taken by
Jacob Sines, who attempted to develop a population of rats that were
ulcer-susceptible (e.g., Sines, 1959, 1963). By exposing animals to immobilization and examining them for lesions without sacrificing them,
Sines selected animals that developed lesions and inbred them. After in-
breeding for six generations, he developed a strain of animals, which,
when exposed to 12 hours of restraint, developed lesions in 100 percent
of the cases. Only 20 percent of normal stock animals developed
lesions in response to this restraint. When Sines mated normal Sprague-
Dawley females with sixth-generation "ulcer-susceptible" males, 88 percent of the offspring from this mating developed lesions in response to
this restraint, showing that the ulcer susceptibility could not be explained
on the basis of the behavior of ulcer-susceptible mothers. A variety
of behavioral characteristics were also found in the ulcer-susceptible animals. Most prominently, the rats were more active in novel situations
and they defecated more in an open field (Sines, 1961). They also more
readily learned a shuttle avoidance-escape response (Sines, Cleeland, and
Adkins, 1963).

Observations such as the behavioral characteristics noted by Sines for ulcer-susceptible rats suggested that animals that developed lesions might be more "emotional" than animals that did not develop lesions. Indeed, Brodie (1963) reported that a number of tranquilizers reduced the development of gastric lesions in immobilized animals. On the other hand, when Ader extensively studied the relationship between several measures of emotionality (such as an animal's reaction to being handled and its performance in an open field), he found no consistent relationship between these measures and development of lesions. Ader (1967b) argued that there was no validity to the supposition that lesions were related to emotionality, using classical tests to define emotionality.

Fear Stimuli

Despite the problems of reliably and validly measuring "emotion," such as are evident from Ader's studies, the idea that emotions are important in the genesis of gastric lesions has continually received attention because of the observation that ulcers seem to develop in people who are experiencing emotional upheaval. Perhaps the simplest test carried out to determine whether emotion affects gastric pathology has been that of exposing animals to fear stimuli and studying development of gastric lesions that result from this condition. Sawrey and Sawrey (1964) reported an early study in which they exposed rats to pairings of a light and buzzer with shock for a number of trials (20 to 80) before restraining the subjects. They found that presenting the light and buzzer (a fear stimulus) to restrained animals increased the incidence of gastric lesions over that produced by restraint alone.

Although the finding by Sawrey and Sawrey might seem obvious and expected, it has not been replicated since the original report. Fear stimuli have been reported to have no effect on gastric lesions (Mikhail, 1969; Gliner and Shemberg, 1971) and even to reduce gastric lesions (Lovibond, 1969). Because fear-producing stimuli characteristically increase sympathetic tone, thereby reducing gastrointestinal motility and acid secretion, fear stimuli thereby reduce some of the factors that promote gastric lesions. However, Mahl (1949, 1952) observed that stomach acid was increased in both dogs and monkeys as the result of exposure to fear stimuli. Mahl's procedures differ markedly from those reported above in that his animals were exposed to the fear conditions for many days. This raises the possibility that long-term or chronic rather than acute exposure to fear stimuli may increase certain aspects of gastric function that would promote lesions. Obviously, this is not true of all factors involved in gastric lesions since chronic exposure to stressful conditions can produce habituation and decrease lesions (see above).

Conflict

Perhaps the first attempt to show clearly the influence of a significant psychological factor on the development of experimental lesions can be seen in a series of "conflict" studies carried out principally by William Sawrey, John Weisz, and John Conger. These pioneering investigators used an experimental situation embodying the concept that had dominated the psychosomatic literature on human ulcer—conflict. The most well known of such formulations was that of Franz Alexander. Alexander (1934) proposed that the ulcer patient experienced a conflict between a perceived necessity to be active and assertive on the one hand and his deep-seated desire to have oral needs passively satisfied on the other. This conflict—demands for activity versus passive desires—led to unconscious expression of the passive oral strivings in the form of gastric hypersecretion, which eventually manifested itself in the somatic symptom, a duodenal ulcer.

In the experimental studies carried out by Sawrey, Weisz, Conger, and their collaborators, a conflict situation was established for experimental animals (rats) between hunger and an aversive condition. Animals lived in a box, such as is shown in Figure 7-6, having a food container at one end and a water tube at the other. The floor, made up of a grid of bars, was roughly divided into three sections, with the two end sections adjacent to the food and water being electrically charged. Thus, the animal could remain safely in a center section of the box, but if it attempted to procure either food or water, it would receive a shock in doing so. In the usual experimental protocol, the animals were subjected to these conditions for 47 of every 48 hours; during the one remaining hour the animal could eat or drink without being shocked for doing so. In most studies, animals were maintained in these conditions for 30 days prior to sacrifice.

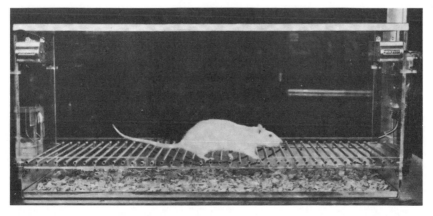

Figure 7-6. Apparatus and subject as used in a "conflict" experiment. Food is available at one end of the chamber and water at the other end, but the grid floor in these areas is electrically charged. (From Ader, 1963a.)

The first report of this method was made by Sawrey and Weisz (1956). They simply compared a group of animals exposed to this conflict condition with a group of control animals that were deprived of food and water for the same periods of time that the conflict condition was in effect. Gastric lesions were found in animals exposed to conflict but not in those exposed to the control condition. However, because the control condition did not include shock, it was not apparent that conflict was responsible for this difference; the effect might have occurred without conflict simply from exposure to food deprivation and shock or even shock alone.

Subsequent studies (Sawrey, Conger, and Turrell, 1956; Weisz, 1957) attempted to correct this inadequacy and also to evaluate the importance of the many factors included in this experimental situation. These factors included conflict, shock, hunger, and thirst. Table 7-1 shows the results reported by Sawrey, Conger, and Turrell (1956) for the various conditions that they examined. They and Weisz (1957) found that animals made hungry and thirsty and exposed to conflict as described by Sawrey and Weisz developed more gastric lesions than animals exposed to any other experimental condition. Most important, animals in the conflict condition developed more severe lesions than "yoked" animals that were also made hungry and thirsty and were shocked whenever a matched animal in the conflict situation received shock. Because these "yoked" animals received similar aversive conditions to those in the conflict situation (deprivation and shock) but did not experience the conflict, the difference between these two groups indicated that conflict could contribute to lesion formation. The other major

Table 7-1. Incidence of ulcers under various experimental conditions

Experimental condition[1]	Number of animals	Percent with ulcers	Number of ulcers	Mean weight loss (g)
C H S T	50	76	434	99.5
NC H S T	20	30	44	79.8
NC H S NT	10	40	26	75.1
NC H NS T	10	0	0	54.7
NC NH S T	10	0	0	42.9
NC H NS NT	10	20	4	54.6
NC NH NS T	10	0	0	25.4
NC NH S NT	10	0	0	10.7
NC NH NS NT	10	0	0	29.2[2]

[1] S: Shock, NS: not shocked, T: thirst, NT: not thirsty, H: hunger, NH: not hungry, C: conflict, NC: no conflict.
[2] This group gained weight.
Source: From Sawrey, W. L., Conger, J. J., and Turrell, E. S. An experimental investigation of the role of psychological factors in the production of gastric ulcers in rats. *Journal of Comparative and Physiological Psychology*, 1956, 49, 457–461.

finding was that groups made hungry (with or without thirst and with or without shock) often developed lesions, which indicated that gastric lesions were highly dependent upon food deprivation.

Investigators subsequently used the conflict technique to study effects of other variables. For example, Ader, Beels, and Tatum (1960b) studied effects of early weaning, the variable recently focused upon by Ackerman and his colleagues. Ader and his associates compared animals weaned at 15 days of age with animals weaned at the usual time of 21 days and found that the animals weaned at an early age were more susceptible to conflict-induced lesions.

Despite the elegance and thoroughness of experimental conditions used in the conflict studies, serious questions about the interpretation of these studies have arisen since their completion. First, the type of lesion generally produced in these experiments was not an erosion in the lower, glandular portion of the stomach such as Selye had observed, but was a lesion that appeared in the upper, rumenal portion of the stomach. This type of lesion was that observed by Shay and his collaborators (1943) following ligation of the pyloric opening at the base of the stomach. Shay's experiments led him to conclude that these rumenal lesions were produced when acid gastric juice came into prolonged contact with the upper, rumenal portion of the stomach, a development that occurred in his studies when the pylorus was closed. The work of Shay and subsequent researchers has made clear that the development of similar rumenal lesion could also occur as the result of severe and prolonged food deprivation in an unligated stomach; apparently the prolonged absence of food contents from the stomach could also bring acidic gastric juice into sufficient contact with the rumen to cause lesions. Because the type of lesion developed in these early conflict studies is now recognized as highly dependent on food deprivation, it must be considered that the lesions found in those experiments could well have been a secondary consequence of the severe food deprivation that took place in those experiments. Thus, the different experimental conditions might well have had their effects on lesion development because they produced corresponding reductions in food intake. In other words, the various conditions may have caused animals to reduce the food intake by some amount, and the animals in each condition then developed lesions depending upon how little they ate. The correlation between weight loss in each group and lesion development (see Table 7-1) is consistent with this possibility.

Another difficulty was pointed out by Miller (1963). He pointed out that Sawrey, Conger, and Turrell (1956) had been quite ingenious in attempting to equate the shock for each animal in the conflict condition and its yoked partner by wiring the grids for these two animals *in series*. Electronically, the two animals therefore appeared as two resistors in the same circuit so that the shock they received was of the same duration and current intensity. But despite this, pointed out Miller, the two animals may still have received the shock through very different areas of their bodies so that the procedure used was not adequate for establishing that both animals received the same shock. For example, a yoked animal might learn to lie on its side so that it hardly felt the shock, whereas the conflict animal would necessarily receive the shock through its sensitive front feet as it moved towards the food. Thus, differences between these groups might be due to differences in the amount of shock received.

As a result of these criticisms, research on the influence of conflict diminished after publication of the original studies. It was not until 1969 that an experiment appeared which could not be questioned on the same basis as the original conflict experiments. At this time, Lovibond published an account of a study in which he immobilized animals and, while they were immobilized, presented the animals with stimuli that had been previously paired with food and shock. His results showed that simultaneous presentation of the stimuli for food and for shock resulted in more lesions than sequential presentation of these stimuli. Lovibond concluded that the presentation of stimuli signaling conflicting drive states could exacerbate gastric lesions. Lovibond's study does not encounter problems of prolonged food deprivation because the lesions were produced by an acute immobilization procedure, as described previously. Also, the different groups should not have received different amounts of shock because shock was administered to all animals under similar conditions before the immobilization procedure. On the other hand, because these animals were immobilized and therefore unable to actually perform appropriate approach and avoidance behaviors, the experiment examined only limited aspects of a normal conflict.

A relatively recent experiment on conflict (Weiss, 1971c) overcame the earlier problems by establishing a conflict without using food to motivate the approach response. Weiss first exposed rats to a situation in which the animal was required to respond (by wheel turning) to avoid or escape a train of shocks to its tail. After 24 hours, the conditions were slightly altered so that the animal thenceforth was given a pulse of shock whenever it performed the wheel-turning response so that responses which avoided or escaped from the train of shocks now also resulted in a brief shock to the tail. Thus, the animal now had to accept a small shock in order to avoid or escape a much larger shock. This conflict condition was maintained for 24 more hours, at the end of which time gastric pathology was determined. A yoked animal, matched to each "conflict" animal, was subjected to all experimental stimuli simultaneously, receiving the same shocks as the conflict subject throughout all phases of the experiment, but its behavior had no effect on the occurrence of shocks so that it was not "in conflict."

Weiss found that animals in the conflict condition developed considerably more severe gastric lesions than did matched yoked animals. The most sensitive measure of pathology was found to be the total length of lesioned tissue observed in the stomach.[1] For animals in the conflict condition, the median total length of gastric lesions was twice as large—5.8 millimeters (mm)—as for the matched yoked subjects (2.9 mm). Because food motivation was not involved in this conflict condition, all animals were completely deprived of food throughout the relatively brief period (48 hours) of the experiment so that differences in food intake could not affect lesions as had occurred in earlier studies. The lesions found by Weiss were all in the lower, glandular portion of the stomach. Also, all shocks were administered to both the conflict subject and its matched yoked subject through electrodes fixed on the animals' tails so that they could not alter the shock by changing their bodily position. Because the electrodes were wired in series, shocks for both the conflict and the yoked animal were identical in duration and current intensity. Weiss concluded that the conflict condition was one of the most ulcerogenic that he had worked with, which is consistent with observations that conflict in animals and humans is particularly ulcerogenic.

Another recent experiment demonstrating a new method for producing gastric lesions also testifies to the pronounced ulcerogenic capacity of conflict. Wald, Desiderato, and MacKinnon (1973) established a situation in which an animal remained on an elevated grid platform surrounded by a continuously charged grid floor, so that an animal would learn to remain on the elevated platform since it received the shock whenever it stepped down. Shocks were delivered periodically to the elevated grid platform, which occasionally drove the animal from it to the electrically charged floor below. Thus, a conflict situation was established because the animal's tendency was to leave the elevated platform when it received shock there, but it then received shock on the floor below. Wald and his colleagues found that this condition could rapidly induce gastric lesions, producing severe lesions within a few hours.

---

[1]Various methods for quantifying gastric lesions have been used. Initially, investigators noted only the presence or absence of lesions, but as it became apparent that the pathological process manifested itself as a continuum of changes, more sophisticated methods were developed. Scales for rating pathology were introduced. Also, in an effort to make scoring less subjective than occurs with scales, lesions have been counted, thereby yielding a "number of lesions" score as the quantification of pathology. Within the recent past, several studies (Ganguly, 1969; Sethbhakdi, Pfeiffer, and Roth, 1970) have used measurements of lesion length or area, showing that this technique can reflect differences that other quantification techniques may not detect. The technique employed in the experiment described here was to measure the length of each lesion in the animal's stomach, add the measurements together, and thereby obtain the "total length of lesioned tissue" for each subject.

Predictability

Prior to studies of conflict, investigators had been primarily concerned with the physiological processes related to gastric lesions and had been content to utilize any stressor condition that would produce the lesions. The studies of conflict marked the beginning of attempts to determine what significant psychological and behavioral factors in stressor conditions affect lesions. Following these investigations, another psychological variable was soon found to have important effects on gastric lesions—predictability of the stressor. Effects of predictability were determined in experiments that compared lesion development in animals that could predict when a stressor would occur with lesion development in animals that could not predict when a stressor would occur.

In one of the first such studies, Seligman (1968) was studying the behavior of animals that were pressing a lever for food. He compared the effects of introducing shock into this lever-press situation, contrasting shock that was preceded by a signal (predictable shock) with shock not preceded by a signal (unpredictable shock). Animals given predictable shock initially stopped lever-pressing but soon began to press again, whereas animals given unpredictable shock completely stopped lever-pressing. After three weeks in the lever-press situation, the animals were sacrificed and examined for gastric lesions. Eight animals that had received unsignaled shock were found to have lesions whereas no animals that received signaled shock showed evidence of lesions.

However, because gastric lesions were not the primary focus of Seligman's experiment, several factors enter this study which make the lesion findings difficult to interpret. First, because the animals were lever-pressing for food, animals in the signaled-shock condition, which recovered lever-pressing early in the experiment, were therefore eating during the test. In contrast, animals given unsignaled shock did not lever-press during the session and therefore were not eating at this time. Because gastric lesions are reduced by food intake and food contents in the stomach (e.g., Brodie and Hanson, 1960), the lesion differences observed could have simply been the result of eating differences that took place in the course of lever-pressing. Second, lesion differences may also have occurred because of systematic differences in the shock received by the groups. The signaled-shock group had a warning before the shock and might have made postural changes on the grid floor to reduce discomfort from the shock. Moreover, the fact that these animals tended to maintain lever-pressing meant that shocks would often be received through their tough rear feet. In contrast to this, animals in the unsignaled-shock group had no warning signal to use to adjust their posture. Because this group ceased lever-pressing completely, these animals are likely to have been standing with all four feet on the grid floor thereby receiving shock through their more sensitive front feet. Thus, the lesion differences might also have been due simply to the fact that animals in the unsignaled-shock condition received more severe shocks than did the animals in the signaled-shock condition.

Weiss (1968b, 1970) contrasted the effects of predictable and unpredictable shock under conditions in which shocks were delivered through fixed tail electrodes wired in series so that shocks were necessarily of the same duration and current intensity regardless of what postural changes the animals might attempt to make. These studies were conducted by exposing "triplets" of animals to the experimental conditions. A triplet consisted of three animals simultaneously exposed to the experimental conditions. In this case, a triplet consisted of one animal that received a signal before shock, one animal that received the same shocks but with the signal given randomly with respect to shock, and a third animal that received no shock. The time between each shock varied with the average interval being one minute; thus, animals could not learn when shocks would occur but depended entirely on the signal to predict them. The animals were maintained in these conditions for 19 hours prior to sacrifice. Because all subjects were completely deprived of food and water through the stress session, there was no possibility that differences in food intake could have played a role in the lesion differences observed.

The experiments showed that unpredictable shock was remarkably more ulcerogenic than predictable shock. Again, the most sensitive measure of pathology was the total length of lesions. The amount of gastric lesions found in subjects given unpredictable shock averaged 8.9 mm, whereas the subjects given predictable shock averaged only 1.5 mm of lesions. The amount of lesions found in non-shock controls was a negligible 0.5 mm. Thus, the stomachs of animals given predictable shock were more like stomachs of unshocked controls than like the stomachs of animals given unpredictable shock. Stomachs from a typical triplet are shown in Figure 7-7. As can be discerned from the figure, the major determinant of gastric lesions in these studies was the psychological factor of predictability, this factor being much more important than whether or not the shock occurred for a subject.

It should be noted at this point that several previous studies had examined effects of shock predictability on loss of body weight and depression of feeding and drinking (Brady, Thorton, and de Fisher, 1962; Paré, 1964; Friedman and Ader, 1965). One would assume that development of gastric lesions and weight loss should parallel one another as indices of "stress." However, the studies of weight loss all showed that predictable shock produced greater weight loss and more suppression of feeding and drinking than did unpredictable shock, which thus seemed opposite to the findings described above where gastric lesions were measured. However, in the earlier studies, shock was delivered through a grid floor, allowing for the possibility that animals could alter shock by changing bodily position. Weiss (1970)

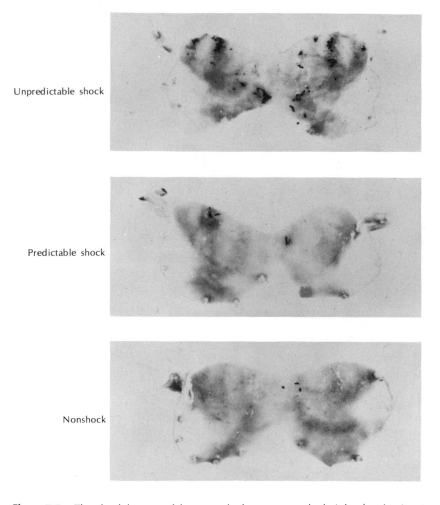

Unpredictable shock

Predictable shock

Nonshock

Figure 7-7. The glandular area of the stomachs from one matched triplet showing (top to bottom) the subject that received unpredictable shock, predictable shock, and no shock. (The lesions appear as intensely dark areas formed by clotted blood at the site of the lesion; the defects on the border of the stomachs are caused by pins holding the stomachs open.) (From Weiss, 1970.)

therefore measured changes in body weight and consummatory behavior with predictable and unpredictable shock delivered through fixed electrodes. This experiment found that greater weight loss and depression of food and water intake occurred in the unpredictable shock condition, a result consistent with the lesion results. Weiss suggested that the methodological difference in how shock was delivered was not a trivial one but, in fact, could reverse completely the results of predictability experiments. He suggested that giving shock through a grid floor could enable animals to practice "inefficient coping attempts" which could cause more pathological changes than would occur if an animal made no coping attempts. Since animals given predictable shock would be better able to initiate such deleterious behavior because of a warning signal, this could explain why the early studies of weight loss had found signaled shock to be more deleterious. He suggested that the use of fixed electrodes eliminated this confounding factor and enabled one to see clearly the effect of predictability.

Mezinskis, Gliner, and Shenberg (1971) confirmed that predictable shock produced more lesions than unpredictable shock when fixed tail electrodes were used. They observed this regardless of whether the unpredictable-shock subjects received no signal at all or a random signal. In addition, they found that it made no difference whether the shocks were always of the same duration or of different durations. Price (1972) also used fixed electrodes, but experimented with unrestrained animals (Weiss and Mezinskis, Gliner, and Shemberg had worked with moderately restrained animals). Price found that predictable shock resulted in less severe gastric lesions and less loss of body weight than did unpredictable shock, an outcome in agreement with that reported by Weiss and by Mezinskis, Gliner, and Shemberg. Thus, in experiments that have used fixed electrodes, the results have been consistent.

Why should predictability result in less pathology than unpredictability? There are obviously two alternatives. Predictability can be beneficial (1) because it tells the subject when the dangerous event is about to occur so that the subject can prepare for the stressor, or (2) because it tells the subject when the dangerous event will *not* occur; that is, it tells the subject when it is safe. Most experiments on predictability offer no basis for selection of either alternative. Seligman (1968) has suggested that the second of these alternatives—that the subject knows when it is safe—is the correct one, basing this conclusion on his behavioral data that showed that the animals given signaled shock would return to lever-pressing when the danger signal was not present. Comparing two different conditions that produced gastric lesions, Weiss (1970) also concluded that the value of a predictive stimulus was to inform the animal when it was safe. In one condition, a single "beeping" tone stimulus occurred before each shock; in the other, a series of tones preceded this beeping tone so as to establish a kind of "external clock." The external clock therefore better informed the subject of exactly when the shock would occur than did the beeping tone alone; thus, shock preceded by the external-clock should be less pathogenic if the benefit of predictability derives from knowing when the stressor will occur. On the other hand, the external-clock contained less safety time than did the single beeping tone because it continuously presented danger (tone) signals; thus, the single beeping tone should prove less pathogenic if the benefits of predictability derive from receiving stimuli that indicate the presence of safety. Weiss found that the single beeping tone resulted in significantly less severe lesions than the external clock, a result which is in agreement with Seligman's hypothesis that the benefits of predictability derive from its enabling the subject to know when it is safe.

Caul, Buchanan, and Hays (1972) also found results that agree with the "safety" hypothesis. They found that the extent of gastric lesions in several conditions was directly proportional to the amount of time that animals were in the presence of stimuli associated with the stressor. Seligman and Meyer (1970) presented further results that indicated predictability was beneficial because it produced safety, but again the primary focus of their experiment was on lever-pressing for food and the ulcer results cannot be interpreted because of differences in food intake, as has been explained before.

Finally, Paré and Livingston (1973) studied the effects of shock predictability on gastric secretion. They found that both the total amount of gastric secretion and the total acid output per hour decreased as a consequence of shock whether it was predictable or unpredictable. This occurred when restrained animals were tested with grid shock and when unrestrained animals were tested with tail shock. Gastric fistulas were used, so that the results were not compromised by possible misplacement of a stomach tube. The investigators' conclusion was that the gastric-lesion differences that develop in predictable-unpredictable shock experiments are the result of factors other than gastric secretions; this conclusion seems warranted.

Coping Behavior

One of the most obvious psychological factors that would seem to be of importance in any stressor condition is control over the stressor. What differences would occur if an animal was in control of a stressor in comparison with having no control over it? The first study specifically addressed to this question has become one of the most widely-read studies in psychosomatic medicine, the "executive" monkey study. These data were originally published by Porter et al. (1958) and by Brady et al. (1958), and the most well-known exposition of the results appeared in *Scientific American* (Brady, 1958).

The executive monkey phenomenon is based on results obtained from four pairs of monkeys. A pair of such monkeys is shown in Figure 7-8. In each pair of monkeys, one animal, called the "executive," was able to press a lever that avoided a strong unsignaled shock. Each lever press postponed shock onset for 20 seconds, so continued responses within 20 seconds of the last response could postpone shock indefinitely. Any failure to respond within 20 seconds resulted in a shock. This procedure, in which responses postpone shocks that are otherwise presented at regular intervals with no warning signal preceding them, is called an unsignaled, or Sidman, avoid-

Figure 7-8. An "executive" or avoidance-escape monkey (left) and a yoked monkey (right) in primate chairs during the avoidance procedure. (From Brady et al., 1958.)

ance schedule. The other monkey in each pair, called the yoked monkey, simply received shock whenever the executive monkey failed to postpone the shock. The yoked monkey in each pair therefore received the same shocks as the executive monkey but had no control over them.

In all four pairs, the executive monkeys developed duodenal ulcers and died whereas the yoked monkeys evidenced no pathology when they were examined. Actually, what occurred was that executive monkeys began dying in the apparatus and the lesions were subsequently discovered on autopsy; yoked animals were then sacrificed and no lesions were found in them. It was not until the last two pairs of monkeys were placed into this experiment that the investigators were clearly aware that the shock-avoidance procedure they were using was apt to cause duodenal ulcers. The excitement generated by these results can be sensed from the fact that the production of duodenal lesions by the shock-avoidance method used appeared to represent a genuine discovery.

Unfortunately, subsequent attempts to replicate the executive monkey experiment failed. When other experimental conditions were attempted, these also did not succeed. A subsequent experiment manipulated the duration of the stress session relative to the rest period but found no duodenal lesions. Other laboratories experienced a similar lack of success. Foltz and Millet (1964) reported that they could not reproduce the original results; in fact, the only pathology they observed appeared in a yoked animal. For over a decade, the executive monkey phenomenon seemed to be an anomaly.

In 1968, Weiss published a report that rats able to control shock (avoidance-escape animals) developed less severe gastric erosions than yoked rats that received the same shocks without having control over them. In this study, as in Weiss's study of predictability, matched triplets of animals were again exposed to experimental conditions simultaneously. A triplet consisted of one animal that could avoid or escape from shock by performing a selected response; a second animal that had no control over shock but was simply shocked whenever the first animal received shock; and a third control animal that was not shocked. A signal was presented (to all animals) 10 seconds before the delivery of shock, so that the shock was preceded by a warning signal in this experiment. Figure 7-9 shows the triplet arrangement.

As stated above, this experiment found that avoidance-escape animals developed less severe gastric lesions than yoked animals. Moreover, the results again showed the importance of psychological factors. The animals that could control shock developed an average of only 1.6 mm of lesions compared with 4.5 mm of lesions in the yoked animals. In comparison with the non-shock animals, which developed a negligible 0.5 mm of lesions, the avoidance-escape animals were therefore more similar to the non-shock controls than they were to their yoked "helpless" partners who had received exactly the same shock. Thus, it was seen that control of shock was a more important variable than whether or not shock occurred for the animal.

These results were, of course, opposite to the findings of the executive monkey study in which the avoidance-escape, or executive, animal had developed the more severe pathology. Weiss (1971a) subsequently published another experiment in which he tested the possibility that differences in the warning signal given before shock were responsible for these opposite findings. Whereas Weiss (1968) had given his avoidance-escape rats a warning signal before shock, the executive monkeys had not had any warning signal. Weiss therefore conducted an experiment in which some triplets of animals (avoidance-escape, yoked, non-shock) were given a warning signal before shock whereas other triplets received no warning signal before shock. Also, a third tone condition (called Progressive Signal) was included in which trip-

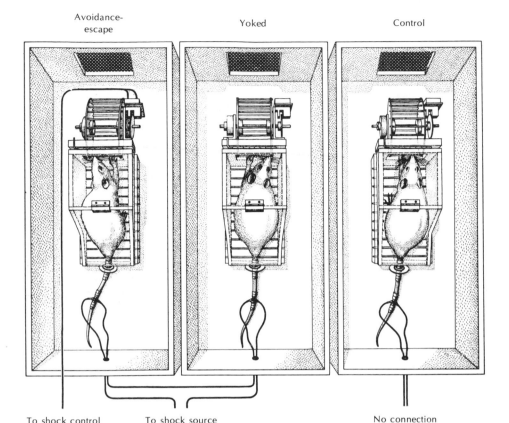

Avoidance-
escape   Yoked   Control

To shock control   To shock source   No connection

Figure 7-9. A matched triplet in a study of coping behavior. At left is the avoidance-escape animal, whose wheel is wired to the shock control. At center is the yoked animal, whose tail electrodes are wired in series with the avoidance-escape subject but whose wheel turns have no effect on shock. At right is the unshocked control subject.

lets received a complex warning signal before shock that formed a kind of external clock. Except for the difference in warning signals, the conditions for all triplets were the same. The results of this experiment are shown in Figure 7-10. Weiss's idea that the absence or presence of a warning signal before shock might reverse the effects of coping behavior was not supported; it can be seen that the avoidance-escape animals developed less severe gastric lesions in all warning signal conditions than did yoked animals.

Several studies have now confirmed that rats in control of shock develop less severe lesions than rats that are not in control. Gliner (1972) combined coping behavior and predictability differences. He gave all rats inescapable shock but allowed one group to choose for itself whether the shock would be preceded by a signal or not. This group developed the least severe lesions, with progressively more lesions developing in groups that were unable (a) to

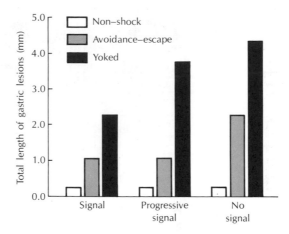

Figure 7-10. The median total length of gastric lesions for the non-shock, avoidance-escape, and yoked groups in the various signal conditions. For some triplets, a warning signal preceeded shock (Signal), for others a series of signals forming an external clock preceeded shock (Progressive Signal), and for others no warning signal preceeded shock (No Signal). (From Weiss, 1971a.)

choose, and (b) to both choose and predict shock. Also, Moot, Cebulla, and Crabtree (1970) showed that animals that could terminate a shock delivered while lever-pressing for food developed significantly less gastric lesions than animals unable to terminate the shock but given shock of the same duration. (Although this study was originally presented as a study of conflict, the experiment failed to show that there was any augmentation of gastric lesions by the conflict condition as contrasted with given inescapable shocks of the same duration to yoked animals. Because this difference must appear in order to establish the conflict condition as being effective [it had appeared in all conflict studies described in that section of this chapter], the study by Moot *et al.* is not relevant to conflict but does demonstrate the effectiveness of controlling a stressor.)

Despite the failure of Weiss's original concept to explain why the executive monkey experiment had found coping behavior to be detrimental, an explanation nevertheless emerged from his studies. Because of the large number of subjects used in the experiment (Weiss, 1971a), it was possible to analyze in detail the relationship between behavior and lesions in each of the different conditions. This analysis led to a formulation which stated that gastric lesions were a function of two variables.

First, gastric lesions were found to increase as the number of responses that animals made increased. On reflection, this was not surprising. When an animal is presented with a stressor stimulus, the animal will make coping attempts. Thus, gastric lesions, or "ulcerogenic stress," were found to be a function of the number of such coping attempts, or responses, that an animal made in a stressful situation.[2] The severity of lesions, however, did not relate to responding alone; it was observed to be equally related to a second variable—the informational feedback that animals received immediately after coping attempts. If responses immediately produced appropriate feedback—that is, if responses immediately brought about stimuli that had no connection with the stressor—then the ulcerogenic condition did not occur. On the other hand, if responses failed to produce such stimuli, then ulcerogenic stress did occur. Weiss referred to the appropriate feedback, which consisted of stress-free stimuli, as "relevant feedback." A non-ulcerogenic coping attempt, then, was one that immediately produced relevant feedback. The second functional relationship stated that the more relevant feedback that occurred from coping attempts, the less the gastric lesions.

It was possible to express these relationships in mathematical form, which is shown in Figure 7-11. This model is generated from the two functional relationships I have described; that is, that gastric lesions increase as the number of responses increases, and that gastric lesions decrease as the amount of relevant feedback increases. The resultant function is a plane; in any condition where the number of responses that an animal makes and the amount of relevant feedback it receives can be determined, the extent of gastric lesions that should develop can be predicted by taking the point of intersection and projecting up to the plane. The height of the plane above the base of the model defines the amount of lesions that are expected.

This model has had a number of applications. First, the data obtained by Weiss (1971a), which is shown in Figure 7-10, fit the model quite well, as is shown in Figure 7-12. Second, the model was used as a basis for carrying out additional experiments. One of these was the conflict experiment described on p. 248. Because the occurrence of a shock immediately after each coping attempt would mean that the relevant feedback from coping attempts would be extremely low, the model predicted that the punishment (or conflict condition) should be highly ulcerogenic, and this was found to be the case. Another experiment (Weiss, 1971b) demonstrated the converse. When a tone stimulus followed a response to increase relevant feedback, gastric lesions were reduced considerably under conditions that were otherwise ulcerogenic.

Third, the model suggested why animals that are in control of stressful situations should develop less severe lesions than animals that have no

---

[2] This does not mean that the responses themselves *cause* lesions but simply that responding and lesion severity can be seen to increase together; that is, that they are correlated. This was pointed out in an article entitled "Psychological Factors in Stress and Disease," by J. M. Weiss (*Scientific American*, June 1972, pp. 104–113).

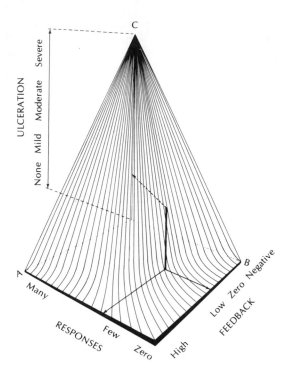

Figure 7-11. This three-dimensional figure describes the proposed relationship between responses, feedback, and gastrointestinal lesions (ulceration). The relationship is a plane which shows how the two independent variables, responses and feedback, are related to the dependent variable, ulceration. The arrows show how this plane is used. Where the number of responses made and amount of feedback obtained for such responding intersect, the amount of ulceration is determined by the height of the plane above this point. (For ease of reading this figure, responses and feedback are labeled across the axes in the foreground. These labels are customarily placed along the axes in the background which are parallel to the ones bearing the labels. It therefore should be noted that feedback designations apply to the axis from Point A to the intersection of the three axes, and response designations apply to the axes from Point B to the intersection.) (From Weiss, 1971a.)

control. Because animals that have no control over a stressor cannot, by definition, produce any relevant feedback by responding, the amount of relevant feedback for such animals is necessarily fixed at zero. These animals therefore develop lesions in direct correspondence to the number of responses that they emit, and since the plane (see Figure 7-12) shows considerable elevation above the zero feedback continuum, these animals lesion severely. In contrast, avoidance-escape animals generally produce relevant feedback that is greater than zero; since the elevation of the plane is considerably lower when feedback exceeds zero, these animals will therefore lesion less severely.

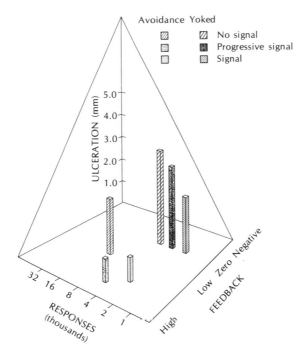

Figure 7-12. Results from Figure 7-10 presented in relation to the model shown in Figure 7-11. For each group that received shock, the amount of ulceration (height of bar) is shown at the point where responding and feedback for that group intersect. (From Weiss, 1971a.)

Finally, the model described above also led to an explanation for the executive monkey results. Since the monkeys developed duodenal ulcers and the rats developed gastric erosions, this explanation obviously rests on the assumption that the psychological and behavioral principles invoked affect both lesions similarly; if this assumption is not correct, the explanation is invalid. The explanation is as follows: Careful inspection of the conditions used in the executive monkey experiment revealed that the monkey in each pair that was made the executive was chosen for this group because it showed a higher rate of responding on an initial pretest than did the other subject, which was made its yoked partner (see Brady et al., 1958). Thus, executive monkeys were selected for a higher rate of responding than yoked subjects, and therefore, according to the theory, were more likely to develop lesions than their yoked partners. Moreover, the Sidman (unsignaled) avoidance schedule provided the executive animals with a relatively low amount of relevant feedback, since there were no external warning signals to be terminated by correct responses. This combination of factors—a high rate of responding and a low amount of relevant feedback—is specified by the theory to be optimal for development of lesions. Weiss (1971b) was able to show that in a similar population of avoidance-escape and yoked pairs of rats, selected for higher responding amongst the avoidance-escape animals, the avoidance-escape animals developed significantly more severe gastric lesions than yoked animals under a Sidman-type avoidance condition. Thus, Weiss concluded that the executive monkey study represented a highly unusual situation in which the normally-beneficial effect of having control over a stressor was reversed, but nevertheless a situation that readily could be explained in accordance with the model shown in Figure 7-11.

Subsequent experiments have also considered issues relevant to the executive monkey phenomenon. Barbaree and Harding (1973) reported that a Sidman schedule could be used to produce more lesions in avoidance-escape animals than in yoked animals even if the avoidance-escape animals were not selected for higher responding at the outset. These investigators found that, in seven pairs of animals, all avoidance-escape animals developed clearly discernible lesions while only one yoked animal showed any evidence (and a minute amount) of gastric pathology. These results differ somewhat from those found by Weiss in that Weiss only obtained this result when he selected high-responding avoidance-escape animals that were matched with low-responding yoked animals. However, inspection of the results reported by Barbaree and Harding indicated that the avoidance-escape subjects in that experiment showed a remarkably high rate of responding while their yoked animals showed a relatively low rate. Using an apparatus similar to that used by Weiss, Barbaree and Harding's avoidance-escape animals responded at a rate 27 times as great as that of their yoked animals, whereas in the studies reported by Weiss, his avoidance-escape animals averaged 3.2 times the response rate of yoked animals. Thus, according to the explanation presented above for the executive monkey phenomenon, the avoidance-escape animals used by Barbaree and Harding should indeed have shown severe pathology. Barbaree and Hardy concluded that their results were consistent with this formulation.

Tsuda and Hirai (1975) have recently shown that by manipulating both responding and feedback characteristics, it was also possible to reverse the normally beneficial effects of having control over shock. Working with matched triplets of animals in an apparatus similar to that shown in Figure 7-9, Tsuda and Hirai required avoidance-escape animals in different triplets to make either 1, 2, 5, or 8 responses in order to avoid or escape shock. As the response requirement increased, the amount of responding obviously increased and the amount of relevant feedback from each response also decreased. Thus, gastric lesions amongst avoidance-escape animals were expected to increase as the response requirement increased. These results, shown in Figure 7-13, were obtained. Avoidance-escape animals showed progressively more lesions in each successive response condition. Yoked

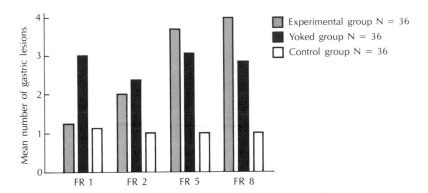

Figure 7-13. Mean number of gastric lesions for the experimental (avoidance-escape), yoked, and control groups in the various conditions. FR stands for fixed ratio, and the numeral denotes the number of responses required to avoid or terminate shock. (From Tsuda and Hirai, 1975.)

animals showed generally similar amounts of lesions in all conditions. Whereas avoidance-escape animals showed significantly less severe lesions than matched yoked animals when only 1 response was required to control shock, avoidance-escape animals showed more severe gastric lesions than yoked animals when 8 responses were required to control shock. The results thus again indicated that the effectiveness of a coping response depends on the rate at which it must be emitted and the relevant feedback received for the response.

Goesling, Buccholz and Carreira (1974) perhaps extended the "response rate" issue to a logical extreme when they required avoidance-escape animals to be inactive in order to control the shock, comparing such animals with yoked subjects. When avoidance-escape animals were required to not move in a wheel in order to avoid shock, they developed significantly less severe lesions than yoked animals; only 3 of 15 avoidance-escape animals developed lesions, whereas 13 out of 15 yoked animals developed lesions.

An ambitious experiment recently carried out by Natelson (1976) studied whether the principles described above could be used to develop chronic lesions in monkeys. A major problem in testing any explanation for the executive monkey phenomenon is that chronic lesions have not been obtainable in monkeys since the original observation. Natelson therefore used conditions designed to be highly stressful in order to simply determine whether chronic lesions could be obtained in the monkey. The experiment consisted of three stages beginning with random unavoidable shocks, progressing to unsignaled shock avoidance-escape (Sidman) sessions, and concluding with the use of several punishment (conflict) paradigms. Stomach pathology was assessed throughout all phases of the experiment by endoscopy carried out twice weekly. Of the eight monkeys studied, one developed no lesions, four developed gastric lesions, and three developed duodenal lesions. In all cases, however, the lesions were short-lived, disappearing in less than a week and in no case classifiable as a chronic ulcer. Lesions were seen more frequently during the conflict condition toward the end of the experiment than in the earlier stages. The investigator reported that there was some tendency for animals with higher response rates to show more pathology than animals with low response rates, but this relationship was quite weak. Natelson's study is of importance in that it employed sophisticated behavioral techniques and continual monitoring of gastric pathology. The experiment confirms that, unfortunately, the executive monkey population was obviously highly susceptible to duodenal ulcers for reasons that are presently unknown, and that such susceptibility does not characterize monkeys now generally used in experimentation.

A small number of studies have examined secretion of acid during avoidance-escape responding. Polish et al. (1962) studied gastric secretion in monkeys on the same avoidance schedule that had been used in the executive monkey experiment. When effects of an acute avoidance session were studied, suppression of acid output and total gastric secretion was seen initially, followed in some cases by an increase in acid output when the avoidance session was terminated. When subjected to four weeks of avoidance conditioning, some of the monkeys showed an elevation in acid output, but the individual differences were quite large. It is interesting to note that the two monkeys that showed the greatest acid output throughout the chronic avoidance procedure were found to have duodenal erosions at the conclusion of the experiment. Paré (1972) found that when animals had previously been trained on a Sidman avoidance schedule for 12 days prior to measurement, the volume of gastric secretion decreased but the total acid output was also found to increase. Overall, the results of experiments that have examined gastric secretion indicate that the initial response to a stressful situation is a decrease in gastric secretory function but that certain long-term procedures, such as Sidman avoidance, may be capable of elevating total acid output in certain subjects.

An intriguing observation also made in the monkey experiments was reported by Brady (1964). One of the monkeys in the gastric secretion study pulled out its fistula, externalizing part of the gastric mucosa which could then be observed by the investigators during the experiment. They observed that, during avoidance-escape periods, the mucosa became engorged with blood and that during "time-out" periods, it blanched. Wolf and Wolff saw similar engorgement develop in their human patient, Tom, during periods of emotional excitement. This change is of particular interest for the present discussion in that engorgement of the mucosa is suspected to occur as part of the pathological sequence leading to erosions in the rat (see p. 239).

Aggression

One study has examined effects of shock-induced fighting on development of gastric lesions. This study, carried out by Weiss, Pohorecky, Salman, and Gruenthal (1976) showed that administration of tail shock to two animals in the same apparatus so that they would fight in response to shock caused these animals to develop less severe gastric lesions than animals which received the same shocks while alone. The results were remarkable. The animals shocked together attacked each other vigorously, as shown in Figure 7-14. But despite the attacks, bites, and wounds, these animals developed less severe lesions than animals shocked simultaneously but alone. The average amount of lesioned tissue found in animals that fought was 3.2 mm whereas the average in animals shocked alone was 8.2 mm. Another pair of animals in each experimental run was also shocked together but with a grid of Plexiglas bars between the two animals; these animals reared up and made aggressive responses toward each other but could not make contact because of the Plexiglas grid between them. Such animals showed a similar reduced amount of lesions (3.9 mm) as did animals that were allowed to fight, showing that the reduction in gastric lesions was not the result of the physical contact that took place during the fight but of the behavioral responses involved in making the aggressive gestures toward the other animal. To rule out the possibility that fighting behavior might reduce gastric lesions simply because it involved shocking two animals in the same location, a second experiment was carried out. This experiment found that if two animals were shocked in the same place but with a solid, opaque barrier between them so that they did not make aggressive gestures toward one another, they developed gastric lesions as severe as those of animals shocked alone. Thus, the presence of two animals receiving shock in the same location was not sufficient to produce the effect; visual contact and the aggressive response were apparently the significant factors.

Conclusion

In 1931, Dr. Harvey Cushing, professor of surgery at Harvard Medical School, stated at the outset of his Balfour lecture (Cushing, 1932):

> It is only in man that ulcers occur spontaneously with any considerable frequency and it is not at all improbable that the prevalence, particularly of duodenal ulcers, has something to do with the strain and stress of modern life; for people today rarely find it possible to enjoy the comparatively placid existence enjoyed by their forebears. All clinicians are familiar with the facts: (1) that "highly-strung" persons are particularly susceptible to "nervous indiges-

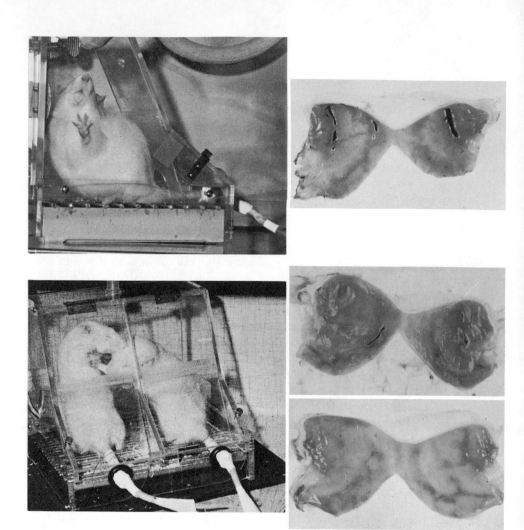

Figure 7-14. On the left side, at the top is shown an animal in an individual apparatus responding to shock, while at the bottom are shown two animals together in a "double" apparatus responding to the same shock by fighting. Opposite, on the right side of the figure, at the top is shown the stomach of the animal shocked individually which shows severe lesions, while at the bottom are shown the stomachs of the two animals that fought in response to the same shock.

tion" and associated ulcer; (2) that ulcers become symptomatically quiescent or even tend to heal when patients are mentally and physically at rest, and (3) that symptoms are prone to recur as soon as the victim of the disorder resumes his former tasks and responsibilities."

This statement, made nearly a half-century ago, attests to the fact that clinicians have long been aware of the potential relationship between stressful conditions and nervousness on the one hand and gastrointestinal disorders on the other. What, then, has experimental animal research contributed to this problem area in the intervening years?

As a result of experimentation, it is no longer necessary to base certain important conclusions on clinical anecdotes. Perhaps the most significant of these conclusions is that psychological factors play a major role in regulating gastric pathology. In adequately designed studies of conflict, predictability, coping behavior, and aggression, the data consistently show that psychological factors can be even more important than a physical stressor in determining the severity of gastric pathology. Figure 7-10, for example, shows this clearly. In this figure, it can be seen that control animals receiving no shock at all developed a negligible amount of pathology (median = 0.5 mm lesions). Considering the animals that did receive shocks, one can see that when the shocks were controllable (avoidable-escapable) and also preceded by a warning signal (second group from left), the amount of pathology that occurred was not much more severe than in the non-shock conditions (median = 1.0 mm). However, for the group shown on the extreme right, wherein the shock was neither controllable nor preceded by a signal, pathology was much more considerable (median = 4.5 mm). Summarizing these results, it is evident that very little of the variability is attributable to the presence or absence of shock; most of the variability is attributable to differences in controllability and predictability, psychological variables in the situation.

Perhaps the most striking confirmation of the importance of psychological factors comes from the recent study of aggression. Animals that were shocked together so that they fought and wounded one another actually developed considerably less severe lesions than animals shocked by themselves. Moreover, animals that displayed the fighting behavior but without physically attacking one another because of a barrier between them showed a similar reduction in lesions to that seen in the animals that fought with physical contact. Thus, in this study, the physical trauma involved in fighting clearly had no measurable effect on the degree of gastric pathology; it (a) certainly did not lead to greater pathology amongst animals that fought in comparison with those receiving the shock alone, and (b) did not produce any difference from animals that engaged in fighting behavior without physical contact. On the other hand, expressing the aggressive response considerably reduced gastric lesions. Thus, these results provide an instance in which a physical stressor of considerable intensity (striking, biting, etc.) made no measurable contribution to the development of gastric lesions, while behavioral/psychological aspects of fighting behavior had considerable influence on pathology.

Beyond establishing the importance of psychological factors, however, the legacy of experimentation becomes more speculative. There are, however, intriguing suggestions. Cushing referred to the "highly-strung" person as being particularly susceptible to gastric pathology. In reviewing the research on the psychological/behavioral basis of gastrointestinal disorders, one continually sees indications from the experimental data that Cushing (and others) have grasped a valid and significant relationship here, however vague. For example, a number of experimenters have noted a relationship between gastrointestinal lesions and elevated motor activity in experimental animals. Ader and his associates found that animals developed more lesions when restrained during periods of the day when they are normally more active than they do when restrained during periods when they are normally less active (Ader, 1967a). Sines and his colleagues, who bred ulcer-susceptible rats, found these rats to be more active in an open field (Sines, 1961) and also superior to normal animals in a type of avoidance task (a shuttle task) that is well-learned by highly active rats (Sines, Cleeland, and Adkins, 1963). Weiss found that gastric lesions were directly related to the number of "coping attempts", or responses, animals emitted in a variety of situations (Weiss, 1971a, b, c). Paré (1975) has now thoroughly investigated a remarkable phenomenon in which food-deprived rats, if allowed to exercise on a running wheel, show inordinately high rates of activity and concurrently develop very severe gastric lesions, whereas animals similarly food-deprived but not allowed to exercise on a running wheel do not develop gastric lesions.

All of these experimental observations suggest that there is some relationship between motor activity and gastric lesions. What seems most likely, of course, is that some aspect of central activation, originating in the brain, results in both the initiation of motor activity and the initiation of physiological processes which, if prolonged, lead to gastric lesions. Thus, skeletal activity would be a correlate of vulnerability to gastric lesions. However, we cannot yet dismiss the possibility that high levels of activity could activate certain brain areas or visceral organs through neural afferents and thereby play some role in promoting lesions. The implausibility of this need not be debated; the issue will be settled by examining gastric lesion development in animals that are in some way paralyzed to eliminate skeletal motor activity.

To speculate a bit further, one of the more intriguing aspects of the data that relates activity to gastric lesions is the possibility that such findings point to a basic biological relationship extending beyond gastric lesions. Does hyperactivity, or what it reflects as occurring in the central nervous system, mark susceptibility to a number of diseases? Friedman, Jenkins, and others (e.g., Friedman and Rosenman, 1959; Jenkins, 1971; Glass, Snyder and Hollis, 1974) have pointed out that continual activity and lack of ability to relax mark individuals with high susceptibility to coronary heart disease. This pattern, which they call the "type A" coronary-prone behavior pattern, is marked by intense striving, impatience, restlessness, and is particularly evidenced by an extreme time pressure to get things done that the individual perceives himself as being under. Whether this profile also can be related to individuals having an increased susceptibility to gastrointestinal disorders remains to be seen, but the descriptions do sound similar to that given, for example, in Cushing's lecture.

This discussion must not end without acknowledging that such patterns which emerge so promisingly have definite exceptions. There is hardly a serious clinical investigator who cannot relate experiences with a well-integrated individual who nevertheless has a history of chronic gastrointestinal disturbance. On the experimental side, well-respected investigators have also failed to find relationships between activation and gastric lesion formation. Bonfils and his associates have reported failures to find that struggling in restraint is consistently related to lesion development (Dubrasquet et al., 1971). Ackerman and his colleagues have also recently found that groups that develop severe lesions in their experiments show little activity during the time when the lesions develop. Clearly, there are basic principles which we do not yet understand so that we are not yet able to reconcile the conflicting results which do not support some of our observations. However, it is through further experimentation that these questions will be answered; the promise lies in the method.

Psychosomatic Disorders and Biofeedback: A Psychobiological Model of Disregulation

Gary E. Schwartz
Yale University

Introduction

This model is about self-regulation and feedback systems in the human brain, and about what happens to the normal adaptive functioning of bodily systems regulated by the brain when the feedback mechanisms are disrupted. This breakdown in feedback mechanisms is termed *disregulation* (Schwartz, unpublished manuscript). I propose that disregulation can contribute to malfunctioning of bodily tissues, referred to as psychosomatic disorders in medical terms. However, to understand how feedback systems break down and produce alterations in biology and behavior, it is first necessary to understand the nature of normal feedback mechanisms and to appreciate their unique role in maintaining the structure and functioning of living systems. Gaarder (1975) has recently said that "the concept of feedback is a major focus around which modern biology has been reorganized." In the future, the same will likely be said to be true for medicine and the behavioral sciences.

The model I will outline has its origins in a broader psychobiological analysis of personality and medicine I have developed (Schwartz, in preparation). The starting point for this analysis is that the final common pathway for coordinating and regulating bodily processes, and therefore overt behavior and subjective experience, is the brain. Because the systematic application of this point of view to psychosomatic disorders is relatively new, the first half of the chapter will be devoted to a general introduction to the brain and its regulation by means of feedback. After briefly reviewing the paradox of brain self-regulation and its relationship to feedback and human consciousness, I will present a more detailed analysis of biological systems and feedback mechanisms. I will then introduce the concept of psychosomatic disorders as a functional illness of disregulation, placing special emphasis on essential hypertension as a model system. I will look at both genetic and experiential factors from the perspective of disregulation, and will analyze biofeedback and other behavioral procedures for correcting disregulation. Finally, I will present a psychobiological analysis of so-called placebo effects and illustrate an unexpected and potentially dangerous consequence of modern drug and surgical therapies—inadvertent perpetuation of disregulation.

The Paradox of Brain Self-Regulation

Although we do not usually think about it, we are constantly regulating complex patterns of our brain processes as part of our interaction with the environment. This capacity for neural self-regulation is extraordinary, especially when we consider the fact that the human brain, consisting of 10 billion neurons, manages to keep track of and coordinate thousands of separate body parts designed for registering information inside and outside the body (here called *input devices*) and influencing the physical and chemical environments inside and outside the body (here called *output devices*). Not only does most of the regulation go on without our normally being aware of the underlying processes, but the brain is so constructed that it is impossible for us to consciously experience these processes, even if we were to choose to do so.

When I talk about the paradox of brain self-regulation, I am referring to the fact that not only does the conscious brain have an inherent inability to be aware of much of the feedback that participates in regulating bodily responses, but it is incapable of experiencing *any* of the feedback involved in regulating itself. I have suggested that this is a core trait of human biopersonality (Schwartz, in preparation) and that it has many philosophical and behavioral implications. This may explain not only why brain feedback and self-regulation concepts have taken so long to be recognized, but also why experienced clinicians and scientists, as well as laymen, find the concept of brain self-regulation so difficult to accept once it has been clearly pointed out.

Recent research in biofeedback and the self-regulation of physiological processes illustrates the paradoxical nature of brain self-regulation. As defined by Miller (1974) biofeedback is

> . . . the use of modern instrumentation to give a person better moment-to-moment information about a specific physiological process that is under the control of the nervous system but not clearly or accurately perceived. In the terminology of servo systems, such information has been called feedback. Such information about a biological process is called biofeedback.

The inability of the conscious brain to recognize and accept the fact of its own self-regulation is illustrated in biofeedback studies where visual or auditory feedback is presented for specific changes in brain wave activity. It has been found that subjects given biofeedback for alpha readily learned to control the predominance of their alpha frequency, an EEG signal of 8-13 hertzes (hz) recorded over the occipital region (reviewed in Beatty, 1977). Initially, this discovery was received with surprise and wonder, because the data implied that subjects could learn to directly control their brain waves. Before this experimental demonstration, no one had actually observed a person regulating his brain waves, so brain regulation was not generally recognized.

The second reaction to brain wave biofeedback studies was equally interesting. When the question was asked, "how were the subjects controlling their brain waves?" the explanations were given in terms of events that could be *consciously* perceived—they tensed their muscles, moved their eyes, thought arousing thoughts, or regulated their attention (Lynch and Paskewitz, 1971). But the conclusion that regulation of occipital EEG is associated, for example, with movements of the eye does not answer the fundamental question, "how does the person control his eyes?" The answer should be that the *brain* regulates much of what the eye does, and the brain performs its regulation based on multiple sources of feedback impinging on it at any one moment—including feedback from the eye itself (Gaarder, 1975). In the process of regulating its eyes, the brain changes its electrochemical configuration, which is expressed electrophysiologically in the EEG. In other words, eye movements and EEG are *two different indexes of the same thing—the brain's self-regulation.*

The approach taken in this model is that the brain constantly regulates itself and thereby controls its multiple output devices, including skeletal muscles, smooth muscles, and glands. This regulation is based on the total configuration or *pattern* of feedback to the brain through its input devices. The reception and mode of processing this input is a function of programming (genetically layed down and then subsequently modified through maturation and learning). If this regulation goes astray, causing specific output devices to be either over- or underactivated, the output devices can develop structural anomalies or injuries diagnosed as disease, and require medical intervention.

Feedback between the Brain and its Body

Situated at the top of the body, encapsulated in a strong, protective structure (the skull), the brain is anatomically limited in that it is capable of directly responding to primarily two kinds of signals—neural and humoral. Despite this limitation, the brain is capable of processing information derived from various forms of energy, such as force, temperature, and molecular vibrations in the air. This sensitivity to multiple forms of energy results from highly sophisticated input devices or transducers that convert these energy forms into neural impulses that it can understand. Although we may say "I see with my eyes" (this is the way we experience our perceptions) what we are actually doing is *using* our eyes so that our *brain* can see. The class of senses providing feedback to the brain about the environment outside of the skin are called *exteroceptors*, the five basic ones being vision, hearing, taste, touch and smell.

A second "environment" to which the brain is sensitive is the set of neural and chemical inputs provided from interoceptors located *inside* the body, but outside of the brain. Experientially, we feel that we *are* our bodies, not our brains (which we cannot normally experience). But structurally, the reverse is actually the case. It is the brain that experiences its body.

A detailed discussion of the brain's inability to recognize at an experiential level that *it* is experiencing the environments under and outside the skin is beyond the scope of this chapter (see Schwartz, in preparation). Nor is it feasible to present a detailed discussion here of the anatomy of the brain and body. The reader should consult a recent introductory book about the structure and function of the human organism (Thompson, 1975; Beatty, 1975; Teyler, 1975). An especially enjoyable presentation of material regarding the brain's role in regulating the body can be found in *The Body Has A Head* by Gustave Eckstein (1969).

It is important to recognize that the normal brain not only processes, but correctly *localizes* the actual *source* of stimulation in the environment. This property has crucial adaptive consequences for survival of both brain and body. If the thumb of the right hand is accidentally broken it is imperative that the brain correctly locate the injury and insure that the thumb is not used until it is sufficiently healed. The interoceptive input devices thus serve as an important feedback mechanism by stimulating the brain to perform the appropriate regulation. As will become clear, when this feedback mechanism breaks down, the health of the body and the brain can deteriorate, and disregulation is said to exist.

Feedback mechanisms between the brain and its body are extremely complicated, and a sizable number cannot be consciously perceived by the brain. Interoceptive input devices providing neural stimulation to the brain include stretch receptors in the muscles, temperature and pressure receptors in a variety of organs including blood vessels, and chemoreceptors responsive to such factors as the concentration of carbon dioxide in the blood. For example, when we voluntarily hold our breath, carbon dioxide builds up in the blood stream and stimulates chemoreceptors feeding into respiratory regulation areas in the lower brain stem. The lower brain stem in turn activates the respiratory output system, thereby causing expansion of the chest, and we take another breath. However, *consciously* we experience neither the actual build-up of carbon dioxide in the blood nor the resulting neural feedback to the lower brain stem. What we experience instead are peripheral proprioceptive sensations activated in the struggle to keep from breathing. If the lower brain stem is "fighting" to force the respiratory apparatus to take another breath, then what system is holding the respiratory apparatus back from doing so? The conclusion must be that some *other* part of the brain must be simultaneously counteracting the lower brain stem reaction. Research suggests that "voluntary" regulation of this type in humans occurs in the highest centers of the cortex, especially the frontal cortex (Luria, 1973).

The brain is capable of influencing the interoceptive and exteroceptive environments by controlling bodily output devices. It activates and coordinates the temporal sequence and force of skeletal muscles that control exteroceptive input devices, such as eye movements, and other skeletal muscles that move the bones and therefore the body; it also orchestrates the myriad visceral and glandular output devices necessary for maintaining the health of the body and of the brain itself. The brain as an organ has no *internal* means of sustaining itself. It has no means, for example, of taking oxygen from the air, combining it with other nutrients, or circulating these life-supporting supplies to its tissues. Rather it closely regulates a set of output devices that are designed to perform a particular function, such as the lungs (for absorbing oxygen from the air), the stomach (for converting foods from the external environment into a form that the tissues can use), and the heart (for pumping the nutrients to each of the individual cells). For the brain to be able to keep track of this complex regulation, it must have the capability of monitoring the actual state of its effectors through interoceptive input (feedback) devices. In this way, the brain not only makes sure that it gets what *it* needs, but also ascertains that all input and output devices of its body are regulated properly.

From this perspective, it becomes clear that the brain has the major responsibility for the care of itself and its body. Its ability to maintain health depends on a capability to register and process feedback signals from the bodily organs. In order to understand and treat functional disorders caused by over- or underactivity of specific organs, medicine is just beginning to recognize that it must look not only at the peripheral manifestations of disease in the body, but also at the brain, the master organ of regulation.

Unfortunately, a major problem is that clinicians experience the same paradox of brain self-regulation as their patients. Consequently, they too are functionally blind to the realization that it is the brain, and not the peripheral organs that is the regulator of much disease. Similarly, physicians do not recognize that teaching a person to control his diet or teaching a person to "think happy thoughts" are fundamentally the same process: both require the patient to regulate his *brain* for the sake of his bodily health. But I will return to this point later.

Feedback, Homeostasis and Biological Systems

Feedback is one of the most important, yet elusive, phenomenon in nature. Feedback applies equally well to both living and nonliving systems. The term *feedback* refers to the process by which information is returned to a regulating system for the purpose of influencing the stability of the system. A simple mechanical example of a nonliving feedback system is the governor of a steam engine (Gaarder, 1975). The purpose of the governor in a steam engine is to keep the speed of the engine constant. If the engine goes too fast, a device is required that will automatically cut the steam to the engine, thereby slowing the engine. Conversely, if the engine goes too slowly, a device is needed to increase the steam pressure to the engine, thereby increasing the speed of the engine. This can be achieved by the use of some very simple feedback mechanisms.

For example, according to one procedure a pair of weights attached to an axle spins in synchrony with the engine. Consequently, the faster the axle spins, the more centrifugal force is produced, and the further the weights are extended from the axle. The weights in turn are connected to a valve controlling the flow of steam to the engine. If the weights are attached so that the farther they extend from the axle, the steam pressure to the engine is less, a negative feedback loop is created. In this way, faster axle turning leads to less steam, and slower axle turning leads to more steam. With this basic device, the speed of a complex steam engine can be finely regulated.

It is not surprising that feedback systems evolved from an engineering tradition employing precise mathematics and models are typically illustrated by block diagrams that depict the components and their interrelationships. For the steam engine example, one would draw two blocks, one representing steam to the engine, the other representing the speed of the engine. (See Figure 8-1.) The relationship between the two blocks is depicted by arrows. Steam to the engine is shown influencing the engine speed. The feedback link is drawn in the opposite fashion, from the speed of the engine to the steam generator. This shows that the engine speed affects the steam to the engine, the direction sometimes indicated by (−) for negative or (+) for positive feedback. It is important to recognize that negative is the condition that leads to stability. Positive feedback produces exactly the opposite effect. If the governor had been connected so that the faster the spin, the more the

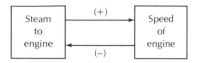

Figure 8-1. Feedback regulation of the speed of a steam engine. (From Gaarder, 1975.)

steam, it would constantly augment whatever change in speed the engine happened to be showing. In other words, positive feedback serves to amplify (rather than inhibit) the function to which it is connected.

Feedback can occur in mechanical, electrical, chemical, or neural forms. All have particular relevance to biological systems. The link between nonliving and living systems was discovered in the 1940s by researchers in cybernetics (Wiener, 1948). *Cybernetics* can be viewed as the science of applying feedback principles. In recent years, *biocybernetics* has emerged; it places special emphasis on the interaction between man and machines, especially computers. In feedback terms, the issue is one of directly providing the computer with feedback of human physiology and behavior in such a way that the computer can alter the person's physiology and behavior in an adaptive fashion. Biofeedback can be seen as a branch of biocybernetics.

The relevance of feedback models to physiology and psychosomatic disorders is found in the notion of homeostasis. *Homeostasis* refers to the biological feedback process by which physiological variables are kept within certain limits for the purpose of survival (Langley, 1965). This process was posited by the French physiologist Claude Bernard in the last century and elaborated by Walter Cannon during the first decade of this century. Cannon's classic volume *The Wisdom of the Body* (1939) states this position beautifully, and the book deserves to be read today for its prose and insight. The emphasis of this chapter on the role of the brain in detecting the state of bodily processes and subsequently regulating these processes for health is a direct extension of the homeostasis concept.

It is unfortunate that homeostasis traditionally is associated with "automatic" and "involuntary" systems, for this association limits its general application to the regulation of physiological systems. For example, whereas the maintenance of blood pressure during periods of "fight or flight" was viewed as a homeostatic mechanism (Cannon, 1939), the regulation of fine motor movements by peripheral and central feedback mechanisms was not. Movement was thought to be under voluntary control. Although establishing a dichotomy between involuntary and voluntary systems may be a useful way of describing which adjustments are more autonomous than others, this does not mean that they act according to different underlying principles. I think that it is more fruitful to consider feedback mechanisms in the regulation of *all* physiological processes and then consider what different neuropsychological mechanisms are possible for processing information and achieving regulation.

Functional Feedback Systems in the Brain

Given that the brain has to deal with *multiple* processes, where does the *organization* of processing and regulation occur? Should we view each neuroanatomical subdivision as separate and independent or is it more appropriate to look for integrations of specific input and output messages to meet specific needs? Current neuropsychology suggests that in order to understand how the brain regulates inputs and outputs, it is necessary to consider the concept of "functional systems", originally described by Anokhin (1935). A recent statement of this position is discussed in Luria's (1973) book *The Working Brain*. Consider first Luria's discussion of functional systems as they relate to complex bodily processes:

> When we speak of the "function of digestion" or "function of respiration", it is abundantly clear that this cannot be understood as a function of a particular tissue. The act of digestion requires transportation of food to the stomach, processing of the food under the influence of gastric juice, the participation of the secretions of the liver and pancreas in this processing, the act of contraction of the walls of the stomach and intestines, the propulsion of the material to be assimilated along the digestive tract, and finally, absorption of the processed components of the food by the walls of the small intestine.
>
> It is exactly the same with the function of respiration. The ultimate object of respiration is the supply of oxygen to the alveoli into the blood. However, for this ultimate purpose to be achieved, a complex muscular apparatus incorporating the diaphragm and the intercostal muscles, capable of expanding and contracting the chest and controlled by a complex of nervous structures in the brain stem and higher centers, is necessary.
>
> It is obvious that the whole of this process is carried out, not as a simple "function", but as a *complete functional system* embodying many components belonging to different levels of the secretory, motor and nervous apparatus (p. 27).

Luria argues that the model of functional systems should be applied equally to the structure of the brain itself. In the same way that respiration cannot be localized solely in the lungs, or digestion solely in the stomach, neither can the neural regulation of breathing be localized solely in a single respiratory "center" in the brain. According to Luria, the brain coordinates *multiple* areas of neural tissues to meet specific functional goals.

Luria goes one step further by providing a foundation for understanding the relationship between cognitive processes and multiple systems in the brain. According to Luria:

> Mental functions, as complex functional systems, cannot be localized in narrow zones of the cortex or in isolated cell groups, but must be *organized in systems of concertedly working zones, each of which performs its role in complex functional systems*, and which may be located in completely different and often far distant areas of the brain (p. 21).

However, how do these processes become organized? Are they all interconnected at birth, or are additional neural functional systems created in the individual brain through experience and feedback from the external environment? Luria is very explicit on this point, emphasizing the special nature of the human brain to modify itself with external feedback.

With Luria's analysis, we come full circle in describing a general model for viewing feedback of multiple processes as functional systems, including external environmental inputs. At this point, it becomes possible to examine the nature of psychosomatic disorders in terms of the psychobiology of brain disregulation.

Psychosomatic Disorders and Disregulation

The term *psychosomatic* has had a long and arduous history. The word is derived from the Greek words "psyche" and "soma". Psyche in ancient times meant soul or mind, although more recently it has come to mean behavior as well. On the other hand, soma typically referred to the physical organism; the body. Thus we see contained in the word psychosomatic the classic split between mind (or behavior) and body. Psychosomatic disorders were considered to be those physical disorders whose etiology could be attributed to psychological causes. (Lachman, 1972.)

The term psychosomatic is often used loosely in everyday language to refer to various aches and pains that are not accompanied by obvious physical damage, and therefore are attributed to existing only in the mind of the person who suffers from them. However, the more appropriate medical term for this condition is *hypochondriasis*. The term psychosomatic should be reserved for only those conditions where organ pathology can be documented.

Another long-standing distinction in medical literature concerns disorders of the autonomic nervous system versus those of the central nervous system. Traditionally, disorders of the autonomic nervous system that had emotional components were considered to be psychosomatic, whereas disorders of the skeletal neuromuscular system were given another diagnosis, such as conversion hysteria (Lachman, 1972). Interestingly, within this distinction headaches having a vascular origin (e.g., migraine) would be classified as psychosomatic, whereas headaches having muscular origin (e.g., tension headache) would not be.

However, these distinctions have outlived their usefulness, particularly from the point of view outlined in this chapter. For example, it is important to distinguish disorders caused directly by local tissue injury (e.g., viruses or physical traumas) from disorders primarily mediated by neural disregulation of the brain. The former are usually classified as biological and the latter psychological. However, this designation carried to an extreme results in an artificial and counterproductive separation. In point of fact, once we accept the important role that the brain plays in regulating bodily functions, it becomes clear that *all* disorders have both a biological and "psychological" component because the ability of a tissue to recover from local traumas depends in part on the brain's capability to recognize the trauma and regulate itself accordingly.

Similarly, although it is important to distinguish between pain initiated at the periphery (so-called real pain) versus pain initiated in the brain itself (sometimes called feigned pain), it is equally important to recognize that in the final analysis, both pains are psychological in that they are perceptions of the brain. Finally, there is value in distinguishing between autonomic versus skeletal neuromuscular disorders to the extent that they represent different tissues with different neural innervations. But to call one psychosomatic and the other something else creates a false dichotomy. Both types of disorders may well develop as a consequence of brain disregulation, and therefore both should fall under the category of psychosomatic.

From this perspective, *all* disease has both a biological and psychological component. More appropriately stated, all disease at the periphery has both a local component and a more central, neural component. This conclusion has been independently drawn by Whatmore and Kohli (1974) in their book *The Physiopathology and Treatment of Functional Disorders.* Their approach emphasizes the importance of neural feedback for the etiology and treatment of functional disorders, and we will later consider their analysis in more detail.

Functional disease can involve any organ system in the body, including the brain itself. Classic examples of psychosomatic disorders having important neural components include essential hypertension (high blood pressure), certain forms of tachycardia and other cardiac arrythmias, Raynaud's disease (peripheral constriction in the hands and feet), hives, ulcers, asthma, migraine headaches, low back pain, colitis, constipation, and vomiting. A more inclusive list emphasizing the contribution of environmental stimuli to the etiology of disorders would contain the hyperventilation syndrome, affective disorders (anxiety, depression and aggression), insomnia, menstrual irregularities, and dysmenorrhea, impotence, and frigidity (Whatmore and Kohli, 1974). However, if the list were to be entirely complete, it would have to include *all* disorders of the body, from the common cold to cancer. Research shows that a person's *susceptibility to all disease* and *speed of recovery* from disease is influenced by his psychobiological state (Bakan, 1968; Graham, 1972).

My theory is that disregulation enters into all these conditions, although it is easiest to illustrate in those disorders whose primary etiology involves the over- or underactivity of the neural systems that govern them (Schwartz, in preparation). The basic model is as follows: When the environment places demands on a person, his brain performs the regulations necessary to meet the specific demands. Depending upon the nature of the environmental demand or stress, certain bodily systems will be activated, while others may be simultaneously inhibited. However, if this process is sustained to the point where the tissue suffers deterioration or injury, the negative feedback loops of the homeostatic mechanism will normally come into play, forcing the brain to modify its directives to aid the afflicted organ. Often this negative feedback loop causes the experience of pain.

For example, if a person is eating while he is very active his stomach may be unable to function properly. Consequently, the stomach may generate negative feedback to the person's brain, which is experienced as a stomach ache. This corrective signal should serve the important function of causing the brain to change its regulation in specific ways, such as to lead the person to slow down and allow digestion to occur more normally. The pain serves a second function in that it "teaches" the brain what it can and cannot do if the stomach is to work properly. The adaptive brain is one that can learn through its mistakes and learn to anticipate the needs of its organs.

Figure 8-2 illustrates this basic process. Stimuli from the external environment (Stage 1) enter the brain (Stage 2) by means of sensory input (not shown) and the brain deals with this stimulation overtly by controlling its motor output (not shown). The stomach (Stage 3) is also regulated by the brain, and it can in turn influence the brain's regulation of itself by its negative feedback loop (Stage 4). However, the brain may not regulate itself effectively to meet the stomach's needs. The reasons for this can be quite varied. There are four major stages where disregulation is thought to occur:

Stage 1: Environmental Demands. The stimuli from the external environment may be so demanding that the brain is forced to ignore the negative feedback from the stomach. A person placed in unavoidable stress must continue to act in certain ways despite the negative feedback that tells him to change his behavior. Many previous theories of psychosomatic disorders have emphasized this stage (see Graham, 1972).

Stage 2: Information Processing of the Central Nervous System (CNS). The brain may be programmed, initially through genetics and subsequently through learning, to respond inappropriately to stimuli present in the external environment (or internal environment). Thus, although the negative feedback from the abused organs may be present, the brain may be disinclined to respond in an appropriate fashion. In other words, the brain may select to act in ways that will lead it to ignore the corrective negative feedback or use that feedback in ways that are deleterious for the peripheral organ.

Stage 3: Peripheral Organ. The organ in question may itself be hyper- or hyporeactive to the neural stimulation coming from the brain. This is the literal translation of what had sometimes been called the "weak organ" theory of psychosomatic disorders. It can explain why, in response to

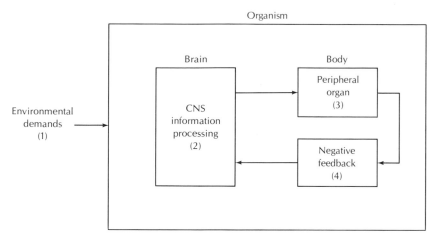

Figure 8-2. Block diagram depicting (1) environmental demands influencing (2) the brain's regulation of its (3) peripheral organs, and (4) negative feedback from the peripheral organ back to the brain. Disregulation can be initiated at each of these stages.

the same environmental stress, different human organs ultimately become dysfunctional (Sternbach, 1966). It is possible that the brain cannot regulate itself to compensate for the altered negative feedback, or finds itself no longer capable of modifying the functioning of a diseased organ (whether the disease initially is caused by Stages 1 and 2, by a local injury, or by a biological agent—for example, a germ).

Stage 4: Negative Feedback. Finally, it is possible that the negative feedback derived from the peripheral organ may itself be inappropriate. In other words, it is possible for the protective negative feedback systems to become less effective and in extreme cases to be inactivated. This would have negative consequences for the health of the organ. The extreme example of this condition can be seen in people born without the normal system to respond to pain (Melzack, 1973). These people are constantly in danger of severely injuring themselves, for they lack the natural protective mechanism for detecting and therefore coping with injury.

Although the etiology of disregulation can occur at any of these four stages, the general consequence of disregulation is the same in each case. By not responding appropriately to negative feedback, the brain fails to maintain stable regulation of the organ in question, and disregulation (with its accompanying instability) emerges. This analogy is an extension of feedback models and cybernetics (Powers, 1973), and has already been shown to be of value in understanding the regulation of sensory and motor processes (Gaarder, 1975).

The concept of disregulation provides a framework for uncovering mechanisms that underlie a disorder regulated by nerves. Not only can disregulation occur at each of the four stages in the system, but problems can occur simultaneously at multiple stages of the system. In the extreme case, if (1) a person was exposed to demanding stimulation in his environment that required continued adaptation (Stage 1) *and* (2) his brain processed the sensory information and reacted inappropriately because of genetic or learning deficiencies (Stage 2) *and* (3) the peripheral organ itself reacted inappropriately because of genetic or maturational deficiencies (Stage 3) *and* (4) the peripheral feedback mechanisms from this organ were also ineffective (Stage 4) this *pattern* of factors would increase the likelihood of the person developing a specific psychosomatic disorder. Because the brain and body are composed of multisystems that must be coordinated in an integrated fashion, it becomes necessary to examine each of the components and then consider how they combine to produce the final outcome we call disease.

The concept of disregulation may be viewed as an extension of current psychobiological theories of psychosomatic disorders. For example, Whatmore and Kohli (1974) have developed a neuropsychological theory linking brain function with peripheral disease. They emphasize the concept of physiological feedback and are among the earliest clinicians to use biofeedback procedures in the treatment of functional disorders. Although they do not make the point explicitly, their analysis implies disregulation of interactions between the brain and the body.

The cornerstone of Whatmore and Kohli's (1974) psychosomatic model is the concept of physiological *signaling*. They propose that disease results from "signaling errors" within the physiologic feedback system. There are two basic kinds of signals: action-potentials (nerve impulses) conducted along neurons, and molecules or ions (chemical signals) transmitted by the blood stream and tissue fluids. Whatmore and Kohli emphasize a special mode of signaling or feedback which they refer to as "ponesis" or "ponetic signaling." Ponesis comes from the word "ponos" meaning effort, work or toil. They summarize the mechanism of ponetic signaling as follows:

> Ponesis consists of action-potential output from the premotor and motor cortex and includes the consequent action-potentials in descending pathways, side branches, lower motor neurons skeletal muscles, and the various feedback pathways . . . Ponetic signalling consists of the signalling effects within an organism that result from ponesis. Since ponesis occurs in covert as well as overt forms, some ponetic signalling is extremely subtle, especially in the human organism (p. 16).

If errors arise in the signaling of any of these systems, dysponesis is said to be present, and functional disorders may develop. Dysponesis, then, is an example of disregulation.

Disregulation and Essential Hypertension

Having considered psychosomatic disorders and disregulation in general terms, it is now possible to apply this approach to specific disorders. Essential hypertension is a good model system because its underlying regulatory mechanisms are fairly well understood. It also illustrates some of the theoretical and practical consequences surrounding the brain self-regulation paradox because its negative feedback system is completely silent and unperceived by the conscious brain.

Essential hypertension refers to high blood pressure of unknown etiology. "Unknown" means that the cardiologist cannot attribute the cause to any local, peripheral injury or disease. This is not to say that he cannot locate where in the plumbing of the cardiovascular system the pressure is being increased, but only that the cause of this localized change is not readily apparent. It is usually implicitly assumed, but not stated, that in these cases the high blood pressure is regulated in part by overactive neural or humoral control (or both) by the brain. Between 90 and 95 percent of all cases of hypertension have no known etiology and therefore are labeled *essential*. High blood pressure is a serious medical problem, estimated to affect between 15 and 30 percent of the population in the United States. Concern with hypertension is largely due to its association with increased risk of coronary artery disease and cerebrovascular accidents (Kannel, Schwartz, and McNamara, 1969), the major causes of death in the United States today.

The cardiovascular system is a closed loop feedback system that has a pump (the heart) for circulating blood through its massive interconnected network of arteries, arterioles, capillaries and veins. This system is incredibly complex and the brain coordinates numerous factors that are a part of it. The average heart over the course of 70 years generates over 3,000,000,000 beats, pumping over 150,000 tons of blood in its lifetime (Eckstein, 1969). Even more amazing is the total length of the capillary beds alone—if connected and laid end to end, they would create a thin pipe reaching several times around the earth.

A simplified, but useful feedback diagram of the physiological mechanisms that regulate arterial blood pressure is shown in Figure 8-3 (from Shapiro and Surwit, 1976). The brain regulates two major systems, the heart and the vascular, with the former having dual innervations of sympathetic and parasympathetic neural fibers, and the latter having only sympathetic fibers. The vascular system is influenced by three pathways, all initially regulated by the brain: the first, a direct sympathetic pathway; the second, the adrenals and kidney; and the third, the skeletal muscles. The heart is regulated by the brain through direct sympathetic and parasympathetic fibers; second, by peripheral respiratory events; and third, by feedback

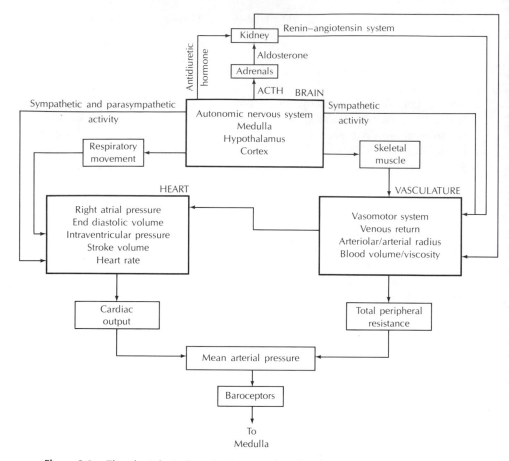

Figure 8-3. The physiological mechanisms employed in the regulation of arterial blood pressure. The diagram oversimplifies the processes in order to provide a general overview of mechanisms most relevant to behavioral manipulation. Boxes labeled Heart, Brain and Vasculature each contain a subset of relevant systems and functions. Although these are not necessarily temporally or functionally related in the order presented, the outside arrows indicate the site at which other systems exert their influence on the system described in the box. The reader should note the numerous and diverse pathways through which behavioral control over blood pressure could be exerted. For example, relaxation techniques acting on the musculature could have their main effect on the vasculature, producing a decrease in peripheral resistance. Yogic exercises emphasizing breath control might have their main effect on cardiac output by changing intraventricular pressure. Although the diagram suggests that a feedback approach including both cardiac and vasculature parameters would be most efficacious, it illustrates how verbal instruction acting on the cortex might also affect blood pressure. (From Shapiro and Surwit, 1976.)

from the vascular beds themselves. It follows that mean arterial pressure is the product of the pressure exerted by the total output of blood ejected by the heart and the resistance it encounters from the peripheral vasculature. Consequently, blood pressure is at all times a complex, constantly changing product of specific cardiac and vascular factors.

The cardiovascular system is sufficiently flexible to provide special circulatory needs to local tissues and organs automatically without awareness on the part of the brain (Schwartz, 1974). For example, if the brain initiates movement in the right hand, local changes in these vascular beds will be elicited to meet the specific metabolic requirements of the hand muscles. The brain achieves this cardiovascular regulation by means of *internal* neural feedback loops within the brain itself, plus additional peripheral feedback from the body that indicates the actual state of the output devices in question. In this way, the cardiovascular system is designed to meet the metabolic needs of the brain and all other tissues of the body. Depending upon the specific *pattern* of bodily responses, the cardiovascular system will be *patterned* by the brain to meet these specific demands in the most effective and effortless manner possible.

The brain receives major neural feedback of mean arterial pressure from specially designed input devices called *baroreceptors*, situated in the carotid sinus arches and in various vessels of the cardiovascular system. These receptors transduce pressure to neural pulses; the higher the pressure (from about 20 to 200 millimeters of mercury (mmHg)), the higher the frequency of the pulses to the brain. The baroreceptors function as a negative feedback loop. The higher the pressure, the greater the neural firing, which leads the brain to regulate the heart to beat more slowly (primarily by increasing parasympathetic firing to the heart), and also to produce dilation of the vasculature (by decreasing sympathetic firing to arterioles). The converse occurs when blood pressure decreases. Thus, with a normally functioning baroreceptor feedback loop, the brain achieves highly stable regulation of its blood pressure.

Neural regulation of blood pressure is highly complex, and it employs multiple pathways in the brain. Cohen and MacDonald (1974) outline six major organizational features of these functional pathways. Although the exact details of their model need not concern us here, two features of their analysis are important for the present discussion. First, an "exercise" pathway originating in the motor cortex can be separated from a "defense" pathway originating in the amygdala. Postulating two relatively separate functional systems helps to explain how a person could have large blood pressure increases during simple exercise (involving no danger) or large increases in pressure in response to a threatening situation (which demands minimal skeletal movement). An example of simple exercise would be jogging relatively leisurely. Examples of "stress" conditions requiring minimal motor exercise would be doing complex cognitive problems under time pressure (e.g., mental arithmetic) or immersing your hand or foot in painfully cold ice water. Although both experiences result in increased cardiovascular functioning, the *pattern* of the increases is *not* identical because they are generated by different neural mechanisms.

The second major point is that the six functional systems do not usually operate independently. Rather, systems may combine their work depending upon the environmental demands placed upon the brain. For example, there is a major difference between running through the forest and running through the forest with a bear in hot pursuit. Whereas the former might primarily involve the exercise system, the latter would likely simultaneously involve both the exercise and defense systems.

Stage 1: Environmental Demands

With this basic information about the regulation of blood pressure, it is possible to examine the literature on the etiology of essential hypertension from the perspective of disregulation. Let us first consider (Stage 1) *the nature of the environmental stimuli that the brain is exposed to, and the demands placed on the brain by the environment for dealing with them.* It is now well documented that many hypertensive patients live in environmental conditions that require the brain to prepare for continued action (exercise) and threats such as danger and pain (Gutmann and Benson, 1971). Herd, Kelleher, Morse and Grose (1974) demonstrated in studies with lower primates that conditioning procedures that require animals to remain vigilant and to continue responding in order to avoid painful stimulation result in marked elevations in their blood pressure. Clinicians have long noted that demanding environments requiring continued behavioral adjustment to avoid threat or danger are associated with stimulus elicited bouts of high blood pressure in humans (Gutmann and Benson, 1971). In light of our interactive analysis of the exercise and defense pathways in the regulation of the cardiovascular system, it is understandable how this particular *combination* of environmental conditions can lead to elevated pressure.

The question remains, however, whether environmental conditions *alone* can ultimately lead the brain to produce sustained hypertension and accompanying organ damage. The answer to this is not known. However, when stressful environmental conditions are *combined* with the other three stages underlying disregulation, the probability of developing hypertension is increased dramatically.

Stage 2: CNS Information Processing

Second, let us consider how negative feedback from the baroreceptors might be used (and misused) by the brain to protect its cardiovascular system and itself. I stated earlier that as the first response to increased baroreceptor findings the brain would act to keep blood pressure levels as low as possible, at the same time meeting the demands made by the environment. However, a second consequence might be reduction of the negative input of the environmental stimuli by dampening of cortical receptivity to the exteroceptive input devices. This notion of a sensory dampening effect is based on the observation that feedback from the baroreceptors not only modulates the lower medullary centers, but can also influence higher cortical centers as well. This mechanism is the foundation of Lacey and Lacey's theory concerning the role of blood pressure and heart rate in modulating attention to environmental stimuli versus attention to such internal stimulation as imagery (Lacey and Lacey, 1974). Lacey and Lacey have argued that in conditions requiring an active processing of stimuli from the environment, it is adaptive for the heart to slow down, thereby reducing baroreceptor firing and thus increasing sensitivity of the cortex. Conversely, it is adaptive for heart rate and blood pressure to increase during performance of complex cognitive tasks that require minimal distraction from environmental stimuli. In this instance feedback from the baroreceptors further inhibits the influence of external stimuli on the cortex.

Although the relevance of this theory to normal heart rate and blood pressure is debated, there is little question that under extreme conditions the mechanism can have a powerful effect. For example, research using decorticated animals has shown that rage reactions can be intensified if the baroreceptors are removed, whereas it is possible to inhibit rage reaction if the baroreceptors are strongly stimulated (Bartorelli et al., 1960). Dworkin has recently suggested that a similar mechanism may apply to hypertensive humans (Miller and Dworkin, 1977). He suggests that placed in an environment that stimulates aggressive tendencies but does not allow the release of these reactions, people may be reinforced for having high blood pressure. Besides aiding in the inhibition of the rage reaction, this would lead to attenuation of the negative inputs from the environment through baroreceptor influence on the cortex. In other words, the brain may inadvertently learn to use this natural feedback loop for a purpose at odds with the needs of the cardiovascular system and thereby lead to its destruction. Miller and Dworkin use the term "anti-homeostasis" to describe this phenomenon, and it closely parallels the general model of disregulation I describe.

To summarize thus far, the brain may learn to disregulate its cardiovascular system, thereby using the negative feedback from the baroreceptors to elicit a coping strategy that is biologically maladaptive to the health of the cardiovascular system. This notion of disregulation illustrates how environmental stimuli and demands (Stage 1 of disregulation) can lead to *learned* alterations in brain adaptation and coping (Stage 2). Many other factors can also contribute to disregulation at Stage 2, including those initially produced through genetics and subsequently modified through experience. It has long been known that hypertension runs in families (e.g., Zinner, Levy, and Kass, 1971) and a genetic contribution has been inferred, although not yet proven. However, a number of genetic studies in lower animals, particularly rats, indicate that rats can be bred for hypertension, its effects apparent as early as 2 days after birth (Jones and Dowd, 1970). Some reports are now indicating that high blood pressure has been observed in young children as well (Zinner, Levy and Kass, 1971).

When we speak of genetic factors, however, we should not consider them as independent of other contributions such as environmental demands (Stage 1). For example, it has long been noted that blacks tend to be more prone toward developing hypertension than whites, but these differences can be attributed in part to the greater stress placed on blacks than whites in the environment of the United States (Gutmann and Benson, 1971). On the other hand, recent data has shown that black newborns have higher resting heart rates than white newborns, suggesting that there may be an initial predisposition for the development of hypertension that is then accentuated by the appropriate environmental demands (Schachter, Kerr, Wimberly and Lachin, 1974).

Observing a genetic difference does not describe the neurophysiological mechanisms underlying its expression. Is the difference due to greater reactivity on the part of the brain to incoming stimuli (Stage 2), is the difference due to alterations at the *periphery* in terms of the structure of the organ itself (Stage 3), or does the difference depend on whether the peripheral feedback mechanisms are intact (Stage 4)—which could, in turn, influence Stage 2 and Stage 3? At the present time, no one knows the answers to these questions.

One clue implicating genetic components to Stage 2 brain processes grows out of personality studies suggesting that hypertensive humans tend to react inappropriately to aggressive or threatening situations (Harris et al., 1953). To the extent that this temperament characteristic has a genetic component (Buss and Plomin, 1975), it is reasonable to hypothesize that the neural systems that express these temperament characteristics partially regulate the cardiovascular system as well. However, the data for such theorizing are not substantial. Until more personality studies on neurophysiology are conducted, the mechanisms that express genetic components will remain a mystery (Schwartz, in preparation).

Little systematic research has been conducted on environmental conditions that lead the brain to *ignore* or *misuse* the negative feedback coming from the baroreceptors and consequently develop disregulation that would be expressed as hypertension. Clinicians have long noted that patients who have essential hypertension appear to be overly inhibited in their expression of anger and anxiety. Alexander's (1939, p. 176) description of this condition is a classic in early psychodynamics:

> According to this assumption, the typical course of essential hypertension might be described as follows: The maturing individual in the course of his life gradually becomes more and more confronted with the complex problems of maintaining his and his family's existence, his social position and prestige. In our present civilization all these tasks unavoidably involve hostile competitive feelings, create fears, and require at the same time an extreme control of these hostile impulses. Those who through constitution or through early life experiences have acquired a greater amount of inhibitions will handle their aggressions less efficiently than others and will tend to repress them. On account of

their inhibitions they cannot find socially acceptable legitimate vents for their aggressive feelings, and thus these hostile impulses become accumulated and increase in intensity. It must also be borne in mind that the neurotic individuals who are more than normally blocked in relieving their hostilities and aggressions usually become inhibited also in many other respects, particularly sexual expression. All these inhibitions make them, in their struggle for life, less effective, create feelings of inferiority in them, stimulate either envy, and increase their hostile feelings toward their more successful, less inhibited competitors. These hostilities again require a greater amount of control and thus lead to greater inhibitions, greater inefficiency, and in turn again stimulate hostile envious, and competitive tendencies.

A number of studies not only provide support for Alexander's description of the hypertensive personality but also provide a foundation for a more psychobiological analysis of this behavioral configuration. In a series of studies, Graham and associates (reviewed in Graham, 1972) showed that hypertensive patients, as compared to patients with other psychosomatic disorders, tend to express the specific attitudes of being threatened and having to be constantly on guard for danger. Furthermore, when these same attitudes are suggested to normal subjects under hypnosis, increases in blood pressure are observed. Hokanson and his colleagues (Hokanson, Burgess and Cohen, 1963) have demonstrated that if normal subjects are angered, their pressure will rise and remain so throughout the experiment unless they are allowed to express their aggression.

A peripheral physiological mechanism for sustaining high blood pressure during a suppressed rage is suggested by the fact that isometric *tension* (which would be found in a person who was continually tensing his muscles) leads to sustained elevations in pressure, whereas isotonic *action* (such as moving one's muscles while running) has less of a pressure increasing effect (Lind et al., 1964). Returning to Figure 8-3, it is reasonable to speculate that conditions that lead to continued skeletal readiness for activation of aggression and behaviors appropriate to danger are associated with elevated cardiac output and peripheral resistance. If this response is not dissipated, blood pressure levels will remain high.

The brain self-regulation paradox is particularly evident in the early development of hypertension, because feedback from high blood pressure is not normally perceptible to either the child who is developing hypertension or to the parents who unknowingly aid in its production. The child experiences no sensation of sustained high blood pressure, nor do his parents recognize that the child may be learning to maintain this high level in order to be accepted by the family. Let us assume that the child in question tends to have a low tolerance for frustration (possibly due to genetic factors). Further assume that he is continually teased and bothered by a younger sibling. This may elicit aggression. However, when the child attempts to express his aggression overtly, either to the sibling or the parents, he is punished. Punishment serves to suppress the aggression, *one* cause of which is increased pressure. To avoid punishment and receive praise, the child learns to inhibit the aggressive response. Unfortunately, unknown to either the child or his parents, he is learning to maintain high blood pressure as part of the inhibition of aggression (Schwartz, 1976). In the process, the child's brain learns to ignore high pressure signals from the baroreceptors or, as hypothesized by Dworkin, to utilize them differently (Miller and Dworkin, 1977). Disregulation of the cardiovascular system is the result in either case.

This capacity of the brain to ignore negative feedback is a major component of early psychodynamic theories of neurosis, psychosomatic disorders, including hypertension (Alexander, 1939). Recently, neuropsychological evidence has provided a mechanism for explaining this phenomenon. In an important paper entitled "Implications for Psychiatry of Left and Right Cerebral Specialization: A Neurophysiological Context for Unconscious Processes" Galin (1974) indicates how mental events in the right hemisphere can be disconnected functionally from the left hemisphere. By the inhibition of neural transmission across the cerebral commisures, which connect the two hemispheres, each half may continue with a life of its own. Because normal, verbal consciousness is localized primarily in the left hemisphere, a functional disconnection would result in the left hemisphere being essentially unconscious of emotional processes occurring in the right. We have recently discovered something that supports Galin's theory. In response to emotional questions, the average person tends to move his eyes to the left (indicating relative right hemisphere activation), whereas in response to nonemotional questions, the person tends to move his eyes to the right (indicating relative activation of the left hemisphere (Schwartz, Davidson, and Maer, 1975). Extending this observation to denial and repression in psychosomatic disorders, Gur and Gur (1975) have reported that people who tend to persistently move their eyes to the left regardless of the type of question score higher on scales of denial *and* report higher incidence of psychosomatic complaints. These data, in combination, suggest the intriguing hypothesis that the brain can, under certain conditions, learn to cope with negative affective physiological states by functionally severing communication across the two hemispheres. The conscious brain would then perceive a reduction in the affective processes. In fact, these processes are actually accentuated because the inhibitory control of these processes by the left hemisphere is no longer being provided, and a state of disregulation exists.

Stage 3: Peripheral Organ, and Stage 4: Negative Feedback

The last two stages of the disregulation model, which concern possible differences in peripheral organ responsivity and the peripheral negative feedback, have received the least systematic analysis. This is partly due to the fact that researchers in psychosomatic medicine have only recently recognized the importance of examining underlying components of complex systems in order to understand normal and disordered regulation. Also, it is extremely difficult to disentangle these last two factors in a living human being. However, we can briefly illustrate their relevance to normal regulation and disregulation because they likely play an important role as functional disorders develop.

For example, it is well known that hypertension develops in stages; the early labile stage is associated with high cardiac output, and the latter stabile stage is associated with sustained peripheral resistance (reviewed in Forsyth, 1974). The sustained peripheral resistance is believed to be a structural change in the vasculature (Stage 3) caused by repeated high pressure initiated by the heart. Consequently, in the early stages of hypertension the brain responds to increased baroreceptor firing by decreasing heart rate and dilating the periphery, thereby effectively lowering the pressure. But later the brain is no longer effective in returning the pressure to normal. The brain's effort to decrease heart rate cannot compensate for the high peripheral resistance that is no longer responsive to the brain's neural or humoral commands. What does the brain do when its output devices are no longer able to perform? One likely effect is that the brain will become fatigued and habituated, and in the process learn that high pressure is now normal. In other words, as a result of a structural change at the periphery (Stage 3) the brain (Stage 2) may end up modifying its *interpretation* of the feedback (Stage 4) accordingly. This in turn accentuates the disregulation and has a further negative consequence on the cardiovascular system.

The sustained pressure can also affect the baroreceptors themselves (Stage 4). The baroreceptors may themselves become fatigued and habituated because of sustained high pressure, and so become less capable of generating the appropriate high rates of neural firing. Consequently, the brain would receive false feedback information suggesting that the blood pressure is lower than it actually is. In turn, the brain would exert less effort in inhibiting the heart and vasculature. The result would be further disregulation and instability of pressure.

To summarize, disregulation of blood pressure can occur at various stages, which when combined, may produce a functional disorder having serious consequences for survival. Beginning with specific conditions imposed on the brain by the outside environment—especially aggressive stimulation (Stage 1)—the environment interacts with the genetic constitution of the brain, leading it to respond in specific ways (Stage 2). The learned changes in the brain can be brought on by environmental training (such as parents reinforcing children for the inhibition of aggression) or self-training (the Dworkin baroreceptor hypothesis). When we consider possible changes at the periphery, including the capability of vasculature to respond to neural innervation by the brain (Stage 3), or the capability of the baroreceptors to correctly generate the negative feedback (Stage 4) we begin to understand how *vicious circles of disregulation* can lead to marked instability of the cardiovascular system.

By considering the role of multiple processes in the etiology of disregulation, we can see how patients with hypertension differ in what has caused the disorder in them. This helps explain how the inhibition of aggression may be present in *some* hypertensive patients, yet not be crucial to *all* hypertensive patients. Consideration of multiple processes allows for an appreciation of the natural time course of disregulation, and of how factors that may have originally *initiated* disregulation may no longer be critical to the later *maintenance* of disregulation. This realization provides the foundation for carefully assessing the etiology and maintenance of disregulation in a given patient, and utilizing different stages of the disregulation in order to bring the disorder back under more regular control.

Treatment of Disregulation in Essential Hypertension

The ultimate test of a good diagnostic procedure is that it successfully matches treatment procedures to each patient's needs. Analyzing psychosomatic disorders in terms of disregulation can provide a framework.

The first thought that the reader may have is that if disregulation is the core problem, then the negative feedback loop should be reinstated, possibly by direct medical intervention. This is the strategy applied by Schwartz and colleagues (Schwartz et al., 1967). They reported that direct electrical stimulation of the carotid nerve in 11 human patients produced a reversal of systemic arterial hypertension. However, they noted that, "it is possible that over a given period of time, the baroreceptor mechanism will reset itself to maintain hypertensive pressure." In other words, the brain may come to habituate to the artificial accentuation of negative feedback impulses elicited by the electrical stimulation.

The question to ask is, "does the disregulation model outlined here predict that *all* patients will be helped by this technique?" The answer is yes, but only in the short run. If disregulation is continually being augmented by environmental stimuli (Stage 1) and maladaptive coping by the brain (Stage 2), then the artificial enhancement of baroreceptors output (Stage 4) will be effective only in the short run because the brain will likely learn to counteract the increased negative feedback—an inappropriate response. It is reasonable to predict that for patients who maintain high blood pressure primarily because they have damaged peripheral baroreceptors (Stage 4) medical augmentation of the baroreceptors should have long-term effectiveness. On the other hand, direct baroreceptor stimulation, coupled with therapy aimed at changing the person's environment (Stage 1) or his lifestyle

(Stage 2) may be especially effective in decreasing the blood pressure of patients suffering chronic, stable hypertension maintained in part by faulty baroreceptors.

Another approach to the treatment of disregulation is to augment the feedback loop using "psychological" procedures. Biofeedback of exogenous origin, which provides the brain with a new form of feedback about the state of organ in question, is one such method. Its relationship to the four major stages of disregulation is diagrammed in Figure 8-4. With this augmented, external feedback (Stage 1) the brain (Stage 2) has an enhanced capability to draw on a variety of neural mechanisms to regulate blood pressure (Stage 3). Hypertension is a unique disorder in that not only does it lack conscious awareness of the baroreceptor feedback that is present but it typically lacks the protective negative feedback about discomfort or pain that many injuries provide. Unlike disorders (e.g., ulcers) that loudly tell the brain to take corrective action, blood pressure (in most instances) lacks this intrinsic motivational feedback. Consequently, even though biofeedback makes it possible to provide subjects with new *information*, thereby enabling them to perceive and therefore regulate their pressure, the biofeedback itself provides no intrinsic, unavoidable constraints that might force the brain to take the information into account. This may explain the difficulty of treating hyper-

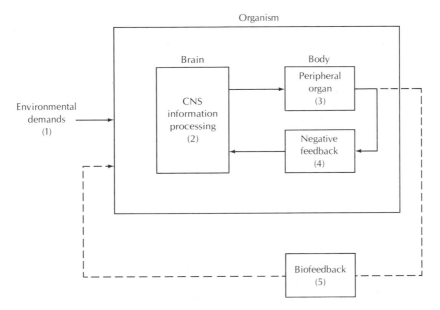

Figure 8-4. Biofeedback (Stage 5) is a parallel feedback loop to Stage 4, detecting the activity of the peripheral organ (Stage 3), and converting it into environmental stimulation (Stage 1) that can be used by the brain (Stage 2) to increase self-regulation.

tensive patients with procedures that require the brain to regulate itself (Schwartz, 1973). We could possibly imagine building a new negative feedback loop into the brain by automatically activating a painful stimulus whenever the person's pressure went too high. However, it is unlikely that this procedure would be chosen by the average person (since the average person does not choose to inflict pain on himself) even if it proved to be effective. Therefore, not only do we have the problem of convincing the patient that he has a major role in determining the state of his blood pressure, but, in addition, we need to convince him that he must take responsibility and act accordingly for the sake of his survival (Schwartz, 1973).

A number of experiments have demonstrated that subjects can learn to control their blood pressure when given biofeedback (simple lights and tones) and rewards (slide of landscapes, attractive nudes or monetary bonuses) for doing so. If subjects are not told what the response is or what direction the response is to change, they rapidly learn to control the specific responses directly associated with feedback. For example, feedback given for relative increases and decreases in systolic pressure (the peak pressure following each heart contraction), leads to voluntary control of systolic blood pressure in the absence of corresponding heart rate changes (Shapiro et al., 1969; Shapiro, Tursky and Schwartz 1970a). Conversely, if subjects are given biofeedback and reward for increasing and decreasing heart rate, they learn to regulate their heart rate in the absence of corresponding blood pressure changes (Shapiro, Tursky and Schwartz, 1970b). In both cases, answers to postexperimental questions indicate an absence of consistent differences in the subjective experience of increasing versus decreasing these cardiovascular responses. Interestingly, most subjects did not believe they had much control over their responses.

However, if subjects receive feedback and reward for specific *patterns* of heart rate and blood pressure (Schwartz, 1972), additional important findings emerge. First, subjects learn to regulate both their blood pressure and heart rate concurrently. When they are required to integrate both responses (increase both or decrease both), their learning occurs more quickly and results in slightly larger changes. Conversely, when subjects are asked to differentiate both responses (increase one and simultaneously decrease the other), their ability to separate the responses is attenuated. In other words, teaching subjects to control a *pattern* of responses uncovers constraints between the systems that are not necessarily apparent when feedback and reward are given for the single systems alone (Schwartz, 1975; 1976).

The most intriguing finding in this experiment was the reply of subjects asked what they were doing, thinking, and feeling while controlling the feedback. Those groups of subjects taught to lower *both* blood pressure and heart rate simultaneously reported sensations of quiet relaxation. Recalling that these subjects received minimal instructions, the emergence of this subjective experience with pattern regulation becomes particularly telling.

General neural relaxation with its corresponding subjective experience does not simply consist of low heart rate or low blood pressure (or low muscle tension or relaxed breathing) but rather the *pattern* or integration of these changes.

The concept that the whole (a pattern) can be *qualitatively different* from the sum of its parts, and yet be dependent upon the organization of its parts for its unique (or *emergent*) properties, is seen at all levels of physics, chemistry, biology, and neuropsychology (Weiss, 1969). Pattern biofeedback research emphasizes the emergent property that patterns of physiological processes can acquire. Once the theoretical relevance of emergent properties in patterns of physiological responses is recognized, we can begin to appreciate how treatment procedures may be effectively patterned or combined to produce results that are improved greatly from those predicted simply by the effects of treating individual physiological events. Luria's (1973) concept of functional systems illustrates the unique integrations that neural tissues can acquire, and the concept of disregulation involving multiple interacting processes (Schwartz, in preparation) provides a complementary framework.

A number of researchers have reported preliminary results applying biofeedback to patients who had essential hypertension. Benson, Shapiro, Tursky and Schwartz (1971) administered multiple sessions of systolic blood pressure biofeedback training to 7 patients who had essential hypertension. Five of these patients responded positively to the treatment, showing decreases in blood pressure of 34, 29, 16, 16, and 17 mmHg with 32, 32, 34, 21, and 12 sessions of training respectively. These basic findings have been replicated in more recent research by Kristt and Engel (1975), who measured blood pressures in the patients' homes as well as the laboratory. However, let me make three basic points about these findings. First, no report published to date has included appropriate control groups to clarify whether the biofeedback was a major, or even relevant cause of the decreases that were obtained. The blood pressure of some patients will decrease because of habituation to the laboratory. We also must consider the so-called placebo effect, which argues that improvement may occur simply because therapist and patient *expect* that treatment will be effective. This complication has particular relevance to psychosomatic disorders (because by definition these disorders are influenced by "psychological" factors — Stages 1 and 2) so we will later discuss psychobiological mechanisms by which disregulation could be reduced through expectancy.

The second point concerns the observation that patients showing the most improvement with biofeedback training were those capable of physiologically modifying the state of their cardiovascular output systems (Stage 3) through neural or humoral regulation—Stage 2 (Schwartz, 1973). Returning to the disregulation model, if the peripheral organ is damaged so that the brain cannot longer regulate it, it is unreasonable to expect biofeedback to have any effect.

Third, we must distinguish between a patient's initial ability to *learn* a self-regulation skill versus his motivation to continue to *use* the skill for the sake of his health. An anecdote from my own experience (Schwartz, 1973, p. 473) might illustrate:

> A good example of this point comes from one of our hypertension patients, who, during the feedback sessions, was successful in lowering his pressure. Over the five daily sessions of a typical week, he might lower his pressure by 20 mmhg and thus earn a total of over $35.00. However, we consistently noticed that after the weekend he would enter the laboratory on Monday with elevated pressure again. In interviews with the patient, the problem became clear. After earning a sizeable amount of money, the patient would go to the race track on the weekend, gamble, and invariably lose. The likelihood of teaching this patient to "relax" while at the race track through simple laboratory blood pressure feedback would seem slim, indicating that there is a need to work on other aspects of the patient's behavior and personality which are related to the high pressure.

Restated in terms of the disregulation model, it may be necessary to change other aspects of Stages 1 and 2 to achieve long-term clinical gains (Stage 3) for such patients. We are now finding that it may be equally, if not more, effective to give biofeedback for systems other than blood pressure in order to lower blood pressure. The disregulation model suggests the necessity of considering the separate components underlying disregulation, and treating them in an integrative fashion. From this perspective, it would be desirable to assess what role various central and peripheral processes play in the production of hypertension. As illustrated in Figure 8-3, if it was determined that high blood pressure was maintained peripherally by chronically tense skeletal muscles, then it would be logical to teach the person to reduce his muscle tension using central mechanisms. This strategy was originally adopted by Whatmore and Kohli in the early 1950s. Their theory of functional disorders centered on signaling errors of the premotor and motor cortex. Such signals were thought to be expressed, for example, in pattern changes in muscle tension. Many of these muscle patterns were below levels of normal awareness and could only be recognized by biomedical recording procedures. Using these procedures, Whatmore and Kohli (1974) administered long-term training in both the *awareness* and *regulation* of these subtle muscle changes.

The role of the skeletal system in cognition and emotion has a long history and is still debated. In the early 1920s, Edmund Jacobson demonstrated very small yet highly reliable changes in specific muscles when subjects engaged in imagery (reviewed in Jacobson, 1973). For example, when subjects imagined that their right hand was moving, their eyes would look to the right and there would be tiny increases in the muscle tension of their forearm extensor. Noticing that anxiety and stress often were accompanied by increases in muscle tension, Jacobson concluded that training subjects to produce *general* muscle relaxation resulted in reduced neural reactivity and improved health. Jacobson has applied his progressive muscle relaxation procedure to various psychosomatic disorders including essential hypertension and he reports it to be effective in many instances.

Although Jacobson was primarily interested in muscle activity, his training required that the subjects regulate a variety of *neural* systems in order to achieve deep muscle relaxation over their entire bodies. In the process of relaxing the major muscle groups, respiration decreased and became more regular. Returning to Figure 8-3, we can see how Jacobson's progressive relaxation procedure would not only regulate multiple skeletal muscles and greatly reduce the requirement for peripheral blood flow, but, by regularizing the respiratory system, would influence cardiac output as well. Jacobson was teaching his patients an integrated multisystem self-regulation procedure that could have major effects in correcting visceral disregulation. However, there are currently no long-term, carefully controlled, clinical studies verifying the effects of deep muscle relaxation for different psychosomatic disorders.

Jacobson's observations of covert muscle response have recently been applied to the generation of emotional imagery. In the process of generating affective imagery, the brain produces discrete patterns of facial muscle activity, "covert" facial expressions. (Schwartz et al., 1976). Figure 8-5

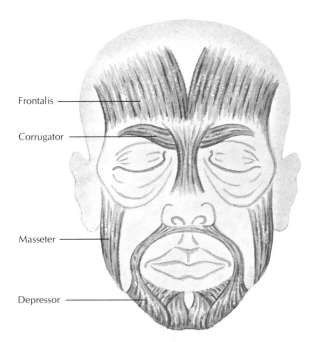

Figure 8-5. The underlying facial muscles and placement of electrodes used in the Schwartz, Fair, Salt, Mandel, and Klerman (1976) experiment.

shows the placement of electrodes in a typical experiment, and Figure 8-6 presents data from 12 normal and 12 depressed subjects. Among the normal subjects, thinking happy thoughts is associated with a specific pattern of facial muscle tension that is different from both thinking sad thoughts and thinking angry thoughts. When these subjects are requested to think about a typical day, they generate a miniature happy pattern.

The results for depressed patients provide some important differences. Whereas depressed subjects readily generate sad and angry patterns comparable to normal subjects, their muscle patterns for happy imagery are markedly attenuated. When the depressed subjects think about a typical day, the resulting muscle pattern appears to be one of sadness.

These data are important for a number of reasons. First, they provide support for recent theory (Izard, 1971) suggesting that the subjective experience of emotion is an emergent property of neural feedback to the brain

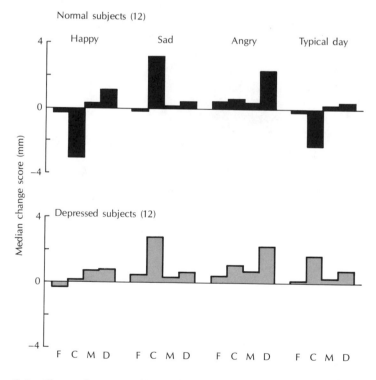

Figure 8-6. Changes in pattern of facial muscle tension in normal and depressed subjects instructed to generate imagery for happiness, sadness, anger, and a typical day. The muscle regions monitored, the frontalis (F), corrugator (C), masseter (M), and depressor (D) are shown in Figure 8-5. The data represent integrated EMG, with 1 mm = 45 microvolts/30 seconds. (From Schwartz, Fair, Salt, Mandel and Klerman, 1976.)

from specific *patterns* of facial and postural muscle tension. Although this theory has not been documented by a developmental study, the configuration of these patterns of muscle tension are probably innately wired in the brain. Consequently, the experience of discrete emotions such as happiness, sadness or anger becomes an emergent property of the specific pattern of firing in question. Second, data support the theory that affective disorders are associated with different patterns of muscle tension which, through the resulting disregulation, lead the brain to generate maladaptive physiological regulation. We can only speculate whether hypertensive patients who are inhibiting (and even denying) hostile impulses, are continually generating covert facial and body patterns of muscle tension of anger and aggression. The release of such muscular tension could have direct consequences on peripheral resistance and therefore blood pressure.

Finally, the imagery data provides an empirical demonstration that the brain is capable of generating discrete patterns of physiological activity associated with the conscious processes of cognition and emotion. If as a result of consciously regulating specific thoughts and emotions, the brain generates specific motor and visceral output devices, we have the psychobiological foundation for teaching a person to regulate his health. From this perspective, it is possible for us to understand how yoga or meditation can reduce premotor and motor firing and be used effectively to treat patients with specific psychosomatic disorders.

Research indicates that the regular practice of meditation procedures such as transcendental meditation (TM) can be associated with decreases in blood pressure in patients who have essential hypertension (Benson, 1975). Like the earlier studies on progressive relaxation, these studies are preliminary and have yet to be documented with appropriate controls.

Benson has suggested that all psychosomatic disorders may be viewed as overactive fight or flight responses (aggression or fear) and that this perpetual mode of over responding can be counteracted by the "relaxation response" (Benson, 1975). Benson's concept of the relaxation response emphasizes the patterning of physiological responses. Furthermore, Benson approaches the induction of relaxation by manipulating multiple components that contribute to disregulation. Benson requires that subjects sit in a quiet place, where there are few disturbing or distracting external stimuli (Stage 1 of disregulation). When the subjects follow these instructions, they are reducing premotor and motor firing to the skeletal muscles, and by attending to their breathing and the generation of a nonaffective simple auditory word, they are eliminating other cognitions that normally would result in the continued elicitation of undesirable motor and visceral reactions. By requiring the subjects to turn their attention inward and to experience the pleasant sensations of their relaxed muscles and quiet breathing, Benson's procedure also accentuates the brain's recognition (Stage 2) of internal feedback (Stage 4) from the periphery (Stage 3). In this manner a deceptively simple relaxation procedure influences *all* stages of disregulation.[1]

Space does not allow a more detailed discussion of other relaxation procedures such as yogic breathing and autogenic theory in the treatment of hypertension (reviewed in Shapiro, Mainardi, and Surwit, 1977). However, unlike Benson who argues that each of these procedures produce the *same* relaxation response, I think that different relaxation procedures employ different combinations of systems in the brain, and thus elicit different patterns of physiological relaxation. As I said in an earlier work (Schwartz, 1975, p. 323):

> When we consider the phenomenon of relaxation still more broadly, it becomes clear that various patterns of cognitive, attentional and somatic strategies can be brought into play, and that different relaxation procedures emphasize the regulation of different combinations of processes. Davidson and Schwartz (1976) have outlined how relaxation paradigms utilize different combinations of strategies, which will be reflected in different patterns of physiological responses. Similarly, it is possible to classify various kinds of anxiety involving combinations of cognitive, visceral and somatic components. The most effective relaxation procedure may depend on the type of anxiety the person is experiencing at the time.
>
> Take for example, a case of high cognitive-low somatic anxiety, in which a person, although physically exhausted, is unable to fall asleep because his mind is racing with disturbing images and thoughts. The age old treatment of this pattern of anxiety is to visualize sheep and count them—a cognitive self-regulation procedure that may be effective because it blocks both unwanted visual (right hemisphere) and verbal (left hemisphere) images at the same time.
>
> Another pattern is exemplified by the person who feels tense and jittery, but can point to no particular cause for his anxiety (no specific images come to mind). For such cases of low cognitive-high somatic anxiety, effective "relaxation" strategies include jogging, gardening, or other self-generated somatic activities that serve to block their undesirable somatic state and use up some of the unwanted metabolism at the same time, thereby producing fatigue.

The reader may begin to wonder whether *all* psychotherapies consist of the retraining of neural patterning and whether all therapies ultimately revolve around the concept of feedback and disregulation. I take that position, although it is far from universally accepted. Although clinicians are somewhat willing to take this perspective when dealing with psychosomatic disorders that have caused overt tissue damage, there is strong resistance to it when the disregulation is of a more central (e.g., cognitive) nature. The

---

[1] Benson (1975) believes that his combined relaxation procedure is equal to, if not more effective than, transcendental meditation as practiced by followers of the Maharishi Mahish Yogi. If this is true, then the expense of obtaining an individual "Mantra" (a word said to be uniquely suited to placing a person "in harmony with his environment") may be avoided without losing the effect by using any word pleasing to the person (Benson uses the word *one*).

reason for this, as suggested before, probably lies in the inherent brain self-regulation paradox that leads us to separate mind and behavior from our brains.

A section on the treatment of hypertension from the perspective of disregulation would be incomplete if it did not mention the relevance of more traditional components of psychotherapy and chemotherapy. If we consider environmental demands (Stage 1), it is clear that efforts directed at either changing a stressful and hostile environment, or helping the patient to decide to leave that environment are important for long-term elimination of disregulation. The body is simply not built to perform in all environments, and a major function of peripheral negative feedback is to stimulate the brain to change the external environment for the body's health. Various forms of psychotherapy may help to change the person's *perceptions* of the environment or his health. A clear example concerns the inhibition of aggression. Various modeling and role-playing procedures, plus assertive training, might be used to help the hypertensive patient to correctly do any or all of these things: (1) recognize that the environment is or is not hostile, (2) respond to the environment in such a way as to change it (e.g., by communicating to one's boss that his behavior is unappreciated and undesirable) and (3) release his hostility in an adaptive manner (e.g., by fantasizing certain actions or performing a skeletal relaxation procedure).

Psychotherapy that directly addresses the question of training a person to *recognize* and *release* his hostility may be particularly valuable for certain types of hypertension. Research described previously indicates that the expression of aggression is often accompanied by the return of blood pressure to normal. Clinicians have reported instances of patients decreasing their blood pressure 40 to 50 mmhg in a single therapy session after a hostility source they previously denied is finally recognized and the hostility is released.

Unfortunately, medicine often takes the approach that if a disorder such as high blood pressure can be regulated with drugs, then the problem has essentially been solved. However, the concept of disregulation points out the fallacy of that approach. If the etiology of the patient's hypertension is due to environment and misuse of information by the brain, then treating the hypertension pharmacologically may lower the pressure, but it will not eliminate the important environmental and life style factors. Consequently, it is likely that under repeated environmental stress and maladaptive coping on the part of the brain, other bodily systems may succumb to disregulation in the future. This is *not* to argue against drug treatment, but rather to argue against the blind use of drug treatment without concern for the total etiology of the disregulation. It is quite possible that certain drugs will be useful in *initially* bringing pressure down. The disregulation model would predict that when combined with self-regulation training and alterations in both the brain and the external environment, it should be possible to reduce the amount of drugs needed to *sustain* low pressures, if not to eliminate the drugs altogether for certain patients.

Similarly, blood pressure biofeedback can be applied much more broadly than simply as a tool for teaching patients to "directly" regulate pressure. Rather, biofeedback can be used to indicate to both the patient and his therapist that the patient is currently thinking, feeling, or doing specific things that are detrimental to his physical or emotional health (see Figure 8-4).

> In the same way that a scale helps direct the therapist and his patient in learning how to reduce food consumption and/or increase exercise in order to control his weight (rather than sitting on the scale for hours at a time trying to lower his weight by thought processes alone), biofeedback for visceral and neural disorders may be so employed as well. By means of immediate augmented feedback (with its associated increased bodily awareness), the patient may be able to learn new ways of coping *behaviorally* with his environment, or he may be able to alter his life style (or environment) in such a way as to keep his physiological processes within safer limits. In this respect, biofeedback is really similar to current psychotherapies, for they all provide corrective feedback. (Schwartz, 1973, p. 673).

The correct application of the disregulation model to psychosomatic disorders should stimulate an eclectic, yet systematic approach to treatment. The disregulation model emphasizes a multisystem, feedback-oriented program involving specific combinations of the separate treatment components tailored to needs of individual patients. Hence, assertive training might be combined with blood pressure biofeedback and deep muscle relaxation training, and all of this might be used while a patient was taking drugs, at least initially. However, this is not meant to imply that treatment programs are to be haphazardly designed without regard to the specific needs of the patient. On the contrary, the model would predict that the most effective treatment regime would be one that best matches the pattern of the disregulation to the individual patient.

Disregulation and the Placebo Effect

A phenomenon that has helped perpetuate the mind and body distinction in psychosomatic disorders, and consequently has plagued its understanding and treatment, is the so-called placebo effect (Shapiro, 1960). The word placebo comes from the Latin verb meaning "I shall please," and is present in all forms of healing. The extreme example is that of the patient who comes to his healer suffering from various disorders (such as hypertension, migraine headaches, or chest pains) and is given an inert substance (e.g., capsule containing plain water), or some other apparently innocuous treatment (e.g., promise from a fortune teller that the future will be bright). Nonetheless, the patient's specific symptoms may actually decrease; not only those of subjective discomfort, but the physical indications of injury as well.

Research on the placebo effect indicates that the optimal condition for recovery is one where both the patient and healer hold a strong belief that the treatment will work (Shapiro, 1960). Factors that increase the likelihood of this occurring include (1) the development of a strong patient-healer relationship, (2) other social variables such as the healer's accreditation and status, (3) the apparent potency of the treatment to the patient (the inert medication may have a strong negative taste) and (4) the introduction of a *new* treatment to both the patient and healer that because of its novelty is enthusiastically received by both parties.

Lacking a framework in which to interpret the placebo response, psychology and medicine have traditionally been reluctant either to accept or utilize the response fully. However, the concept of disregulation, if it is to be consistent and inclusive, should be able to elucidate the mechanisms underlying positive responses to placebos.

Two psychobiological mechanisms underlying the placebo response can be posited and evaluated scientifically. The first concerns the initial effect that diagnosis and treatment can have on reducing stress in the patient, regardless of whether they are ultimately correct. The worried patient generates various thoughts that can cause maladaptive muscular tensing and activation of the sympathetic defense system, which in turn results in increased pressure in the vasculature. This state is not an optimal environment for the brain to coordinate maximal physiological regulation and health. If the patient is provided a plausible diagnosis and a plausible treatment, reductions in maladaptive thoughts and accompanying muscular tensions and visceral reacting may occur, thereby increasing the likelihood that the biochemical processes necessary to healing will take place. Such a general change in the immune system, this could contribute to the healing of numerous disorders—however, its role would depend on the responsiveness of the particular peripheral disorder to normal bodily restorative processes, which can vary markedly. Simply stated, a major component of placebo treatments could be that they elicit a generalized relaxation response that has beneficial effects on the regulation of bodily processes.

This mechanism can lead to healing of the peripheral injury and therefore decreases in subjective discomfort. However, the latter may also be aided by a second major mechanism underlying the placebo treatment: the redirection of attention. The worried patient, anxious about his health, continually attends to his discomfort, with the result being an increase in the intensity of that discomfort. Normally we can regulate our own attention to some degree, and our conscious experience depends in part on the degree to which we attend. Placed in a more psychobiological perspective, the brain only consciously registers a certain number and intensity of sensory inputs at any one time, and consequently its response to these inputs depends in part on whether correct registration occurs. When the healer provides a diagnosis and treatment, he essentially communicates to the patient's brain that continual monitoring of the symptom's sensation is no longer necessary. Rather, the brain should redirect itself toward attending to other more adaptive stimuli and processes. Not surprisingly, if the healer's directions are followed, the conscious brain will almost immediately experience a decrement in the symptom. This will reinforce the belief that the treatment is actually working, and thereby initiate a positive feedback cycle.

When the two mechanisms of relaxation and attention redirection are activated concurrently, the result can be an interactive self-perpetuating feedback loop. Since the valence of the effects are positive (e.g., reduction in discomfort) the positive feedback loop further augments the direction of the healing process. By increasing relaxation *and* redirecting attention, both mechanisms reduce the subjective experience of distress. Consequently, the brain is reinforced to continue redirecting its attention and maintain a more relaxed state. This in turn reduces the brain's *perception* (Stage 2) of negative feedback (Stage 4) emanating from the organ (Stage 3) and also reduces the brain's *production* (Stage 2) of the maladaptive visceral response (Stage 3), the latter aiding peripheral healing. This decreases the negative feedback (Stage 4) emanating from the organ itself (Stage 3). Hence, complex disregulation can revert back to self-regulation when the proper set of brain processes are placed in motion.

From the perspective of the disregulation model, it follows that this combination of mechanisms can be an *indirect* consequence of *all* treatment procedures, particularly those that employ a sensitive therapist who responds to the personal needs of his patient. However, this hypothesis has yet to receive empirical investigation, so it should be viewed as tentative.

Perpetuation of Disregulation by the Traditional Medical Model

A model if it is to be useful should be capable not only of integrating previously disparate data and phenomenon, but of uncovering new phenomena not previously recognized or appreciated. I have illustrated how the concept of disregulation integrates diverse theories about both the psychology and biology of functional disease and have extended the model to help explain mechanisms underlying important related phenomena such as the placebo effect. In this final section let us consider a novel, and somewhat disturbing, implication of the disregulation model for the logic and ultimate utility of the traditional medical model. The strict medical model implies the use of direct biological intervention (surgical or pharmacological) to correct injury or disease that results in tissue damage. The disregulation model predicts that because of incomplete diagnosis and treatment of disregulation, the strict medical model inadvertently leads to its perpetuation—not only for bodily disease but for man's social behavior as well.

The basic premise of the disregulation model is that the brain has primary responsibility for maintaining the health of itself and its body and that it succeeds in this task by altering or regulating itself to meet the needs of specific organs. Because the body, as any complex physical device, can only work effectively within certain tolerances, the brain must continually ascertain that all components are working effectively. If any component begins to break down, the brain must adjust itself to bring the disregulation back into balance.

As we have discussed, disregulation can be initiated and perpetuated at four stages. Often, the disregulation is initiated by exogenous stimulus demands (Stage 1) and the brain's reaction to them (Stage 2). If the brain is exposed to environmental conditions that ultimately lead to the breakdown of a given organ system (Stage 3) and a functional disorder develops, appropriate internal negative feedback loops are activated (Stage 4), many of which generate pain. This negative stimulus "drives" the brain to take corrective action. Even if the brain is busy attending to other stimuli and fails to recognize the breakdown of a given organ, at some point the organ will generate sufficient negative feedback (if the loop is intact) to redirect the brain's attention. Anyone who has experienced a really strong stomach ache caused by overeating or eating the wrong food knows well the power that negative feedback can have in commanding his attention and altering his subsequent behavior.

The fundamental question is, what should the brain's response to this internal stimulation be? From a psychobiological perspective, the brain *should* either direct a change in the outside environment, leave the environment, or modify its interactions with the environment. Consequently, the intrinsic pain of the disturbed stomach keeps our behavior in check by forcing us to stop eating, or to not eat the dangerous food again.

However, for many sociological reasons, man is no longer content to follow his initial biological heritage. He may no longer feel competent to change either his environment or his behavior—perhaps he simply lacks the motivation. However, because of his superior cortical structures and the consequential development of culture, man is no longer constrained to deal with disregulation by responding in the natural way. Instead, the typical patient would rather change his body than change his lifestyle or his environment, the two factors (Stages 1 and 2) that together augment or cause the bodily dysfunctions in the first place (Schwartz, 1973). Simply stated, man may choose instead to modify Stage 3 or 4 or both by extrinsic biological intervention. According to the disregulation model, if the negative feedback mechanisms are removed artificially, the brain is freed to continue behaving in maladaptive ways that ultimately may be deleterious to survival and satisfaction. Lacking the stabilizing impact of negative feedback regulation, the brain thus goes increasingly out of control (Schwartz, in preparation).

Consider a simple stomach ache. Today human culture strongly reinforces the practice of taking drugs to eliminate stomach aches caused by the brain's disregulation. Antacid commercials exemplify this twentieth century value system. They depict an obese man stuffing himself with apple pies or spaghetti. When a functional stomach ache follows, the obvious conclusion should be that the stomach and the rest of the body were not meant to be fed like that. The man's stomach ache represents the biological feedback mechanism necessary to keep him from further abusing his body. Instead what we hear is: "Eat, and if you get a stomach ache, don't change your environment or behavior. Rather, eliminate the discomfort by taking a pill."

Or they depict a family at Christmas time, surrounded by crowds, trying with great difficulty to hold packages, rushing from counter to counter, continually inhibiting the resentment they feel at being bumped or otherwise offended. In the process, one member of the family develops a stomach ache. The conclusion according to the disregulation model is that the stomach and the rest of the body were not meant to live like that. The person's stomach ache represents the biological feedback mechanism necessary to keep him from further abusing his body. But this is not the message of the commercial. Rather, what we hear is "Shop, and if you get a stomach ache, don't go home or change your behavior. Rather, eliminate the discomfort by popping a pill."

Simple antacids are a mild drug, and they do not always work. When they don't, other stronger medication is often prescribed to quell the pain. Then when the organ becomes so abused that an ulcer develops and internal bleeding occurs, does the person listen to his stomach and radically change his external environment and behavior? Often times no. What he does instead is go to his twentieth century surgeon for repair. Medicine is developing new and finer means of bypassing normal adaptive feedback mechanisms. A patient can have a vagotomy and eliminate the brain's capability to regulate the stomach neurally at all. And if the trend in modern medicine continues, people can look forward to the day when, if their stomachs continue to be an obstacle, they can simply go to their local surgeon and obtain an artificial stomach.

Then the brain would no longer be constrained by the needs of a natural stomach. According to the disregulation model, this brain would be free to continue and even expand upon the inappropriate disregulation that was the initial cause of the problem (Schwartz, unpublished manuscript). The stomach is only one organ, however, whereas modern medicine is using the same strategy for all systems of the body. Our culture continually reinforces the idea that if the brain and its body cannot cope with the external environment, they will simply have to undergo medical alternation to adjust. According to the disregulation model, this prospect carried to its extreme will have dire consequences for the ultimate survival of the human species as we now know it.

The reader should not conclude that I am opposed to all medicine. On the contrary, the disregulation model clearly indicates under what specific conditions medical intervention is adaptive, not only in the short run, but, more important, in the long run. My point is that we should not come to the overly simplistic conclusion that the correction of Stages 3 and 4 of disregulation by medical procedures should be the *sole* approach to treatment. Rather, to keep the health and behavior of the human species intact it may be necessary to accept both the limitations and wisdom of the body as it is, even though this may require more active self-regulation on the part of our brains.

The Neonatal Split-Brain Kitten: A Laboratory Analogue of Minimal Brain Dysfunction

Jeri A. Sechzer
The New York Hospital—Cornell Medical Center

Introduction

The Minimal Brain Dysfunction (MBD) syndrome is characterized by hyperactivity, incoordination, impulsivity, decreased attention span, impaired learning and memory, diminished ability to experience pain and pleasure (anhedonia), and the "paradoxical" response to amphetamine. It occurs in four times as many males as females. MBD has become the most common syndrome seen by child psychiatrists; it occurs in 5 to 10 percent of school children. Recent evidence suggests that MBD is frequently an antecedent of common, more severe psychiatric conditions that appear in late adolescence or adult life. Thus, not only is MBD one of the most common disorders of childhood, but its relation to adult psychopathology might make it one of the most significant childhood disorders as well.

The experimental work from my laboratory was supported by National Science Foundation Grant GB-33469. Some of the data reported here have been presented before elsewhere (Sechzer, 1973; Sechzer et al., 1974; Sechzer et al., 1976a). I thank my colleagues S. E. Folstein, E. H. Geiger, R. F. Mervis, S. M. Meehan, and P. G. Kessler for their participation in the behavioral tests and observations described in this chapter. I am grateful to Mrs. Marion Jacobson and Mrs. Gisela Wrubel for typing the manuscript, to Ms. Lisa Kaplan for her assistance in editing, and to Ms. Elaine Rossinoff for preparation of the histological sections.

History

Minimal brain dysfunction was first described by Bond (1922) and Hohman (1922) following the World War I pandemic of von Economo's encephalitis. They noted that after recovery from illness children underwent a "profound change in character and behavior" and became "irritable, restless, quarrelsome, disobedient, no longer amenable to discipline, emotionally unstable, capriciously moody, and given to truancy, lying, and stealing." Because these behavioral alterations had developed following encephalitis they were attributed to injury or infection of the brain.

Strecker and Ebaugh (1924) and Kasanin (1929) reported similar behavior patterns, and in 1937 Blau identified the essential characteristic to be the "complete reversal of personality from that of a normal child to an unsocial, unmanageable one who was unyielding to any form of training." Later reports also associated this syndrome with whooping cough (Lurie and Levy, 1942), lead poisoning or lead exposure (Thurston, Middlekamp, and Mason, 1955; David, Clark, and Voeller, 1972; Needleman, 1973; Baloh et al., 1975), pre- and post-partum complications and prematurity (Montagu, 1962; Knoblock and Pasamanick, 1965; Werry, 1968). These children also showed an increased occurrence of minor or "soft" neurological signs but not of major or "hard" neurological signs. Soft neurological signs are slight and inconsistent, and they are not distinctly associated with a neuroanatomical site of lesion. Such signs are characterized by *incoordination*—poor visuomotor coordination, poor balance, clumsiness, choreiform movements (which are involuntary, irregular, and jerky), and poor speech. Hard neurological signs are prevalent and persistent, and they can be associated with a neuroanatomical site or lesion. Such signs include paresis, paralysis, anesthesia, and reflex changes.

Many terms have been used to describe minimal brain dysfunction. Because the syndrome was initially attributed to brain injury, descriptive terms such as "postencephalitic behavior disorder," "minimal brain damage," and "minimal cerebral palsy" still include a reference to this presumed etiology. Other terms like "hyperkinetic behavior syndrome," "hyperactive child syndrome," "choreiform syndrome," and "maturational lag" emphasize behavioral and developmental characteristics. The most recent terms, "minimal cerebral dysfunction" and "minimal brain dysfunction," emphasize functional alterations in the central nervous system.

According to Wender (1971), each term presents its own problem. "Postencephalitic behavior disorder," "minimal brain damage," and "minimal cerebral palsy" make etiological assumptions when in many cases there are no obvious signs of neurological damage. "Hyperkinetic behavior syndrome," "hyperkinetic child syndrome," and "choreiform syndrome" designate a salient attribute but ignore or deemphasize emotional and intellectual deficits. "Maturation lag" again has etiological assertions (i.e. delayed myelination of the central nervous system) of a self-limited delay in development, which may be unjustified. "Minimal cerebral dysfunction" and "minimal brain dysfunction" imply an alteration in central nervous system function without specifying its nature or cause. In agreement with Wender (1971) I find these last two terms the least offensive, and use the latter because "minimal brain dysfunction" (MBD) avoids the connotation of specific localization in the central nervous system.

Characteristics of Minimal Brain Dysfunction

Some MBD symptoms are evident in infancy, whereas others become apparent as a child develops. They may be inconsistent, exacerbated more or less by various stimuli and may not exist with equal intensity in every child.

Hyperactivity. An increase in motor behavior is one of the most salient characteristics of MBD. Parents commonly depict a child who was restless in infancy, stood and walked at an early age, and was "into everything." As the child developed, he or she became unmanageable, was incessantly in motion, fidgeted constantly, and was unable to sit still for even a few minutes. This hyperactivity is manifested in constant and focusless locomotion rather than excessive bursts of directed activity. The striking feature is not just the total amount of activity children display but rather their inability to inhibit activity appropriately.

Incoordination. Soft neurological signs associated with *incoordination* are more prevalent in children who have MBD. As I have said before, MBD children may present one or more of the following symptoms: poor visuomotor coordination, impaired fine motor coordination, poor balance, clumsiness, choreiform movements, and poor speech. Although 50 percent of MBD children exhibit soft signs, the incidence of hard neurological signs (paresis, paralysis, anesthesia, and reflex changes) is no greater than that of a randomly selected population of children who do not have MBD.

Impulsivity. Defective impulse control is exhibited in many ways by MBD children. They show little perseverance at challenging tasks. Their planning and judgment are poor and they begin activities on the spur of the moment without thinking them through. MBD children display less forethought and organizational ability than would be appropriate for children their age. MBD children are more likely than most children to expend energy in several directions at once without thinking of the consequences of their actions. Many of them are reckless and apparently accident-prone, and they are frequently injured. MBD children sometimes express social impulsivity or antisocial behavior through compulsive stealing, lying, pyromania, and wanton destruction of property.

Decreased Attention Span. A shortened attention span and poor ability to concentrate are other striking abnormalities associated with MBD children. The children are easily distracted by extraneous sounds and sights and are attracted to irrelevant details and objects. Attention and concentration deficits become very evident once school begins. They definitely play an important role in academic underachievement.

Impaired Learning and Memory. Underachievement in school is a hallmark of the MBD syndrome. MBD children have difficulty in learning to read, and some MBD children also have problems in writing, comprehension, and arithmetic. Yet MBD children score in the normal range on intelligence tests and have positive school experiences (Paine, Werry, and Quay, 1968). However, their retention of classroom material is also sometimes impaired. Material learned one day is often completely forgotten the next (Strauss and Lehtinen, 1947; Laufer and Denhoff, 1957; Wender, 1971, 1972). Whether this reflects an impairment in recall or in long-term acquisition has not yet been determined.

Anhedonia. Anhedonia is the diminished intensity of experienced pain and pleasure and the decreased responsiveness to negative and positive reinforcement. Although not always conspicuous, this symptom is usually present in children who have MBD. Parents consistently report that the children habitually appear dissatisfied and discontented. Disobedience is difficult to control with punishment or with social pressures, not surprising in view of their depressed hedonic level.

The "Paradoxical" Amphetamine Response. The "paradoxical" response to amphetamine and amphetamine-like drugs (amphetamines produce increased activity, tension, and often euphoria) was first recognized by Bradley in 1937 and has been the basis of various drug treatments ever since. In MBD children, amphetamine *decreases* activity, increases attention span and concentration, and improves learning and memory. I will discuss this phenomenon in detail in the sections on drug management and theories of MBD.

Electroencephalographic Studies. Most studies of MBD children have reported an increased incidence of electroencephalographic (EEG) abnormalities (Capute, Neidermayer, and Richardson, 1968; Satterfield, 1973; Wender, 1971). An EEG tracing is classified abnormal if it contains either excessive slow-wave (theta or delta) activity, generally accompanied by fair to poor wave organization (lack of rhythmicity) and reduced amplitude, or frequent epileptiform (sharp or spike wave) discharges (Satterfield et al., 1974), or both. The usefulness of the EEG is limited as an aid in diagnosing minimal brain dysfunction by the incidence of abnormal findings in normal children. For instance, Capute et al. (1968) found EEG abnormalities in 43 percent of MBD children and in 17 percent of normal children. In addition, because the EEG provides at best a very crude measure of brain dysfunction, the significance of an abnormal EEG in MBD children is not clear. However, Satterfield (1973) has suggested that an EEG may gauge the response of MBD children to drug treatment. He found that 83 percent of MBD children with abnormal EEGs respond to methylphenidate (an amphetamine-like drug), compared with 59 percent of MBD children with normal EEG's.

Management of the Minimal Brain Dysfunction Syndrome

Because the prevention or cure for minimal brain dysfunction has not yet been established, treatment is aimed at minimizing and reversing the child's symptoms to enable intellectual and psychosocial growth. Once a diagnosis of minimal brain dysfunction is made, three approaches to treatment may be considered: environmental manipulation, psychotherapy, and medication. The three treatments can also be used in varying combinations. Although the first two types of management are far from irrelevant, they appear to be of secondary importance when compared to the effectiveness of drug treatment.

Drug Management. The most effective drugs used in the treatment of MBD are stimulants, and of these amphetamines and methylphenidate (Ritalin) are used most commonly. Because amphetamines were originally associated with the treatment of MBD, other drugs with similar effects are referred to as amphetamine-like drugs.

In 1937, Bradley reported the surprising paradoxical and therapeutic effects of benzedrine sulfate (*dl*-amphetamine) on a group of children in a residential treatment center whose behavioral disorders included increased motor activity, learning disabilities, disturbed school behavior, aggressiveness, and schizoid behavior. The drug brought "spectacular" improvement in the academic performance of half the children. Their motor activity decreased and they became emotionally subdued (less noisy, aggressive, and domineering), although more interested in their surroundings. In the majority of children the drug effects appeared 30 to 45 minutes after oral ingestion; they were at their height during the second and third hours, and they gradually disappeared over a 6 to 12 hour period.

By paradoxical, Bradley referred to the fact that amphetamine, which produces greater activity and tension and often euphoria in adults, will decrease activity, sedate, and even alter intellectual and social functions in MBD children. Strangely, the scientific and clinical world took little notice of Bradley's work. Then in 1950, before the syndrome was clearly defined,

Bradley reviewed his 12 years of amphetamine treatment with 350 children suffering a variety of behavior disorders (Bradley, 1950). Between 50 and 85 percent of the children improved and showed the paradoxical response to amphetamine. Since 1950, many studies have independently confirmed the effectiveness of amphetamine treatment for childhood disorders that have the symptom complex associated with MBD (Laufer, Denhoff, and Solomans, 1957; Knobel, 1962; Eisenberg et al., 1963; Burks, 1964). The mechanisms by which amphetamine induces the paradoxical response in MBD children (but not in normal children (Snyder and Myerhoff, 1973) or adults) is still unknown, although various researchers have proposed neurochemical mechanisms. Amphetamine is effective with 66 to 75 percent of MBD children (O'Malley and Eisenberg, 1973). The optimal dosage ranges from 0.1 mg/kg of body weight to 1.5 mg/kg of body weight and treatment is continued depending on symptoms.

According to Wender (1971), approximately 25 percent of MBD children show a therapeutic response to amphetamine. The common responsiveness of a symptom complex to amphetamines constituted one of the reasons for placing a seemingly heterogeneous group of children under the term *minimal brain dysfunction*. Rather than just suppressing these symptoms, amphetamine also appears to promote intellectual and social development. An appropriate dose diminishes hyperactivity and quiets a child without producing drowsiness. It increases attentiveness and persistence and decreases distractibility. Impulsivity diminishes and children become more sensitive to reward and punishment. Social assertiveness is lessened, and learning and memory may be remarkably improved. Whether amphetamine acts directly on mechanisms of learning and memory or whether it indirectly alleviates motor, attentional, or motivational symptoms is unknown.

Groups of drugs other than the amphetamines have proved useful in treating MBD children. Methylphenidate (Ritalin) is a drug so similar in effect to amphetamine that it is used equally as much in management of the MBD syndrome (Millichap, 1973). Pemoline (Cylert), a weak central nervous system stimulant, Imiprimine (Tofranil), an antidepressant, and diphenylhydantoin (Dilantin), an anticonvulsant, reportedly have been used for MBD with some success (Millichap, 1973).

Environmental Manipulation. The symptoms of an MBD child improve in a structured environment where the amount of extraneous stimulation is decreased, social situations are avoided, and where the child's alternatives are limited. Careful selection of a school capable of meeting the special needs of the MBD child is essential. Psychological testing is useful in determining needs such as remedial reading, individual tutoring, degree of isolation and structure in the classroom and involvement in group activities supervised by an adult.

Psychotherapy.   Individual psychotherapy can be useful as an accessory to other methods in the treatment of MBD. The child may need assistance in understanding his or her problem. Poor self-image and low self-esteem are often correlated with MBD; they may require treatment. Psychotherapy can help the child on medication to accept a new role, to attempt more appropriate behaviors, and to acquire healthy peer relationships in an academic and social situation.

Family counseling and therapy may become very important once the child is on medication. They help the family to understand the child's behavior and to guide him or her in establishing a different position in the family group as improvement continues.

The need to use all three approaches in the management of the MBD child cannot be overstated. Although drug treatment appears to be the most effective, environmental manipulation and psychotherapy are valuable and important adjuncts.

Patterns of Minimal Brain Dysfunction

From infancy through adolescence symptoms of minimal brain dysfunction emerge, interact with, and effect intellectual and psychosocial growth and development. This is in marked contrast with growth and development in normal children.

Changes With Age.   Although there is not one set of patterns or group of symptoms in all MBD children, characteristic features of the syndrome present themselves as the child grows.

The most conspicuous symptom of MBD in infants is hyperalertness and irritability. Later on, toddlers (2–4 years) display behavior traits of destructiveness, unmanageability, and lack of response to parental discipline. They also appear less coordinated than normal and exhibit immature speech patterns.

Hyperactivity increases as children near school age and usually causes a bevy of social and adjustment problems. When children are in the third or fourth grade (9–10 years), learning disorders related to reading, arithmetic, and writing and antisocial traits such as stealing, lying, and firesetting emerge.

During preadolescence and early adolescence antisocial behavior develops further in MBD children and often causes this normally difficult maturational stage to be tumultuous. These problems, combined with existing learning difficulties, produce an MBD child whose academic ability may be generally or severely retarded.

It is usual for hyperactivity and other MBD symptoms to abate after puberty. It was thought that the MBD children outgrew their problems as they reached physiological maturity but now the future of the MBD child after adolescence and during adulthood is uncertain. Longitudinal and retrospective studies indicate that if untreated, MBD results in an increased risk of psychopathology in later life—ranging from poor social adjustment, underachievement, and social failure to juvenile delinquency and psychosis.

Prognosis of the MBD Syndrome. Clinical literature suggests that the MBD syndrome diminishes with age and generally disappears between the ages of 12 to 18 years (Bradley, 1950; Laufer, and Denhoff, 1950). The most obvious improvement is that children who had MBD come to engage in normal amounts of activity. However, the syndrome does not diminish with the disappearance of its overt symptoms. Recently, there has been an increasing awareness of the relationship between MBD in childhood and later adult psychopathologies. Consequently, the long-term prognosis of minimal brain dysfunction is beginning to receive a considerable amount of attention.

Two techniques have been used to evaluate the outcome of this disorder. Anterospective (longitudinal) studies provide an assessment at the initial referral and repeated testing during periodic follow-up examinations. These scores are used to assess the progress of a child diagnosed as having MBD and to estimate how much change has occurred during a specific time. Retrospective or cross-sectional studies investigate present status by assessing people from different populations who were diagnosed as having MBD when they were children. Both studies require a properly matched control group to serve as a standard with which to evaluate group differences or change. Quite often, follow-up studies combine the techniques.

Anterospective Studies. Weiss, Minde, Werry, Douglas and Nemeth (1971) conducted a five-year follow-up study of 64 children between 10 and 18 years of age (mean age = 13.34 years). Longitudinal and cross-sectional procedures were used to measure both change and current status. The investigators reported that compared to the initial examination (five years before) hyperactivity, distractibility, and aggressiveness had diminished greatly and remained a serious problem in only a minority of the subjects. Other major symptoms persisted, however. Disorders in concentration and attention and chronic underachievement in school were still unchanged despite the youths' normal or even above normal intelligence. A high proportion of them still manifested significant psychopatholgoy five years later, as evidenced by emotional immaturity, inability to maintain goals, poor self-image, and significant feelings of hopclessness. The children in this study had received drug therapy at one time but not during the follow-up period. (Results of cross-sectional measures will be discussed in the next section).

A 25-year longitudinal study was carried out by Menkes, Rowe and Menkes (1967) on 14 children who had initially been diagnosed as having

MBD, but who had not received drug therapy. At the time of reexamination, four subjects were institutionalized, diagnosed as psychotic; two were clearly retarded and living dependent lives with their families; eight were self-supporting. Of the eight who were self-supporting, four had spent some time in a psychiatric institution. These data must be interpreted cautiously because the sample is small and the criteria for diagnosis 25 years ago was inconsistent and may have included patients with maximal rather than minimal brain dysfunction. Morris, Escoll, and Wexler (1956), reported the results of a 20- to 30-year follow-up study on 68 children who had been diagnosed between the ages of 4 and 15 years as having an "aggressive behavior disorder." These children, although diagnosed long ago, appeared to be severely disturbed and antisocial MBD children, yet there was no evidence of brain damage. Of the 68 children followed until age 18 or older, only 14 to 20 percent were considered to have made good adjustments. The remainder exhibited significant psychiatric disturbances.

A most recent study by Huessy and Cohen (1976) evaluated the progress of children with hyperkinetic behaviors and learning disabilities over a seven-year period, from the second to the ninth grades. A teacher questionnaire was designed to measure social maturity, neuromuscular development, academic performance, and general attitude and behavior. Their data appear to confirm the notion that children who are identified early as having behavioral and learning problems risk developing academic as well as social adjustment problems in adolescence.

Retrospective Studies: Results of a cross-sectional study by Weiss et al. (1971) complement the longitudinal measures I have mentioned. When the current status of the MBD subjects was compared with that of a normal control group, it was found that although hyperactivity, distractibility, and aggressiveness had diminished somewhat over five years, behavior was still not normal. Scores of MBD subjects on scales of behavioral and social adjustment, oral reading, arithmetic, and writing, were still significantly inferior to those of the control group. Compared to normal children MBD subjects manifested significant psychopathology.

In another study, Hartocollis (1968) described the childhood characteristics of a group of 15 adult psychiatric patients who were in the hospital. Their early history showed many symptoms commonly associated with minimal brain dysfunction: hyperactivity, clumsiness, aggressiveness, temper tantrums, poor intellectual performance, and adolescent deviant behavior that included lying and stealing. As adults, these patients were classified as either schizophrenic, depressed, or infantile.

Although the findings in these two classes of studies are suggestive, not conclusive, they have important implications. First, although hyperactivity and several symptoms of MBD may diminish or disappear near puberty, other perhaps more serious characteristics of the syndrome persist. Second, the MBD syndrome may be an early manifestation of psychiatric disorders of late adolescence and adulthood—which include underachievement, character disorders, sociopathy, and schizophrenia. Finally, the MBD syndrome could conceivably disappear around puberty; the antisocial or abnormal behavior that remains may be present because of learning variables. Perhaps during early life, while the child presented MBD symptoms, parents, teachers, peers, and other persons reacted to him (or her) in such a way that conditions were set up for later abnormal or antisocial behavior. The fact that diagnosis and treatment of MBD in infants and young children is very difficult may be an important contribution to later adult psychopathology. If identification and management of the disorder began early enough then perhaps what appears to be a more serious prognosis could be modified. The work of Prechtl (1967) suggests that in some children MBD could be identified shortly after birth, which would permit the development of a preventative program. Although recent evidence of Mackay, Beck, and Taylor (1973) implies that long-term pharmacotherapy may be beneficial for adolescents who have the MBD syndrome, it remains to be seen whether such medication will permanently correct the symptoms.

The Neonatal Split-Brain Preparation as an Animal Model for Minimal Brain Dysfunction

Criteria for an Animal Model

Although symptoms, characteristics, and treatments of minimal brain dysfunction have been extensively reported, its nature and cause still remain a mystery. One major obstacle to our defining them is the lack of a suitable animal model, which would aid us in sorting out perplexing problems of etiologies, diagnostic criteria, and the efficacy of various treatments. Techniques derived from an animal model could be developed to explore for responsible neuroanatomical and neurochemical systems that could explain to us the "paradoxical" response to amphetamines. Conditions developed for studying and treating the model could then be adapted for children.

Criteria for an appropriate animal model for minimal brain dysfunction have been selected (Sechzer, Faro, and Windle, 1973), which require that:

1. Symptoms should be evident, in part, from birth.
2. Other symptoms should appear at ages comparable to those at which they appear in children.
3. The symptoms should be ameliorated by amphetamine or amphetamine-like drugs and the animals should respond (as children do) with a decrease in activity and an improvement in attention, learning, and memory.

4. The brains of the animals should be analyzed for pathologic changes through classical histological techniques, histofluorescent methods, and biochemical assays.

The Neonatal Split-Brain Preparation

My colleagues and I became interested in an animal model for minimal brain dysfunction while observing the behavioral development of kittens that had surgical division of the corpus callosum and commissure of the fornix (hippocampal commissure or psalterium) at or close to birth.

The corpus callosum is the largest and most important commissure in the central nervous system. This commissure, connecting the two brain halves, can be seen as a a broad thick plate of fibers in the interhemispheric space. Axons of the corpus callosum interconnect the neocortices of the two hemispheres. This commissure has been implicated in the transfer of learning and memory from one hemisphere to the other (Myers and Sperry, 1958; Meikle and Sechzer, 1960; Sperry, 1964). Not only is the interhemispheric transfer of these processes abolished after corpus callosum section but acquisition time is prolonged and retention impaired (Sechzer, 1970). Thus, one of the conclusions of split-brain experiments is that interaction between the two cerebral hemispheres through the corpus callosum is essential for normal learning and memory. Physiologically, the corpus callosum has been associated with the interhemispheric mediation of an epileptic discharge. Midsagittal surgical section of the callosum in humans who have intractable epilepsy has ameliorated these seizures (Bogen, Fisher, and Vogel, 1962).

The commissure of the fornix, or psalterium, a small flattened sheet of fibers, is just beneath the splenium (tail) of the corpus callosum. The fornix constitutes the main efferent system of the hippocampal formation, deep within the anterior portion of the temporal lobe (or within its homologous structure in animals lacking complete development of this area). The commissure of the fornix contains axons of the large pyramidal cells of the hippocampal cortex and interconnects the hippocampal cortices of each hemisphere. Although the hippocampus has been associated with recent memory (Scoville and Milner, 1957; Kaada, Rasmussen, and Kveini, 1961; Green, 1964), the commissure of the fornix has not been sectioned alone to determine whether it is important in mediating memory or some other process between the two hemispheres. Because of its proximity to the callosum, the two structures are usually sectioned together both in animals and humans.

Two small pathways cross in the corpus callosum and are sectioned along with it. The first, the striate-striate pathway, arises in the caudate nucleus of one hemisphere, crosses in the anterior part of the callosum, and terminates in the caudate nucleus of the opposite hemisphere (Mensah and Deadwyler,

1974). The second pathway, the cortico-striate pathway, arises in the sensorimotor cortex (in rats, rabbits and cats) or the cingulum (in monkey and man) of one hemisphere and crosses in the callosum to the caudate nucleus of the other hemisphere (Webster, 1965; Carman, Cowan, and Webster, 1956; Locke, Kruper, and Yakovlev, 1964; Locke and Yakovlev, 1965). Whether these two transcallosal pathways participate in interhemispheric transfer has not yet been determined.

Split-brain animal experiments have revealed the important role for the corpus callosum (but not yet for the other pathways sectioned with it) in the interhemispheric transfer of learning and memory and for the interaction of the two hemispheres for normal acquisition and retention. However, these experiments have all been conducted with animals in which split-brain surgery was performed during adult life—long after the maturation of the callosum and the development of adaptive and intellectual processes. Presumably, by this time the interaction between the two hemispheres has completely developed. My colleagues and I attempted to disconnect the two hemispheres in newborn kittens by commissurotomy. In this way, each brain half would develop without callosally mediated interaction. Such a preparation would permit us to investigate the role of each hemisphere in the normal development of learning, memory, and other behaviors.

Eighteen kittens from five mothers bred in my animal colony served as subjects. The mothers were under close observation during the last seven days of gestation so that birth of the kittens would be closely timed.[1] The corpus callosum and the psalterium of 11 kittens were sectioned within 24 hours after birth. The procedure was carried out on two kittens on the third postnatal day (72 hours old), and the remaining five kittens were controls.

Split-brain surgery was performed under general anesthesia using aseptic techniques. Details of the surgical procedure are published elsewhere (Sechzer et al., 1976a).

Observations and tests were conducted with nine 24-hour split-brain kittens, one 72-hour split-brain kitten, and five normal kittens. Litters were usually spaced four to five months apart and no more than two of them were born at close intervals. Two of the 24-hour split-brain kittens and one 72-hour split-brain kitten died.

Observations and Behavioral Tests

Home Orientation. We used a procedure similar to that described by Rosenblatt, Turkewitz, and Schneirla (1969) to observe how an infant kitten finds its mother and home area; that is, the area of the cage where the kitten is nursed. For each test session, the mother remained alone in the home

---

[1] Gestation period for the cat is 65 ± 4 days.

area after the littermates were removed. The kitten to be tested was placed in the corner of the cage diagonal to the home area (see Figure 9-1). The path it took to return to the home area and its mother is shown in Figure 9-1. Normal kittens represented in Figures 9-1A and 1C took a direct path back to

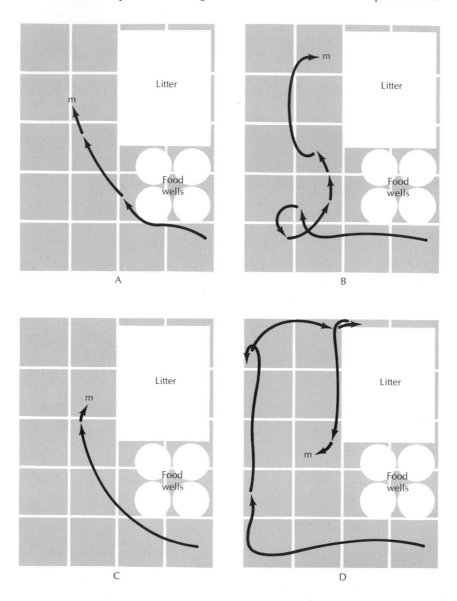

Figure 9-1. Orientation of displaced kittens towards home area and mother. A and C, left, represent direct path taken by normal kittens in order to return to mother, m, in home quadrant. B and D, right, represent circuitous path taken by neonatal split-brain kittens.

the home area and their mother. On the other hand, split-brain kittens (Figures 9-1B and 1D) took a circuitous path of greater distance that required more time.

Hyperactivity

0–6 Weeks. Within a few days after surgery the split-brain kittens showed increased activity. Although normal kittens remained huddled together and sleeping, the split-brain kittens roamed the cage, climbing over their mother's body. This behavior persisted even after their eyes opened at about the end of the first week.

By six weeks of age the split-brain animals appeared hyperactive. When they were exercised in our animal quarters, they engaged in constant, random, and focusless behavior rather than the excessive bursts of activity typical of normal kittens. The animals were easily distracted and they hurried from one object to the next. The control group paid attention to fewer objects but remained with each one for a longer time.

6 Months. We wanted to determine whether amphetamine would diminish hyperactivity in the split-brain group as it does in hyperactive children (the paradoxical response). When the animals were five to six months old, we measured their activity when they were undrugged and again when they were under the influence of *d*-amphetamine.[2] The measures of activity we used were subjective and included: locomotion, ease of handling, exploration, and alertness (response to sounds, sudden light changes, moving objects, people, and other animals). Each behavior was rated from −4 to +4 and the mean score was plotted. For example, in locomotion measure: −4 = lying quietly, 0 = walking about and exploring objects, and +4 = constant, random, and focusless locomotion.

Activity before and after amphetamine administration is shown in Figure 9-2. Before amphetamine injection, normal kittens were rated +1 and split-brain kittens were rated +3 on the same scale. With increasing dosage, the normal kittens became more active. In contrast, with increasing dosage, the split-brain kittens became less active and at an average dose of .7 mg/kg of body weight hyperactivity was dramatically diminished.

Split-brain kittens curled up or sat quietly in their cages, a behavior we had never observed before. When removed from their cages, they either stayed in one place or walked about slowly. They were less distracted by sudden sounds or movements and seemed to attend to various objects about them for longer periods. Within two hours after amphetamine administration they began to return to their usual hyperactive state.

---

[2]*d*-Amphetamine was supplied through the courtesy of Smith, Kline, and French Laboratories, Philadelphia, Pa.

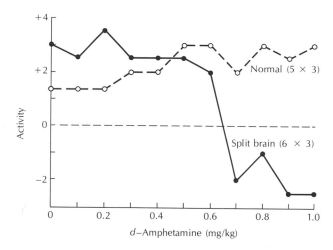

Figure 9-2. Effect of increasing doses of *d*-amphetamine on activity of normal (open circles) and of neonatal split-brain (closed circles) kittens. Five normal kittens were tested 3 times on each dose (5 x 3) and six split-brain kittens were tested 3 times on each dose (6 x 3) at 48-hour intervals. Saline injections in normal and split-brain kittens did not alter behavior.

Open Field. Open field tests were also conducted when the animals were six months of age. The open field apparatus consisted of a 150 × 150 centimeter wood floor with a wood fence 90 centimeters high. The wood floor was marked into 25 square divisions of 30 square centimeters each. *In the first test*, the number of squares traversed and the pattern of activity shown by each kitten were recorded during several 3-minute test series. *In a second test series*, toys were introduced and the kittens' attention to them was recorded for 10 minutes. All observations were made from a 3-foot distance using a convex mirror so that the kittens could not see the observers. Each series was conducted four times and the mean score was plotted. Figures 9-3 and 9-4A and 4B depict the results of one split-brain kitten and its normal littermate.

Squares Crossed. The mean number of squares crossed in the open field is represented in Figure 9-3. Without amphetamine, the normal kitten crossed 106 squares during the 3-minute test in the open field, and the split-brain kitten crossed 161 squares. After 0.2 mg of amphetamine/kg of body weight, the normal kitten crossed 200 squares, the split-brain kitten, 55 squares. After 0.5 mg amphetamine/kg of body weight, the normal kitten crossed 239 squares (more than double that of its preamphetamine score), the split-brain kitten, 92. Although the normal kittens increased their activity by 89 and 125 percent with 0.2 and 0.5 mg of amphetamine/kg of body weight respectively, the activity of the split-brain kittens decreased by 66 and

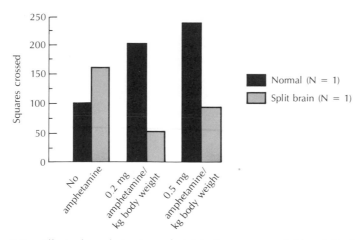

Figure 9-3. Effect of amphetamine administration on open-field activity for a 6-month-old neonatal split-brain kitten and its control littermate. Ordinate indicates number of squares crossed during a 3-minute test session.

43 percent after the same amphetamine dosage.[3] The activity of the split-brain kitten under the effect of amphetamine is comparable to the activity of the normal kitten without amphetamine.

Objects Handled. Figures 9-4A and 4B represent the mean number of objects handled and the number of seconds spent with each object before and after amphetamine. A paper ball, a plastic cup and hanging paper streamers were placed in the open field. During a 10-minute test without amphetamine the normal kitten transferred its attention from toy to toy an average of 7.7 times (Figure 9-4A), spending 16.9 seconds (Figure 9-4B) with each object or a total of 130 seconds. For the remainder of the 10 minutes the normal kitten walked about, ran, or groomed itself. The split-brain kitten transferred its attention from toy to toy an average of 14.2 times (Figure 9-4A), spending only 0.65 seconds with each one (Figure 9-4B). The split-brain kitten played for a total of only 9 seconds and spent most of the remaining time running about and leaping at the sides of the box.

After either 0.2 or 0.5 mg of amphetamine/kg of body weight, the normal kitten actually transferred its attention more (15 times), played with each toy for shorter periods (6.5 and 4.3 sec.), and had a total playtime of only 67.5 and 97.5 seconds. In contrast to the performance of the normal kitten with amphetamine, the split-brain kitten spent more time with each object. At a

---

[3] Repeated dosage with amphetamine results in tolerance. The greater number of squares crossed at 0.5 mg/kg amphetamine than at 0.2 mg/kg amphetamine reflects the tolerance this animal developed following closely repeated doses of amphetamine.

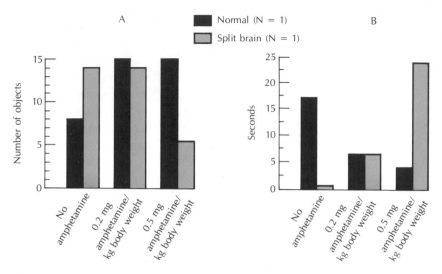

Figure 9-4. Effect of amphetamine administration on open-field activity with play objects of a 5-month-old neonatal split-brain kitten and its control littermate. 4A demonstrates the mean number of objects attended, and 4B, the mean number of seconds spent with each object, in the open field during a 10-minute observation period.

dose of 0.5 mg/kg of body weight the kitten transferred its attention from toy to toy only 6.0 times during the 10-minute test, spending 24 seconds with each object, and had a total playtime of 144 seconds.

Learning and Memory

Procedure. When the animals were one year old, their learning and retention were tested. Each animal was trained to make a visual pattern discrimination in order to obtain food. The animals were adapted to and then trained in a visual discrimination apparatus that consisted of a start box and a runway, at the end of which two translucent plastic doors hung side by side. A small compartment behind each door held a food cup and served as a goal box. The pairs of visual stimuli to be discriminated by the animals were identical in shape and differed only in orientation: either upright or inverted triangles or horizontal or vertical stripes. One pair of stimuli was affixed to each plastic door. The unlocked door represented the positive or correct stimulus, and the locked door held the negative or incorrect stimulus. Each animal learned to leave the start box, proceed down the alley to the pair of patterned doors, select one, and push it back to obtain food in the goal box. When a cat pushed on the unlocked door it received immediate access to the food cup. A push on the incorrect door yielded a bumped head. Cats that bumped their heads subsequently learned to correct their response to the opposite side. Training was continued until each animal performed correctly 90 percent of the time for three consecutive days. The experiments were conducted every other day in a semidarkened room and the animals were deprived of food for approximately 23 hours. The cats were rewarded with small pieces of raw spleen for pushing back the correct door. The same procedure was used when training was carried out under amphetamine.[4] During this part of the experiment, training started 55 minutes after amphetamine was administered. (Because we wanted to minimize any residual effect of amphetamine, we tested the cats every other day.)

Training was carried out first without amphetamine, and then two months later the cats were trained with amphetamine on a second and different pattern discrimination. Another group of cats were trained in reverse order.

Results. Regardless of the order of the testing, the results were the same. Neonatal split-brain cats took longer than normal cats to learn without amphetamine, but with amphetamine they learned more quickly. Figure 9-5 represents these mean differences. Split-brain cats trained first without amphetamine took an average of 780 trials to reach the 90 percent criterion of learning for three consecutive days. With amphetamine they learned the second task, which was equal in difficulty with the first, in only 520 trials, an improvement of 33 percent. Under the reversed circumstances, split-brain cats trained first with amphetamine needed only 560 trials to reach the 90 percent criterion of learning but needed 810 trials to reach the same criterion without amphetamine. This represents a 31 percent improvement in learning when amphetamine is used. Normal cats took only 450 trials without amphetamine and 550 trials with amphetamine to reach 90 percent scores.

The every other-day performance of normal and split-brain cats revealed two different patterns of behavior. The performance of normal cats on each training session improved. Forty-eight hours later, when next tested, their initial performance indicated they remembered most or all of the previous test session. However, the responses of split-brain cats suggested a time-dependent memory deficit. Although performance improved by the end of a day's session, initial performance on the next test day had decreased mark-

---

[4]The animals were maintained at 80 percent of their body weight. On this feeding schedule animals are very hungry and so they develop anorexia in response to amphetamine at much higher doses than when they are on a 100 percent feeding schedule. On the other hand, lower doses of amphetamine result in increased activity and increased arousal in normal cats and decreased activity and decreased arousal in split-brain cats. Without producing anorexia it is possible to obtain an effect on activity with amphetamine and still train the cats to learn a discrimination on the basis of motivation for food. We give our cats the remainder of their daily food portions immediately after each test session and have never found them to be satiated.

edly; it appeared as if animals responded correctly only by chance. This pattern of behavior was repeated throughout a large segment of the test. Thus, prolonged training was necessary for split-brain animals to reach the goal we had set.

Without amphetamine, habituation to the test apparatus was prolonged, and during training it was extremely difficult to persuade the split-brain cats to work throughout the 30 trials of a day's session. The animals were easily distracted by the slightest noise and they frequently jumped out of the testing apparatus after about 15 trials.

When training with amphetamine was started, the animals' behavior changed. It became relatively easy to complete a 30-trial session and the cats no longer tried to escape from the test apparatus. Day-to-day retention increased and learning was faster. Thus, the improvements in learning and retention could be said to be a result of amphetamine treatment.

Histology

When these experiments were completed, the brains of the animals were perfused with 8.5 percent sucrose followed by a 7.5 percent sucrose and 10 percent formalin solution. Then they were removed from the skull. After being embedded in celloidin, alternate sections of 30 microns (μ) were stained with thionine by Weil's method. The corpus callosum and the commissure of the fornix showed complete midsagittal section in all the

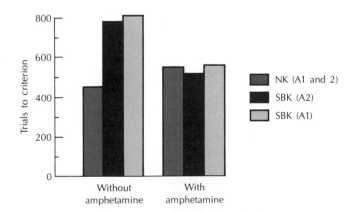

Figure 9-5. Effect of amphetamine administration on learning a pattern discrimination task to a 90 percent criterion in 1-year-old neonatal split-brain cats (SBK) and their normal littermates (NK). A1 indicates learning with amphetamine on the first task; A2 indicates learning with amphetamine on the second task and A1 and 2 indicates that results from first and second task were combined. There were four split-brain cats in each amphetamine group and four normal cats in the control group.

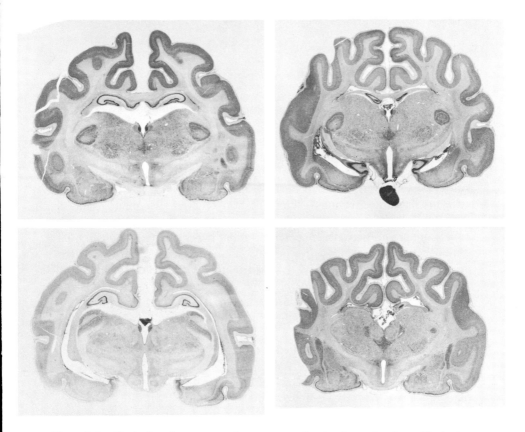

Figure 9-6. The brains of one group of cats were perfused at 6 months of age. The brains of a second group of cats were perfused at 2 years of age. *Left:* Brain sections of 2-year-old cats. The upper section is the brain of a normal animal; the lower section is that of a split-brain cat whose corpus callosum was sectioned 24 hours after birth. *Right:* Brain sections of 6-month-old cats. The upper section is taken from a normal control animal; the lower section from a split-brain cat whose corpus callosum was sectioned 72 hours after birth.

animals but one. In the brain of this cat, approximately 2 millimeters of the anterior callosum remained intact. However, this animal's performance did not differ from the others in any of the tests. Figure 9-6 shows thionine-stained coronal sections through the hippocampal area of the brains of two neonatal split-brain cats and their normal littermates. Sections on the left were obtained from a two-year-old normal cat (upper) and a two-year-old split-brain cat (lower) that had its corpus callosum sectioned 24 hours after birth. Those on the right represent a 6-month-old normal cat and a 6-month-old split-brain cat that had its corpus callosum sectioned 72 hours after birth. The sections of the normal cats show an intact corpus callosum and commissure of the fornix, connecting the two cerebral hemispheres. In the sections of the split-brain cats the corpus callosum and commissure of the fornix are completely absent in the midline. There is also no evidence of surgical damage to the dorsal or medial cortical areas, to the subcallosal surface, or to subjacent structures.

Discussion

It is possible to use the neonatal split-brain kitten as an experimental analogue or model of minimal brain dysfunction because it mimics many of the symptoms shown by children who have MBD. Hyperactivity appears within a few days after neonatal split-brain surgery, while decreased attention span and deficits in learning and memory become apparent as the kittens develop. These can be readily observed in an open field and in standard learning situations. Administration of d-amphetamine results in decrease in activity and in improvement in attention, learning, and memory. Some preliminary evidence indicates that hyperactivity in these animals diminishes with maturity as it does in children who have MBD and that despite the decrease in activity, deficits in attention, learning, and memory persist. Table 9-1 shows the striking behavioral similarities between neonatal split-brain kittens and MBD children.

Two attempts to develop an animal model for hyperactivity were reported by Corson and his colleagues (Corson et al., 1972, 1973) and by Silbergeld and Goldberg (1974). They studied a group of adult dogs that were hyperkinetic, untrainable, aggressive, and violent. Because their early history was unknown, the investigators had no information about the onset and development of hyperactivity. Amphetamine and methylphenidate administration, in the same dose range used for children (0.1 to 1.5 mg/kg of body weight), had the paradoxical effect of calming the animals so that they could be handled easily and conditioned with classical Pavlovian procedures. Although these results are pertinent, there are two major differences between the dogs Corson examined and MBD children on drug therapy. First, the hyperactive dogs that he examined were mature and well past puberty, whereas the average hyperactive MBD child is prepubertal. Second, although hyperkinesis reappeared when drug treatment was stopped, the aggression and violence that were extinguished during the treatment period did not reappear when medication was withdrawn. However, drug withdrawal in MBD children usually results in the reappearance of hyperactivity as well as aggression and other MBD symptoms. In addition, Corson's model is primarily concerned with hyperactivity and not with other prominent MBD symptoms.

Silbergeld and Goldberg imply that they have developed a neonatal model of "minimal brain dysfunction hyperactivity" in lead-treated mice. In their experiments, new mother mice were given lead acetate solutions (2, 5, or 10 mg/ml) in place of drinking water. Some offspring were removed from lead at weaning and others were maintined on it until at least 40 days of age. Subsequent testing showed heightened motor activity in lead-treated mice as compared to controls. Treatment with central nervous stimulants— amphetamine and methylphenidate—increased the activity of control mice but produced a paradoxical effect in hyperactive mice; it significantly reduced their activity. Although parallels between the classical description of MBD hyperactivity and the symptoms appearing in lead-treated mice exist, the relevance of these findings to the actual MBD child is dubious. The hyperactivity of MBD children is a prepubertal phenomenon, Silbergeld and Goldberg observed hyperactivity in postpubertal mice only. Mice reach puberty at about 35 days of age. In addition, during tests of motor activity, amphetamine and methylphenidate produced an initial increase in activity before an ultimate suppression. This contrasts the immediate suppression of hyperactivity in MBD children by the same drugs.

To obtain suppression of activity in mice, extremely large doses of amphetamine (10 mg/kg of body weight) and of methylphenidate (40 mg/kg of body weight) were required. These doses are much larger than that used for treating MBD children (the average daily dose of amphetamine for children being 1.5 to 5 mg/kg of body weight and for methylphenidate, 10 to 30 mg/kg of body weight (Millichap, 1973).

The discrepancies between the two previous studies and MBD children emphasize the need for adequate criteria in developing an experimental model of minimal brain dysfunction. A relevant animal model need not show every characteristic of the human disorder (especially emotional charactcristics that can be observed only in humans) but its salient attributes should be evident.

Hyperactivity, decreased attention span, deficits in learning and memory, and the paradoxical response to amphetamine are the core characteristics of MBD that should be represented in the model.

One major advantage of an animal model for a suspected central nervous system disorder is that the brains of the selected animals can be studied with a variety of techniques, which can contribute crucial information about the possible etiology (or etiologies) of the disorder. All of these conditions were considered in the establishment of criteria for an appropriate animal model for minimal brain dysfunction (Sechzer et al., 1973). We used these criteria to corroborate our belief that neonatal split-brain kittens would fulfill that function.

It is uncertain how callosal section in the neonatal kitten leads to the symptom complex we have described but it does appear to be one way of producing a syndrome of *mild* brain dysfunction in the young of this species.[5] The animals become hyperactive, they learn poorly, and they have short attention spans, but they do not have gross neurological abnormalities and their rate of motor development is not slowed (Sechzer, Folstein, and Mervis, unpublished data).

Neonatal commissurotomy in kittens may reduce the number of neurons and synaptic connections that participate in organized behaviors. The reduction could come about in several ways. First, division of the corpus callosum

---

[5] Corpus callosum section in the adult cat does not produce this syndrome of behaviors.

Table 9-1 Comparison of Results Shown by MBD Children and by Neonatal Split-Brain Kittens

	CHARACTERISTICS OF MINIMAL BRAIN DYSFUNCTION		BEHAVIORAL STUDIES WITH NEONATAL SPLIT-BRAIN KITTENS (NSBK)	
Behavior	Disorder in Children	Disorder in Neonatal Split-Brain Kittens	Experimental Method	Experimental Results with NSBK
Motor Activity	* Hyperactivity: constant, random and focusless activity; fidgeting	* Hyperactivity: constant, random, and focusless activity; constant pacing in cage; fidgeting; unmanageability	Home orientation Activity rating Open field: squares crossed, objects handled, time spent with objects	Home orientation: NSBK take a longer and more circuitous route to home area and mother than controls take. Activity rating: On scale from +4 to −4 NSBK were rated +3 and controls +1.25 Open field: NSBK crossed more squares (161) than controls (106), attended more objects, and spent less time with them than controls; slight sounds interfered with test session
Attention	* Decreased attention span Poor concentration ability Distractibility	* Decreased attention span Distractibility	Open field Habituation to test apparatus Learning tasks	Open field: NSBK attended 14.2 objects/10 minutes; controls attended 7.7 objects/10 minutes, spending an average of .62 seconds and 16.9 seconds, respectively, with each Habituation and learning task: NSBK constantly explored box and jumped out during test session
Learning and Memory	* Impairments in learning * Deficits in memory Academic underachievement	* Impaired learning * Deficits in memory Poor habituation	Habituation to test apparatus Learning tasks: brightness and pattern discrimination Retention (24- and 48-hour)	Habituation and learning take longer (almost 2 times) with NSBK than with controls Retention for 24 and 48 hrs. is poor with NSBK
Emotionality	Anhedonia Chronic discontent Aggressiveness, uncontrollability, defiance	Aggressiveness, uncontrollability Decreased responsiveness to positive reinforcement (Does this involve emotionality or is this an attentional or motivational deficit?)	Activity rating Habituation and learning with positive reinforcement	Activity rating: NSBK are aggressive and are hard to control Habituation and learning: animal may not be responsive to positive reinforcement

Impulse Control	Impulsivity (defective impulse control): little perseverance at tasks; defective organization ability; recklessness, compulsive stealing and lying	Difficulty completing trial session, even when hungry (Does this represent a defect in impulse control?)	Learning tasks	Learning: NSBK jump out of test box They have difficulty completing test session (Does this represent a defect in impulse control?)
Coordination	Incoordination: visuomotor incoordination, fine motor incoordination, poor balance, clumsiness, immature speech patterns	Mild to moderate incoordination: visuomotor incoordination, fine motor incoordination, poor balance Disappears usually by 6 months of age	Home orientation Open field Climbing in cage	Home orientation: NSBK show poor balance Open field: NSBK have difficulty striking at objects Climbing in cage: shows NSBK to be incoordinated and to have poor balance Symptoms are mild-moderate and disappear within 6 months
Response to Amphetamine	*Paradoxical response: decrease in activity, distractibility and aggression; improvements in attention, learning and memory; some increased responsiveness to positive and negative reinforcement	*Paradoxical: activity, distractibility and aggression decrease; improvements in attention, learning, and memory; apparent increased responsiveness to positive and negative reinforcement	Activity rating Open field Habituation Learning tasks Retention Reinforcement	Activity rating with Amphetamine: activity decreases in NSBK to −2; controls increase activity to +3 Open field with Amphetamine: NSBK crossed less squares (92), handled less objects (6) for a longer time (24 seconds); controls crossed more squares (239), handled more objects (15) for a shorter time (4.3 seconds) Habituation: in NSBK is faster with amphetamine Learning: by NSBK improves by 31 to 33 percent with amphetamine Retention: (24- and 48-hour) in NSBK improves Positive reinforcement: may be more effective in NSBK with amphetamine
Postpuberty	Decrease in hyperactivity; distractibility and aggression; persistent deficits in attention, learning and memory; adult psychopathology	Decrease in activity, distractibility and aggression; persistence of deficits in attention, learning and memory	Activity rating Habituation Learning	Activity rating: Postpubertal NSBK are less active (0 – +1) Habituation and learning: NSBK are less distracted but inattention and deficits in learning and memory persist

* Salient attributes

generally isolates the cortical neuronal processes of the two hemispheres from each other. Second, callosal section causes degeneration of callosal fibers and perhaps the cells from which they are derived. Third, neonatal commissurotomy in kittens may disrupt and limit the interplay of excitatory and inhibitory processes that, according to Purpura (1973), are so important for the development of normal physiological operations. Fourth, severing two transcallosal pathways (the striate-striate and the cortico-striate) that occurs in sectioning of the corpus callosum may play a role in the production of this behavior.

I do *not* wish to imply that children with minimal brain dysfunction are split-brained or have callosal deficits, but I do want to speculate that MBD children may have a similar or related reduction in the number of functional neuronal processes. Some support for this idea comes from the paradoxical results of amphetamine treatment of MBD children. In addition to decreased activity, the treated children show improvement in attention, learning, and memory (Stewart, Ferris, and Pitts, 1966; Wender, 1971). Stewart and his associates have hypothesized a deficit in central nervous system norepinephrine to account for the effects of amphetamine. According to them, the release of this neurotransmitter is impaired in MBD children. Amphetamine facilitates the release of neuronal norepinephrine and its precursor, dopamine (Schildkraut and Kety, 1967) and thereby increases the ease of synaptic transmission. The number of functional neuronal processes that participate in organized behavior increases. Observations that both children and neonatal split-brain kittens respond to amphetamine with a decrease in activity and an improvement in attention, learning, and memory suggest that the primary sensory and perceptual pathways involved may be deficient but are not permanently damaged. They can be restored temporarily to a normal functional level by amphetamine therapy. Thus, a reduction in the number of functional neuronal processes, brought about by deficient catecholamine systems injured at birth or deficient from genetic dispositions in MBD children, could account for the early appearance of this disorder.

This neuronal-reduction theory is based on data derived from tests and observations of neonatal split-brain kittens, from the responses of MBD children to amphetamine and the implication of dysfunction in catecholamine systems. Other theories of MBD—genetic; prenatal, perinatal, or paranatal; and biochemical deficiency—are not contradicted by this hypothesis.

Well-documented studies have associated birth and pregnancy complications with appearance of MBD symptoms. Knobloch and Pasamanick (unpublished data) studied children who were premature or who had perinatal difficulties and paranatal medical complications. These children developed abnormalities, including hyperactivity, and they resembled other children who had the MBD syndrome. Werry (1968) examined children who had the hyperkinetic syndrome and found that a large proportion had an abnormal perinatal history. Denhoff (1973) also reported atypical perinatal histories in 11 percent of MBD children.

Wender favors a theory of genetic and biochemical etiology. Genetic transmission theory is based upon the occurrence of MBD among siblings whose parents had a history of the disorder. A biochemical basis for MBD is suggested by the responses of MBD children to amphetamines, which may increase the functional activity of catecholamine transmitters (norepinephrine and dopamine) that are genetically deficient (Wender, 1971, 1973).

Altered genetic transmission, abnormal pregnancy, birth complications such as anoxia, and neonatal illness or trauma could bring about a reduction in functional neuronal processes that might account for the early appearance of MBD symptoms. If the reduction was caused by a biochemical deficit in central catecholamine systems, behaviors that include motor activity, attention, learning and memory, coordination, impulse control, and responsivity to positive and negative reinforcement—all of which may be dependent upon catecholamines—would not evolve normally. As the child develops, these behaviors may become disordered and result in hyperactivity, decreased attention span, impaired learning and memory, incoordination, impulsivity, and anhedonia. Amphetamine administration would facilitate the release of central catecholamines, raise their presynaptic concentration, increase synaptic activity, and thereby augment the number of neuronal processes that participate in organized behavior. The sum of these pharmacological actions would be the paradoxical response.

All of these theories could be explained by a neuronal-reduction hypothesis. However, Kinsbourne (1973) has proposed a theory that "neurodevelopmental lag" is the cause of MBD. This theory specifies a delay in neurological maturation and implies that when the central nervous system finally matures, the MBD syndrome will disappear. Although the theory can account for the early appearance of MBD and the developmental decline in hyperactivity, it is contradicted by recent evidence that the MBD child does not completely outgrow the disorder. Postpubertal MBD children frequently display symptoms similar to more serious adult psychopathology.

Some psychological theories of MBD cannot account for either the early appearance of the disorder or for the paradoxical response of MBD children to amphetamines. Readers can find information about them in a book edited by de la Cruz, Fox, and Roberts (1973).

Tonic Immobility: Evolutionary Underpinnings of Human Catalepsy and Catatonia

Gordon G. Gallup, Jr.
State University of New York at Albany

Jack D. Maser
National Institute of Mental Health

Animal hypnosis has not exactly been in the mainstream of modern psychology. The phenomenon is well documented, but until recently it was poorly understood. Figure 10-1 depicts a chicken in the so-called hypnotic state. Note the unusual posture and the peculiar position of its legs and neck.

Although interest in animal hypnosis dates back at least to the Old Testament, the subject was popularized by an Austrian monk who published one of the first detailed accounts of the reaction in 1646 (see Völgyesi, 1966). He alleged he had hypnotized a chicken by holding its head on the ground and forcing the animal to fixate on a line drawn away from its beak. This and subsequent demonstrations attracted considerable attention and interest; Pavlov and Darwin were prompted to speculate about the possible significance of animal hypnosis. However, early interest in the phenomenon turned to speculation rather than experimentation, and well-controlled studies on animal hypnosis did not begin to appear until the 1950s. To avoid the historical preconceptions associated with the word hypnosis, many investigators now use *tonic immobility* as a more neutral and descriptive label (Crozier, 1923). For the interested reader, reviews of the literature that

Figure 10-1. A chicken exhibiting tonic immobility.

emphasize different theoretical points of view are provided by Gallup (1974a), Gilman and Marcuse (1949), Klemm (1971), Ratner (1967) and Volgyesi (1966).

Characteristics of Tonic Immobility

Many techniques for producing tonic immobility were devised and then maintained superstitiously—farmers place a bird's head under its wing, alligator wrestlers rub their opponents' stomachs, and a magician strokes a rabbit into acquiescence. However, almost all effective procedures incorporate some form of physical restraint. Under conditions of manual restraint, the typical laboratory procedure, the experimenter simply holds the animal down on a flat surface (see Figure 10-2). The animal reacts by struggling and attempting to escape, as you might expect. But if you persist and hold firmly for about 15 seconds, these frantic responses will subside and the animal will assume a relatively motionless, immobilized posture that it will maintain even in the absence of any further restraint. Restraint is necessary for the initiation of the reaction, but not for its continuation.

As implied by this description, tonic immobility represents a catatonia-like paralysis that initially takes the form of muscular rigidity, but may be followed by hypotonicity. Other characteristics include suppression of vocal behavior, changes in heart and respiration rate, altered electroencephalographic patterns, muscle tremors in the legs that resemble those of Parkinsonism, and diminished responsiveness to external stimulation. Animals may also close their eyes intermittently during an immobility episode and

Figure 10-2. A chicken being subjected to manual restraint as a means of inducing tonic immobility.

appear to be asleep or dead. Because of the tremor, eye closure, occasional head turns, and vocalizations, the behavior could not be described as absolute immobility. There is clearly a profound state of response inhibition, but that state is subject to environmental events and a surprisingly dynamic internal physiology.

Tonic immobility may last from only a few minutes to over several hours. Although in chickens the average is around 500–600 seconds, the record duration of a single uninterrupted immobility reaction in our laboratory is 5 hours and 45 minutes. In lizards the response has been known to last for 8 hours or more (Prestrude, 1975).

Despite its unusual or even abnormal appearance, tonic immobility is a robust, naturally occurring response found in a wide variety of animals. To date, the reaction has been documented in scores of different species, including such diverse groups as insects, crustaceans, fish, amphibians, reptiles, birds, lower mammals, and even primates. The published literature on tonic immobility consists of over 600 reports, but until only a few years ago the reaction had escaped much systematic attention in this country. Tonic immobility has been attributed to death feigning, fear, cortical inhibition, sleep, spatial disorientation, and hypnosis (see Gallup, 1974a; Ratner, 1967). In keeping with the latter interpretation, which has been by far the most popular, the phenomenon was designated animal hypnosis.

Hypnosis

The attempt to ascribe the response to some kind of hypnotic state has probably been an impediment to both research and conceptualization. Although perhaps intuitively appealing, the hypnotic model has never succeeded in generating much scientific data. Even hypnosis as a special state in man remains elusive and debatable (Spanos and Barber, 1974). Trying to relate one poorly understood phenomenon to another that is equally intangible provides very little in the way of a heuristic advantage. The label "animal hypnosis" has tended to attract people satisfied with impressionistic data, and it has probably caused many reputable scientists to ignore or avoid reference to the phenomenon. Even today, however, there continue to be investigators (e.g., Draper and Klemm, 1967; Hoskovec and Svorad, 1969) who advocate using tonic immobility as a model or prototype for studying hypnosis in man.

As evidence for the conceptual confusion that has continued to plague a clearer understanding of the phenomenon, consider the labels that have been attached to it: akinesis, fascination, terror paralysis, monoideism, rho, letisimulation, paroxysmal inhibition, bewitchment, thanatosis, mesmerism, entrancement, Totstell reflex, sham death, and still reaction.

Catatonia, Catalepsy, and Cataplexy

Although our initial interest in tonic immobility was unrelated to questions of psychotic behavior in man, the reaction resembles a constellation of symptoms often ascribed to catatonic schizophrenia, catalepsy, and cataplexy.[1] In practice these constitute somewhat overlapping diagnostic categories, but they all share as one of their most prominent symptoms some degree of motor involvement.

---

[1] Others (e.g., Klemm, 1971; Svorad, 1957) have also noted that tonic immobility may bear a relationship to psychotic states in man, but these suggestions have not been accompanied by substantial documentation or elaboration. A recent article by Stille and Sayers (1975), however, argues in much more detail for morphine-induced immobilization in rats as a model for catatonia. The present chapter differs principally from the Stille and Sayers position in that we discuss a *naturally occurring* case of animal catatonia.

Catatonic schizophrenia or *catatonia* is but one of five or six different kinds of schizophrenia. The symptoms, however, make it an easily distinguishable subcategory. In contrast to many other kinds of psychoses, there is no intellectual impairment in catatonia. Moreover, the onset of a catatonic reaction usually occurs much more suddenly than other types of schizophrenia (Coleman, 1964), and catatonic patients are often characterized by alternate periods of stupor and agitated excitement. During the stuporous phase a patient assumes a motionless and occasionally atypical posture, a catatonic trance. While in the trance the patient appears oblivious to the world around him: remaining mute, motionless and unresponsive to external events, often staring out into space at nothing in particular. This immobilized or paralyzed condition can be accompanied by waxy-flexibility or *catalepsy*, which means that the patient's posture can be molded into new and unusual positions without disrupting the trance. Such positions have reportedly been maintained unchanged for several hours. Similar postures may also appear with rigid, rather than flexible musculature—this is called *rigid catalepsy*. Catalepsy is considered by most psychiatrists to be a classical symptom of catatonic schizophrenia, but only about 20–30 percent of such patients exhibit catalepsy.

A somewhat related condition called *cataplexy* is characterized by a temporary loss of muscle tone and weakness, which causes a person to suddenly become incapable of moving and to literally sink to the ground. Some cases of cataplexy are triggered by an acute emotional crisis. *Narcolepsy* is frequently discussed in conjunction with cataplexy, and it consists of sudden and uncontrollable onset of brief periods of sleep, often under inappropriate conditions. Cataplexy differs symptomatically from narcolepsy in that there is no loss of consciousness in the former. There is no loss of awareness in catatonia either.

Tonic Immobility as a Model for Catatonia

This cursory overview should suffice to show that tonic immobility appears curiously reminiscent of certain symptoms of so-called psychopathology in man. Nowhere is the correspondence more striking than in catatonia. Characteristics common to catatonic schizophrenics (Gjessing, 1974; Weiner, 1958) and tonically immobile animals (Gallup, 1974a) include: (1) rapid onset, (2) Parkinsonian-like tremors, (3) muscular rigidity, (4) a hypnotic or stuporous gaze, (5) mydriasis, (6) exopthalmus, (7) waxy flexibility, (8) no loss of consciousness, (9) sudden termination, (10) the absence of vocal behavior, (11) agitated aggressive and defensive reactions following recovery, (12) the fact that both are occasionally fatal, and (13) the onset of both reactions in association with emotional stress.

Partly because of these similarities tonic immobility might be a useful laboratory analog or research model for catatonia. For the past several years we have been collaborating on an interdisciplinary program of research in an effort to pinpoint the behavioral antecedents and biological bases for tonic immobility. In this chapter we will attempt to briefly summarize our findings, and then will discuss the implications of these data in terms of the model.

Fear Potentiation

The onset of catatonia in man can be associated with emotional stress (e.g., Milici, 1949). A common observation among clinicians is that catatonics give the impression of being overcome with fear; as a result catatonia has been characterized as a "panic reaction" (Hoskins, 1946). Patients corroborate these impressions; upon recovery from the catatonic trance, often report that they had been afraid to move or that they felt paralyzed with fear (Rosen, Fox, and Gregory, 1972). Catatonia aside, we have all heard reports of people being "scared stiff."

Tonic immobility also seems to be a fear reaction. Fear was one of the early causes to which tonic immobility was attributed, but before we began our work (1970) there had been no formal attempts to test the fear hypothesis directly. An inspection of the autonomic and psychophysiological data suggest that quite contrary to its appearance, the tonically immobile animal is undergoing considerable arousal. For instance, in chickens, respiration rate rises dramatically following immobility onset, whereas heart rate and body temperature drop (Nash, Gallup, and Czech, 1976). Carli (1974) finds similar cardiac changes in rabbits, and Klemm (1971) has noted considerable EEG activation during immobility.

Our initial attempt to test the fear hypothesis focused on the effects of electric shock. There is considerable precedent in psychology for viewing shock as a means of inducing fear, and we consistently find that pretreatment with a brief electric shock increases the duration of immobility in chickens (Gallup, Creekmore, and Hill, 1970; Gallup, Nash, Potter, and Donegan, 1970). Not only does shock prolong immobility, but, as shown in Figure 10-3, the more intense the shock the longer the reaction (Gallup, 1973b).[2] Indeed, it is not unusual for animals receiving shock before induction to remain immobile from 10 to 20 times longer than unshocked controls. Abrupt exposure to loud noise as an alternative means of inducing

---

[2] For a more detailed discussion of some of the shock effects on tonic immobility see Nash and Gallup (1975b).

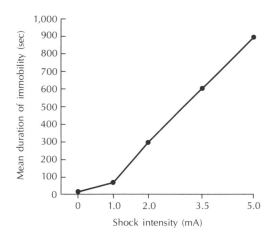

Figure 10-3. Duration of tonic immobility as a function of the intensity of a 2-second preinduction shock. (From Gallup, 1973b.)

fear also produces accentuated immobility in such animals as lizards, frogs and chickens (Edson and Gallup, 1972; Gallup, Nash, Potter, and Donegan, 1970; Nash, Gallup, and McClure, 1970).

Although the fact that tonic immobility is accentuated by both shock and noise might seem to provide strong support for fear potentiation, the skeptic could argue that in neither case is fear necessarily implicated. Electric shock produces considerable physiological and motoric involvement, such as tetanizing effects, which could conceivably prolong immobility irrespective of fear. Similarly, remote tendencies toward audiogenic seizure could complicate a fear interpretation of the effects of loud noise. In an attempt to preclude the confounding effects of any intense stimulus, we turned to the conditioned or learned fear paradigm in which neutral cues are systematically paired with shock. When presented with a CS on the test trial, which two days earlier had been paired with shock, birds remained immobile over five times longer than those receiving an equivalent number of unpaired shocks (Gallup, Rosen, and Brown, 1972). Also, as would be expected, the effect of a conditioned aversive stimulus on tonic immobility is proportional to the intensity of shock used during training (Gallup, 1973b).

Considering the influential work by Seligman and his associates on learned helplessness (Model 3) it is also interesting to note that repeated exposure to inescapable shock (see Table 10-1) serves to potentiate tonic immobility by about 4.5 times, as compared to yoked controls that can escape shock (Maser and Gallup, 1974). In other words, whether subjects

Table 10-1 Duration of Immobility Following 70 Trials with Escapable or Inescapable Shock

Treatment	Mean Duration	Standard Deviation
Inescapable Shock	794.25	849.70
Escapable Shock	173.58	326.31
No Shock	17.33	35.71

Source: From Maser and Gallup, 1974.

have experienced a series of controllable or uncontrollable aversive events before immobility testing seems to exert an important influence on the time course of the immobility reaction.

Even suspension over a visual cliff, with the implied threat of an impending fall, is sufficiently fear provoking to lengthen time of immobility (Gallup and Williamson, 1972). But all of these data could be construed as being a bit circular. Rather than using the duration of immobility to measure the effects of different fear manipulations, it would be better to define fear and the behavior it is supposed to explain independently. In an attempt to assess the aversive properties of the induction procedure, we found that tonic immobility could be used as a punisher if induction was made contingent upon the emission of a previously learned, appetitively motivated instrumental response (Nash and Gallup, 1975a). In other words, just like other aversive stimuli that are made response contingent, immobility induction produced long-lasting response suppression. It appears to be the induction of immobility that is aversive, however, and not immobility itself. Birds given response-contingent immobilization and allowed to remain immobile for 240 seconds showed no more of a punishment effect than chickens permitted to remain immobile for only 15 seconds.[3]

Adrenalin injections exacerbate the immobility reaction in chickens, lizards, and frogs, which might point to chemical underpinnings of fear (e.g., Braud and Ginsburg, 1973). High concentrations of adrenalin and adrenalin metabolites have been found in the blood of catatonics shortly after the onset of the stuporous phase (Gjessing, 1974). To the extent that serum adrenalin is a marker of stress, the parallel between tonic immobility and catatonia continues to hold.

---

[3]Chickens from strains that show prolonged immobility also show much more evidence for heightened emotionality in an open-field maze, as measured by latency to ambulate, ambulation scores and defecation (Gallup, Ledbetter, and Maser, 1976). This provides independent support for the notion that fear is involved.

Fear Alleviation

Procedures designed to increase fear all share the capacity to prolong tonic immobility, but do opposite procedures also have the opposite effect? To qualify as a fear reaction, procedures known to reduce fear ought to antagonize the immobility response. It is well established that handling, taming and familiarization are potent immobility antagonists (e.g., Gilman, Marcuse, and Moore, 1950), which explains why the reaction is not typically found in household pets. Paradoxical as it might seem, aversive conditioning techniques can also be used to reduce fear. The rationale for this is quite simple. If the receipt of shock is fear producing, then there ought to be something about the termination of shock that is fear reducing. A cue that consistently precedes and predicts shock should come to elicit anticipatory or conditioned fear. However, a cue that is paired with shock *offset* and that predicts a shock-free interval should come to serve in the capacity of a "safety signal" (Seligman, Maier, and Solomon, 1971). Using two groups of birds trained under one or the other of these conditions, we subdivided them into two additional groups before testing: one group (controls) in each condition was comparably trained but received no stimulation during the test (Maser, Gallup, and Barnhill, 1973). In spite of the fact that all birds received an equivalent number of shocks during training, they differed appreciably on the test trial. Subjects to which the fear signal was presented before induction showed a tenfold increase in duration of immobility as compared to controls, whereas those shown the safety signal evidenced a 95 percent reduction in immobility compared with similarly conditioned but unstimulated controls.

Tranquilizers also reduce fear and apprehension, and their effects should apply to tonic immobility. To test this we used a tranquilizer (metoserpate HCl) specifically designed for use with domestic fowl. We found that as dosage increased the duration of immobility decreased (Gallup, Nash, and Brown, 1971). Not only did tranquilized chickens show briefer reactions, they were also more difficult to immobilize.

Pretreatment with tranquilizers also neutralizes the effect of conditioned fear on tonic immobility (Gallup, Rosen, and Brown, 1972). Heavy doses of thorazine (chlorpromazine), which has been widely used in the treatment of schizophrenia, attenuate immobility reactions (Maser et al., 1974). In low doses, however, chlorpromazine produces an unusual potentiation effect, which may be comparable to the phenothiazine-induced catalepsy often found in animals and occasionally reported in psychotic human patients (May, 1959; Williams, 1972).

Is tonic immobility subject to other pharmacological manipulations known to affect similar symptoms in man? Imipramine hydrochloride, a tricyclic antidepressant, has been described by medical practitioners as the drug of choice for treating catapletic behaviors in man. In our work with this drug we have found further support for the applicability of the model. We have found that imipramine is a potent immobility antagonist, which at high doses virtually eradicates tonic immobility (see Figure 10-4), if subjects are tested shortly after peripheral administration (Maser and Gallup, 1974). Moreover, as shown by Thompson et al. (1974), scopolamine, which has also been described as an anticataleptic, yields considerably diminished immobility duration in chickens.

Fear or Arousal?

In a recent paper Leftwich and May (1974) argued that "fear and arousal are inextricably confounded" in most studies of tonic immobility. In other words, differences in immobility duration may simply reflect non-specific changes in generalized arousal rather than fear. Attempts to manipulate arousal while preventing fear from intensifying, however, fail to support this contention. Food deprivation is profoundly arousing, particularly to birds because of their higher metabolic rate, but 24 hours without food leaves tonic immobility unaffected. Hungry birds show immobility reactions identical to those of birds given continuous access to food (Gallup and Williamson, 1972). Similarly, we have been unable to show an effect of frustration, induced by the omission of an expected food reward, on tonic immobility. Although some psychologists might argue that frustration is aversive, few would contend that frustration produces fear. Finally, d-amphetamine, which is widely acknowledged to heighten arousal, actually decreases rather than increases the duration of tonic immobility (Boren and Gallup, 1976; Thompson, Piroch, and Hatton, 1973). Thus, mere changes in arousal would appear to be unrelated in any systematic way to changes in

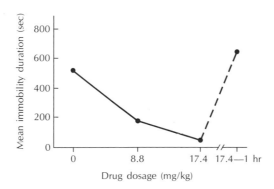

Figure 10-4. Effect of imipramine HCl on tonic immobility. (Maser and Gallup, 1974.)

tonic immobility. Applying tonic immobility as a clinical model, we would suggest that the catatonic's level of arousal is not the primary cause of his psychomotor debilitation.

Learned Helplessness

Since the question will inevitably be raised in the context of the present volume, it is worth mentioning that tonic immobility shows some obvious similarities to learned helplessness, as evidenced by the profound effects of inescapable shock on both. Indeed, manual restraint would seem capable of producing helplessness in its own right because under conditions of restraint any attempts to escape are ineffectual. While restrained, the animal, in effect, has no control. But tonic immobility differs from learned helplessness in some very fundamental ways. First of all, it is not learned. Tonic immobility occurs in the absence of complex, or even simple training regimes. Moreover, whereas atropine and septal lesions apparently immunize organisms against the debilitating effects of learned helplessness (Model 3), we have been unable to find an effect of atropine (Maser, Gallup, and Hicks, 1975) or septal lesions (Maser, Klara, and Gallup, 1973) on the immobility reaction in chickens.

However, Woodruff and Lippincott (1976) have reported septal lesions enhanced immobility in rabbits. The chicken has a relatively small and undefined septal region, but the rabbit's is large and often used as a model in limbic system research. But if tonic immobility was a reflection of learned helplessness, one would predict a decrease, not an increase in duration. Clearly learned helplessness as an explanation of tonic immobility is contrary to physiological and behavioral evidence. Uncontrollable shock does potentiate immobility, but there is no contradiction here for several reasons. First, uncontrollable shock may be more aversive and stressful than escapable shock. Second, inescapable shock is *not the cause* of tonic immobility. Physical restraint is the necessary condition for immobility.

Neurological Correlates

The neuroanatomical basis for tonic immobility has received considerable attention in recent years. Klemm (1971) says that using electrophysiological data and brain transection studies, he has identified an anatomical locus for tonic immobility which resides in the medullary portion of the brainstem. He reports that surgical transections as far back as the eighth cranial nerve in frogs leave the response intact, as do transections behind the forebrain ganglia and thalamus in both guinea pigs and rats. Further, Klemm (1969) found increased unit activity in the brainstem during tonic immobility.

Pavlov thought tonic immobility was a consequence of cortical inhibition, and there does seem to be cortical involvement. However, rather than causing immobility, the cortex appears to antagonize it. As compared to intact controls, decorticate rats are more susceptible to tonic immobility and show longer reactions (McGraw and Klemm, 1969). A 25 percent solution of potassium chloride applied directly to the surface of the rat's cortex produces a condition of functional decortication by depressing cortical electrical activity. Animals so treated show greater susceptibility and much longer immobility reactions, as illustrated in Figure 10-5 (Teschke, Maser, and Gallup, 1975). Similarly, lesions of the anterior two-thirds of the chicken archistriatum, which is thought to be embryologically comparable to mammalian neocortex (Karten, 1969), provide for greatly enhanced immobility durations (Maser, Klara, and Gallup, 1973).

In spite of the overall lack of responsiveness, epileptiform EEG activity has been observed in both tonically immobile animals (Klemm, 1971) and catatonic patients (Hill and Rowntree, 1949), suggesting a kind of behavioral-EEG dissocation. There is no question that both reactions are principally efferent in nature, and there is little or no evidence of afferent inhibition—sensory and associative processes remain functional and unaffected. For example, the catatonic schizophrenic seems detached and totally unaware of his environment during the stuporous phase, but later many catatonic patients recount the events that were occurring around them in surprisingly vivid detail. Animals also continue to monitor their surrounds during tonic immobility and are capable of recording and processing consid-

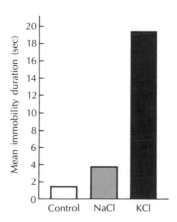

Figure 10-5. Effect of spreading cortical depression on tonic immobility in rats. (From Teschke, Maser, and Gallup, 1975.)

erable information. In fact, several recent studies show evidence for "post-hypnotic" retention of information acquired during the immobility episode (see Gallup, 1974a).

Pharmacology and Neurochemistry

Given the surge of interest in chemotherapy over the last 25 years and the current attempts to identify a biochemical basis for different behavioral disorders (see Model 11), the neuropharmacology of tonic immobility may also bear on the development of our model.

Tonic immobility is sensitive to a variety of other chemical agents in addition to tranquilizers. Indeed, we think that the simplicity and objectivity of the reaction make it an excellent behavioral preparation for studying drug effects. Table 10-2 summarizes a small part of our work on over 20 drugs as they relate to the duration of immobility. In all instances we have collected dose-response curves for each compound, and we have also collected time-delay data for many. Let us emphasize that rather than inducing catalepsy, these drugs were used to *modify* an already existing response tendency. That is, we are dealing with something other than mere drug-induced catalepsy.

Cholinergic Effects

Many of the drugs we have used are thought primarily to affect one or more of at least three basic synaptic systems involving different neurotransmitters: cholinergic (acytelcholine), adrenergic (epinepherine and norepinepherine), and serotonergic (serotonin). As Table 10-2 indicates, drugs such as sco-polamine and physostigmine have opposing influences on tonic immobility (Thompson et al., 1974) and they are known to have opposite cholinergic effects. However, cholinergic effects do not necessarily mean that immobility is mediated by the cholinergic system. Rather, recent data suggest that the cholinergic system may be involved in fear. For example, scopolamine appears to have tranquilizing properties (e.g., Plotnik, Mollenauer, and Snyder, 1974), and because of fear involvement any cholinergic influence on tonic immobility may be less than direct. Moreover, atropine, a relatively specific cholinergic blocker, has no effect on immobility even in unusually large doses (Maser, Gallup, and Hicks, 1975). Any cholinergic influence on tonic immobility is further complicated by the fact that the effects of scopolamine and physostigmine may be species specific. Effects of cholinergic compounds on tonic immobility in rabbits are the opposite of those produced in chickens (Hatton, Woodruff, and Meyer, 1975).

Table 10-2   Drug Effects on the Duration of Tonic Immobility in
Chickens

Increase	No Effect	Decrease
LSD-25	Atropine	Chlorpromazine
BOL-148	p-CPA	Imipramine
Chlorpromazine	Tetrabenazine	Serotonin
Adrenalin	l-LSD	d-Amphetamine
Morphine	Alcohol	Scopolamine
Δ^9 THC	5-HTP	Metoserpate HCl
Δ^8 THC	Reserpine	
Δ^3 THC	Methylscopolamine	
Physostigmine	Norepinephrine	
Iproniazid	Dopamine Beta-	
Pargyline	hydroxylase	
Tryptophan	Inhibitors	

Adrenergic Effects

The adrenergic system has been implicated in learned helplessness (see
Model 3), and norepinepherine (NE) depletion has been correlated with
some of the symptoms commonly associated with inescapable shock. However, in contrast to their effect on learned helplessness, agents thought to
produce NE depletion (e.g., tetrabenazine) have no consistent effect on
tonic immobility. In fact, repeated attempts to block NE synthesis, as well as
injections of NE itself, have failed to produce any reliable effects on tonic
immobility (Thompson, Scuderi, and Boren, 1974).

Serotonergic Effects

Of the remaining monoamines affected by many of these compounds, the
putative neurotransmitter and indoleamine, serotonin, may account for
much of the data (Maser, Gallup, and Hicks, 1975). Figure 10-6 illustrates
the biosynthetic pathway of serotonin projected onto a pre- and postsynaptic
neuron, and the numbers in parentheses summarize some of our attempts at
experimental intervention. Injections of tryptophan (1), a naturally occurring
amino acid that is the dietary precursor to serotonin, enhanced the duration
of tonic immobility; and chickens fed a specially prepared tryptophan-free
diet demonstrated practically no immobility at all (Gallup et al., 1977).[4]

---

[4] In light of these data, it would be most intriguing to see if catatonics might show a reduction
of symptoms following dietary depletion of tryptophan.

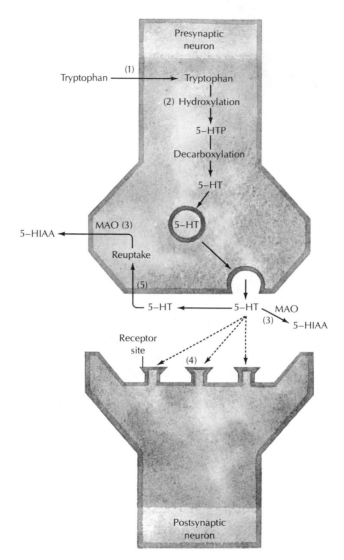

Figure 10-6. The biosynthetic pathway of serotonin (5-HT) projected onto a pre- and postsynaptic neuron.

Monoamine-oxydase (MAO) inhibitors (3), such as pargyline and iproniazid, prevent the breakdown of serotonin in the synaptic cleft and allow for its accumulation; they also prolong tonic immobility. Similarly LSD-25 (4), which is thought to compete with serotonin for postsynaptic receptor sites and which reduces the activity of serotonergic neurons, lengthens immobility time (see Figure 10-7). Thus, increases in brain serotonin seem

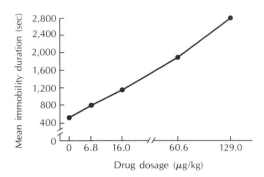

Figure 10-7. Dose-dependent relationship between LSD-25 and tonic immobility. (From Maser, Gallup, and Hicks, 1975.)

to be associated with prolonged reactions, whereas decreases in serotonin lead to abbreviated immobility times. On the other hand, imipramine, which is believed to block the uptake of serotonin back into the presynaptic neuron (5), and serotonin itself both reduce immobility when injected peripherally. Elsewhere in the body serotonin is intimately associated with muscular activity, and because imipramine potentiates the peripheral effects of serotonin, these results may be due to motoric confounding. We have recent evidence for this interpretation; when either imipramine or serotonin is injected directly into the ventricles of the brain to avoid systemic effects, tonic immobility subsequently increases rather than decreases.

Morphine, a widely used sedative and analgesic, has the seemingly paradoxical effect of potentiating immobility. In fact, birds receiving a fairly small dose (10 mg/kg) show average reactions that last more than 80 minutes. The basis for this effect is not obvious because morphine has been implicated in affecting many different neurochemical systems. However, pretreatment with parachlorophenylalanine (PCPA), a powerful depletor of brain serotonin that prevents the hydroxylation of tryptophan into 5-hydroxytryptophan (2), abolishes the morphine-induced enhancement of tonic immobility (Hicks et al., 1975). Pretreatment with PCPA also blocks the amphetamine-induced attenuation of tonic immobility (Boren and Gallup, 1976).

As further evidence for serotonergic involvement, there is a striking parallel between our work with chickens and electrophysiological data on rats from Aghajanian's laboratory (e.g., Aghajanian, Foote, and Sheard, 1970; Aghajanian and Haigler, 1973). Aghajanian finds that the electrical activity of the raphé nuclei, which are composed almost entirely of serotonergic cells, is suppressed by many of the same compounds we have found to potentiate tonic immobility. Also in support of the parallel, d-amphetamine increases raphé electrical activity and, as previously noted, decreases tonic immobility. Perhaps the electrical activity of raphé nuclei, which is affected by changes in serotonin level, is intimately involved in tonic immobility. It may be more than merely coincidental that many of these nuclei are found in roughly the same area of the brainstem as Klemm's (1971) neurological control center for tonic immobility. On the basis of our pharmacological work we think that one of the neural mechanisms responsible for the motoric components of catatonia may be localized in the brainstem, specifically in the raphé nuclei.

Genetic Underpinnings

Human psychopathology has distinct genetic correlates (e.g., Heston, 1970). There also appears to be a genetic component to tonic immobility. We have found large differences in tonic immobility among chickens of different strains, in spite of the fact that they were all reared under identical conditions. White Leghorns, for instance, typically remain immobile from three to four times longer than Production Red chickens, and hybrid offspring derived from crossbreeding these two strains show immobility durations that lie between the two (Gallup, Ledbetter, and Maser, 1976). More direct evidence of a genetic influence comes from the fact that we have been able to selectively breed chickens on the basis of immobility differences (Gallup, 1974b). In only one generation birds derived from parents that had long reactions remained immobile over four times longer than chicks with parents that exhibited brief reactions. By merely manipulating breeding patterns we achieved considerable control over the mean expression of the trait. McGraw and Klemm (1973) also report both strain differences and similar effects of selective breeding for tonic immobility in rats.

Evolutionary Considerations

Because of the demonstration of genetic involvement we might inquire into the possible evolutionary basis for tonic immobility and speculate on its appearance in humans. Does tonic immobility have any natural biological significance? We could cogently argue that much of the previous data might be an artifact of laboratory conditions involving ecologically irrelevant manipulations. Consider electric shock. In spite of its current popularity among psychologists, we know of no contemporary terrestrial animal that has evolved under exposure to electric shock.[5]

---

[5] The applicability, or at least generalizability, of learned helplessness to many organisms outside the laboratory could be called into question on these grounds. In the case of predator-prey relationships, repeated exposure to inescapable aversive stimulation is probably an atypical situation in the natural environment, since repetition would be precluded by death.

We have reported the effect of shock, drugs, noise, and brain lesions, but why do organisms exhibit tonic immobility in the first place? Is tonic immobility just an accident? If it is a mere curiosity, then it is a very unusual one. Why is the response found in such an amazing diversity of species with very different evolutionary histories? Until recently most psychologists have ignored these kinds of questions. To tease out the stimulus antecedents through experimentation and gain some appreciation for the physiological substrate of behavior only answers questions in a proximate and mechanistic sense. Unlike molecules, organisms are not absolute. Life has an evolutionary as well as an ontogenetic history. Evolutionary questions focus on functional significance; that is, if behavior contributes to reproductive success then the genetic basis for such responses will be selected for and perpetuated. It is important to recognize that evolution is concerned with the survival of genes, not individuals. Fitness only contributes to evolution to the extent that it aids and abets reproductive success.

Not unrelated to the idea of tonic immobility as a fear reaction is the long-standing Darwinian notion that it may represent an evolved defense against predators. In addition to the need to eat, drink and sleep, many animals share the everpresent threat of predation. An advocate of the predatory view, Ratner (1967), argued that many prey can be shown to progress through four fairly distinct behavioral stages during a predatory encounter (see Figure 10-8). First, the prey freezes, but as distance decreases between predator and prey this is followed by flight and eventually fighting and struggling at close quarters. Finally, after extended contact, tonic im-

Figure 10-8. A diagram of Ratner's (1967) defensive distance hypothesis of tonic immobility.

mobility ensues as the prepotent response. Tonic immobility may be the terminal defensive reaction in a series of distance-dependent defenses. It is interesting to note that scopolamine, which reduces immobility, has recently been shown to greatly diminish the rat's predatory fear of cats (Plotnik, Mollenauer, and Snyder, 1974).

Simulated Predation

As a preliminary test of predatory involvement we exposed chickens to a natural fear stimulus in the form of a stuffed hawk. Even though the chickens had never seen a hawk before, their periods of tonic immobility were magnified 5 to 6 times in its presence (see Figure 10-9) (Gallup et al., 1971). The effect depended on proximity of predator and prey—as distance from the hawk increased the duration of immobility decreased.

Next, we attempted to find out what in a stuffed hawk could possibly be so frightening. We manipulated its facial features one at a time and we discovered that only visual contact with the hawk's eyes brought about longer periods of immobilization. A hood over the hawk's head or even small pieces of black tape over his eyes caused the reaction to change dramatically. Without eyes the hawk had little or no effect on the chickens.

Figure 10-9. A chicken immobilized in the presence of a stuffed Cooper's hawk. (From Gallup, Nash, Donegan, and McClure, 1971.)

Figure 10-10. The eyespot patterns on an Io moth.

The hawk affected lizards in a similar way (Gallup, 1973a), and again, when the hawk's eyes were occluded periods of immobility were of much shorter duration.

Since contrived experiences with a predator prolong tonic immobility, one might conjecture that in all laboratory studies of tonic immobility the researcher is in effect simulating a predatory encounter every time he grabs an animal and applies manual restraint. We have found that when both chickens and lizards are tested from behind an opaque partition that obscures the presence of the experimenter, immobility reactions are reduced (e.g., Edson and Gallup, 1972). Even eye contact with humans functions much like eye contact with a hawk because staring at immobilized chickens reliably prolongs the response (Gallup, Cummings, and Nash, 1972). The pervasive influence of eye contact is best represented by the fact that artificial glass eyes, suspended by themselves on wooden dowels, yield striking potentiation effects on immobility in chickens and crabs (Gallup, Nash, and Ellison, 1971; O'Brien and Dunlap, 1975). Thus, the chicken's fear of eyes would appear to be independent of its appearing in the context of other facial and body features of potential predators.[6] The avian fear of eyes has had some curious ecological repurcussions. As a consequence of this aversion, certain insects commonly preyed upon by birds have evolved intricate eyespot patterns (see Figure 10-10) that serve to intimidate and repel would-be predatory birds. The insect's defense against predation is to simulate predation.

---

[6]Although it may not be directly related, gaze avoidance and a general aversion to eye contact tend to be a common reaction among schizophrenics (Rutter and Stephenson, 1972; Williams, 1974).

Animals typically show intense escape reactions at the conclusion of an immobility reaction (Ratner and Thompson, 1960)—as further evidence of some kind of predatory involvement—and under conditions of simulated predation many exhibit agitated aggressive behavior following recovery from tonic immobility (Gallup, Nash, and Ellison, 1971). Mirroring the behavior of animals, human patients have also been known to go into manic, hyperaggressive states after recovery from catatonic stupors. The abrupt onset of such behaviors and the frenzy of the attacks can make catatonics very dangerous (Coleman, 1964).

Survival Value

It is not enough, however, to show that the mere threat of predation affects tonic immobility. To view the response as an evolved predator defense presumes that the reaction somehow contributes to survival; are immobile animals really less likely to succumb to predation? Consider the proverbial cat and mouse. As long as the mouse remains motionless following initial capture, the probability of further attack is reduced. In fact, many predators are highly sensitive to movement by prey, and without such stimulus support they often lose interest and become distractable (e.g., Herzog and Burghardt, 1974; MacDonald, 1973). Data now exist on a number of species (e.g., Sargeant and Eberhardt, 1975) that show under both laboratory and field conditions that tonic immobility can minimize stimulation for further attack and allow for escape when the predator is distracted.

Implications for Human Psychopathology

As a possible model of catatonia, tonic immobility represents a naturally occurring phenomenon, rather than a contrived laboratory analogue. The immobility reaction has been taken into the laboratory for analysis, not created in the laboratory by complex training procedures, social deprivation, or drug treatments. We have nothing against contrived laboratory models. Many of the other models in this book describe research that has contributed profound insights into the etiology of human suffering. But most human behavioral disorders occur outside of the laboratory, and it is reassuring to know that there might be some natural models as well.

We think that tonic immobility shows some striking similarities to catatonic states in man, and that it has much to recommend it as a research preparation (see Table 10-3). Using a broad interdisciplinary approach we have been able to achieve considerable control over the reaction. We now have behavioral, genetic, neurological, ecological, and pharmacological

Table 10-3   Outline Summary of Tonic Immobility

Origin	*Symptoms*
Evolved predator defense?	Rapid onset
	Muscular rigidity
	Hypnotic gaze
Etiology	Lack of responsiveness
Fear	No loss of consciousness
Chronic stress	Waxy flexibility
Elements of	Parkinsonian-like tremors
helplessness?	Occasionally fatal
	Defensive reaction
Biological Bases	upon termination
Brain stem mechanisms	
(raphé nuclei?)	*Therapy*
Cortical factors	Imipramine
Cholinergic effects	Tranquilizers
Monoaminergic effects	Behavior therapy
Genetic influence	

information on tonic immobility. Whether this information could be extended to instances of human psychotic states is an unanswered question, but one we feel may be worthy of future research. As they stand, however, the implications of our model for man are more conceptual than practical.

Nomenclature

It is now widely acknowledged that many of the diagnostic labels used to categorize mental patients carry negative and counterproductive expectations, which not only influence the patient's reaction to his problem but the clinician's perception of the patient (e.g., Rosenhan, 1973). More generally, the whole concept of *psychopathology* may be grossly misleading when applied to behavior in the traditional way. Pathology implies the action of pathogens, disease-causing entities usually associated with infectious microorganisms. Clearly most behavioral problems are not physically contagious. There is no evidence that someone can be vaccinated against schizophrenia, or that visitors to mental hospitals should wash their hands when they leave for fear of contracting mental illness. Germs and viruses have little to do with the problems experienced by most mental patients, so why persist in using inappropriate and potentially damaging concepts like psychopathology? Some behaviors fit the pathology concept, such as the psychotic symptomatology associated with syphilis in its advanced stages (general paresis), but these have not been the general subject of most psychological research.

Genetic Predispositions

Given the fact that medical models of behavior problems are often inappropriate and misleading, we are usually left with the alternative that the behaviors are somehow learned; that is, that they are a product of experience. Although it is appropriate to speak of learned responses as acquired, learning itself is not an acquired phenomenon. The capacity for learning is genetically determined. Moreover, it can be shown that learning presupposes innate behavior. Classical conditioning is predicated on an already existent unconditioned stimulus—unconditioned response connection, and in instrumental conditioning reinforcement only serves to strengthen responses that already have some probability of occurrence. A blank slate would always remain blank if learning was the only basis for behavior. Furthermore, it is now apparent that what organisms learn is not arbitrary, and that there may be genetic and evolutionary constraints on the specifics of what gets learned (Seligman, 1970). Organisms whose survival is critically dependent upon learning can ill afford to let its direction be determined by chance factors.

Human Evolution

We have tried to show that unlike other models of mental and emotional problems, tonic immobility may have an evolutionary basis. Much of man's behavior evolved in response to environmental, ecological, and reproductive contingencies that may no longer be applicable. In the past few thousand years, man has emancipated himself from many of the conditions that gave rise to his existence. The kinds of selective pressures operating during the Pliocene epoch bear little resemblance to many of those we confront today. A number of ethologists (e.g., Tinbergen, 1968) say they think that cultural evolution has outstripped our biological ability to keep pace. Could it be that some of our previously adaptive behaviors have become maladaptive? Have some mental patients in effect been victimized by preprogrammed behaviors that are inappropriate to the demands of crowded living in a stressful and complex technological society? Campbell (1975, p. 1,106), summarizes our position most eloquently, ". . . the wisdom produced by an evolutionary system is always wisdom about past worlds, a fitness to past selective systems. If those worlds have changed, the adaptations may no longer be useful, may in fact have become harmful."

There is growing evidence for the existence of evolutionary overtones to behavior problems. For example, Seligman (1971) has shown that the objects of many human phobias are not arbitrary, contrary to modern learning theory, but highly specific to situations that may have been critical to our evolution and survival. Contrast common human phobias for the dark, heights, closed spaces, snakes, and spiders with household objects such as hammers, electric outlets, doors, stoves and parents. Most children suffer much more abuse and pain in association with objects in this latter category, yet there are few, if any, people who have a hammer phobia.

Perhaps the *symptoms* as well as the objects of behavioral problems also reflect evolutionary influences. During their evolution humans were probably not immune to the effects of predation. Maybe there are elements contained in catatonia that represent fragments of primitive defenses against predators that now misfire under conditions of exaggerated stress. Today man is not prey but predator and the veneer of civilization may obscure many of his natural defenses. It is only under conditions of unusual stress, combined with a particular constitutional makeup that tonic immobility may be triggered in man. Possibly such situations prevail on the field of battle, in situations in which the person is "frozen with fear," and in some unfortunate person's overall aversive life conditions—where withdrawal from social intercourse takes the form of depressed motoric involvement as a predominant defense against an experience containing elements of predation.[7]

When viewed from the evolutionary perspective we have been advocating, some behavior problems may only be situationally abnormal and not fundamentally so. To simply accept the notion that normality and abnormality lie on a continuum may obscure the possibility that much of so-called abnormal behavior may be a normal response to an abnormal situation. Prevailing views of mental illness would be quite different were we to accept the notion that clinical symptoms might have a basis in normality and evolution. The conceptual basis for treatment would certainly be changed. It would make no sense to use drugs, electroconvulsive shock, or brain surgery. How do you cure a pupillary reflex to bright light, an eyeblink, or a patellar reflex? Obviously the question is inappropriate, and may be equally inappropriate when applied to certain behavior problems. The important questions may relate to minimizing the probability of the reoccurrence of so-called maladaptive behavior or abbreviating an ongoing behavioral episode, rather than to cures or rehabilitation.

---

[7]For a much more extreme view of possible evolutionary influences on schizophrenia in general, the reader should consult Jonas and Jonas (1975).

Movement and Madness. Towards a Biological Model of Schizophrenia

Steven M. Paul
Laboratory of Clinical Science
National Institute of Mental Health

Biological Research and Psychiatry

Psychiatry is the branch of medicine that assumes both the diagnosis and treatment of human psychopathology. This is no small task because nowhere in clinical medicine can the disease concept itself be so convincingly challenged as in psychiatry (Szasz, 1961). It is still not uncommon to hear fervent debate among psychiatrists, lawyers, and lay people about exactly what emotional and behavioral factors constitute mental illness—or, for that matter, mental health (Moore, 1975). Only within the last five years have systematic attempts been made to test the validity and reliability of diagnosing psychiatric illness (Woodruff, Goodwin, and Guze, 1974), which is one reason why attempts at establishing biological correlates to such illnesses have been generally unsuccessful. Nevertheless, the philosophy that basic neurobiological mechanisms subserve most forms of behavior and that aberrant behavioral and emotional states result from deviations in these basic mechanisms has managed to flourish within the broad scope of dynamic psychiatry.

This dichotomy in psychiatric epistemology has led to a distinction between the so-called organic illnesses, presumably a result of some metabolic

The author would like to thank Dr. John Raftery, Dr. Ara Yeretzian, Dr. Martin Irwin, Ms. Jann Paul, MSW, and Ms. Lela Louis for their comments and help with the manuscript.

perturbation within the brain, and the so-called functional diseases presumed to have their origins in pathological psychosocial development. Such rigid concepts of human behavior are irrevelant; one could say, for example, that all behavior is in essence "biological," as behavior itself merely represents the sum of neuronal events leading to an observable set of coordinated motor movements. Similarly, what psychological process (e.g., sensory perception, memory, affect, or emotion) could be without some accompanying biochemical change within the nervous system? The question is not whether biological processes are a part of human psychopathology, but whether they can be identified and used in the diagnosis and treatment of such disorders.

Etiology and Psychiatric Disease

The question of causality in psychiatric illness (and for that matter in any medical illness) is central to a discussion of biological psychiatry. As defined by Guze (1970), a cause is any event, A, that increases the likelihood of another event, B; in psychiatry, the latter event represents a specific illness, such as schizophrenia. Causes, therefore, can be characterized either as necessary and sufficient for the occurrence of some event, as necessary but insufficient, or as predisposing but neither necessary nor sufficient. Few diseases in medicine fall into the first category, and most have causes that are necessary but insufficient without other simultaneously occurring metabolic or genetic factors. For example, phenylketonuria, often considered a purely genetic disease dependent on a single autosomal recessive allele, can be greatly reduced in severity by administration of low phenylalanine diets. Thus, the phenotypic expression of "pure genetic defects" is often dependent on simple environmental factors, in this instance diet. Correspondingly, infectious diseases like tuberculosis and poliomyelitis, otherwise thought to be caused by an environmentally transmitted organism, are also dependent on variables such as malnutrition and genetic predisposition. The manifestation of such environmentally transmitted conditions are many times dependent on constitutional or genetic factors as well. Rather imprecise boundaries exist between nature and nurture; a concept many times employed in discussions on psychiatric diseases like schizophrenia.

It is also well recognized that no medical affliction is purely dependent on biological variables and that a variety of psychological and sociological factors surround most, if not all, diseases. This has led to the recent upsurge in eclectic theories of psychiatric illness, specifically for the group of schizophrenias (Meyer, 1951). Proponents of this eclectism argue for multicausality: they say that all three factors (sociological, biological, and psychological) contribute uniquely to the development of schizophrenia in each person who suffers from it. Such a concept is not unique to medicine or psychiatry. Before the application of modern biological methods, many diseases were considered to be the result of multiple complex variables such as impoverished socioeconomic class and disordered psychological functioning. Sociological factors, for example, have been given preeminent status in the etiology of schizophrenia because it is well known that the incidence of schizophrenia among persons of low socio-economic class is greater than would occur by chance alone (Faris and Dunham, 1939). Recent genetic studies, however, suggest that the lower socioeconomic class among schizophrenics may be a result of the illness rather than a cause of it (Goldberg and Morrison, 1963). However, the question still remains controversial (Mishler and Scotch, 1963).

Stress and Schizophrenia

What then is the relationship between psychological or sociological factors and schizophrenia? It is well known that psychotic episodes among schizophrenics are often related to periods of emotional turmoil and environmental change (Smythies, 1963), so it would appear that life events are important contributing factors in the pathogenesis of schizophrenia. The question of whether there is a direct cause-and-effect relationship is as yet unanswered. It would be neither surprising nor unique for schizophrenia if psychological stress were in fact intimately related to the development of its symptoms. Many examples of such mind–body dualism exist in medicine. Diabetes mellitus, an endocrine disorder in which daily insulin replacement is usually necessary for prevention of hyperglycemia, is a good example of a disease in which psychological factors are not simply manifestations of the illness, but relate to both its clinical course and overall prognosis. A heretofore well-controlled diabetic may have a greater need for insulin during periods of stress; yet this does not imply that stress causes diabetes. Examples such as these help to provide impetus for studying schizophrenia within the framework of a medical model. As we shall see, the analogy between diseases like diabetes or hypertension and schizophrenia is striking and it serves to emphasize the prominent biological aspect of the illness.

Biological Factors in Psychosis

The identification of biological causes for psychiatric illness has precedent. At the turn of the century a significant proportion (20 percent) of psychiatric hospital beds were occupied by patients suffering from either pellagra (Walther, 1953) or neurosyphilis—general paresis of the insane (Brune, 1970). Recognition of pellagra as a vitamin deficiency and neurosyphilis as an infectious disease has all but eliminated these conditions as serious psychiatric and medical problems. We can only speculate about how many cases of thyroid disease, collagen disease, and various infectious diseases of the central nervous system would still be diagnosed as functional psychiatric conditions if present-day diagnostic techniques were not available. Many of these diseases could not be satisfactorily separated clinically from present-day functional psychoses until the development of more sophisticated diagnostic techniques (e.g., serologic tests for neurosyphilis).

Looking at history, it should not surprise us that theories on schizophrenia have named every cause from the "stress" of poor socio-economic class, chaotic family life, and numerous pathological parent-child relationships (Weiner, 1967) to diverse biological theories of endogenously produced hallucinogens, abnormal serum proteins, autoimmunity, vitamin deficiency, toxic dietary constituents, cerebral allergy, and, more recently, slow viruses (Himwich, 1970). However, there is no unequivocal evidence that any one of these factors taken alone is the most important etiological variable. This list is by no means inclusive but it emphasizes the complexity and frustration surrounding the attempts at unraveling psychological as well as biological causes for the group of schizophrenias.

The inevitable question of why the *biological* factors in schizophrenia have remained so elusive can be answered quite simply. Our understanding of the basic neurobiological mechanisms mediating behavior and emotion is still in its infancy. Only recently has knowledge of the brain's neurotransmitters (those small molecules that presumably jump from synapse to synapse mediating neuronal conduction) been viewed as applicable to human disease states. Recent advances in our understanding of the neurochemical defects in various movement disorders such as Parkinson's disease and Huntington's chorea, along with the discovery of effective drugs for the treatment of schizophrenia, have provided a link between movement and madness. This biochemical and pharmacological link has provided a foot in the door for developing a biological model of schizophrenia based on testable hypotheses. The causes of schizophrenia are far from being solved, but circumstantial evidence implicates at least some neurotransmitters in the development of schizophrenia. This conclusion is derived from biochemical and pharmacological studies discussed in following paragraphs. When combined with recent genetic findings, these studies provide the most compelling evidence to date of a biological etiology for schizophrenia.

The Phenomenology of Schizophrenia: Diagnostic Criteria

Classification of psychiatric disorders into recognizable syndromes (symptom complexes) that follow reproducible and consistent clinical courses has been a process fraught with uncertainty. The final classification of any illness must await an understanding of its etiology; so it is not surprising that the classification of psychiatric diseases has been especially difficult. In the absence of such knowledge, empirical criteria must be used. But many specific syndromes in clinical medicine were recognized long before their exact causes were known. Some like scarlet fever and chicken pox have subsequently been shown to be true diseases in that one etiological variable or cause can be demonstrated. Others like diabetes mellitus and hypertension are recognized as syndromes with multiple etiologies, and they probably represent more than one disease.

It is highly unlikely that all the clinical states currently being diagnosed as schizophrenia are in fact one illness with a single etiology. For this reason, any model of schizophrenia, biological or otherwise, will depend on the diagnostic orientation of the investigator and the emphasis he places on specific symptoms.

Schizophrenia, an affliction that has remained both a diagnostic and therapeutic enigma since recorded medical history, is but one of a group of psychoses for which no underlying pathological mechanism has been unequivocally delineated. This symptom complex is characterized by a profound thought disorder with either hallucinations, delusions, or extreme conceptual disorganization. Various investigators have emphasized different diagnostic criteria, but in general diagnostic consistency exists between experienced clinicians (Hordern, Sandifer, Green, and Tinbury, 1968). There are, however, major qualitative as well as quantitative differences in the diagnosis of schizophrenia between English-speaking countries; a fact possibly related to a selective emphasis on different symptomatology.

Although some of the schizophrenics' signs and symptoms may represent involvement of some final common pathway in psychotic behavior, the onset, clinical course, and mode of transmission of this disease separate it from other psychotic processes.[1] Evidence for this final common pathway derives from the many demonstrable neuropathological conditions that mimic the psychoses of schizophrenia (Davison and Bagley, 1969). These diseases, referred to in this model as the somatic or organic psychoses, provide valuable information about the neuroanatomical and neurochemical basis of psychotic behavior and allow insight into the mechanisms underlying schizophrenic behavior.

Although many references were made to schizophrenic behavior as early as the first and second centuries A.D., it was not until 1896 that Emil Kraepelin separated schizophrenia from other forms of psychoses and modern-day attempts at its classification began (Kraepelin, 1925). Kraepelin also coined the term *dementia praecox* to indicate that schizophrenia is primarily a disease of young people and that it rarely begins after the age of

---

[1] A symptom is an abnormal sensation perceived by the patient, and a sign is something that can be observed by an examiner.

40. Kraepelin advocated a conservative, rather narrow view of schizophrenia, now accepted by most European psychiatrists, which assumed a very poor prognosis in nearly all cases. This view is more descriptive than explanatory, and it emphasizes the readily observable and consistent features of this complex syndrome.

The name *schizophrenia* itself was introduced by Eugene Bleuler—along with a more liberal approach to its diagnosis (Bleuler, 1964). Bleuler thought that not all schizophrenic patients were incurable and that the condition improved significantly in many cases. He based his diagnostic criteria on a theory that schizophrenia represented a "splitting of psychic functions and personality." This rather broad hypothesis is similar to the psychoanalytic concept of schizophrenia commonly employed in this country. Bleuler's theory and classification were undoubtedly influenced by Freud's view of psychological development. Consequently, many psychiatrists believe that schizophrenia is a manifestation of a "weak ego" (Beres and Obers, 1950), and that because of this the schizophrenic is unable to utilize important homeostatic ego defenses in handling psychosexual drives. Without ego defenses, the schizophrenic succumbs to a "primitive form of behavior" (i.e., primary process behavior) manifested by "thought disorder, affective poverty, disorganization, and an inability to conform to the demands of reality" (Brenner, 1955). Such a broad concept, even if correct, would be difficult to confirm, or for that matter, to refute.

One of Bleuler's major contributions was that he established a hierarchy of schizophrenic symptoms that he thought were inherent to and characteristic of the illness. These broad diagnostic criteria (Table 11-1) were subsequently expanded upon, and they form the basis for present day phenomenological approaches. The phenomenological-existential classification of schizophrenia emphasizes that certain schizophrenic experiences are psychologically irreducible, and thus are phenomena in their own right. It makes no concerted attempt at explaining these experiences by way of preconceived theoretical concepts. This approach can be used to delineate and study a more homogeneous population of schizophrenics; something that is vital for reproducible biological research. Nevertheless, all such classification methods depend on introspective techniques and thus may be useless except in the study of human beings. Therein lies the most obvious obstacle to developing an experimental animal model for almost any category of human psychopathology.

Table 11-1 lists the major diagnostic criteria commonly employed in diagnosing schizophrenia. It seems clear from this table that differences in such criteria lie primarily in the *emphasis* placed on specific symptoms rather than in differing symptomatology. For example, auditory hallucinations are almost characteristic of schizophrenia under Schneiderian criteria, but are no more than accessory symptoms under Bleuler's schema. Individual symptoms in Table 11-1 can be categorized into one of four areas of

Table 11-1 Symptoms and Signs of Schizophrenia

Schnieder's First Rank Symptoms
(one necessary for diagnosis)

1. *Auditory Hallucinations*
   a. Audible thoughts (voices speaking patient's thoughts aloud)
   b. Voices arguing (two or more voices arguing usually about patient—refer to patient in third person)
   c. Voices commenting on patient's actions

2. *Delusional Experiences*
   a. Bodily sensations imposed on patient by some external source
   b. Thoughts being taken from his mind
   c. Thoughts ascribed to others
   d. Diffusion of thoughts (patient's thoughts experienced as all around him)
   e. Feelings, impulses, and acts of volition imposed on him or under the control of external sources

3. *Delusional Perception* (private meaning of a concensually validated perception)

Diagnostic and Statistical Manual of Mental Disorders, 2nd Ed.
American Psychiatric Association, (Psychoanalytic influence)

1. *Disturbances in thinking*—marked by alterations of concept formulation leading to misinterpretation of reality and sometimes Delusions and Hallucinations
2. *Mood changes* including ambivalent, constricted, and inappropriate emotional responsiveness and loss of empathy
3. *Behavior* which is withdrawn and regressive and bizarre

Bleuler's Criteria
(Only fundamental symptoms necessary)

1. *Fundamental Symptoms*
   a. Thought disorder
   b. Blunted affect
   c. Ambivalence or withdrawal
   d. Autism

2. *Accessory or Secondary Symptoms*
   a. Hallucinations
   b. Paranoid ideation
   c. Grandiosity
   d. Hostility and belligerence

psychological dysfunction characteristic of schizophrenia: disorders of perception; disorders of thinking; disorders of emotional expression; and disorders of movement or motor behavior (Fish, 1967). In order to compare any experimental mode of schizophrenia with the disease itself, it is necessary to have more than a cursory understanding of the clinical syndrome. For this reason, a brief outline of these four major areas of psychological dysfunction in schizophrenia will follow.

Disorders of Perception

Auditory hallucinations and disturbances of body image are among the most common perceptual disturbances in schizophrenia. The schizophrenic experience of hearing voices varies. For some schizophrenics these voices are easily discernible, whereas for others they are indistinct and may be perceived as voices "in the mind." The latter, called a pseudohallucination, is usually regarded as having no special prognostic significance. In some patients, auditory hallucinations have little effect on everyday functioning, but in others they seriously interfere with normal behavior—even with such tasks as personal hygiene and verbal communication. Unequivocal auditory hallucinations are considered by many a core symptom, and if no organic basis is found for them, they are highly suggestive of schizophrenia. For this reason, any valid biological model of schizophrenia must include auditory hallucinations. Visual hallucinations are reported by a small percentage of schizophrenics, but they are more common in organic states such as drug toxicity.

Many schizophrenics experience disturbances in body image; their perception of the size of various body parts (e.g., hands, nose, feet) is altered. Patients commonly report sudden changes in the size of body parts, and many attach special significance to these changes. Consider this case history from my own experience:

> A twenty-two year old white male was referred to the psychiatrist from the dermatology clinic because he was now convinced that he was, in fact, a woman. After a long interview, he disclosed that he perceived his breasts to be larger than they had been previously and that his hands were smaller. Since these features were characteristic of women, he then began thinking he had somehow been transformed into a female. He had initially sought confirmation from the dermatologist for these perceived changes.

Auditory hallucinations and altered body image are themselves indicative of schizophrenia, but they must be interpreted within the context of other symptoms. Perceptual changes can be used in a biological model because they can be produced by a variety of methods (e.g., hallucinogenic drugs).

Disorders of Thinking

Schizophrenic thought disorder is characterized by an inability to organize thoughts for communicating in a comprehensible manner. Listening to a schizophrenic can be a puzzling experience; although individual words and phrases can be understood, the overall train of thought makes no sense because the associations between phrases are loose or disjointed. I once treated a twenty-four-year old black male who, when asked just how he came to be admitted to a psychiatric unit, replied: "I'm not sure, but sometimes birds respond with kindness, so why shouldn't it be that way?"

In addition to looseness of associations, schizophrenics commonly express feelings of persecution. They feel they are being spied upon or pursued. Many schizophrenics feel that their thoughts are being controlled (thought control) or broadcasted to others (thought broadcasting). Paranoid delusions are usually quite detailed and are very realistically perceived by the patient. An eighteen-year-old college sophomore recently admitted to a psychiatric unit reported the following experience:

> "I walked down 56th Street from the library onto Kimbark. On the other side of the street from me were three guys dressed in very odd costumes. They wore black coats, which was strange for April of 1973, and underneath were white bulky coveralls that covered their entire bodies. They began engaging in telepathic communication with me and laughed quite heartily at me. They said they had just teleported from another university and that I was utterly dead and that I revealed myself to be utterly crazy."

Although the paranoid delusions typical of the schizophrenic's thought disorder can be brought on by certain toxic drug states, the entire thought disorder has yet to be reproduced. The incomprehensible speech and the typical loose cognitive associations do not apparently occur as a result of hallucinogenic drug abuse. For this reason, development of a biological model which includes the schizophrenic's thought disorder has eluded researchers.

Disorders of Emotional Expression

Schizophrenic patients characteristically have great difficulty in expressing emotions. Their emotional tone or affect appears blunted or flat even while they are experiencing intense feelings. Not uncommonly, schizophrenics sit totally disinterested and expressionless; at other times, they may demonstrate inappropriate laughing and giggling (hebephrenia). It is also common for patients who experience frightening auditory hallucinations or paranoid delusions to be rather depressed or even suicidal. The relationship between affective symptoms and "pure" schizophrenia is not well understood. Whether or not affective symptoms are part of a schizophrenic's core symptomatology, are caused by the illness, or simply occur simultaneously with schizophrenic thought disorder are questions currently being debated. What is clear, however, is that in schizophrenia, the overt expression of emotion is many times out of tune with the feelings being experienced. Catatonia is believed by many to be an extreme example of this incongruity between feelings and emotion. I once encountered an eighteen-year-old white male with a good academic record who had become increasingly withdrawn and isolated during his senior year of high school. Three days prior to his admission to a psychiatric hospital he became mute and displayed episodes of bizarre posturing in which he remained in fixed positions of immobility for long hours. After several days' treatment with antipsychotic medication, the patient became responsive and related his experiences during the previous three days. He described very intense feelings of disorganization in which individual thoughts could not be deciphered nor acted upon. He also experienced frightening perceptual changes, including the sensation of "bugs crawling under his skin," yet he was unable to move or ask for help.

Aside from the extreme example of catatonia, defects in emotional expression among schizophrenics are difficult to study or produce experimentally.

Disorders of Movement

Abnormal movements are characteristic of many psychotic states, including schizophrenia. They also occur as side effects of many drugs commonly used in the treatment of schizophrenia, so it is difficult to estimate their natural incidence. Although they are of little diagnostic significance, their value may lie in their use as a behavioral bridge between the human disease and an experimental animal model. As we shall discuss in following sections, many types of abnormal movement observed in schizophrenic patients (e.g., sterotypies, catatonia) can be produced in animals by experimental methods.

The movement disorders commonly observed among neuropsychiatric patients have been categorized by Fish (1967). Let us discuss them now with regard to schizophrenia. They include the following five categories:

1. Disorders of adaptive movement
2. Nonadaptive movements
3. Motor speech disorders
4. Disorders of posture
5. Abnormal complex patterns of behavior

Disordered adaptive movements, such as those involved in emotional expression, occur in many schizophrenics and are most prominent in *catatonia*. They include the marked loss of facial expression and a paucity of expressive limb movements—for example, gestures and arm and leg movements. Disordered adaptive movements similar to those commonly observed in the catatonic patient are observed in people who have Parkinson's disease and other degenerative neurological illnesses. Schizophrenics display another more common form of disordered adaptive movement— they have difficulty completing certain motor acts. This is called *blocking* or *obstruction* and it usually results in a considerable delay between the initiation and completion of a motor task. During the lapse, the patients appear preoccupied with other thoughts, but they complain of having no thoughts at all.

Nonadaptive movements are the bizarre spontaneous movements characteristic of the hospitalized, chronic schizophrenic. They are also characteristic of many neurological disorders such as Huntington's chorea, for which they are of more diagnostic significance. One form of the nonadaptive movement observed quite typically in schizophrenic patients is called *stereotypy*. *Stereotypic movements are nonadaptive movements that occur as repetitive behaviors which show little variation.* Stereotypic movements are not goal directed and many times take the form of repetitive limb movements, grimaces, and rituals.

Motor-speech abnormalities are not uncommon among schizophrenics; they include mutism, negativism, verbal stereotypies (repeated phrases), changes in inflection and rhythm, perseveration, and echolalia (an echoing of words presented to the patient).

Postural abnormalities among schizophrenics are difficult to categorize, but almost all who are familiar with their behaviors agree that the abnormalities are quite common. Many times schizophrenic patients assume bizarre postures as a result of specific delusions or perceptual changes. A good example is a patient of mine who continually walked with his upper torso tilted 45° to the left because he perceived the hospital walls to be tilting in the same direction. Once outside, this posture ceased.

Many other complex forms of abnormal motor behavior occur in schizophrenia. These are usually characteristic of small numbers of patients and thus cannot be called core symptoms. Catatonic stupor, catatonic excitement, hebephrenic behavior, periodic catatonia and "simple" schizophrenic behavior are good examples of more complex types of abnormal motor behavior seen in schizophrenia.

Genetic Transmission of Schizophrenia

Perhaps the most compelling evidence in support of any biological theory of schizophrenia is the unequivocal contribution of genetic factors to the transmission of the illness. It has long been recognized that schizophrenia tends to run in families (Kallmann, 1946); however, the studies that best distinguish environmental (including psychosocial) factors from genetic ones have been accomplished only within the last decade. The more recent studies using adopted and cross-fostered children (born of schizophrenic parent or parents) have solidified opinion that a genetic predisposition is a major determinant for the development of the illness (Rosenthal et al., 1975). Such data has provided further impetus for the development of experimental models of psychosis based on genetic correlations.

Early epidemiological studies established that the incidence of schizophrenia in the general population is approximately 1 percent (for a review of older literature, see Slater, 1968). This incidence is the same regardless of culture and despite great dissimilarities in the standard of living among various countries; the epidemiologic data provides indirect evidence for a significant genetic contribution. In addition, it is now generally accepted that children of schizophrenic parents are 15 times more likely to develop the illness than other members of the population (Shields, 1968). Studies of identical and nonidentical twins, where one twin has schizophrenia, have revealed that the concordance rate (the percentage in which both twins are affected) for schizophrenia is four to five times greater in monozygotic (identical) than dizygotic, or nonidentical (Gottesman and Shields, 1966). In addition, the concordance rate between dizygotic twins is no greater than among other siblings. Although this data is *strong* evidence for a genetic transmission, it does not rule out environmental variables (Rosenthal, 1968).

Heston and his coworkers at the Oregon State Psychiatric Hospital designed an ingenious study in which the children of schizophrenic mothers (who were raised within a few days of birth by adopted parents or foster care facilities) were later studied for the development of psychopathology (Heston, 1970). A comparable control group consisting of children born to normal mothers and raised in a similar manner was also studied. The psychiatric evaluation of each subject was done blindly (i.e., the examiner did not know which children belonged to which group of mothers) and independently by two psychiatrists. The study revealed that the incidence of psychopathology among children born of schizophrenic mothers and reared apart was much greater than in the control group. Five of 47 children in the experimental group eventually developed schizophrenia, but no cases had been found in the control group at the time this study was published. Heston's results have been replicated by a number of investigators (Karlsson, 1966; Rosenthal et al., 1968) and they provide the strongest evidence yet for a biological (i.e., genetic) basis for schizophrenia. Nevertheless, for a number of reasons, adoption, sibling, and twin studies will never be considered definitive. The interested reader should consult Shields (1968) for a discussion of the methodological inadequacies of these studies. Along with ethical considerations only one will be mentioned here. This is that before they adopt a child, one (or both) of whose biological parents were schizophrenic, the foster parents are usually informed of this fact. It is now believed that whatever their good intentions, foster parents who knowingly adopt such a child may themselves show borderline, subclinical psychopathology. The literature on the genetics of schizophrenia has been reviewed by a number of authors (Rosenthal and Kety, 1968; Heston, 1970) and it is too voluminous to be adequately discussed here. Suffice it to say that a careful search for natural gene products such as central nervous system neurotransmitters and their respective biosynthetic and metabolic enzymes could prove valuable in elucidating the basis of a genetic predisposition for schizophrenia.

Dopamine: Biochemical Link
Between Movement and Madness

Two of the most widely heralded therapeutic advances in medicine during the past 20 years have been the introduction of phenothiazines as the first effective antipsychotic agents in the treatment of schizophrenia (Courvoisier et al., 1953) and the use of levodopa (L-Dopa) for the treatment of Parkinson's disease (Cotzias, Papavasiliou, and Gellene, 1969). Although the drugs were discovered and developed independently—the former by serendipity, the latter by deductive reasoning—a subsequent understanding of their behavioral and pharmacological effects has helped to unravel the relationship between abnormal motor behavior and psychosis. Antipsychotic drugs, for example, have two unique properties: they can effectively ameliorate schizophrenic symptoms; and at the same time they are capable of producing a Parkinson-like movement disorder. L-Dopa (the amino acid precursor of dopamine), although quite effective in reducing the movement abnormality of Parkinson's disease, can itself produce psychiatric symptoms including a clinically indistinguishable schizophreniform psychosis (Celesia and Barr, 1970). Other drugs such as amphetamine and methylphenidate, which are known to have major effects on the dopamine-containing neurons of the brain, have been shown to produce a paranoid psychosis that is very similar (if not identical) to that seen in some schizophrenics (Ellinwood, 1967). These drugs, although rarely used therapeutically, are also effective in the treatment of Parkinson's disease (Miller and Nieburg, 1973).

The observation that drugs effective in reducing psychotic symptoms may also lead to a clinically apparent movement disorder (while anti-Parkinsonian agents can also precipitate a psychosis) has prompted speculation that common neurochemical mechanisms exist for both the control of extrapyramidal movement and psychotic behavior. Similarly, the fact that other extrapyramidal disorders, such as Huntington's chorea, often are present with a schizophreniform psychosis, strengthens the argument that these two phenomena are more than coincidentally related (Heathfield, 1967).

The most convincing evidence for a neurochemical common denominator in the control of both movement and madness derives from a wide variety of basic and clinical studies that implicate the neurotransmitter substance *dopamine*. This data forms the basis of what has now become known as the "Dopamine Hypothesis of Schizophrenia" (Snyder, 1972; Klawans, Goetz and Westheimer, 1972; Meltzer and Stahl, 1976), which in its simplest form postulates a relative excess of dopamine (either actual or functional) at specific dopamine receptor sites within the central nervous system. A brief review of the basic biochemistry, anatomy, and pharmacology of the dopamine-containing systems within the brain will be important in developing this concept.

Dopamine: Distribution,
Synthesis, Metabolism and Function

Dopamine (DA) is but one of a group of biochemical compounds known as catecholamines that are found in varying concentrations within the brains of almost all species—including man. Dopamine is not uniformly distributed throughout the brain, but exists in discrete anatomical areas that are connected to one another by DA-containing pathways or tracts. In humans, the highest concentrations of dopamine are found in the caudate nucleus, putamen, globus pallidus, and substantia nigra; areas that compose part of the extrapyramidal motor system (Sourkes, 1972). Other closely related structures such as the nucleus accumbens and olfactory tubercle contain great concentrations of dopamine as well (Cooper, Bloom, and Roth, 1974).

Dopamine is chemically similar to the other naturally occurring catecholamines—norepinephrine (NE) and epinephrine (E)—which differ only in the substitution of a hydroxyl group (i.e., NE) and a methyl group (i.e., E) on the carbonyl side chain, as illustrated in Figure 11-1. The figure

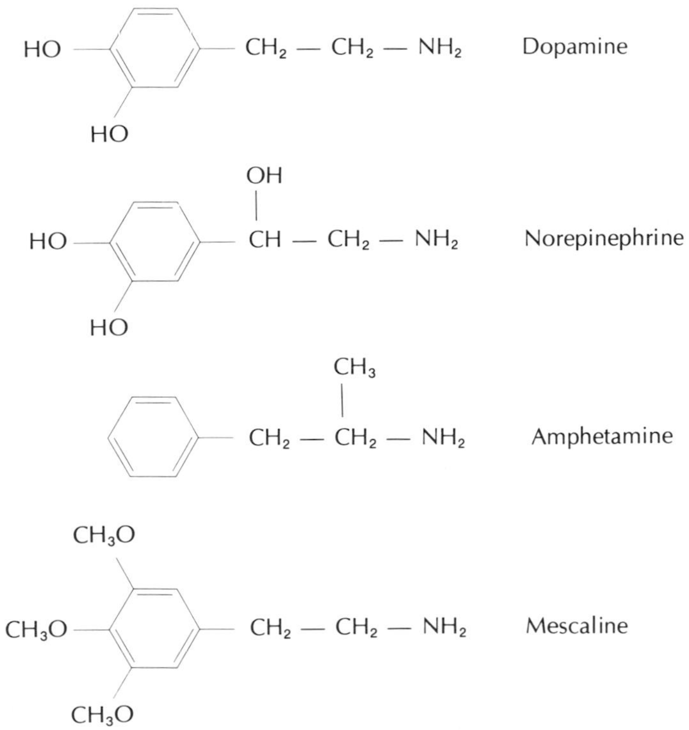

HO — [benzene ring] — $CH_2 — CH_2 — NH_2$ Dopamine
HO

HO — [benzene ring] — $CH(OH) — CH_2 — NH_2$ Norepinephrine
HO

[benzene ring] — $CH_2 — CH_2 — NH_2$ with CH_3 Amphetamine

CH_3O
CH_3O — [benzene ring] — $CH_2 — CH_2 — NH_2$ Mescaline
CH_3O

Figure 11-1. The structural similarities among dopamine and other closely related psychoactive compounds.

also illustrates the close structural similarities between dopamine and the psychoactive compounds amphetamine and mescaline. Dopamine, like other catecholamines, is formed enzymatically from the dietary amino acid precursor tyrosine (Figure 11-2). The rate-limiting step in its synthesis occurs

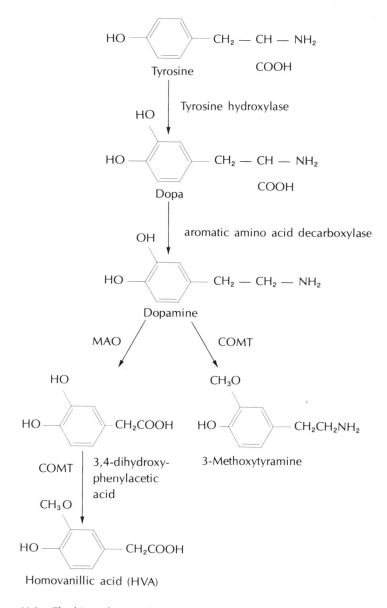

Figure 11-2. The biosynthesis and metabolism of dopamine, beginning with tyrosine, a natural dietary constituent.

with the hydroxylation of tyrosine to dopa by the enzyme tyrosine hydroxylase. Dopa is then decarboxylated by an aromatic amino acid decarboxylase to form dopamine itself. Dopamine can apparently be synthesized entirely within the nerve ending or terminal (Snyder, 1972), where it is then stored within granules or synaptic vesicles, prior to release (Figure 11-3). Storage in synaptic vesicles not only provides a depot for the transmitter, but prevents premature degradation by catabolic enzymes.

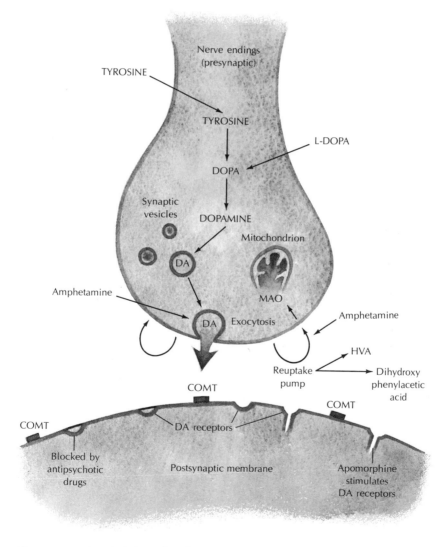

Figure 11-3. A typical dopaminergic neuron.

The release of dopamine from nerve endings within the central nervous system is less well understood than transmitter release in the peripheral nervous system; but it probably involves the process of exocytosis. During the periods of axonal depolarization dopamine is released into the synaptic cleft where it comes into contact with specific postsynaptic receptors. Recently, presynaptic "autoreceptors," which are believed to be important in the regulation of dopamine synthesis, have been described (Roth, Walters, and Morgenroth, 1974). The physiological action of dopamine is terminated by either the process of "reuptake" (back into the presynaptic terminal) or metabolic degradation near the postsynaptic membrane. A diagram of a typical dopaminergic nerve ending is shown in Figure 11-3. Various psychoactive drugs have been shown to interfere with this process at specific steps. For example, amphetamine causes both the release of dopamine from the nerve ending and blockade of its reuptake. The net effect of amphetamine's action, therefore, is to prolong the activity of dopamine at the hypothetical dopamine receptor. Antipsychotic drugs, on the other hand, preferentially block postsynaptic dopamine receptors (Creese, Burt, and Synder, 1976) as well as presynaptic dopamine receptors (Seeman and Lee, 1975), a fact that adds to the growing body of evidence in support of the Dopamine Hypothesis. Metabolic breakdown of dopamine occurs as a result of two enzymes: monoamine oxidase (MAO) and catechol-O-methyl-transferase (COMT). The major metabolic products include dihydroxyphenylacetic acid (DOPAC) and homovanillic acid (HVA) (Figure 11-2).

From a number of histochemical and biochemical studies there is evidence for at least five dopamine-containing pathways within the brain. They include: *the nigrostriatal tract; mesolimbic tract; tuberoinfundibular tract; mesocortical tract;* and a recently described *incerto-hypothalamic tract* (Figure 11-4).

Cell bodies of the *nigrostriatal pathway* originate in a nucleus called the pars compacta of the substantia nigra and project to the caudate-putamen of the basal ganglia, or neostriatum (Ungerstedt, 1971). The terminals of these dopamine neurons project to neostriatal interneurons that are believed to be cholinergic in nature. The nigrostriatal pathway is undoubtedly the best studied dopamine tract because of its well-known relationship to Parkinson's disease. In Parkinson's disease, a degeneration of this pathway results in associated movement and behavioral abnormalities, most of which can be reversed by treatment with L-Dopa (Calne and Sandler, 1970). Dopamine itself, is thought to have inhibitory effects on neostriatal cells (Bloom, Costa, and Salmoiraghi, 1965), but evidence of its having an excitatory role exists as well (Feltz, 1971).

The basal ganglia are believed to serve in the regulation of "slow voluntary smooth movement of different speed" (Kornhuber, 1974). The extrapyramidal dopamine system can be thought of as "regulating the re-

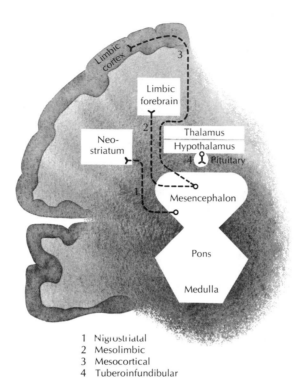

Figure 11-4.   Four major dopamine tracts of the brain (Meltzer and Stahl, 1976). (1) Substantia nigra to the caudate-putamen complex (striatum), (2) limbic forebrain to midbrain tegmentum, (3) midbrain to limbic cortex, and (4) connecting stalk between the hypothalamus and the pituitary gland.

sponsiveness of the basal ganglia to the motor commands of the cortex" (Matthysse, 1974). Thus, in diseases like Parkinsonism, where there is a deficiency of extrapyramidal dopamine, there is also a delay in the *initiation of movement.* Conversely, too much dopamine in such a system may result in movements (like the repetitive movements of stereotypy or chorea) that would normally have been filtered out or "dampened." Pharmacologic stimulation of these dopamine tracts in humans (with either L-Dopa or the dopamine-agonist apomorphine) exacerbates the choreiform movements of both Huntington's disease (Klawans, 1970) and tardive dyskinesia, which will be discussed in following paragraphs (Klawans, 1973). In animals both drugs characteristically produce stereotypic behavior (Ernst, 1967).

Cell bodies of the *mesolimbic dopamine tract* originate near the interpeduncular nucleus of the ventral tegmentum and project to both the nucleus accumbens and olfactory tubercle (Ungerstedt, 1971). Very little is currently known about the function of dopamine in this pathway. Because the rostral termination of this system (along with that of mesocortical tract) includes many of the limbic areas known to effect emotional behavior, it is therefore of great interest. Hokfelt and coworkers (Hokfelt, Ljungdahl, Fuxe, and Johansson, 1974) were the first to demonstrate the distribution of dopamine-containing terminals in the limbic cortex. These areas include the cingulate gyrus, hippocampus, amygdaloid cortex, and entorhinal cortex.

There is considerable indirect evidence suggesting that certain areas within the mesolimbic tract are relevant to the pathogenesis of schizophrenia (Stevens, 1973). Stimulation of the dorsal hippocampus by electrical or chemical means, for example, has been reported to produce hallucinations and disturbances in thinking (Horowitz and Adams, 1970). Torrey and Peterson (1974) have summarized the behavioral and perceptual changes observed after stimulation or ablation of the limbic system in humans. They include: paranoid ideation, depersonalization, perceptual changes, catatonic-like behavior, and disturbances of mood and emotion. Heath and coworkers (Heath, 1954) were the first to directly record electrical activity (EEG) by use of depth electrodes implanted in various subcortical structures of schizophrenic patients. Characteristic abnormal epileptiform activity was consistently recorded from subcortical sites in the rostral forebrain (septal region) of schizophrenic patients. The activity was not found in controls. This finding has been replicated by Hanley (1972) and it provides the only direct evidence for abnormal brain activity in schizophrenia. These "dysfunctional" subcortical sites correspond to dopamine-containing structures within the rostral projection of the mesolimbic dopamine tract.

The *tuberoinfundibular dopamine tract* consists of cell bodies originating in the arcuate nucleus of the hypothalamus and extending to the outer layer of the median eminence (Fuxe and Hokfelt, 1966). This pathway is active in the regulation of both synthesis and secretion of at least two pituitary hormones. One of these, prolactin, is under tonic inhibitory control by dopamine within this tract. Thus, any drug that effectively blocks dopamine receptors in this area undoubtedly increases the concentration of prolactin in the blood. Clinically effective antipsychotic agents have been shown to be potent releasers of prolactin (Meltzer and Fang, 1975).

A closely related dopamine tract, the *incertohypothalamic tract* includes cell bodies that originate in the posterior hypothalamus and project diffusely to the anterior hypothalamus and zona incerta (Bjorkland, Lindvall, and Nobin, 1975). Also included are cell bodies located in the periventricular nucleus of the hypothalamus, which gives rise to terminal projections in the septal, preoptic, and anterior hypothalamic areas. An neuroendocrine function has been postulated for this pathway as well.

Are Antipsychotic Drugs Specific?

If antipsychotic drugs are truly *antischizophrenic compounds*, then an understanding of their underlying mechanism of action could aid us in delineating the biochemical changes that occur during the illness. Following the introduction and widespread use of these compounds in this country, a number of large collaborative studies were designed to test and compare their clinical efficacy (Klein and Davis, 1969). Initially, some investigators suspected that the antipsychotic phenothiazines were no more than super-sedatives, rather than specific antischizophrenic drugs. For this reason, very potent sedatives such as phenobarbitol were studied as well for possible antipsychotic properties. The results of the National Institute of Mental Health-Veterans Administration collaborative studies revealed the phenothiazines to be quite effective as antipsychotic agents when compared to either placebo or phenobarbitol. In fact, phenobarbitol itself was found to be no more effective than placebo, which suggests that sedation is not a requisite for antipsychotic activity.

A further analysis of the "psychotic" symptoms most affected by the phenothiazines revealed a marked specificity in their activity. Table 11-2 lists the response of "core" schizophrenic symptoms to commonly used phenothiazine compounds. Bleuler's fundamental symptoms (see Table 11-1) for example, were most beneficially influenced by these drugs, whereas the accessory or secondary symptoms were less influenced. Nonspecific schizo-

Table 11-2 Response of Schizophrenic Symptoms to Phenothiazines

Bleuler's Schema	Response
Fundamental	
Thought disorder	Marked
Blunted affect	Marked
Withdrawal	Marked
Autistic behavior	Marked
Accessory	
Hallucinations	Significant
Paranoid ideation	Significant
Grandiosity	Significant
Hostility and belligerence	Significant
Nonschizophrenic	
Anxiety and tension	Not significant
Guilt	Not significant

From Klein and Davis (1969).

phrenic symptoms such as anxiety and tension were relatively unaffected. These results indicate that the underlying mechanism of action of these compounds may indeed relate to the pathogenic mechanisms of psychosis. However, it is quite conceivable that these drugs may act by mechanisms far removed from those relevant to schizophrenia.

There are many clinically effective and chemically unrelated antipsychotic compounds currently employed for the treatment of schizophrenia. These agents differ primarily in their relative therapeutic dosage (i.e., clinical potencies) and associated side effects, as no clear-cut differences in antipsychotic properties have been demonstrated.[2] All antipsychotic compounds are capable of producing movement abnormalities but some are more potent in this regard than others.

The Role of Dopamine
in Drug-Induced Extrapyramidal Disorders

Antipsychotic compounds, regardless of major differences in their chemical structure, produce a number of clinically apparent extrapyramidal movement abnormalities. These include a *Parkinsonian syndrome*, an *acute dyskinesia or dystonia*, and a late onset or *tardive dyskinesia*.

Parkinson's Syndrome. All of the signs and symptoms characteristic of the Parkinsonian triad can be seen in drug-induced or *pseudo parkinsonism*. This triad of symptoms consists of *tremor, rigidity,* and *bradykinesia*. Patients with Parkinson's disease characteristically present with a stiffness or rigidity of muscle groups (flexor greater than extensor), a "pill-rolling" tremor of the arms or legs, an expressionless face, hypersalivation, loss of many adaptive movements (e.g., facial expression, gait, etc.) and subtle motor speech abnormalities. Parkinsonism has a number of causes. *Primary* or *idiopathic* Parkinson's disease is the prototype of the disorder and is associated with degenerative changes in the striatal-nigral dopamine tract. Possibly the most common type of Parkinsonism, however, results from the use of antipsychotic drugs such as the phenothiazines or butyrophenones. Signs of Parkinsonism usually begin within a few days of initiating antipsychotic medication (Ayd, 1961; Freyhan, 1957) and are almost always apparent within three months. The incidence of Parkinsonism among patients treated with either phenothiazines or butyrophenone ranges from 10-60 percent (Goldman, 1961; Chase, 1972), although scientists who use very sensitive detection methods estimate that it may be as high as 90 percent (Haase and Janssen, 1965).

---

[2]The exact differences in therapeutic efficacy among antipsychotic drugs have not yet been demonstrated for groups of patients.

The discovery of decreased concentrations of dopamine in the basal ganglia of patients dying of Parkinson's disease (Ehringer and Hornykiewicz, 1960) initiated a new era in the understanding of the biochemical basis of extrapyramidal movement. Loss of dopaminergic input to the striatum, secondary to a degeneration of dopamine cell bodies in the substantia nigra, is believed responsible for the typical triad of Parkinsonian symptoms. An important outgrowth of these studies was the eventual use of L-Dopa in the treatment of Parkinsonism. It is generally accepted that L-Dopa provides at least 60 percent improvement in roughly 80 percent of patients. Large doses of L-Dopa, from 3 to 8 grams per day, are usually necessary for amelioration of symptoms. Other drugs, notably the *anticholinergic* compounds (Trihexyphenidyl and Benztropine) are also effective, but to a somewhat lesser degree. The fact that anticholinergic drugs are effective in the treatment of Parkinson's disease indicated that central cholinergic hyperactivity may be responsible for at least part of the illness. Some researchers have postulated that a "dopaminergic-cholinergic balance" within the basal ganglia is necessary for normal extrapyramidal function. Thus, in Parkinson's disease, loss of striatal dopamine leads to an *imbalance* between these two neurotransmitters (Weintraub and VanWoert, 1971). Although much indirect evidence exists to support the "dopaminergic-cholinergic imbalance" hypothesis, it has recently been demonstrated that the clinically effective anticholinergic drugs are also potent inhibitors of the presynaptic dopamine "reuptake" pump (Figure 11-3) (Coyle and Snyder, 1969). It is therefore conceivable that these drugs may act by increasing dopamine at the postsynaptic receptor. In this regard other dopamine releasers or reuptake blockers such as amphetamine and methylphenidate are also effective in reducing Parkinsonian symptoms (Miller and Nieburg, 1973).

The mechanism of drug-induced Parkinsonism is most likely related to successful competitive blockade of postsynaptic dopamine receptor sites (Hornykiewicz, 1972). This conclusion can be drawn from a number of independent observations. First, neurophysiological studies of striatal neurons indicate that the phenothiazines and related antipsychotic agents block the inhibitory effects of iontophorised dopamine (Bunney and Aghajanian, 1975). In addition, as first demonstrated by Carlsson and Lindquist (1963), the acute administration of antipsychotic phenothiazines increases dopamine metabolites in the rat brain. Subsequent investigation of this phenomena has attributed this increase to a postsynaptic blockade of dopamine receptors with a compensatory increase in dopamine synthesis, release, and metabolism (i.e., in dopamine turnover). In a series of investigations Nyback and associates (1968) have shown that the increase in dopamine turnover following the administration of antipsychotic drugs is roughly proportional to their clinical efficacy. Some of the exceptions to this relationship include the antipsychotic drugs that are also associated with a lower incidence of extrapyramidal side effects in humans (i.e., thioridazine and clozapine). Recently, Miller and Hiley (1974) as well as Snyder, Greenberg, and Yamamura (1974) have provided strong evidence that differences among antipsychotic drugs in their capacity to produce extrapyramidal symptoms result from differences in their anticholinergic properties. Thus, although antidopamine effects are responsible for the Parkinsonian movement disorder, the potent *anticholinergic* properties of certain antipsychotic agents may, in fact, attenuate this side effect.

Clinical studies have shown that drugs that increase the availability of dopamine or that directly stimulate dopamine receptors (e.g., L-Dopa, amphetamine, apomorphine) will alleviate the drug-induced extrapyramidal symptoms (Barbeau, 1969; Miller and Nieburg, 1973). Similarly, drugs that decrease the availability of dopamine or directly block the dopamine receptor itself will exacerbate these symptoms (Hornykiewicz, 1972).

More direct evidence for involvement of dopamine in drug-induced extrapyramidal symptoms comes from biochemical studies on the so-called dopamine receptor. All neurotransmitters are thought to bring about their physiological effects through interaction with a specific receptor. For dopamine, this receptor is believed by many to be the enzyme *adenylate cyclase* (Robison, Butcher, and Sutherland, 1971). Upon activation by the neurotransmitter, this enzyme catalyzes the conversion of adenosine triphosphate (ATP) to cyclic-adenosine monophosphate (AMP), which in turn has a variety of intracellular effects. Cyclic AMP acts as a second chemical messenger to promote phosphorylation of intracellular proteins. This chain of events is responsible for initiating dopamine-related physiological activity within the neuron, such as changes in ionic permeability and depolarization.

In an elegant set of studies, Kebabian and Greengard (1971) have isolated and identified a dopamine-sensitive adenylate cyclase from the basal ganglia. This enzyme is stimulated by very low concentrations of dopamine and by other dopamine agonists such as apomorphine. Most of the clinically effective antipsychotics have been shown to be potent inhibitors of the dopamine-stimulated adenylate cyclase, but some well known antipsychotic agents (e.g., haloperidol and spiroperidol) are relatively weak inhibitors (Miller, Horn, and Iverson, 1974). This discrepancy has led some investigators to challenge the hypothesis that antipsychotic drugs exert their therapeutic effects by blocking postsynaptic dopamine receptors. Indeed, Seeman and Lee (1974) have suggested that the clinical potency of these compounds correlates best to the inhibition of dopamine *release* rather than with any postsynaptic effect. Whether or not the dopamine-sensitive adenylate cyclase is actually the dopamine receptor itself is still undecided (Arbuthnott et al., 1974). More recently, specific dopamine "receptor binding" to brain membrane preparations has been demonstrated (Seeman et al., 1975; Burt et al., 1975). This binding correlates very closely to the known pharmacological properties of the hypothetical dopamine receptor and thus is likely to be a better estimate of dopamine receptor activity. All the clinically effective antipsychotics that have been tested so far have been shown to be potent inhibitors of this dopamine binding; their capacity to inhibit closely parallels their potency (Creese, Burt, and Snyder, 1976). It is likely therefore that the production of extrapyramidal movements (as well as the amelioration of psychotic symptoms) by antipsychotic drugs is related to their effects on post-synaptic dopamine receptors.

Acute Dyskinesia

Acute dyskinesias or dystonias occur soon after treatment with antipsychotic drugs and consist primarily of "intermittent and sustained muscular spasms and/or abnormal postures" (Marsden, Tarsy, and Baldessarini, 1975). Generally, the muscles of the head and neck, including the eyes (e.g., blinking and blepharospasm), the mouth (e.g., protrusion of tongue) and the face (e.g., grimacing), are affected. Acute dyskinesias appear before the other drug-induced movement disorders, and they can occur within a few hours following a single dose of an antipsychotic drug. Dystonias also occur most infrequently as compared with other drug-induced extrapyramidal symptoms, probably in less than 10 percent of treated cases (Chase, 1972).

The biochemical events responsible for acute dyskinesias are not well understood. Dystonias are usually reversed quite readily by anticholinergic drugs such as those used in Parkinsonism and there are also a few reports of beneficial effects with apomorphine and methylphenidate (Fann, 1966; Gessa, Tagliamonte, and Gessa, 1973). These results implicate a blockade of the dopamine receptor in the pathogenesis of acute dyskinesias, but the results so far are inconclusive.

Tardive Dyskinesia

Tardive dyskinesia (late onset or persistent dyskinesia) consists of involuntary, rhythmic, stereotyped movements that typically occur within the bucco-linguo-masticatary muscles, the oral and facial muscles (Crane, 1973; Klawans, 1973). These movements usually develop after prolonged treatment with an antipsychotic drug and rarely occur before a patient has had six months of continuous treatment. Symptoms of tardive dyskinesia characteristically appear following the reduction or complete withdrawal of the drug. The reported prevalance of tardive dyskinesia in chronically hospitalized schizophrenics is somewhere between .5 and 50 percent. Crane (1973) estimates that between .5 and 40 percent of asymptomatic patients develop tardive dyskinesia following discontinuation of their medication after prolonged treatment. The relationship between drug exposure or dosage and the development of tardive dyskinesia is quite variable and highly idiosyncratic, although it is clear that most patients who develop symptoms have been treated with relatively high doses for extended periods of time (Ayd, 1967).

A number of clinical observations have indicated that tardive dyskinesia may in fact represent a state of *dopaminergic hypersensitivity*. Drugs that decrease dopamine activity (e.g., reserpine, tetrabenazine, or alpha-methyl tyrosine) or that further block the effects of dopamine at the receptor (e.g., higher dosages of antipsychotics) will almost always suppress symptoms. On the other hand, both direct (e.g., L-Dopa) and indirect (e.g., amphetamine) acting dopamine antagonists exacerbate tardive dyskinesia (Chase, 1972). The close similarity between tardive dyskinesia and the dyskinesias produced by L-Dopa in patients with Parkinson's disease strengthens these observations.

If the capacity of antipsychotic drugs to produce extrapyramidal side effects were closely related to an amelioration of schizophrenic symptoms, then it would be more likely that some common underlying mechanism exists. The high incidence of extrapyramidal side effects among successfully treated schizophrenic patients led early investigators to postulate that they were in fact *necessary* for the drugs' therapeutic effects (Denham and Carrick, 1961; Deniker, 1960). Later, more controlled studies have now established that antipsychotic effects can occur without apparent extrapyramidal symptoms (Bishop, Gallant, and Sykes, 1965; Cole and Clyde, 1961). Nevertheless, a complete separation of antipsychotic effects and extrapyramidal symptoms has to date proved impossible. It is likely that mutually antagonistic pharmacological properties (e.g., anticholinergic vs. antidopaminergic) are responsible for the variability between antipsychotic drugs in the incidence of their extrapyramidal side effects.

The Role of Dopamine in Drug-Induced Psychoses

The possibility that certain drug-induced psychoses could in fact be experimental models for various human psychotic states has for many years been an attractive one. (The close structural similarities between many hallucinogenic drugs and certain endogenous neurotransmitters, which Figure 11-1 illustrates has made this an active area of research.) Although potent hallucinogens such as LSD and mescaline are capable of reproducing some of the schizophrenic's symptoms (e.g., visual hallucinations), in general, the clinical picture is quite different (Hollister, 1962). There is probably no acute drug state that closely resembles schizophrenia. However, the chronic use of certain psychostimulants such as amphetamine ("speed") or phencyclidine ("angel dust") has long been recognized as a producer of a paranoid psychosis that can be indistinguishable, at times, from schizophrenia. In addition, chronic amphetamine abuse results in a number of movement abnormalities, such as the stereotypes and rituals that are commonly observed among schizophrenic patients.

Clinical studies of human amphetamine abusers have revealed that chronic concentrated doses of amphetamine can produce a psychotic state that closely resembles that of acute paranoid schizophrenia (Connell, 1958). In fact, many cases of amphetamine psychosis are misdiagnosed as paranoid schizophrenia until more careful drug histories are taken. Classically, the psychosis of chronic amphetamine abusers includes marked paranoid delusions, auditory hallucinations, and visual hallucinations. The characteristic thought disorder of schizophrenia is not as common a finding in amphetamine psychosis, but nonetheless it has been reported (Kalant, 1966).

Schizophrenic patients themselves are much more sensitive to the psychotomimetic properties of amphetamines and related compounds (Janowsky et al., 1973). Relatively small doses of amphetamine, or of the closely related analogue methylphenidate, can bring out symptoms in a relatively asymptomatic patient. This finding has led to speculation that amphetamines' effect might simply be related to a provocation of latent schizophrenia among chronic abusers. However, Griffith and coworkers (Griffith, Oates, and Cavanaugh, 1968) as well as Angrist and Gershon (1970) have been able to induce a paranoid psychosis by chronically administering amphetamine to volunteers who had no previous history of schizophreniform illness. Thus, it is highly unlikely that amphetamine psychosis is unique only to those who had a predisposition towards developing schizophrenia. There are many good descriptive reviews on the clinical similarity between amphetamine psychosis and schizophrenia (Kalant, 1966). These clinical similarities have prompted some investigators to propose amphetamine psychosis as a good heuristic model for schizophrenia (Kety, 1972; Snyder, 1974).

The pharmacological effects of amphetamine are also believed to involve the catecholamine-containing neurons in the brain (Snyder, 1972). Amphetamine has a number of biochemical effects, including the potentiation of catecholamine release, the blockade of the presynaptic reuptake "pump," and a weak inhibitory effect on MAO (see Figure 11-3; Carlsson, 1970). All of these effects have the combined action of promoting dopamine activity at the postsynaptic receptor. We have already discussed how amphetamine itself can effect a number of naturally occurring or iatrogenic extrapyramidal movement disorders. Amphetamine can also produce various abnormal movements in normal individuals, including stereotypies and choreiform movements (which are also thought to be a result of increased dopaminergic activity within the striatum). Finally, most effective antipsychotics are capable of ameliorating amphetamine psychosis, a fact that strengthens the analogy to schizophrenia (Angrist, Lee, and Gershon, 1974).

There are also many dissimilarities between amphetamine psychosis and schizophrenia. For example, the incidence of visual hallucinations is much greater among amphetamine abusers than among schizophrenics. The degree of apparent psychomotor stimulation is also considerably greater in amphetamine psychosis than in most cases of schizophrenia (e.g., chronic schizophrenia). In addition, characteristic symptoms of amphetamine psychosis rarely include the many nonparanoid features of schizophrenia (Table 11-1) such as a "flattened" affect or "looseness" of associations. Snyder (1972), who has critically reviewed the differences between schizophrenia and amphetamine psychosis, maintains that these may in part be due to amphetamine's pharmacological effects on other neurotransmitter amines within the brain.

Several drug states can be mistaken for schizophrenia as well. Cocaine psychosis is a predominantly paranoid state that includes both auditory and visual hallucinations. Phencyclidine, an infrequently used general anesthetic and common "street" drug, produces an altered state of consciousness that includes marked concreteness, bizarre thought content, and delusions (Meltzer et al., 1972). There is experimental evidence that both cocaine and phencyclidine act by strongly inhibiting the reuptake of dopamine. Their psychotomimetic actions have not unequivocally been elucidated.

Finally, it is quite likely that there is no *pure* "schizophrenic" drug just as there is probably no perfect human model psychosis. However, this does not diminish the value of these drugs as potential probes for dissecting the biochemical events of psychosis, but rather emphasizes the uniqueness of the human affliction we call schizophrenia.

Summary and Conclusions

The validity of any experimental model of human psychopathology will naturally depend on the similarities between the model itself and the clinical disorder. For this reason the difficulties inherent in defining schizophrenia as a unitary disorder, or in simply identifying core symptoms, will undoubtedly continue to plague future attempts at developing such a model. At the present time we could safely surmise that there is *no* adequate experimental model for schizophrenia in that there is no known experimental procedure that can reproduce even a small percentage of what we now believe composes the schizophrenic syndrome. What this means is that the success of future attempts at producing a model psychosis will also depend on our sharpening our diagnostic acumen and deciphering which observable schizophrenic behaviors are truly characteristic of the disease process itself.

Nonetheless, there has been much written on the biological cause or etiology of schizophrenia. It is thus problematic for the student and scientist

Table 11-3   The Pharmacology of Movement and Madness

Drugs	Parkinson's	Acute Dyskinesia	Tardive Dyskinesia (or chorea)	Psychosis	Major Dopamine (DA) Effect
L-Dopa	Better	Better?	Worse	Worse	Increases DA synthesis
Antipsychotic Phenothiazines	Worse	Worse	Better	Better	Blocks post-synaptic DA effects
Anticholinergic	Better	Better	Worse	Worse	Inhibits DA reuptake
MAO Inhibitors	Better	(?)	Worse	Worse	Inhibits metabolism of DA
Amphetamine	Better	Better	Worse	Worse	Causes DA release and blocks reuptake
Reserpine	Worse	Worse	Better	Better	Depletes nerve endings of DA
α-Methyl-p-tyrosine	Worse	Worse	Better	Better	Inhibits DA synthesis

to separate what is fact from what is artifact. As Daniel X. Freedman so aptly stated, "biological psychiatrists have the habit of discovering either the cause or the cure of schizophrenia approximately every two years—a cycle of discovery so dependable that it can be correlated with the course and severity of the Canadian winters.[3]" The hypothesized biological causes for schizophrenia now number in the hundreds and include almost every conceivable pathological mechanism known to afflict mankind. Our scanty understanding of its real etiology is not due to lack of imagination. Out of this chaos, however, has come a few consistent and almost irrefutable facts. First, there appears to be a strong genetic predisposition is those people who develop the disease. Therefore, it is likely that some biological diathesis is necessary for the development of schizophrenia. Second, we now have certain drugs that are quite specific in their task of ameliorating the schizophrenic psychosis. Although these agents also produce undesirable side effects, even these side effects may be of importance in understanding how the drugs work. Although they were once thought of as being epiphenomenon, they have now given us valuable clues about the biochemical events that may underlie psychosis.

The pharmacologic data presented in this paper are summarized in Table 11-3. These observations are consistent with the theory that a relative

---

[3] Dedication, Connecticut Mental Health Center, October 1966.

hyperactivity of the dopamine-containing neurons of the brain may be central to the schizophrenic process. Similarly, it is now known that dopamine-related mechanisms are also important in the pathogenesis of the movement disorders commonly associated with schizophrenia. However, much of this data has been derived indirectly and *few* direct measurements can be found to substantiate this hypothesis in schizophrenic patients themselves (see Meltzer and Stahl, 1976).

In addition, a "one transmitter" theory of any disorder is probably overly simplistic, as it is now recognized that many complex interrelationships exist between individual neurotransmitters. Finally, although the dopamine hypothesis is an attractive one and accounts for many clinical observations, it still does not answer the question of etiology. For example, antipsychotic drugs may be as irrelevant to our understanding of the pathogenesis of schizophrenia as digitalis is to our understanding of the development of atherosclerotic heart disease. The uniqueness of this hypothesis, however, lies in the wealth of information it has already generated and, undoubtedly, will continue to generate, about the basic neurobiological mechanisms of behavior.

Sexual Diversity

Ingeborg L. Ward
Villanova University

Introduction

When considering sexuality, most of us tend to think in terms of a dichotomy. Individuals are viewed as fitting into one of two distinct categories—either male or female. Associated with each of these sexual stereotypes is a characteristic chromosome composition, anatomy, physiology, gender identity (self-concept), and a set of sexually dimorphic behaviors. For example, normal males have the XY complement of sex chromosomes, females have an XX. Anatomical males have a penis, prostate, and androgen-secreting testes, and females have a clitoris, vagina, uterus, and ovaries that release estrogen. The stereotype of the male assumes him to be assertive, aggressive, to engage in behaviors that require considerable energy expenditure, and to take the active role during copulation. Females, on the other hand, are seen as being submissive, supportive, and less extravagant in their energy expenditure, and they supposedly assume a more passive role during sexual intercourse.

Despite such popular beliefs, regardless of whether one attempts to define sexuality in genetic, anatomical, or behavioral terms, there are people who fall somewhere between the two stereotypic extremes (see Money and Ehrhardt, 1972, for comprehensive coverage of this topic). Moreover, the number of persons in whom the usual correlations between physical structures and behavior do not hold is substantial. After illustrating the diversity found within and among the several dimensions of sexuality, I shall deal in this chapter with theories of their etiology.

The assistance of O. Byron Ward, Jr. in the writing and editing of this manuscript and the helpful comments of John Money are gratefully acknowledged. Preparation of this article was supported in part by Grant HD-04688 from the National Institute of Child Health and Human Development and by Research Scientist Development Award, Type II 1-K2-MH-00049 from the National Institute of Mental Health.

Intersexuality

The term *intersexuality* pertains to persons in whom the anatomical, chromosomal, and behavioral characteristics of typical males and females are intermingled. I will discuss ambiguities within each of these three dimensions of sexuality separately.

Chromosomal Sex

Some people cannot be classified as either male or female on the basis of their chromosome composition. The Turner and Klinefelter syndromes are examples of variability in the combination of sex chromosomes. In the Turner syndrome, the second sex chromosome is missing, leaving a single unpaired X. Persons who have the Turner syndrome are anatomically and behaviorally feminized, but they lack ovaries. They also are short in stature. Because they lack functional gonads, they are irreversibly sterile. However, if a maintenance dosage of ovarian hormone is administered beginning at the age of puberty, the behavioral and physical characteristics of an adult female can be induced and maintained in them.

In the Klinefelter syndrome there is one extra chromosome, an extra X (47, XXY). Persons who have the Klinefelter syndrome are anatomical males with underdeveloped testes and external genitals. The testes are sterile. Pubertal masculinization may be weak and may benefit from supplemental androgen treatment. Whereas the Turner syndrome is associated with ultrafeminine behavior, some people who have the Klinefelter syndrome have problems of male gender identity.

Morphological Sex

The development of male and female sex structures, with the exception of the gonads, is dependent on the presence or absence of testicular hormones during fetal ontogeny. If the gonads, which differentiate under the influence of the sex chromosomes, become testes, they normally become functioning endocrine glands early in the prenatal period and produce male hormones (androgen). These androgens are secreted into the bloodstream and circulated in the developing fetus, masculinizing sensitive target tissues. The first to be affected is the internal duct system, so that under the influence of various testicular secretions (e.g. testosterone, Müllerian inhibiting substance), the vas deferens and seminal vesicles develop while differentiation of the Fallopian tubes and uterus is suppressed. Similarly, at a slightly later time, the external morphology becomes the penis and scrotum rather than the clitoris, labia majora, and vagina. Conversely, if the gonads become ovaries, very little gonadal hormone is released during fetal life. The absence of testicular hormones constitutes the conditions necessary for the development of the female anatomy. In the human, differentiation of the sexual morphology is relatively completed by the end of the first three months of pregnancy.

Several points are important to our discussion of morphology. First, the critical factor that determines whether the sexual morphology is masculinized or feminized is *hormonal*, not genetic. Second, the timing of the testicular hormones is very important. The direction in which any one component of the morphology develops depends on the hormonal milieu that exists at the point in embryonic or fetal life during which that structure evolves. Differentiation cannot be influenced by conditions that exist before or after the critical period, nor can it be reversed after its completion—at least by hormonal means. Thus, if hormonal concentrations fluctuate abnormally during early stages of fetal development, the infant may be born with incompletely differentiated male or female structures. Two examples illustrate the consequences of such a flaw in prenatal hormone release.

Androgen is secreted not only by the testes but also by the adrenal cortex. During fetal development, this endocrine gland normally releases insufficient quantities of androgen to influence the course of sexual differentiation. However, in the adrenogenital syndrome an inherited enzymatic flaw interferes with the normal synthesis of adrenal cortisol. This results in an overproduction of its precursor hormone, which is androgenic. The presence of adrenal androgen in genetic females partially mimics the hormonal conditions normally present in fetal males and makes the androgen-sensitive tissues masculine. The extent to which the female is masculinized depends on the severity of the disorder. Typically the ovaries, Fallopian tubes, and uterus are normal, and the external morphology consists of an empty scrotum and a penis or masculinized clitoris. The external orifice of the vagina generally is absent or malformed. If the disorder is diagnosed at birth, the hormonal balance can be corrected by lifelong cortisone treatment and the genitals surgically reconstructed to be congruent with the gonadal and genetic sex. Because the ovaries are not impaired, a normal feminizing puberty occurs, although it may be somewhat delayed. If the disorder is not diagnosed, the person may be further masculinized because of continued postnatal exposure to adrenal androgen. The result is a severely masculinized adult female. Sometimes the condition is not identified until puberty, at which point a genetic and gonadal female has been reared as a male. Typically, such people choose to continue in male roles as adults. Removal of the ovaries and lifelong treatment with androgen plus cortisone make this a realistic possibility, but fertilization is impossible.

The reverse of the masculinized female occurs in the androgen insensitivity syndrome, an inherited disorder in which a chromosomal male is unable to utilize the androgen that the testes secrete in normal amounts. The biochemical flaw responsible for this disorder is still unknown but one of its consequences is a failure of the cells to bind androgen. Predictably, the tissue insensitivity to androgen results in the feminization of many components of the sexual apparatus, including the external genitals. Even if diagnosed at birth, the condition is now irreversible. Instead, such chromosomal males are reared as girls. They spontaneously undergo a feminizing puberty mediated by the estrogen that the testes secrete in small amounts even in normal men. (In normal males, androgen effectively counteracts testicular estrogen, thus preventing feminization at puberty.) Although people who have the androgen insensitivity syndrome are unable to conceive, having neither ovaries nor a uterus, they are feminine in their behavior. Many marry and adopt children.

Behavioral Sex

By far the most numerous instances of sexual ambiguity among human beings are to be found in behavior. This includes homosexuals and transsexuals, who genetically and anatomically appear normal but who manifest behavior more characteristic of the opposite sex.

Homosexuality is defined as erotic arousal and sexual interaction to the point of orgasm with a member of the same anatomical sex. Although this definition appears to apply to a clearly distinguishable and homogeneous group, people displaying such behavior or preference constitute a heterogeneous population that has many subcategories. First, environmental conditions may facilitate the appearance of intersexed behavior. Certain institutional settings, such as prisons and sex-segregated boarding schools, prevent or severely limit normal social contact between males and females. Not infrequently under such restrictions, homosexual interaction occurs among people who before and after being institutionalized are heterosexual. This phenomenon is referred to as *facultative homosexuality*. Second, there are *bisexuals*, who live in a normal social environment and who are capable of being erotically aroused by members of either sex. They may be married and have children while continuing to maintain occasional or regular homosexual contacts. Finally, there are *obligative homosexuals*, who are incapable of erotic arousal by members of the opposite sex and who find sexual satisfaction exclusively with partners of the same sex. For some people homosexuality represents a lifelong pattern, just as for others it constitutes only a chapter in their total life history.

Homosexuals also may be categorized according to the preferred role of each of the partners in a male homosexual relationship. For example, some homosexuals assume the active role, in which chiefly "male" behavior is exhibited, but toward another male. By contrast, some homosexuals prefer the passive role, traditionally considered a "female" role. Third, some have no particular preference and alternate roles depending on their partner and on other conditions. Analogous examples exist among lesbians.

Some homosexuals are indistinguishable from heterosexuals aside from their sexual preference. Others, regardless of their preferred role during copulation, exhibit effeminacy, or in the case of lesbians, masculinity, in dress, social behavior, grooming habits, speech patterns, occupation, and recreational interests.

Transexualism is a somewhat different syndrome. Whereas the male homosexual considers himself to be a male with different sexual interests from those of heterosexual males, the male-to-female transexual is firmly convinced that he is really a female trapped in a male body. This dilemma causes such intense distress that he becomes obsessed with the desire to have his anatomical and hormonal sex altered to conform with his psychological sex. The reverse is true of female transexuals. Transexuals are not particularly attracted to homosexuals, but rather want to change themselves to become acceptable to heterosexual members of their former sex. Many surgically reassigned transexuals lead normal lives, in which their former identities are unknown and unsuspected.

Etiology of Intersexed Behavior

Psychosocial Theories

Little empirical data exist about the etiology of homosexuality and even less exist about transexuality. Most theorizing has been done by clinicians based on data drawn from patients. To the extent that the clinical subgroup may not be representative of the general population of intersexed individuals, such theories are limited. Most leading theories view intersexed behaviors as disorders and lean heavily toward psychoanalytic or behavioristic interpretations. The most commonly cited causes of homosexuality are overidentification with or patterning after the parent of the opposite sex during early childhood. A variety of reasons for such an inappropriate course of development have been proposed. For example, a young boy may pattern himself after his mother if she is the stronger and more dominant parent; presumably she is a more attractive figure to imitate than a weak and submissive father. Paradoxically, it has been postulated that a child identifies with a relatively submissive mother if his father is overbearing and abusive toward his wife and offspring. Apparently, the child rejects him as an example of appropriate adult behavior. Third, a strong male figure may be absent altogether from the immediate family structure, so that only females act as adult models. Data in support of each of these interpretations have been generated.

However, all of these theories are weak in that they are not as predictive as one might wish. One can point to numerous examples of homosexuals whose family background contains none of these family constellations. Moreover, many heterosexual people were reared by domineering mothers or in families without fathers, including the normal siblings of homosexuals.

Although intersexed behavior has long been recognized in all Western cultures, it was not until the late 1940s that its pervasiveness began to be appreciated. At that time, Alfred Kinsey and his associates published their now classic books surveying the sexual habits of human males and females (Kinsey, Pomeroy, and Martin, 1948; Kinsey et al., 1953). To the chagrin of a society that had designated such behaviors taboo, it was revealed that 37 percent of the male and 13 percent of the female population of the United States had had at least one homosexual experience between adolescence and old age that culminated in orgasm. Kinsey considered this a possible under-estimation of the true incidence, at least in males. Furthermore, these data were relatively consistent, regardless of social and economic class, and regardless of whether they were gathered in large metropolitan centers, small towns, or rural areas. This statistic becomes especially significant if con-trasted with legal sanctions imposed against homosexual contacts. Even today, few states (e.g. Connecticut and Illinois) allow intercourse between consenting adults of the same sex. The penalties range from fines to life imprisonment. Although extreme sentences are rarely imposed, society nevertheless punishes people known to engage in such practices by stigmatiz-ing them or even making them social outcasts. Such penalties and social sanctions reflect the commonly held assumption that intersexed behavior is the result of a free personal choice and that with a little self-discipline and will power it could be inhibited. In fact, however, few data substantiate such a position. Indeed, no known treatments for these syndromes have a suffi-ciently lasting effect or are effective for a sufficient number of people to be designated as a cure. Even in people who badly want to change their behavior, homosexual behavior may persist, despite legal punitive measures, psychoanalysis, group therapy, or any of the various behavior modification techniques that attempt to extinguish or recondition behavior using basic learning principles. These treatments assume that sexual patterns are ac-quired or shaped by early childhood and adolescent experiences and are reversible. If adult behavior patterns are undesirable, the task of the thera-pist, as presently conceived, is to identify and counteract early pathological environmental influences.

Prenatal Hormonal Organization of Behavior

On closer inspection, it appears that the environmental viewpoint may be overly simplistic. Recently, considerable animal data have shown that pre-natal hormones determine adult reproductive behavior potentials. Although embryologists and anatomists long ago had established that a single hormonal principle determines the direction in which sexual anatomy differentiates, it was not until 1959 that a similar mechanism was found also to influence the development of sexually dimorphic behavior. In a now classic study, Phoenix, Goy, Gerall, and Young (1959) injected pregnant guinea pigs with the male hormone testosterone propionate (TP), correctly assuming that the steroid would pass from the mother's bloodstream into that of the developing fetuses. Although this treatment had no remarkable effects on the male offspring, it masculinized the morphology and behavior of their sisters. This was ascertained in the following manner. Untreated control and prenatally androgenized females were allowed to grow to adulthood, at which time their ovaries were removed in order to eliminate the endogenous gonadal hormone supply that could not be controlled by the experimenter. Half of the animals in each group then were injected with a standard dose of estrogen and progesterone and tested with vigorous males for their ability to show normal female receptivity. The hormone treatment insured that all guinea pigs had adequate and equivalent amounts of the appropriate hormones needed to activate female behavior, if a potential for it existed. Compared to the control group, TP-treated animals showed greatly impaired female sexual behavior. Even repeated administration of ovarian hormones did not rectify the deficiency. A second set of control and androgenized females received daily injections of TP and periodically were given access to a receptive female in order to test their capacity to behave like males in copulation. The control females were unresponsive but the androgenized females engaged in frequent and vigorous mounting and pelvic thrusting.

This basic experiment has been replicated and extended to a variety of mammalian species including rats, mice, hamsters, gerbils, beagles, and rhesus monkeys. Indeed, it can be demonstrated that if genetic females are exposed to sufficiently large quantities of androgen during a sufficiently lengthy period of fetal development, behavior is so totally masculinized that they are even capable of ejaculating and expelling semen (minus sperm) (Ward, 1969; Beach et al., 1972; Eaton, Goy, and Phoenix, 1973). Conversely, even a single injection of androgen, if timed exactly right, can block the development of female behavior potentials in genetic female rats (Barraclough and Gorski, 1962).

The reverse also is true. If androgen is withheld from fetal males through castration, behavioral potentials are demasculinized and feminized. This can be demonstrated especially well in the rat, which, unlike many other commonly studied laboratory animals, is born in a relatively immature state so that the process of sexual differentiation spans the last week of prenatal life and the first ten days after birth. As shown in Table 12-1, male rats gonadectomized 1, 5, and 10 days after birth or as adults (90 days) show strikingly different potentials for male and female sexual behavior (Grady, Phoenix, and Young, 1965; Gerall et al., 1967). Castration on the day of birth totally blocks the ability to ejaculate, even if prolonged androgen

Table 12-1. Male and female sexual behavior shown by male rats castrated at various ages after birth (All groups were given daily injections of TP as adults while being tested for male behavior, and they received weekly injections of estrogen and progesterone while tested for female behavior.)

Age of castration	Percentage ejaculating	Female behavior score*
Day 90 females	0	79
Day 1 males	0	57
Day 5 males	25	18
Day 10 males	88	3
Day 90 males	86	4

Source: After K. L. Grady, C. H. Phoenix, and W. C. Young, *J. Comp. Physiol. Psychol.* 59 (1965): 176.
* Female behavior was scored as a lordosis quotient, which is the ratio of lordosis responses to the number of times the animal was mounted expressed as a percentage.

replacement treatment is given in adulthood. However, if estrogen and progesterone are injected, such males will show sexual behavior similar to that of normal females. If castration is delayed until day 10 of postnatal life or any time thereafter, the males are normal, displaying the complete male copulatory pattern when given androgen in adulthood and very little propensity for female behavior, even after extensive and prolonged treatment with female hormones. The behavior of animals castrated on day 5 falls somewhere between these two extremes, with some increase in female patterns and a general attenuation but not total absence of male behavior. The normal rat copulatory pattern is illustrated in Figure 12-1. The receptive (estrous) female responds to the male's mount by displaying lordosis, an arching of her back and raising of the neck and pudental area.

This extensive series of experiments indicates that the general rules found to govern the differentiation of reproductive morphology also apply to the development of sexually dimorphic behaviors. If androgen is present during critical fetal and, in a few species, neonatal stages, the tissues destined to mediate adult sexual behavior are masculinized. (Specific pathways and nuclei of the spinal cord and brain and peripheral sensory receptors such as those located in the genitals control sexual behavior.) In the absence of androgen, female potentials are formed. The relative degree to which one set of behavior is established to the exclusion of the other is a function of both *the amount of prenatal hormone and the timing.* Because various behaviors develop at different times, the onset and duration of appreciable androgen levels is critical in determining the particular aggregate of adult potentials. For example, although the development of male and female potentials overlaps, the induction of masculine patterns, as compared with female, appears to begin and end at slightly earlier stages. Furthermore, various components of a complete pattern seem to evolve independently so

Figure 12-1. In the typical rat copulatory sequence, the male mounts the female from behind, palpates her flanks, and engages in vigorous pelvic thrusting. This elicits the lordosis reflex from the female—a characteristic arching of the back.

that in the rat, for example, a potential for ejaculation is established by the presence of early postnatal androgen, and male mounting is determined by prenatal androgen. Theoretically, by properly regulating the administration and withdrawal of fetal androgen, it is possible to produce organisms that either are asexual or exhibit forms of behavior characteristic of both sexes. As with morphology, the critical variable is the relative hormonal environment existing at the time when the tissues controlling a response develop. Androgen before or after that point has no consequences.

Sexually Dimorphic Social Behavior

Even more relevant than rodent experiments to our understanding of human sexuality is a longitudinal study conducted at the Oregon Regional Research Center on the development of sexually dimorphic behavior patterns in rhesus monkeys. In the Oregon study, comparisons were made from birth to adulthood among normal male and female monkeys and a group of genetic females treated with androgen in utero, that is, whose mothers were injected with TP during pregnancy. The importance of this study lies in its use of a primate species, which can be expected to yield data that can be generalized more readily to man. Unlike the more frequently studied rodents, rhesus monkeys have a prolonged infancy, childhood and adolescence, each with its own set of developmental behavioral stages. Thus it becomes possible to assess the effect of fetal androgen not only on adult behavior but also on juvenile social behavior. Observation of the same group of animals over a seven-year period confirmed that adult female monkeys, androgenized during fetal life, copulate to the point of ejaculation when placed with receptive females, much as do their rodent counterparts. Furthermore, they are clearly distinguishable from normal females at much earlier ages—from childhood on they engage in forms of play and aggressive behavior that characterize their male rather than female peers (Phoenix, Goy, and Resko, 1968; Goy, 1970; Eaton, Goy, and Phoenix, 1973). The frequency with which a number of characteristic forms of behavior are displayed by young monkeys differs between males and females. One of these patterns is rough-and-tumble play, which, as Figure 12-2 indicates, is distinguishable between the sexes at 3½ months of age. The frequency with which prenatally androgenized females engage in this behavior falls between that of normal males and normal females. Similar curves were generated for stereotyped threat expression, play initiation, chasing, and prepuberal mounting. Males and prenatally androgenized females did not show identical levels of behavior probably because they were not exposed to the same level of testosterone during precisely the same stages of prenatal development, nor for the same length of time. The mothers of the females had been injected during only a limited portion of pregnancy, beginning on day 39 and continuing through

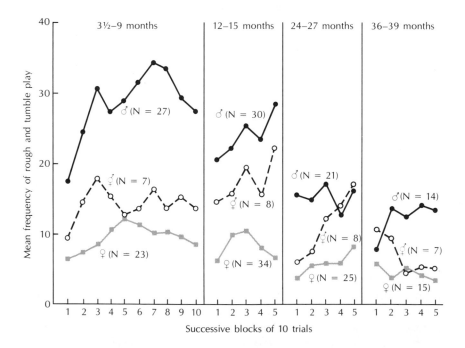

Figure 12-2. Average frequency of rough-and-tumble play shown by males (♂), females (♀), and prenatally androgenized females (♀̣) during the first 39 months of life. (From Goy, R. W., 1970.)

day 69 or 105. The length of the gestation period in the rhesus monkey is about 168 days. Normal male fetuses are not dependent on experimenter-delivered androgen, having their supply constantly replenished by their own testes.

The masculinized juvenile play patterns seen in androgenized female monkeys have an analog in the human adrenogenital syndrome. Money and Ehrhardt (1972) have completed a detailed analysis of the childhood and adolescent behavior of fetally androgenized human females, who display a very predictable and homogeneous behavioral syndrome. Most are tomboys to an extreme degree, with all of the characteristics associated with such a label. They expend a great deal of physical energy, preferring vigorous outdoor activities and often joining boys in team sports. Although not particularly aggressive, they defend themselves well if attacked. Their dress preferences are for slacks and skirts rather than frilly dresses. Unlike control girls, they have little interest in dolls, real infants, or the idea of one day having children of their own—attitudes interpreted to indicate decreased parentalism. If asked about their future goals, androgenized girls anticipate careers, which may or may not be combined with marriage. Control females typically list marriage as a major goal, with a career subordinated to this primary objective. This general behavioral syndrome was characteristic of even those adrenogenital girls in whom the disorder was discovered and treated at birth, indicating that its roots reach back to prenatal exposure to androgen.

Stress and Psychosexual Differentiation

Although at first glance the intersexed behavior shown by animals subjected to various prenatal hormonal manipulations would appear to have direct implications for psychosexual development in man, there has been a general reluctance to make such a generalization—and for good reason. Although hormones delivered prenatally by means of a hypodermic syringe or withdrawn by means of castration can readily be shown to alter behavior, the overwhelming majority of human beings displaying intersexed behaviors have no established history of hormonal imbalance during prenatal life. Furthermore, the extreme manipulations typically employed in animal experiments result in alterations of sexual morphology as well as behavior. By contrast, most human beings who might be considered to display behavioral syndromes analogous to these animals have a normal sexual anatomy and physiology. The burden of proof is on the animal experimenters to demonstrate that sufficient variability can be induced within a basically normal endocrine system by natural means (i.e. employing no known pathology, hormone ingestion, or surgical intervention) to cause changes in behavior but not in morphology.

Such an animal model may now exist for males. It recently has been shown that if pregnant rats are subjected to intense chronic stress, the subsequent adult behavior of their male offspring is demasculinized and feminized without any associated detectable change in adult reproductive morphology or physiology (Ward, 1972; 1974). As shown in Figure 12-3, gravid females were placed into small Plexiglas restrainers illuminated by floodlights. This procedure was repeated three times daily during the last week of the rat's three-week gestation period. No further treatment was given after birth, and the mother and her litter were not disturbed until weaning. When the pups reached adulthood—60 days of age in the rat—males and females both were tested for sexual behavior. The females were found to be normal, showing neither deficiencies in female estrous behavior nor a propensity for male copulatory patterns. Their male siblings were another

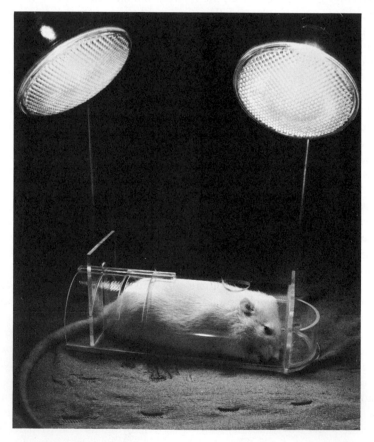

Figure 12-3. Pregnant rats were stressed by being restrained in Plexiglas holders illuminated by floodlights.

story. When placed together with receptive females, most prenatally stressed males failed to initiate copulation, even after many weeks of testing. Conversely, if castrated and injected with estrogen and progesterone, these males readily lordosed when mounted by a vigorous male. A summary of these data is presented in Table 12-2.

In a separate experiment, I (Ward, 1974) evaluated the reversal in sexual behavior potential by giving prenatally stressed males daily TP injections in adulthood. This procedure had a limited therapeutic effect on male behavior in that without such treatment only 10 percent of the animals had ejaculated, whereas after 5 weeks of daily treatment, 50 percent had done so. In addition, tests for female lordosis were given. No control male ever lordosed following treatment with androgen, but 80 percent of the prenatally stressed males repeatedly displayed the female lordotic sexual pattern—a far larger percentage than had shown male behavior. The tests for male and female behavior were given consecutively—only the sexual partner with which the experimental animal was to interact was changed. This fortuitous arrangement of tests revealed the extent to which environmental conditions determine which dimorphic behavior the bipotential organism will exhibit at any moment. Following prolonged androgen treatment, 40 percent of prenatally stressed males showed either the male ejaculatory or the female lordotic pattern, depending on the stimulus animal placed into the cage. Furthermore, they could alternate from one pattern to the other within a matter of minutes, responding differently and appropriately to either a receptive female or a vigorous male.

That androgen induces female behavior in prenatally stressed male rats is especially interesting because human male homosexuals respond similarly to hormones. Androgen injections are still proposed by some physicians as a treatment for various forms of male sexual inadequacies, including impotence and homosexuality. Limited success has been achieved in heightening male libido in heterosexuals. However, in a homosexual it enhances sexual drive for a male partner. Androgen treatment does not make behavior more heterosexual but rather intensifies the existing homosexual drive state, thus aggravating the symptoms it was intended to alleviate (Money, 1961).

Table 12-2 Male and female behavior shown by control and prenatally stressed male rats

Prenatal treatment	Percentage ejaculating	Mean lordosis responses
Control	64	2.7
Stress	21	8.8

Source: From I. L. Ward, *Science* 175 (1972): 82.

Prenatally stressed rats and human male homosexuals have yet another characteristic in common. The reproductive anatomy and physiology of both groups appears indistinguishable from that of heterosexual controls. We have compared body weights, development of the external genitalia, size of the testes, and various internal organs such as the prostates of control and prenatally stressed males at various times in postnatal development. No significant differences are detectable. Furthermore, histology of the testes revealed that prenatally stressed male rats produce viable sperm in adulthood. A review of the clinical literature yields similar results for human male homosexuals. Although reports exist that homosexuals have reduced testosterone output (Loraine, et al., 1970; Loraine et al., 1971; Kolodny, 1971), decreased sperm count (Kolodny et al., 1971), or differ from heterosexuals in other physical dimensions (Evans, 1973), attempts to replicate such findings usually fail (Doerr et al., 1973; Birk et al., 1973; Brodie et al., 1974); some studies are discounted because of methodological errors or sampling biases. At the present time, there are no reliable indexes by which either prenatally stressed rats or human males showing feminized-demasculinized behavior patterns can be distinguished physically from heterosexuals.

Possible Mechanism of Action

The mechanism by which stressing of gravid females alters the sexual behavior of male offspring still remains to be identified, but there is a promising lead. A series of recent studies has demonstrated that adult males of a variety of mammalian species, including man, show reductions in concentration of androgen in their blood if exposed to severe and chronic stress. A representative study is that of Kreuz, Rose, and Jennings (1972). These investigators compared plasma testosterone levels of young men at various stages of training in the U.S. Army's Officer Candidate Course. This course was designed not only to impart the basics of military science, but also to place the prospective officers under considerable psychological pressure, and thus to gauge their ability to function effectively under stressful conditions. Typically, about 30 percent of the candidates fail to complete the program. Figure 12-4 shows clearly that during the early period of the program (stress), concentrations of testosterone in blood plasma were markedly smaller than those shown a few weeks later when the same men were in the less demanding final phase (recovery) of training. The concentrations of testosterone during stress also were lower than those obtained from a control group of prison volunteers and a group of regular army recruits. Changes in testis size and androgen concentrations also have been reported for male rhesus monkeys exposed to demanding electric shock avoidance schedules (Mason et al., 1968); for male mice housed in overcrowded cages

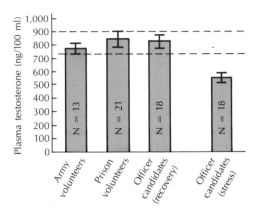

Figure 12-4. Mean concentrations of testosterone in blood plasma of soldiers during the early (stress) and late (recovery) periods of training in the United States Army's Officer Candidate Course compared to groups of prison and nonstressed army volunteers. (From L. E. Kreuz, Rose, R. M., and Jennings, J. R., 1972.)

(Christian, 1955); and for men exposed to the stress of major surgery (Matsumoto et al., 1970). Numerous studies indicate that the suppression of gonadal hormones can be triggered by a variety of stresses, ranging from physical to social and psychological.

It has not yet been verified that fetal males respond in a similar manner. If they do, a possibly important variable in the organization of sexual behavior has been identified. Because sufficient concentrations of androgen in the fetus are a prerequisite for proper masculinization, any stress-induced attenuation should have direct consequences on adult behavior—provided that the onset, severity, and duration of the stress fall within the critical period during which psychosexual differentiation occurs. In adult males androgen levels and androgen-mediated functions return to normal once the stress ceases. Such recovery in fetal males, however, would not be able to reverse the atypical programming of the nervous system induced by even short periods of depressed gonadal output.

If this hypothesized mechanism of action eventually is substantiated by empirical data, it will raise another question. How is the alteration in behavior achieved without a detectable change in morphology? There are at least two possible explanations. Perhaps the neural pathways that mediate behavior are more sensitive to relatively limited reductions in androgen than is peripheral anatomy. One must recall from Figure 12-4 that in adult males stress attenuates but does not altogether eliminate testicular output. Alternatively, the testes secrete several different androgens, of which testosterone is only one, albeit the most prevalent and potent. Although stress has been shown to decrease testosterone, its effects on other androgens are less well known. Conceivably, there could be a selective suppression of the particular hormone most critical in the organization of behavior, leaving sufficient quantities of other, less potent androgens to adequately masculinize the evolving morphology.

Another major question asks precisely how stressors acting on the mother are able to reach the fetus, sequestered and presumably protected within the uterus. The mother undergoes a variety of hormonal changes during stress (e.g. increased adrenalin, adrenal corticoids, ACTH), any one or combination of which could cross the placental barrier and trigger a stress response within the fetus. Actually, the distinction between the mother and fetus might best be viewed as semantic because they constitute a single biological unit. Although several substances (e.g. selected hormones) do not cross freely from the mother's bloodstream into that of the fetus, many others do. Indeed, biologically active substances also travel from the fetus to the mother.

There is no direct evidence indicating a correlation between fetal stress and the occurrence of homosexuality in human beings. We have no knowledge of what conditions might prove sufficiently stressful to a pregnant woman that they would alter critical hormone levels in the developing fetus, nor will it be easy to establish correlations between such prenatal events and a behavioral syndrome that may not appear until many years later. Furthermore, if the prenatal stress syndrome found in rats is to serve as an animal model for conditions predisposing human males towards intersexuality, we would have to assume that the factors responsible for female intersexuality are different. Although fetal stress feminizes the behavior pattern of male rats, it does not masculinize their female siblings.

Summary and Conclusions

Taken as a whole, animal studies do not begin to provide an all-inclusive explanation of human sexual behavior. However, they indicate that there are various physiological variables, heretofore unknown or ignored, that mold the somatic and neural substrate upon which traditionally accepted psychosocial factors act to produce the diversity of sexual patterns that human beings display. During prenatal life, gonadal secretions organize sexually dimorphic behaviors. In fetal males, the release of such hormones (androgens) is not necessarily an automatic event but rather can be suppressed by aversive environmental conditions acting on the mother during pregnancy.

After birth, the gonads of both sexes become relatively dormant until puberty. During infancy and childhood, social experience and learning probably either reinforce and strengthen or weaken and countermand existing behavioral predispositions. If there is a fairly high correlation between anatomical sex, prenatally determined behavioral predispositions, and pre-puberal socialization, a stable heterosexual personality emerges. If the three are not congruous some degree of conflict or abnormality might be expected in the final makeup of behavioral capabilities and preferences. This interaction becomes even more complicated if one recognizes that social behaviors believed to act as relevant stimuli are often elicited—at least in part. Thus female and feminized male infants may evoke a totally different set of responses towards themselves from their caretakers than do normal males or masculinized females. It later becomes difficult to evaluate to what degree the behavior parents exhibited towards a particular child actually critically shaped the child's eventual adult sexual behavior. We can only speculate about the extent to which tendencies induced by fetal hormonal conditions can be overridden or reversed by postnatal socialization.

Finally, complete with a repertoire of behavioral potentials, a child reaches puberty. The gonads again become active and the resultant rise in gonadal secretions activates latent sexual patterns. Two points are important. First, postpubertal sexual behavior requires the presence of adequate amounts of adult hormones and of an appropriate stimulus partner. Second, only already existing potentials can be activated at this late stage in development. For example, if a potential for female behavior does not exist, no amount of estrogen nor even the most attractive and persuasive of male partners will evoke it. However, if the potential is fully organized, its threshold might be sufficiently low that it could be activated by any gonadal hormone, androgen or estrogen, provided that a receptive sexual partner also is available.

In summary, four critical factors acting at different stages of development determine what sexual behavior the adult will manifest. These are the prenatal hormonal milieu, prepubertal socialization, pubertal and adult hormones, and the nature of available sexual partners. Generally, these four reinforce one another, resulting in exclusively heterosexual behavior. However, considering the variety of ways in which these factors can interact it is not reasonable to expect all members of society to conform to one of two sexual stereotypes.

Bibliographic Index

Bracketed numbers at the end of each entry indicate pages on which the entry is referred to in text.

Abrams, P. S.   Age and effect of separation on mother and infant rhesus monkeys *(Macaca mulatta)*. (Paper presented at the meeting of the American Association of Physical Anthropologists, Mexico City, 1969.) [143]

Ackerman, S. H., Hofer, M. A., and Weiner, H.   Age at maternal separation and gastric erosion susceptibility in the rat. *Psychosomatic Medicine*, 1975, 37, 180–184. [242]

Ackerman, S. H., and Weiner, H.   Peptic ulcer disease: Some considerations for psychosomatic research. In O. W. Hill (Ed.), *Modern trends in psychosomatic medicine* (Vol. 3). London: Butterworth, 1976. Pp. 363–381. [237]

Ader, R.   Susceptibility to gastric lesions in the rat. *Journal of Neuropsychiatry*, 1963, 4, 399–408. (a) [243, 245]

Ader, R.   Plasma pepsinogen levels in rat and man. *Psychosomatic Medicine*, 1963, 25, 218–220. (b) [243]

Ader, R.   Behavioral and physiological rhythms and the development of gastric erosions in the rat. *Psychosomatic Medicine*, 1967, 29, 345–353. (a) [268]

Ader, R.   Emotional reactivity and susceptibility to gastric erosions. *Psychological Reports*, 1967, 20, 1188–1190. (b) [244]

Ader, R., Beels, C. C., and Tatum, R.   Social factors affecting emotionality and resistance to disease in animals: II. Susceptibility to gastric ulceration as a function of interruptions in social interactions and the time at which they occur. *Journal of Comparative and Physiological Psychology*, 1960, 53, 455–458. (a) [243]

Ader, R., Beels, C. C., and Tatum, R.   Blood pepsinogen and gastric erosions in the rat. *Psychosomatic Medicine*, 1960, 22, 1–12. (b) [247]

Adolph, E. F.   Urges to eat and drink in rats. *American Journal of Physiology*, 1947, *151*, 110–125. [29]

Aghajanian, G. K., Foote, W. E., and Sheard, M. H.   Action of psychotogenic drugs on single midbrain raphe neurons. *The Journal of Pharmacology and Experimental Therapeutics*, 1970, *171*, 178–187. [349]

Aghajanian, G. K., and Haigler, H. J.   Direct and indirect actions of LSD, serotonin and related compounds on serotonin-containing neurons. In J. Barchas and E. Usdin (Eds.), *Serotonin and behavior*. New York: Academic Press, 1973. [349]

Agras, W. S., Chapin, H. N., and Oliveau, D. C.   The natural history of phobias: Course and prognosis. *Archives of General Psychiatry*, 1972, 26, 315–317. [180]

Agras, W. S., Sylvester, D., and Oliveau, D.   The epidemiology of common fears and phobias. *Comprehensive Psychiatry*, 1969, *10*, 151–156. [180, 182]

Ainsworth, M. D. S.   Discussion of Suomi and Bowlby by chapters. In G. Serban and A. Kling (Eds.). *Animal models in human psychobiology*. New York: Plenum Press, 1976, pp. 37–47. [143]

Akiskal, H. S., and McKinney, W. T.   Overview of recent research in depression. *Archives of General Psychiatry*, 1974, 32, 285–305. [136, 148, 162, 163, 172]

Akiyama, M.   Effects of extinction techniques on avoidance response. *Bulletin of the Faculty of Education, Hiroshima University*, 1968, *17*, 173. [203, 205]

Akiyama, M.   Relation between extinction techniques and extinction of avoidance response in albino rats. *Japanese Annual of Animal Psychology*, 1969, *19*, 15–16. [203]

Akiyama, M.   Relation of CR and competing responses in avoidance learning. *Bulletin of the Faculty of Education, Hiroshima University*, 1971, 20, 208–209. [205]

Alarcon, R. D., and Cori, L.   The precipitating event in depression. *Journal of Nervous and Mental Disease*, 1972, *155*, 379–391. [123]

Alexander, F.   The influence of psychological factors upon gastrointestinal disturbances: General principles, objectives, and preliminary results. *Psychoanalytic Quarterly*, 1934, 3, 501–539. [232, 245]

Alexander, F. Emotional factors in essential hypertension. *Psychosomatic Medicine*, 1939, *1*, 153–216. [288, 290]

Anand, B. K.   Nervous regulation of food intake. *Physiological Reviews*, 1961, *41*, 677–708. [27]

Anand, B. K., Sharma, K. W., and Dua, S.   Activity of single neurons in the hypothalamic feeding centers: Effect of glucose. *American Journal of Physiology*, 1964, *207*, 1146–1154. [28]

Anderson, D. C., Cole, J. O., and McVaugh, W.   Variations in unsignaled inescapable preshock as determinants of responses to punishment. *Journal of Comparative and Physiological Psychology* (Supplement), 1968, *65*, 1–17. [109]

Anderson, D. C., and Paden, P.   Passive avoidance response learning as a function of prior tumbling trauma. *Psychonomic Science*, 1966, *4*, 129–130. [109]

Anderson, O. D., and Parmenter, R. A long-term study of the experimental neurosis in the sheep and the dog. *Psychosomatic Medicine Monographs,* 1941, 2, 1–150. [19]

Angel, J. L. Constitution in female obesity. *American Journal of Physical Anthropology,* 1949, 7, 433–471. [48]

Angrist, B. M., and Gershon, S. The phenomenology of experimentally-induced amphetamine psychosis. *American Journal of Psychiatry,* 1970, 126, 95–107. [383]

Angrist, B. M., Lee, H. K., and Gershon, S. The antagonism of amphetamine-induced symptomatology by a neuroleptic. *American Journal of Psychiatry,* 1974, 131, 817–819. [383]

Anokhin, P. K. *Problems of centre and periphery in the physiology of nervous activity.* Gorki: Gosizdat, 1935. (Russian) [277]

Arbuthnott, G. W., Attree, T. J., Eccleston, D., Loose, R. W., and Marten, M. J. Is adenylate cyclase the dopamine receptor? *Medical Biology,* 1974, 52, 350–353. [380]

Astwood, E. B. Presidential address: The heritage of corpulence. *Endocrinology,* 1962, 71, 337–341. [49]

Ayd, F. J., Jr. A survey of drug-induced extrapyramidal reactions. *Journal of the American Medical Association,* 1961, 175, 1054–1060. [378]

Ayd, F. J., Jr. Persistent dyskinesia: A neurologic complication of major tranquilizers. *Medical Sciences,* 1967, 18, 32–40. [382]

Baile, C. A., and Forbes, G. B. Control of food intake and regulation of energy balance in ruminants. *Physiological Review,* 1972, 54, 160–214. [30]

Bakan, D. *Disease, pain and sacrifice.* Chicago: University of Chicago Press, 1968. [279]

Baloh, R., Sturm, R., Green, B., and Gleser, G. Neuropsychological effects of chronic asymptomatic increased lead absorption. *Archives of Neurology,* 1975, 32, 326–328. [309]

Barbaree, H. E., and Harding, R. K. Free-operant avoidance behavior and gastric ulceration in rats. *Physiology and Behavior,* 1973, 11, 269–271. [262]

Barbeau, A. Levodopa therapy in Parkinson's disease: A critical review of nine years' experience. *Canadian Medical Association Journal,* 1969, 101, 791–800. [380]

Baron, J. M. Gastric secretion in relation to subsequent duodenal ulcer and family history. *Gut,* 1962, 3, 158–161. [237]

Barraclough, C. A., and Gorski, R. A. Studies on mating behaviour in the androgen-sterilized female rat in relation to the hypothalamic regulation of sexual behaviour. *Journal of Endocrinology,* 1962, 25, 175–182. [393]

Bartorelli, C., Bizzi, E., Libretti, A., and Zanchetti, A. Inhibitory control of sinocarotid pressoceptive afferents on hypothalamic autonomic activity and sham rage behavior. *Archives Italiennes de Biologie,* 1960, 98, 308–326. [287]

Baum, M. Extinction of an avoidance response following response prevention: Some parametric investigations. *Canadian Journal of Psychology,* 1969, 23, 1–10. (a) [201]

Baum, M. Extinction of an avoidance response motivated by intense fear: Social facilitation of the action of response prevention (flooding) in rats. *Behavior, Research and Therapy*, 1969, 7, 57–62. (b) [201]

Baum, M. Extinction of avoidance responding through response prevention (flooding). *Psychological Bulletin*, 1970, 74, 276–284. [201, 202, 204]

Baum, M. Avoidance training in both alcohol and non-drug states increases the resistance to extinction of an avoidance response in rats. *Psychopharmacologia*, 1971, 19, 87–90. [202]

Baum, M. Flooding (response prevention) in rats: The effects of immediate vs. delayed flooding and of changed illumination conditions during flooding. *Canadian Journal of Psychology*, 1972, 26, 190–200. (a) [201]

Baum, M. Repeated acquisition and extinction of avoidance in rats using flooding (response prevention). *Learning and Motivation*, 1972, 3, 272–278. (b) [201, 202, 205]

Baum, M. Extinction of avoidance behaviour: Comparison of various flooding procedures in rats. *Bulletin of the Psychonomic Society*, 1973, 1, 22–24. (a) [201]

Baum, M. Extinction of avoidance in rats: The effects of chlorpromazine and methylphenidate administered in conjunction with flooding (response prevention). *Behavior, Research and Therapy*, 1973, 11, 165–169. (b) [201]

Baum, M. Instrumental learning. In M. P. Feldman and A. Broadhurst (Eds.), *Theoretical and experimental bases of the behaviour therapies*. New York: Wiley, 1976. [201]

Baum, M., and Gordon A. Effects of a loud buzzer applied during response in rats. *Behavior, Research and Therapy*, 1970, 8, 287–292. [203]

Baum, M., and Myran, D. D. Response prevention (flooding) in rats: The effects of restricting exploration during flooding and of massed vs. distributed flooding. *Canadian Journal of Psychology*, 1971, 25, 138–146. [203]

Beach, F. A., Kuehn, R. E., Sprague, R. H., and Anisko, J. J. Coital behavior in dogs: XI. Effects of androgenic stimulation during development on masculine mating responses in females. *Hormones and Behavior*, 1972, 3, 143–168. [393]

Beagley, G. H. Septal facilitation and inhibition of responses elicited from subcortical structures in the cat. (Unpublished Master's thesis, Bryn Mawr College, 1972.) [225]

Beatty, J. *Introduction to physiological psychology*. Monterey: Brooks/Cole, 1975. [273]

Beatty, J. Learned regulation of alpha and theta frequency activity in the human electroencephalogram. In G. E. Schwartz and J. Beatty (Eds.), *Biofeedback: Theory and research*. New York: Academic Press, 1977, pp. 351–370. [272]

Beaudoin, R., and Mayer, J. Food intakes of obese and non-obese women. *Journal of the American Dietetic Association*, 1953, 29, 29–33. [52, 60]

Beck, A. T. *Depression: Clinical, experimental, and theoretical aspects*. New York: Hoeber, 1967. [111, 112, 113, 115, 122, 126, 154, 230]

Beck, A. T. Cognitive therapy: Nature and relation to behavior therapy. *Behavior Therapy*, 1970, 1, 184–200. (a) [122, 126]

Beck, A. T. The phenomena of depression: A synthesis. In D. Offer and D. X. Freedman (Eds.), *Clinical research in perspective: Essays in honor of Roy R. Grinker, Sr.* New York: Basic Books, 1970. (b) [122]

Beck, A. T., and Hurvich, M. S. Psychological correlates of depression: I. Frequency of masochistic dream content in a private practice sample. *Psychosomatic Medicine*, 1959, *21*, 50–55. [114]

Beck, A. T., and Ward, C. H. Dreams of depressed patients: Characteristic themes in manifest content. *Archives of General Psychiatry*, 1961, *5*, 462–467. [114]

Becker, E. *The revolution in psychiatry*. London: Free Press of Glencoe, Collier-MacMillian, 1964, pp. 108–135. [135]

Behrend, E. R., and Bitterman, M. E. Sidman avoidance in the fish. *Journal of the Experimental Analysis of Behavior*, 1963, *13*, 229–242. [107]

Benjamin, S., Marks, I. M., and Huson, J. Active muscular relaxation in desensitization of phobic patients. *Psychological Medicine*, 1972, *2*, 381–390. [203]

Benson, H. *The Relaxation Response*. New York: William Morrow and Co., 1975. [299, 300]

Benson, H., Shapiro, D., Tursky, B., and Schwartz, G. E. Decreased systolic blood pressure through operant conditioning techniques in patients with essential hypertension. *Science*, 1971, *173*, 740–742. [295]

Berblinger, K. W. Obesity and psychotic stress. In N. L. Wilson (Ed.), *Obesity*. Philadelphia: Davis, 1969. [33]

Beres, D., and Obers, S. J. The effects of extreme deprivation in infancy on psychic structure in adolescence. *Psychoanalytic Study of the Child*, 1950, *5*, 212–235. [363]

Berlyne, D. The affective significance of uncertainty. In *Psychopathology of human adaptation*. Serban, G. (Ed.). New York: Plenum Press, 1977, pp. 319–341. [211]

Berman, J. S., and Katzev, R. D. Factors involved in the rapid elimination of avoidance behavior. *Behavior, Research and Therapy*, 1972, *10*, 247–256. [202, 203]

Bianchi, G. H. Origins of disease phobia. *Australian and New Zealand Journal of Psychiatry*, 1971, *5*, 241. [199, 200]

Bibring, E. The mechanism of depression. In Greenacre, P. (Ed.), *Affective disorders*. New York: International Universities Press, 1953. [115, 122, 126]

Birk, L., Williams, G. H., Chasin, M., and Rose, L. I. Serum testosterone levels in homosexual men. *The New England Journal of Medicine*, 1973, *289*, 1236–1238. [400]

Bishop, M. P., Gallant, D. M., and Sykes, T. F. Extrapyramidal side effects and therapeutic response. *Archives of General Psychiatry*, 1965, *13*, 155–162. [382]

Bjorkland, A., Lindvall, O., and Nobin, A. Evidence of an incerto-hypothalamic dopamine neurone system in the rat. *Brain Research*, 1975, 89, 29–41. [376]

Blau, A. Mental changes following head trauma in children. *Archives of Neurology and Psychiatry*, 1937, *35*, 723–769. [309]

Bleuler, E. *Dementia praecox, or The group of schizophrenias* (J. Zinkin, trans.). New York: International Universities Press, 1964. [8, 363, 364]

Bloom, F. E., Costa, E., and Salmoiraghi, G. C. Anesthesia and the responsiveness of individual neurons of the caudate nucleus of the cat to acetylcholine, norepinephrine, and dopamine administered by microelectrophoresis. *Journal of Pharmacology and Experimental Therapeutics*, 1965, *150*, 244–252. [375]

Bockus, H. L., Glassmire, C., and Bank, J. Fractional gastric analysis. *American Journal of Surgery*, 1931, *12*, 6–17. [237]

Bogen, J. E., Fisher, E. P., and Vogel, P. S. Cerebral commissurotomy: A second case report. *The Journal of the American Medical Association*, 1962, *174*, 1328–1329. [318]

Bond, E. D. Postencephalitic, ordinary and extraordinary children. *Journal of Pediatrics*, 1922, *1*, 310–314. [309]

Bonfils, S., Liefooghe, G., Gellé, Z., Dubrasquet, M., and Lambling, A. "Ulcère" expérimental de contrainte du rat blanc: III. Mise en évidence et analyse du rôle de certains facteurs psychologiques. *Revue française d'études cliniques et biologiques*, 1960, *5*, 571–581. [241, 269]

Bonfils, S., Richir, C., Potet, F., Liefooghe, G., and Lambling, A. "Ulcère" expérimental du contrainte du rat blanc: II. Anatomopathologie des lésions gastriques et de la différentes lésions viscérales. *Revue française d'études cliniques et biologiques*, 1959, *4*, 888–894. [239, 241]

Bonfils, S., Rossi, G., Liefooghe, G., and Lambling, A. "Ulcère" expérimental du rat blanc: I. Méthodes. Fréquence des lésions. Modifications par certains procédés techniques et pharmacodynamics. *Revue française d'études cliniques et biologiques*, 1959, *4*, 146–150. [237]

Boren, J., and Gallup, G. G., Jr. Amphetamine attenuation of tonic immobility in chickens. *Physiological Psychology*, 1976, *4*, 429–432. [343, 349]

Bortz, W. M. Metabolic consequences of obesity. *Annals of Internal Medicine*, 1969, *71*, 833–843. [43]

Bourne, P. G. (Ed.). *Addiction.* New York: Academic Press, 1974. [67]

Bowden, D., and McKinney, W. T. Behavioral effects of peer separation, isolation, and reunion on adolescent male rhesus monkeys. *Developmental Psychobiology*, 1972, *5*, 353–362. [150, 152]

Bowers, M. G., Jr., and Freedman, D. X. Psychedelic experiences in acute psychosis. *Archives of General Psychiatry*, 1966, *15*, 240–248. [8]

Bowlby, J. Grief and mourning in infancy and early childhood. *The Psychoanalytic Study of the Child*, 1960, *15*, 9–52. [136, 138, 139]

Bowlby, J. *Separation: Anxiety and anger.* New York: Basic Books, 1973. [136, 137, 141, 142, 143, 146, 147, 148, 161]

Brackbill, G. A. Studies of brain dysfunction in schizophrenia. *Psychological Bulletin*, 1956, *53*, 210–226. [15]

Bradley, C. The behavior of children receiving benzedrine. *American Journal of Psychiatry*, 1937, *94*, 577–585. [311, 312]

Bradley, C. Benzedrine and dexedrine in the treatment of children's behavior disorders. *Pediatrics*, 1950, *5*, 24–36. [312, 313, 315]

Brady, J. P., Thornton, D. R., and deFisher, D. Deleterious effects of anxiety elicited by conditioned pre-aversive stimuli in the rat. *Psychosomatic Medicine*, 1962, *24*, 590–595. [251]

Brady, J. V. Ulcers in "executive" monkeys. *Scientific American*, October 1958, 95–100. (Offprint 425.) [254]

Brady, J. V. Experimental studies of psychophysiological responses to stressful situations. In *Symposium On Medical Aspects of Stress in the Military Climate* (22–24 April 1964). Washington, D.C.: Walter Reed Army Institute of Research. [264]

Brady, J. V., Porter, R. W. Conrad, D. G., and Mason, J. W. Avoidance behavior and the development of gastroduodenal ulcers. *Journal of the Experimental Analysis of Behavior*, 1958, *1*, 69–72. [254, 255, 261]

Braud, W. G., and Ginsburg, H. J. Effect of administration of adrenalin on immobility reaction in domestic fowl. *Journal of Comparative and Physiological Psychology*, 1973, *83*, 124–127. [341]

Braud, W. G., Wepmann, B., and Russo, D. Task and species generality of the "helplessness" phenomenon. *Psychonomic Science*, 1969, *16*, 164–165. [107, 109]

Bray, G. A. The myth of diet in the management of obesity. *American Journal of Clinical Nutrition*, 1970, *23*, 1141–1148. (a) [45, 64]

Bray, G. A. Measurement of subcutaneous fat cells from obese patients. *Annals of Internal Medicine*, 1970, *73*, 565–569. (b) [46]

Bray, G. A. Lipogenesis in human adipose tissue: Some effects of nibbling and gorging. *Journal of Clinical Investigation*, 1972, *51*, 537–548. [50]

Bray, G. A., and York, D. A. Genetically transmitted obesity in rodents. *Physiological Reviews*, 1971, *51*, 598–646. [49]

Breese, G. R., Prange, A. J., Howard, J. L., Lipton, M. A., McKinney, W. T., Bowman, R. E., and Bushnell, P. 3-methoxy-4-hydroxyphenylglycol excretion and behavioral changes in rat and monkey after central sympathectomy with 6-hydroxy-dopamine. *Nature New Biology*, 1972, *240*, 286–287. [167]

Bregman, E. An attempt to modify the emotional attitude of infants by the conditioned response technique. *Journal of Genetic Psychology*, 1934, *45*, 169–198. [7]

Brenner, D. *Elementary textbook of psychoanalysis*. New York: International Universities Press, 1955. [363]

Bresnahan, E. L. Effects of intradimensional and extradimensional equivalence training, and extradimensional discrimination training upon stimulus control. (Paper presented at the meeting of the American Psychological Association, Washington, D.C., September 1969.) [120]

Breuer, J., and Freud, S. *Studies on hysteria*. J. Strachey (Ed.), (*Complete Psychological Works*, Standard Edition, Vol. II). London: Hogarth Press, 1957, pp. 215–222. (Originally published, 1895.)

Bridger, W. H., and Gantt, W. H. The effect of mescaline on differentiated conditional reflexes. *American Journal of Psychiatry*, 1956, *113*, 352–358. [17]

Brito, T. de, Montenegro, M. R., Leite, O. C., Berquo, E., and Vasconcellos, E. The relations between gastritis, peptic ulcers, and gastric carcinoma in surgically resected stomachs. *Gastroenterologia*, 1961, *95*, 341–351. [238]

Broadhurst, P. L. Abnormal animal behavior. In H. J. Eysenck (Ed.), *Handbook of abnormal psychology* (1st ed.). New York: Basic Books, 1960. [10]

Broadhurst, P. L. Animal studies bearing on abnormal behaviour. In H. J. Eysenck (Ed.), *Handbook of abnormal psychology* (2nd ed.). San Diego: Robert K. Knapp, 1973. [18]

Broadhurst, P. L., and Bignami, G. Correlative effects of psychogenetic selection: A study of the Roman high and low avoidance strains. *Behavior, Research and Therapy*, 1965, *2*, 273–280. [194]

Brobeck, J. R. Mechanisms of the development of obesity in animals with hypothalamic lesions. *Physiological Reviews*, 1946, *26*, 541–559. [27, 59]

Brobeck, J. R.   Food and temperature. *Recent Progress in Hormone Research*, 1960, *16*, 439–366. [27]

Brodie, D. A.   Literature review of restraint-induced ulcers. *Journal of Neuro-psychiatry*, 1962, *4*, 388–390. [237, 241, 242]

Brodie, D. A.   Literature review of restraint induced ulcers. *Journal of Neuro-psychiatry*, 1963, *4*, 388–390. [244]

Brodie, D. A., and Hanson, H. M.   A study of the factors involved in the production of gastric ulcers by the restraint technique. *Gastroenterology*, 1960, *38*, 353–360. [237, 239, 241, 242, 250]

Brodie, H. K., Gartrell, N., Doering, C., and Rhue, T.   Plasma testosterone levels in heterosexual and homosexual men. *American Journal of Psychiatry*, 1974, *131*, 82–83. [400]

Brooks, C. McC., Lockwood, R. L., and Wiggins, M. L.   A study of the effects of hypothalamic lesions on the eating habits of the albino rat. *American Journal of Physiology*, 1946, *147*, 735–741. [27, 59]

Brookshire, K. H., Littman, R. A., and Stewart, C. N.   Residue of shock trauma in the white rat: A three factor theory. *Psychological Monographs*, 1961, *75*, 10. [109]

Brown, C.   *Manchild in the promised land.* New York: Macmillan, 1965. [94]

Brown, J. S.   *The motivation of behavior.* New York: McGraw-Hill, 1961. [79]

Bruch, H.   Transformation of oral impulses in eating disorders: A conceptual approach. *Psychiatric Quarterly*, 1961, *35*, 458–481. [33, 39, 58]

Bruch, H.   *Eating disorders.* New York: Basic Books, 1973. [33, 39, 42, 58]

Brune, G. G.   The somatically determined psychoses. In H. Himwich (Ed.), *Biochemistry, schizophrenia, and affective illness.* Baltimore: Williams & Wilkins, 1970, pp. 43–78. [360]

Bullen, B. A., Reed, R. B., and Mayer, J.   Physical activity of obese and nonobese: Adolescent girls appraised by motion picture sampling. *American Journal of Clinical Nutrition*, 1964, *14*, 211–223. [60]

Bunney, B. S., and Aghajanian, G. K.   Evidence for drug actions on both pre- and post-synaptic catecholamine receptors in the CNS. In E. Usdin and W. Bunney, Jr. (Eds.), *Pre- and post-synaptic receptors.* New York: Marcel Dekker, 1975. [379]

Burdon, A. P., and Paul, L.   Obesity: A review of the literature, stressing the psychosomatic approach. *Psychiatric Quarterly*, 1951, *25*, 568–580. [33, 34]

Burgess, E.   The modification of depressive behavior. In R. Rubin and C. Franks (Eds.), *Advances in behavior therapy.* New York: Academic Press, 1968. [126, 127]

Burks, H. F.   Effects of amphetamine therapy on hyperkinetic children. *Archives of General Psychiatry*, 1964, *11*, 604–609. [313]

Burt, D. R., Enna, S. J., Creese, I., and Snyder, S. H.   Dopamine receptor binding in the corpus striatum of mammalian brain. *Proceedings of the National Academy of Sciences*, 1975, *72*, 4655–4659. [380]

Buss, A. H., and Plomin, R.   *A temperament theory of personality development.* New York: Wiley, 1975. [288]

Cabanac, M., Minaire, Y., and Adair, E.   Influence of internal factors on the pleasantness of gustative sweet sensation. *Communications in Behavioral Biology*, Part A, 1968, *1*, 77–82. [29]

Cahnan, W. J. The stigma of obesity. *Sociology Quarterly*, 1968, 9, 283–299. [42]

Cairns, R. B. Attachment behavior of mammals. *Psychological Review*, 1966, 73, 409–426. [148]

Calne, D. B., and Sandler, J. L-dopa and parkinsonism. *Nature*, 1970, 226, 21–24. [374]

Campbell, D., Sanderson, R. E., and Laverty, S. G. Characteristics of a conditioned response in human subjects during extinction trials following a single traumatic conditioning trial. *Journal of Abnormal and Social Psychology*, 1964, 68, 627–639. [207]

Campbell, D. T. On the conflicts between biological and social evolution and between psychology and moral tradition. *American Psychologist*, 1975, 30, 1103–1126. [356]

Cannon, W. B. *The wisdom of the body*. New York: W. W. Norton, 1939. [276]

Cappon, D., and Banks, R. Distorted body perception in obesity. *Journal of Nervous and Mental Disease*, 1968, 146, 465–466. [34]

Capute, A. J., Niedermayer, E. F. L., and Richardson, F. The electroencephalogram in children with minimal cerebral dysfunction. *Pediatrics*, 1968, 41, 1104–1114. [311]

Carli, G. Blood pressure and heart rate in the rabbit during animal hypnosis. *Electroencephalography and Clinical Neurophysiology*, 1974, 37, 231–237. [339]

Carlisle, H., and Stellar, E. Caloric regulation and food intake preference in normal, hyperphagic, and aphagic rats. *Journal of Comparative and Physiological Psychology*, 1969, 69, 107–114. [60]

Carlson, M. J., and Black, A. H. Traumatic avoidance learning: The effects of preventing escape responses. *Canadian Journal of Psychology*, 1957, 14, 21–28. [107]

Carlsson, A. Amphetamine and brain catecholamines. In E. Costa and S. Garatini (Eds.), *Amphetamines and related compounds*. New York: Raven Press, 1970, pp. 289–300. [383]

Carlsson, A., and Lindquist, M. Effect of chlorpromazine or haloperidol on formation of 3-methoxy-tyramine and normetanephrine in mouse brain. *Acta Pharmacologica et Toxicologica*, 1963, 20, 140–144. [379]

Carman, J. B., Cowan, W. M., Powell, T. P. S., and Webster, K. E. A bilateral corticostriate projection. *Journal of Neurological Surgery and Psychiatry*, 1965, 28, 71–77. [319]

Carney, M. W. P., Roth, M., and Garside, R. F. The diagnosis of depressive syndromes and the prediction of E. C. T. response. *British Journal of Psychiatry*, 1965, 111, 659–674. [127]

Carpenter, K. L., and Mayer, J. Physiologic observations on yellow obesity in the mouse. *American Journal of Physiology*, 1958, 193, 499–504. [49]

Carroll, M. E., Dinc, H. I., Levy, C. J. and Smith, J. C. Demonstration of neophobia and enhanced neophobia in the albino rat. *Journal of Comparative and Physiological Psychology*, 1975, 89, 457–467. [191]

Catania, A. C. Elicitation, reinforcement, and stimulus control. In R. Glaser, (Ed.), *The Nature of reinforcement*. New York: Academic Press, 1971, pp. 196–220. [117]

Caul, W. F., Buchanan, D. C., and Hays, R. C. Effects of unpredictability of shock on incidence of gastric lesions and heart rate in the immobilized rat. *Physiology and Behavior*, 1972, 8, 669–672. [254]

Celesia, G. G., and Barr, A. N.   Psychosis and other psychiatric manifestations of levodopa therapy. *Archives of Neurology,* 1970, *23,* 193–200. [370]

Chambers, C. D.   *Drug use in the New York State labor force.* Report of New York State Narcotic Control Commission, Division of Research, 1971. [67]

Chase, T. N.   Drug-induced extrapyramidal disorders. *Research Publication Association of Nervous and Mental Disorders,* 1972, *50,* 448–471. [378, 381, 382]

Chesters, J. K., and Will, M.   Some factors controlling food intake by zinc-deficient rats. *British Journal of Nutrition,* 1973, *30,* 555–566. [29]

Chinn, S., Garrow, J. S., and Miall, W. B.   The long-term stability of body weight in a randomly selected sample of the adult population in South Wales. In J. S. Garrow (Ed.), *Energy Balance and Obesity in Man.* London: North-Holland Publishing Co., Ltd., 1972. [30]

Chirico, A., and Stunkard, A.   Physical activity and human obesity. *New England Journal of Medicine,* 1960, *263,* 935–940. [60]

Cho, C. H., Ogle, C., and Dai, S.   Acute gastric ulcer formation in response to electrical vagal stimulation in rats. *European Journal of Pharmacology,* 1976, *35,* 215–219. [239]

Christian, J. J.   Effect of population size on the adrenal glands and reproductive organs of male mice in populations of fixed size. *American Journal of Physiology,* 1955, *182,* 292–300. [400]

Church, R. M.   Response suppression. In B. A. Campbell and R. M. Church (Eds.), *Punishment and aversive behavior.* New York: Appleton-Century-Crofts, 1969. Pp. 111–156. [117]

Clark, P. J.   The heritability of certain anthropometric characters as ascertained from measurement of twins. *American Journal of Human Genetics,* 1956, *8,* 49–54. [48]

Cobb, S., and Lindemann, E.   Neuropsychiatric observation after the Coconut Grove fire. *Annals of Surgery,* 1943, *117,* 814–824.

Cohen, D. H., and MacDonald, R. L.   A selective review of central neural pathways involved in cardiovascular control. In P. A. Obrist, A. H. Black, J. Brener, and L. V. DiCara (Eds.), *Cardiovascular psychophysiology.* Chicago: Aldine, 1974. [285]

Cole, J. O.   Therapeutic efficacy of antidepressant drugs. *Journal of the American Medical Association,* 1964, *190,* 448–455. [114, 115]

Cole, J. O., and Clyde, D. J.   Extrapyramidal side effects and clinical response to the phenothiazines. *Revue Canadienne de Biologie,* 1961, *20,* 565–574. [382]

Coleman, J. C.   *Abnormal psychology and modern life.* Glenview, Illinois: Scott, Foresman, 1964. [338, 354]

Comstock, G. W., and Stone, R. W.   Changes in body weight and subcutaneous fat thickness related to smoking habits. *Archives of Environmental Health,* 1974, *24,* 271–276. [30]

Connell, P. H.   *Amphetamine psychosis.* (*Maudsley Monographs* (No. 5), *Institute of Psychiatry.*) London: Chapman & Hall, Ltd., 1958. [383]

Connolly, J., Hallam, R. S. and Marks, I. M.   Selective association of fainting with blood-injury fear. *Behavior Therapy,* 1976, 7 (1), 8. [184]

Cooper, J. R., Bloom, F. E., and Roth, R. H.   *The biochemical basis of neuropharmacology* (2nd ed.). New York: Oxford University Press, 1974. [371]

Corbit, J., and Stellar, E. Palatability, food intake, and obesity in normal and hyperphagic rats. *Journal of Comparative and Physiological Psychology*, 1964, *58*, 63–69. [60, 61]

Corson, S. A., Corson, E. O'L., Kirilcuk, V., Arnold, E. L., Knopp, W., and Kirilcuk, J. Comparative responses to amphetamines by naturally occurring hyperkinetic, aggressive, and normal dogs (Discussion). *Annals of the New York Academy of Sciences*, 1973, *205*, 132–138, 262–266. [328]

Corson, S. A., Corson, E. O'L., Kirilcuk, V., Kirilcuk, J., Knopp, W., and Arnold, L. E. Interaction of amphetamines and psychosocial therapy in the control of violence and hyperkinesis in dogs. *Psychopharmacologia*, 1972, *26*, 55–56. [328]

Cotzias, G. C., Papavasiliou, P. S., and Gelene, R. Modification of parkinsonism-chronic treatment with L-dopa. *New England Journal of Medicine*, 1969, *280*, 337–345. [370]

Courvoisier, S., Fournel, J., Ducrot, R., Kolsky, M., and Koetschet, P. Properties pharmacodynamiques du chlorhydrate de chloro-3 (dimethylamino-3-propyl) -10 phenothiazine (4650 R.P.). *Archives of International Pharmacodynamics*, 1953, *92*, 301–305. [370]

Cowgill, G. R. The energy factor in relation to food intake: Experiments on the dog. *American Journal of Physiology*, 1928, *85*, 45–64. [29]

Coyle, J. T., and Snyder, S. H. Antiparkinsonian drugs: Inhibition of dopamine uptake in the corpus striatum as a possible mechanism of action. *Science*, 1969, *166*, 899–901. [379]

Craddock, D. *Obesity and its management*. London: Livingstone, 1969. [33]

Crane, G. E. Persistent dyskinesia. *British Journal of Psychiatry*, 1973, *122*, 395–405. [381]

Creese, I., Burt, D. R., and Snyder, S. H. Dopamine receptor binding predicts clinical and pharmacological potencies of antischizophrenic drugs. *Science*, 1976, *192*, 481–483. [374, 381]

Crisp, A. H. Premorbid factors in adult disorders of weight, with primary reference to primary anorexia nervosa: A literature review. *Journal of Psychosomatic Research*, 1970, *14*, 1–22. [33]

Crozier, W. J. Reflex immobility and the central nervous system. *Proceedings of the Society for Experimental Biology and Medicine*, 1923, *21*, 55–56. [334]

Cushing, H. Peptic ulcers and the interbrain. *Surgery, Gynecology, and Obstetrics*, 1932, *55*, 1–34. [239, 265, 267, 268]

Dai, S., Ogle, C. W., and Lo, C. H. The effects of metiamide on gastric secretion and stress ulceration in rats. *European Journal of Pharmacology*, 1975, *33*, 277–282. [237]

D'Amato, M. R. Derived motives. In *Annual Review of Psychology*, Vol. 25. Palo Alto, Calif., Annual Reviews, 1974. Pp. 83–106. [69]

David, O., Clark, J., and Voeller, K. Lead and hyperactivity. *The Lancet*, Vol. II, 1972, 7783, 900–903. [309]

Davidson, R. J., and Schwartz, G. E. Psychobiology of relaxation and related states: A multi-process theory. In D. Mostofsky (Ed.), *Behavior control and modification of physiological activity*. Englewood Cliffs, N.J.: Prentice-Hall, 1976. [300]

Davis, J. Efficacy of tranquilizing and antidepressant drugs. *Archives of General Psychiatry*, 1965, *13*, 552–572. [115]

Davison, G. C., and Neale, J. M. *Abnormal psychology: An experimental clinical approach*. New York: Wiley, 1974. [10]

Davison, K., and Bagley, C. R. *Schizophrenia-like psychosis associated with organic disorders of the central nervous system: A review of the literature*. (British Journal of Psychiatry Special Publication No. 4) Ashford, Kent: Headley Brothers, 1969. [362]

Decke, E. Effects of taste on the eating behavior of obese and normal persons. In S. Schachter (Ed.), *Emotion, obesity, and crime*. New York: Academic Press, 1971. [56, 60]

De La Cruz, F., Fox, B. H., and Roberts, R. H. (Eds.). *Annals of the New York Academy of Sciences*, 1973, *205*, 5–396. [333]

Delprato, D. J. An animal analogue to systematic desensitization and elimination of avoidance. *Behaviour Research and Therapy*, 1973, *11*, 49–55. (a) [202, 203]

Delprato, D. J. Exposure to the aversive stimulus in an animal analogue to systematic desensitization. *Behaviour Research and Therapy*, 1973, *11*, 187–192. (b) [203]

Delprato, D. J., and Jackson, D. E. Counterconditioning and exposure only in the treatment of specific (conditioned) suppression. *Behaviour Research and Therapy*, 1974, *11*, 453–461. [203]

Denham, J., and Carrick, D. J. Therapeutic value of thioproperazine and the importance of the associated neurological disturbances. *Journal of Mental Science*, 1961, *107*, 326–345. [382]

Denhoff, E. The natural life history of children with minimal brain dysfunction. *Annals of the New York Academy of Sciences*, 1973, *205*, 188–205. [332]

Deniker, P. Experimental neurological syndromes and the new drug therapies in psychiatry. *Comprehensive Psychiatry*, 1960, *1*, 92–102. [382]

de Wied, D., Bohus, B., and Greuen, H. M. Influence of pituitary and adrenocortical hormones on conditioned avoidance behaviour in rats. In R. P. Michael (Ed.), *Endocrinology and human behaviour*. (Proceedings of a conference held at the Institute of Psychiatry, May 1967.) Oxford: Oxford University Press, 1968. [197]

de Wied, D., Sarantakis, D., and Weinstein, B. Behavioral evaluation of peptides related to scotophobia. *Neuropharmacology*, 1973, *12*, 1109–1115. [197]

Dickie, M. M., and Woolley, G. W. The age factor in weight of yellow mice. Weight reduction of aging yellow and "thin-yellows" revealed in littermate comparisons. *Journal of Heredity*, 1946, *37*, 365–368. [49]

Djahanquiri, L. R., Taubin, H. L., and Landsberg, L. Increased sympathetic activity in the pathogenesis of restraint ulcer in rats. *Journal of Pharmacology and Experimental Therapeutics*, 1973, *184*, 163–168. [239]

Dmitruk, V. M. "Experimental neurosis" in cats: Fact of artifact? *Journal of Abnormal Psychology*, 1974, *83*, 97–105. [22]

Doerr, P., Kockott, G., Vogt, H. J., Pirke, K. M., and Dittmar, F. Plasma testosterone, estradiol, and semen analysis in male homosexuals. *Archives of General Psychiatry*, 1973, *29*, 829–833. [400]

Dole, V. P. Relation between non-esterified fatty acids in plasma and metabolism of glucose. *Journal of Clinical Investigation*, 1956, 35, 150. [43]

Dollard, J., and Miller, N. E. *Personality and psychotherapy*. New York: McGraw-Hill, 1950. [24]

Dorworth, T. R. The effect of electroconvulsive shock on "helplessness" in dogs. (Unpublished doctoral dissertation, University of Minnesota, 1971.) [125]

Dragstedt, L. R. Gastric secretion and duodenal ulcer. In T. K. Shnitka, J. Gilbert, and R. C. Harrison (Eds.), *Gastric secretion: Mechanisms and control*. New York: Pergamon, 1967, pp. 241–253. [237]

Dragstedt, L. R., Ragins, H., Dragstedt, L. R., III, and Evans, S. O. Stress and duodenal ulcer. *Annals of Surgery*, 1956, 144, 450–463. [238]

Dragstedt, L. R., and Woodward, E. R. Appraisal of vagotomy for peptic ulcer after seven years. *Journal of the American Medical Association*, 1951, 145, 795–800. [239]

Draper, D. C., and Klemm, W. R. Behavioral responses associated with animal hypnosis. *The Psychological Record*, 1967, 17, 13–21. [337]

Dubrasquet, M., Sergent, D., Lewin, M., and Bonfils, S. Relationship between circadian rhythms, spontaneous activity, and restraint ulcer in the rat. In C. J. Pfeiffer (Ed.), *Peptic ulcer*. Philadelphia: Lippincott, 1971, pp. 105–112. [269]

Dweck, C. S., and Reppucci, N. D. Learned helplessness and reinforcement responsibility in children. *Journal of Personality and Social Psychology*, 1973, 25, 109–116. [116]

Dworkin, S. Conditioning neuroses in dogs and cats. *Psychosomatic Medicine*, 1939, 1, 388–396. [215]

Dwyer, J. T., Feldman, J. J., and Mayer, J. The social psychology of dieting. *Journal of Health and Social Behavior*, 1970, 11, 269–287. [31]

Eaton, G. G., Goy, R. W., and Phoenix, C. H. Effects of testosterone treatment in adulthood on sexual behavior of female pseudohermaphrodite rhesus monkeys. *Nature New Biology*, 1973, 242, 119–120. [393, 396]

Eckstein, G. *The body has a head*. New York: Harper & Row, 1969. [273, 283]

Edson, P. H., and Gallup, G. G., Jr. Tonic immobility as a fear response in lizards (*Anolis carolinensis*). *Psychonomic Science*, 1972, 26, 27–28. [340, 353]

Edwards, A. E., and Acker, L. E. A demonstration of the long-term retention of a conditioned GSR. *Psychosomatic Medicine*, 1962, 24, 459–463. [17]

Ehringer, H., and Hornykiewicz, O. Verteilung von Noradrenalin und Dopamin in Gehirn des Menschen und ihr Verhalten bei Erkrankungen des extrapyramidalen Systems. *Klinische Wochenschrift*, 1960, 38, 1236–1239. [379]

Eichelman, B. Effect of subcortical lesions on shock-induced aggression in the rat. *Journal of Comparative and Physiological Psychology*, 1971, 74, 331–339. [60]

Eisenberg, L., Lachman, R., Molling, P., Lockner, A., Mizelle, J. D., and Conners, C. K. A psychopharmacologic experiment in a training school for delinquent boys: Methods, problems, findings. *American Journal of Orthopsychiatry*, 1963, 33, 431–437. [313]

Eiserer, L. A., and Hoffman, H. S.   Priming of ducklings' responses by presenting an imprinted stimulus. *Journal of Comparative and Physiological Psychology*, 1973, 82, 345–359. [76, 78]

Ellinwood, E. H. Jr.   Amphetamine psychosis. I. Description of the individuals and process. *Journal of Nervous and Mental Disease*, 1967, 144, 273–283. [370]

Engberg, L. A., Hansen, G., Welker, R. L., and Thomas, D. R.   Acquisition of key-pecking via autoshaping as a function of prior experience. *Science*, 1972, 178, 1002–1004. [121]

English, H. B.   Three cases of the "conditioned fear response." *Journal of Abnormal and Social Psychology*, 1929, 34, 221–225. [7, 193]

Ernst, A. M.   Mode of action of apomorphine and dexamphetamine on gnawing compulsion in rats. *Psychopharmacologia*, 1967, 10, 316–323. [375]

Erwin, J., Brandt, E. M., and Mitchell, G.   Attachment formation and separation in heterosexually naive preadolescent rhesus monkeys (*Macaca mulatta*). *Developmental Psychobiology*, 1973, 6, 531–538. [148, 149]

Erwin, J., Mobaldi, J., and Mitchell, G.   Separation of rhesus monkey juveniles of the same sex. *Journal of Abnormal Psychology*, 1971, 78, 134–139. [152]

Esser, A. H.   (Personal communication, 1974.) [138] .

Evans, G.   Septal inhibition of aversive emotional states. (Unpublished Master's thesis, Bryn Mawr College, 1974.) [226]

Evans, R. B.   Biological factors in male homosexuality. *Medical Aspects of Human Sexuality*, 1973, 7, 12–33. [400]

Fábry, P., Hejda, S., and Cerný, K.   Effect of meal frequency in school children. Changes in weight-height proportion and skinfold thickness. *American Journal of Clinical Nutrition*, 1966, 18, 358–361. [50]

Fann, W. E.   Use of methylphenidate to counteract acute dystonic effects of phenothiazines. *American Journal of Psychiatry*, 1966, 122, 1293–1294. [381]

Faris, R. E. L., and Dunham, H. W.   *Mental disorders in urban areas*. Chicago: University of Chicago Press, 1939. [360]

Feinberg, I.   A comparison of the visual hallucinations in schizophrenics with those induced by mescaline and LSD-25. In L. J. West (Ed.), *Hallucinations*. New York: Grune and Stratton, 1962. [8]

Feldman, S., Conforti, N., Chowers, I., and Davidson, J.   Pituitary-adrenal activation in rats with medial basal hypothalamic islands. *Acta Endocrinologica*, 1970, 63, 405–414. [241]

Feltz, P.   Monoamines and the excitatory nigro-striatal linkage. *Experentia*, 1971, 27, 2. [374]

Ferster, C. B.   Classification of behavioral pathology. In L. Krasner and L. P. Ullman (Eds.), *Research in behavior modification*. New York: Holt, Rinehart and Winston, 1965, pp. 6–26. [154]

Ferster, C. B.   Animal behavior and mental illness. *Psychological Records*, 1966, 16, 345–346. [123]

Ferster, C. B.   A functional analysis of depression. *American Psychologist*, 1973, 28, 857–870. [123]

Ferster, C. B., and Skinner, B. F.   *Schedules of reinforcement*. New York: Appleton-Century-Crofts, 1957. [117]

Fish, F. *Clinical psychopathology signs and symptoms in psychiatry.* Bristol: John Wright & Sons, Ltd., 1967. [364, 367]

Fodor, J. A. *Psychological explanation: An introduction to the philosophy of psychology.* New York: Random House, 1968. [5]

Foltz, E. L., and Millett, F. E. Experimental psychosomatic disease states in monkeys: I. Peptic "ulcer-executive" monkeys. *Journal of Surgical Research,* 1964, *4,* 445–453. [256]

Forsham, P. H. Some endocrine anomalies in obesity. In *Obesity.* Postgraduate Medicine Symposiums, 1974. [43]

Forsyth, R. P. Mechanisms of the cardiovascular responses to environmental stressors. In P. A. Obrist, A. H. Black, J. Brener, and L. V. DiCara (Eds.), *Cardiovascular psychophysiology.* Chicago: Aline, 1974. [291]

Frazier, L. E., Wissler, R. W., Steffee, C. H., Wollridge, F. L., and Cannon, P. R. Studies in amino acid utilization. I. The dietary utilization of mixtures of purified amino acids in protein-depleted adult albino rats. *Journal of Nutrition,* 1947, *33,* 65–84. [29]

Freedman, D. Hereditary control of early social behaviour. In B. M. Foss (Ed.), *Determinants of infant behaviour* (Vol. 3). London: Methuen, 1965. Pp. 149–159. [194, 196]

French, J. D., Porter, R. W., Cavanaugh, E. D., and Longmire, R. L. Experimental gastroduodenal lesions induced by stimulation of the brain. *Psychosomatic Medicine,* 1957, *19,* 209–220. [239]

Freud, S. Mourning and melancholia. In *Collected papers* (Vol. 4). London: Hogarth Press, 1950, pp. 152–172. (Originally published, 1917.) [148, 161]

Freyhan, F. A. Psychomotility and parkinsonism in treatment with neuroleptic drugs. *Archives of Neurology and Psychiatry,* 1957, *78,* 465–472. [378]

Friedhoff, A. J., and van Winkle, E. Isolation and characterization of a compound from the urine of schizophrenics. *Nature,* 1962, *194,* 897–898. [9]

Friedman, A. S. Minimal effects of severe depression on cognitive functioning. *Journal of Abnormal Psychology,* 1964, *69,* 237–243. [113]

Friedman, M., and Rosenman, R. H. Association of specific overt behavior patterns with blood and cardiovascular findings. *Journal of the American Medical Association,* 1959, *169,* 1286–1296. [268]

Friedman, S. B., and Ader, R. Parameters relevant to the experimental production of stress in the mouse. *Psychosomatic Medicine,* 1965, *27,* 27–30. [251]

Freimark, S. J. Effects of electrical stimulation of the brain on the formation of acute gastric lesions. *Physiology and Behavior,* 1973, *11,* 855–859. [239]

Fuxe, K., and Hokfelt, T. Further evidence of tuberoinfundibular dopamine neurons. *Acta Physiologica Scandinavia,* 1966, *66,* 245–246. [376]

Gaarder, K. R. *Eye movements, vision, and behavior.* Washington, D.C.: Hemisphere Publishing Corporation, 1975. [270, 272, 275, 276, 281]

Galin, D. Implications of left-right cerebral lateralization for psychiatry: A neurophysiological context for unconscious processes. *Archives of General Psychiatry,* 1974, *9,* 412–418. [290]

Gall, F. J. Sur les fonctions du cerveau et sur celles de chaunce de ses parties. Paris, 1825. Translation in *Gall's Works,* Vol. IV, VI (Winslow Lewis, translator). Boston, 1835. [2]

Gallup, G. G., Jr. Simulated predation and tonic immobility in lizards *(Anolis carolinensis)*. *Copeia*, 1973, 3, 623–624. (a) [353]

Gallup, G. G., Jr. Tonic immobility in chickens: Is a stimulus that signals shock more aversive than the receipt of shock? *Animal Learning and Behavior*, 1973, 1, 228–232. (b) [339, 340]

Gallup, G. G., Jr. Animal hypnosis. Factual status of a fictional concept. *Psychological Bulletin*, 1974, 81, 836–853. (a) [335, 337, 338, 346]

Gallup, G. G., Jr. Genetic influence on tonic immobility in chickens. *Animal Learning and Behavior*, 1974, 2, 145–147. (b) [350]

Gallup, G. G., Jr., Creekmore, H. S., and Hill, W. E., III. Shock-enhanced immobility reactions in chickens: Support for the fear hypothesis. *The Psychological Record*, 1970, 20, 243–245. [339]

Gallup, G. G., Jr., Cummings, W. H., and Nash, R. F. The experimenter as an independent variable in studies of animal hypnosis in chickens *(Gallus gallus)*. *Animal Behaviour*, 1972, 20, 166–169. [353]

Gallup, G. G., Jr., Ledbetter, D. H., and Maser, J. D. Strain differences in tonic immobility: Evidence for an emotionality component. *Journal of Comparative and Physiological Psychology*, 1976, 90, 1075–1081. [341, 350]

Gallup, G. G., Jr., Maser, J. D., Wallnau, L. B., Boren, J. L., Gagliardi, G. J., and Edson, P. H. Tryptophan and tonic immobility in chickens: Effects of dietary and systemic manipulations. *Journal of Comparative and Physiological Psychology*, 1977. [347]

Gallup, G. G., Jr., Nash, R. F., and Brown, C. W. The effects of a tranquilizer on the immobility reaction in chickens: Additional support for the fear hypothesis. *Psychonomic Science*, 1971, 23, 127–128. [342, 352]

Gallup, G. G., Jr., Nash, R. F., Donegan, N. H., and McClure, M. K. The immobility response: A predator-induced reaction in chickens. *The Psychological Record*, 1971, 21, 513–519. [352]

Gallup, G. G., Jr., Nash, R. F., and Ellison, A. L., Jr. Tonic immobility as a reaction to predation: Artificial eyes as a fear stimulus for chickens. *Psychonomic Science*, 1971, 23, 79–80. [353, 354]

Gallup, G. G., Jr., Nash, R. F., Potter, R. J., and Donegan, N. H. Effect of varying conditions of fear on immobility reactions in domestic chickens *(Gallus gallus)*. *Journal of Comparative and Physiological Psychology*, 1970, 73, 442–445. [339, 340]

Gallup, G. G., Jr., Nash, R. F., and Wagner, A. M. The tonic immobility reaction in chickens: Response characteristics and methodology. *Behavior Research Methods and Instrumentation*, 1971, 3, 237–239. [336]

Gallup, G. G., Jr., Rosen, T. S., and Brown, C. W. Effect of conditioned fear on tonic immobility in domestic chickens. *Journal of Comparative and Physiological Psychology*, 1972, 78, 22–25. [340, 342]

Gallup, G. G., Jr., and Williamson, G. T. Effect of food deprivation and a visual cliff on tonic immobility. *Psychonomic Science*, 1972, 29, 301–302. [341, 343]

Gamzu, E., and Williams, D. R. Classical conditioning of a complex skeletal response. *Science*, 1971, 171, 923–925. [121]

Ganguly, A. K. A method for quantitative assessment of experimentally produced ulcers in the stomach of albino rats. *Experientia*, 1969, 25, 1224. [249]

Gantt, W. H.   *Experimental basis for neurotic behavior.* New York: Harper, 1944.
[16, 216]

Gantt, W. H.   The physiological basis of psychiatry: The conditional reflex. In J.
Wortis (Ed.), *Basic problems in psychiatry.* New York: Grune & Stratton,
1953. [16, 216]

Gantt, W. H.   Factors involved in the development of pathological behavior: Schizokinesis and autokinesis. *Perspectives in Biology and Medicine,* 1962, 5, 473–
482. [17]

Gantt, W. H.   Experimental basis for neurotic behavior. In H. D. Kimmel (Ed.),
Experimental psychopathology: Recent research and theory. New York: Academic Press, 1971. [17, 215, 216]

Garb, J. L., and Stunkard, A. J.   Taste aversions in man. *American Journal of
Psychiatry,* 1974, *131,* 1204–1207. [191]

Gellerman, L. W.   Chance orders of alternating stimuli in visual discrimination
experiments. *Journal of Genetic Psychology,* 1933, 42, 207–208. [219]

Gerall, A. A., Hendricks, S. E., Johnson, L. L., and Bounds, T. W.   Effects of
early castration in male rats on adult sexual behavior. *Journal of Comparative
and Physiological Psychology,* 1967, *64,* 206–212. [393]

Gershon, E., Dunner, D., and Goodwin, F.   Toward a biology of effective disorders: Genetic contributions. *Archives of General Psychiatry,* 1971, 25, 1–15.
[135]

Gessa, R., Tagliamonte, A., and Gessa, G. L.   Blockade by apomorphine of
haloperidol-induced dyskinesia in schizophrenic patients. *Lancet,* 1973, 2,
395. [381]

Gibbon, J., Berryman, R., and Thompson, R. L.   Contingency spaces and measures in classical and instrumental conditioning. *Journal of the Experimental
Analysis of Behavior,* 1974, *21,* 585–605. [117]

Gibbs, J., Young, R. C., and Smith, G. P.   Cholecystokinin decreases food intake
in rats. *Journal of Comparative and Physiological Psychology,* 1973, *84,* 488–
495. [29]

Gibson, A. R., and Gazzaniga, M. S.   Hemispheric differences in eating behavior
in split-brain monkeys. *Physiologist,* 1971, *14,* 150. [63]

Gibson E. J., and Walk, R. D.   The "Visual Cliff." *Scientific American,* April
1960, pp. 64–71. (Offprint 402.) [179]

Gilman, T. T., and Marcuse, F. L.   Animal hypnosis. *Psychological Bulletin,*
1949, *46,* 151–165. [335]

Gilman, T. T., Marcuse, F. L., and Moore, A. U.   Animal hypnosis: A study in
the induction of tonic immobility in chickens. *Journal of Comparative and
Physiological Psychology,* 1950, *43,* 99–111. [342]

Gittelman-Klein, R., and Klein, D. F.   Controlled imipramine treatment of school
phobia. *Archives of General Psychiatry,* 1971, *25,* 204–207. [188]

Gjessing, L. R.   A review of periodic catatonia. *Biological Psychiatry,* 1974, 8,
23–45. [338, 341]

Glass, D. C., Snyder, M. L., and Hollis, J. F.   Time urgency and the type A
coronary-prone behavior pattern. *Journal of Applied and Social Psychology,*
1974, *4,* 125–140. [268]

Gliner, J. A.   Predictable versus unpredictable shock: Preference behavior and
stomach ulceration. *Physiology and Behavior,* 1972, 9, 693–698. [257]

Gliner, J. A., and Shemberg, K. M.   Conditioned fear and gastric pathology in a continuing stress-rest paradigm in rats. *Journal of Comparative and Physiological Psychology*, 1971, 74, 20–22. [257]

Gluck, J. P., Harlow, H. F., and Schiltz, K. A.   Differential effect of early enrichment and deprivation on learning in the rhesus monkey. *Journal of Comparative and Physiological Psychology*, 1973, 84, 598–604. [164]

Glucksman, M. L., and Hirsch, J.   The response of obese patients to weight reduction: A clinical evaluation of behavior. *Psychosomatic Medicine*, 1968, 30, 1–11. [40, 41]

Glucksman, M. L., Hirsch, J., and McCully, R. S.   The response of obese patients to weight reduction. II. A quantitative evaluation of behavior. *Psychosomatic Medicine*, 1968, 30, 359–373. [41]

Goesling, W. J., Buchholz, A. R., and Carreira, C. J.   Conditioned immobility and ulcer development in rats. *Journal of General Psychology*, 1974, 91, 231–236. [263]

Goldberg, E. M., and Morrison, S. L.   Schizophrenia and social class. *British Journal of Psychiatry*, 1963, 109, 785–802. [360]

Goldman, D.   Parkinsonism and related phenomena from administration of drugs: Their production and control under clinical conditions and possible relation to therapeutic effect. *Revue Canadienne de Biologie*, 1961, 20, 549–560. [378]

Goldman, R., Jaffa, M., and Schachter, S.   Yom Kippur, Air France, dormitory food, and eating behavior of obese and normal persons. *Journal of Personality and Social Psychology*, 1968, 10, 117–123. [52]

Goldstein, A.   Opioid peptides (endorphins) in pituitary and brain. *Science*, 1976, 193, 1081–1086.

Gordon, A., and Baum, M.   Increased efficacy of flooding (response prevention) in rats through intracranial stimulation. *Journal of Comparative and Physiological Psychology*, 1971, 75, 68–72. [203]

Gottesman, I. I., and Shields, J.   Schizophrenia in twins: 16 years' consecutive admissions to psychiatric clinic. *British Journal of Psychiatry*, 1966, 112, 809–818. [369]

Goy, R. W.   Early hormonal influences on the development of sexual and sex-related behavior. In F. O. Schmitt (Ed.), *The neurosciences: Second study program*. New York: The Rockefeller University Press, 1970. [396]

Grady, K. L., Phoenix, C. H., and Young, W. C.   Role of the developing rat testis in differentiation of the neural tissues mediating mating behavior. *Journal of Comparative and Physiological Psychology*, 1965, 59, 176–182. [393, 394]

Graff, H., and Stellar, E.   Hyperphagia, obesity, and finickiness. *Journal of Comparative and Physiological Psychology*, 1962, 55, 418–424. [61]

Graham, D. T.   Psychosomatic medicine. In N. S. Greenfield and R. A. Sternbach (Eds.), *Handbook of psychophysiology*. New York: Holt, Rinehart and Winston, 1972. [279, 280, 289]

Graham, P.   Controlled trial of behaviour therapy vs. conventional therapy: A pilot study. (Unpublished D.P.M. dissertation submitted to the University of London, 1964.) [182]

Granville-Grossman, K.   The early environment in affective disorder. In A. Copen and A. Walk (Eds.), *Recent developments in affective disorders*. London: Headley Brothers, 1968, pp. 65–79. [148]

Gray, J. A. *Pavlov's typology.* New York: The Macmillan Company, 1964. [13, 215]

Green, J. D. The hippocampus. *Physiological Reviews,* 1964, *44,* 561–608. [318]

Grey Walter, W. The contingent negative variation is an aid to psychiatric diagnosis. In Kietzman, M. L., Sutton, S. & Zubin, J. (Eds.), *Experimental Approaches to Psychopathology.* N.Y.: Academic Press, 1975, p. 198. [198]

Griffin, G. A., and Harlow, H. F. Effects of 3 months of total deprivation on
social adjustment and learning in the rhesus monkey. *Child Development,*
1966, *37,* 533–547. [143]

Griffith, J. J., Oates, J., and Cavanaugh, J. Paranoid episodes induced by drugs.
Journal of the American Medical Association, 1968, *205,* 39. [383]

Griggs, R. C., and Stunkard, A. J. The interpretation of gastric motility: Sensitivity
and bias in the perception of gastric motility. *Archives of General Psychiatry,*
1964, *11,* 82–89. [55]

Grinker, J., Hirsch, J., and Levin, B. The affective response of obese patients to
weight reduction: A differentiation based on age of onset of obesity. *Psychosomatic Medicine,* 1973, *35,* 57–62. [40]

Grinker, R., Sr., Miller, J., Sabshin, M., Nunn, R. J., and Nunally, J. C. *The
phenomena of depression.* New York: Hoeber, 1961. [111, 115]

Gross, L. The effects of early feeding experience on external responsiveness. (Unpublished doctoral dissertation, Columbia University, 1968.) [58, 59]

Grossman, S. P. The VMH: A center for affective reactions, satiety, or both? *Journal of Physiology and Behavior,* 1966, *1,* 1–10. [63]

Grossman, S. P. Aggression, avoidance, and reaction to novel environment in
female rats with ventromedial hypothalamic lesions. *Journal of Comparative
and Physiological Psychology,* 1972, *78,* 274–283. (a) [60]

Grossman, S. P. Cholinergic synopses in the limbic system and behavioral inhibition. In I. J. Koplin (Ed.), *Neurotransmitters.* Baltimore: Williams & Wilkins,
1972. (b) [226]

Grossman, S. P. Role of the hypothalamus in the regulation of food and water
intake. *Psychological Review,* 1975, *82,* 200–224. [28]

Grosz, C. R., and Wu, R. T. Stress ulcers: A survey of the experience of a large
general hospital. *Surgery,* 1967, *61,* 853–857. [236]

Gur, R., and Gur, R. Defense mechanisms, psychosomatic symptomology, and
conjugate lateral eye movements. *Journal of Consulting and Clinical Psychology,* 1975, *43,* 416–420. [290]

Guth, P. H., and Hall, P. Microcirculatory and mast cell changes in restraint-
induced gastric ulcer. *Gastroenterology,* 1966, *50,* 562–570. [239]

Guth, P. H., and Mendick, R. The effect of chronic restraint stress on gastric
ulceration in the rat. *Gastroenterology,* 1964, *46,* 285–286. [242]

Gutmann, M. C., and Benson, H. Interaction of environmental factors and systemic arterial blood pressure: A review. *Medicine,* 1971, *50,* 543–553. [286,
288]

Guze, S. B. The need for tough-mindedness in psychiatric thinking. *Southern
Medical Journal,* 1970, *63,* 662–671. [359]

Haase, H. J., and Janssen, P. A. H. *The action of neuroleptic drugs.* Amsterdam:
North Holland, 1965. [378]

Hagman, E.   A study of fears of children of pre-school age. *Journal of Experimental Education*, 1932, *1*, 110–130. [180]

Hall, W. H., and Smith, G. P.   Gastric secretory response to chronic hypothalamic stimulation in monkeys. *Gastroenterology*, 1969, *57*, 491–499. [239]

Hamburg, D. A., Hamburg, B. A., and Barchas, J. D.   Anger and depression in perspective of behavioral biology. In L. Levi (Ed.), *Parameters of emotion*. New York: Raven Press, 1974. [138]

Hamburger, W. W.   Emotional aspects of obesity. *Medical Clinics of North America*, 1951, *35*, 483–499. [32]

Hanley, J.   Automatic recognition of EEG correlates of behavior in a chronic schizophrenic patient. *American Journal of Psychiatry*, 1972, *128*, 1524–1528. [376]

Hanley, T., Lewis, J. G., and Knight, G. J.   The influence of fatness in the plasma NEFA response to glucose ingestion. *Metabolism*, 1969, *16*, 324. [43]

Hannum, R. D., Rosellini, R. A., and Seligman, M. E. P.   Retention of learned helplessness and immunization in the rat from weaning to adulthood. *Developmental Psychology*, 1976, *12*, 449–454. [108, 129]

Hansen, E. W.   The development of maternal and infant behavior in the rhesus monkey. *Behaviour*, 1966, *27*, 107–149. [140]

Hanson, H. M.   Restraint and gastric ulcers. *Journal of Neuropsychiatry*, 1963, *4*, 390–396. [237, 239]

Hare, E. H.   Masturbatory insanity: The history of an idea. *The Journal of Mental Science*, 1962, *108*, 1–25. [2]

Harlow, H. F.   The development of affectional patterns in infant monkeys. In B. M. Foss (Ed.), *Determinants of infant behavior*. London: Methuen, 1961. [196]

Harlow, H. F., Dodsworth, R. O., and Harlow, M. K.   Total social isolation in monkeys. *Proceedings of the National Academy of Sciences*, 1965, *54*, 90–96. [133]

Harlow, H. F., and Harlow, M. K.   The affectional systems. In A. Schrier, H. Harlow, and F. Stollnitz (Eds.), *Behavior of nonhuman primates* (Vol. 2). New York: Academic Press, 1965, pp. 287–334. [138, 149, 150]

Harlow, H. F., and Harlow, M. K.   Effects of various mother-infant relationships on rhesus monkey behaviors. In B. M. Foss (Ed.), *Determinants of infant behavior* (Vol. 4). London: Methuen, 1969, pp. 15–36. [133]

Harlow, H. F., Harlow, M. K., and Suomi, S. J.   From thought to therapy: Lessons from a primate laboratory. *American Scientist*, 1971, *59*, 538–549. [109]

Harlow, H. F., and Suomi, S. J.   Production of depressive behaviors in young monkeys. *Journal of Autism and Childhood Schizophrenia*, 1971, *1*, 246–255. [156, 157, 158]

Harlow, H. F., and Suomi, S. J.   Induced depression in monkeys. *Behavioral Biology*, 1974, *12*, 273–296. [141, 145, 146]

Harlow, M. K.   Nuclear family apparatus. *Behavior Research Methods and Instrumentation*, 1971, *3*, 301–304. [138, 163]

Harper, A. E., Benevenga, N. J., and Wohlhueter, R. M.   Effects of ingestion of disproportionate amounts of amino acids. *Physiological Review*, 1970, *50*, 428–558. [29]

Harper, A. E., and Spivey, H. E. Relationship between food intake and osmotic effect of dietary carbohydrate. *American Journal of Physiology*, 1958, *193*, 483–487. [29]

Harris, W. R. E., Sokolow, M., Carpenter, L. G. Jr., Freeman, M., and Hunt, S. P. Response to psychologic stress in persons who are potentially hypertensive. *Circulation*, 1953, *7*, 874–879. [288]

Hartocollis, P. The syndrome of minimal brain dysfunction in young adult patients. *Bulletin of the Menninger Clinic*, 1968, *32*:2, 102–114. [316]

Hase, T., and Moss, B. Microvascular changes of gastric mucosa in the development of stress ulcer in rats. *Gastroenterology*, 1973, *65*, 224–234. [239]

Haslerud, G. M. The effect of movement of stimulus objects upon avoidance reactions in chimpanzees. *Journal of Comparative Psychology*, 1939, *25*, 507–528. [179]

Hatton, D. C., Woodruff, M. L., and Meyer, M. E. Cholinergic modulation of tonic immobility in the rabbit *(Oryctolagus cuniculus)*. *Journal of Comparative and Physiological Psychology*, 1975, *89*, 1053–1060. [346]

Heath, R. G. (Ed.) *Studies in schizophrenia*. Cambridge: Harvard University Press, 1954. [376]

Heathfield, K. W. G. Huntington's chorea: Investigation into the prevalence of this disease in the area covered by the North East Metropolitan Regional Hospital Board. *Brain*, 1967, *90*, 203–232. [370]

Hebb, D. O. Spontaneous neurosis in chimpanzees: Theoretical relations with clinical and experimental phenomena. *Psychosomatic Medicine*, 1947, *9*, 3–16. [10]

Hebb, D. O., and Thompson, W. R. The social significance of animal studies. In G. Lindzey (Ed.), *Handbook of social psychology* (Vol. I). Cambridge, Mass.: Addison-Wesley, 1954. [178]

Herd, J. A., Kelleher, R. T., Morse, W. H., and Grose, S. A. Sympathetic and parasympathetic activity during behavioral hypertension in the squirrel monkey. In P. A. Obrist, A. H. Black, J. Brener, and L. V. DiCara (Eds.), *Cardiovascular psychophysiology*. Chicago: Aldine, 1974. [286]

Herman, C. P., and Polivy, J. Anxiety, restraint, and eating behavior. (Unpublished manuscript. Northwestern University, 1974.) [39]

Hersen, M. Self-assessment of fear. *Behavior Therapy*, 1973, *4*, 241–257. [180]

Herson, M., Eisler, R. M., Alford, G. S., and Agras, W. S. Effects of token economy on neurotic depression: An experimental analysis. *Behavior Therapy*, 1973, *4*, 392–397. [126]

Herzog, H. A., Jr., and Burghardt, G. M. Prey movement and predatory behavior of juvenile western yellow-bellied racers, *Coluber constrictor mormon*. *Herpetologica*, 1974, *30*, 285–289. [354]

Hess, E. H. *Imprinting*. Reinhold, N.Y.: Van Nostrand, 1973. [195]

Hess, W. R. Diencephalon: *Autonomic and extrapyramidal functions*. New York: Grune and Stratton, 1954. [225]

Heston, L. L. The genetics of schizophrenic and schizoid disease. *Science*, 1970, *167*, 249–256. [350, 369]

Hetherington, A. W., and Ranson, S. W. Hypothalamic lesions and adiposity in the rat. *Anatomical Record*, 1940, *78*, 149–172. [27]

Hicks, L. E., Maser, J. D., Gallup, G. G., Jr., and Edson, P. H. Possible serotonergic mediation of tonic immobility: Effects of morphine and serotonin blockade. *Psychopharmacologia*, 1975, *42*, 51–56. [349]

Hill, D., and Rowntree, D. The spontaneous variability of the EEG in some schizophrenics. *EEG Clinical Neurophysiology*, 1949, *1*, 117–124. [345]

Himwich, H. E. In *Biochemistry, schizophrenia and affective illnesses*. Baltimore: Williams & Wilkins, 1970. [361]

Hinde, R. A. The use of differences and similarities in comparative psychopathology. In G. Serban and A. Kling (eds.), *Animal models in human psychobiology*. New York: Plenum Press, 1976, pp. 187–202. [141]

Hinde, R. A., and Davies, L. Removing infant rhesus from mother for 13 days compared with removing mother from infant. *Journal of Child Psychology and Psychiatry*, 1972, *13*, 227–237. [144, 146, 154]

Hinde, R. A., and Spencer-Booth, Y. Individual differences in the responses of rhesus monkeys to a period of separation from their mothers. *Journal of Child Psychology and Psychiatry*, 1970, *11*, 159–176. [143]

Hinde, R. A., and Spencer-Booth, Y. Effects of brief separations from mothers on rhesus monkeys. *Science*, 1971, *173*, 111–118. [144]

Hinde, R. A., Spencer-Booth, Y., and Bruce, M. Effects of 6-day maternal deprivation on rhesus monkey infants. *Nature*, 1966, *210*, 1021–1033. [140]

Hinton, J. *Dying*. London: Pelican Press, 1967. [181]

Hiroto, D. S. The relationship between learned helplessness and the locus of control. *Journal of Experimental Psychology*, 1974, *102*, 187–193. [108, 116, 127]

Hiroto, D. S., and Seligman, M. E. P. Generality of learned helplessness in man. *Journal of Personality and Social Psychology*, 1975, *31*, 311–327. [107, 108, 109, 112, 116]

Hirsch, J. The regulation of food intake (Discussion). *Advances in Psychosomatic Medicine*, 1972, *7*, 229–242. [30]

Hirsch, J., and Han, P. W. Cellularity of rat adipose tissue, effects of growth, starvation, and obesity. *Journal of Lipid Research*, 1969, *10*, 77. [46]

Hirsch, J., and Knittle, J. L. Cellularity of obese and nonobese human adipose tissue. *Federation of American Societies for Experimental Biology: Federation Proceedings*, 1970, *29*, 1516–1521. [46, 47]

Hoebel, B. G., and Teitelbaum, P. Weight regulation in normal and hypothalamic hyperphagic rats. *Journal of Comparative and Physiological Psychology*. 1966, *61*, 189–193. [44]

Hoffman, H. S., Eiserer, L. A., Ratner, A. M., and Pickering, V. L. Development of distress vocalization during withdrawal of an imprinting stimulus. *Journal of Comparative and Physiological Psychology*, 1974, *86*, 563–568. [74]

Hoffman, H. S., and Ratner, A. M. A reinforcement model of imprinting: Implications for socialization in monkeys and men. *Psychological Review*, 1973, *80*, 527–544. [74]

Hoffman, H. S., Searle, J. L., Toffey, S., and Kozma, F., Jr. Behavioral control by an imprinted stimulus. *Journal of the Experimental Analysis of Behavior*, 1966, *9*, 177–189. [72]

Hoffman, H. S., and Solomon, R. L. An opponent-process theory of motivation: III. Affective dynamics in imprinting. *Learning and Motivation*, 1974, *5*, 149–164. [69, 72]

Hohman, L. B. Post encephalitic behavior disorders in children. *Johns Hopkins Hospital Bulletin*, 1922, *380*, 372–375. [309]

Hokanson, J. E., Burgess, M. and Cohen, M. F. Effects of displaced aggression on systolic blood pressure. *Journal of Abnormal and Social Psychology*, 1963, *67*, 214–218. [289]

Hokfelt, T., Ljungdahl, A., Fuxe, K., and Johansson, O. Dopamine nerve terminals in the rat limbic cortex: Aspects of the dopamine hypothesis of schizophrenia. *Science*, 1974, *184*, 177–179. [376]

Hollenberg, C. H., Vost, A., and Patten, R. L. Regulation of adipose mass: Control of fat cell development and lipid content. *Recent Progress in Hormone Research*, 1970, *26*, 463–495. [46]

Hollister, L. E. Drug-induced psychoses and schizophrenic reactions: A critical comparison. *Annals of the New York Academy of Sciences*, 1962, *96*, 80–89. [8, 9, 382]

Honig, W. H. (Ed.). *Operant behavior: Theory and research*. New York: Appleton-Century-Crofts, 1966. [117]

Hordern, A., Sandifer, M. G., Green, L. M., and Tinbury, G. C. Psychiatric diagnosis: British and North American concordance on stereotypes of mental illness. *British Journal of Psychiatry*, 1968, *114*, 935–944. [362]

Hornykiewicz, O. Neurochemistry of prakinsonism. In A. Lajtha (Ed.), *Handbook of neurochemistry* (Vol. 7). New York: Plenum, 1972, pp. 465–501. [379, 380]

Horowitz, M. J. Intrusive and repetitive thoughts after experimental stress. *Archives of General Psychiatry*, 1975, *32*, 1457–1463. [186]

Horowitz, M. J., and Adams, J. E. Hallucinations on brain stimulation: Evidence for revision of the Penfield hypothesis. In W. Keup (Ed.), *Origins and mechanisms of hallucinations*. New York: Plenum, 1970, pp. 13–22. [376]

Horton, E. S., Danforth, E., Jr., Sims, E. A. H., and Salans, L. B. Correlation of forearm muscle and adipose tissue metabolism in obesity before and after weight loss. *Clinical Research*, 1972, *20*, 548. [45]

Hoskins, R. G. *The biology of schizophrenia*. New York: Norton, 1946. [339]

Hoskovec, J., and Svorad, D. The relationship between human and animal hypnosis. *American Journal of Clinical Hypnosis*, 1969, *11*, 180–182. [337]

Huessy, H. R., and Cohen, A. H. Hyperkinetic behaviors and learning disabilities followed over seven years. *Pediatrics*, 1976, *57*, 4–10. [316]

Hunt, J. McV. The effect of infant feeding frustration upon adult hoarding in the albino rat. *Journal of Abnormal and Social Psychology*, 1941, *36*, 338–360. [58]

Hunt, W. A., and Matarazzo, J. D. Habit mechanisms in smoking. In W. A. Hunt (Ed.), *Learning mechanisms in smoking*. Chicago: Aldine, 1970, pp. 65–90. [93]

Hunt, W. A., and Matarazzo, J. D. Three years later: Recent developments in the experimental modification of smoking behavior. *Journal of Abnormal Psychology*, 1973, *81*, 107–114. [86, 93, 101]

Hurvich, L. M., and Jameson, D. Opponent processes as a model of neural organization. *American Psychologist*, 1974, 29(2), 88–102. [72]

Irwin, S., and Seevers, M. H. Altered responses to drugs in the post addict *(Macaca mulatta)*. *Journal of Pharmacology and Experimental Therapeutics*, 1956, *116*, 31–32. [89]

Isaacson, R. L. *The limbic system*. New York: Plenum Press, 1974. [199]

Itard, J. *The wild boy of Aveyron*. Trans. by G. Humphrey and M. Humphrey. New York: Appleton-Century-Crofts, 1962. (Originally published, 1932.) [14, 133]

Ivanov-Smolensky, A. G. *Essays on the patho-physiology of the higher nervous activity*. Moscow: Foreign Languages Press, 1954. [215]

Ivy, A. C., Grossman, M. I., and Bachrach, W. H. *Peptic Ulcer*. Philadelphia: Blakiston, 1950. [239]

Izard, C. E. *The face of emotion*. New York: Appleton-Century-Crofts, 1971. [298]

Jacobs, H. L., and Sharma, K. N. Energy balance and palatability: The effect of food deprivation on the intake of positively and negatively flavored solutions. *Physiologist*, 1964, 7, 166. [58]

Jacobs, H. L., and Sharma, K. N. Taste versus calories: Sensory and metabolic signals in the control of food intake. *Annals of the New York Academy of Sciences*, 1969, *157*, 1084–1125. [29]

Jacobson, E. Electrophysiology of mental activities and introduction to the psychological process of thinking. In F. J. McGuigan and R. A. Schoonover (Eds.), *The psychophysiology of thinking*. New York: Academic Press, 1973. [296, 297]

Jaffe, J. H. Drug addiction and drug abuse. In L. Goodman and A. Gilman (Eds.), *The pharmacological basis of therapeutics* (3rd ed.). New York: Macmillan, 1965. Pp. 285–311. [67, 68, 89, 95]

Jaffe, J. H., and Sharpless, S. K. The rapid development of barbiturate physical dependence and its relation to pharmacological denervation supersensitivity. *Pharmacologist*, 1963, 5, 249. [85]

Jaffe, J. H., and Sharpless, S. K. Pharmacological denervation supersensitivity in the central nervous system: A theory of physical dependence. In A. Wikler (Ed.), *The addictive states*. Williams & Wilkins, Baltimore, 1968, pp. 226–243. [85]

Janowsky, D. S., El-Yousef, M. K., Davis, J. M., Hubbard, B., and Sekerke, H. J. Cholinergic reversals of manic symptoms. *Lancet*, 1972, *1*, 1236–1237. [115, 127]

Janowsky, D. S., El-Yousef, M. K., Davis, J. M., and Sekerke, H. J. Provocation of schizophrenic symptoms by intravenous methylphenidate. *Archives of General Psychiatry*, 1973, 28, 185–191. [383]

Jenkins, C. D. Psychologic and social precursors of coronary disease. *New England Journal of Medicine*, 1971, 284, 244–255 and 307–317. [268]

John, E. A study of the effects of evacuation and air raids on pre-school children. *British Journal of Education and Psychology*, 1941, *11*, 173–182. [180]

Johnson, M. L., Burke, B. S., and Mayer, J. Relative importance of inactivity and overeating in the energy balance of obese high school girls. *American Journal of Clinical Nutrition*, 1956, *4*, 37–44. [60]

Jonas, A. D., and Jonas, D. F. An evolutionary context for schizophrenia. *Schizophrenia Bulletin*, 1975, *12*, 33–41. [357]

Jones, B. C., and Clark, D. L. Mother-infant separation in squirrel monkeys living in a group. *Developmental Psychobiology*, 1973, *6*, 259–269. [141]

Jones, D. R., and Dowd, D. A. Development of elevated blood pressure in young genetically hypertensive rats. *Life Sciences*, 1970, *9*, 247–250. [287]

Jordan, H. A., Stellar, E., and Duggan, S. Z. Voluntary intragastric feeding in man. *Communications in Behavioral Biology*, 1968, *1*, 65–67.

Kaada, B. R., Rasmussen, E. W., and Kveini, O. Effects of hippocampal lesions on maze learning and retention in rats. *Experimental Neurology*, 1961, *3*, 333–355. [318]

Kaada, B. R., Rasmussen, E. W., and Kveim, O. Impaired acquisition of passive avoidance behavior by subcallosal, septal, hypothalamic, and insular lesions in rats. *Journal of Comparative and Physiological Psychology*, 1962, *55*, 661–670. [60]

Kahn, M. W. The effect of severe defeat at various age levels on the aggressive behavior of mice. *Journal of Genetic Psychology*, 1951, *79*, 117–130. [109]

Kalant, O. J. *The amphetamines: Toxicity and addiction.* Springfield: Charles C. Thomas, 1966. [383]

Kalisch, B. J. The stigma of obesity. *Journal of American Dietetic Association*, 1972, *72*, 1124–1127. [42]

Kallmann, F. J. The genetic theory of schizophrenia: An analysis of 691 schizophrenic index families. *American Journal of Psychiatry*, 1946, *103*, 309–322. [368]

Kannel, W. B., Schwartz, M. J., and McNamara, P. M. Blood pressure risk of coronary heart disease: The Framingham study. *Diseases of the chest*, 1969, *56*, 43. [283]

Kaplan, H. I., and Kaplan, H. S. The psychosomatic concept of obesity. *Journal of Nervous and Mental Disease*, 1957, *125*, 181–189. [33, 39]

Kaplan, J. The effects of separation and reunion on the behavior of mother and infant squirrel monkeys. *Developmental Psychobiology*, 1970, *3*, 43–52. [141]

Karlsson, J. L. *The biologic basis of schizophrenia.* Springfield: Charles C. Thomas, 1966. [369]

Karsh, E. B. Fixation produced by conflict. *Science*, 1970, *168*, 873–875. [25]

Karten, J. H. The organization of the avian telencephalon and some speculation on the phylogeny of the anmiote telencephalon. *Annals of the New York Academy of Sciences*, 1969, *167*, 164–179. [345]

Kasanin, J. Personality changes in children following cerebral trauma. *Journal of Nervous Mental Disorders*, 1929, *69*, 385–406. [309]

Katcher, A. H., Solomon, R. L., Turner, L. H., LoLordo, V. M., Overmier, J. B., and Rescorla, R. A. Heart-rate and blood pressure responses to signalled and unsignalled shocks: Effects of cardiac sympathectomy. *Journal of Comparative and Physiological Psychology*, 1969, *58*, 163–174. [73, 75]

Katzev, R. D.   Extinguishing avoidance responses as a function of delayed warning-signal termination. *Journal of Experimental Psychology*, 1967, 75, 339. [203]

Katzev, R. D., and Miller, S. V.   Strain differences in avoidance conditioning as a function of the classical CS-US contingency. *Journal of Comparative and Physiological Psychology*, 1974, 87, 661–671. [107]

Kaufman, I. C.   Mother-infant separation in monkeys: An experimental model. In J. P. Scott and E. Senay (Eds.), *Separation and depression: Clinical and research aspects.* (AAAS #94) Washington, D.C.: American Association for the Advancement of Science, 1973, pp. 33–52. [146]

Kaufman, I. C., and Rosenblum, L. A.   The reaction to separation in infant monkeys: Anaclitic depression and conservation-withdrawal. *Psychosomatic Medicine*, 1967, 29, 648–675. [123, 140]

Kaufman, I. C., and Rosenblum, L. A.   The waning of the mother-infant bond in two species of macaque. In B. M. Foss (Ed.), *Determinants of infant behavior* (Vol. 4). London: Methuen, 1969. [140, 143, 144]

Kebabian, J. W., and Greengard, P.   Dopamine-sensitive adenyl cyclase: Possible role in synaptic transmission. *Science*, 1971, 174, 1346–1348. [380]

Kemler, D., and Shepp, B.   The learning and transfer of dimensional relevance and irrelevance in children. *Journal of Experimental Psychology*, 1971, 90, 120–127. [121]

Kennedy, G. C.   The role of depot fat in the hypothalamic control of food intake in the rats. *Proceedings of the Royal Society of London*, 1953, 140, 578–592. [28]

Kety, S. S.   Toward hypotheses for a biochemical component in the vulnerability to schizophrenia. *Seminars in Psychiatry*, 1972, 4, 233–238. [383]

Keys, A., Brozek, J., Henschel, A., Mickelson, O., and Taylor, H.   *The biology of human starvation* (2 vols.). Minneapolis: University of Minnesota Press, 1950. [41, 58]

Kiell, N.   *The psychology of obesity.* Springfield: Charles C. Thomas, 1973. [32]

Kiloh, L. C., and Garside, R. F.   The independence of neurotic depression and endogenous depression. *British Journal of Psychiatry*, 1963, 109, 451–463. [121]

Kimmel, H. D.   Pathological inhibition of emotional behavior. In: H. D. Kimmel (Ed.), *Experimental Psychopathology*. N.Y.: Academic Press, 1971. [81]

Kinsbourne, M.   Minimal brain dysfunction as a neuro-developmental lag. *Annals of the New York Academy of Sciences*, 1973, 205, 268–273. [333]

Kinsey, A. C., Pomeroy, W. B. and Martin, C. E.   *Sexual behavior in the human male.* Philadelphia: W. B. Saunders, 1948. [392]

Kinsey, A. C., Pomeroy, W. B., Martin, C. E., and Gebhard, P. H.   *Sexual behavior in the human female.* Philadelphia: W. B. Saunders, 1953. [392]

Klawans, H. L.   A pharmacologic analysis of Huntington's chorea. *European Neurology*, 1970, 4, 148–163. [375]

Klawans, H. L.   The pharmacology of tardive dyskinesias. *American Journal of Psychiatry*, 1973, 130, 82–86. [375, 381]

Klawans, H. L., Goetz, C., and Westheimer, R.   Pathophysiology of schizophrenia and the striatum. *Diseases of the Nervous System*, 1972, 33, 711–719. [370]

Klein, D. C., Fencil-Morse, E., and Seligman, M. E. P.   Learned helplessness, depression, and the attribution of failure. *Journal of Personality and Social Psychology*, 1976, 33, 508–516. [108, 112, 113, 116, 123]

Klein, D. C., and Seligman, M. E. P. Reversal of performance deficits and perceptual deficits in learned helplessness and depression. *Journal of Abnormal Psychology,* 1976, *85,* 11–26. [108, 113, 116, 123, 126, 127, 128]

Klein, D. F. Delineation of two drug-responsive anxiety syndromes. *Psychopharmacologia,* 1964, *5,* 397–408. [188]

Klein, D. F., and Davis, J. M. In *Diagnosis and drug treatment of psychiatric disorders.* Baltimore: Williams & Wilkins, 1969. [377]

Klein, D. F. and Fink, M. Psychiatric reaction patterns to imipramine. *American Journal of Psychiatry,* 1962, *119,* 432–438. [188]

Klemm, W. R. Mechanisms of the immobility reflex ("animal hypnosis") II. EEG and multiple unit correlates in the brain stem. *Communications in Behavioral Biology,* 1969, *3,* 43–52. [345]

Klemm, W. R. Neurophysiologic studies of the immobility reflex ("animal hypnosis"). In S. Ehrenpreis and O. C. Solnitzky (Eds.), *Neurosciences Research* (Vol. 4). New York: Academic Press, 1971. [335, 337, 339, 344, 345, 350]

Klerman, G. L., and Cole, J. O. Clinical and pharmacology of imipramine and related antidepressant compounds. *Pharmacological Review,* 1965, *17,* 101–141. [114]

Klinger, E. Consequences of commitment to and disengagement from incentives. *Psychological Review,* 1975, *82,* 1–25. [124]

Knittle, J. Early influences on development of adipose tissue. In G. A. Bray (Ed.), *Obesity in perspective.* Washington, D.C.: U.S. Government Printing Office, 1975. [45, 47]

Knittle, J. L. and Ginsberg-Fellner, F. The effect of weight reduction on in vitro adipose tissue lipolysis and cellularity in obese adolescents and adults. *Diabetes,* 1972, *21,* 754. [46]

Knittle, J. L. and Hirsch, J. Effect of early nutrition on the development of rat epididymal fat pads: Cellularity and metabolism. *Journal of Clinical Investigation,* 1968, *47,* 2091. [45, 46]

Knobel, M. Psychopharmacology for the hyperkinetic child. *Archives of General Psychiatry,* 1962, *6,* 198–202. [313]

Knobloch, H., and Pasamanick, B. Prospective studies on the epidemiology of reproductive causality: Methods, findings and some implications. (Presented at the Merrill Palmer Institute Conference on Research and Teaching of Infant Development, 11 February 1965, unpublished.) [309, 332]

Kollar, E. J., and Atkinson, R. M. Responses of extremely obese patients to starvation. *Psychosomatic Medicine,* 1966, *28,* 227–245. [40]

Kolodny, R. C., Masters, W. H., Hendryx, J., and Toro, G. Plasma testosterone and semen analysis in male homosexuals. *The New England Journal of Medicine,* 1971, *285,* 1170–1174. [400]

Konorski, J. The role of prefrontal control in the programming of motor behavior. In J. D. Maser (Ed.), *Efferent organization and the integration of behavior.* New York: Academic Press, 1973, pp. 179–180. [190]

Kornhuber, H. H. Cerebral cortex, cerebellum, and basal ganglia: An introduction to their motor functions. In F. O. Schmitt, and F. Worden (Eds.), *The neurosciences third study program.* Cambridge, Mass.: MIT Press, 1974, pp. 267–280. [374]

Kraepelin, E.   *Dementia praecox and paraphrenia* (translated from 8th German edition). Edinburgh: Livingstone, 1925. [362, 363]

Kraepelin, E.   Manic-depressive insanity and paranoia. In his *Textbook of psychiatry* (Trans. R. M. Barclay). Edinburgh: Livingstone, 1913. [121, 363]

Kraepelin, E.   *Psychiatrie.* Leipzig: Barth, 1910. [7, 363]

Kraines, S. H.   *Mental depressions and their treatment.* New York: Macmillan, 1957. [114, 121]

Krasnogorski, N. I.   The conditioned reflexes and children's neuroses. *American Journal of Diseases of Children,* 1925, 30, 753–768. [13]

Kreisberg, R. A., Boshell, B. R., DiPlacido, J., and Roddam, R. F.   Insulin secretion in obesity. *New England Journal of Medicine,* 1967, 276, 314. [44]

Kretschmer, E.   *Physique and character.* London: Routledge and Keyan, 1925. [2]

Kreuz, L. E., Rose, R. M., and Jennings, J. R.   Suppression of plasma testosterone levels and psychological stress. *Archives of General Psychiatry,* 1972, 26, 479–482. [400, 401]

Kristt, D. A., and Freimark, S. J.   Histopathology and pathogenesis of behaviorally induced gastric lesions in rats. *American Journal of Pathology,* 1973, 73, 411–420. [239]

Kristt, D. A., and Engel, B. T.   Learned control of blood pressure in patients with high blood pressure. *Circulation,* 1975, 51, 370–378. [295]

Lacey, B. C., and Lacey, J. I.   Studies of heart rate and other bodily processes in sensorimotor behavior. In P. A. Obrist, A. H. Black, J. Brener, and L. V. DiCara (Eds.), *Cardiovascular psychophysiology.* Chicago: Aldine, 1974. [287]

Lachman, S. J.   *Psychosomatic Disorders.* New York: Wiley, 1972. [278]

Lader, M. H. and Marks, I. M.   *Clinical anxiety.* London: Heinemann Medical, 1972. [176, 199]

Lader, M. H. and Wing, L.   *Physiological measures, sedative drugs, and morbid anxiety.* (Maudsley Monograph No. 14.) London: Oxford, 1966. [195]

Langley, L. L.   *Homeostasis.* New York: Reinold, 1965. [195]

Larsen, S. R.   Strategies for reducing phobic behaviour. (Doctoral dissertation, Stanford University, 1965.) [192]

Laufer, M. W., and Denhoff, E.   Hyperkinetic behavior syndrome in children. *Journal of Pediatrics,* 1957, 50, 463–473. [311, 315]

Laufer, M. W., Denhoff, E., and Solomans, J.   Hyperkinetic impulse disorder in childrens' behavior problems. *Psychosomatic Medicine,* 1957, 19, 38–49. [313]

Lautch H.   Dental phobia. *British Journal of Psychiatry,* 1971, 119, 151–158. [200]

Lazarus, A. A.   Learning theory and the treatment of depression. *Behavior Research and Therapy,* 1968, 6, 83–89. [154]

Leaf, R. C.   Avoidance response evocation as a function of prior discriminative fear conditioning under curare. *Journal of Comparative and Physiological Psychology,* 1964, 58, 446–449. [107]

Lederhendler, I., and Baum, M.   Mechanical facilitation of the action of response prevention (flooding) in rats. *Behavior Research Therapy,* 1970, 8, 41–48. [203]

Leftwich, D., and May, J.   The effects of conditioned aversive stimuli presented during tonic immobility in guinea pigs. *Journal of Comparative and Physiological Psychology*, 1974, 87, 513–516. [343]

Leon, G. R., and Chamberlain, K.   Emotional arousal, eating patterns and body image as differential factors associated with varying success in maintaining a weight loss. *Journal of Consulting and Clinical Psychology*, 1973, 40, 474–480. [41]

Lepkovsky, S.   Newer concepts in the regulation of food intake. *American Journal of Clinical Nutrition*, 1973, 26, 271–284. [30]

Lessac, M., and Solomon, R. L.   Effects of early isolation on the later adaptive behavior of beagles: A methodological demonstration. *Developmental Psychology*, 1969, 1, 14–25. [129]

Levine, R. J., and Senay, E. C.   Histamine in the pathogenesis of stress ulcers in the rat. *Psychosomatic Medicine*, 1970, 43, 61–65. [237]

Levine, S., and Soliday, S.   The effects of hypothalamic lesions on conditioned avoidance learning. *Journal of Comparative and Physiological Psychology*, 1960, 53, 497–501. [60]

Lewinsohn, P. M., Weinstein, M. S., and Shaw, D.   Depression: A clinical research approach, in R. D. Rubin and C. M. Franks (Eds.), *Advances in behavior therapy*. New York: Academic Press, 1969. Pp. 231–240. [126]

Lewis, J. K., and McKinney, W. T.   Effects of electroconvulsive shock on the behavior of normal and abnormal rhesus monkeys. *Behavioral Psychiatry*, 1976, 37, 687–693. [171]

Liberman, R. P., and Raskin, D. E.   Depression: A behavioral formulation. *Archives of General Psychiatry*, 1971, 24, 515–523. [123]

Lichko, A. E.   Conditioned reflex hypoglycemia in man. *Pavlov Journal of Higher Nervous Activity*, 1959, 9, 731-739. [81]

Lichtenberg, P.   A definition and analysis of depression. *Archives of Neurology and Psychiatry*, 1957, 77, 516–527. [122]

Liddell, H. S.   Conditioned reflex method and experimental neurosis. In J. McV. Hunt (Ed.), *Personality and the behavior disorders* (Vol. 1). New York: Ronald Press, 1944. [18, 19, 215, 216]

Liddell, H. S.   *Emotional hazards in animals and man.* Springfield: Charles C Thomas, 1956. [18, 19]

Lind, A. R., Taylor, S. H., Humphreys, P. W., Kennelly, B. M., and Donald, K. W.   The circulatory effects of sustained voluntary muscle contraction. *Clinical Science*, 1964, 27, 222–224. [289]

Lindesmith, A. R.   *Addiction and opiates.* Chicago: Aldine, 1968. [89]

Lindner, M.   *Hereditary and environmental influences upon resistance to stress.* (Doctoral dissertation, University of Pennsylvania, 1968.) [110]

Locke, J.   *Some Thoughts Concerning Education.* Ward, Lock & Co. London: 1693. [187]

Locke, S., Kruper, D. C., and Yakovlev, P. I.   Limbic nuclei of thalamus and connections of limbic cortex. *Archives of Neurology*, 1964, 11, 571–582. [319]

Locke, S., and Yakovlev, P. I.   Transcallosal connections of the cingulum of man. *Archives of Neurology*, 1965, 13, 471–476. [319]

Looney, T. A., and Cohen, P. S.   Retardation of jump-up escape responding in rats pretreated with different frequencies of noncontingent electric shocks. *Journal of Comparative and Physiological Psychology*, 1972, 78,317–322. [107, 108]

Loraine, J. A., Adamopoulos, D. A., Kirkham, K. E., Ismail, A. A. A., and Dove, G. A.   Patterns of hormone excretion in male and female homosexuals. *Nature*, 1971, *234*, 552–556. [400]

Loraine, J. A., Ismail, A. A. A., Adamopoulos, D. A., and Dove, G. A.   Endocrine function in male and female homosexuals. *British Medical Journal*, 1970, *4*, 406–409. [400]

Louderback, L.   *Fat power: Whatever you weigh is right*. New York: Hawthorn Books, 1970. [34]

Lovibond, S. H.   Effect of patterns of aversive and appetitive conditioned stimuli on the incidence of gastric lesions in the immobilized rat. *Journal of Comparative and Physiological Psychology*, 1969, *69*, 636–639. [244, 248]

Lundquist, G.   Prognosis and course in manic-depressive psychosis. *Acta Psychiatrica Neurologica* (Supplement), 1945, *35*. [114]

Luria, A. R.   *The working brain*. New York: Basic Books, 1973. [274, 277, 278, 295]

Lurie, L. A., and Levy, S.   Behavior disorders—personality changes and behavior disorders of children following pertussis. *The Journal of the American Medical Association*, 1942, *120B*, 890–894. [309]

Lykken, D.   A study of anxiety in the sociopathic personality. *Journal of Abnormal and Social Psychology*, 1957, *55*, 6–10. [37]

Lynch, J. J., and Paskewitz, D. A.   On the mechanisms of the feedback control of human brain-wave activity. *Journal of Nervous and Mental Disease*, 1971, *3*, 205–207. [272]

Lynn, R.   Aging and expressive movements: An interpretation of aging in terms of Eysenck's construct of psychotism. *Journal of Genetic Psychology*, 1962, *100*, 77–84. [15]

Lynn, R.   Russian theory and research on schizophrenia. *Psychological Bulletin*, 1963, *60*, 486–498. [15]

MacDonald, L.   Attack latency of *Constrictor constrictor* as a function of prey activity. *Herpetologica*, 1973, *29*, 45–48. [354]

MacGregor, F. C., Abel, F. M., Bryt, A., Lauer, E., and Weisman, S.   *Facial deformities and plastic surgery: A psychosocial study*. Springfield: Charles C Thomas, 1953. [34]

MacKintosh, N. J.   Selective attention in animal learning. *Psychological Bulletin*, 1965, *64*, 124–150. [120]

MacKintosh, N. J.   Stimulus selection: Learning to ignore stimuli that predict no change in reinforcement. In R. A. Hinde and J. Stevenson-Hinde (Eds.), *Constraints on learning*. New York: Academic Press, 1973, pp. 75–100. [121]

Mackay, M., Beck, L., and Taylor, B.   Methylphenidate for adolescents with minimal brain dysfunction. *New York State Journal of Medicine*, 1973, *73*, 550–555. [317]

Mahl, G. F.   Effect of chronic fear on the gastric secretion of HCl in dogs. *Psychosomatic Medicine*, 1949, *11*, 30–44. [244]

Mahl, G. F.   Relationship between acute and chronic fear and gastric acidity and blood sugar levels in *Macaca mulatta* monkeys. *Psychosomatic Medicine*, 1952, *14*, 182–210. [244]

Maier, N. R. F.   *Frustration*. Ann Arbor: University of Michigan Press, 1949. [23, 24, 121]

Maier, N. R. F.   Frustration theory: Restatement and extension. *Psychological Review*, 1956, *63*, 370–388. [24, 25]

Maier, S. F.   Failure to escape traumatic shock: Incompatible skeletal motor responses or learned helplessness? *Learning and Motivation*, 1970, *1*, 157–170. [107, 119, 128]

Maier, S. F., Albin, R. W., and Testa, T. J.   Failure to learn to escape in rats previously exposed to inescapable shock depends on the nature of the escape response. *Journal of Comparative and Physiological Psychology*, 1973, *85*, 581–592. [107, 108]

Maier, S. F., Anderson, C., and Lieberman, D. A.   Influence of control of shock on subsequent shock-elicited aggression. *Journal of Comparative and Physiological Psychology*, 1972, *81*, 94–100. [109]

Maier, S. F., and Seligman, M. E. P.   Learned helplessness: Theory and evidence. *Journal of Experimental Psychology: General*, 1976, *105*, 3–46. [110, 120]

Maier, S. F., Seligman, M. E. P., and Solomon, R. L.   Pavlovian fear conditioning and learned helplessness. In B. A. Campbell and R. M. Church, *Punishment and aversive behavior*. New York: Appleton-Century-Crofts, 1969. Pp. 299–342. [117]

Maier, S. F., and Testa, T. J.   Failure to learn to escape by rats previously exposed to inescapable shock is partly produced by associative interference. *Journal of Comparative and Physiological Psychology*, 1975, *88*, 554–564. [120]

Malin, D. H.   Synthetic scotophobin: Analysis of behavioural effects on mice. *Pharmacology, Biochemistry & Behavior*, 1974, *2*, 147–153. [197]

Malin, D. H., Radcliffe, G. J., Jr. and Osterman, D. M.   Stimulus specific effect of scotophobin on mouse plasma cortecoids. *Pharmacology, Biochemistry & Behavior*. 1976, *4* (4), 481–483. [197]

Marks, I. M.   *Patterns of meaning in psychiatric patients: Semantic differential responses in obsessives and psychopaths.* (Maudsley Monograph No. 13.) London: Oxford, 1965. [182]

Marks, I. M.   *Fears and phobias*. London: Academic Press, 1969. [7, 177, 178, 179, 182, 190, 191]

Marks, I. M.   Behavioral treatments of phobic and obsessive-compulsive disorders: A critical appraisal. In R. Hersen et al. (Eds.), *Progress in behavior modification*. New York: Academic Press, 1975. [187, 202, 203, 207]

Marks, I. M.   The conquest of fear. New York: Mc-Graw Hill, In press.

Marks, I. M., Birley, J. L. T., and Geider, M. G.   Modified leucotomy in severe agoraphobia: a controlled serial inquiry. *British Journal of Psychiatry*, 1966, *112*, 757–769.

Marks, I. M., and Herst, E. R.   A survey of 1,200 agoraphobics in Britain. *Social Psychiatry*, 1970, *5*, 16–24. [180, 189]

Marks, I. M., Hodgson, R., and Rachman, S.   Exposure in vivo treatment of chronic obsessive-compulsive neurosis: A 2-year followup and issues in treatment. *British Journal of Psychiatry*, 1975, *127*, 349–364. [186, 187]

Marks, I. M., Viswanathan, R., and Lipsedge, M. S.   Enhanced extinction of fear by flooding during waning diazepam effect. *British Journal of Psychiatry,* 1972, *121,* 493–505. [184]

Marsden, C. D., Tarsy, D., and Baldessarini, R. J.   Spontaneous and drug-induced movement disorders in psychotic patients. In D. F. Benson and D. Blumer (Eds.), *Psychiatric aspects of neurological disease.* New York: Grune & Stratton, 1975, 219–266. [381]

Marshall, J.   Increased orientation to sensory stimuli following medial hypothalamic damage in rats. *Brain Research,* 1975, *86,* 373–387. [28, 63, 64]

Martin, I., and Rees, L.   Reaction time and somatic reactivity in depressed patients. *Journal of Psychosomatic Research,* 1966, *9,* 375–382. [114]

Maser, J. D., and Gallup, G. G., Jr.   Tonic immobility in the chicken: Catalepsy potentiation by uncontrollable shocks and alleviation by imipramine. *Psychosomatic Medicine,* 1974, *36,* 199–205. [107, 340, 341, 343]

Maser, J. D., Gallup, G. G., Jr., and Barnhill, R.   Conditioned inhibition and tonic immobility: Stimulus control of an innate fear response in the chicken. *Journal of Comparative and Physiological Psychology,* 1973, *83,* 128–133. [342]

Maser, J. D., Gallup, G. G., Jr., and Hicks, L. E.   Tonic immobility: Possible involvement of monoamines. *Journal of Comparative and Physiological Psychology,* 1975, *89,* 319–328. [346, 347, 349]

Maser, J. D., Gallup, G. G., Jr., Hicks, L. E., and Edson, P. H.   Chlorpromazine dosage and duration of tonic immobility: Biphasic effects. *Pharmacology Biochemistry & Behavior,* 1974, *2,* 119–121. [342, 344]

Maser, J. D., Klara, J. W., and Gallup, G. G., Jr.   Archistriatal lesions enhance tonic immobility in the chicken *(Gallus gallus). Physiology and Behavior,* 1973, *11,* 729–733. [344, 345]

Mason, J. W., Kenion, C. C., Collins, D. R., Mougey, E. H., Jones, J. A., Driver, G. C., Brady, J. V., and Beer, B.   Urinary testosterone response to 72-hr. avoidance sessions in the monkey. *Psychosomatic Medicine,* 1968, *30,* 721–732. [400]

Masserman, J. H.   *Behavior and neurosis: An experimental psychoanalytic approach to psychobiologic principles.* Chicago: University of Chicago Press, 1943. [20, 21, 201, 216, 217]

Masserman, J. H.   The principle of uncertainty in neurotigenesis. In H. D. Kimmel (Ed.), *Experimental psychopathology: Recent research and theory.* New York: Academic Press, 1971. Pp. 13–32. [20]

Masserman, J. H., Arieff, A., Pechtel, C., and Klehr, H.   Effects of direct interrupted electroshock on experimental neuroses. *Journal of Nervous and Mental Disease,* 1950, *112,* 384–392. [21]

Masserman, J. H., and Jacques, M. G.   Effects of cerebral electroshock on experimental neuroses. *American Journal of Psychiatry,* 1947, *104,* 92–99. [21]

Masserman, J. H., and Pechtel, C.   How brain lesions affect normal and neurotic behavior: An experimental approach. *American Journal of Psychiatry,* 1956, *112,* 865–872. [21]

Masserman, J. H., and Yum, K. S.   An analysis of the influence of alcohol on experimental neuroses in cats. *Psychosomatic Medicine,* 1946, *8,* 36–52. [21]

Masserman, J. H., Yum, K. S., Nicholson, M. R., and Lee, S. Neurosis and alcohol: An experimental study. *American Journal of Psychiatry*, 1944, *100*, 389–395. [21]

Matsumoto, K., Takeyasu, K., Mizutani, S., Hamanaka, Y., and Uozumi, T. Plasma testosterone levels following surgical stress in male patients. *Acta Endocrinologica*, 1970, *65*, 11–17. [401]

Matthysse, S. Schizophrenia: Relationship to dopamine transmission, motor control, and feature extraction. In F. O. Schmitt and F. Worden (Eds.), *The neurosciences third study program.* Cambridge, Mass.: MIT press, 1974, pp. 733–740. [375]

Maurer, D. W., and Vogel, M. P. H. *Narcotics and narcotic addiction.* Springfield: Charles C Thomas, 1967. [88, 89, 92]

May, R. H. Catatonic-like states following phenothiazine therapy. *American Journal of Psychiatry*, 1959, *115*, 1119–1120. [342]

Mayer, J. Genetic, traumatic, and environmental factors in the etiology of obesity. *Physiological Reviews*, 1953, *33*, 472–508. [50]

Mayer, J. Inactivity as a major factor in adolescent obesity. *Annals of the New York Academy of Sciences*, 1965, *131*, 502–506. [60]

Mayer, J. *Overweight: Causes and control.* Englewood Cliffs, N.J.: Prentice-Hall, 1968. [33]

McAdam, D. W., and Kaelber, W. W. Differential impairment of avoidance learning in cats with ventromedial hypothalamic lesions. *Experimental Neurology*, 1966, *15*, 293–298. [60]

McCulloch, T. L., and Bruner, J. S. The effect of electric shock upon subsequent learning in the rat. *Journal of Psychology*, 1939, *7*, 333–336. [109]

McGraw, C. P., and Klemm, W. R. Mechanisms of the immobility reflex ("animal hypnosis") III. Neocortical inhibition in rats. *Communications in Behavioral Biology*, 1969, *3*, 53–59. [345]

McGraw, C. P., and Klemm, W. R. Genetic differences in susceptibility of rats to the immobility reflex ("animal hypnosis"). *Behavior Genetics*, 1973, *3*, 155–161. [350]

McKenna, R. J. Some effects of anxiety level and food cues on the eating behavior of obese and normal subjects. *Journal of Personality and Social Psychology*, 1972, *22*, 311–319. [39]

McKenzie, J. C. Profile on slimmers. *Commentary*, 1967, *9*, 77–83. [31]

McKinney, W. T. Animal models in psychiatry. *Perspectives in Biology and Medicine*, 1974, *17*, 529–541. [132, 153, 167]

McKinney, W. T., and Bunney, W. E. Animal model of depression: Review of evidence and implications for research. *Archives of General Psychiatry*, 1969, *21*, 240–248. [123, 132, 134, 167]

McKinney, W. T., Eising, R. G., Moran, E. C., Suomi, S. J., and Harlow, H. F. Effects of reserpine on the social behavior of rhesus monkeys. *Diseases of the Nervous System*, 1971, *32*, 735–741. [167]

McKinney, W. T., Kliese, K. A., Suomi, S. J., and Moran, E. C. Can psychopathology be reinduced in rhesus monkeys? *Archives of General Psychiatry*, 1973, *29*, 630–634. [163]

McKinney, W. T., Suomi, S. J., and Harlow, H. F. Repetitive peer separation of juvenile-age rhesus monkeys. *Archives of General Psychiatry*, 1972, 27, 200–203. (a) [152]

McKinney, W. T., Suomi, S. J., and Harlow, H. F. Vertical chamber confinement of juvenile-age rhesus monkeys. *Archives of General Psychiatry*, 1972, 26, 223–228. (b) [160]

Meichenbaum, D. H. *Cognitive behaviour modification*. (University Program Modular Studies.) Morristown, N.J.: General Learning Press, 1974. [212]

Meikle, T. H., and Sechzer, J. A. Interocular transfer of brightness discrimination in split-brain cats. *Science*, 1960, 132, 734–735. [318]

Melges, F. T., and Bowlby, J. Types of hopelessness in psychopathological process. *Archives of General Psychiatry*, 21, 1969, 240–248. [115, 122, 126]

Mello, N. K. A review of methods to induce alcohol addiction in animals. *Pharmacology, Biochemistry and Behavior*, 1973, 1, 89–101.

Meltzer, H. Y., and Fang, V. S. Serum prolactin levels in schizophrenia: Effect of anti-psychotic drugs: A preliminary report. In E. J. Sachar (Ed.), *Hormones behavior and psychopathology*. New York: Raven Press, 1975. [376]

Meltzer, H. Y., Holzman, P. S., Hassan, S. Z., and Guschwan, A. Effects of phencyclidine and stress on plasma creatine phosphokinase (CPK) and adolase activities in man. *Psychopharmacologia*, 1972, 26, 44–53. [384]

Meltzer, H. Y., and Stahl, S. The dopamine hypothesis of schizophrenia. *Schizophrenia Bulletin*, 1976, 2, 19–76. [370, 375, 386]

Melvin, K. B. Vicious circle behaviour. In H. D. Kimmel (Ed.), *Experimental psychopathology: Recent research and theory*. New York: Academic Press, 1971. Pp. 95–115. [204]

Melzack, R. *The puzzle of pain*. New York: Basic Books, 1973. [281]

Mendels, J. *Concepts of depression*. New York: Wiley, 1970. [111, 135]

Mendels, J., and Frazer, A. Brain biogenic amine depletion and mood. *Archives of General Psychiatry*, 1974, 30, 447–451. [115]

Menkes, M., Rowe, J. S., and Menkes, J. H. A twenty-five-year follow-up study of the hyperkinetic child with minimal brain dysfunction. *Pediatrics*, 1967, 39, 393–399. [315]

Mensah, P., and Deadwyler, S. The caudate nucleus of rat: Cell types and demonstration of a commissural system. *Journal of Anatomy*, 1974, 117, 281–293. [318, 319]

Meyer, A. Fundamental conceptions of dementia praecox. In his *Collected papers* (Vol. 2). Baltimore: Johns Hopkins Press, 1951. Pp. 432–437. [359]

Meyer, D. R. Access to engrams. *American Psychologist*, 1972, 27, 124–133. [171]

Mezinskis, J., Gliner, J., and Shemberg, K. Somatic response as a function of no signal, random signal, or signalled shock with variable or constant durations of shock. *Psychonomic Science*, 1971, 25, 271–272. [253]

Mikhail, A. A. Relationship of a conditioned anxiety to stomach ulceration and acidity in rats. *Journal of Comparative and Physiological Psychology*, 1969, 68, 623–626. [244]

Mikhail, A. A. Effects of acute and chronic stress situations on stomach acidity in rats. *Journal of Comparative and Physiological Psychology*, 1971, 74, 23–27. [237]

Mikhail, A. A.   Stress and ulceration in the glandular and nonglandular portions of the rat's stomach. *Journal of Comparative and Physiological Psychology*, 1973, 85, 636–642. [240]

Milici, P.   Affectivity, inhibition, introversion—catatonic stupor. *Psychiatric Quarterly*, 1949, 23, 486–501. [339]

Miller, E., and Nieburg, H. A.   Amphetamines: Valuable adjunct in treatment of Parkinsonism. *New York State Journal of Medicine*, 1973, 73, 2657–2661. [370, 379, 380]

Miller, J. J., and Mogenson, G. J.   Modulary influences of the septum on lateral hypothalamic self-stimulation. *Experimental Neurology*, 1971, 33, 671–683. [225]

Miller, J. J., and Mogenson, G. J.   Projection of the septum to the lateral hypothalamus. *Experimental Neurology*, 1972, 37, 229–243. [225]

Miller, N. E.   Animal experiments on emotionally induced ulcers. *Proceedings of the Third World Congress of Psychiatry* (Vol. 3). Toronto: Univ. of Toronto Press, 1963, pp. 213–219. [247, 248]

Miller, N. E.   Biofeedback: Evaluation of a new technique. *New England Journal of Medicine*, 1974, 290, 684–685. [272]

Miller, N. E., Bailey, C. J., and Stevenson, J. A. F.   Decreased hunger but increased food intake resulting from hypothalamic lesions. *Science*, 1950, 112, 256–259. [60]

Miller, N. E., and Dworkin, B. R.   Critical issues in therapeutic applications of biofeedback. In G. E. Schwartz and J. Beatty (Eds.), *Biofeedback: Theory and research*. New York: Academic Press, 1977, pp. 129–162. [287, 290, 291]

Miller, R. J., and Hiley, C. R.   Anti-muscarinic properties of neuroleptics and drug-induced parkinsonism. *Nature*, 1974, 248, 596–597. [380]

Miller, R. J., Horn, A. S., and Iverson, L. I.   The action of neuroleptic drugs on dopamine-stimulated adenosine cyclic 3′, 5′ monophosphate production in rat neostriatum and limbic forebrain. *Molecular Pharmacology*, 1974, 10, 759–766. [380]

Miller, W. R.   Psychological deficit in depression. *Psychological Bulletin*, 1975, 82, 238–260. [112, 114]

Miller, W. R., and Seligman, M. E. P.   Depression and the perception of reinforcement. *Journal of Abnormal Psychology*, 1973, 82, 62–73. [113, 127]

Miller, W. R., and Seligman, M. E. P.   Learned helplessness and depression in man. *Journal of Abnormal Psychology*, 1975, 84, 228–238. [108, 112, 113, 116, 123]

Miller, W. R., and Seligman, M. E. P.   Learned helplessness, depression, and the perception of reinforcement. *Behaviour Research and Therapy*, 1976, 14, 7–17. [108, 113, 116, 123]

Miller, W. R., Seligman, M. E. P., and Kurlander, H. M.   Learned Helplessness, depression, and anxiety. *Journal of Nervous and Mental Disease*, 1975, 161, 347–357. [113, 116]

Millichap, J. G.   Drugs in the management of minimal brain dysfunction. *Annals of the New York Academy of Sciences*, 1973, 205, 321–334. [313, 329]

Minsky, M. L.   Matter, mind, and models. In M. L. Minsky (Ed.), *Semantic information processing*. Cambridge, Mass.: The MIT Press, 1968. [3]

Mirsky, I. A. Physiologic, psychologic, and social determinants in etiology of duodenal ulcer. *American Journal of Digestive Diseases*, 1958, 3, 285–314. [232]

Mishler, E. G., and Scotch, N. A. Sociocultural factors in the epidemiology of schizophrenia. *Psychiatry*, 1963, 26, 315–351. [360]

Mitchell, G. D., Harlow, H. F., Griffin, G. A., and Møller, G. W. Repeated maternal separation in the monkey. *Psychonomic Science*, 1967, 8, 197–198.

Mitchell, G. D., Raymond, E. J., Ruppenthal, G. C., and Harlow, H. F. Long-term effects of total social isolation upon behavior of rhesus monkeys. *Psychological Reports*, 1966, 18, 567–580.

Mittlemann, B., and Wolff, M. G. Emotions and gastroduodenal function. Experimental studies on patients with gastritis, duodenitis, and peptic ulcer. *Psychosomatic Medicine*, 1942, 4, 5–61. [232]

Money, J. Components of eroticism in man: I. The hormones in relation to sexual morphology and sexual desire. *The Journal of Nervous and Mental Disease*, 1961, 132, 239–248. [399]

Money, J., and Ehrhardt, A. A. *Man & Woman, Boy & Girl*. Baltimore: The Johns Hopkins University Press, 1972. [387, 397]

Montagu, A. *Prenatal influences*. Springfield: Charles C Thomas, 1962. [309]

Moore, M. E., Stunkard, A., and Srole, L. Obesity: Social class, and mental illness. *Journal of the American Medical Association*, 1962, 181, 962–966. [31]

Moore, M. S. Some myths about mental illness. *Archives of General Psychiatry*, 1975, 32, 1483–1497. [358]

Moot, S. A., Cebulla, R. P., and Crabtree, J. M. Instrumental control and ulceration in rats. *Journal of Comparative and Physiological Psychology*, 1970, 71, 405–410. [258]

Morris, H. H., Escoll, P. J., and Wexler, R. Aggressive behavior disorders of childhood: A follow-up study. *American Journal of Psychiatry*, 1956, 112, 991–997. [316]

Moscovitch, A., and LoLordo, V. M. The role of safety in the Pavlovian backward conditioning procedure. *Journal of Comparative and Physiological Psychology*, 1968, 66, 673–678. [73, 81]

Mowrer, O. H., and Viek, P. An experimental analogue of fear from a sense of helplessness. *Journal of Abnormal Social Psychology*, 1948, 43, 193–200. [110]

Murphree, O. D., Dykman, R. A. and Peters, J. E. Objective measures of behaviour in two strains of the pointer dog. (Paper presented at the Symposium on Higher Nervous Activity, IV World Psychiatry Congress. Madrid, September 1966.) [194]

Myers, R. E., and Sperry, R. W. Interhemispheric communication through the corpus callosum: Mnemonic carryover between the hemispheres. *Archives of Neurology and Psychiatry*, 1958, 80, 298–303. [318]

Nash, R. F., and Gallup, G. G., Jr. Aversiveness of the induction of tonic immobility in chickens (*Gallus gallus*). *Journal of Comparative and Physiological Psychology*, 1975, 88, 935–939. (a) [341]

Nash, R. F., and Gallup, G. G., Jr. Effect of different parameters of shock on tonic immobility. *Behavior Research Methods and Instrumentation*, 1975, 7, 361–364. (b) [339]

Nash, R. F., Gallup, G. G., Jr., and Czech, D. A. Psychophysiological correlates of tonic immobility in the domestic chicken *(Gallus gallus)*. *Physiology and Behavior*, 1976, *17*, 413–418. [339]

Nash, R. F., Gallup, G. G., Jr., and McClure, M. K. The immobility reaction in leopard frogs *(Rana pipiens)* as a function of noise-induced fear. *Psychonomic Science*, 1970, *21*, 155–156. [339, 340]

Natelson, B. The "executive" monkey revisited. (Paper presented at the Symposium on Nerves and the Gut. Philadelphia, Pennsylvania, August 1976. To be published in F. P. Brooks (Ed.), *Nerves and the Gut*, in press.) [263, 264]

Nebylitsyn, V. D., and Gray, J. A. (Eds.). *Biological bases of individual behavior*. New York: Adacemic Press, 1972. [215]

Needleman, H. Lead poisoning in children: Neurologic implications of widespread subclinical intoxication. In S. Walzer, and P. H. Wolff (Eds.), *Minimal cerebral dysfunction in children*, New York: Grune & Stratton, 1973, pp. 47–54. [309]

Newburgh, L. H. Obesity: Energy metabolism. *Physiological Reviews*, 1944, *24*, 18–45. [43]

Newburgh, L. H., and Conn, J. W. A new interpretation of hyperglycemia in obese middle aged persons. *Journal of American Medical Association*, 1939, *112*, 7. [44]

Ngui, P. W. The koro epidemic in Singapore. *Australian and New Zealand Journal of Psychiatry*, 1969, *3*, 263–266. [199]

Nisbett, R. E. Determinants of food intake in human obesity. *Science*, 1968, *159*, 1254–1255. (a) [57]

Nisbett, R. E. Taste, deprivation, and weight determinants of eating behavior. *Journal of Personality and Social Psychology*, 1968, *10*, 107–116. (b) [51, 60]

Nisbett, R. E. Hunger, obesity, and the ventromedial hypothalamus. *Psychological Reviews*, 1972, *79*, 433–453. [57]

Nisbett, R. E., and Kanouse, D. Obesity, food deprivation, and supermarket shopping behavior. *Journal of Personality and Social Psychology*, 1969, *12*, 289–294. [58]

Novak, M. A. Fear-attachment relationships in infant and juvenile rhesus monkeys. (Doctoral dissertation, University of Wisconsin, 1973.) [148]

Novin, D., VanderWeele, D. A., and Rezek, M. Infusion of 2-deoxy-D-glucose into the hepatic portal system causes eating: Evidence for peripheral glucoreceptors. *Science*, 1973, *181*, 858–860. [29]

Nyback, H., Borzecki, Z., and Sedvall, G. Accumulation and disappearance of catacholamines formed from tyrosine ^{14}C in mouse brain: Effect of some psychotropic drugs. *European Journal of Pharmacology*, 1968, *4*, 395–403. [379]

O'Brien, T. J., and Dunlap, W. P. Tonic immobility in the blue crab *(Callinectes sapidus*, Rathbun): Its relation to threat of predation. *Journal of Comparative and Physiological Psychology*, 1975, *89*, 86–94. [353]

Öhman, A., Eriksson, A., Fredriksson, M., Hugdahl, K., and Oloffson, C. Habituation of the electrodermal orienting reaction to potentially phobic and supposedly neutral stimuli in normal human subjects. *Biological Psychology*, 1974, *2*, 85–92. [192, 210]

Öhman, A., Erixon, G., and Lofberg, I.   Phobias and preparedness: Phobic versus neutral pictures as conditioned stimuli for human autonomic responses. *Journal of Abnormal Psychology*, 1975, *84*, 41–45. [210]

Oi, M., Oshida, K., and Sugimura, A.   The location of gastric ulcer. *Gastroenterology*, 1959, *36*, 45–56. [233]

Oler, I., and Baum, M.   Facilitated extinction of an avoidance response through shortening of the inter-trail interval. *Psychonomic Science*, 1968, *11*, 323–324. [202]

Olgilvie, R. F.   Sugar tolerance in obese subjects: A review of 65 cases. *Quarterly Journal of Medicine*, 1935, *4*, 345. [43]

Ollerenshaw, D.   Classification of functional psychoses. *British Journal of Psychiatry*, 1973, *122*, 517–530. [135]

O'Malley, J. E., and Eisenberg, L.   The hyperkinetic syndrome. In S. Walzer and P. H. Wolff (Eds.), *Minimal Cerebral Dysfunction in Children*. New York: Grune & Stratton, 1973, pp. 95–104. [313]

Oomura, Y.   Effects of glucose and free fatty acid in chemosensitive neuron in the rat hypothalamus. In D. Novin, W. Wyrwicka, and G. A. Bray (Eds.), *Hunger: Basic mechanisms and clinical implications*. New York: Raven Press, 1975. [28, 29]

Orbach, J., Traub, A. C., and Olson, R.   Psychophysical studies of body image. *Archives of General Psychiatry*, 1966, *12*, 41–47. [34]

Osmond, H., and Smythies, J. R.   Schizophrenia: A new approach. *Journal of Mental Science*, 1952, *98*, 309–315. [8]

Overmier, J. B.   Interference with avoidance behavior: Failure to avoid traumatic shock. *Journal of Experimental Psychology*, 1968, *78*, 340–343. [107, 109]

Overmier, J. B., and Seligman, M. E. P.   Effects of inescapable shock upon subsequent escape and avoidance responding. *Journal of Comparative and Physiological Psychology*, 1967, *63*, 23–33. [104, 106, 107, 109, 125, 222]

Padilla, A. M., Padilla, C., Ketterer, T., and Giacalone, D.   Inescapable shocks and subsequent avoidance conditioning in goldfish, *Carrasius avaratus. Psychonomic Science*, 1970, *20*, 295–296. [109]

Paine, R. S., Werry, J. S., and Quay, H. C.   A study of minimal cerebral dysfunction. *Developmental Medicine and Child Neurology*, 1968, *10*, 505–520. [311]

Panksepp, J.   Hypothalamic regulation of energy balance and feeding behavior. *Federation Proceedings*, 1974, *33*, 1150–1165. [29]

Paré, W.   The effect of chronic environmental stress on stomach ulceration, adrenal function, and consummatory behavior in the rat. *Journal of Psychology*, 1964, *57*, 143–151. [251]

Paré, W. P.   Conditioning and avoidance-responding effects on gastric secretion in the rat with chronic fistula. *Journal of Comparative and Physiological Psychology*, 1972, *80*, 150–162. [237, 264]

Paré, W. P.   The influence of food consumption and running activity on activity-stress ulcer in the rat. *American Journal of Digestive Diseases*, 1975, *20*, 262–273. [268]

Paré, W. P., and Livingston, A., Jr.   Shock predictability and gastric secretion in the chronic gastric fistula rat. *Physiology and Behavior*, 1973, *11*, 521–526. [237, 254]

Paré, W. P., and Temple, L. J.   Food deprivation, shock stress, and stomach lesions in the rat. *Physiology and Behavior*, 1973, *11*, 371–375. [240]

Parmenter, R.   The influence of degrees of freedom upon stereotyped conditioned motor reflexes in the sheep. *Journal of General Psychology*, 1940, *23*, 47–54. [19]

Partridge, M.   Some reflections on the nature of affective disorders arising from the results of prefrontal leucomoty. *Journal of Mental Science*, 1949, *20*, 295–296. [121]

Paskind, H. A.   Brief attacks of manic-depressive depression. *Archives of Neurological Psychiatry*, 1929, *22*, 123–124. [114]

Paskind, H. A.   Manic-depressive psychosis in private practice: Length of attack and length of interval. *Archives of Neurological Psychiatry*, 1930, *23*, 789–794. [114]

Pavlov, I. P.   *Conditioned reflexes* (G. V. Anrep, trans.). London: Oxford University Press, 1927. [214, 215]

Pavlov, I. P.   *Lectures on conditioned reflexes.* New York: International Publishers, 1928. [216]

Pavlov, I. P.   *Lectures on conditioned reflexes: Vol. 2, Conditioned reflexes and psychiatry* (W. H. Gantt, trans.). New York: International Publishers, 1941. [9, 12, 13]

Pavlov, I. P.   *Psychopathology and psychiatry: Selected works* (S. Belsky and D. Myshne, trans.). Moscow: Foreign Languages Publishing House, 196?. [12]

Payne, R. W.   Cognitive abnormalities. In H. J. Eysenck (Ed.), *Handbook of abnormal psychology.* New York: Basic Books, 1961, pp. 193–261. [114]

Peters, J. E., Murphree, O. D., Dykman, R. A. and Reese, W. G.   Genetically determined abnormal behaviour in dogs. (Paper presented to the Symposium on Higher Nervous Activity: IV World Psychiatry Congress. Madrid, September 1966.) [194]

Phoenix, C. H., Goy, R. W., Gerall, A. A., and Yong, W. C.   Organizing action of prenatally administered testosterone propionate on the tissues mediating mating behavior in the female guinea pig. *Endocrinology*, 1959, *65*, 369–882. [393]

Phoenix, C. H., Goy, R. W., and Resko, J. A.   Psychosexual differentiation as a function of androgenic stimulation. In M. Diamond (Ed.), *Perspectives in reproduction and sexual behavior.* Bloomington: Indiana University Press, 1968. [396]

Pincus, H. H., and Tucker, G. J.   *Behavioral neurology.* London: Oxford University Press, 1974.

Pliner, P., Mayer, P., and Blankstein, K.   Responsiveness to affective stimuli by obese and normal individuals. *Journal of Abnormal Psychology*, 1974, *83*, 74–80. [34]

Plotnik, R., Mollenauer, S., and Snyder, E.   Fear reduction in the rat following central cholinergic blockade. *Journal of Comparative and Physiological Psychology*, 1974, *86*, 1074–1082. [346, 352]

Polish, E., Brady, J. V., Mason, J. W., Thach, J. F., and Niemack, W.   Gastric contents and the occurrence of duodenal lesions in the Rhesus monkey during avoidance behavior. *Gastroenterology*, 1962, *43*, 193–201. [237, 238, 264]

Poresky, R. Noncontingency detection and its effects. (Paper presented at Eastern Psychological Association, Atlantic City, April 1970.) [117]

Porter, R. W., Brady, J. V., Conrad, D., Mason, J. W., Galambos, R., and Rioch, D. Some experimental observations on gastrointestinal lesions in behaviorally conditioned monkeys. *Psychosomatic Medicine*, 1958, *20*, 379–394. [254]

Powell, P. A., and Creer, T. L. Interaction of developmental and environmental variables in shock-elicited aggression. *Journal of Comparative and Physiological Psychology*, 1969, *69*, 219–225. [109]

Powers, W. T. *Behavior: The control of perception.* Chicago: Aldine, 1973. [281]

Prechtl, H. F. B. Neurological findings in newborn infants after pre- and paranatal complications. (Paper presented at Nutricia Symposium on Aspects of Praematurity and Dysmaturity, Groningen, May 1967.) [317]

Premack, D. Reinforcement theory. In D. Levine, (Ed.), *Nebraska Symposium on Motivation*, (Vol. 13). Lincoln: University of Nebraska Press, 1965. Pp. 123–188. [117]

Preston, D. G., Baker, R. P., and Seay, B. M. Mother-infant separation in Patas monkeys. *Developmental Psychology*, 1970, *3*, 298–306. [140]

Prestrude, A. M. Parasympathetic concommitants of tonic immobility. (Paper presented at the Southwestern Psychological Association, Houston, April 1975.) [336]

Price, J., and Kasriel, J. Touch aversions. (Paper presented at the 25th Annual Meeting of Indian Psychiatric Society, Chandigharh, India, 1973.) [177]

Price, K. P. Predictable and unpredictable shock: Their pathological effects on restrained and unrestrained rats. *Psychological Reports*, 1972, *30*, 419–426. [253]

Purpura, D. P. Analysis of morphophysiological developmental processes in mammalian brain. In J. I. Nurnberger (Ed.), *Biological and environmental determinants of early development.* (Association for Research in Nervous and Mental Diseases, Proceedings, Vol. 51.) Baltimore: Williams & Wilkins, 1973, pp. 79–112. [332]

Rabinowitz, D. Some endocrine and metabolic aspects of obesity. *Annual Review of Medicine*, 1970, *21*, 241–258. [43]

Racinskas, J. R. Maladaptive consequences of loss or lack of control over aversive events. (Doctoral dissertation, Waterloo University, Ontario, Canada, 1971.) [108, 116]

Randle, P. J., Garland, P. B., Newsholme, E. A., and Hales, C. N. The glucose fatty acid cycle: Its role in insulin sensitivity and the metabolic disturbances of diabetes mellitus. *Lancet*, 1963, *1*, 785. [43]

Ratner, S. C. Comparative aspects of hypnosis. In J. Gordon (Ed.), *Handbook of clinical and experimental hypnosis.* New York: Macmillan, 1967. [335, 337, 351]

Ratner, S. C., and Thompson, R. W. Immobility reactions (fear) of domestic fowl as a function of age and prior experience. *Animal Behaviour*, 1960, *8*, 186–191. [354]

Redmond, D. E., Maas, J. W., Kling, A., and Dekirmenjian, H.   Changes in primate social behavior following treatment with alpha-methylparatyrosine. *Psychosomatic Medicine*, 1970, 32, 551. [167]

Reich, T., Clayton, T., and Winokur, G.   Family history studies. V. The genetics of mania. *American Journal of Psychiatry*, 1969, 125, 1359–1368. [135]

Reisinger, J. J.   The treatment of "anxiety-depression" via positive reinforcement and response cost. *Journal of Applied Behavior Analysis*, 1972, 5, 125–130. [126]

Reite, M., Kaufman, I. C., Pauley, J. D., and Stynes, A. J.   Depression in infant monkeys: Physiological correlates. *Psychosomatic Medicine*, 1974, 36, 363–367. [153]

Rescorla, R. A.   Pavlovian conditioning and its proper control procedures. *Psychological Review*, 1967, 74, 71–80. [117]

Rescorla, R. A.   Probability of shock in the presence and absence of the CS in fear conditioning. *Journal of Comparative and Physiological Psychology*, 1968, 66, 1–5. [117]

Rescorla, R. A., and Skucy, J.   Effect of response independent reinforcers during extinction. *Journal of Comparative and Physiological Psychology*, 1969, 67, 381–389. [123]

Reynierse, J. H. and Wiff, L. I.   Effects of temporal placement of response prevention of avoidance on extinction of avoidance in rats. *Behaviour Research and Therapy*, 1973, 11, 119–124. [202, 203]

Ricciuti, H. N.   Fear and the development of social attachments in the first year of life. Lewis, M., and Rosenblum, L. A. (Eds.), *The Origins of Fear*. New York: John Wiley, 1974. [196]

Richter, C. P.   Experimentally produced behavior reactions to food poisoning in wild and domestic rats. *Annals of the New York Academy of Sciences*, 1953, 56, 225–239. [29]

Rie, H. E.   Depression in childhood. *Journal of the American Academy of Child Psychiatry*, 1966, 5, 653–685. [137]

Robert, A., and Nezamis, J.   Histopathology of steroid-induced ulcers. *Archives of Pathology*, 1964, 77, 407–423. [237]

Robert, A., and Stout, T.   Production of duodenal ulcers in rats. *Federation Proceedings*, 1969, 28, 323. [236]

Robert, A., Stout, T. J., and Dale, J. E.   Production by secretagogues of duodenal ulcers in the rat. *Gastroenterology*, 1970, 59, 95–102. [234, 236]

Robertson, J., and Robertson, J.   Young children in brief separation: A fresh look. *Psychoanalytic Study of the Child*, 1971, 26, 264–315. [137]

Robertson, J., and Robertson, J.   Quality of substitute care as an influence on separation responses. *Journal of Psychosomatic Research*, 1972, 16, 261–265. [146]

Robins, L.   *The Viet Nam drug abuser returns*. New York: McGraw-Hill, 1974. [67]

Robinson, S., and Winnik, H. Z.   Severe psychotic disturbances following crash diet weight loss. *Archives of General Psychiatry*, 1973, 29, 559–562. [40]

Robison, G. A., Butcher, R. W., and Sutherland, E. W.   *Cyclic AMP*. New York: Academic Press, 1971. [380]

Rodin, J.   Effects of distraction on the performance of obese and normal subjects. *Journal of Comparative and Physiological Psychology*, 1973, 83, 68–78. [53, 54]

Rodin, J.   Shock avoidance behavior in obese and normal subjects. In S. Schachter and J. Rodin (Eds.), *Obese humans and rats*. Washington, D.C.: Erlbaum/ Wiley, 1974. [53]

Rodin, J.   The effects of obesity and set point on taste responsiveness and ingestion in humans. *Journal of Comparative and Physiological Psychology*, 1975, 89, 1003–1009. [60]

Rodin, J.   The relationship between external responsiveness and the development and maintenance of obesity. In D. Novin, W. Wyrwicka, and G. A. Bray (Eds.), *Hunger: Basic mechanisms and clinical implications*. New York: Raven Press, 1976. [56, 61]

Rodin, J., Elman, D., and Schachter, S.   Obese humans and rats. Washington, D.C.: Erlbaum/Wiley, 1974. [34, 35, 53]

Rodin, J., Herman, C. P., and Schachter, S.   Obesity and various tests of external sensitivity. In S. Schachter and J. Rodin, *Obese humans and rats*. Washington, D.C.: Erlbaum/Wiley, 1974. [54]

Rodin, J., Moskowitz, H. R., and Bray, G. A.   Relationship between obesity, weight loss and taste responsivity. *Physiology and Behavior*, 1976, 17, 591–597. [29]

Rodin, J. and Slochower, J.   Fat chance for a favor: Obese-normal differences in compliance and incidental learning. *Journal of Personality and Social Psychology*, 1974, 29, 557–565. [34, 54]

Rodin, J., and Slochower, J.   Externality in the nonobese: The effects of environmental responsiveness on weight. *Journal of Personality and Social Psychology*, 1976, 33, 338–344. [61]

Rolls, E. T., Burton, M. J., and Mora, F.   Visual responses of neurones in the lateral hypothalamus and substantia inominata. (Unpublished manuscript, University of Oxford, 1975.) [28]

Rosellini, R. A., Bazerman, M. H., and Seligman, M. E. P.   Exposure to noncontingent food interferes with the acquisition of a response to escape shock. *Journal of Experimental Psychology: Animal Behavior Processes*, unpublished manuscript (1976). [121]

Rosellini, R. A., and Seligman, M. E. P.   Frustration and learned helplessness. *Journal of Experimental Psychology: Animal Behavior Processes*, 1975, 104, 149–157. [109]

Rosellini, R. A., and Seligman, M. E. P.   Failure to escape shock after repeated exposure to inescapable shock. *Bulletin of the Psychonomic Society*, 1976, 7, 251–253. [110]

Rosen, E., Fox, R. E., and Gregory, I.   *Abnormal psychology*. Philadelphia: Saunders, 1972. [339]

Rosenblatt, J. S., Turkewitz, G., and Schneirla, T. C.   Development of home orientation in newly born kittens. *Transactions of the New York Academy of Sciences*, 1969, 31, 231–250. [319]

Rosenblum, L. A.   Relations among infants and juveniles in man and related animals. In M. Lewis and L. Rosenblum (Eds.), *Friendship and peer relations* (The origins of behavior, Vol. 4). New York: Wiley, 1975.

Rosenhan, D. L. On being sane in insane places. *Science,* 1973, *179,* 250–258. [357]

Rosenthal, D. The hereditary-environment issue in schizophrenia: Summary of the conference and present status of our knowledge. In D. Rosenthal and S. Kety (Eds.), *The transmission of schizophrenia.* Oxford: Pergamon Press, 1968, pp. 413–428. [369]

Rosenthal, D., and Kety, S. (Eds.) *The transmission of schizophrenia.* Oxford: Pergamon Press, 1968. [369]

Rosenthal, D., Wender, P. H., Kety, S. S., Shulsinger, F., Welner, J., and Oslergaard, L. Schizophrenics' offspring reared in adoptive homes. In D. Rosenthal and S. Kety (Eds.), *The transmission of schizophrenia.* Oxford: Pergamon Press, 1968, pp. 377–391. [369]

Rosenthal, D., Wender, P. H., Kety, S. S., Schulsinger, F., Welner, J., and Reider, R. Parent-child relationships and psychopathological disorder in the child. *Archives of General Psychiatry,* 1975, *32,* 466–476. [368]

Ross, L. D. Cue and cognition controlled eating among obese and normal subjects. (Doctoral dissertation, Columbia University, 1969.) [52, 53]

Ross, L. D., Pliner, P., Nesbitt, R., and Schachter, S. Patterns of externality in the eating behavior of obese and normal college students. In S. Schachter, *Emotion, obesity, and crime.* New York: Academic Press, 1971. [52, 53, 60]

Roth, R. H., Walters, J. R., and Morgenroth, V. H. Effects of alterations in impulse flow on transmitter metabolism in central dopaminergic neurons. In E. Usdin (Ed.), *Advances in biochemical psychopharmacology* (Vol. 12). New York: Raven Press, 1974, pp. 369–384. [374]

Roth, S., and Bootzin, R. R. The effects of experimentally induced expectancies of external control: An investigation of learned helplessness. *Journal of Personality and Social Psychology,* 1974, *29,* 253–264. [108]

Roth, S., and Kubal, L. The effects of noncontingent reinforcement on tasks of differing importance: Facilitation and learned helplessness effects. *Journal of Personality and Social Psychology,* 1975, *32,* 680–691. [109, 116]

Ruppenthal, G. C., Harlow, M. K., Eisele, C. D., Harlow, H. F., and Suomi, S. J. Development of peer interactions of monkeys reared in a nuclear-family environment. *Child Development,* 1974, *45,* 670–682. [164]

Rutter, D. R., and Stephenson, G. M. Visual interaction in a group of schizophrenic and depressive patients. *British Journal of Social and Clinical Psychology,* 1972, *11,* 57–65. [353]

Rutter, M., and Hemming, M. Individual items of deviant behavior through prevalence and clinical significance. In M. Rutter, J. Tizard and K. Whitmore (Eds.), *Education, health and behaviour.* London: Longmans, 1970. [182]

Sackett, G. P. Monkeys reared in isolation with pictures as visual input: Evidence for an innate learning mechanism. *Science,* 1966, *154,* 1468–1472. [143, 195, 196]

Salans, L. B., Cushman, S. W., and Wisemann, R. E. Studies of human adipose cell size and number in nonobese and obese patients. *Journal of Clinical Investigation,* 1973, *52,* 929. [46]

Salans, L. B., Knittle, J. L., and Hirsch, J. The role of adipose tissue cell size and adipose tissue insulin sensitivity in the carbohydrate intolerance of human obesity. *Journal of Clinical Investigation*, 1968, 47, 153. [46]

Sargeant, A. B., and Eberhardt, L. E. Death feigning by ducks in response to predation by red foxes *(Vulpes fulva)*. *American Midland Naturalist*, 1975, 94, 108–119. [354]

Sargant, W. *Battle for the mind: A physiology of conversion and brain-washing.* New York: Doubleday, 1957. [11]

Sartory, G., and Eysenck, H. J. Strain differentials in acquisition and extinction of fear responses in rats. *Psychological Reports*, 1976, 38, (1), 163–187. [175]

Satterfield, J. H. EEG issues in children with minimal brain dysfunction. In S. Walzer and P. H. Wolff (Eds.), *Minimal cerebral dysfunction in children.* New York: Grune & Stratton, 1973, pp. 35–46. [311]

Satterfield, J. H., Cantwell, D. P., Saul, R. E., and Yusin, A. Intelligence, academic achievement, and EEG abnormalities in hyperactive children. *American Journal of Psychiatry*, 1974, 131, 391–393. [311]

Sawrey, W. L., Conger, J. J., and Turrell, E. S. An experimental investigation of the role of psychological factors in the production of gastric ulcers in rats. *Journal of Comparative and Physiological Psychology*, 1956, 49, 457–461. [246, 247]

Sawrey, W. L., and Sawrey, J. M. Conditioned fear and restraint in ulceration. *Journal of Comparative and Physiological Psychology*, 1964, 57, 150–151. [244]

Sawrey, W. L., and Weisz, J. D. An experimental method of producing gastric ulcers. *Journal of Comparative and Physiological Psychology*, 1956, 49, 269–270. [245, 246]

Schachter, J., Kerr, J. L., Wimberley, F. C., and Lachin, J. M. Heart rate levels of black and white newborns. *Psychosomatic Medicine*, 1974, 36, 513–524. [288]

Schachter, S. *Emotion, obesity, and crime.* New York: Academic Press, 1971. [50]

Schachter, S., Goldman, R., and Gordon, A. Effects of fear, food deprivation, and obesity on eating. *Journal of Personality and Social Psychology*, 1968, 10, 91–97. [38, 51]

Schachter, S., and Gross, L. Manipulated time and eating behavior. *Journal of Personality and Social Psychology*, 1968, 10, 98–106. [51–52]

Schachter, S., and Rodin, J. (Eds.) *Obese humans and rats.* Washington, D.C.: Erlbaum/Wiley, 1974. [50, 52, 59, 60, 61]

Schemmel, R., Mickelson, O., and Gill, J. L. Dietary obesity in rats: Body weight and body fat accretion in seven strains of rats. *Journal of Nutrition*, 1970, 100, 1041–1048. [49]

Schildkraut, J. J. The catecholamine hypothesis of affective disorders: A review of supporting evidence. *American Journal of Psychiatry*, 1965, 122, 509–522. [114, 167]

Schildkraut, J. J., and Kety, S. S. Pharmacological studies suggest a relationship between brain biogenic amines and affective state. *Science*, 1967, 156, 21–30. [332]

Schindler, R., and Baxmeier, R. I. Mucosal changes accompanying gastric ulcer: A gastroscopic study. *Annals of Internal Medicine*, 1939, 13, 693–699. [238]

Schlottmann, R. S., and Seay, B. M. Mother-infant separation in the Java monkey (*Macaca irus*). *Journal of Comparative and Physiological Psychology*, 1972, 29, 334–340. [140, 144]

Schonfeld, W. A. Gynecomastia in adolescence: Effect on body image and personality adaptation. *Psychological Medicine*, 1962, 24, 379–389. [34]

Schwartz, G. E. Voluntary control of human cardiovascular integration and differentiation through feedback and reward. *Science*, 1972, 175, 90–93. [294]

Schwartz, G. E. Biofeedback as therapy: Some theoretical and practical issues. *American Psychologist*, 1973, 29, 666–673. [294, 295, 296, 302, 305]

Schwartz, G. E. Toward a theory of voluntary control of response patterns in the cardiovascular system. In P. A. Obrist, A. H. Black, J. Brener, and L. V. Di Cara (Eds.), *Cardiovascular psychophysiology*. Chicago: Aldine, 1974. [285]

Schwartz, G. E. Biofeedback, self-regulation, and the patterning of physiological processes. *American Scientist*, 1975, 63, 314–324. [294, 300]

Schwartz, G. E. Self-regulation of response patterning: implications for psychophysiological research and therapy. *Biofeedback and Self-Regulation*, 1976, 1, 7–30. [290, 294]

Schwartz, G. E., Davidson, R. J., and Maer, F. Rights-hemisphere lateralization for emotion in the human brain: Interactions with cognition. *Science*, 1975, 190. 286–288. [290]

Schwartz, G. E., Fair, P. L., Salt, P., Mandel, M. R., and Klerman, J. L. Facial muscle patterning to affective imagery in depressed and nondepressed subjects. *Science*, 1976, 192, 489–491. [297, 298]

Schwartz, S. I., Griffith, L. S. C., Neistadt, A., and Hagfors, N. Chronic carotid sinus nerve stimulation in the treatment of essential hypertension. *American Journal of Surgery,1*1967, 144, 5–15. [292]

Scott et al. (1960) [239]

Scott, H. W., Herrington, J. L., Edwards, L. W., Shull, H. J., Stephenson, S. E., Sawyers, J. L., and Clossen, K. L. Results of vagotomy and antral resection in surgical treatment of duodenal ulcer. *Gastroenterology*, 1974, 39, 590–597. [162]

Scoville, W. B., and Milner, B. Loss of recent memory after bilateral hippocampal lesions. *Journal of Neurology, Neuro-Surgery, and Psychiatry*, 1957, 20, 11–21. [318]

Seay, B. M., Hansen, E. W., and Harlow, H. F. Mother-infant separation in monkeys. *Journal of Child Psychology and Psychiatry*, 1962, 3, 123–132. [138, 139, 140, 144, 154]

Seay, B. M., and Harlow, H. F. Maternal separation in the rhesus monkey. *Journal of Nervous and Mental Disease*, 1965, 140, 434–441. [144, 154]

Sechzer, J. A. Prolonged learning and split-brain cats. *Science*, 1970, 169, 889–892. [317]

Sechzer, J. A. The neonatal split-brain kitten as an animal model for minimal brain dysfunction. (Paper presented at the Third Annual Meeting of the Society for Neuroscience, 1973.) [308]

Sechzer, J. A., Faro, M. D., and Windle, W. F. Studies of monkeys asphyxiated at birth: Implications for minimal brain dysfunction. In S. Walzer and P. H. Wolff (Eds.), *Minimal cerebral dysfunction in children*, New York: Grune & Stratton, 1973, pp. 19–34. [317, 329]

Sechzer, J. A., Folstein, S. E., Geiger, E. H., and Mervis, R. F. The split-brain neonate: A surgical method for corpus callosum section in newborn kittens. *Developmental Psychobiology*, 1976, 9, 377–388. (a) [308, 319]

Sechzer, J. A., Kessler, P. G., Folstein, S. E., and Geiger, E. H. Implications of early hemispheric disconnection for minimal brain dysfunction. (Paper read at the Symposium on Behavioral and Electrophysiological Effects of Central Nervous System Lesions in Mammals: 82*nd Annual Convention of the American Psychological Association*, 1974.) [308]

Sechzer, J. A., Kessler, P. G., Folstein, S. E., Geiger, E. H., and Meechan, S. M. An animal model for the minimal brain dysfunction syndrome. In D. V. S. Sankar (Ed.), *Mental health in children* (Vol. II). New York: P. J. D. Publications, 1976. [308]

Sechzer, J. A., Turner, S. G., and Liebelt, R. A. Motivation and learning in mice after goldthioglucose-induced hypothalamic lesions. *Psychonomic Science*, 1966, 4, 259–260. [60]

Seeman, P., and Lee, T. The dopamine-releasing actions of neuroleptics and ethanol. *Journal of Pharmacology and Experimental Therapeutics*, 1974, 190, 131–140. [380]

Seeman, P., and Lee, T. Antipsychotic drugs: Direct correlation between clinical potency and presynaptic action of dopamine neurons. *Science*, 1975, 188, 1217–1219. [374]

Seeman, P., Wong, M. D., Tedesco, J., and Wong, K. Brain receptors for antipsychotic drugs and dopamine: Direct binding assays. *Proceedings of National Academy of Science*, 1975, 72, 4376–4880. [380]

Seligman, M. E. P. Chronic fear produced by unpredictable shock. *Journal of Comparative and Physiological Psychology*, 1968, 66, 402–411. [120, 250, 253]

Seligman, M. E. P. On the generality of the laws of learning. *Psychological Review*, 1970, 77, 406–418. [356]

Seligman, M. E. P. Phobias and preparedness. *Behavior Therapy*, 1971, 2, 307–320. [7, 356]

Seligman, M. E. P. *Helplessness*. San Francisco: W. H. Freeman and Company, 1975. [109, 218, 222]

Seligman, M. E. P., and Beagley, S. Learned helplessness in the rat. *Journal of Comparative and Physiological Psychology*, 1975, 88, 534–541. [107, 108, 227]

Seligman, M. E. P. and Binik, Y. Safety signal hypothesis. In H. Davis and H. Hurwitz (Eds.), *Pavlovian and Operant Interactions*. Hillsdale, New Jersey: Lawrence Erlbaum Associates. In press. [115]

Seligman, M. E. P., and Groves, D. Non-transient learned helplessness. *Psychonomic Science*, 1970, 19, 191–192. [107, 109, 129]

Seligman, M. E. P., and Hager, J. *The biological boundaries of learning*. New York: Appleton-Century-Crofts, 1972. [190, 191]

Seligman, M. E. P., and Johnston. A cognitive theory of avoidance learning. In F. S. McGuigan and D. Lumsden (Eds.), *Contemporary approaches to conditioning and learning*. Washington, D.C.: V. H. Winston & Sons, 1973. [204]

Seligman, M. E. P., Klein, D. C., and Miller, W. R. Depression. In H. Leitenberg (Ed.), *Handbook of behavior modification and behavior therapy*. Englewood Cliffs, N.J.: Prentice-Hall, 1976. [126, 135]

Seligman, M. E. P., and Maier, S. F. Failure to escape traumatic shock. *Journal of Experimental Psychology*, 1967, 74, 1–9. [106, 107, 119, 128, 129, 222, 225]

Seligman, M. E. P., Maier, S. F., and Geer, J. The alleviation of learned helplessness in the dog. *Journal of Abnormal Psychology*, 1968, 73, 256–262. [104, 107, 109, 124]

Seligman, M. E. P., Maier, S. F., and Solomon, R. L. Unpredictable and uncontrollable aversive events. In F. R. Brush (Ed.), *Aversive conditioning in learning*. New York: Academic Press, 1971. [105, 117, 342]

Seligman, M. E. P., and Meyer, B. Chronic fear and ulcers in rats as a function of the unpredictability of safety. *Journal of Comparative and Physiological Psychology*, 1970, 73, 202–207. [250]

Seligman, M. E. P., Rosellini, R. A., and Kozak, M. J. Learned helplessness in the rat: Time course, immunization and reversibility. *Journal of Comparative and Physiological Psychology*, 1975, 88, 542–547. [107, 109, 125, 129]

Seltzer, C. C. Genetics and obesity. In J. Vague and R. M. Denton (Eds.), *Physiopathology of adipose tissue* (Excerpta Medica Monograph). Amsterdam: Excerpta Medica, 1969, pp. 325–334. [48]

Selye, H. A syndrome produced by diverse nocuous agents. *Nature*, 1936, 138, 32. [240, 241, 247]

Senay, E. C. Toward an animal model of depression. *Journal of Psychiatric Research*, 1966, 4, 65–71. [148]

Sethbhakdi, S., Pfeiffer, C. J., and Roth, J. L. A. Gastric mucosal ulceration following vasoactive agents: A new experimental approach. *American Journal of Digestive Diseases*, 1970, 15, 261–270. [249]

Seward, J. P., and Humphrey, G. L. Avoidance learning as a function of pretraining in the cat. *Journal of Comparative and Physiological Psychology*, 1967, 63, 338–341. [107]

Seyffert, W. A., Jr., and Madison, L. L. Physiologic effects of metabolic fuels on carbohydrate metabolism. I. Acute effect of elevation of plasma free fatty acids on hepatic glucose output, peripheral glucose utilization, serum insulin, and plasma glucagon levels. *Diabetes*, 1967, 16, 765. [43]

Shapiro, A. K. A contribution to a history of the placebo effect. *Behavioral Science*, 1960, 5, 109–135. [302, 303]

Shapiro, D., Mainardi, J. A., and Surwit, R. S. Biofeedback and self-regulation in essential hypertension. In G. E. Schwartz and J. Beatty (Eds.), *Biofeedback: Theory and research*. New York: Academic Press, 1977, pp. 313–350. [300]

Shapiro, D., and Surwit, R. S. Learned control of physiological function and disease. In H. Leitenberg (Ed.), *Handbook of behavior modification and behavior therapy*. Englewood Cliffs: Prentice-Hall, 1976. [283, 284]

Shapiro, D., Tursky, B., Gershon, E., and Stern, M. Effects of feedback and reinforcement on the control of human systolic blood pressure. *Science*, 1969, 163, 588–590. [294]

Shapiro, D., Tursky, B., and Schwartz, G. E. Control of blood pressure in man by operant conditioning. *Circulation Research* (Supplement I), 1970, 26–32. (a) [294]

Shapiro, D., Tursky, B., and Schwartz, G. E. Differentiation of heart rate and systolic blood pressure in man by operant conditioning. *Psychosomatic Medicine*, 1970, 32, 417–423. (b) [294]

Sharpless, S. K.   Hypnotics and sedatives. In L. S. Goodman and A. Gilman (Eds.), *The pharmacological basis of therapeutics* (3rd ed.). New York: The Macmillan Company, 1965. [13]

Shay, H., Komorov, S. A., Fels, F. F., Moranze, D., Gruenstein, M., and Siplet, H. A.   A simple method for the uniform production of gastric ulceration in the rat. *Gastroenterology*, 1945, 5, 43–61. [239, 240, 247]

Shearman, R. W.   Response-contingent CS termination in the extinction of avoidance learning. *Behaviour Research and Therapy*, 1970, 8, 227–239. [202]

Shenger-Krestovnikova, N. R.   Contributions to the question of differentiation of visual stimuli and the limits of differentiation by the visual analyzer of the dog. *Bulletin of the Lesgaft Institute of Petrograd*, 1921, 3, 1–43. [11, 214, 216, 217]

Shields, J.   Summary of the genetic evidence. In D. Rosenthal and S. Kety (Eds.), *The transmission of schizophrenia*. Oxford: Pergamon Press, 1968, pp. 95–126. [369]

Shields, J.   (Paper presented to The Interdisciplinary Society of Biological Psychiatry, Amsterdam, September, 1975.) [195]

Shipman, W. G., and Plesset, M. R.   Anxiety and depression in obese dieters. *Archives of General Psychiatry*, 1963, 8, 530–535. [35]

Shorvan, H. J., and Richardson, J. S.   Sudden obesity and psychological trauma. *British Medical Journal*, 1949, 2. [33]

Shreeve, W. W.   Transfers of carbon-14 and tritium from substrates to CO_2 water, and lipids in obese and diabetic subjects. *Annals of the New York Academy of Sciences*, 1964, 131, 464. [43]

Shurman, A. J., and Katzev, R. D.   Escape avoidance responding in rats depends on strain and number of inescapable preshocks. *Journal of Comparative and Physiological Psychology*, 1975, 88, 548–553. [107]

Siegel, A., and Skog, D.   Effects of electrical stimulation of the septum upon attack behavior elicited from the hypothalamus of the cat. *Brain Research*, 1970, 23, 371–380. [225]

Siegel, S.   Morphine tolerance as an associative process. *Journal of Experimental Psychology: Animal Behavior Processes*, 1977, 3, 1–13. [80, 98]

Siegel, S.   Conditioning insulin effects. *Journal of Comparative and Physiological Psychology*, 1975, 89, 189–199. [80, 81, 98]

Siegel, S.   Morphine analgesic tolerance: Its situation specificity supports a Pavlovian conditioning model. *Science*, 1976, 193, 323–325. [98]

Sidman, M.   Avoidance conditioning with brief shock and no exteroceptive warning signal. *Science*, 1953, 118, 157–158. [200]

Siegeltuch, M., and Baum, M.   Extinction of well-established avoidance responses through response prevention (flooding). *Behaviour Research and Therapy*, 1971, 9, 103–108. [202]

Silbergeld, E. K., and Goldberg, A. M.   Lead-induced behavioral dysfunction: An animal model for hyperactivity. *Experimental Neurology*, 1974, 42, 146–157. [328]

Silverstone, J. T., and Solomon, T.   Psychiatric and somatic factors in the treatment of obesity. *Journal of Psychosomatic Research*, 1965, 9, 247–255. [35]

Sims, E. A. H., Danforth, E., Jr., Horton, E. S., Bray, G. A., Glennon, J. A., and Salans, L. B. Endocrine and metabolic effects of experimental obesity in man. *Recent Progress in Hormone Research*, 1973, 29, 457–496. [44]

Sims, E. A. H., Goldman, R. F., Gluck, C. M., Horton, E. S., Kelleher, P. C., and Rowe, D. W. Experimental obesity in man. *Transactions of the Association of American Physicians*, 1968, 81, 153–170. [44]

Sims, E. A. H., and Horton, E. S. Endocrine and metabolic adaptation to obesity and starvation. *American Journal of Clinical Nutrition*, 1968, 21, 1455–1470. [44, 45]

Sines, J. O. Selective breeding for development of stomach lesions following stress in the rat. *Journal of Comparative and Physiological Psychology*, 1959, 52, 615–617. [243]

Sines, J. O. Behavioral correlates of genetically enhanced susceptability to stomach lesion development. *Journal of Psychosomatic Research*, 1961, 5, 120–126. [243, 268]

Sines, J. O. Physiological and behavioral characteristics of rats selectively bred for susceptibility to stomach lesion development. *Journal of Neuropsychiatry*, 1963, 4, 396–398. [243]

Sines, J. O., Cleeland, C., and Adkins, J. The behavior of normal and stomach lesion susceptible rats in several learning situations. *Journal of Genetic Psychology*, 1963, 102, 91–94. [243, 268]

Skillman, J. J., and Silen, W. Acute gastroduodenal "stress" ulceration· Barrier disruption of varied pathogenesis. *Gastroenterology*, 1970, 59, 479–482. [235]

Skillman, J. J., and Silen, W. Stress ulcers. *Lancet*, 1972, 2, 1303–1306. [236, 237, 239]

Slater, E. A review of earlier evidence on genetic factors in schizophrenia. In D. Rosenthal and S. Kety (Eds.), *The transmission of schizophrenia*. Oxford: Pergamon Press, 1968, pp. 15–26. [369]

Slochower, J. Emotional labeling and overeating in obese and normal weight individuals. (Doctoral dissertation. Columbia University Teachers College, 1975.) [40]

Smart, R. Conflict and conditioned aversive stimuli in the development of experimental neurosis. *Canadian Journal of Psychology*, 1965, 19, 208–223. [22]

Smith, M. P., and Duffy, M. The effects of intragastric injection of various substances on subsequent bar pressing. *Journal of Comparative and Physiological Psychology*, 1955, 48, 387–391. [28]

Smythies, J. R. Biochemistry of schizophrenia. *Postgraduate Medical Journal*, 1963, 39, 26–33. [360]

Snyder, S. H. Catecholamines in the brain as mediators of amphetamine psychosis. *Archives of General Psychiatry*, 1972, 27, 169–179. [370, 373, 383, 384]

Snyder, S. H. Catecholamines as mediators of drug effects in schizophrenia. In F. O. Schmitt and F. G. Worden (Eds.), *The neurosciences third study program*. Cambridge, Mass.: MIT Press, 1974, pp. 721–732. (a) [8]

Snyder, S. H. *Madness and the brain*. New York: McGraw-Hill, 1974. (b) [7, 383]

Snyder, S. H., Greenberg, D., and Yamamura, H. I. Antischizophrenic drugs and brain cholinergic receptors: Affinity for muscarinic sites predicts extrapyramidal effects. *Archives of General Psychiatry*, 1974, 31, 58–61. [380]

Snyder, S. H., and Myerhoff, J.   How amphetamine acts in minimal brain dysfunction. *Annals of the New York Academy of Sciences,* 1973, *205,* 310–320. [313]

Solomon, R. L., and Corbit, J. D.   An opponent-process theory of motivation: I. Temporal dynamics of affect. *Psychological Review,* 1974, *81,* 119–145. [69, 70, 71, 75, 79]

Solomon, R. L., and Corbit, J. D.   An opponent-process theory of motivation: II. Cigarette addiction. *Journal of Abnormal Psychology,* 1973, *81,* 158–171. [69]

Solomon, S. S., Ensinck, J. W., and Williams, R. H.   Effect of starvation on plasma immunoreactive insulin and nonsuppressible insulin-like activity in normal and obese humans. *Metabolism,* 1968, *17,* 528. [44]

Solow, C., Silberfarb, P. M., and Swift, K.   Psychosocial effects of intestinal bypass surgery for severe obesity. *New England Journal of Medicine,* 1974, *290,* 300–304. [41]

Solyon, L., Heseltine, G. F. D., McClure, D. J., Solyon, C., Ledridge, B. and Steinberg, G.   Behavior therapy versus drug therapy in the treatment of phobic neurosis. *Canadian Psychiatric Association Journal,* 1973, *18,* 25–31. [188]

Sourkes, T. L.   Parkinson's disease and other disorders of the basal ganglia. In R. W. Albers, G. J. Siegal, R. Katzman, and B. W. Agranoff (Eds.), *Basic neurochemistry.* Boston: Little, Brown and Company, 1972, pp. 565–578. [371]

Spanos, N. P., and Barber, T. X.   Toward a convergence in hypnosis research. *American Psychologist,* 1974, *29,* 500–511. [337]

Spence, K.   Theoretical interpretations of learning. In S. S. Stevens (Ed.), *Handbook of experimental psychology.* New York: Wiley, 1951. [205]

Spencer-Booth, Y., and Hinde, R. A.   The effects of separating rhesus monkey infants from their mothers for 6 days. *Journal of Child Psychology and Psychiatry,* 1967, *7,* 179–197. [143]

Sperry, R. W.   The great cerebral commissure. *Scientific American,* January 1964, 42–54. (Offprint 174.) [318]

Spiegel, T.   Calorie regulation of food intake in man. *Journal of Comparative and Physiological Psychology,* 1973, *83,* 24–37. [55]

Spitz, R. A.   Anaclitic depression. *The Psychoanalytic Study of the Child,* 1946, *2,* 313–347. [136, 137, 138, 139, 144, 146]

Srole, L., Langner, T. S., Michael, S. T., Opler, M. K., and Rennie, T. A. C. *Mental health in the metropolis: The MIDTOWN Manhattan study* (Vol. 1). New York: McGraw-Hill, 1962. [31]

Starr, M.   (Unpublished research paper, 1974.) [76, 77]

Starr, M.   Unpublished Doctoral Dissertation. University of Pennsylvania, 1976. [76, 77, 79]

Stern, R. S. and Marks, I. M.   A comparison of brief and prolonged flooding in agoraphobics. *Archives of General Psychiatry,* 1973, *28,* 210–216. [202]

Sternbach, R. A.   *Principles of psychophysiology.* New York: Academic Press, 1966. [281]

Stewart, M., Ferris, A., and Pitts, N.   The hyperkinetic child syndrome. *American Journal of Orthopsychiatry,* 1966, *36,* 861–867. [332]

Stille, G., and Sayers, A.   Die Immobilisationreaktion der Ratte als tierexperimentelles Modell für die Katatonie. *Pharmakopsychiatrie Neuro-Psychopharmakologie*, 1975, 8, 105–114. [337]

Strauss, A. A., and Lehtinen, L. E.   *Psychopathology and education of the brain-injured child* (Vol. I). New York: Grune & Stratton, 1947. [311]

Strecker, E. A., and Ebaugh, F.   Neuropsychiatric sequelae of cerebral trauma in children. *Archives of Neurology and Psychiatry*, 1924, 12, 443–453. [309]

Stricker, E. M., and Zigmond, M. J.   Brain catecholamines and the lateral hypothalamic syndrome. In D. Novin, W. Wyrwicka, and G. A. Bray (Eds.), *Hunger: Basic mechanisms and clinical implications.* New York: Raven Press, 1976. [64]

Stunkard, A. J.   The dieting depression incidence and clinical characteristics of untoward responses to weight reduction regimens. *American Journal of Medicine*, 1957, 23, 77–86. [40, 41]

Stunkard, A. J., and Koch, C.   The interpretation of gastric motility: I. Apparent bias in the reports of hunger by obese persons. *Archives of General Pyschiatry*, 1964, 11, 74–82. [51]

Stunkard, A. J., and Mendelson, M.   Obesity and the body image. *American Journal of Psychiatry*, 1967, 123, 1296–1300. [34, 35]

Suomi, S. J.   Experimental production of depressive behavior in young monkeys. (Unpublished doctoral dissertation, University of Wisconsin, 1971.) [148]

Suomi, S. J.   Repetitive peer separation of young monkeys: Effects of vertical chamber confinement during separation. *Journal of Abnormal Psychology*, 1973, 83, 1–10. [149, 159]

Suomi, S. J.   Social interactions of monkeys reared in a nuclear family environment versus monkeys reared with mothers and peers. *Primates*, 1974, 15, 311–320. [164]

Suomi, S. J.   Factors affecting responses to social separation in rhesus monkeys. In G. Serban and A. Kling (Eds.), *Animal models in human psychobiology*. New York: Plenum Press, 1976, pp. 9–26. [144, 148]

Suomi, S. J., Collins, M. L., and Harlow, H. F.   Effects of permanent separation from mother on infant monkeys. *Developmental Psychology*, 1973, 9, 376–384. [143, 145, 146, 147, 164]

Suomi, S. J., Collins, M. L., Harlow, H. F., and Ruppenthal, G. C.   Effects of maternal and peer separations on young monkeys. *Journal of Child Psychology and Psychiatry*, 1976, 17, 101–112. [149, 154]

Suomi, S. J., Eisele, C. J., Grady, S. A., and Harlow, H. F.   Depression in adult monkeys following separation from nuclear family environment. *Journal of Abnormal Psychology*, 1975, 84, 576–578. [164, 166]

Suomi, S. J., Eisele, C. J., Grady, S. A., and Tripp, R.   Social preferences of monkeys reared in an enriched laboratory environment. *Child Development*, 1973, 44, 451–460.

Suomi, S. J., and Harlow, H. F.   Apparatus conceptualization for psychopathological research in monkeys. *Behavior Research Methods and Instrumentation*, 1969, 1, 247–250. [155]

Suomi, S. J., and Harlow, H. F.   Depressive behavior in young monkeys subjected to vertical chamber confinement. *Journal of Comparative and Physiological Psychology*, 1972, 80, 11–18. (a) [157]

Suomi, S. J., and Harlow, H. F. Social rehabilitation of isolate-reared monkeys. *Developmental Psychology*, 1972, 6, 487–496. (b) [133]

Suomi, S. J., and Harlow, H. F. Effects of differential removal from group on social development of rhesus monkeys. *Journal of Child Psychology and Psychiatry*, 1975, 16, 149–158. [149, 160]

Suomi, S. J., and Harlow, H. F. The facts and functions of fear. In M. Zuckerman & C. Speilsburger (Eds.), *Emotions and anxiety: New concepts, methods, and applications.* New York: Halsted Press, 1976. [143]

Suomi, S. J., Harlow, H. F., and Domek, C. J. Effect of repetitive infant-infant separation of young monkeys. *Journal of Abnormal Psychology*, 1970, 76, 161–172. [149, 150, 151, 167]

Suomi, S. J., Harlow, H. F., and Kimball, S. D. Behavioral effects of prolonged partial social isolation in the rhesus monkey. *Psychological Reports*, 1971, 29, 1171–1177. [160]

Suomi, S. J., Harlow, H. F., and Novak, M. A. Reversal of social deficits produced by isolation-rearing in monkeys. *Journal of Human Evolution*, 1974, 3, 527–534. [133]

Suomi, S. J., Sprengel, R. D., and Harlow, H. F. Social rehabilitation of depression in monkeys. (Paper presented at the meeting of the American Psychiatric Association, Anaheim, California, May, 1975.) [167, 169]

Sussman, K. E. Effect of prolonged fasting on glucose and insulin metabolism in exogenous obesity. *Archives of Internal Medicine*, 1966, 117, 343. [43]

Swanson, D. W., and Dinello, F. A. Follow-up of patients starved for obesity. *Psychosomatic Medicine*, 1970, 32, 209–214. [40]

Szasz, T. S. *The myth of mental illness.* New York: Harper & Row, 1961. [358]

Tan, E., Marks, I. M. and Marset, P. Modified leucotomy in obsessive-compulsive neurosis. *British Journal of Psychiatry*, 1971, 118, 155–164. [198]

Taulbee, E. S., and Wright, H. W. A psycho-social-behavioral model for therapeutic intervention. In C. D. Spielberger (Ed.), *Current topics in clinical and community psychology III.* New York: Academic Press, 1971. [126]

Teitelbaum, P. Sensory control of hypothalamic hyperphagia. *Journal of Comparative and Physiological Psychology*, 1955, 48, 156–163. [60]

Teitelbaum, P. Random and food-directed activity in hyperphagic and normal rats. *Journal of Comparative and Physiological Psychology*, 1957, 50, 486–490. [60]

Teitelbaum, P., and Campbell, B. A. Ingestion patterns in hyperphagic and normal rats. *Journal of Comparative and Physiological Psychology*, 1958, 51, 135–140. [60]

Teplov, B. M. Problems in the study of general types of higher nervous activity in man and animals. In J. A. Gray (Ed.), *Pavlov's typology.* New York: Macmillan, 1964. [12]

Teschke, E. J., Maser, J. D., and Gallup, G. G., Jr. Cortical involvement in tonic immobility ("Animal hypnosis"): Effect of spreading cortical depression. *Behavioral Biology*, 1975, 13, 139–143. [345]

Teyler, T. J. *A primer of psychobiology.* San Francisco: W. H. Freeman and Company, 1975. [273]

Thomas, D. R., Freeman, F., Sviniki, J. G., Burr, D. E., and Lyons, J. Effects of extradimensional training on stimulus generalization. *Journal of Experimental Psychology*, 1970, 83, 1–22. [120]

Thompson, H. Gastritis in partial gastrectomy specimens. *Gastroenterology*, 1959, 36, 861. [238]

Thompson, R. J. *Introduction to physiological psychology*. New York: Harper & Row, 1975. [273]

Thompson, R. W., Piroch, J., and Hatton, D. The effect of sympatholytic and sympathomimetic drugs on the duration of tonic immobility (animal hypnosis) in chickens. (Paper presented at the meeting of the Midwestern Psychological Association, Chicago, May 1973.) [343]

Thompson, R. W., Piroch, J., Fallen, D., and Hatton, D. A central cholinergic inhibitory system as a basis for tonic immobility (animal hypnosis) in chickens. *Journal of Comparative and Physiological Psychology*, 1974, 87, 507–512. [343, 346]

Thompson, R. W., Scuderi, R., and Boren, J. The effect of the catecholamines on tonic immobility (animal hypnosis). (Paper presented at the Rocky Mountain Psychological Association, Denver, May 1974.) [347]

Thorndike, E. L. *The psychology of wants, interests, and attitudes*. London: Appleton-Century, 1935. [193]

Thornton, J. W., and Jacobs, P. D. Learned helplessness in human subjects. *Journal of Experimental Psychology*, 1970, 83, 1–??. [116]

Thurston, D. L., Middlekamp, J. N., and Mason, E. The late effects of lead poisoning. *Journal of Pediatrics*, 1955, 42, 120–128. [309]

Tinbergen, N. On war and peace in animals and man. *Science*, 1968, 160, 1411–1418. [356]

Torrey, E. F., and Peterson, M. R. Schizophrenia and the limbic system. *Lancet*, 1974, 2, 942–946.

Traub, A. C., and Orbach, J. Psychophysical studies of body image. *Archives of General Psychiatry*, 1964, 11, 53–66. [34]

Tsuda, A., and Hirai, H. Effects of psychological factor on stress pathology in rats: The difficult effect of coping response task. *Japanese Psychological Research*, 1975, 17, 119–132. [262, 263]

Turner, S. G., Sechzer, J. A., and Liebelt, R. A. Sensitivity to electric shock after ventromedial hypothalamic lesions. *Experimental Neurology*, 1967, 19, 236–244.

Ungar, G. Is there a chemical memory trace? *Israel Journal of Chemistry*, 1976. [189, 197]

Ungar, G., Desiderio, D. M. and Park, W. Isolation, identification, and synthesis of a specific-behavior-inducing brain peptide. *Nature*, 1972, 238, 198–202. [197]

Ungerstedt, U. Stereotaxic mapping of the monoamine pathways in the rat brain. *Acta Physiologica Scandinavia* (Supplement) 1971, 397, 1–48. [374, 375]

U.S. Department of Health, Education, and Welfare. *First Special Report to the U.S. Congress on Alcohol and Health from the Secretary of Health, Education, and Welfare, December 1971*. (DHEW Pub. No. (HSM) 73-9031.) Washington, D.C.: U.S. Government Printing Office, 1971. [67, 83, 85, 87]

U.S. Department of Health, Education, and Welfare. *Second Special Report to the U.S. Congress on Alcohol and Health from the Secretary of Health, Education, and Welfare, June 1974*. (DHEW Pub. No. (ADM) 57-212.) Washington, D.C.: U.S. Government Printing Office, 1975. [67]

U.S. Public Health Service, Division of Chronic Disease. *Obesity and health: A sourcebook of current information for professional health personnel*. (Public Health Service Publication #1485.) Washington, D.C.: U.S. Government Printing Office, 1966. [31]

Uno, T., Greer, S. E. and Goates, L. Observational facilitation of response prevention. *Behaviour Research and Therapy*, 1973, *11*, 207–212. [202]

Valentine, C. W. The innate bases of fear. *Journal of Genetic Psychology*, 1930, *37*, 394–419. [193]

Vandenberg, S. G., Clark, P. J. and Samuels, I. Psychophysiological reactions of twins: Hereditary factors in galvanic skin resistance, heartbeat, and breathing rates. *Eugenics Quarterly*, 1965, *12*, 7–10. [195]

Vanzant, F. R., Alvarez, W. C., Berkson, J., and Eusterman, C. B. Changes in gastric acidity in peptic ulcer, cholecystitis, and other diseases. *Archives of Internal Medicine*, 1933, *52*, 616–631. [237]

Venables, P. The effect of auditory and visual stimulation on skin potential response of schizophrenics. *Brain*, 1960, *83*, 77–92. [15]

Volgyesi, F. A. Hypnosis of man and animals (2nd ed.). Baltimore: Williams & Wilkins, 1966. [334, 335]

von Verschuer, O. II. Die vererbungsbiologische zwillingforschung Ihrg biologischen Grunlagen. *Ergebnisse der inneren Medizin und Kinderheilkunde*, 1927, *31*, 35–120. [48]

Wadd, W. *Cursory remarks on corpulence*. London: 1816. [32]

Wagner, A. R. Stimulus selection and a "modified continuity theory." In G. H. Bower, and J. T. Spence, (Eds.), *The psychology of learning and motivation, III*. New York: Academic Press, 1969. [117]

Wald, E., Desiderato, O., and Mackinnon, J. R. Production of gastric ulcers in the unrestrained rat. *Physiology and Behavior*, 1973, *10*, 825–827. [249]

Wallace, A. F. C. Mazeway disintegration: The individual's perception of sociocultural disorganization. *Human Organization*, 1957, *16*, 23–27. [104, 114]

Walters, G. C. and Glazer, R. D. Punishment of instinctive behavior in the Mongolian gerbil. *Journal of Comparative and Physiological Psychology*, 1971, *75*, 331–340. [191]

Walther, E. Zur Klinik und Pathogenese de Pellagra-psychosen. *Nervenarzt*, 1953, *24*, 367–377. [360]

Wangensteen, S. C., and Golden, G. T. Acute "stress" ulcers of the stomach: A review. *American Surgeon*, 1973, *39*, 562–567. [235]

Ward, I. L. Differential effect of pre- and postnatal androgen on the sexual behavior of intact and spayed female rats. *Hormones and Behavior*, 1969, *1*, 25–36. [393]

Ward, I. L. Prenatal stress feminizes and demasculinizes the behavior of males. *Science*, 1972, *175*, 82–84. [398, 399]

Ward, I. L.   Sexual behavior differentiation: Prenatal hormonal and environmental control. In R. C. Friedman, R. M. Richart, and R. L. VandeWiele (Eds.), *Sex differences in behavior.* New York: Wiley, 1974. [398, 399]

Watson, J., and Marks, I. M.   Relevant vs. irrelevant flooding in the treatment of phobias. *Behaviour Therapy,* 1971, 2, 275–293. [188]

Watson, J. B., and Rayner, R.   Conditioned emotional reactions. *Journal of Experimental Psychology,* 1920, 3, 1–14. [6, 193]

Watson, J. S.   Memory and "contingency analysis" in infant learning. *Merrill-Palmer Quarterly Behavioral Development,* 1967, 13, 55–67. [117]

Watson, R. E.   Experimentally produced conflict in cats. *Psychosomatic Medicine,* 1954, 16, 340–347. [217]

Webster, K. E.   A cortico-striatal projection in the cat. *Journal of Anatomy,* 1965, 99, 329–337. [319]

Weeks, J. R., and Collins, R. J.   Patterns of intravenous self-injection by morphine-addicted rats. In A. Wikler (Ed.), *The addictive states.* Baltimore: Williams & Wilkins, 1968, pp. 288–298. [90]

Weinberger, N. M.   Effect of detainment on extinction of avoidance responses. *Journal of Comparative Physiological Psychology,* 1965, 60, 135–138. [201]

Weiner, H.   Diagnosis and symptomatology. In L. Bellak (Ed.), *Schizophrenia: A review of the syndrome.* New York: Logos Press, 1958. [338]

Weiner, H.   Schizophrenia, III: Etiology. In A. M. Freedman and H. I. Kaplan (Eds.), *Comprehensive textbook of psychiatry.* Baltimore: Williams & Wilkins, 1967. [361]

Weiner, H., Thaler, M., Reiser, M. F., and Mirsky, I. A.   Etiology of duodenal ulcer. I. Relation of specific psychological characteristics to rate of gastric secretion (serum pepsinogen). *Psychosomatic Medicine,* 1957, 19, 1–10. [232, 243]

Weintraub, M. I., and VanWoert, M. H.   Reversal of cholinergic hypersensitivity in Parkinson's disease by levadopa. *New England Journal of Medicine,* 1971, 284, 412–415. [379]

Weisman, R. G., and Litner, J. S.   Positive conditioned reinforcement of Sidman avoidance behavior. *Journal of Comparative and Physiological Psychology,* 1969, 68, 597–603. (a) [73]

Weisman, R. G., and Litner, J. S.   The course of Pavlovian excitation and inhibition of fear in rats. *Journal of Comparative and Physiological Psychology,* 1969, 69, 667–672. (b) [73, 81]

Weiss, G., Minde, K., Werry, J. W., Douglas, V., and Nemeth, E.   Studies on the hyperactive child. VIII. Five-year follow-up. *American Journal of Psychiatry,* 1971, 24, 409–414. [315, 316]

Weiss, J. M.   Effects of coping responses on stress. *Journal of Comparative and Physiological Psychology,* 1968, 65, 251–260. (a) [109, 110, 117, 256]

Weiss, J. M.   Effects of predictable and unpredictable shock on development of gastrointestinal lesions in rats. In *Proceedings, 76th Annual Convention, American Psychological Association,* 1968, pp. 263–264. (b) [115]

Weiss, J. M.   Somatic effects of predictable and unpredictable shock. *Psychosomatic Medicine,* 1970, 32, 397–408. [251, 252, 253]

Weiss, J. M.   Effects of coping behavior in different warning-signal conditions on stress pathology in rats. *Journal of Comparative and Physiological Psychology,* 1971, 77, 1–13. (a) [115, 256, 258, 259, 260, 261, 268]

Weiss, J. M.   Effects of coping behavior with and without a feedback signal on stress pathology in rats. *Journal of Comparative and Physiological Psychology*, 1971, 77, 22–30. (b) [115, 259, 261, 268]

Weiss, J. M.   Effects of punishing the coping response (conflict) on stress pathology in rats. *Journal of Comparative and Physiological Psychology*, 1971, 77, 14–21. (c) [115, 248, 249, 268]

Weiss, J. M.   Psychological factors in stress and disease. *Scientific American*. June 1972, 104–113. [259]

Weiss, J. M., Glazer, H. I. and Pohorecky, L. A.   Coping behavior and neurochemical changes: an alternative explanation for the original "learned helplessness" experiments. In G. Serban and A. Kling (Eds.), *Animal models of human psychobiology*. New York: Plenum Press, 1976, pp. 141–173. [110, 125]

Weiss, J. M., Pohorecky, L. A., Salman, S., and Gruenthal, M.   Attenuation of gastric lesions by psychological aspects of aggression in rats. *Journal of Comparative and Physiological Psychology*, 1976, 90, 252–259. [265]

Weiss, J. M., Stone, E. A., and Harrell, N.   Coping behavior and brain norepinephrine level in rats. *Journal of Comparative and Physiological Psychology*, 1970, 72, 153–160. [110]

Weiss, P. A.   The living system: Determinism stratified. In A. Koestler and J. R. Smythies (Eds.), *Beyond Reductionism: New perspectives in the life sciences*. Boston: Beacon Press, 1969. [295]

Weisz, J. D.   The etiology of experimental gastric ulceration. *Psychosomatic Medicine*, 1957, 19, 61–73. [245, 246]

Welker, R. L.   Acquisition of a free-operant-appetitive response in pigeons as a function of prior experience. (Doctoral dissertation, University of Colorado, 1974.) [121]

Wender, P. H.   *Minimal brain dysfunction in children*. New York: Wiley, 1971. [309, 310, 311, 313, 332, 333]

Wender, P. H.   The minimal brain dysfunction syndrome in children. *Journal of Nervous and Mental Disease*, 1972, 155, 55–71. [311]

Wender, P. H.   Some speculations concerning a possible basis of minimal brain dysfunction. *Annals of the New York Academy of Sciences*, 1973, 205, 18–28. [333]

Werkman, S. L., and Greenberg, E. S.   Personality and interest patterns in obese adolescent girls. *Psychosomatic Medicine*, 1967, 24, 72–75. [33]

Werry, J. S.   Studies on the hyperactive child: An empirical analysis of the minimal brain dysfunction syndrome. *Archives of General Psychiatry*, 1968, 19, 9–16. [309, 332]

Whatmore, G. B., and Kohli, D. R.   *The physiopathology and treatment of functional disorders*. New York: Grune & Stratton, 1974. [279, 282, 296]

Wheatley, M. D.   The hypothalamus and affective behavior in cats. *Archives of Neurology and Psychiatry*, 1944, 52, 296–316. [60]

Wiener, N.   *Cybernetics or control and communication in the animal and in the machine*. Cambridge, Mass.: MIT Press, 1948. [276]

Wikler, A.   Some implications of conditioning theory for problems of drug abuse. *Behavioral Science*, 1971, 16, 92–97. [82, 89, 98]

Wikler, A., and Pescor, F. J. Classical conditioning of a morphine-abstinence phenomenon, reinforcement of opisid-drinking behavior and "relapse" in morphine-addicted rats. *Psychopharmacologia*, 1967, *10*, 255–284. [89]

Wilcoxon, H. C. "Abnormal fixation" and learning. *Journal of Experimental Psychology*, 1952, *44*, 324–331. [24]

Williams, E. An analysis of gaze in schizophrenics. *British Journal of Social and Clinical Psychology*, 1974, *13*, 1–8. [353]

Williams, P. An unusual response to chlorpromazine therapy. *British Journal of Psychiatry*, 1972, *121*, 439–440. [342]

Williams, D. The structure of emotions reflected in epileptic experiences. *Brain*, 1956, *79*, 29–67.

Williams, T. A., Friedman, R. J., and Secunda, S. K. *The depressive illness.* (Special report.) Washington, D.C.: National Institute of Mental Health, 1970. [104, 134]

Wing, L. The syndrome of childhood autism. *British Journal of Hospital Medicine*, 1970, *4*, 381–392. [170]

Wing, L., and Wing, J. Multiple impairments in early childhood autism. *Journal of Autism and Childhood Schizophrenia*, 1971, *1*, 256–266. [171]

Winokur, G. Types of affective disorders. *Journal of Nervous and Mental Disease*, 1973, *156*, 82–96. [135]

Wishner, J. On deviant behaviour, diagnostic systems, and experimental psychopathology. *International Review of Applied Psychology*, 1969, *18*, 79–82. [10]

Withers, R. Problems in the genetics of human obesity. *Eugenics Review*, 1964, *56*, 81–90. [48]

Wittgenstein, L. *Philosophical investigations.* New York: Macmillan, 1953. [105]

Wolf, S., and Wolff, H. G. *Human gastric function.* New York: Oxford University Press, 1947. [235, 264]

Wolff, H. G., Wolf, S., Grace, W. J., Holmes, T. E., Stevenson, I., Straub, L., Goodell, H., and Seton, P. Changes in form and function of mucous membranes occurring as part of protective reaction patterns in man during periods of life stress and emotional conflict. *Transactions of the Association of American Physicians*, 1948, *61*, 313–334. [235]

Wolpe, J. Experimental neuroses as learned behavior. *British Journal of Psychology*, 1952, *43*, 243–268. [217]

Wolpe, J. *Psychotherapy by reciprocal inhibition.* Stanford University Press, 1958. [21]

Wolpe, J. The practice of behavior therapy. New York: Pergamon Press, 1969. [126]

Wolpe, J., and Lazarus, A. *Behavior therapy techniques.* Oxford: Pergamon Press, 1968. [126]

Woodruff, M. L., and Lippincott, W. I. Hyperemotionality and enhanced tonic immobility after septal lesions in the rabbit. *Brain, Behavior and Evolution*, 1976, *13*, 22–33. [344]

Woodruff, R. A., Goodwin, D. W., and Guze, S. B. *Psychiatric diagnosis.* New York: Oxford University Press, 1974. [358]

Woods, S. C., Decke, E., and Vasselli, J. R.   Metabolic hormones and regulation of body weight. *Psychological Review*, 1974, *81*, 26–43. [29]

Wooley, O. W.   Long-term food regulation in the obese and nonobese. *Psychosomatic Medicine*, 1971, *33*, 436–444. [55]

Wooley, O. W., Wooley, S. C., and Dunham, K. B.   Can calories be perceived and do they affect hunger in obese and nonobese humans? *Journal of Comparative and Physiological Psychology*, 1972, *80*, 250–258. [55]

Wurtman, R. J., and Fernstrom, J. D.   Effects of the diet on brain neurotransmitters. *Nutrition Reviews*, 1974, *32*, 193–200. [28]

Yalow, R. S., Glick, S. M., Roth, J., and Berson, S. A.   Plasma insulin and growth-hormone levels in obesity and diabetes. *Annals of the New York Academy of Sciences*, 1965, *131*, 357. [44]

Yarrow, L. M.   Maternal deprivation: Toward an empirical and conceptual re-evaluation. *Psychological Bulletin*, 1961, *58*, 459–490. [134]

Yerkes, R. M., and Yerkes, A. W.   Nature and conditions of avoidance (fear) response in chimpanzees. *Journal of Comparative Psychology*, 1936, *21*, 53–66. [179]

Young, C. M., Scanlan, S. S., and Topping, C. M.   Frequency of feeding, weight reduction, and body composition. *Journal of American Dietetic Association*, 1971, *59*, 466–472. [50]

Young, J. P. R., Lader, M. H., and Fenton, G. W.   A twin study of the genetic influences on the electroencephalogram. *Journal of Medical Genetics*, 1972, *9*, 13–16. [195]

Young, L. D., Lewis, J. K., and McKinney, W. T.   Response to maternal separation: A reconsideration. (Paper presented at the meeting of the American Psychiatric Association, Anaheim, California, May 1975.) [142, 154]

Young, L. D., McKinney, W. T., Lewis, J. K., Breese, G. R., Smither, R. D., Mueeler, R. A., Howard, J. L., Prange, A. J., and Lipton, M. A.   Induction of adrenal catecholamine synthesizing enzymes following mother-infant separation. *Nature New Biology*, 1973, *246*, 94–96. [153]

Young, L. D., Suomi, S. J., Harlow, H. F., and McKinney, W. T.   Early stress and later response to separation. *American Journal of Psychiatry*, 1973, *130*, 400–405. [162]

Zborowski, M.   Cultural components in response to pain. *Journal of Social Issues*, 1952, *8*, 16–30. [199]

Zinner, S. II., Levy, P. S., and Kass, E. H.   Familial aggregation of blood pressure in childhood. *New England Journal of Medicine*, 1971, *284*, 401–404. [287]

SUBJECT INDEX